The *Irwin Professional Publishing* HANDBOOK
of Telecommunications

Second Edition

James Harry Green

IRWIN
Professional Publishing
Burr Ridge, Illinois
New York, New York

This book is dedicated to my wife, Pat, whose support and devotion made this work possible.

Sponsoring editor: Susan Stevens, Ph.D.
Project editor: Karen J. Nelson
Production manager: Ann Cassady
Jacket Designer: Renee Klyczek Nordstrom
Printer: Arcata Graphics/Hawkins

Library of Congress Cataloging-in-Publication Data

Green, James H. (James Harry)

 The IRWIN *Professional Publishing* handbook of telecommunications
/ James Harry Green. 2nd ed.

  p. cm.

 Includes bibliographical references and index.

 ISBN 1–55623–333–7

 1. Telecommunication systems—Handbooks, manuals, etc.

2. Business—Communication systems—Handbooks, manuals, etc.

I. Title.

TK5101.G722 1991

621.382—dc20   91–29126

Printed in the United States of America

5 6 7 8 9 0 K 8 7 6 5 4

Preface

Almost a decade has passed since AT&T and the Department of Justice signed the historic agreement that ripped apart the Bell System and opened the long distance network to competition. Has experience validated the theory that led to divestiture? Has competition led to greater innovation and lower prices? Would the average consumer have been better off under the old system? The jury is still out on these questions. There can be little doubt that innovation in both equipment and services has boomed in the past 10 years. The cost of long distance service has dropped by at least one-third—even more for large companies. End user access charges, which are effectively just an increase in local service costs, have accompanied the drop in long distance prices. In most areas, the cost of local lines has increased even more than the access charge component. The average consumer doesn't use enough long distance to offset higher local service costs, so there is at least one class of user that is worse off than before.

How much of the innovation and price change would have occurred without divestiture? That is a subject for speculation because, as Heraclitus said, you cannot step twice in the same river. The one indisputable fact about divestiture is that it has made life a great deal more complex and interesting for those who make their living managing telecommunications systems. The key issue is system integration. Although some vendors accept responsibility for designing, installing, and maintaining a company's entire telecommunication system, the cost of such service is high. In most companies, the owner retains the burden of assuring compatibility and determining which vendor is responsible for clearing trouble.

In theory, the telecommunication system should work as well after divestiture as it did before. With the technological advances—primarily the surge toward end-to-end digital connectivity—has come improved service. In practice, however, several events have occurred in the past few years that potentially worsen service. Chapter 2, which deals with transmission performance, relates a case in point. Regulatory commissions have permitted many local exchange carriers (LECs) to charge their customers for "improved transmission performance." The quality of transmission, therefore, depends on the individual economic judgments of many companies, some of which may weigh the cost of service more heavily than the quality. Another case in point are voice compression systems, which cram more voice signals into narrower bandwidth—at reduced cost and diminished quality.

Before divestiture, a company could consume telecommunications services without understanding the technology. For small companies, that is still the case, but for large companies the risk of making an error or missing an opportunity is too great to leave to vendors. Someone within the company must know how to manage the technologists who apply the services and equipment that comprise the telecommunication system. Managing outside experts requires some knowledge of the building blocks and how they work. This book's objective is to further that understanding. It does not cover the technologies in depth because each chapter discusses subjects that are deep enough to warrant a full book. The book is intended to help you understand enough about the technologies to apply them intelligently.

Telecommunications has at least as many buzz words and as much jargon as the computer industry, except that its history is longer and the body of knowledge has been more closely held. Before divestiture, telecommunications technology was rarely taught outside the telephone companies, and as a result, telecommunications knowledge is not widespread. A second objective of this book is to explain the industry's jargon in a context that requires little or no technical education to comprehend.

This book consists of five parts. Part 1, Principles of Telecommunications Systems, discusses the underlying principles of voice and data communications that are common to all systems. Part 2 discusses the principles of switching technology, including some older techniques that are giving way to more advanced digital switching systems. The third part covers transmission systems, which include such technologies as radio, fiber optics, and satellite systems, which glue the networks together. Part 4 deals with equipment, such as private branch exchanges, key telephone equipment, automatic call distributors, and facsimile machines, that resides on the customer's premises. The final part discusses the voice and data networks that tie these elements together, including wide area, metropolitan, and local area networks. The book concludes with a short chapter on future trends in telecommunications. Reference material is scattered throughout and included in the appendices, which deal with information that does not fit logically into one of the chapters. A bibliography, a glossary, and an index complete the book.

Only five years separate the first and second editions of this book, but the changes in telecommunications are so vast that at least half of the material in this edition is new. Many underlying principles do not change, but in the last half of the 1980s, telecommunications service in the United States was transformed by several factors, some of which are practically invisible to the consumer. First, the nationwide fiber optic systems that were in the planning stages in 1985 are complete, resulting in improved long distance service and reduced costs. Telephone service is becoming less and less distance sensitive, and because of different regulatory jurisdictions, it is not unusual to pay less to call across the country than across a state.

The second major factor in the past five years has been growth in local area networks. Although the evolution is far from complete, the stand-alone computer is becoming less prevalent today. In the future, data networks are likely to become networks of interconnected LANs with the division between voice, data, and video apparent only at the source. In the network, the different forms of information transport are merged as high speed digital signals.

The revolution is far from over. The next five years will see changes at least as great as those the last five have seen as the transition to digital service is carried to the desktop and as greater bandwidth is demanded to eliminate the barriers to effective communication that the networks of the past have imposed. Fiber optics continues to prevail as the transmission medium of choice, eventually finding its way to the home and directly to the desktop.

The symbiotic relationship between telecommunications and the computer continues into the future, with neither able to exist without the other.

Table of Contents

List of Figures

List of Tables

1

Principles of Telecommunications Systems

For the first 100 years of its existence, the telephone system was a single-owner monopoly. Interconnection to the Bell System's network was permitted to independent telephone companies that offered public service in a franchised territory, but the connection of privately owned equipment was prohibited by tariffs. Then, starting with the Carterfone case in 1968, the fully integrated Bell System gradually disintegrated. In 1984, it was divided into the seven regional Bell Holding companies (RBHCs), which furnish exchange service, and AT&T, which retained the long distance service and manufacturing arms.

The breakup of the Bell System was wholeheartedly approved by competing manufacturers and long distance carriers but was greeted less than enthusiastically by many users. The question of whether divestiture is beneficial or not will never be answered because the results are irreversible. One certain result is an urgent need for every organization to understand telecommunications technology to a depth never required before.

The technology is not drastically different from computer technology, and in fact, many of the same components and techniques are used in both. Most companies have developed staffs that understand computers and manage their resources because they have never had the alternative of turning their entire computing resource over to one company, as many organizations once did with their telephone service.

Since divestiture, many companies have enhanced their internal resources for dealing with telecommunications technology. Unlike a computer, which can be understood as a stand-alone device, a telecommunications system is connected to what has been called the largest time-shared computer in the world. Many telecommunications managers deal only with customer premises equipment: the PBXs, multiplexers, station sets, and modems that connect over leased lines and trunks to the rest of the network. An understanding of the entire network is necessary, however, to make intelligent purchase decisions and to determine the probable cause of trouble when something fails.

The first part of this book explains the major building blocks of the telecommunications system and how the elements fit together. It also covers common concepts of analog and digital communications, transmission theory, and data communications theory. Outside plant, which forms the local loops that connect users to the central office, is also discussed in this part. Part 1 concludes with a discussion of voice compression equipment, which is a technology that will help speed the evolution of the all-digital network.

An understanding of basic electricity is essential for comprehending many concepts discussed in this book. Readers who do not understand alternating and direct current and radio may wish to start by reading Appendix A, in which these principles are explained.

1

Introduction to Telecommunications

To the user on the end of a telephone, the telecommunications network looks like a single monolithic entity—a black box with telephone lines that somehow mysteriously get connected to one another. It is a tribute to the inventive genius of the thousands of scientists, engineers, and technicians who design, install, and maintain the many parts of the network that it functions exactly as if it were a black box. In reality, however, the network is composed of countless assemblies of circuits, switching systems, radio and fiber optic systems, signaling devices, and telephone instruments that act as part of a coordinated whole. Every day, the industry adds new devices to the network, and they must function with other devices that were designed and installed more than 30 years ago.

The word *network* has become an ambiguous term. It can describe the relationship of a group of broadcasting stations or a social fabric that binds people of similar interests. In telecommunications the usage is somewhat more specific, but the precise meaning of the term must be derived from context, and this can be confusing to those outside the industry. In its broadest sense a telecommunications network is the combination of all the circuits and equipment that enable users to communicate. All the switching apparatus, trunks, subscriber lines, and auxiliary equipment that support communication can be classified as elements of the network. In another sense, the word narrows to mean the switching circuits that interconnect the inputs and outputs of a switching machine. At the circuit level a third meaning describes the interconnection of components to form a filter or level-reducing attenuator. The only way the ambiguity can be dealt with is to become familiar enough with the technology to take the meaning of the term from its context.

The direct interconnection of two stations meets the definition of a network in the strictest sense of the word, but this is a restrictive kind of private network because it lacks accessibility. In a broader sense, public networks provide the capability for a station to reach another station anywhere in the world without the need for complex addressing.

Over the years, telecommunications apparatus has grown increasingly complex, shrunk dramatically in size and power consumption, and become more trouble-free. The industry successfully integrates such new technologies as lightwave and satellite communications with coaxial cable systems designed before World War II.

To understand the systems discussed in this book, it is necessary to understand how they fit together as part of a coordinated whole. This chapter describes the major building blocks of the telecommunications network without explaining how or why they work. Many terms are introduced and explained in detail only later in the book. You are cautioned that despite its origins in rigid scientific disciplines, the vocabulary of telecommunications is frequently highly ambiguous, and the meaning of many of its terms must be taken from context. Therefore, when we use terminology, we will define it in context to illustrate its meaning.

Just as the human body can be viewed either as a unit or as an assembly of systems, including digestion, respiration, and circulation, the telecommunications network can be understood by examining its systems. We will first discuss the major systems in broad terms, and in subsequent chapters will examine them in greater detail.

The Major Telecommunications Systems

Figure 1.1 shows the major classes of telecommunications equipment and how they fit together to form a communications network. In the telecommunications industry, as in the computer industry, the manufacturers often set the standards, and compli-

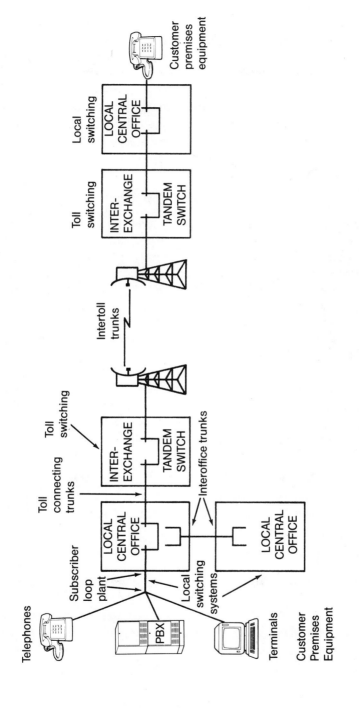

Figure 1.1   The major classes of telecommuncations equipment.

ance with equipment standards set by others is voluntary. In the past few years, international standards-setting organizations have been uncommonly active, so we are now threatened by too many, rather than too few, standards. This topic is examined in more detail in a later section. Unlike the systems of the human body, the systems in telecommunications are not tightly bound to one another. Each element in Figure 1.1 is largely autonomous. The telecommunications network is created by the systems' exchanging signals across the interfaces.

Customer Premises Equipment

Located on the user's premises, *station*, or *terminal*, equipment is the only part of the telecommunications system with which users normally come in contact directly. It includes the telephone instrument itself, and the wiring in the user's building that connects to Local Exchange Carrier (LEC) equipment. For our purposes, station equipment also includes other apparatus, such as *private branch exchanges* (PBXs) (sometimes also called computer branch exchanges or private automatic branch exchanges), and local area networks (LANs) that normally belong to a single organization. It also includes multiple-line key telephone equipment used to select, hold, and conference calls. Data equipment, such as modems and multiplexers, and auxiliary equipment, such as speaker phones, automatic dialers, and answering sets, also falls into the station equipment classification.

Customer premises equipment has two primary functions. It is used for intraorganizational communication within a narrow range, usually a building or campus, and it connects to private or common carrier facilities for communication over a wider range.

Subscriber Loop Plant

The *subscriber loop*, also known as the *local loop*, consists of the wire, poles, terminals, conduit, and other outside plant items that connect customer premises equipment to the LEC's central office. Before deregulation, LECs had a monopoly on the local loop. Now, however, alternatives are becoming available. For some services it is possible to transport information over cable television and in other cases to use privately owned facilities such as microwave radio or privately owned fiber optics to bypass LEC equipment.

Local Switching Systems

The objective of the telecommunications system is to interconnect users, whether they are people communicating over a telephone line, or systems communicating over specially designed data circuits. These connections are either dialed by the user or wired in the LEC's central office where they remain connected until the service is discontinued. This latter kind of circuit is called a *private*, or *dedicated*, line.

The local switching office (often called an *end office*) is the point at which local loops terminate. Loops used for switched services are wired to systems that can switch to other loops or to *trunks*, which are channels to other local or long distance switching offices. Loops used for private line services are directly wired to other loops or to trunks to distant central offices.

Interoffice Trunks

Because of the huge concentrations of wire that converge in local switching offices, there is a practical limit to the number of users that can be served from a single office or wire center. Therefore, in major metropolitan areas, the LECs strategically place multiple central offices according to population density and connect them with interoffice trunks. Central offices exchange signals and establish talking connections over these trunks to set up paths to addresses corresponding to telephone numbers dialed by the users.

Tandem Switching Offices

As the number of central offices in a region increases, it becomes impractical to connect every office to every other office with trunks. For one thing, the number of groups of trunks would be unmanageable. Also, some central offices have too little traffic demand between them to justify the cost of directly connected trunks. To solve these problems, the telephone network is equipped with tandem switches to interconnect trunks. Local tandem switches connect local trunks, and toll tandem, also called interexchange tandem, switches connect central offices to inter-exchange trunks leading outside the free calling area. A special type of tandem switch known as a *gateway* interconnects the telephone networks of different countries when their networks are incompatible.

Privately owned tandem switches also may interconnect circuits under the control of a single organization. Before the breakup of the Bell System, the telephone companies owned the toll tandem switches. Now, with multiple interexchange carriers (IECs) offering service, each carrier connects tandem switches to the end office or to an LEC-owned *exchange access tandem*.

Interexchange Trunks

LECs divide their serving areas into classifications known as *exchanges*. Most exchanges correspond roughly to the boundaries of cities and their surrounding areas. Interexchange trunks that connect offices within the free calling area are known as *extended area service* (EAS) trunks, while those that connect outside the free calling area are called *toll* trunks. Trunks that connect the LEC to an IEC are called *interLATA connecting trunks*.

Transmission Equipment

The process of transporting information in any form, including voice, video, and data, between users is called *transmission* in the telecommunications industry. The earliest transmission took place over open wire suspended on poles equipped with cross-arms and insulators, but that technique has now largely disappeared. For short ranges, some trunks are carried on pairs of copper wire that are twisted into cables of as many as 3600 pairs. For longer ranges, interoffice and interexchange trunks are transported over twisted pair wire, terrestrial microwave radio, fiber optic light guides, or satellites. *Multiplexing* equipment divides these backbone transmission facilities into voice channels.

Fundamentals of Multiplexing

The basic building block of the telephone network is the *voice grade* communications channel occupying 300 to 3300 Hz of

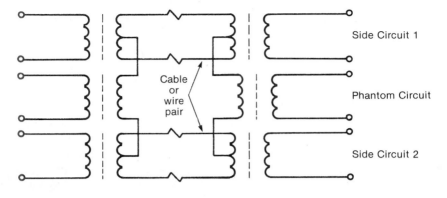

Figure 1.2 **Phantom telephone circuit.**

bandwidth. This bandwidth is far from the bandwidth of high fidelity systems, which typically reproduce 30 to 20,000 Hz, but for ordinary voice transmission a voice grade circuit is entirely satisfactory. For the first six or seven decades of telephony, open wire and multiple-pair cables were the primary transmission media. At first, each pair of wires carried one voice channel. However, these media, known as *facilities* in telecommunications vernacular, have enough bandwidth to carry several channels. For example, most stereo systems use twisted pair wire between the amplifier and the speaker, and they have bandwidths six times that of a voice grade channel.

The telecommunications industry has always invested heavily in research and development. Much of it has been directed toward how to impose an increasing amount of information on a single transmission medium. The process of placing multiple voice channels over one facility is known as *multiplexing*.

The term multiplexing is as broad in meaning as the capacity of the transmission medium it seeks to expand. In its earliest and simplest form, multiplexing did not even require electronic equipment. Telecommunications engineers found that two identical circuits connected as shown in Figure 1.2 could carry a third circuit. The resulting circuit, known as a *phantom*, was of even higher quality than the two original side circuits. For the price of a simple transformer (telephone people call it a *repeat coil*), the carrying capacity of a pair of wires could be increased by 50%.

Frequency Division Multiplexing

Even the phantom circuit, however, left much bandwidth unused. With the arrival of the vacuum tube in the 1920s, another form of multiplexing, known as *carrier,* became possible. The earliest carrier systems increased the capacity of a pair of wires by a technique known as frequency division multiplexing (FDM). Broadcast radio is an example of FDM in action (except that it does not allow two-way communication). In an FDM carrier system, as Figure 1.3 shows, each channel is assigned a transmitter-receiver pair or modem (a term derived from the words modulator and demodulator). These units operate at low power levels and are connected to a cable rather than an antenna; therefore they do not radiate as a radio does. Otherwise, the concepts of radio and carrier are identical.

FDM carrier systems in use today range in capacity from one additional voice or data channel over a pair of wires to as many as 10,800 voice channels on a broadband coaxial cable.

Time Division Multiplexing

Although FDM is an efficient way of increasing the capacity of a transmission medium, the techniques used in its manufacture do not lend themselves to large scale integration. Therefore, FDM is gradually being replaced by *time division multiplexing* (TDM), which uses techniques similar to those used in computers. In TDM, shown conceptually in Figure 1.4, instead of the bandwidth of the transmission medium being divided into frequency segments, each user has access to the full bandwidth of the system for a small amount of time. As Figure 1.4 shows, electronic equipment distributes a digitized voice signal from each user to an appropriate time segment of the transmission medium. The capacity of the transmission medium is so great that users are not aware that they are sharing it. Chapter 4 describes the concept of time division multiplexing in more detail.

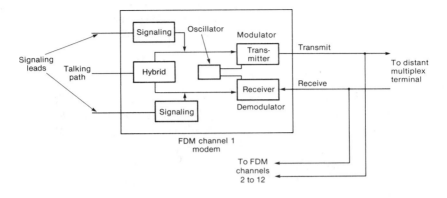

Figure 1.3 **Frequency division multiplexing system.**

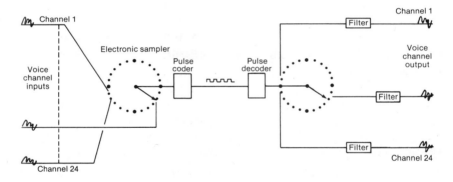

Figure 1.4 **Time division multiplexing system.**

Higher Order Multiplexing

The basic building block of both analog and digital multiplexing systems is the *group*. A group has 12 voice grade circuits combined into a band of analog frequencies, or into a stream of digital data. Groups are formed in equipment called a *channel bank*. Analog channel banks consist of 12 circuits; digital channel banks derive 24 circuits known as a *digroup*. Higher order multiplexing combines the output of channel banks into hundreds and thousands of circuits that can be transmitted over broadband facilities such as coaxial cable, microwave radio, and fiber optics.

Data Multiplexing

When data communications people speak of multiplexing, they are usually using the word in a different sense from that used above. Data multiplex equipment subdivides a voice channel into several lower bandwidth data channels. In later chapters this multiplexing will be described in more detail. For now it is important to know that "multiplex" must be understood in context, for it is a term that has many different meanings.

Analog and Digital Transmission Concepts

When a person speaks into a telephone instrument, the voice actuates a transmitter to cause current flowing in the line to vary proportionately, or *analog*ously, to the changes in sound pressure. Because people speak and hear in analog, there was, until recent years, little reason to convert an analog signal to digital. Now, there are three primary reasons digital transmission is important. First, digital equipment is less expensive to manufacture than analog; second, an increasing amount of communication takes place between digital terminal equipment such as computers; and third, digital transmission provides higher quality in most respects than analog transmission.

The higher quality of digital signals results from the difference in the methods of amplifying the signal. In analog transmission, an audio amplifier, known as a *repeater,* boosts the signal along with any noise on the line. With digital transmission, regenerators detect the incoming bit stream and create an entirely new signal that is identical to the original. If a digital signal is regenerated before noise causes errors to occur, the result is a channel that is practically noise-free.

The system for transmitting telephone signals digitally is known as *pulse code modulation (PCM)*. A PCM channel bank samples the voice, converts it to an eight-bit digital word, and transmits it over a line interspersed with digital signals from 23 other channels. Repeaters spaced at appropriate intervals regenerate the 24-channel signal.

The theory of PCM is not new; an IT&T scientist in England developed it in 1938. Though the system was technically feasible then, however, it was not economical because of the high cost of the electronics needed to make the analog-to-digital conversion. With the invention of the transistor, the development of solid state electronics, and particularly large scale integration, the economics shifted in favor of digital transmission. PCM is replacing analog techniques in all parts of the telecommunications system except at the source, the telephone. Telephone sets in which the voice is digitized in the instrument, however, are common in PBXs. At present, digital telephone sets are not practical in public telephone networks for technical and economic reasons, but the drawbacks will disappear in time.

Switching Systems

For many applications, fixed circuits between points, known as *point-to-point,* or *dedicated,* circuits, are desirable. Usually, however, the real value of a telecommunications system lies in its ability to access a wide range of users wherever they are located. This is the role of telephone switching systems.

Early Switching Systems

The earliest switching systems were manually operated. Telephone lines and trunks were terminated on jacks, and operators interconnected lines by inserting plug-equipped cords into the jacks. Figure 1.5 shows a manual toll switchboard from 1926. Note the headsets worn by the operators and the large clock mechanism used for timing calls.

In 1891, a Kansas City undertaker named Almon B. Strowger patented an electromechanical switch that could be controlled by pulses from a rotary dial. The Strowger system, also known as *step-by-step*, is still in use in the United States today. Although step-by-step has disappeared in large metropolitan areas, many small offices serving rural communities still use this system. The distinguishing feature of step-by-step is that electrical pulses

Figure 1.5   A 1926 toll switchboard.
  Courtesy, AT&T Corporation.

created by a dial directly control the motion of the switches. The switching system has no intelligence and limited ability to vary the destination of the call. This point will be important to remember when we discuss limitations in providing completely uniform telecommunications services between users and IECs that competed with AT&T before divestiture.

Common Control Switching Offices

All switching offices have a common characteristic: they contain a limited amount of equipment that many users share. With manual and step-by-step systems, all the equipment used to establish a talking path remains connected for the duration of the call. As technology advanced, it developed that keeping the equipment occupied for the duration of the call is not the most economical way to switch. More important, it is also inflexible. As a call progresses through the switching system, if it encounters blockage, the system is incapable of rerouting the call to a different path. It can only signal the user to hang up and try again. These drawbacks can be overcome by *common control* switching systems.

Common control switching equipment sets up the talking path through a switching network and releases when the connection is established. The common control equipment is not called on again until the connection is to be taken down. In this respect, common control equipment serves a function similar to that served by the human manual switchboard operator. Although common control equipment is more complex than directly controlled switching, it is also more efficient and much faster.

In contrast to step-by-step where the user builds a connection gradually with pulls of the dial, under common control the user transmits dial or tone pulses into a circuit that registers the digits. An advantage of this method is that when dialing is complete, logic circuits can inspect the digits, determine the destination of the call, and choose an alternative route if all trunks in the preferred route are busy. This capability, known as *alternate routing*, is shared by all modern switching systems.

The earliest common control equipment, introduced in the 1920s, was a system known as *panel*, followed about two decades later by the *crossbar* system. The systems take their names from the method of interconnecting lines and trunks. Panel equipment has all but disappeared, but crossbar equipment is still in use in the United States and is discussed in more detail in Chapter 8.

Computer Controlled Switching Systems

Common control offices use electromechanical relays in their logic circuits. Relays have an electronic counterpart, the logic gate. Both gates and relays are binary logic devices. That is, they are either on or off, and if a decision can be reduced to a series of yes/no responses to outside conditions, both logic gates and relays can do the same functions.

The electronic equivalent of a common control central office was a natural outgrowth of computer and switching technology. Early electronic switching systems used wired logic; that is, they were not programmable. In the middle 1960s, the age of the stored program control (SPC) central office was born. The Western Electric No. 1 ESS, which is in widespread use today, has a reed relay switching network driven by a software program.

Digital Central Offices

When large scale integrated circuits were perfected in the 1970s, it became technically feasible to develop a digital switching network to replace the electronic network in SPC central offices. The current state-of-the-art of central office technology has a digital switching network controlled by a programmable central processor. Most modern switching equipment, ranging from small PBXs to large toll tandem switches that can handle thousands of trunks, uses this technology. Now, further research is underway to develop even less costly switching systems that are capable of switching light streams rather than electrical pulses.

Numbering Systems

Switching systems route calls between themselves and selected terminating stations by *addressing*. Station addresses in North America consist of an area code and a telephone number. From overseas locations, a country code is added. Without controlled assignment of telephone numbers, the telephone system could

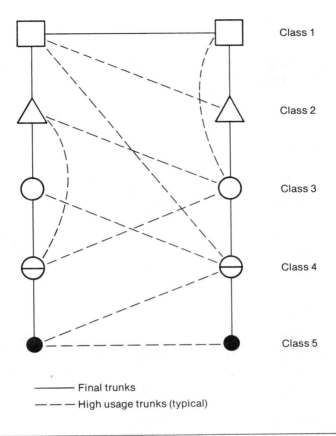

Class 1

Class 2

Class 3

Class 4

Class 5

————— Final trunks

— — — High usage trunks (typical)

Figure 1.6 **Switching hierarchy used by the Bell System before divestiture.**

not function. In this section we will look briefly at how telephone numbering operates both in this country and worldwide.

The Switching Hierarchy

The public telephone network operated by AT&T and connecting LECs was divided into five classes of switching systems as illustrated in Figure 1.6. Since divestiture, AT&T and other IECs have reduced the number of levels in the switching hierarchy, but the class designation remains for Class 5 central offices, the lowest class in the hierarchy. Class 5 offices, also known as *end offices*, are the systems that directly serve subscriber lines. Higher class offices are tandem offices used for connecting toll trunks.

Trunks between switching systems are classified as either *high usage* or *final* trunks. Within certain limits, high usage trunks can be established between any two offices if the traffic volume justifies it. Common control switching systems contain the intelligence to enable them to decide what group of trunks to choose to route calls to the destination, always attempting first to connect to a distant central office over a high usage trunk. Calls progress from system to system until the terminating office is reached. Systems route calls by exchanging signals over either the trunk that provides the talking path or a separate data network.

Figure 1.6 shows that if all high usage trunks were busy, a call from a Class 5 office could theoretically be routed over as many as nine final trunks in tandem before it reached the terminating Class 5 office. In practice, this rarely, if ever, happens.Traffic engineers monitor the amount of traffic flowing between terminating points and order the proper quantity of trunks to cause calls to complete over the most economical route. At present, AT&T uses a system known as Dynamic Nonhierarchical Routing (DNR) to route calls between nodes on the interexchange network. The larger IECs use a similar method of routing calls.

The Nationwide Numbering Plan

Every telephone line in the United States and Canada has a unique 10-digit address. The first division is a three-digit *area code*. This code is also sometimes called the *numbering plan area* (NPA) code. Within the area, each central office is assigned at least one three-digit *central office code*. Within the central office, each customer has a *line number* between 0000 and 9999. Each central office code, therefore, can support 10,000 lines. In larger cities it is common for a single switching system to serve multiple central office codes. Appendix F lists the North American dialing codes.

The Worldwide Numbering Plan

Not all nations in the world use the same numbering plan as the United States. This is of little consequence if the gateway offices that interconnect the countries can translate the dialed digits to their destination. Each nation in the worldwide plan is assigned a two- or three-digit country number. Worldwide dialing is accomplished without operators by dialing an international direct distance dialing (IDDD) access code, a country code, and the terminating telephone number. Appendix F includes the country codes for the world-wide dialing plan.

Interexchange Carrier Access to Local Networks

The 10-digit telephone addresses discussed here allow completing a call to any telephone in the country after access to the IEC selected to handle the user's long distance calls has been obtained. Until the 1984 breakup of the Bell System, AT&T through its Long Lines division, the Bell Operating Companies, and independent telephone companies owned the only public switched network that spanned the country. The Bell Operating Companies generally handled intercity communications within state boundaries and, in a few instances, between states. The bulk of the interstate calling, however, was handled by Long Lines.

The toll network was accessed by dialing 1. In the early years of user-dialed long distance calls, operators identified the calling telephone number by bridging on the call momentarily and asking the calling party for the billing number. This process was called *operator number identification* (ONI). Gradually, the LECs added *automatic number identification* (ANI) equipment to identify the billing number.

In 1976, the Federal Communications Commission (FCC), which regulates interstate telephone service, opened long distance telephone service to competition from other IECs. These IECs gained access to the local telephone network through an ordinary seven-digit telephone number. This form of access had technical drawbacks that resulted in poorer quality transmission for reasons that Chapter 2 explains. An equally important drawback is the necessity of dialing a seven-digit telephone number for access to the long distance network instead of the digit 1 that all callers used for access to AT&T's network. Also, automatic number identification was not feasible with this method of access, so users had to dial a personal identification number (PIN). With a five- or six-digit PIN, this form of access required the caller to dial up to 22 or 23 digits to reach the terminating telephone number.

Equal Access

In 1982, AT&T and the Department of Justice signed a consent decree that resulted in AT&T's divesting itself of its operating telephone companies. An element of the decree required the LECs to give equal access to all IECs. Under equal access, all carriers have connections that are technically equivalent to AT&T's connection to end offices. When a user originates a call, the switching equipment must decide which IEC the user wants to handle the call. The selected IEC is known in the industry as the *primary interexchange carrier* (PIC). In central offices equipped with stored program controllers that are programmed for equal access, each user presubscribes to a preferred IEC. The central office routes the call to that IEC when the user dials 1. Callers can reach other IECs by dialing a five-digit code, 10XXX, where XXX is a number assigned to the IEC. Automatic number identification is a standard equal access feature, so PIN dialing is not required.

As required by the consent decree between AT&T and the Department of Justice, the Bell companies programmed equal access into most SPC offices by 1986, In many locations, equal access tandem offices allow access to multiple IECs. It should be understood,however, that except for GTE, independent telephone companies are not required to provide equal access, though many of them have voluntarily done so. GTE agreed in 1983 to provide equal access from its central offices as a condition imposed by the Department of Justice in permitting GTE to purchase Sprint. Subsequently, GTE divested itself of Sprint.

Another significant feature of the agreement between AT&T and the Department of Justice is the subdivision of the country into service areas called local access transport areas (LATAs). Under the terms of the agreement, the local Bell Operating Companies can offer toll telephone service only within the LATA. Between LATAs, AT&T and any other authorized IEC can furnish long distance services.

Private Telephone Systems

Many organizations operate private telecommunications systems. These systems range in size from the Federal Telephone System (FTS), which is larger than the telecommunications systems in many countries, to small PBXs.

Private networks normally must be connected to the public network so users can place calls to points that the private network does not cover and so people outside the private network can reach them. This is done by connecting to an end office in a manner similar to the pre-equal access connection described for IECs. These connections are usually switched through a PBX or through private tandem switching systems.

Private network operators design them to transmission and numbering plan criteria similar to networks operated by the LECs. There is no reason that private systems must conform to the nation-wide numbering plan. If they do not, however, the result is often a dual numbering system—one for calls placed on the private network and another for calls placed on the public network.

Standards

The close interrelatedness of the telecommunications network requires standards that enable devices to communicate with one another. Unfortunately, the need for standards and the need for technical progress sometimes conflict because standards often are not set until the technology has been proven in practice, and the only way to prove the technology is through extensive use. Therefore, when it comes time to set a standard, a large base of installed equipment designed to proprietary standards is already in place. The policies of many standards-setting organizations preclude their adopting proprietary standards, even if the manufacturer is willing to make them public. Also, competing manufacturers are represented on the standards-setting bodies of the United States, which is an incentive for bodies to not accept proprietary standards. As a result, even after standards are adopted, a considerable amount of equipment exists that does not conform to the standard.

Some standards are set before they are tested in commercial applications. A good example is the Open Systems Interconnect (OSI) model of the International Standards Organization (ISO), which is discussed in Chapter 3. The model was developed first, well before any practical demonstration of its technical feasibility. Vendors have adopted standards from one or more of its seven layers, but at the time of this writing, no commercial products use the entire model.

How Standards Are Developed

The list of participants in the standards-setting process is long and sometimes not well coordinated. A standard passes through four key stages as it moves from conception to adoption:

- Conceptualization.
- Development.
- Influence.
- Promulgation.

In the United States, just about anyone can conceptualize the need for a standard. Before development begins, however, some recognized body must accept responsibility for the task. For example, local area network standards could have been developed by several different organizations; the Institute of Electrical and Electronic Engineers (IEEE) accepted the task. The Electronics Industries Association (EIA) is another organization that has developed many standards that the American National Standards Institute (ANSI) has accepted.

The development of a standard is usually assigned to a committee within the organization. If the committee is not broadly represented across interest groups, the standards work may never begin. Participation is largely voluntary and is usually funded by the standards influencers, who are the companies or associations with the most to gain or lose. Governmental organizations also wield influence in the standards process. For example, the General Services Administration decreed under its Government OSI Profile (GOSIP) that all data communications purchased by the federal government after 1990 must comply with the OSI model. Companies with vast market power also fill the role of standards influencers. Often, their influence is enhanced because they have already demonstrated technical feasibility of the standard in practice.

The standards promulgators are the agencies that can accredit standards and produce the rules and regulations for enforcing them. In the United States ANSI is the chief organization that accredits standards developed by other organizations such as IEEE and EIA.

Standards Organizations

In the United States and internationally, many organizations and associations are involved in the standards process. The following is a brief description of the role of the most influential of these.

International Telecommunications Union (ITU). The International Telecommunications Union (ITU) was formed in 1865 to promote compatibility of the communications systems that were then emerging. The ITU, now a United Nations-sponsored organization to which 160 countries belong, distributes international standards through its two consultative committees. The International Radio Consultative Committee (CCIR) is responsible for frequency allocations and sponsors international agreements to promote the use of radio and to prevent interference.

The International Telephone and Telegraph Consultative Committee (CCITT) is the primary international standards body for telecommunications. CCITT does its work through some 13 study groups that work in four-year sessions. After a four-year session, the study groups present their work to a plenary assembly for approval. Plenary assemblies will meet in 1992 and 1996. The principal standards adopted by the 1988 and earlier assemblies are listed in Appendix B.

In some countries, where state-owned agencies operate the telecommunications system, CCITT recommendations bear the force of law. In the United States, compliance is largely voluntary, although the standards of the ITU are accepted by international treaty.

International Standards Organization (ISO). The International Standards Organization (ISO) is an association of standard-setting organizations from the various nations that participate in the process. In the United States, ANSI is the ISO representative and advisor to the State Department on ITU standards. The most familiar ISO standards in the telecommunications industry are the standards that support the OSI model.

International Electrotechnical Commission (IEC).   The IEC accredits standards on much the same basis as does the ISO. In contrast to ISO standards, which are primarily logical, IEC promulgates electrical standards.

American National Standards Institute (ANSI).   ANSI is the standards body in the United States that promulgates standards of all types, not just information processing and telecommunications. ANSI is a nongovernmental, nonprofit organization comprising some 300 standards committees. The ANSI X.3 committees handle information-related standards; T1 committees handle telecommunications standards. Both consumers and manufacturers are represented on ANSI committees, and cooperating trade groups that follow ANSI procedures do much of the work. The Institute of Electrical and Electronic Engineers (IEEE) and the Electronic Industries Association (EIA) are two prominent organizations that promulgate standards through ANSI.

Industry and Professional Associations

Two of the most important industry and professional associations are IEEE and EIA. EIA has produced many standards that are important to the telecommunications industry. For example, most data terminal devices use the EIA-232-C interface standard in their interconnection with circuit equipment. The IEEE is a professional association that has had an important effect on standards activities, such as the local area network standards that its 802 committee developed. These standards, discussed in more detail in Chapter 27, use the framework of ISO's Open Systems Interconnect model and CCITT protocols to develop three local network alternatives. IEEE is also responsible for metropolitan area network standards that are presently under development.

Other associations include the Corporation on Open Systems (COS), an industry group that is promoting open architectures;

Computer and Business Equipment Manufacturing Association, Exchange Carrier's Association, Open Software Forum, and in Europe, the Standards Promotion and Applications Group (SPAG).

De Facto Standards

Large companies such as IBM and AT&T have enough market power to set proprietary standards, which others must follow to be compatible. IBM's Systems Network Architecture (SNA) is the most widely used data communications architecture in the world. Yet, SNA is not an international standard, although it is closely aligned in concept to OSI.

The voice networks in the United States are largely designed to AT&T's proprietary standards. Before divestiture, AT&T released these standards to other manufacturers through the United States Independent Telephone Association (now United States Telephone Association). Sometimes others manufactured equipment through cross-licensing agreements with AT&T, but usually compatibility information was unavailable until several years after AT&T successfully introduced the technology.

Sometimes, CCITT has adopted AT&T standards. For example, the standards for the United States version of digital multiplex is a CCITT recommendation, but it is not compatible with the European version, which is also a CCITT standard. In other cases, CCITT standards and AT&T proprietary standards conflict. For example, signaling between AT&T's long distance switching offices for several years used a protocol known as Common Channel Interoffice Signaling (CCIS). The international standard is CCITT Signaling System No. 7, which is incompatible with CCIS.

The Importance of Standards

In the years before the FCC and the courts opened AT&T's network to interconnection and competition, users could avoid compatibility problems (except in data communications where incompatible protocols were a frequent problem) by turning the responsibilities over to the LEC. Now that station equipment is no longer owned by the LEC and long distance networks are a complex combination of common carrier and private facilities, compatibility is a concern of almost every user. The need for compatibility thrusts the issue of standards to the forefront because users' options are limited if manufacturers' interfaces remain proprietary.

Appendix B lists many standards published and used worldwide. Appendix D tells where to obtain information from the organization that published the standard. For the most part, these are the standards of public bodies such as CCITT and EIA. Some of the information Bellcore (the research arm of the seven Bell Operating regions) publishes is also listed because of its widespread acceptance as a de facto standard.

Summary

One cannot help being awed by the intricacy of the nation's telecommunications system. The complexity is evident from this brief overview, but it becomes even more impressive as the details emerge. The marvel is that the system can cover such a vast geographical area, can be administered by hundreds of thousands of workers and contain countless pieces of electrical apparatus, and still function as reliably as it does. As we discuss these elements in greater detail, the techniques that create this high quality service will become more understandable.

2

Voice Transmission Principles

Before the dissolution of the Bell System, telecommunications managers and users had little reason to concern themselves with transmission quality. Over the years, quality gradually improved, and as it did, users' expectations grew. The improvements did not, however, simply happen. They occurred because engineers and scientists, principally from the Bell Laboratories, developed procedures for measuring transmission quality, and equipment that delivered an increasing degree of freedom from the principal enemies of good transmission: loss, noise, and echo.

Today the idea of a unified network transmission design no longer exists. The former Bell Operating Companies through their research and development arm, Bell Communications Research, develop and publish the standards to which the local exchange networks are designed. Interexchange carriers are free to design their networks to any standard they choose, but most follow the standards previously published by AT&T.

Private networks are under no transmission restrictions, other than the acceptance of their users, and with the mixture of circuits and equipment that is available today, there is a real risk that users will find certain connections unacceptable. This chapter discusses the fundamentals of transmission design and explains how common carriers achieve quality in their networks. Most of the principles are equally applicable to private networks.

In common carrier and private telecommunications systems, systematic maintenance, careful circuit design, and high quality equipment help assure quality. Transmission quality is entirely

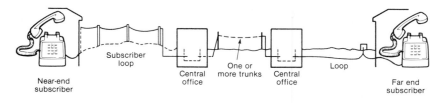

Figure 2.1   Typical telecommunication circuit.

different from switching system quality. Switching systems are go/no-go devices. The connection is either established or it isn't. With transmission systems, quality is a statistical measure. The telecommunications system always introduces some impairments into the talking path between users. Transmission design is a compromise between quality and cost. Although it is possible to build a telecommunications system that will reproduce voices with near-perfect fidelity and clarity, such quality is neither necessary nor economical.

Transmission Impairments

For voice communication, four variables are particularly important in ensuring the adequacy of communications: level or volume, noise, bandwidth, and echo. For data communications, which comprises an increasingly large portion of telecommunications traffic, envelope delay and amplitude distortion are also important.

Volume or Level

Consider the simple telecommunications circuit illustrated in Figure 2.1. The telephone instrument converts the changes in sound pressure from a talker's voice to a varying electrical current that is an analog of the acoustic signal. (Refer to Chapter 18 for an explanation of how the telephone instrument functions.) The electrical characteristics of the circuit between the sending and receiving telephones modify the signal to reduce its volume (or increase its loss), change the bandwidth of the signal, and introduce extraneous signals such as noise, crosstalk, and distortion.

The unit of loss is the *decibel* (dB). A decibel is a logarithmic unit that expresses the relationship between the power or voltage levels of signals. Appendix A discusses the decibel in more detail for those who are unfamiliar with it.

An increase in signal volume that doubles the power of the signal is a 3 dB increase. Similarly, a drop in signal power that halves the signal is a 3 dB reduction. The smallest change that the human ear can detect is about 1 dB; a 3 dB change is apparent to a listener concentrating on hearing the change. It is essential to understand that the dB is not an absolute unit of measurement as are the volt, the ampere, and the watt. The dB measures only the ratio of two quantities of the same unit. A signal power of one milliwatt is an almost universally used standard power against which other power levels are compared. The dB is often used to express power levels compared to one milliwatt; for example, 0 dBm = 1 mw.

The amount of loss that users can tolerate in a circuit depends on noise impairments, the tolerance of the listener for weak signals, and other distortions that alter the character of the received signal. This, of course, depends greatly on individual preference and varies widely among users, ranging from those with hearing impairment to those with acute hearing sensitivity. Because of the wide differences in preference, transmission objectives are statistically based with signal and noise standards designed to satisfy most users.

Amplification easily overcomes loss in telecommunications circuits. Amplifiers, or *repeaters*, however, may introduce undesired side effects along with the desired effect of reducing loss. Not only do they add cost to the circuit, but they add distortion as limited bandwidth, additional noise, and other undesirable changes to the signal they amplify. Designers attempt to minimize the use of repeaters to the greatest extent possible, particularly in local subscriber loops. With more than 150 million subscriber loops in the United States, the cost of amplifying more than a small fraction of them would be substantial. Instead, designers provide amplification for trunks, which all users share, and for some long loops. The characteristics and economics of the ordinary telephone and the subscriber loop drive the design of the elements of the telecommunications network, which Chapters 6 and 18 discuss.

Increasingly, the use of digital trunk facilities minimizes loss and noise impairments. The vast majority of the subscriber loops are still analog, however, and are the source of a large share of the transmission impairments in today's connections. In the future integrated services digital networks, which Chapter 26 discusses, digital subscriber loops will permit end-to-end digital connections. With these, transmission impairments will be controlled by designers and will be of little concern to users.

Noise

Noise is any unwanted signal in a circuit. Hum, crackling or frying, and crosstalk from adjacent circuits are all examples of unwanted signals that careful design and maintenance of a circuit can control. There are definite trade-offs between the various noise impairments and the quality of the signal as the listener perceives it. A uniform level of hiss, for example, may be tolerable if no other impairments exist and the signal level is high. The most important measurement of noise is the signal-to-noise ratio (expressed in dB).

Data signals exhibit an entirely different tolerance to noise than do humans. A data signal may be satisfactory in the presence of uniform steady hissing noise (white noise) that would be bothersome to humans. On the other hand, impulse noise (clicks, pops, or sometimes frying noise) will destroy a data signal on a circuit that might be acceptable for speech communication.

Circuit noise originates from three primary sources. The first is interference from external sources. Electric power lines, lightning, industrial apparatus such as electric motor commutators, crosstalk from adjacent circuits, and other sources can cause circuit noise.

The second source is thermal noise developed within the telecommunications apparatus itself. Any conductor carrying current at a temperature higher than absolute zero (-273° C), generates noise from internal electron movement. Some types of circuit elements, such as vacuum tubes, generate more thermal noise than others, but it is present in all circuit elements, including such passive elements as wire.

The third source of noise is distortion generated by non-linearities in circuit elements, primarily amplifiers. Amplifiers do not precisely reproduce their input signals. The small imperfections in an amplifier's transfer characteristic (the output of the amplifier compared to the input) distort the amplified signal so that extra components appear in the output signal. The effect is aggravated by operating the amplifier beyond its design capability. Chapter 5 discusses this effect, which is called *intermodulation distortion.*

Bandwidth

Bandwidth is the circuit attribute that, with frequency response, controls the naturalness of transmitted speech. As with level, this is a subjective evaluation. The human ear can detect tones between about 20 Hz and 16,000 Hz, but because the voice has few frequency components below about 300 Hz or above 3500 or 4000 Hz, a telephone circuit that transmits a band of frequencies in this range is adequate for voice communication. Channels for voice transmission are usually designed to pass a nominal bandwidth of 300 Hz to 4000 Hz. Telephone receivers are designed to be most sensitive to the frequency spectrum between 500 Hz and 2500 Hz, because research has shown that most of the frequency components of ordinary speech fall into this range.

Because of the technical difficulty of constructing filters and amplifiers with uniform transmission at all frequencies within the pass band, the high and low frequency ends of the transmitted spectrum suffer more loss or attenuation than frequencies in the center of the band. Circuits that carry program audio or high speed data transmission have much wider bandwidths than those used for voice transmission.

Echo

When telephone signals traverse a transmission facility, they move with a finite, although very high, speed. Electrical signals propagated in free space, a radio broadcast signal for example, travel at the speed of light (300,000,000 meters per second). Signals on a physical transmission circuit, on the other hand, propagate at about 50 to 80% of the speed of light, depending on the type of transmission medium and the amount of amplification or filtering

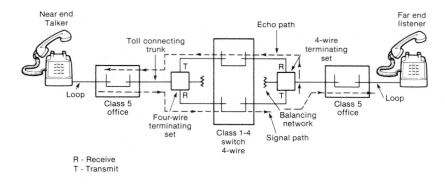

Figure 2.2   Typical long haul connection.

applied to the circuit. A signal is delayed, therefore, as it transits any type of network.

If, in traversing the circuit, the electrical signal encounters an impedance irregularity, a reflection will occur just as a reflection occurs to a sound propagated in a large, empty room. The reflected signal returns to the sending end of the circuit and sounds to the talker like the echo from a long, hollow pipe. The greater the distance from the talker to the irregularity, the greater the time delay in the reflected signal.

Echo is detrimental to transmission in proportion to the amount of delay suffered by the signal and the amplitude of the echoed signal. A communication circuit that displays even a small amount of echo is unfit for service if the delay is too long. On the other hand, a small amount of echo occurs in the ordinary telephone where the user hears it as *sidetone*, which is the sound of the speaker's voice in his or her receiver. Because sidetone is not delayed, it does not interfere with communication. In fact, designers deliberately introduce a certain amount of sidetone in a telephone to help the talker regulate his or her voice level. A lack of sidetone gives the talker the perception that the instrument is dead, while a sufficient amount causes talkers to lower their voices somewhat. The most serious form of echo in communications circuits arises from *four-wire terminating sets*, or *hybrids*. These are devices that convert the transmission circuit from four-wire to two-wire as Figure 2.2 shows. Economics impels the designer to make as much of a communications network two-wire as possible to minimize costs. Carrier and radio systems inherently transmit in only one direction so that a separate path or channel is required in each direction to obtain two-way transmission. The two directions of transmission must be combined into a single two-way two-wire circuit at each end by a four-wire terminating set, or hybrid, for extension through two-wire switching systems and to two-wire local loops.

In digital networks the hybrid is still required at the two-to-four-wire junction point, such as the line circuit where the two-wire loop connects to the switching network in a digital switching system. The hybrids in a digital switch serve the same purpose as they do in an analog switch, but the hybrid circuitry is digital instead of analog. In today's networks, most of the interexchange circuits and switches are digital, and most of the local switching systems are analog. An interexchange call will usually be four-wire and digital from the interLATA access trunks of the local switch to the interLATA access trunks of the local switch at the distant end. The only opportunity for echo to occur, therefore, is in the hybrids at each end of the connection.

In a hybrid the two-wire portion of a circuit is balanced against a network that approximates the electrical characteristics of the two-wire transmission line. When the balancing network is identical with the transmission line, the hybrid is in balance, and energy received over the four-wire transmission path is coupled to the two-wire path. Because the balancing network fails to match the two-wire line, a signal feeds back to the talker at the distant end as an echo. The farther away from the talker the echo occurs, the greater the time delay introduced into the return signal and the greater the impediment to good transmission. Figure 2.2 shows the configuration of a typical analog long distance circuit showing four-wire terminating sets, four-wire transmission facilities, and the echo path.

The loss of a signal traversing a circuit, through the hybrid and back to the sending end is called *return loss*. If the return loss of the circuit does not equal or exceed the amplification in both paths of the four-wire circuit, oscillation, or *singing*, occurs. This is the same effect observed when the volume is advanced on a public address system until the system squeals or sings. The hybrid's balancing network must be adjusted to at least 10 dB more loss than needed to prevent the circuit from singing. Adjustments to the hybrid balance network become more important as the circuit becomes longer. At about 2000 miles, the round trip delay on a circuit becomes excessive and any appreciable echo becomes disturbing to the talkers. *Echo suppressors* in analog circuits and *echo cancelers* in digital circuits control echo.

Echo suppressors are devices that automatically insert loss in the return path of a four-wire circuit. The echo suppressor switches back and forth between the two transmission paths following first one talker then the other. Properly adjusted, an echo suppressor inserts only enough loss in the circuit to allow the listener to interrupt the talker, but otherwise attenuates the reflected signal by approximately 15 dB. Long circuits such as satellite circuits with round trip delays of about 0.5 second require a more effective method of eliminating echo. On such circuits, echo cancelers are used. Echo cancelers perform the same function as echo suppressors but operate by creating a replica of the near-end signal and subtracting it from the echo to cancel the echo.

Circuit loss is adjusted in shorter circuits to control echo. The whole subject of loss and echo control is embodied in the *via net loss plan*, which is a set of design rules that optimize transmission performance and economics in an analog telecommunications network. The advent of modern digital transmission and switching facilities has caused the loss plan to evolve toward a fixed loss plan that integrates zero loss digital transmission facilities and digital echo cancelers into the network. The via net loss plan is discussed in a later section.

Amplitude Distortion

Telecommunications channels rarely have a perfectly flat response across the voice frequency band. Figure 2.3a shows an equalized channel; Figure 2.3b shows the frequency response characteristic of a channel before equalization. Although equipment used in voice frequency channels is manufactured to close tolerances, the accumulated small deviations inherent in the manufacturing process produce the irregular response illus-

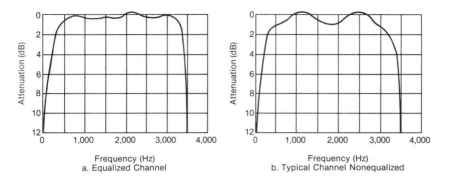

Figure 2.3   Voice channel attenuation.

trated. The channels can be brought into close tolerance by adding equalizers where the demands of the service justify the extra cost.

Envelope Delay Distortion

The design of electronic amplifiers and multiplexers requires components that introduce varying amounts of delay to frequencies within the voice frequency pass band. This varying delay is known as *envelope delay*. Envelope delay has no discernible effect on voice frequency signals, but for data signals, which are composed of complex voice frequency tones, envelope delay results in tones arriving at the receiver slightly out of phase with one another. So high speed modems, which use phase characteristics to encode the data signal, may not operate properly. Envelope delay distortion can be compensated by the addition of delay equalizers either in the telecommunications circuit or in the data terminal equipment.

Elements of Transmission Design

Transmission design is the process of balancing loss, noise, and echo against circuit costs. The fourth variable, bandwidth, is not adjustable; it is inherent in the design of amplifiers and multiplex equipment. The remainder of this chapter discusses transmission from the point of view of the quality requirements of voice frequency circuits. Data circuits traveling over the switched telephone network must accept the characteristics of the circuits as they are, but as the network evolves toward all-digital, it is increasingly congenial toward data. On analog private line data circuits, transmission can be controlled more closely by *conditioning*, which Chapter 25 discusses.

Telecommunications circuits are either switched or dedicated; that is, the user dials the connection and releases it on call termination, or the circuit is permanently connected between two or more points. The characteristics of dedicated or private line circuits can be specifically designed for the application, but because of the random originations and terminations and the variation of the characteristics of switched circuits, design control is less exact. Switched circuit design is a compromise based on the probability of the user's receiving a connection that is of satisfactory quality a high percentage of the time.

Each switched connection is composed of three types of circuits: a subscriber loop on each end, a toll-to-local office connecting trunk (interLATA connecting trunk) on each end, and one or more inter-office trunks (intertoll trunks) between. These types of circuits are designed using different rules. Each circuit type is allocated a share of the end-to-end impairment, with the objective of providing a total connection of satisfactory quality to the user.

Variables in Transmission Quality

In the preceding sections, we introduced several terms that are essential to understanding transmission quality. In this section, we introduce additional terminology and discuss the methods of measuring and controlling transmission quality.

It is important to remember the difference between loss and level in a circuit. Level is a measurement of signal power at a specified point in the circuit known as a *transmission level point* (TLP). Loss is the difference in level between TLPs. A voice frequency signal is a complex amalgam of tones that vary widely in frequency and amplitude. Broadcast engineers often measure such a complex signal as *volume units* (VU) using a meter with a highly damped movement to smooth out the peaks and valleys of

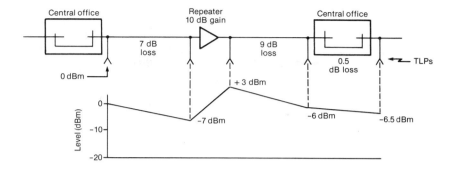

Figure 2.4   Transmission levels and transmission level points.

the voice signal. Other than the dynamic characteristics, a VU meter is the same as a dB meter.

A voice frequency signal is impractical for measuring level and making adjustments to circuits, in which level is adjusted in 0.1 dB increments. Level is measured by applying a 1004 Hz single frequency tone to the circuit at a standard TLP and then measuring the test tone at another TLP. The measured tone is then compared to a standard one milliwatt (0.001 watt) test source to establish a test tone level. Most transmission testing equipment is calibrated against a one milliwatt source so that measurements can be made directly with the test set. The test tone frequency is set at 1004 Hz because a frequency of 1000 Hz is an exact submultiple of many carrier frequencies used in multichannel carrier systems. These tones may interact with carriers to produce confusing effects on the measurements made at the distant end of the circuit. Figure 2.4 illustrates the concept of TLPs, loss, and gain.

Transmission Level Points

Several measurement points in circuits are traditionally set at a specified level. For example, the output of a switch is considered a 0 TLP. This does not, however, mean that signals leave the switch at 0 dBm; usually they are less. For example, if a 0 dBm signal is inserted at the end of a subscriber loop that has 5 dB of loss and if the switch inserts an additional 0.5 dB of loss, the output measurement at the 0 TLP will be -5.5 dBm.

Carrier channels are normally designed with TLPs of -16 dBm into the transmitting port and +7 dBm out of the receiver. Thus, a carrier system introduces into the circuit 23 dB of gain that can be used to overcome other circuit losses. If this is more gain than needed, it is adjusted with fixed loss attenuators, which are known as *pads*.

Insertion Loss

Circuit design is simplified by treating certain elements as black boxes with identifiable loss characteristics. For example, when a connection traverses a switching machine, it is generally assumed to have a 0.5 dB loss. Some PBXs have a loss of as much as 6 dB between lines. Circuit designers call this *insertion loss,* or *inserted connection loss* (ICL). Insertion losses are additive. If two trunks, each with 5 dB of loss, are connected into a circuit, they will introduce 10 dB of loss into the connection.

Reference Noise

Noise is measured with respect to an arbitrary reference noise (rn) level of -90 dBm. This level, defined as 0 dBrn, is at the threshold of audibility. As mentioned earlier, not only the level, but also the frequency of noise determines its interfering effects. If noise is evenly distributed across a voice frequency band (called white noise), the noise in the 500 Hz to 2500 Hz range will be more annoying to the listener than low and high frequency noise because both the ear and the telephone are more sensitive to these middle frequencies. Therefore, noise is measured through a *C message weighting* filter. This weighting, shown in Figure 2.5, passes noise in roughly the same proportion as the sensitivity of the human ear. The interfering effect of noise on voice communication is usually expressed as dBrnc, with the c indicating the use of a C message weighting filter. When noise is measured at a 0 TLP or mathematically adjusted to a 0 TLP, it is expressed as dBrnc0. Special service circuits, such as data and broadcast audio, do not have the same tolerance for high and low frequency noise. Therefore, they are measured without the C message weighting filter.

A noise measurement is a measure of the noise power in a connection and is not directly additive in the same way as loss.

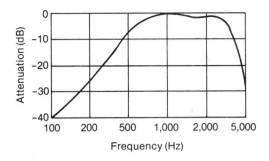

Figure 2.5   C message weighting response curve.

Doubling the noise power in a circuit increases the noise by 3 dB. If two circuits, each with 20 dBrn of noise, are connected in tandem, the result will be a noise level of 23 dBrn.

Echo Return Loss

As mentioned previously, listeners are most sensitive to interference in the frequency spectrum between about 250 Hz and 2500 Hz. Measuring a circuit's return loss in that band produces a value called *echo return loss*. The measurement is made by transmitting a band of white noise limited by filters to 250 Hz to 2500 Hz, and measuring the returned noise energy. A useful companion measurement is the *singing point* in which an amplifier is inserted into the circuit to increase the gain to the point at which the circuit just begins to oscillate, or sing. The circuit sings at the frequency at which it has the poorest return loss. Measurements of echo return loss, singing loss, and singing frequency are important indicators of circuit performance.

Subscriber Loop Transmission

Of the circuit elements, subscriber loop transmission is the most difficult to control because of the varying distance of users from the telephone central office and the varying composition of the circuits that serve them. Subscriber loop losses vary from 0 dB (some are inside the telephone central office) to as much as 8 or 10 dB. It is technically possible to design all subscriber loops to some target figure, say 5 dB. This could be done by inserting resistance networks (pads) into shorter loops and amplifiers into loops with more than 5 dB of loss. With so many subscriber loops, however, the cost of designing them all to a fixed loss is prohibitive while the network remains analog. With an all-digital network, fixed loss loops will become a reality.

Loop Loss

Designers select cable gauge and loop length with the objective of allowing at least 23 milliamps of current to flow in the combination of the telephone set, cable circuit, and central office battery feed circuitry. Of these elements, the loss of the cable is the most variable because its resistance varies with the wire gauge and the length of the loop. Cables are built to design objectives that typically result in circuits of 8 dB of loss or less. Except for those few that are derived on multiplex equipment, subscriber loops are connected to the central office with twisted pair cable. Loop design balances cost against transmission quality. To the greatest extent possible, fine gauge cable is used because its cost is lower and its smaller diameter fits into conduit more readily. Most loops leave the central office in cables composed of 26 gauge wire. This provides adequate transmission to about 15,000 feet from the central office. The effects of loss in longer loops are overcome by using coarser gauge cable—24 gauge, 22 gauge, and, rarely, 19 gauge.

The frequency response of cable is reasonably linear. Cable loss is a composite of resistance and capacitance loss. Cable pairs, acting like large capacitors, attenuate the high more than the low frequencies. The effects of high frequency loss are overcome in loops more than 18,000 feet long by using inductance coils in series with the conductors. This technique, known as *loading*, improves the loss of the loop at the expense of frequencies above 4 KHz, which the load coils attenuate. Figure 2.6 shows the frequency response of loaded and nonloaded cable pairs. While loading improves the voice frequency characteristics of cable, it precludes the use of limited distance modems on the circuit. These modems, which are discussed in Chapter 3, are inexpensive devices that permit data transmission at 19.2 kb/s.

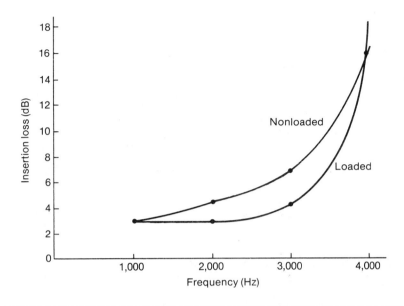

Figure 2.6   Loss-frequency response of 10,000 feet of 26-gauge cable.

Shielding

Properly constructed loops are enclosed in shielded cables and are not greatly affected by external noise. Many loops in the United States are built jointly with electric power transmission lines, which are a potential source of noise. Continuity of the metallic shield that surrounds cable pairs must be strictly maintained if noise influence is to be minimized. Failure to attend to shielding and balance, described in the next section, accounts for most noise problems in telephone circuits.

Balance

Induction, by itself, is not necessarily detrimental to telephone circuits. In rural areas, unshielded open wires often share pole lines with electric power circuits without interference. The degree of interference depends on the *balance* of the telephone circuit. In a balanced environment, each wire in the cable has the same amount of exposure to interference; interference induced in one wire of the pair is cancelled by the interference induced in the second wire. As Figure 2.7a shows, when the two wires of a cable

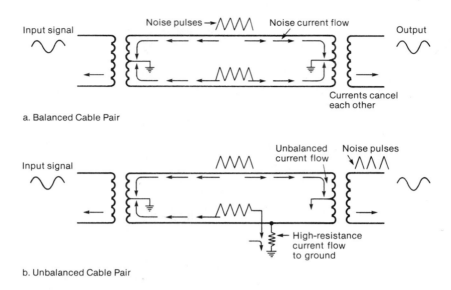

Figure 2.7   Noise current flow in a cable.

pair are identically balanced in resistance and isolation from ground, induced voltages are equal when measured from each side of the pair to ground. Telephone sets and amplifiers, which detect voltages across the two wires of a pair, are insensitive to these balanced voltages, but any imbalance results in noise in the output circuit as Figure 2.7b shows. Chapter 6 describes how cable balance is controlled. For now it is necessary only to understand its effects. Noise on most subscriber loops should be in the order of 5 or 10 dBrnc0. When the noise exceeds 20 dBrnc0, corrective action is usually required.

Loops exist in a hostile environment. They are exposed to weather, flooded manholes, icing, winds, disruptions by excavation; the hazards are many and difficult to avoid. Therefore, this portion of a connection exhibits the greatest variability in transmission performance. Bandwidth, envelope delay, and amplitude distortion are less affected by the hazards that confront subscriber loops, but the variability of subscriber loops greatly affects loss and noise.

InterLATA Connecting Trunks

Trunks connecting an IEC's switching office to an LEC's end office are called *interLATA connecting trunks*. These trunks connect directly from the IEC's point of presence to the LEC's end office, or they connect through an access tandem. InterLATA connecting trunks are the circuits that connect the user to an IEC's operator and to recording and billing equipment for directly dialed calls, and that terminate calls from a distant IEC's switching office to the local central office. Some of these trunks are connected over voice frequency cable circuits, but the majority are digital carrier. In any event, these trunks almost invariably have adjustable gain, and loss, therefore, can be controlled within close limits. The design objectives for interLATA connecting trunks as prescribed by *Notes on the BOC Intra-LATA Networks—1986* range from 3.0 dB for digital trunks to 4.0 dB for analog trunks without gain.

Noise on interLATA connecting trunks is also controllable. Trunks connected over analog carrier facilities are subject to thermal and intermodulation noise. Voice frequency trunks are subject to the same external interfering effects as subscriber loops, although their cables are usually installed in a less hostile environment and are more carefully balanced.

All such trunks are subject to interference from within the telephone central office. In electromechanical central offices, relays and switches are a source of interference that affects all types of trunks. This interference usually takes the form of impulse noise, which has short spikes of noise that have little effect on voice communication, but are a serious source of errors in data transmission.

Intertoll Trunks

Intertoll trunks are circuits that interconnect IEC switching offices. These trunks are, with rare exception, deployed over carrier facilities where the loss and gain are controllable, and the causes of noise found in cables are of small concern.

Intertoll circuits are designed with loss according to via net loss design rules to aid in controlling the interfering effects of echo. Analog intertoll trunks, which are rapidly disappearing, operate with a variable amount of loss determined by via net loss rules and are tested with 2 dB pads in each end to optimize the signal level with respect to the TLPs. Similarly, digital trunks operate at zero loss and are tested with 3 dB pads in the receiving path at each end to provide consistency with the analog environment. When analog circuits are connected in tandem to build up a long circuit, the overall connection of intertoll trunks operates at via net loss. Similarly, digital circuits operate at zero loss when connected in tandem.

Via Net Loss

The variable component in trunk design is determined by a factor known as the via net loss factor (VNLF) of the circuit. A VNLF of 0.0015 dB per mile is used for analog terrestrial carrier circuits; for example, a circuit 1000 miles long would require 1.5 dB of loss. In practice, designers add somewhat more loss than this for administrative reasons. The amount is unimportant for this discussion.

The IECs administer intertoll circuit loss. Private network users who obtain circuits from a carrier are provided with circuits with a net loss that the carrier designs and controls.

The net loss of circuits is subject to variation because of maintenance actions, component aging, and equipment troubles. Statistically, the variations between circuits should compensate for one another. However, because of the random nature of connections through the switching network, it is possible for some connections to be established with either so much loss that it is difficult to hear or so little that the circuit sounds hollow or, in the worst case, oscillates or sings.

Noise Sources

Intertoll circuits are susceptible to the same noise sources as interLATA connecting trunks. A primary advantage of lightwave circuits is that, because the signals are digital and are regenerated at every repeater point, noise is not a problem. The noise levels of long haul digital circuits are not appreciably higher than those of local digital circuits, and as a result, cross-country circuit quality has improved dramatically as the IECs have shifted their circuits from the older microwave radio and coaxial cable to lightwave.

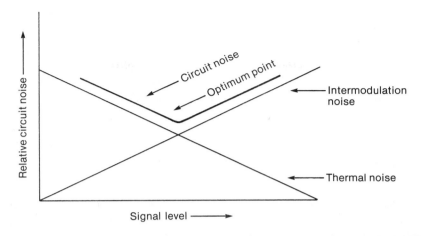

Figure 2.8   Effects of thermal and intermodulation noise on circuit noise.

Some analog circuits remain, however, and the analog microwave and the multiplex equipment used on microwave and coaxial cable is subject to intermodulation noise. As mentioned earlier, both thermal noise and intermodulation noise are present in electronic communications systems. The overall noise effect on a circuit is the sum of both types of noise. The effect of noise is optimized by adjusting the operating level of the signal applied to the circuit. When the signal level is very low, the thermal noise becomes controlling, and when the signal level is high, a high level of intermodulation noise is apparent. As Figure 2.8 shows, there is an optimum operating level for the signals where the noise from both sources is at a minimum.

Microwave radio systems are also susceptible to other noise sources, particularly noise in the first receiver amplifier stages. This noise becomes perceptible when the received radio signal fades. As the received signal falls, it approaches the noise level generated in the front end of the receiver. This noise is then amplified with the desired signal and appears as a deteriorated signal-to-noise ratio. Microwave systems are usually equipped with standby transmitters and receivers that can take over when the regular channel fades or fails. Chapter 14 discusses protection, or diversity, more fully.

Echo Control

Echo is an important variable in intertoll network design. As previously mentioned, echo of short time delay is controlled by introducing a small amount of loss proportional to the delay of the circuit. Beyond a delay in the order of 10 to 20 milliseconds, however, the loss begins to be too great for satisfactory transmission, and echo suppressors or cancelers must be inserted in the circuit.

Local Interoffice Trunks

In a metropolitan network composed of more than one central office, the end or local central offices are linked by local interoffice trunks. These trunks are normally designed to a nominal loss of 3 dB, but the loss may be as high as 5 dB. They are used for calls within a local calling area and are not used for access to interexchange facilities. Therefore, loss and noise are less critical than in interLATA connecting trunks, and echo is of no consequence. Balance is still important because a poor return loss results in hollowness or singing. The facilities and equipment used in interoffice trunks are identical with equipment used in interLATA connecting trunks, and the same loss and noise considerations apply.

Special Purpose Trunks

LECs and IECs use a variety of trunks for special applications. Examples are directory assistance, intercept (used for recorded announcements and operator transfer of disconnected numbers), repair service, and verification (used by operators to verify busy/idle status of lines). The design of these trunks is wholly within the purview of the LEC and is of little concern to the user. *Notes on the BOC Intra-LATA Networks—1986* covers these design variables in detail.

Private networks may employ special purpose trunks for a variety of applications. Examples are PBX tie lines, WATS lines, 800 (INWATS) lines, point-to-point voice and data, broadcast audio, wired music, and telemetering. These circuits are deployed over private facilities within the user's premises, over private or common carrier facilities in a metropolitan area, or over leased or common carrier facilities world-wide. Satisfactory transmission quality is obtained only by careful design of these circuits. Common carriers usually offer design assistance. However, the common carrier often lacks knowledge of the total makeup of a circuit and cannot control transmission variables. It is, therefore, essential that all users of special services understand the effects of transmission design on the systems they are purchasing.

Loss and Noise Grade of Service

Transmission measurements can be made with precision, and with modern equipment a high degree of level stability and noise performance is achievable. This does not answer the question of how good a circuit must be to satisfy its users because telephone connections are subjectively evaluated. A person who is hard-of-hearing finds perfectly satisfactory a connection that others complain is too loud and is dissatisfied with circuits that others find acceptable. Clearly, transmission quality must be evaluated against a widely varying base of opinion.

Transmission objectives are based on the results of many opinion samples measured by Bell Laboratories. In these tests, varying amounts of loss and noise were introduced into connections and users rated the quality. The result of these samples is a family of loss/noise grade of service curves. These opinion curves are translated into design and maintenance objectives for both loss and noise. Figure 2.9 is a set of curves that show the rating assigned by users to connections with varying combinations of loss and noise. Note the relationship between loss and noise. Generally, more noise is tolerable if accompanied by less loss, and more loss is acceptable if the noise level is low.

Designers assure transmission quality by controlling three elements:

- Circuit design.
- Circuit maintenance.
- Overall connection evaluation.

In circuit design, loss is the only adjustable characteristic. The other variables, principally noise and echo, are functions of how well telecommunications circuits and equipment are designed and maintained. It is unrealistic to expect equipment design and maintenance to overcome the effects of poor circuit design.

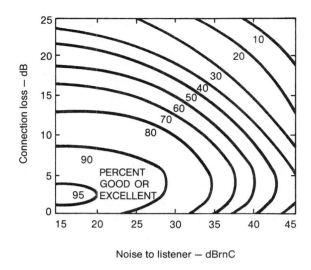

Figure 2.9   Loss-noise grade-of-service curves.

Circuits with excessive loss will produce connections with excessive noise. Circuits with too little loss will result in singing, increases in intermodulation noise, and complaints from users of excessive level or hollowness.

Conversely, properly designed circuits cannot be expected to provide satisfactory transmission service when equipment is not maintained to high standards. The nation's telecommunications networks are composed of equipment ranging from new to more than 40 years old. Although most new equipment provides excellent transmission performance with minimum maintenance, regular testing is required to ensure satisfactory performance.

Equipment and circuit maintenance are not enough to ensure that most connections will be satisfactory to the user. In both public and private networks, a regular sampling program of end-to-end connection quality is an important quality assurance technique. By making repeated loss and noise measurements to terminating locations resembling the calling patterns of the users, irregularities can be detected before they result in user complaints.

Transmission Measurements

Transmission quality assurance requires systematic measurement with accurately calibrated test equipment. This section describes transmission measurement techniques and equipment.

Loss Measurements

Loss is measured with a transmission measuring set (TMS) that has a tone generator, or oscillator, and a level detector with a meter or digital readout. Many TMSs also include noise measuring apparatus. A TMS measures level at specified TLPs and at impedances that match the impedance of the TLP. Loss is nominally specified at 1000 Hz. In practice, measurements are made at 1004 Hz to prevent interference with digital carrier equipment.

Measurements are made by sending a single tone into the circuit at a transmitting TLP and measuring the level at a receiving TLP. Levels are adjusted by either changing physical pads or setting software pads so the design loss is achieved within specified limits. A TMS can also measure the equalization of a circuit by sending and receiving a band of frequencies instead of a single tone.

Most common carrier and many private networks are equipped to make automatic transmission measurements on circuits. Both the transmitting and receiving ends have testing systems that automatically send and measure test tones in both directions. Equipment at the far end, known as a *responder*, records measurements from the near end and reports the results over a data circuit. Most automatic test equipment also measures noise and tests signaling.

Noise Measurements

Noise is measured with a noise measuring set that can be either a separate instrument or part of a TMS. Noise measurements are made at a TLP with the far end terminated in its characteristic impedance. If the circuit is used for voice communication, measurements are made through a C message filter. If the TLP is not a 0 level point, noise measurements are adjusted to 0 and expressed as dBrnc0. For example, if noise measures 27 dbrnc at a

+7 TLP, the 7 dB gain would be subtracted and the circuit noise expressed as 20 dBrnc0.

Return Loss Measurements

Return loss measurements are made by sending a signal into the input port of a four-wire terminating set and measuring the signal returned to the output port. If a 1 KHz tone is used for the test signal, the resulting measurement may not reveal the worst-case return loss, because the hybrid balance is never uniform across the voice frequency spectrum. To find the degree of hybrid balance in a working circuit it is necessary to measure return loss at enough frequencies across the voice band to permit plotting a return loss curve that shows the worst-case frequency.

To simplify testing, a white noise source in the band of 250 Hz to 2500 Hz is used as a test signal. Typical return loss measuring instruments are equipped with a white noise source, band limiting filters, and high and low pass filters so return loss measurements can be made over the entire voice frequency band.

Envelope Delay Measurements

Envelope delay measurements are made with test sets that send a pair of closely spaced frequencies from the sending end of the circuit to a synchronized test set at the receiving end. The combination measures directly the relative delay of signal frequencies at various points within the circuit pass band. The ideal circuit would display linear delay across the pass band so that all components would be transmitted in a perfect phase relationship.

Applications

A satisfactory transmission grade of service must be designed into every common carrier and private network. This chapter has discussed transmission in only the broadest terms to give the reader an understanding of the importance and principles of transmission quality control. In public networks, transmission design is under the control of the company supplying the service. When only one network existed in the United States, AT&T and its subsidiaries controlled transmission design. The independent companies connected to the network designed their circuits to the same objectives, so the network could be considered a single entity. Private networks were composed primarily of circuits obtained from telephone companies and were also designed to AT&T-specified standards and objectives.

Today, the nation's telecommunications system is composed of a multitude of networks designed and controlled by the seven RBHCs, the independent telephone companies within their territories, and many IECs of which AT&T, although the dominant carrier, is only one. Although the networks of AT&T and its ex-affiliates are not significantly changed from their pre-divestiture designs, the shape of the remaining network is changing. Each IEC sets its own transmission objectives, and the quality is therefore not necessarily uniform.

Users need to be aware that the facilities offered by the carrier of their choice may offer different grades of service. This is not to imply that the service will be unsatisfactory. The nature of today's network is to provide choices at different cost levels, and for some applications, lower transmission quality may be acceptable. It is important to evaluate quality and to understand the implications of the different alternatives.

The most important implication of the multiple networks of the kind we have in the United States today is that the vendor may not assume responsibility for end-to-end circuit performance. If the user has telephone sets made by one vendor, cable by another, a PBX by a third vendor, connected by circuits provided by a LEC and one or more IECs, it may be difficult to find which vendor is at fault when transmission quality is impaired. This makes it imperative to develop a network transmission design before procuring equipment and circuits.

The design of a telecommunications network must include performance specifications for each element. For example, in designing a PBX tie trunk to a particular net loss, it is important to know how much of each impairment to assign to the loops, the PBXs, the interexchange access lines, and the long haul trunks provided by the IEC. If calculations are made in advance and each vendor agrees to provide equipment and services that meet these specifications, offending circuit elements can be readily identified.

Designers should not assume that shortcomings in one part of a circuit can be compensated for in another part. For example, if the interexchange trunk has excessive loss, it cannot be made up by amplifiers at the station. To do so would likely result in noise in the receiving direction and excessive output level in the transmitting direction. Excessive output causes crosstalk and distortion.

Standards

Transmission standards are derived from a variety of experiments and studies performed by AT&T and CCITT. In the United States, suppliers of telecommunications circuits and services are free to design their networks to whatever criteria they choose. Users should be alert to differences in transmission quality and may wish use CCITT recommendations as references in comparing alternative sources.

Transmission Traps for the Unwary

This section presents examples of some common causes of unsatisfactory transmission in private networks. We do not attempt to describe all the traps that can occur; the purpose is to show that users must be alert to avoid telecommunications services that provide unsatisfactory results.

Add-On Conferencing

Local loops are designed to a maximum loss of 8 dB to 10 dB. With these losses, most connections will be satisfactory, depending on the talker's volume, circuit noise, and room noise. Many PBXs and key telephone systems allow multiparty conferencing by directly connecting lines together. When two lines are tied together, the received signal power divides equally between them. This introduces 3 dB of loss, turning a loop with 8 dB of loss into one with 11 dB of loss. Depending on the loop loss, the number of stations tied together, and the loss of the circuits connecting them, this form of conferencing may be satisfactory; however, the results are not dependable because of the variability in the end-to-end circuit loss.

The most reliable, although more expensive, way to handle multiport conferencing is through special apparatus known as *conference bridges.* These devices are mounted in the LEC's central office where they can be dialed up, or on the user's premises where they can be connected by dialing or by a PBX operator. Bridges insert gain into the legs of the conference circuit and ensure that circuits are properly terminated so that gain can be regulated without hollowness or singing.

High Loss PBX Switching Networks

Modern digital PBXs use four-wire switching networks. In contrast to older two-wire electromechanical PBXs, these machines have hybrids in all line interface circuits. To reduce costs, the hybrids often insert 2 dB of loss in each line circuit, so on line-to-line connections, the loss across the switching network is 4 dB. Trunk hybrids are usually zero loss, so the line-to-trunk loss is 2 dB. For connections within most offices, the amount of cross-PBX loss is inconsequential. Several special situations can, however, result in transmission problems.

The first case involves a PBX with many off-premises lines. If lines to these distant stations have, say, 5 dB of loss, users in that location will experience 14 dB of line-to-line loss (two 5 dB loops plus 4 dB switching loss). This loss is tolerable to most talkers, provided the room and circuit noise are not too high. With high noise, these connections are apt to be the source of complaints. Calls from long subscriber loops (up to 10 dB) connected to the PBX through a trunk that may have 5 dB of loss and out to an off-premises station (5 dB of loss plus 2 dB loss through the PBX) will encounter losses of up to 22 dB.

As Figure 2.9 shows, only half the users will rate such a connection as good at low noise levels. As noise increases, the degree of user satisfaction drops rapidly. It is important, in choosing a PBX that must serve many off-premises stations, to ensure that the PBX inserts a negligible amount of loss into an off-premises line port.

A contrast in volume is also a frequent source of complaint. Users at the off-premises location may find it difficult to understand why connections to phones in the main PBX location are better than to phones in the next room.

When the PBX includes WATS lines or tie trunks to a distant machine, the extra loss from the PBX may result in complaints. Such trunks are designed to a net loss of about 5 dB. The quality of the connection depends on noise and other losses in the circuit. When long loops are present in both ends of the connection, loss is likely to be excessive. When add-on conferencing is used with these trunk calls, transmission is almost certain to be poor.

The electronic hybrids used in some PBXs are also a source of noise. In a noisy environment, room noise feeds into the telephone transmitter and is amplified in the hybrid. The circuit noise is therefore increased by the room noise.

The solution to PBX transmission problems is careful evaluation of the system before purchase. The PBX should be evaluated in an environment similar to that in which it will be used. Transmission calculations should be made on all worst-case combinations of line and trunk connections. When services are procured from interexchange carriers and the local telephone company, the companies' transmission specifications should be obtained. Sometimes it may be necessary to purchase a higher grade of service to obtain satisfactory transmission. In other cases it may be necessary to make regular end-to-end loss and noise measurements to ensure that circuit elements are meeting their specifications. Sometimes it is necessary to insert variable gain amplifiers into the connection. These devices vary the amount of gain based on the signal level.

Improved Transmission Performance Charges

Before divestiture, LECs were responsible for total transmission performance and designed their circuits accordingly. Residence and business classes of service were nominally designed to have a maximum loop loss of 8.0 dB to 8.5 dB. PBX trunks, Centrex lines, off-premises extensions, and other special services were designed to a loss of 3.0 dB to 5.0 dB. In most LECs, if the loss exceeded the maximum allowable threshold, amplification was added to reduce the loss to the lowest practical limit—generally approximately 3.0 dB.

After divestiture, several LECs changed their tariffs to levy an additional charge for "improved transmission performance." The old objective of 8.0 dB to 8.5 dB loss for residence and business lines was left intact and applied to all classes of service. Customers, including PBX customers whose circuits formerly were designed to no more than 5.0 dB of loss, were guaranteed loops that did not exceed 8.5 dB; if lower loss was required, the customer paid an extra charge.

With the responsibility for transmission performance put on the shoulders of the user, it is important that telecommunications managers understand the alternatives. First, it is not necessary to pay the improved transmission performance charge to the LEC; gain devices can be installed at the customer's premises—usually with equally good results. Determine from the LEC what the expected transmission loss will be without gain devices and consider adding enough gain to reduce the circuit loss to 3.0 dB to 5.0 dB.

A second option is to live with the loss as designed. If a PBX has no off-premises extensions and uses T-1 carrier for the connection to the IEC, the chances are excellent that a loss of up to 8.5 dB will not be objectionable. Determine what the line-to-trunk loss of the switch is. If it is or can be adjusted to zero loss, the overall loss probably will not be objectionable. If a few off-premises extensions are connected to the PBX, they may experience poor transmission without gain devices on the trunks. If there are fewer off-premises extensions than trunks, voice regulating repeaters can be added to the extensions. Refer to Chapter 18 for a description of network channel terminating equipment (NCTE).

The third option applies to PBXs that are far enough from the central office that they are beyond the 8.5 dB limit. In some LECs, circuits that existed before divestiture are charged for improved transmission performance even though the circuit loss would exceed the limit without it. It should be possible to have the charge for improved transmission performance removed while retaining the equipment because it is necessary to meet the LEC's standards.

It is important to understand that loss is only one of several criteria affecting subscriber loop performance. Loop current is an even more important consideration, because with insufficient current, PBXs and DTMF dials will not work. Refer to Chapter 31 for a discussion of loop current calculations.

Satellite Services

Geostationary satellites orbit the earth at an altitude of 22,300 miles. Although the cost of satellite circuits may often be less than the cost of terrestrial circuits, the 0.25 second path delay of a satellite circuit makes it unsatisfactory for certain types of communication. Voice communication users usually become accustomed to the delay and are not adversely affected by it, but many data protocols will not function over a satellite. Sometimes, two satellite connections may be required. Most users find that amount of delay intolerable for normal conversations.

Voice Compression Circuits

With the arrival of inexpensive voice compression equipment, more private circuits are being implemented over circuits that may cause transmission impairments. First, there is a limit to the number of times a circuit can be converted between analog and digital. With pulse code modulation (see Chapter 4) as many as seven analog-to-digital conversions may be made without affecting voice transmission. Manufacturers use several proprietary methods to compress voice into much narrower bandwidths than the 64 kb/s bandwidth of PCM, however. The narrower the bandwidth, the less natural the connection will sound, and connecting several highly compressed circuits in tandem may make them unsatisfactory for voice transmission. Telecommunications managers should be aware that most compressed voice algorithms can transmit facsimile or data only at speeds of 4800 b/s or less.

Off-Premises Extension Network

The experience of a rural school district illustrates the transmission problems that can occur with off-premises extensions. The district originally had Centrex service, in which the local loops were designed to have a maximum loss of 5.0 dB, even for the longest loops, which were some eight miles long. Residence lines in the same area were designed to have a maximum loss of 8.5 dB. A call from a residence to the neighboring school would have a maximum loss, therefore, of 13.5 dB, which is generally acceptable.

The school installed a new PBX and served the elementary schools over off-premises extensions, which the LEC designed to

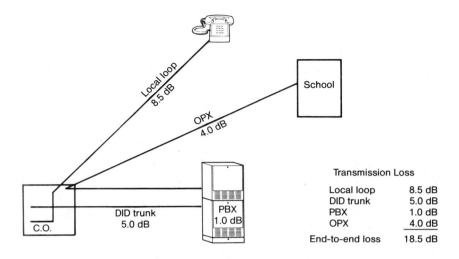

Figure 2.10   Transmission problems with off-premise equipment.

have a maximum loss of 4.0 dB. As shown in Figure 2.10, however, a call placed from a residence to the school encountered the loop loss of 8.5 dB, a DID trunk of 4.0 dB, an off-premises extension of 4.0 dB, and the loss of the PBX and wiring, which averaged 1.0 dB. Altogether, the loss of the call was now at least 17.5 dB and the result was complaints from parents, who had difficulty in calling the school, although it was only a short distance away. Calls from within the PBX or from other schools were satisfactory.

The school district solved the problem by installing gain-regulating repeaters on the off-premises lines at the PBX. These repeaters, which sense the volume of the talker's voice, automatically insert gain or loss to regulate volume on the service.

3

Data Communications Systems

Data communication began with Samuel F. B. Morse's invention of the telegraph in 1844. For nearly 40 years, the telegraph was our sole means of electromechanical communication. It demanded a skill, however, that was not widely possessed, so the telegraph remained simply a message delivery system, not a system designed for personal use. The telephone, on the other hand, matched the public's communication needs and, except where the sender needed a record of the message, the telephone superseded the telegraph as the preferred means of communication.

Now, the pendulum is swinging the other direction. No one knows, or particularly cares, what portion of the nation's telecommunication resources are used for data communication as opposed to voice. As the network evolves toward all-digital, the issue becomes irrelevant because the two forms are indistinguishable from each other except by terminal equipment that is programmed to decode the signals.

Several factors caused the current explosion in data communication, the most important being the dramatic drop in computer prices. Applications that formerly required expensive mainframe computers can now be processed on microcomputers, bringing computing power closer to the end user. As the white collar work force increasingly turns to computers for help, the demand for computing resources has burgeoned, and this demand has in turn spawned a need for shared data bases that are accessed over telecommunications facilities.

Meanwhile, we are left with a network that is part analog and part digital, and the issue of how best to carry out data communication remains very much alive. Data is far more complex than voice and is likely to remain so for several reasons. First, data demands a precision that is totally unnecessary in voice communication. There is so much redundancy in a voice session that a few audible noise bursts on an analog circuit or thousands of missing bits in a digital circuit have little effect on the intelligibility of the message. Besides, if the message is garbled, the receiving party simply asks the sender to repeat, and both parties are satisfied, unless the noise is excessive, in which case they hang up and try another circuit. With data, on the other hand, a single missing bit can cause a serious problem, and every effort is made to get error-free transmission.

The second difference is the lack of standards in data communications. The major computer manufactures have developed proprietary networking systems, and although progress is being made toward developing international standards, proprietary standards are still the order of the day.

The third difference lies in the nature of the network itself. Voice communication lends itself to circuit switching, in which the parties to a session are connected with a physical circuit that is exclusively theirs until the session ends, at which time the circuit returns to a pool. Some forms of data communications (facsimile, for example) are suited to circuit switching. Other forms, such as remote terminals connected to a host, are unsuited for any form of switching. For these applications, dedicated circuits are required. Other forms of data communication, such as multiple remote terminals feeding a single host, operate effectively under packet switching, which provides time-shared access to a network of dedicated circuits.

Telecommunications and the computer are partners in a marriage that is changing the way people store, access, and use information. The merger of the computer and telecommunications makes possible many new applications, including automatic teller machines, airline reservation systems, and credit card verification networks. The telephone network was designed and constructed for voice, however, which means that the computer, a digital device, must adapt to a network that is now partially analog and will remain so for the next few years. This chapter is concerned with data communications equipment and methods. Chapter 25 covers the methods of implementing private and public networks from such equipment. Chapter 27 and Chapter 28 cover local area data networks, which are privately owned networks that communicate over a narrow range.

Data Network Facilities

Facilities is the generic term used to describe the combination of local loops and long haul circuits that support communications. For data applications that require nearly full-time use of a channel between fixed points, *dedicated*, or *private line*, facilities are the most economical. Many applications, however, require switching because they transmit data between multiple points or send only a few short messages each day.

The variety of data communications applications means that no single facility type is universally suitable. For example, the following types of applications illustrate the need for a variety of facilities:

- *Automatic Teller Machines.* These devices are available in nearly all banks and in many public locations such as shopping centers and airports. They demand near-perfect transmission, high security, and rapid response. The transactions are short, and even a heavily used machine makes use of only a fraction of the data-carrying capacity of a circuit.

- *Credit Card Verification.* Nearly every retail establishment has a credit card machine, and many of these verify each transaction. The applications vary from large department stores with dozens of terminals to small, remote stores with a single, seldom-used terminal. For the former a high speed dedicated line is needed; for the latter a dial-up line is more cost-effective.

- *Single Host Supporting Multilocation Terminals.* This application is typical of many large businesses, such as airlines, banks, and order bureaus, that use a mainframe computer linked to terminals over wide area networks.

Since input is from a keyboard, the data rate is limited to typing speed, yet near-instantaneous communication is required. This application needs a network of shared lines to reduce circuit costs.

- *Point-of-Sale Terminals.* Large department stores with multiple locations are typical of this application. Data is transmitted at high speed, but each terminal is used only a fraction of the time. High security and near-perfect accuracy are essential.

- *Electronic Mail.* Several nationwide carriers such as CompuServe, AT&T, and MCI offer electronic mail services to the public. The messages can originate from and be retrieved from any residence or business in the nation. The dial-up telephone network is the most practical facility to support this kind of application.

Private line networks can be constructed over all-digital facilities, but for the next decade most switched data communications will be handled over analog voice facilities. Many applications do not use the full capacity of a circuit, so the only economical way they can be implemented is by sharing the capacity of the circuit. Generally, the facilities they share can be classed as one of five types: point-to-point, multidrop, circuit switched, message switched, or packet switched.

Point-to-Point Circuits

A *point-to-point* circuit, shown in Figure 3.1, is directly wired between the stations on the network. Point-to-point circuits are cost-effective for high speed communications between two processors but are expensive for most keyboard applications. For slower or keyboard-driven applications, the circuit capacity can be shared by subdividing it with a *multiplexer*, which is discussed later.

Low speed point-to-point *voice grade* circuits are known in the industry as 3002 circuits, following the nomenclature used in the AT&T and LEC tariffs. Voice grade circuits can carry data from the slowest speed up to 19.2 kb/s. With data compression, even greater speeds can be carried. Digital circuits can carry data at 2.4, 4.8, 9.6, 19.2, 56, and 64 kb/s. Digital circuits are not technically

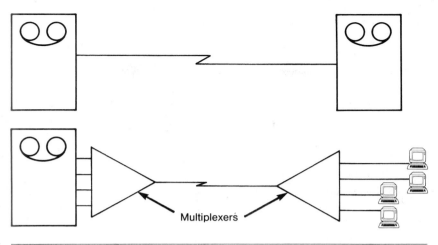

Multiplexers

Figure 3.1   A point-to-point circuit.

voice grade, but they can be used to carry either voice or data as discussed in Chapter 4.

Multidrop Circuits

The simplest point-to-point circuits connect directly between two stations that share exclusive access to the circuit. More complex configurations are multidrop circuits such as that shown in Figure 3.2, in which a station can transmit only when polled. The host computer or an attached unit called a front end processor does the polling. The processor sends a polling message to each station in turn. If the station has traffic, it sends it. Otherwise, it responds negatively. The central unit also sends output messages to the remote stations.

The intelligence to respond to polling messages is sometimes built directly into the terminal. In other configurations the terminals connect through a controller. A polling system keeps circuits fully occupied. Much circuit time is consumed with polling messages and negative responses, however, and these messages, which are collectively known as *overhead*, do not contribute to information flow. In a widely distributed network, where no single station takes up more than a fraction of the circuit time, a multidrop circuit is an effective way of sharing capacity.

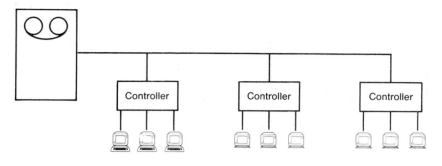

Figure 3.2   A polled multidrop circuit.

Circuit Switching

In a *circuit switched* network, a central switch is connected to stations in a star configuration as shown in Figure 3.3. Communication is between the stations and the switch, or the switch establishes circuits between two or more stations. The stations signal the switch to set up the connection, and when the stations have sent their traffic, they signal the switch to disconnect the circuit. The switch can be a data PBX, a voice/data PBX, or a telephone central office, all of which are discussed later in this book.

In circuit switched networks, the circuits to the stations (called *loops*) are not fully occupied. When the circuits are short, the cost of idle time is acceptable, but with long circuits costs may be excessive if usage is light. Utilization can be improved by using a hierarchical network. In a hierarchical network, the switch is placed close to the stations so the circuits can be short and less costly. The more costly long circuits between the switches (called *intermachine trunks*) are engineered for a higher occupancy rate.

Message Switching

Message switching networks are sometimes called *store-and-forward*. Stations home on a computer that accepts messages, stores them, and delivers them to their destination. The storage turnaround time can be either immediate for interactive applications, or the message may be delayed for forwarding when circuits are idle, rates are lower, or a busy device becomes available.

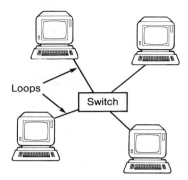

Single Node Network

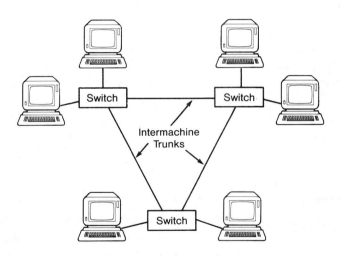

Multinode Hierarchial Network

Figure 3.3   A circuit switched network.

In its earliest form, message switching existed as a torn tape system. Teletypewriter messages were punched into paper tape by a perforator. The tape was torn at the end of the message and transmitted over another circuit, sometimes after being clipped to the wall and stored for a time. Magnetic storage media made paper tape systems obsolete, but the principle remains of receiving messages, formatting them, storing them (if only for an instant), and forwarding them to another location. Message switches route and queue messages, clearing them to their destinations at the scheduled delivery times according to the priority the sender establishes.

Store-and-forward networks include private networks and both domestic and international Telex. Access may be through public value-added networks such as MCI Mail, AT&T Mail, or Western Union's Easy Link. Most networks offer speed and code conversion and may also offer protocol conversion.

Packet Switching

A *packet switched* network has control nodes that host the stations as Figure 3.4 shows. In a packet network, nodes are interconnected by sufficient trunks to support the traffic load. Data travels from the station to the node in *packets*, which are blocks of data characters delimited by header and trailer records. The node moves the packet toward its destination by handing it off to the next node in the chain. Nodes are controlled by software, with algorithms that determine the route to the next station. In contrast to a circuit switched network, where circuits are physically switched between stations, a packet switched network establishes *virtual circuits* between stations.

A virtual circuit is one that appears to the user as if it exists, but does not exist except as a defined path through a shared facility. Virtual circuits are of two types. In a *permanent virtual circuit* mode, the routing between stations is fixed and packets always take the same route. In a *switched virtual circuit* mode, the routing is determined with each packet.

Data Communications Fundamentals

The devices in a data network that originate and receive data are collectively called *data terminal equipment* (DTE). These can range from computers to simple receive-only terminals. DTE is

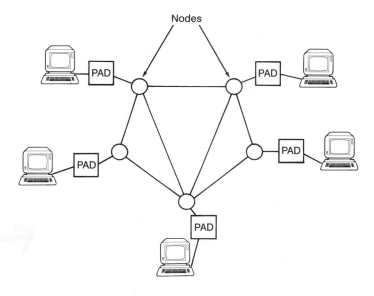

Nodes

PAD — Packet Assembler/Disassembler

Figure 3.4   A packet switched network.

coupled to the telecommunications network by *data circuit terminating equipment* (DCE), which includes any device that converts the DTE output to a signal suitable for the transmission medium. DCE ranges from line drivers to complex modulator/demodulators (*modems*) and multiplexers.

The basic information element processed by a computer is the binary digit, or *bit*. A bit is the smallest information element in the binary numbering system and is represented by the two digits, 0 and 1, corresponding to two different voltage states within the DTE. Processors manipulate data in groups of eight bits known as *bytes* or *octets*. Within the computer's circuits, bytes travel over parallel paths that may be extended to output ports for connection to peripherals such as printers.

The range of parallel ports is limited to a few feet. Although the range can be extended with electronic regenerators, extending eight circuits in parallel over long distances is uneconomical because one circuit would be required for each parallel path. Therefore, most DTE is equipped with an interface to convert the

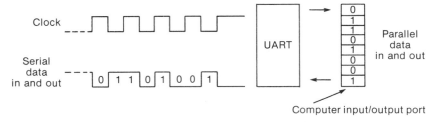

UART = Universal Asynchronous Receiver/Transmitter

Figure 3.5   Parallel and serial data conversion.

eight parallel bits into a serial bit stream as Figure 3.5 shows. This serial bit stream can be coupled to telecommunications circuits through a modem or line driver or directly to circuits up to about one kilometer.

Coding

The number of characters that can be encoded with binary numbers depends on the number of bits in the code. Early teletypewriters used a five-level code called *baudot* that had a capacity of 2^5 or 32 characters. A five-level code limits communications, because there are insufficient combinations to send a full range of upper and lower case plus special characters. In the baudot code, upper and lower case are indicated by shift characters. The receiving device continues in upper or lower case mode until it receives a case-shifting character. If it misses a shift character for some reason, the transmission will be garbled, because special characters are shifted numeric characters in the baudot code.

To overcome this limitation, a seven-level code known as the American Standard Code for Information Interchange (ASCII) was introduced. This code, which Table 3.1 shows, provides 2^7 or 128 combinations. In ASCII transmissions, although seven bits are used for characters, eight bits are transmitted. The eighth bit is used for error detection as described later.

Several other codes are used for data communications. The most prominent is the Extended Binary Coded Decimal Interchange Code (*EBCDIC*), which Table 3.2 shows. EBCDIC is an eight-bit code, allowing a full 256 characters to be encoded. It is used extensively in IBM applications.

Table 3.1   American Standard Code for Information Exchange

b7 b6 b5 b4 b3 b2 b1	000	001	010	011	100	101	110	111
0000	NUL	DLE	SP	0	@	P	'	p
0001	SOH	DC1	!	1	A	Q	a	q
0010	STX	DC2		2	B	R	b	r
0011	ETX	DC3	#	3	C	S	c	s
0100	EOT	DC4	$	4	D	T	d	t
0101	ENQ	NAK	%	5	E	U	e	u
0110	ACK	SYN	&	6	F	V	f	v
0111	BEL	ETB	'	7	G	W	g	w
1000	BS	CAN	(	8	H	X	h	x
1001	HT	EM	)	9	I	Y	i	y
1010	LF	SUB	*	:	J	Z	j	z
1011	VT	ESC	+	;	K	[	k	{
1100	FF	FS	,	<	L	\	l	|
1101	CR	GS		=	M	]	m	}
1110	SO	RS	.	>	N	^	n	~
1111	SI	US	/	?	O	_	o	DEL

Code compatibility between machines is essential. Because EBCDIC and ASCII are both widely used, in some applications code conversion will be required. Most intelligent terminals can be programmed for code conversion, but with non-programmable terminals, external provisions are necessary. This can be a separate code converter or a value-added function of the network.

Data Communications Speeds

Table 3.3 shows the range of speeds for typical data communication applications. The speed that a circuit can support depends on its bandwidth, which as Chapter 2 explains, is 300 to 3300 Hz over voice frequency telephone channels. Where wider bandwidths are required, special service or digital circuits must be obtained over private facilities or through common carrier tariffs.

Table 3.2 Extended Binary Coded Decimal Interchange Code (EBCDIC)

BITS 8765 \ 4321	0000	0001	0010	0011	0100	0101	0110	0111	1000	1001	1010	1011	1100	1101	1110	1111
0000	NUL	SOH	STX	ETX	PF	HT	LC	DEL			SMM	VT	FF	CR	SO	SI
0001	DLE	DC1	DC2	DC3	RES	NL	BS	IL	CAN	EM	CC		IFS	IGS	IRS	IUS
0010	DS	SOS	FS		BYP	LF	EOB	PRE			SM			ENQ	ACK	BEL
0011			SYN		PN	RS	UC	EOT					DC4	NAK		SUB
0100	SP										¢	.	<	(	+	|
0101	&										!	$	*	)	;	¬
0110	-	/										,	%	_	>	?
0111											:	#	@	'	=	□
1000		a	b	c	d	e	f	g	h	i						
1001		j	k	l	m	n	o	p	q	r						
1010			s	t	u	v	w	x	y	z						
1011																
1100		A	B	C	D	E	F	G	H	I						
1101		J	K	L	M	N	O	P	Q	R						
1110			S	T	U	V	W	X	Y	Z						
1111	0	1	2	3	4	5	6	7	8	9						

PF Punch Off
HT Horizontal Tab
LC Lower Case
DEL Delete
SP Space

UC Upper Case
RES Restore
NL New Line
BS Backspace
IL Idle

PN Punch On
EOT End of Transmission
BYP Bypass
LF Line Feed
EOB End of Block

PRE Prefix (ESC)
RS Reader Stop
SM Start Message
Others Same as ASCII

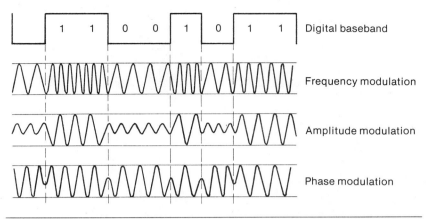

Figure 3.6   Data modulation methods.

Two terms used to express the data-carrying capacity of a circuit are *bit rate* and *baud rate.* Bit rate and baud rate are often used interchangeably, but to do so is not technically accurate. The bit rate of a channel is the number of bits per second the channel can carry. For example, with complex modulation schemes, a voice grade channel can carry 19,200 bits per second or more. The baud rate of a channel describes the number of cycles or symbols per second the channel can handle. The 3000 Hz bandwidth of a voice channel can pass a 2400 baud signal with the extra bandwidth used for guard bands between signals. If the data is encoded at one bit per Hz, the channel is limited to 2400 b/s. Higher bit rates are transmitted by encoding more than one bit per Hz. A 19,200 b/s signal can be carried on a voice grade channel, for example, by encoding eight bits per Hz.

Modulation Methods

A data signal leaves the serial interface of the DTE as a series of baseband voltage pulses as Figure 3.6 shows. Baseband means that the varying voltage level from the DTE is impressed without modulation directly on the transmission medium. Baseband pulses can be transmitted over limited distances from the serial interface or over longer distances by using a limited distance modem or a line driver that matches the serial interface to the cable. For transmission over voice-grade channels, a modem modulates the pulses into a combination of analog tones and

Table 3.3 Data Transmission Speeds and Applications

	50 b/s	75 b/s	100 b/s	150 b/s	300 b/s	1200 b/s	2.4 kb/s	4.8 kb/s	7.2 kb/s	9.6 kb/s	19.2 kb/s	56 kb/s	64 kb/s	1.5 mb/s	10 mb/s	100+ mb/s
Telemetry	↕	↕														
Telex	↕	↕														
Teleprinters			↕	↕	↕	↕										
Interactive Terminals					↕	↕	↕	↕	↕	↕	↕					
Medium-Speed Data							↕	↕	↕	↕	↕					
High-Speed Data											↕	↕	↕	↕		
Digital Video												↕	↕	↕	↕	
Local Area Networks														↕	↕	↕
Image Transmission														↕	↕	↕

amplitude and phase changes that fit within the pass band of the channel.

The digital signal modulates the *frequency,* the *amplitude,* or the *phase* of an audio signal as Figure 3.6 shows. Amplitude modulation by itself is the least used method because it is susceptible to noise-generated errors. It is frequently used, however, in conjunction with frequency and phase changes. Frequency modulation is an inexpensive method used with low speed modems. To reach speeds of more than 300 b/s, phase shift modems are employed.

Quadrature Amplitude Modulation

Modems use increasingly complex modulation methods for encoding multiple bits per Hz to reach speeds approaching the capacity of a voice grade circuit. Since an analog channel is limited to 2400 Hz, or symbols per second, to send 9600 b/s, for example, four bits per Hz must be encoded. The resulting 2^4 encoding yields a total of 16 combinations that each symbol can represent. High speed modems use *quadrature amplitude modulation* (QAM) to send multiple bits per Hz. In QAM two carrier tones combine in quadrature to produce the modem's output signal. The receiving end demodulates the quadrature signal to recover the transmitted signal. Each symbol carries one of 16 signal combinations. As Figure 3.7 shows, any combination of four bits can be encoded into a particular pair of X-Y plot points, which represent a phase and amplitude combination. This combination modulates the carrier signals. This two-dimensional diagram is called a *signal constellation.*

The receiving modem demodulates the signal to determine what pair of X-Y coordinates was transmitted, and the four-bit signal combination passes from the modem to the DTE. If line noise or phase jitter affects the signal, the received point will be displaced from its ideal location, so the modem must make a best guess which plot point was transmitted. If the signal is displaced far enough, the receiver makes the wrong guess, and the resulting signal is in error.

Even higher rates can be modulated, with each additional bit doubling the number of signal points. A 64 QAM signal encodes 2^6 bits per symbol, and a 128 QAM signal results in 2^7 combinations, bringing the signal points closer together and increasing the susceptibility of the modem to impairments. As discussed later, the performance of the modem can be improved by using forward error correction to process the incoming bit stream.

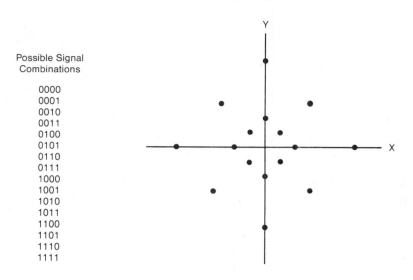

Figure 3.7 **Plot points in a 16-bit (2⁴) quadrature amplitude modu-**
lated signal.

Trellis-Coded Modulation

Trellis-coded modulation (TCM) is a more reliable method of encoding data signals. In a 14,400 b/s modem, for example, data is presented to a TCM modulator in six-bit groups. Two of the six bits are separated from the signal, and a code bit is added. The resulting signal is two groups, one three-bit and one four-bit. These are combined, and the resulting 2^7 bits are mapped into a signal point and selected from a 128-point signal constellation. Since only six of the seven bits are required to transmit the original signal, not all the 128 points are needed to transmit the signal, and only certain patterns of signal points are defined as valid. If a line impairment results in an invalid pattern at the receiver, the decoder selects the most likely valid sequence and presents it to the DTE. TCM reduces the signal's susceptibility to line impairments, but as discussed later, some means of correcting errors must be added to the session.

Full and Half Duplex Mode

Full duplex circuits transmit data in both directions simultaneously. *Half duplex* circuits transmit in only one direction at a time; the channel reverses for transmission in the other direction.

Full duplex circuits use separate transmit and receive paths on a *four-wire* circuit or a *split channel modem* on a *two-wire* circuit. Two- and four-wire circuits refer to the type of facility that the local and interexchange carriers furnish. In the interexchange portion circuits are inherently four-wire, and the two directions of transmission travel over separate paths. It is possible, however, to purchase two-wire local loops, in which case the two directions of transmission must be combined in a single path.

Split channel modems provide the equivalent of four-wire operation by dividing the voice channel into two frequency segments, one for transmit and one for receive. The 2400 baud bandwidth of a channel limits a full duplex modem to 1200 b/s in each direction when straight frequency modulation is used. Modems with more sophisticated modulation are available at higher cost to provide 2400 b/s full duplex communication over two-wire circuits using the CCITT V.22 *bis* modulation method, and 9600 b/s using V.32 modulation.

Synchronizing Methods

All data communications channels require synchronization to keep the sending and receiving ends in step. The signal on a baseband data communications channel is a series of rapid voltage changes, and synchronization enables the receiving terminal to determine which pulse is the first bit in a character.

The simplest synchronizing method is *asynchronous,* sometimes called stop-start synchronization. Asynchronous signals, illustrated in Figure 3.8, are in the one or mark state when no characters are being transmitted. A character begins with a start bit at the zero or *space* level followed by eight data bits and a stop bit at the one level. The terms mark and space are carried over from telegraphy, where current flowed in the line to a teletypewriter to hold it closed when it was not receiving characters. Current loop lines have largely disappeared from public networks because they generate noise. Many asynchronous terminals, however, still operate in a current loop state because their range is greater than the range of EIA serial interfaces.

Asynchronous signals are transmitted in a character mode; that is, each character is individually synchronized. The chief drawback of asynchronous communication is the extra two bits per byte that carry no information. These non-information bits are called *overhead* bits.

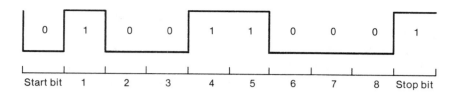

Figure 3.8   Asynchronous data transmission.

To reduce the amount of overhead, data can be transferred in a *synchronous* mode as illustrated in Figure 3.9. Synchronous data is sent in a block mode with information characters sandwiched between header and trailer records. The header and trailer contain the overhead bits; the information bits are transferred without start and stop bits. A clock signal that the modem extracts from the incoming bit stream keeps the two terminals in synchronization.

The drawbacks of synchronous signals are their complexity and their lack of standardization. Variables in the data block, such as block length, error checking routine, and structure of the header and trailer records, are functions of the *protocol*. Although there are some standard protocols, such as High Level Data Link Control (HDLC) recommended by CCITT, many data manufacturers have their own protocols, which are incompatible with one another.

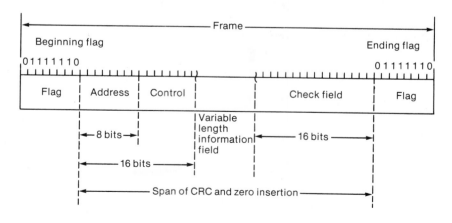

Figure 3.9   Synchronous data transmission (IBM SDLC frame).

Whereas asynchronous data terminals can communicate with each other if the speed, code, and error checking conventions are identical, synchronous terminals require protocol compatibility and intelligence in the DTE or terminal controller. Synchronous data communication systems have offsetting advantages of greater throughput and the ability to use sophisticated error correction techniques that are not compatible with the character mode of transmission.

Error Detection and Correction

Errors occur in all data communications circuits. Where the transmission is text that people will interpret, a few errors can be tolerated because the meaning can be derived from context. In many applications, such as those involving transmission of bank balances, computer programs, and other numerical data, errors can have catastrophic effects. In these applications nothing short of complete accuracy is acceptable. This section discusses causes, detection, and correction of data communication errors.

Causes of Data Errors

The type of transmission medium and the modulation method have the greatest effect on the error rate. Any transmission medium using analog modulation techniques is subject to external noise, which affects the amplitude of the signal. Atmospheric conditions, such as lightning, that cause static bursts can induce noise into data-carrying analog radio and carrier systems. Relay and switch operations in electromechanical central offices, switching to standby channels in microwave, fiber optics, and carrier systems all cause momentary interruptions that result in data errors. Changes in the phase of the received signal, which can be caused by instability in carrier supplies or radio systems also can cause errors because the modem is incapable of determining accurately which of many signal patterns was transmitted.

Any communication circuit is subject to errors during maintenance actions and external damage or interruption by vandalism. Even local networks within a single building are subject to occasional interruptions due to equipment failure or damage to the transmission medium. Whatever the causes, errors are a fact of life in data circuits. The best error mitigation program is a design that reduces the susceptibility of the service to errors. Following that, the next most important consideration is to design the application to detect, and, if possible, correct the errors.

	BIT 8	BIT 7	BIT 6	BIT 5	BIT 4	BIT 3	BIT 2	BIT 1
ASCII a		1	1	0	0	0	0	1
Even Parity	1	1	1	0	0	0	0	1
Odd Parity	0	1	1	0	0	0	0	1

Figure 3.10   Character parity.

Parity Checking

The simplest way of detecting errors is *parity checking*, or *vertical redundancy checking* (VRC), a technique used on asynchronous circuits. In the ASCII code set, the eighth bit is reserved for parity. Parity is set as odd or even, referring to the number of 1s bits in the character. As Figure 3.10 shows, DTE adds an extra bit, if necessary, to cause each character to match the parity established for the network.

Most asynchronous terminals can be set to send and receive odd, even, or no parity. When a parity error occurs, the terminal registers some form of alarm. Parity has two drawbacks: there is no way to tell what the original character should have been, and worse, if an even number of errors occurs, parity checking will not detect the error at all. Therefore, parity is useful only for showing that an error occurred; it is ineffective when transmission accuracy is required.

In terminals operating at 300 or 1200 b/s or more, characters arrive so fast that it is difficult to determine which character was in error when the parity alarm was registered. DTE can be programmed to flag an error character by substituting a special character, such as an ampersand, in its place. The error can be corrected by communication with the sending end.

Echo Checking

Over full duplex circuits, errors can be detected by programming the receiving device to retransmit the received characters to the sending end. This technique, called *echo checking*, is suitable for detecting errors in some forms of text. It is, however, subject to all the drawbacks of proofreading; it is far from infallible. Besides, an error in an echoed character is as likely to have occurred on the return trip as in the original transmission. At 300 b/s, a reader can keep up with echoed characters, but with machine transmission at 1200 b/s or more

Table 3.4   Commonly Used Asynchronous File Transfer Protocols

PROTOCOL	DEFINITION
Xmodem	A half duplex file transfer protocol that has been widely accepted since the late 1970s.
Ymodem	A protocol similar to Xmodem, but with larger data blocks, which results in higher throughput on low error rate circuits.
Zmodem	A refinement of Xmodem and Ymodem, offering greater efficiency in file transfers.
Kermit	A file transfer protocol that is widely supported by personal computers, mainframes, and minicomputers.
Sealink	A full duplex version of Xmodem.
CompuServe B	An efficient file transfer protocol used on CompuServe's network.

it is impossible to read with any degree of reliability. The DTE can be programmed to make the echo check automatically, but correcting errors is just as difficult as with parity. Echo checking is widely used in asynchronous computer and terminal combinations.

Although several systems are used for error detection and correction in the asynchronous mode, there is no universal standard, which is a drawback of asynchronous transmissions. Several protocols, as listed in Table 3.4, are widely supported by telecommunications programs and value added carriers for end-to-end error correction. These protocols operate on an automatic repeat request (ARQ) much the same as synchronous error-correcting protocols, which are described below. Most popular telecommunications software packages support one or more of these protocols. They are required for most transfers of binary files and are easy to use; the user specifies the file to be up- or downloaded. The protocol automatically takes care of the transfer, signaling the user when the transfer is completed. The most effective method of transferring asynchronous data without errors is to use modems that include an error checking protocol such as Microcom Networking Protocol (MNP), which we will discuss later.

Longitudinal Redundancy Checking

Longitudinal redundancy checking (LRC) is a system used for error detection and correction in a block transmission mode. As Figure

BIT POSITION	DATA CHARACTERS						BLOCK PARITY*
	1	2	3	4	5	6	
1	0	1	0	1	1	0	1
2	1	1	0	0	1	1	0
3	0	1	0	1	1	0	1
4	0	0	1	0	1	1	1
5	1	0	1	1	0	1	0
6	0	1	0	1	0	1	1
7	1	0	1	0	1	1	0
p*	1	0	1	0	1	1	0

Direction of transmission

*Even parity

Figure 3.11   Longitudinal redundancy checking.

3.11 shows, each character is checked for parity, and each bit position within the block is also checked. The last character in the block is a parity character that the protocol creates to establish odd or even parity in each bit position in the block. If the block is received in error, the receiving end instructs the transmitting end to resend the block. The block is resent until it is received without error or until the protocol signals an alarm.

Although LRC is more reliable than simple parity checking and offers the additional advantage of error correction, it suffers from the same inability to detect all parity errors and is rarely used today. For example, if the same two bits were received in error in two characters in a block, the error would not be detected. The probability, however slight, is not acceptable for applications that need assurance of data integrity.

Cyclical Redundancy Checking

Most synchronous data networks use cyclical redundancy checking (CRC). All the characters in a block are processed against a complex polynomial that always results in a remainder. The 16-bit remainder is entered in an error check block that is transmitted following the data block. The synchronous data block illustrated in Figure 3.9 contains a CRC field in the trailer record.

At the receiving end the data block is processed against the same polynomial to create another CRC field. If the locally created CRC field fails to match the field received in the data block, the protocol causes the block to be retransmitted. The probability of an uncorrected error with CRC is so slight that it can be considered error-free. The process used by synchronous data link protocols to initiate retransmission of an errored block is known as *automatic repeat request* (ARQ).

When a block is received in error, it makes no difference how many bit errors were received; the entire block must be retransmitted. Therefore, the block error rate (BLER) is the best measure of the quality of a data link. BLER is calculated by dividing the number of errored blocks received over a period of time by the total number of blocks transmitted. A device such as a front end processor or a protocol analyzer can compute BLER.

Forward Error Correction

When the BLER of a circuit is excessive, *throughput*, which is the number of information bits correctly transferred per unit of time, may be reduced to an unacceptable level. The error rate can be reduced by a technique known as *forward error correction* (FEC). In FEC systems, an encoder on the transmitting end processes the incoming signal and generates redundant code bits. The transmitted signal contains both the original information bits and the additional bits. At the receiving end, the redundant bits are regenerated from the information bits and compared with the redundant bits that were received. When a discrepancy occurs, the FEC circuitry on the receiving end uses the redundant bits to generate the most likely bit combination and passes it to the DTE. Although FEC is not infallible, it reduces the block error rate and the number of retransmissions.

Throughput

The critical measure of a data communication circuit is its throughput, or the number of information bits correctly transferred per unit of time. Although it would be theoretically possible for the throughput of a data channel to approach its maximum bit rate, in practice this can never be realized because of overhead bits and the retransmission of error blocks. The following are the primary factors that limit the throughput of a data channel:

- Modem speed. Within a single voice channel, modems ranging from 50 b/s to 19.2 kb/s can be accommodated.
- Half or full duplex mode of operation.
- Circuit error rate.
- Modem reversal time, which is the time required for a half duplex modem to change from the sending to the receiving state.
- Protocol, including quantity of overhead bits and method of error handling such as selective retransmission or "go back N."
- Overhead bits, including start and stop bits, error checking, and forward error correction bits.
- Size of data block. The shorter the data block, the more significant the protocol as a percentage of information bits. When the data block is too long, each error requires retransmitting considerable data. Proper block length is a balance between time consumed in overhead and in error retransmission.
- Propagation speed of the transmission medium.

The throughput of a data channel is optimized by reaching a balance between the above variables using complex formulas. Because of the volume of calculations required to optimize the network, a computer program is generally required to generate throughput curves similar to those in Figure 3.12. Throughput formulas and the method of calculating them are discussed in *The Dow Jones-Irwin Handbook of Telecommunications Management*.

Data Communication Protocols

Protocol is the name given to the software functions that manage information transfer in a data communications network. Typical functions of a protocol are:

- Establishes mutual compatibility of the DTE at both ends of the circuit.
- Establishes the session as half or full duplex.
- Establishes the send and receive modem frequencies.
- Synchronizes the transmitting and receiving terminals

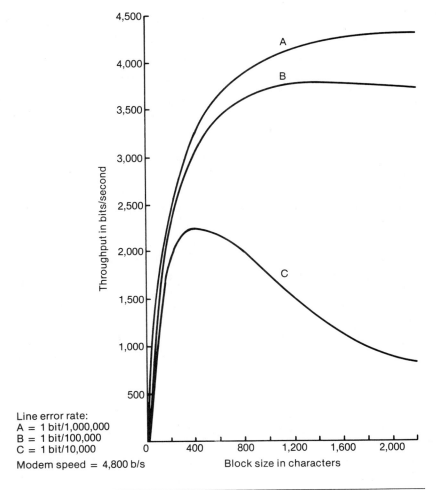

Figure 3.12   Effects of line error rate on throughput.

- Defines the physical interface between DTE and the network.
- Conveys the length of the data block to the receiving DTE.
- Selects the route for transmitting frames.
- Detects errors.
- Acknowledges receipt of frames.
- Arranges retransmission of errored frames.
- Verifies the authenticity of parties to the session.

- Terminates the session.
- Recovers from circuit failures.
- Determines charging and billing for the session.

Protocol compatibility and standardization are the most important issues in data communications. Most major computer manufacturers have developed proprietary protocols that are incompatible with those of other manufacturers. Even standard protocols developed by international agencies, such as CCITT's HDLC and X.25, provide multiple options and are not always interchangeable between applications.

Incompatible protocols can communicate with each other through *protocol converters*. A protocol converter known as a *gateway* communicates with both connecting protocols using their languages. Certain value added networks also offer protocol conversion. They communicate with the DTE using that DTE's own protocol, convert it to the network protocol, and transport it to the distant DTE in its own language. The incompatibility of protocols has long been a stumbling block in the path of full interconnectability of data networks. Although international standards have progressed significantly, the problems of incompatibility are likely to remain for many years.

The Open Systems Interconnect Model

The most significant standardization efforts in protocols have revolved around developing layered protocols. A layer is a discrete set of functions the protocol is designed to accomplish. The International Standards Organization (ISO) has published a seven-layer protocol model, the Open Systems Interconnect (OSI) model, which is illustrated in Figure 3.13.

Controlling communications in layers adds some extra overhead because each layer communicates with its counterpart through header records, but layered protocols are easier to administer than simpler protocols and provide opportunity for standardization. Although protocols are complex, functions in each layer can be modularized so the complexity can be dealt with separately by system designers. Layered control offers an opportunity for standardization and interconnection between the proprietary architectures of different manufacturers. Generally, the degree of standardization is greatest at the first layer, and becomes increasingly disparate in the higher layers. The seven OSI layers

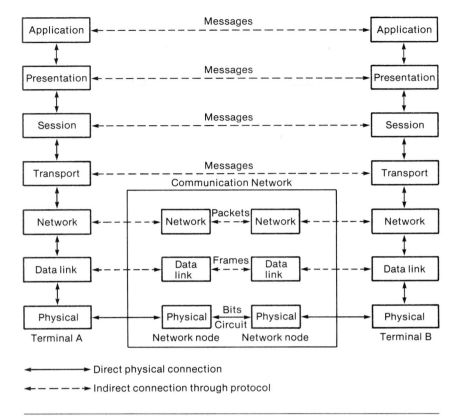

Figure 3.13   International Standards Organization Open Systems Interconnection model.

are defined below. Table 3.5 lists the OSI layers and the principal international standards that apply to each layer.

Layer 1—Physical.   The first layer describes the method of physical interconnection over a circuit. The physical layer contains the rules for the transmission of *bits* between machines and standardizes pin connections between DCE and DTE.

Layer 2—Data Link.   Data link protocols are concerned with the transmission of frames of data between devices. The protocol in the data link layer detects and corrects errors so the user gets an error-free circuit. The data link layer takes raw data characters, creates frames of data from them, and processes acknowledgement messages from the receiver. When frames are lost or muti-

Table 3.5   Principal Standards in the OSI Model

LAYER	STANDARD
Layer 1 Physical	RS232 V.35 RS 449 G.703 X.21 ISDN 1.430 ISDN 1.431
Layer 2 Data Link	802.3 802.4 802.5 High Level Data Link Control (HDLC) Link Access Protocol B (LAPB) ISDN 1.441
Layer 3 Network	CCITT X.25 ISP 8473 Internet ISO 8208 ISDN 1.451 Internet Protocol (IP)
Layer 4 Transport	ISO 8073 CCITT X.224 Transport Control Protocol (TCP)
Layer 5 Session	ISP 8327 Session Protocol ISO 8827 ISO 9548 CCITT X.225
Layer 6 Presentation	ISO 8823 ISO 9576 CCITT X.409

Layer 7 Application	CCITT X.400 Electronic Mail
	CCITT X.500 Directory Services
	ISO 8571 File Transfer, Access, and
	  Management (FTAM)
	ISO 9506 Manufacturing Message
	  Specification (MMS)
	ISO 9040 Virtual Terminal (VT)

lated, the logic in this layer arranges retransmission. Protocols contain flags and headers so DTE can recognize the start and end of a frame. A frame of information, as Figure 3.9 shows, has flags to signal the beginning and ending of the frame, a header containing address and control information, an information field, and a trailer containing CRC bits for error correction.

Layer 3—Network. The network layer accepts messages from the higher layers, breaks them into *packets*, routes them to the distant end through the link and physical layers and reassembles them in the same form in which the sending end delivered them to the network. The network layer controls the flow of packets, controls congestion in the network, and routes between nodes to the destination.

Layer 4—Transport. The transport layer controls end-to-end integrity between DTE devices, establishing and terminating the connection. The transport layer provides network management functions because of the many types of network over which data may travel. The transport layer provides a standard service despite the characteristics of the network. It does its function by communicating with its corresponding layer in the distant machine through message headers and control messages.

Layer 5—Session. The user communicates directly with the session layer, furnishing an address that the session layer converts to the address the transport layer requires. The conventions for the session are established in this layer. For example, the validity of the parties can be verified by passwords. The session can be established as a full duplex or a half duplex session. The session layer determines whether machines can interrupt one another. It establishes how to begin and terminate a session, and how to restore or terminate the connection in case a failure interrupts the session.

Layer 6—Presentation. This layer interprets the character stream that flows between terminals during the session. For example, if encryption or bit compression is used, the presentation layer may provide it. Other machine control functions, including skipping, tabbing, form feed, and cursor movement, are presentation layer functions.

Layer 7—Application. The application layer is the interface between the network and the application running on the computer. The most important application layer functions now are CCITT's

CCITT's X.400 Electronic Mail Protocol and ISO File Transfer, Access, and Management (FTAM).

The OSI objective of the reference model is to establish a framework that will allow any conforming system or network to connect and exchange signals, messages, packets, and addresses. The model makes it possible for communications to become independent of the manufacturer that devised the technology. It should be understood that although the OSI model can be used to develop standards, it is not a standard itself. Manufacturers are increasingly announcing support for OSI, and as Chapter 25 discusses, proprietary networks may eventually merge into compatible standard networks.

Data Communication Equipment

An effective data communication network is a compromise involving many variables. The nature of data transmission varies so greatly with the application that designs are empirically determined. The network designer arrives at the most economical balance of performance and cost, evaluating equipment alternatives as discussed in this section.

Terminals

Terminals can be grouped into three classes—dumb, smart, and intelligent. They are also categorized as synchronous and asynchronous or ASCII terminals. This section discusses the characteristics of terminals and how they differ.

Dumb Terminals

Dumb terminals are so called because they contain no processing power. They are not addressable and, therefore, cannot respond to polling messages. They have no error correcting capability and so are most often located near the host computer. Or they operate behind a controller or multiplexer that has addressing and error correction capability. Most dumb terminals do support parity checking and can flag when errors are occurring. Since they are not addressable, dumb terminals are incapable of line sharing.

Smart Terminals

Smart terminals are nonprogrammable devices, but they are capable of addressing and can be used on a multidrop line. Unlike asynchronous terminals that transmit one character at a time, smart terminals can often store data in a buffer and transmit in block mode. In block mode the terminal can detect errors and, through an ARQ process, retransmit errored blocks. A smart terminal contains only limited processing capability. For example, it may have limited editing capability, but it relies on the host for processing.

Intelligent Terminals

An intelligent terminal contains its own processor and can run application programs. The most common type of intelligent terminal is the personal computer (PC), although PCs do not always operate in intelligent terminal mode.

An intelligent terminal, being capable of running application programs on its own, provides better line utilization than dumb and smart terminals. Certain tasks can be delegated from the host to the terminal, which reduces the amount of data that flows between the two. It is important to note that some kind of communication software must run in an intelligent terminal. By changing applications software, the operator can function with different applications on the host.

Terminal Emulation

As the prices of PCs have fallen over the past few years, many companies have begun to use them instead of terminals. Depending on the applications program running on the PC, it can emulate any of the three classes of terminal.

Since a serial (EIA-232) port is a standard feature of most PCs, it is simple for a PC to emulate an asynchronous terminal. Telecommunications software ranges in features from simple dumb terminal emulation to full-featured intelligent terminal applications. In the latter category, a PC can upload and download files from and to its own disk, select and search for files on the host, and even interact with the host without a human attendant.

Interaction with a synchronous host is considerably more complex. Not only is the protocol specialized and more difficult to implement, the physical interface is likely to be something other than EIA-232; coaxial cable and twinax are common. In such a case, terminal emulation involves placing an interface board in a PC expansion slot and running emulation software in the PC. Emulation boards and software are available for most of the

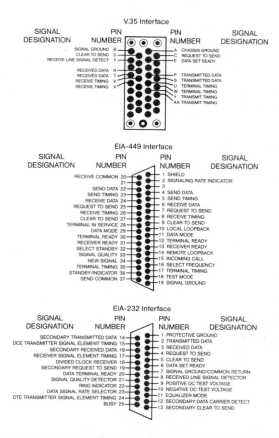

Figure 3.14   CCITT V.35, EIA-232, and EIA 449 interfaces.

popular synchronous protocols such as IBM's Synchronous Data Link Control (SDLC).

Modems

Since the early 1980s, modems have undergone a striking evolution. To understand modems, it is useful to classify them as dial-up and private line. In the latter category, there is considerable risk of incompatibility between modems of different manufacture, although more and more modems are being built to CCITT standards. In the dial-up category, modems have almost become a commodity, although there are a few in the 9600 b/s range that use proprietary signaling formats.

The primary issue in selecting modems is compatibility. The interface between DTE and the modem is standardized in the

United States, with the predominant interfaces the EIA-232, EIA-449, and CCITT V.35. Figure 3.14 illustrates these interfaces. EIA and CCITT standards specify the functions of the interface circuits but do not specify the physical characteristics of the interface connector. Connectors have been adopted by convention; for example, the DB-25 connector has become a de facto standard for the EIA-232 interface. Not all the 25 pins of the DB-25 are necessary in most applications. Therefore, many manufacturers use fewer pins as a way of conserving chassis space. The DB-9 nine-pin connector has become common in AT-type personal computers. The physical connector is only a minor problem to users because units can be easily interconnected with adapters if they are electrically compatible.

Modem compatibility is often related to the Bell System modem numbering plan. Modems may be designated as compatible with a Bell modem, which means they are end-to-end compatible, or they may be designated as equivalent, which means that they perform the same functions but are not necessarily end-to-end compatible with the Bell modem of that number. Table 3.6 lists the most common Bell and CCITT modem standards.

Dial-Up Modems

Like other telecommunications products, modems have become faster, cheaper, and smarter. The ready availability of inexpensive personal computers has expanded the demand for modems, and where a few years ago 1200 b/s modems were the norm, now 2400 b/s is common, and in a few years when prices fall, 9600 b/s dial-up modems will undoubtedly become the standard. Chips containing the circuitry to support the V.22 or V.32 format are the essence of modems, with most vendors also supporting the Hayes command set. Figure 3.15 shows a Microcom QX/V.32C modem.

The Hayes command set is a proprietary group of instructions that receives commands preceded by the letters AT from the DTE and translates these into instructions to handle functions such as dialing a number and hanging up when the session ends. Matched with telecommunications software, dial-up modems enable users to upload and download files, converse with data bases, access packet switching networks, exchange files, and perform other functions that once required a highly trained operator.

Dial-up modems either plug into a personal computer expansion slot or are self-contained devices that plug into the

Table 3.6   Bell and CCITT Model Compatibility Chart

TYPE	SPEED (B/S)	SYNCHRONIZATION	MODE
103 A/J	300	Asynch	FDX Dial-up
113 A/D	300	Asynch	FDX Dial-up
103 F	300	Asynch	FDX P/L
212 A	1200	Synch/Asynch	FDX Dial-up
202 S	1200	Asynch	HDX Dial-up
202 T	1800	Asynch	FDX/HDX/P/L
201 B	2400	Synch	FDX P/L
201 C	2400	Synch	HDX P/L
208 A	4800	Synch	FDX P/L
208 B	4800	Synch	HDX Dial-up
V.21	300	Asynch	FDX Dial-up
V.22	1200	Synch/Asynch	FDX Dial-up P/L
V.22 bis	2400	Synch/Asynch	FDX Dial-up P/L
V.23	1200	Asynch	FDX P/L
V.24	2400	Synch/Asynch	FDX/HDX Dial-up P/L
V.26	2400	Synch	FDX P/L
V.26 bis	2400	Synch	HDX Dial-up
V.27	4800	Synch	FDX P/L
V.27 bis	4800	Synch	HDX Dial-up
V.29	9600	Synch	FDX P/L
V.32	9600	Synch/Asynch	FDX Dial-up
V.33	14,400	Synch	FDX P/L

FDX = Full Duplex
HDX = Half Duplex
P/L = Private Line

computer's serial port. Most dial-up modems have few features beyond the Hayes command set. Some modems, however, support the MNP error correction protocol and are therefore useful between devices that lack error correction capability. Some modems also include more extensive processing capability and storage, which permits them to operate independently of a computer.

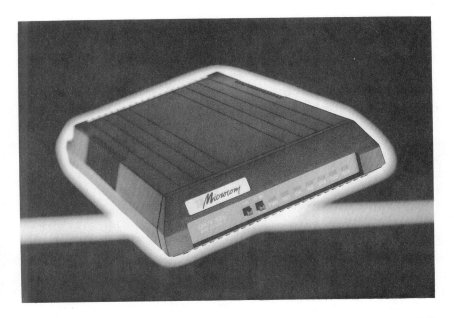

Figure 3.15   Microcom QX/V.32C protocol modem.
Courtesy, Microcom, Inc.

Such devices can place or answer a modem call and upload and download information.

The switched telephone network carries a considerable share of asynchronous data communication. Therefore, many modem features are designed to emulate a telephone set. The most sophisticated modems, in combination with a software package in an intelligent terminal, are capable of fully unattended operation. Modems designed for unattended, and many designed for attended, operation include these features:

- Dial tone recognition.

- Automatic tone and dial pulse dialing.

- Monitoring call progress tones such as busy and reorder.

- Automatic answer.

- Call termination.

Dial-up modems operate in a full duplex split-channel mode. The modem answers an incoming call by sending a tone to indicate whether it will send on the high or low frequency segment of the channel. Either the other modem adjusts automatically or the operator must manually set the modem to the receive frequency.

One consideration in choosing a dial-up modem is whether it is directly or acoustically coupled to the telephone network. An acoustically coupled modem provides a cradle for the handset to rest in. Acoustic coupling is subject to errors and interference from room noise, defective telephone handsets, and poorly seated connections between the handset and the coupler. Direct coupling, which requires the modem to be registered with the FCC or applied through a registered coupler, is much more effective and has replaced most acoustically coupled modems. Acoustic coupling is still useful in some applications, however, including sending data from hotel rooms and pay telephones, which do not provide direct access to the line.

Two CCITT standards provide important capabilities for users of dial-up 2400 b/s modems. V.42 defines methods to ensure error-free transmission over dial-up lines. A companion standard, V.42 *bis,* provides a standard method of data compression. The V.42 standard includes the error-control methods of MNP, but the V.42 *bis* standard does not use the MNP data compression scheme that has been popular in many modems manufactured in the United States.

Private Line Modems

Like dial-up modems, private line modems have dropped in price and improved in functionality, but there is such a diversity of features that they have not reached commodity status, and probably never will. Different manufacturers use proprietary formats to encode the signal, to compress data, and more important, to communicate network management information.

Private line modems can be classed as synchronous or asynchronous, half or full duplex, and two-wire or four-wire, with the latter being the most common. When synchronous modems are used at speeds above 4800 b/s they may require line conditioning from the common carrier. Line conditioning is not available on the switched voice telephone network, but most manufacturers offer modems equipped with *adaptive equalization*, which is circuitry that automatically adjusts the modem to compensate for irregularities in the telephone channel. Adaptive equalization substitutes for line conditioning and enables the use of 9600 b/s on a voice grade private line.

Circuit throughput can be improved by using data compression, a system that replaces the original bit stream with a stream that has fewer bits. With data compression techniques and adaptive equalization, it is possible to operate at 19.2 kb/s or higher over non-conditioned voice grade lines.

The following is a list of the most important features of private line modems. Not all manufacturers use these terms to describe their features.

Adaptable Inbound Rate.   On multidrop circuits where the modems contain adaptive rate capability, one drop suffering from impairments can bring the speed of the entire line down to the speed of the worst-case drop. With adaptable inbound rate, each modem establishes its own rate with the host and transmits at the maximum supportable speed.

Adaptive Line Rate Capability.   This feature enables a modem to sense line conditions and adjust its transmission speed to the maximum speed the line will support.

Fast Reversal.   In half duplex circuits, the modem flip-flops between send and receive. The time required to reverse itself is an important factor in determining throughput. A fast reversal modem minimizes turnaround time.

Internal Diagnostics.   With this feature the modem automatically runs real-time diagnostics and displays information about its status. Some models also display the condition of the communications facility.

Loop-Around.   Line troubles can be isolated by forcing the modem into a loop-back configuration as discussed in Chapter 32. Most modems permit looping the analog and digital sides of the signal to isolate whether a problem is on the line, in the modem, or in the DTE.

MNP Error Control.   The Microcom Network Protocol has become a widely accepted method of obtaining data integrity and data compression on asynchronous lines. Modems equipped with MNP monitor incoming data for errors and request retransmission of errored frames.

Modem Sharing Capability.   A modem sharing unit separates the transmission line into two or more channels, providing multiple slow-speed channels without the use of a multiplexer. For example, a modem with a bandwidth of 9600 b/s could support four 2400 b/s channels.

Network Management.   Many proprietary network management systems collect information from modems and other devices in real time. The modem provides a narrow channel for transmitting network management information such as analog line parameters back to the host for continuous line quality evaluation. With this capability, the network administrator or network management software can test, monitor, and reconfigure the modem from a central site.

Reverse Channel Capability.   In half duplex applications, it is sometimes desirable to send a small amount of information in the reverse direction. For example, it may be necessary to interrupt a transmission. Reverse channel capability provides a narrow band of frequencies for slow speed operation in the reverse direction, while the forward direction transmits wider band data.

Signal Constellation Generator.   The bit patterns of the modem's signal constellation are brought out to test points for monitoring with external test equipment.

Special Purpose Modems

The market offers many modems that fulfill specialized requirements. This section discusses some of the equipment that is available.

Data Over Voice Modems.   Simultaneous voice and data operation is desirable in many applications. A special type of modem called *data over voice* (DOV) multiplexes data and voice on the same point-to-point circuit. A DOV modem applies a full duplex data channel to a carrier frequency above the voice channel. The carrier shifts at speeds up to 19.2 kb/s with filters separating the data and voice signals. The range of DOV modems is limited to about three miles, which is the voice transmission range of a non-loaded cable pair. DOV modems are frequently used in local networks to impose a data signal over a PBX loop.

Dial-Backup Modems.   A dial backup modem contains circuitry to restore a failed leased line over a dial-up line. The restoral may be automatically initiated on failure of the dedicated line. The modem may simulate a four-wire private line over a single dial-up line, or two dial-up lines may be required.

Fiber Optic Modems.   Where noise and interference are a problem, fiber optic modems can provide high bandwidth at a moder-

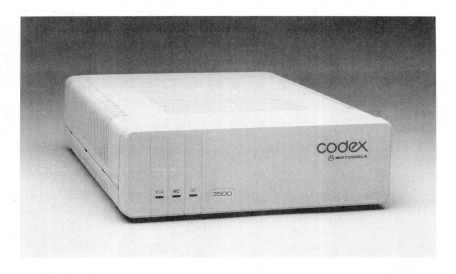

Figure 3.16   The Codex 3500 series CSU/DSU.
Courtesy, Codex Corporation, a subsidiary of Motorola.

ate cost. Operating over one fiber optic pair, these modems couple directly to the fiber optic cable.

Limited Distance Modems.   Many LECs offer limited distance circuits, which are essentially a bare nonloaded cable pair between two points within the same wire center. LDMs are inexpensive sive modems operating at speeds of up to 19.2 kb/s. Where LDM capability is available, the modems are significantly less expensive than long haul 19.2 kb/s modems.

Line Drivers.   A modem is not required for data transmission over some wire circuits. Line drivers are satisfactory over nonloaded facilities over ranges of about 10 miles and at speeds of up to 19.2 kb/s. Many telephone companies offer limited distance data services (LDDS), which are non-multiplexed channels that are provided where nonloaded metallic facilities are available.

Data Service Units

A data service unit (DSU), as illustrated in Figure 3.16, connects DTE to a digital data service (DDS) channel. Operating at the standard DDS rates of 2.4, 4.8, 9.6, 19.2, 56, and 64 kb/s, DSUs are full duplex devices. They are available for both point-to-point and multidrop lines.

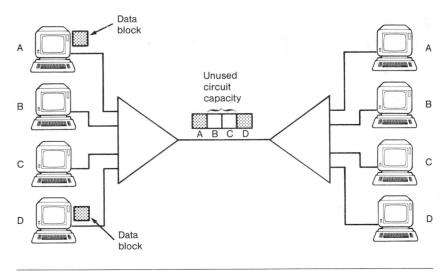

Figure 3.17   **Time division multiplexing.**

Multiplexers and Concentrators

Many data applications, by their nature, are incapable of fully using a data circuit. Rather than flowing in a steady stream, data usually flows in short bursts with long idle periods intervening. To make use of this idle capacity, data *multiplexers* are employed to collect data from multiple stations and combine it into a single high speed bit stream.

Data multiplexers are of two types, *time division multiplexers* (TDM) and *statistical multiplexers* (statmux). In a TDM, each station is assigned a time slot, and the multiplexer collects data from each station in turn. If the station has no data to send, its time slot goes unused. TDM operation is illustrated in Figure 3.17. Figure 3.18 shows a Codex 6216 time division multiplexer.

A statmux, illustrated in Figure 3.19, makes use of the idle time periods in a data circuit by assigning time slots to pairs of stations according to the amount of traffic they have to send. The multiplexer collects data from the DTE and sends it to the distant end with the address of the receiving terminal.

Statistical multiplexers improve circuit utilization by minimizing idle time between transmissions. They are more costly than TDMs, however, and must be monitored to prevent overloads, with stations added or removed to adjust the load to the maximum the circuit will handle while meeting response time objectives.

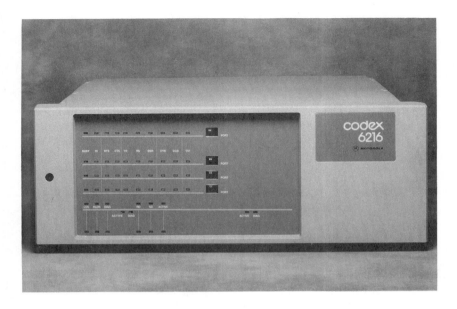

Figure 3.18   Codex 6216 time-division multiplexer.
Courtesy, Codex Corporation, a subsidiary of Motorola

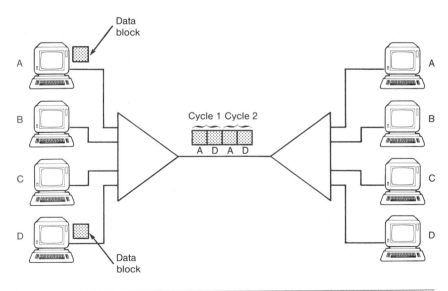

Figure 3.19   Statistical multiplexing.

Analog, or frequency division, multiplexers are also available to divide a voice channel into multiple segments for data transmission. These devices assign each data channel to a frequency and use frequency shift techniques similar to those used in a modem. Their primary use is to connect multiple slow speed data terminals over voice channels.

A *concentrator* is similar to a multiplexer, except that it is usually a single-ended device. At the terminal end, devices connect to the concentrator exactly as they would connect to a multiplexer, and the concentrator connects to the facility. At the host end, the facility is routed directly into the host or front end processor. A concentrator matches the characteristics of the host processor.

The primary application for multiplexers is in data networks that use asynchronous terminals. Since many of these devices cannot be addressed and have no error correction capability, they are of limited use by themselves in remote locations. The multiplexer provides end-to-end error checking and correction and circuit-sharing to support multiple terminals.

Multiplexer Features

Multiple Multiplexer Support.   Some statistical multiplexers have the capability of talking to more than one distant multiplexer in the network. Lacking this capability, multiplexers must be implemented in pairs.

Alternate Routing.   Multiplexers with alternate routing capability can transmit data around network congestion and circuit failures.

Terminal-to-Host Mapping.   With this feature, users can log onto a network and address any host. The multiplexers determine the route.

Network Management Capability.   With this feature a remote network management system can monitor the network through an interface into the multiplexers. It is possible to perform such functions as determining system status, changing port assignments, and diagnosing trouble.

Packet Switching Equipment

Packet switching can be implemented on either public or private networks. A device known as a packet assembler/disassembler

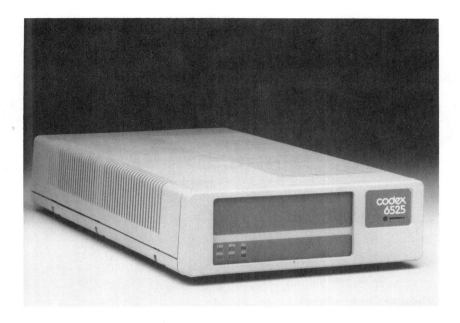

Figure 3.20   Codex 6525 packet switch with integrated packet assembler/disassembler(PAD).
Courtesy, Codex Corporation, a subsidiary of Motorola

(PAD) creates the packets. The PAD accepts a data stream from the DTE and slices it into packets of a length that the network designer determines. The packets are handed off to a packet node, which terminates the circuits and routes packets to the destination. The nodes may be specialized computers or devices that closely resemble multiplexers such as the Codex Packet Switch with an integrated PAD, shown in Figure 3.20. The interface between the PAD and the packet node is CCITT X.25. The standard does not establish the protocol between nodes, so most networks are assembled from nodes of identical manufacture.

Packet networks are usually interconnected in a mesh configuration with at least two alternate routes for handing off traffic. The network uses one of several routing algorithms, which Chapter 25 discusses, to deliver packets to the next node. The transmission is checked for errors in each link and packets are sequenced and handed off to the PAD. The PAD disassembles received packets and presents the original bit stream to the receiving device.

A packet switching network is robust compared to other data communications facilities. Because of its alternate routing capability, the network can usually survive a link failure, although throughput may be diminished. The end-to-end transmission delay through a packet network is usually greater than through a multiplexer network because of the processing time required in each node. Packet networks were developed for a time when circuit error rates were high and speeds were low. With today's digital circuits, packet switching technology is giving way to techniques such as fast packet, which Chapter 7 discusses. Some observers believe that packet switching in its present form will probably not survive beyond the turn of the century.

Ancillary Equipment

This section discusses the ancillary equipment that is available on the market to aid the user in assembling unique applications.

Protocol Converters

When incompatible devices must be used on the same data network, it is often necessary to use a protocol converter. The most common conversion is between synchronous and asynchronous devices. For example, an ASCII to SDLC convertor can be used to enable asynchronous terminals to function on an IBM network. Protocol converters to enable asynchronous and synchronous devices to communicate with X.25 networks are also becoming important. Special types of protocol converters known as gateways are often used to interconnect incompatible networks. A gateway physically connects to each network and implements all the protocol functions of each, making the incompatibility transparent to the users. Gateways also enable local area networks to interface with host computers.

Modem Sharing Devices

The total bandwidth of a circuit is often greater than a single attached device requires. A modem sharing device performs much the same function as a multiplexer, but it is less complex to purchase and administer. It receives information from the line and directs it to the appropriate device, which could be a terminal or a printer. It accepts data from the attached computer and buffers it, if necessary, until line capacity is available to receive it.

Dial Backup Units

Dial backup capability to provide continuity of service if a dedicated line fails is either contained in a modem or provided as a stand-alone device. As discussed in Chapter 33, a dial backup unit normally requires two dial lines to provide the equivalent of full duplex private line capacity. The service may be established manually, or the dial backup unit may monitor the dedicated line and automatically switch with a short interruption in service when a failure occurs.

Bridges

Multidrop circuits are established by *bridging* multiple point-to-point lines. A bridge terminates each line in its characteristic impedance and may provide amplification to make up for bridging losses. The LEC or IEC often provides bridging, but it also may be installed on the customer's premises. Customer premises bridging is effective when a network of T-1 private lines is available and in a campus environment where twisted pair cable supports multiple controllers. It is important to understand that this type of bridge is different from bridges used in local area networks. A LAN bridge is used to extend the range of a network.

Applications

Unlike voice applications, which usually can be handled by equipment vendors and common carriers with little participation by the customer, data applications require direct involvement of the manager. Few applications have a single solution. It is usually possible to design an array of solutions to any problem, with the principal tradeoffs being ease of use, cost, maintainability, and survivability in case of failure. The manager needs a fully defined set of requirements and objectives to select the most effective alternative. This section discusses some important considerations in evaluating data communications services and equipment.

Standards

ANSI, EIA, and CCITT are the principal data communications standards agencies affecting equipment used in the United States. Although much of the data communications equipment being manufactured today conforms to CCITT standards, a considerable amount of nonconforming equipment is in use. For example, dial-up modems operating at less than 2400 b/s use AT&T standards. Many data communications systems operate under proprietary protocols such as IBM's Binary Synchronous Communication (BSC) and Synchronous Data Link Control (SDLC).

Evaluation Considerations

This section discusses considerations in evaluating the major items of data communications equipment. Some factors, including the following, are common to all classes of equipment:

- Compatibility with standards.
- Compatibility with existing equipment.
- Support of the manufacturer and its representatives.
- Compatibility with network management systems.

Evaluating Modems

The following are the most important considerations in choosing a modem.

Dial-up vs. Private Line.   Although some modems are designed for both dial-up and private line use, most models are designed for one or the other. Units that are designed for both are more expensive than single purpose units.

Standards Compatibility.   Many of today's modems conform to one or more CCITT standards, older Bell standards, or both. If modems that do not conform to one of these standards are chosen, they will probably be compatible only with modems of the same manufacture. Consider, in choosing a modem, whether true V.32 capability is required. The V.32 standard calls for full duplex operation at 9600 b/s over a dial-up channel. Less expensive modems offer 9600 b/s in one direction with a reduced speed in the other. For many applications, this capacity is sufficient.

Another important consideration in standards compatibility is what form of data compression and error correction capability the modem supports. Many manufacturers support the MNP protocol. The recently adopted CCITT V.42 and V.42 *bis* standards are compatible with MNP's error correction method but not with its data compression method.

Modem Reversal Time.   Half duplex modems require a finite time to reverse the line from send to receive. This variable is specified as turnaround time or RTS/CTS delay. Fast reversal modems have delay times of less than 10 ms. Other modems may have reversal times as high as 100 ms.

Modulation Method.   The modulation method normally will be a function of the CCITT or Bell compatibility specification if the modem conforms to one of those standards. Since nearly all dial-up modems conform to a standard, the modulation method depends on speed. Private line modems may follow a proprietary modulation scheme, but most will be frequency shift keying (FSK), phase shift keying (PSK), quadrature amplitude modulation (QAM), or trellis-coded modulation (TCM).

Speed. Next to standards compatibility, speed is the primary factor in selecting a modem. Generally, the higher the speed, the higher the price. To save money, choose the lowest speed that meets response time and throughput requirements.

Operating Mode. Modems operate in either full or half duplex mode, synchronous or asynchronous. The application often drives the mode. For example, IBM's BISYNC protocol is inherently half duplex synchronous. Dual-mode modems are available and are generally more expensive than single-mode modems.

Equalization Method. Most modems are equalized to match the characteristics of the transmission facility. Equalization is either fixed or adaptive. The latter is more expensive, but it may enable the modem to function over an unconditioned line, which will save recurring costs on leased circuits.

Diagnostic Capability. Most external modems display the status of the line and major signal leads on the front panel. More elaborate models display status information on alphanumeric readouts. The most elaborate private line modems include network management information that can be linked to a diagnostic center.

Evaluating Multiplexers and Concentrators

Multiplexers can be classified in several ways. First is the time division versus statistical multiplexer classification. Statistical multiplexers are divided into two classes, high end multiplexers that support multiple lines and 30 or more ports and can wrap around line failures, and low end units that simply permit multiple devices to share a single line. This section discusses evaluation considerations of multiplexers and concentrators.

Line Speed. Most multiplexers on the market can support 9600 b/s analog and digital lines. Increasingly, higher speeds including 19.2 kb/s, 56 kb/s, and 64 kb/s are available. An important factor is whether the multiplexer can be upgraded to higher speeds by replacing a card.

Number and Speed of Ports Supported.   The multiplexer must be evaluated based on the number of EIA input devices it can support. Also, the speed of the input ports is important. In some multiplexers, port contention permits multiple input devices to contend for access to a group of ports, which effectively increases the port capacity of the system.

Redundancy.   High end multiplexers have redundant power supplies and processors, which makes them less vulnerable to equipment failures.

Protocol Support.   Multiplexers usually support asynchronous devices. Some applications require support of other protocols such as SDLC and BSC. Some multiplexers support X.25 connections from packet assembler/disassemblers (PADs) and X.25 connections to a packet node.

Security.   Multiplexers may require users to log in and enter a password, adding a second level of security to the host environment.

Network Management Capability.   The multiplexer may be required to support a network management protocol to simplify the task of managing the network and its resources.

Evaluating Packet Switching Equipment

Evaluation considerations for packet switching equipment and multiplexers are equivalent. The same factors discussed in the preceding section should be considered.

Absolute Delay.   Absolute delay affects throughput. The more nodes a signal traverses, the greater the delay and the lower the throughput. A packet switch vendor should be able to quote the absolute delay through its packet switching equipment.

Access Method.   Packet networks are accessed by one of three methods: dial-up to a PAD located on the vendor's premises, a dedicated circuit to a vendor-supplied PAD, or an X.25 connection from the user's PAD to the node. The link between the user's premises and the node may not be protected from errors in the first two access methods. Unless an X.25 circuit from the premises to the node is employed, an error correcting protocol between terminal devices may be required.

Network Certification.   Although X.25 is a standard protocol, there are many variations that network vendors can support. The PAD function may be implemented in a host computer or as a stand-alone device. In either case, the vendor must be prepared to obtain certification from the network vendor that the PAD is compatible.

Selected Data Communications Equipment Manufacturers

Modems

Note: This is only a partial list of the most prominent manufacturers of private line modems and high speed dial-up modems. The list omits many manufacturers of dial-up modems.

Anderson-Jacobson
AT&T Paradyne
Case Communications
Cermetek Microelectronics, Inc.
Codex Corporation
Concord Data Systems, Inc.
Data Race
Databit Inc.
Datec Inc.
Digital Equipment Corporation
Fairchild Data Corp.
Gandalf Technologies, Inc.

General Datacomm, Inc.
Hayes Microcomputer Products, Inc.
IBM Corporation
Micom Communications Corp.
Microcom, Inc.
Mitel Datacom, Inc.
NEC America Inc.
Network Equipment Technologies, Inc.
Penril DataComm
Prentice Corp.

Packet Switching Equipment

BBN Communications Corporation
BT Tymnet Corp.
Case/Datatel, Inc.
Digital Communications Assoc.
Dynatech Communications, Inc.
Gandalf Data, Inc.
Hewlett-Packard Co.
Hughes Network Systems, Inc.

Infotron Systems Corp.
M/A COMM DCC Packet Switching
Micom Communications Corp.
Network Equipment Technologies, Inc.
Sprint Telenet
Tellabs, Inc.
Timeplex, Inc.

Communications Processors

Advanced Computer Communications, Inc.

Amdahl Communications

AT&T Paradyne

Computer Communications, Inc.

Control Data Corp. Communications Systems Div.

Digital Equipment Corp.

IBM Corp.

Micom Communications Corp.

Unisys Corp.

Protocol Converters

Codex Corporation

Data General Corporation

Datapoint Corporation

Digital Communications Assoc.

Gandalf Data Inc.

IBM Corporation

Micom Communications Corp.

Timeplex, Inc.

Time Division and Statistical Multiplexers

AT&T Paradyne Corp.

BBN Communications

Canoga-Perkins Corp.

Case/Datatel Inc.

Codex Corporation

Digital Communications Associates, Inc.

Digital Equipment Corporation

Gandalf Technologies, Inc.

General Datacomm, Inc.

Hewlett-Packard Co.

Infotron Systems Corp.

Micom Communications Corp.

Multi-Tech Systems, Inc.

Network Equipment Technologies, Inc.

OST

Penril DataComm

Prentice Corp.

Racal-Vadic, Inc.

Telindus, Inc.

Tellabs, Inc.

Timeplex, Inc.

Universal Data Systems Inc.

Video Display Terminals

AT&T Corp.

Data General Corp.

Digital Equipment Corp.

Harris Corp.

IBM Corp.

Link Technologies, Inc.

TeleVideo Systems, Inc.

Wang Laboratories, Inc.

Wyse Technology

Unisys Corp.

4

Pulse Code Modulation

From its beginnings as the basic modulation method for T-1 carrier pulse code modulation (PCM) has developed into the fundamental building block of today's switching and transmission systems. Almost every telephone session outside the bounds of the user's serving central office is carried over a system that converts voice into a digital stream of eight-bit words.

Alec Reeves, an ITT scientist in England, first patented the PCM method of multiplexing voice circuits on digital facilities. Although the system was technically conceivable then, it wasn't economically feasible. Pulse generating and amplifying circuits required vacuum tubes, and their size and power consumption consigned PCM to the shelf for another 20 years. Following the development of the transistor, PCM became commercially feasible in the 1960s, and with the development of large scale integration the following decade, cost, size, and power consumption continued to drop, even in the face of high inflation.

Today, digital technology has all but replaced analog technology in transmission systems and is rapidly replacing it in switching systems. Besides the lower cost of integrated circuitry, digital systems have the added advantage of directly interfacing digital switching systems and data circuits without an intervening voice frequency conversion. Digital multiplex is compact, with a per-circuit density more than four times as great as equivalent analog systems. Digital circuits are also less susceptible to noise. In analog circuits, noise is additive, increasing with system length, but in digital carrier the signal is regenerated at each repeater. Over a properly engineered system, the signal arrives at the receiving terminal with quality unimpaired.

Digital transmission has one primary disadvantage: a digital carrier requires several times more bandwidth than an analog carrier. Where an analog carrier transports a voice signal in 4 KHz of bandwidth, a digital voice channel requires 64 kb/s. Even in digital microwave radios with sophisticated modulation techniques, the density of digital signals is about half that of analog signals. As fiber optic transmission facilities replace coaxial cable and microwave, the bandwidth problem becomes insignificant. Also, as subsequent chapters explain, voice and data compression methods reduce the required bandwidth to the point that sometimes digital facilities are more efficient than analog.

Digital Carrier Technology

Carrier systems produced by the Bell System were sequentially lettered, beginning with A and continuing through P carrier. The assigned letters lacked significance until T carrier, which, unlike earlier frequency division systems, uses time division multiplex. In the strictest sense of the word, T-1 carrier refers to the twisted pair line, regenerators, and terminating equipment that carry a 1.544 mb/s signal between two terminal points. In practice, T-1 describes a transport service offered by nearly every common carrier.

A T-1 digital carrier system samples a voice signal, converts it to an eight-bit coded digital signal, interleaves it with 23 other voice channels, and transmits it over a line that regenerates the signal approximately once per mile. The digital signal is encoded and decoded in a digital central office or one of several types of terminal devices. A *channel bank* combines 24 voice and data circuits into a T-1 bit stream. Figure 4.1 is a photograph of a Newbridge 3624 Mainstreet 24-channel bank. A *T-1 multiplexer*, which is described later, breaks the T-1 bit stream into smaller increments than a channel bank and supports both voice and data signals. T-1 lines can be directly connected into digital PBXs and a variety of other devices such as automatic call distributors, all of which are discussed in later chapters.

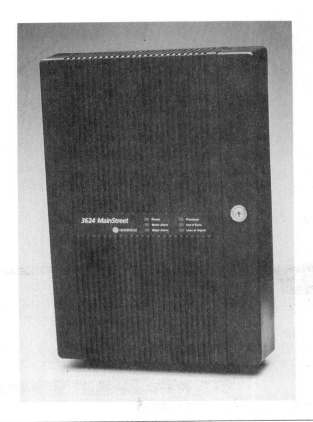

Figure 4.1 Newbridge 3624 MainStreet channel bank.
Courtesy, Newbridge Networks, Inc.

A digital signal is developed by a five-step process, consisting of the following:

- Sampling.
- Quantizing.
- Encoding.
- Companding.
- Framing.

Sampling

According to Nyquist's Theorem, if an analog signal is sampled at a rate twice the highest frequency contained within its bandwidth,

if r = 2x, enough intelligence retained in samples to reconstruct signal output = PAM

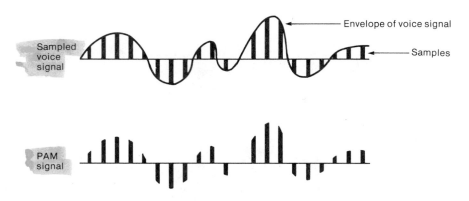

Figure 4.2   Voice sampling.

enough intelligence is retained in the samples to reconstruct the original signal. The range of human hearing is approximately 20 Hz to 20,000 Hz, but the frequency range in a voice signal is much narrower. Communications channels filter the voice to a nominal bandwidth of 4000 Hz (actually 300 to 3300 Hz). Therefore, a sampling rate of 8000 times per second would be sufficient to encode a voice signal for communications purposes. A PCM channel bank does exactly this. The output of the sampling process is a *pulse amplitude modulated* (PAM) signal, shown in Figure 4.2.

Quantizing, Encoding, and Companding

The amplitude of the pulses from the sampling circuit is encoded into an eight-bit word by a process called *quantizing*. The eight-bit word provides 2^8 or 256 discrete steps, each step corresponding to the instantaneous amplitude of the speech sample. The output of the encoder is a stream of octets, each representing the magnitude of a single sample.

The quantizing process does not exactly represent the amplitude of the PAM signal. Instead, the output is a series of steps, which, as shown in Figure 4.3a, does not precisely represent the original waveform. The error is audible in the voice channel as *quantizing noise*, which is present only when a signal is being transmitted. The effects of quantizing noise are greater with low amplitude signals than with high. To overcome this effect, the

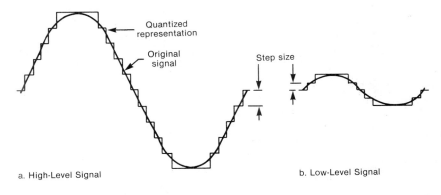

a. High-Level Signal   b. Low-Level Signal

Figure 4.3   Companding in a PCM channel bank.

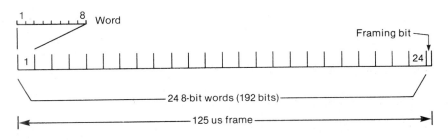

Figure 4.4   PCM frame.

encoded signal is compressed to divide low level signals into more steps and high level signals into fewer steps as shown in Figure 4.3b. When the signal is decoded at the receiving terminal, it is expanded by reversing the compression process. The combination of expansion and compression is called *companding*. In the United States companding follows a formula known as *mu law* coding. In Europe, the companding formula is a slightly different form known as *A law* coding. Although the two laws are incompatible, they differ only slightly.

Framing

The PAM voice signal is encoded in the channel bank and merged with 23 other voice channels. Each channel generates a bit rate of

64 kb/s (8000 samples per sec. x 8 bits per sample). The 24 channels produce the frame format shown in Figure 4.4. A single framing bit, required in earlier systems for synchronization of the terminal equipment, is added to the 192 bits that result from the 24 eight-bit words. A 193-bit frame, 125 microseconds in duration, results. The frame repeats 8000 times per second for a total line rate of 1.544 mb/s. The framing bits follow a fixed pattern of zeros and ones throughout 12 frames. This repetitive sequence of 12 frames is called a *super frame*. The 1.544 mb/s rate results from the following:

$$
\begin{array}{r}
8000 \text{ samples per second} \\
\underline{\times\ 8} \text{ bits per sample} \\
64,000 \text{ bits per channel} \\
\underline{\times\ 24} \text{ channels} \\
1,536,000 \text{ bits per second} \\
\underline{+\ \ 8000} \text{ framing bits per second} \\
1,544,000 \text{ bits per second total}
\end{array}
$$

European digital carrier systems use the same 64 kb/s channel bit rate but multiplex to 32 rather than 24 channels for a 2.048 mb/s bit rate. Of the 32 channels, 30 are used for voice. One channel is used for frame alignment, and one for signaling. Companding and bit rate differences make North American and European digital carrier systems incompatible.

Bit-Robbed Signaling

T-1 carrier's original purpose was interoffice trunking in metropolitan areas. Analog carrier systems required, with a few exceptions, outboard devices to signal over the channel. Since signaling is a binary function, it was economical to use a portion of the T-carrier signal itself to convey the on-hook or off-hook status of the channel. See Chapter 11 for further discussion of how signaling systems work.

The original digital channel banks used the least significant bit in every sixth frame for signaling. This technique is known as *bit robbing*. Within a super frame, the bit robbed from the sixth frame is called the *a bit*. The bit that is robbed from the 12th frame is called the *b bit*. The distortion resulting from bit robbing has no effect on voice signals or data signals modulated with a modem. The error rate would be unacceptable, however, for a 64 kb/s digital data signal. Therefore, a conventional channel bank can handle direct digital input at a maximum of 7 bits x 8000 samples per second, or 56 kb/s per channel. Many manufacturers provide channel units called *dataport* units, which allow data to be applied directly to the digital bit stream without a modem.

Extended Super Frame

Within a super frame, the framing bits synchronize the channels and signal, but otherwise carry no intelligence. Also, the signaling bits reduce the data-carrying capacity of a T-1 channel by 8000 bits per second. As the LECs and IECs convert to common channel signaling, the inband signaling capability of T-1 is no longer required. *Clear channel* capability, which is one of ISDN's features, eliminates the bit-robbed signaling and introduces a revised T-1 format known as *extended super frame* (ESF). Under ESF, the 8000 b/s framing signal, also called the Fe channel, is multiplexed to provide 2000 b/s for six-bit cyclical redundancy checking (CRC) on the data. A 4000 b/s facility data link (FDL) is used for end-to-end diagnostics, network control, and maintenance functions such as forcing loopback of a failed channel. The remaining 2000 b/s are used for framing and signaling. ESF is supported by ANSI as the T1.403 standard.

The CRC code operates in the same manner as data link error detection, which is discussed in Chapter 3. It does not, however, correct errors; it only detects them. The CRC code is calculated at the source and then again at a terminal or intermediate point. If an error is detected, the equipment can flag the fault before a hard failure occurs. The receiving equipment calculates the performance of the facility from the CRC results and sends the information back to the originating equipment over the FDL.

ESF requires a change in channel bank facilities. Some ancillary equipment, such as the channel service unit (CSU), which is described later, can be designed to operate under either SF or ESF rules. ESF requires a change in the line coding, using a coding

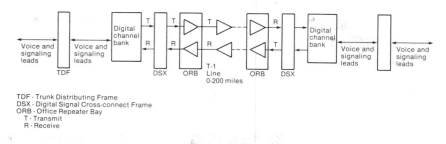

TDF - Trunk Distributing Frame
DSX - Digital Signal Cross-connect Frame
ORB - Office Repeater Bay
 T - Transmit
 R - Receive

Figure 4.5   Block diagram of a T-1 carrier system.

method known as bipolar with 8-zero substitution (B8ZS), which is discussed later.

Digital Transmission Facilities

The basic digital transmission facility is a T-1 line, which has an office repeater at each end feeding twisted pair wire, with digital regenerators spaced every 6000 feet. The function of the office repeater is to match the output of the channel bank to the impedance of the line and to feed power over the line to the repeaters. The line repeaters regenerate the incoming pulses to eliminate distortion caused by the cable. The 6000-foot spacing was selected because manholes are placed at 6000-foot intervals to match the spacing of load coils in voice frequency cables.

Digital signals are applied to twisted pair wire in groups of 24, 48, and 96 channels called T-1, T-1C, and T-2. The signals for all three originate in channel banks, digital central offices, T-1 multiplexers, PBXs, and other T-1 compatible devices. The higher bit rates of T-1C and T-2 are developed by higher order multiplexing as described later. Digital signals also can be applied to fiber optics, microwave radio, or coaxial cable for transmission over longer distances. Digital transmission over these facilities is described in Chapters 13, 14, and 17.

Digital Signal Timing

T-1 signals are synchronized by loop timing, in which synchronizing pulses are extracted from the incoming bit stream. The PCM output of a channel bank is encoded in the bipolar format that is

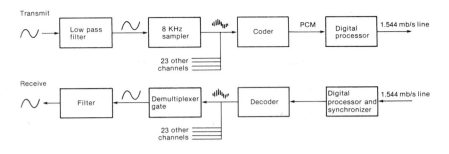

Figure 4.6   Block diagram of a PCM channel bank.

described later. The transition of each 1s bit is detected by the repeaters and the receiving terminals and is used to keep the system in synchronization. If more than 15 consecutive zeros are transmitted on a digital facility, the receiving end may lose synchronization. To prevent this, the channel bank inserts a unique bit pattern that is detected by the receiving end and restored to the original pattern. This technique, called *bit stuffing*, is used by digital carrier systems to prevent loss of synchronization.

The T-1 Carrier System

Figure 4.5 is a block diagram of a T-1 carrier system. The primary elements of the system are the channel banks and the repeaters. The other elements, distributing frame and digital crossconnect frame, are provided for ease of assignment and maintenance.

Channel Banks

A basic digital channel bank consists of 24 channels called a *digroup*. Most manufacturers package two digroups in a 48-channel framework. Five modes of operation are common in the industry:

- Mode 1—A 48-channel mode operating over a T-1C line.

- Mode 2—A 48-channel mode operating over a T-1C line but with the digroups separately timed for operation with an external multiplexer.

- Mode 3—Independent 24-channel digroups operating over two T-1 lines.

Table 4.1   Digital Carrier Typical Channel Unit Types

CODE	FUNCTION
2W E&M	Two-wire E&M signaling trunk
4W E&M	Four-wire E&M signaling trunk
SDPO	Sleeve control dial pulse originating
DPO	Dial pulse originating
DPT	Dial pulse terminating
2W FXO	Two-wire foreign exchange office
4W FXO	Four-wire foreign exchange office
2W FXS	Two-wire foreign exchange subscriber
4W FXS	Four-wire foreign exchange subscriber
2W DX	Two-wire duplex signaling
4W DX	Four-wire duplex signaling
2W ETO	Two-wire equalized transmission only
4W ETO	Four-wire equalized transmission only
2W FXO/GT	Two-wire foreign exchange office with gain transfer
2W FXS/GT	Four-wire foreign exchange office with gain transfer
4W SF	Four-wire single-frequency signaling
PLR	Pulse link repeater
PG	Program
RD	Ringdown
PLAR	Private line automatic ringdown
OCU DP	OCU dataport

- Mode 4—Dual 48-channel banks combined to operate over a T-2 line.

- Mode 5—Dual 48-channel banks combined to operate over a fiber optic pair.

The 48 channels share a common power supply and other common equipment, failure of which can interrupt all 48 channels simultaneously. Figure 4.6 is a block diagram of a digital channel bank.

The channel bank has a metal framework with backplane wiring designed to accept plug-in common equipment and channel units. In the United States, the electrical characteristics of a T-1 signal were developed from information released into the public domain by AT&T through the United States Telephone Association. All T-1 channel banks sold for domestic use conform to the electrical characteristics of the AT&T plan and are therefore end-to-end compatible, but each manufacturer develops its own mountings. Channel and common equipment plug-ins are therefore not physically compatible unless the manufacturer has specifically designed them to plug into the mounting of another manufacturer.

A major advantage of digital channel banks over their analog counterparts is the availability of many channel unit plug-ins. Integrated in these plugs are electrical functions that require external equipment in analog carrier systems. These functions include integrated signaling, voice frequency gain, wide band program transmission, and data transmission capability. Table 4.1 lists the channel units available from most major manufacturers. Most of these special service units have unique signaling options, which are explained in Chapter 11; the transmission functions are covered in this chapter.

Dataport Channel Units

As mentioned earlier, dataport channel units enable direct access to a T carrier bit stream without using a modem or digital-to-analog conversion. Dataport units compatible with the bit-robbed signaling of T-carrier are available in speeds of 2.4, 4.8, 9.6, 19.2, 56, and 64 kb/s. The 64 kb/s capability is available only with ESF carrier systems. Since data circuits do not require signaling, the A and B signaling bits are set to 1 to help retain synchronization. Each channel unit occupies a mounting slot in the channel bank and uses the entire capacity of the bit stream. To access the entire 64 kb/s bandwidth of a voice channel with multiple slow speed data channels, external multiplexers can be used. Some manufacturers also produce channel units with built-in data multiplexers.

Dataport channel units are used in both common carrier and private networks. In private networks they are mounted at the

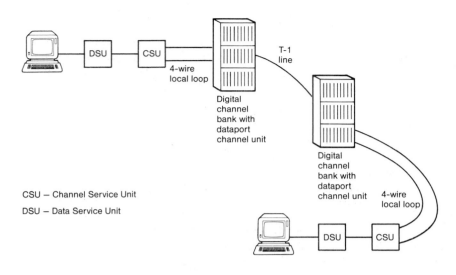

Figure 4.7   Block diagram of dataport application.

user's premises with digital lines run to the DTE through a data service unit (DSU) or channel service unit (CSU), which provide a standard interface to the DTE. The CSU is a line driver and receiver that terminates a four-wire data loop at the user's premises. It equalizes the cable, provides loop-around testing access, and includes electrical protection. A CSU is used when the DTE or a separate DSU provides zero suppression capability, clock recovery, and regeneration. The DSU performs all the functions of the CSU and is functionally equivalent to a modem in that it performs all the line functions needed to connect DTE over a data network. Figure 4.7 is a block diagram of a T carrier dataport system.

Special Transmission Functions

The plug-in units listed in Table 4.1 provide several special transmission functions in addition to the signaling functions that will be described in Chapter 11. Foreign exchange (FX) service is a combination of special signaling and transmission service. It is used by LECs to connect a telephone line in one exchange to a station located in another. FX channel units are also used in PBXs to connect the PBX to off-premises station lines or to foreign exchange trunks extended between PBXs. FX channel units are equipped for direct connection to metallic loops and have provisions for ringing telephones and for adding gain to long loops (gain transfer option).

Program (PG) channel units replace two or more voice channel units and use the added bit stream to accommodate a wider channel for use by radio and television stations, wired music companies, and other applications that require a wide audio band. Program channels with 5 KHz bandwidth replace two voice channels, and 15 KHz units replace six voice channels.

Transmission Only (TO) channel units are used for circuits that do not require signaling and for data services in which signaling is part of the application. TO channel units are also used to connect channels in channel banks wired back-to-back. Back-to-back wiring is used at intermediate points on a T carrier line when it is necessary to drop off individual voice channels.

Intelligent Channel Banks

Although the variety of channel units is a major advantage of digital channel banks, the use of this flexibility requires a large inventory of channel units to ensure that the required units are available for spares and growth. The latest generation of channel banks, typified by Newbridge's 4624 Mainstreet and AT&T's D5 Digital Termination System (DTS), includes intelligence in the channel bank and its channel units. The DTS has a System Controller and up to 20 D5 channel banks of 96 voice channels each.

The D5 channel bank can be accessed remotely over a data facility, and through its controller, the channel units can be remotely adjusted. Channel unit control settings and option selections are typed into a Craft Interface Unit that is either colocated with the DTS or located at the network control center. With this system, channel units can be remotely configured as one of several types by combining more than 25 channel unit types into four, greatly simplifying the inventory management task. Also, through this remote device, transmission levels can be set and maintenance tests made without a technician at the terminal, which reduces the cost of maintaining the system.

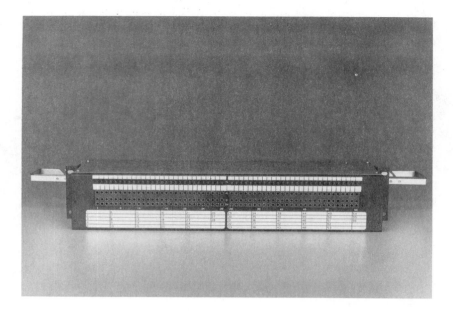

Figure 4.8   ADC digital signal crossconnect (DSX) panel.
Courtesy, ADC Telecommunications Corporation

Digital Crossconnect Panel

In most multiple channel bank installations a digital signal cross-connect (DSX) panel, shown in Figure 4.8, is provided. The transmit and receive circuits of the channel bank are wired through jacks in this panel to provide test access and to enable the channel bank to be connected to another T-1 carrier line. The transfer of the T-1 bit stream to another line is called *patching* and is used for rearranging circuits and for manually transferring to a spare line when repeaters fail.

The ability to patch to spare lines is a vital part of service restoration in common carrier applications and is provided in most installations. In private networks the DSX panel is useful for temporary rearrangement of facilities. For example, a T-1 facility might be used for multiple low speed point-to-point terminal communications during working hours and patched to a high speed multiplexer for transfer of data after hours.

Automatic protection switching is often used for manual patching where rapid restoral is essential and where one or both terminals are unattended. The automatic protection system monitors the bit stream of the protected channel banks and switches automatically to a spare line when the working line fails.

Distributing Frame

The voice frequency side of a channel is wired to crossconnect blocks on a distributing frame, which is discussed in Chapter 12. A crossconnect block provides a convenient location for concentrating lines between the channel banks and their interfacing equipment. Where temporary rearrangements are needed, the voice frequency and signaling leads of a channel are wired through jacks. These jack panels are a convenient place for rapidly restoring circuits and for temporarily rerouting equipment to another channel.

T Carrier Lines

T-1 carrier lines can be extended on twisted pair wire for about 200 miles, although most private and common carrier applications are considerably shorter because longer circuits are usually deployed over radio or fiber optic facilities. A T carrier line accepts a *bipolar* signal from the channel bank as shown in Figure 4.9. A bipolar signal, also called *alternate mark inversion*, assigns 0s to a zero voltage level. Ones signals are alternately + 3 volts. The bipolar signal offers two advantages. First, the line signaling rate is only half the data rate of 1.544 mb/s because in the worst case of a signal composed of all 1s, the signal would alternate at only 772 kb/s. The second advantage is the ability of a bipolar signal to detect line errors. If interference or a failing repeater adds or subtracts 1s bits, a bipolar violation results, which indicates a fault in a T carrier system. A bipolar violation occurs when two 1s bits of the same polarity arrive in sequence.

Clear channel capability requires the T carrier system to support any pattern of bits, including long strings of 0s. ESF systems replace the straight bipolar signal with a coding scheme known as *bipolar with 8-zero substitution* (B8ZS). In this system, any string of eight 0s is replaced with an intentional bipolar

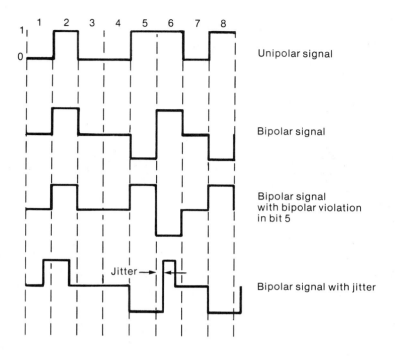

Figure 4.9   T-1 carrier line signals and faults.

violation at the fourth and seventh bits. The receiving equipment, normally the channel service unit, detects the bipolar violation and replaces it with a string of eight 0s. The B8ZS coding scheme is not compatible with earlier T carrier lines, which may correct bipolar violations, but most modern regenerators, office repeaters, and channel service units are ESF-compatible.

Office Repeaters and Channel Service Units

An office repeater terminates the T-1 line at each central office. In the receiving direction, the office repeater performs normal repeater functions, but it is passive in the transmit direction. Its transmit function is to couple the bipolar signal to the line and to feed power to the line repeaters. A special type of office repeater

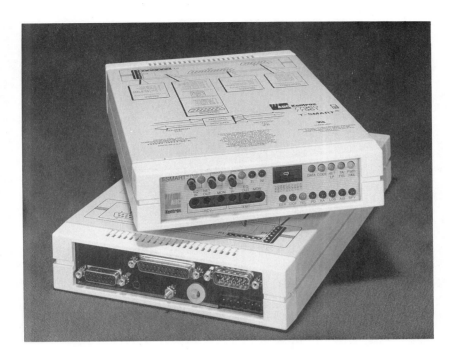

Figure 4.10   ADC Kentrox T-Smart T-1 Carrier channel service unit.
Courtesy, ADC Kentrox Corporation

called a channel service unit (CSU) terminates the customer end of a T-1 line feeding customer premises. Not to be confused with a CSU that operates on a single DDS channel, a T-1 CSU terminates the entire T-1 line. Figure 4.10 shows an ADC Kentrox T-Smart T-1 CSU.

The CSU was considered part of the network before divestiture, but the FCC has ruled that the CSU is network channel terminating equipment (NCTE) and is therefore to be furnished by the customer. Unlike a DDS signal where a DSU is required to convert the line signal from bipolar to the unipolar signal required by the terminal equipment, the bipolar signal is produced by the T-1 multiplexer or channel bank. Increasingly, the CSU function is built into the channel bank or the multiplexer. The CSU fulfills the following functions:

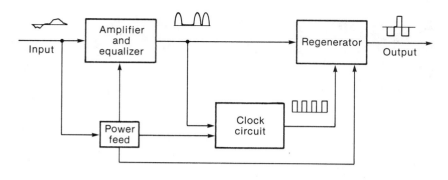

Figure 4.11   Block diagram of a T-1 repeater.

- Terminates the circuit, including lightning and surge protection.
- Regenerates the signal.
- Loops the digital signal back to the originating end upon command.
- Monitors the incoming line for bipolar violations.
- Generates a signal—usually all 1s—to maintain synchronization on the line if the terminal equipment fails.
- Maintains the 1s density requirement of the line.
- Provides signal lamps and line jacks for testing and monitoring.
- Provides line build-out (LBO) if necessary.

Line Repeaters

Line repeaters are mounted in an apparatus case holding 25 units. Apparatus cases are watertight for mounting on poles and in manholes. Repeaters, shown in a block diagram in Figure 4.11, perform these functions:

- Amplify and equalize the received signal.
- Generate an internal timing signal.
- Decide whether incoming pulses are 0s or 1s.
- Regenerate pulses and insert them in the correct output time slot.

Incoming pulses are received in one of three states—plus, minus, or 0. If the incoming pulse, which has been distorted by the electrical characteristics of the line, exceeds the plus or minus threshold, the repeater generates a 1 output pulse. Otherwise it registers a 0.

Phase deviations in the pulse, which are additive along a T carrier line, are known as *jitter*. Excessive jitter, as illustrated in Figure 4.9, can cause errors in data signals. Errors occur when the receiver in a repeater or a terminal incorrectly interprets the incoming signal.

The transmit and receive paths of T-1 signals must be isolated to prevent crosstalk coupling. If excessive crosstalk occurs between the high level pulses of a repeater's output and the low level received pulses of adjacent repeaters, errors will result. These are prevented by assigning the transmit and receive directions to separate cables, to partitions within a specially screened cable, or to separate binder groups within a single cable. Cable binder groups are explained in Chapter 6.

T-1C and T-2 lines operate on the same general principles as T-1 lines except that their bit rates are higher and greater isolation between the pairs prevents crosstalk. Design rules for these systems require either a screened cable, which contains a shield to separate transmit and receive pairs, or separate transmit and receive cables.

T-1 Carrier Synchronization

When T-1 carrier is used in a private network that carries end-to-end digital signals, it is important that the network be kept in synchronization. To understand why, consider the timing diagram shown in Figure 4.12. If the clock of one terminal device runs slightly faster or slower than the clock at the other end, a point will be reached where an extra bit will be inserted or a bit will be lost, and the entire frame will lose synchronization momentarily. This condition is known as a *slip*.

When T-1 carrier was introduced, the circuits riding on the network were mostly analog, and synchronization between the two ends of a circuit was not important. The two directions of transmission were independent of each other, and the receiving

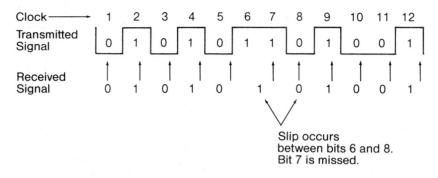

Figure 4.12   Slip in digital transmission.

end extracted timing from the line. If a slip occurred, it was heard as a slight pop and had little effect on voice transmission. With the advent of end-to-end digital circuits, however, slips became a matter of great concern because the loss of one frame of 193 bits causes one or more data blocks to be rejected. To prevent slips and consequent data errors, the entire digital network must be kept locked in synchronization.

In a private network of only two devices linked by T-1, one device is a master and the other is a slave. A precise clocking rate is not important. If the slave extracts clocking from the 1s bits in the received signal, synchronization is maintained. The more nodes that are added to the network, the more critical the provision of a master clock becomes. When the network is connected to a common carrier network, as with a T-1 long distance service, it is vital that the entire network slave from the common carrier because the carrier is tied to a higher level in the national clocking structure.

Nationally, digital network synchronization is maintained through a four-level hierarchy of clocks. ANSI standard T1.101 defines the four levels, which are known as Stratum 1 through Stratum 4 timing levels. Stratum 1 clocks use highly accurate oscillators using Cesium and Rubidium clocks with a maximum drift of 1×10^{-11}. Stratum 2 clocks, which are used in common carriers' toll centers, are slightly less accurate—1×10^{-10} in the short term (one day)—but if synchronization is lost with the Stratum 1 clock, it will still maintain an acceptable amount of stability. Stratum 3 and 4 are less stable and generally depend on

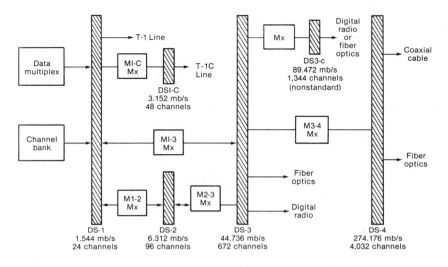

Figure 4.13   North American digital signal hierarchy.

synchronization from higher levels to maintain an acceptable degree of performance. Private network equipment generally contains Stratum 3 or 4 clocking.

The Digital Signal Hierarchy

Digital signals from a T-1 source are multiplexed to higher rates. Figure 4.13 shows the bit rates of the North American digital hierarchy. T-1 signals are applied to a standard repeatered line as described in the next section. Higher rate signals are applied to wire, coaxial cable, fiber optics, and digital microwave radio.

A family of multiplexers raises the basic digital group to higher bit rates. Multiplexers are designated according to the digital signal levels they interface. For example, an M1-3 multiplexer connects DS-1 to DS-3. An M1-3 multiplexer accepts 28 DS-1 inputs and combines them into a single 45 mb/s bit stream. (The bit stream is 44.736 mb/s, but it is commonly called 45 mb/s in the industry.) Multiplexer output can be directly connected to a digital radio or to a fiber optic system.

The primary use of the DS-4 signal level is to feed T-4 coaxial cable. The DS-4 signal speed is too high to apply to the limited bandwidth of a digital microwave, which is currently limited to carrying three DS-3 signals. Lightwave systems, described in Chapter 13, can easily support 274 mb/s, but their bandwidth can transport much higher bit rates, so most manufacturers are producing equipment that operates at bit rates of 1 gb/s or more and are undefined in the digital hierarchy. This ambiguity will eventually be corrected as the world adopts synchronous optical network (SONET) standards, which are discussed in Chapter 13.

Digital Crossconnect Systems

Short haul carrier systems converge in central offices in both private and common carrier networks for connection to long haul facilities. If 24-channel digroups are connected through the office to a single terminating point, no channel bank is required. Instead the incoming T-1 line is connected to the outgoing line with an express office repeater with channel banks needed only at the terminating ends. If fewer than 24 channels are needed, or if channels from a single originating point must be split to separate terminating points, back-to-back channel banks or a drop-and-insert multiplexer must be used to access the bit stream for channel crossconnection.

Back-to-back channel banks are undesirable for several reasons:

- Cost of the channel banks.
- Channel banks are an added source of potential circuit failure.
- Labor cost of making channel crossconnections.
- Extra analog-to-digital conversions, which are a source of distortion.

For smaller networks, a drop-and-insert multiplexer, which splits a certain number of channels out of the T-1 bit stream, can be used. For larger networks, the *digital crossconnect system* (DCS) is a specialized electronic switch that terminates T-carrier lines without channel banks and routes the individual channel bit streams to the desired output line. Figure 4.14 is a photograph of a Tellabs T-1 digital crossconnect system. Unlike the electronic digital switches covered in Chapters 8, 9, and 10, a DCS establishes a semi-permanent path for the bit stream through the switch. This path remains connected until it is disconnected or changed by programmer order or administrative action.

The DCS system eliminates most of the labor associated with rearrangement, eliminates extra analog-to-digital conversions, and offers a high degree of flexibility in rerouting circuits. Also, routing changes can be controlled from a central location over a data link. If the organization uses a mechanized data base to maintain records of facility assignments, the same source that updates the data base can drive the DCS assignments. DCS is a space-saving system because it eliminates the distributing frame blocks and wire required to interconnect the large numbers of voice frequency and signaling leads that back-to-back channel banks would require.

DCS is the key to implementing the intelligent digital network described in Chapter 25. Linked to the user's network control system, DCS allows the user to reconfigure the network to meet changes in demand or to accommodate changes that occur with time, such as assigning network capacity to a voice switch during normal working hours and to a computer center for high speed data transfer during off hours.

Private network managers are increasingly becoming attuned to the problem of network restoral, a function in which DCS plays a key role. When a major switch node fails, a DCS system can quickly reroute traffic around the point of failure. It also increases the traffic carried by T-1 systems. Many of today's T-1 networks are only partially filled. With DCS it is feasible to combine channels to fill a T-1, though it may mean routing a circuit over greater distance than it would otherwise span.

Privately owned DCS systems are not the only alternative available to network operators who need DCS capability. Most large LECs offer DCS as a contracted or tariffed service. Since the T-1 lines may extend through the LEC's central office anyway, using a centralized DCS may make sense technically and economically. The principal issue, however, is the degree of control the LEC provides over the DCS facility. If the network operator has full control over circuit configuration, the use of private versus common carrier DCS is primarily an economic issue.

Figure 4.14   Tellabs T-1 digital crossconnect system.
Courtesy, Tellabs, Inc.

Figure 4.15   General Datacom Megamux TNS T-1 multiplexer.
Courtesy, General Datacomm, Inc.

T-1 Multiplexers

Channel banks are somewhat inflexible devices for subdividing the T-1 bit stream. Voice channels and data occupy a full 64 kb/s each, though the data channels may operate at speeds as slow as 2400 b/s. Also, even intelligent channel banks lack the ability to switch and reroute signals. A more versatile (and expensive) device is the T-1 multiplexer, which uses TDM techniques to combine multiple low speed bit streams into a 1.544 mb/s signal. By using external multi-plexers, it is possible to divide the bandwidth of a single T-1 into more than 2000 fragments. Figure 4.15 shows the General DataC-omm Megamux TNS T-1 multiplexer.

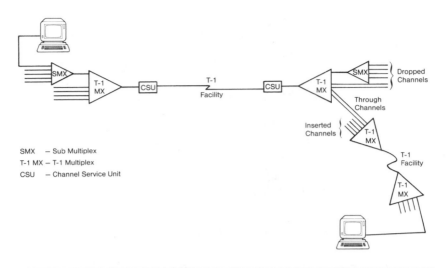

Figure 4.16   T-1 multiplexer layout showing drop-and-insert capability and submultiplexing low-speed channels.

T-1 multiplexers contain control logic to provide clocking, generate frames, and enable testing. The control logic and the power supply are common to the entire multiplexer and may be redundant to improve reliability. The diagnostic capabilities include alarm and loop-back facilities and may include a built-in test pattern generator to help in trouble diagnosis. Multiplexers can generally handle synchronous data from 50 b/s to 1.544 mb/s, and asynchronous data from 50 b/s to 19.2 kb/s. Voice input is accommodated by using PCM or voice compression methods, such as adaptive differential pulse code modulation (ADPCM), or delta modulation, both of which are described in Chapter 7. ADPCM compresses the voice into 32 kb/s, and delta modulation compresses voice into either 32 kb/s or 16 kb/s.

T-1 multiplexers divide the bit stream into a series of sub-slots. Some provide slow speed sub-slots; others provide larger sub-slots, which require external multiplexers to use the capacity of the sub-slot for low speed data. Figure 4.16 shows how a network might be constructed by multiplexing data over T-1 lines. It also shows drop-and-insert capability, another feature of multiplexers. This allows the multiplexer to extract selected channels while extending others on to another destination.

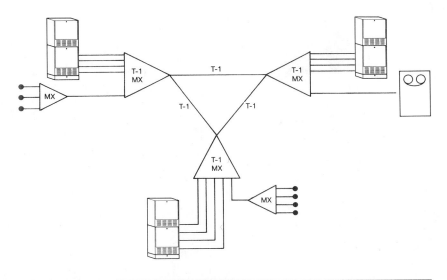

Figure 4.17 Networked T-1 multiplexers.

T-1 multiplexers are more expensive than channel banks. Some products cost two to four times the price of a channel bank, but multiplexers offer significantly increased functionality. Multiplexers can be networked, as Figure 4.17 shows, to form an integrated voice and data network with alternate routing capability and sophisticated network management. A channel bank can theoretically derive as many channels from a T-1 line as a multiplexer can, but to do so would require external data multiplexers and voice compression equipment. The external equipment would be more costly than providing the same facilities in a multiplexer, and the channel bank would still lack the management capabilities and flexibility of a multiplexer.

A valuable feature of T-1 multiplexers is their network management capability. Some multiplexers have the capability of monitoring multiple points in the network, reporting malfunctions and keeping the network manager supplied with usage and performance information from all the nodes. Another vital feature of many multiplexers is their ability to reroute circuits during failure or congestion. Two different systems are used to keep data flowing. A *table-based* system is composed of fixed routing tables that instruct the multiplexer how to act in the face of a failure. A

Figure 4.18   Newbridge 3630 MainStreet multiplexer.
Courtesy, Newbridge Networks, Inc

parameterized, or rule-based, system develops a global view of
the network and responds flexibly.

Drop-and-Insert Multiplexers

Drop-and-insert multiplexers have been available for more than a
decade, but the recent growth of private T-1 systems has made
them increasingly attractive to end users. In concept, a drop-and-
insert multiplexer is similar to an ordinary channel bank with
respect to the channels that are dropped or inserted. These are
connected as individual channels or as a portion of the T-1
bandwidth to a host computer of similar device. A portion of the
T-1 line is connected straight through the multiplexer, usually
continuing on to the next terminal point or terminating in a PBX

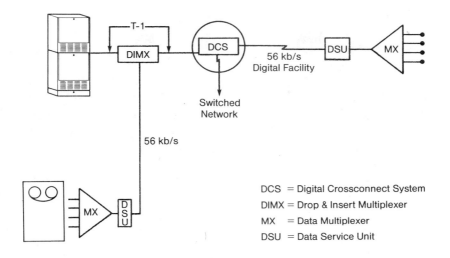

Figure 4.19 **Sharing a voice and data T-1 entrance facility on a single T-1.**

as shown in Figure 4.19. Drop-and-insert capabilities may also be contained in a T-1 multiplexer. A Newbridge 3630 multiplexer is shown in Figure 4.18. This device can be equipped with one or two T-1 interfaces.

T Carrier Line Expansion Systems

Many systems designed to increase the capacity of a carrier line beyond the basic 24 channels of T-1 are proposed or already in use. These can be roughly grouped into two categories: those that use different coding systems on the carrier line to increase its carrying capacity and those that use data compression techniques to encode voice in fewer than the 64 kb/s used by PCM. The former type of system is discussed in this section; voice compression systems are covered in Chapter 7.

T Carrier Line Encoding

The carrying capacity of a T-1 line can be doubled or quadrupled by using different coding schemes to replace the bipolar T-1 line signal. We have discussed T-1C, which employs bipolar line signaling at double the T-1 rate. In addition, there are other systems that are proprietary to their manufacturers. A product called T-1G offered by AT&T encodes the carrier line at 3.22175 mb/s to compress 96 channels into a cable designed for T-1C service.

Unlike T-1, which is standardized among all manufacturers, these systems are proprietary and therefore are compatible only with like equipment. The increase in capacity is achieved at some disadvantage; to expand existing T carrier lines requires replacing repeaters and, sometimes, the apparatus cases that house them. The design rules are more stringent because of crosstalk considerations. Also, this line equipment is usable only on metallic cable facilities. It cannot be used to expand the carrying capacity of radio and fiber optic facilities.

Fractional T-1

Digital service users have, until recently, been faced with two alternatives: leasing service one channel at a time or leasing a full 24-channel T-1 line. With the advent of fractional T-1, a much wider choice is available. For example, AT&T's fractional T-1 offering, Accunet Spectrum of Digital Services (ASDS), provides service at 56 , 64 , 128 , 256 , 512 , and 768 kb/s. Other vendors offer fractional T-1 in multiples of 64 kb/s. The basic building block is the DS-0 channel. Higher bandwidths are available for services such as slow speed digital conferencing, high speed data, and bridging local area networks.

Technically, fractional T-1 is little different from a full T-1 channel. The IEC simply subdivides an existing T-1 channel with a digital crossconnect system (DCS) or a drop-and-insert multiplexer, both of which are discussed earlier in this chapter. Until the LECs file fractional tariffs, the local loop portion of the service will receive the bandwidth of a full T-1 service though less than a full T-1 is used. The most cost-effective way for many companies to use fractional T-1 is to bring the data channels in over the same T-1 that carries incoming and outgoing long distance service. At the customer's premises the T-1 is connected to a drop-and-insert multiplexer to separate the voice and data channels. The voice channels are connected directly to the PBX, and the data channels to a computer or multiplexer, as Figure 4.19 illustrates.

Although fractional T-1 was not viewed as a replacement for analog services when it was introduced, its pricing is low enough that many users will be encouraged to migrate from analog private line services. AT&T, which provides the bulk of the analog private lines in the nation and therefore leads the pricing structure, has priced its ASDS service much lower than Dataphone Digital Service (DDS) and often lower than analog private lines. The additional digital bandwidth, which can be used for compressed voice or multiple data private lines, makes fractional T-1 attractive to most companies.

T-3 Service

The major IECs are offering T-3 service at a cost that is considerably lower than the cost of 28 separate T-1 channels. Any company that needs 10 or more T-1 lines between two cities will find T-3 an attractive option. If the LEC has fiber optic service capability, the T-3 is delivered as a single intact 44.736 mb/s bitstream. Lacking fiber optic capability, the T-3 must be delivered as 28 separate T-1 lines, which is less economical.

Applications

Digital carrier systems have wide application in both common carrier and private networks. Most metropolitan common carrier networks use digital carrier today, with analog carrier confined to expansion of existing systems. Satellite common carriers also offer digital circuits, which are multiplexed with T-1 equipment.

Standards

T carrier standards are primarily set by manufacturers in North America with voluntary adherence to the standards originally developed by Bell laboratories. Many North American standards have been adopted by CCITT and are listed in Appendix B. Extended super frame standards are supported by ANSI as the T1.403 standard, and T carrier synchronization standards are published as ANSI standard T1.101.

Evaluating Digital Transmission Equipment

Originally, digital transmission equipment was used almost exclusively by common carriers. With deregulation of the telecommunications industry, private networks are increasingly composed of digital facilities. Terminal equipment is owned by the network user, and digital lines are implemented over common carrier or privately owned facilities. The criteria for evaluating digital transmission equipment are the same for both private and public ownership.

Reliability

The failure rate of terminal and line equipment is the primary concern in any network. Because the common equipment in the channel bank, T-1 multiplexer and line repeaters, is common to many channels, a single failure disrupts a considerable amount of service. Therefore, strict attention should be paid to the failure rate of these components.

Manufacturers quote failure rates as mean time between failures (MTBF). MTBF is the number of hours between service-affecting interruptions. Although the MTBF figure is an average, it offers a convenient way of calculating the expected frequency of failure by weighting the failure rates of the individual components. For example, if a manufacturer quotes 10,000 hours MTBF on the common equipment for a channel bank and since a failure of a channel bank at either end of the circuit disrupts service, the MTBF for both channel banks together will be half the quoted rate, or 5000 hours. If repeater failures are estimated at 20,000 hours per repeater and the line has four repeaters, the MTBF of the line will be 20,000/4 = 5000 hours. If the line and the channel banks each have an MTBF of 5000 hours, the failure rate of the entire system is 2500 hours. This does not, of course, include failures of the transmission medium or failures from causes external to the equipment.

Availability of Special Service Features

T carrier channel banks can be equipped with a range of special services channel units to match the user's requirements. Most private networks will require dataport and foreign exchange channel units plus a variety of voice channel units to match the

PBX or station equipment they interface. Compatibility with the extended super frame should be considered for all equipment purchased. Even if ESF is not used now, it will likely be required for future applications.

Maintenance Features

The design and layout of a T carrier system has a substantial effect on the cost of administering and maintaining it. Channel banks and line equipment should be equipped with an alarm system that registers local alarms, which can be interfaced to telemetry for unattended operation. Test equipment needed to keep the system operative also should be considered. Typically this has a bit error rate monitor, repeater test sets, a T-1 signal source, and extender boards to obtain access to test and level monitor points on the plug-in units.

The physical layout of the system should be designed to aid maintenance. Voice frequency and signaling leads should be terminated on a distributing frame. If more than one T carrier line is terminated, DSX jacks should be provided. If temporary re-arrangements will be made, voice frequency and signaling leads should be jack-equipped.

Spare channel and common equipment plug-in units should be provided for rapid restoral, with quantities related to the number of units in service and the failure rate of the system. Carrier group alarm (CGA) may be required to lock out switching systems from access in case of channel bank failure. CGA should restore circuits automatically when the failure is corrected.

Power Consumption

Differences in power consumption are found between products of the various manufacturers. Digital carrier is normally left operating continually, so any saving in power will involve a substantial cost saving over the life of the system. Power consumption varies with the mix of channel units installed in the channel bank, so if alternative products are being evaluated, economic comparisons should be made assuming a similar mix of channel units.

Backup Power

Most digital channel banks require -48 volts DC to match the storage batteries in telephone central offices. Converters to power the equipment from commercial AC sources are available. If continuous service during power outages is required, a battery plant should be provided. T-1 multiplexers that use random access memory to store the multiplexer configuration should be equipped with battery power to prevent loss of the configuration when the power fails. See Chapter 12 for power plant and common equipment considerations.

Operating Temperature Range

The operating temperature range of a digital channel bank is rarely a consideration in either private or common carrier networks. Most digital channel banks can operate between about 0° and 50° C, which is well within the limits of most operating environments. T-1 multiplexers, which are not usually designed for a telephone central office environment, may have narrower limits that should be evaluated against the environment in which they will be installed. Forced air circulation may be required for reliable operation at higher temperatures.

Density

Digital channel banks vary in the number of channels that can be installed in a given mounting space. If floor space is plentiful, this is not a matter of great concern, but when many channel banks or multiplexers are being installed, the density and mounting method are factors to consider.

Compatibility

T-1 channel banks built for use in the United States are generally compatible with each other and with the standard T-1 line format. T carrier repeaters are not only compatible with the signal, but are also plug-compatible so that any manufacturer's repeater fits in the same slot in an apparatus case. Other than these two elements, compatibility is a matter of concern. Any T-1 multiplexer will be compatible only with itself unless it was specifically designed to be compatible with that of another manufacturer. Voice compression systems that follow CCITT standards are compatible; other systems are proprietary and will be found incompatible with one another. Any system purchased today should be compatible with the ESF frame format or it will be obsolete before the end of its service life. Compatibility with fractional T-1 is also a concern in devices such as multiplexers and CSUs.

Evaluating T-1 Multiplex

Several features are unique to T-1 multiplexers and should be considered along with the above factors:

- *Vendor support.* Multiplexers are normally deployed over a wide area and in locations where the company may not have staff. Vendor support is critical to minimize outage time.

- *Granularity.* This is the bandwidth of a single time slot and affects the ability of the multiplexer to use the total bandwidth of the T-1 line.

- *Minimum bandwidth required.* Wide bandwidths may require submultiplexers to use lower speed DTE. Some multiplexers provide narrow bandwidth channels that require no submultiplexing.

- *Data channel interface.* The multiplexer will normally support cards of different types to interface EIA-232, V.35, asynchronous, and other standard interfaces.

- *Bypass or nodal delay.* This variable refers to the propagation delay that occurs between nodes on a T-1 multiplexer network.

- *Rerouting capability.* This is the ability to reroute traffic automatically when the primary link fails. The routing method, table routing or parameterized routing, and the time required to effect a reroute are important.

- *Channel bypass and drop-and-insert.* These capabilities may be required to enable flexible use of time slots.

- *Redundancy.* The amount of redundancy in the power supply and central logic improves reliability. Also, the type of redundancy in the power supply is important. Load sharing supplies are more reliable than hot standby supplies, which must switch when the working supply fails.

- *Configuration backup.* Determine whether configuration is maintained in software or hardware. PROM memory tends to be inflexible; RAM memory is flexible but can be lost during power failures. If RAM memory is used, a backup method of restoring the configuration, such as booting from floppy disk or tape should be provided. Also, nondisruptive reconfiguration, which is the ability to reconfigure channels without affecting other channels in service, is important.

- *Circuit trace.* This is the capability to trace the lines and nodes through which a circuit passes.

- *Network management.* This capability provides at least performance reporting, configuration management, and problem diagnosis.

- *Voice compression capability.* The type of modulation used for voice channels is important. The use of ADPCM limits analog data to 4.8 kb/s; the use of delta modulation limits analog data to 2.4 kb/s. ADPCM generally offers better voice quality than other compression methods.

- *Self-diagnostic capability.* The more capability the multiplexer has to diagnose its own trouble, the more rapid restoral will be.

Evaluating Channel Service Units

The following features should be considered in evaluating CSUs for T-1 or fractional T-1 service:

- *Diagnostic capability.* Loopback capability should be a feature of any CSU. Some CSUs permit more advanced testing, particularly when devices of the same manufacture are on both ends of the circuit. ESF-compatible circuits can take advantage of accumulated statistical information, which evaluates the overall health of the circuit. ANSI T1.403 standards, published in 1989, establish the reporting capabilities of the CSU. A CSU that is ESF-compatible may not be compatible with T1.403 standards, and may or may not be capable of reporting line variables such as clock synchronization and framing errors.

- *Powering.* When CSUs were part of the network, they were usually powered from the T-1 line. The main reason for line powering was to use the CSU to maintain synchronization if the terminal equipment lost its power. Many LECs no longer furnish power, in which case the end user must provide power for the CSU.

- *Monitoring capability.* The CSU should contain 1s density and bipolar violation monitoring capability. Discrepancies should be reported to an outboard management system, displayed on panel lamps, or both.

Selected Digital Carrier Equipment Manufacturers

Channel Banks

ADC

AT&T

Aydin Monitor System Digital Communications Group

Hubbell Pulsecom Division

Newbridge Networks

Northern Telecom Inc.

Reliance Comm/Tec

Telco Systems Network Access Corp.

Digital Crossconnect Systems

ADC Telecommunications

AT&T

Augat

Coastcom

Cook Electric

Compunetics Inc., Communications Systems Div.

DCA/Cohesive

Digital Transmission Systems

DSC Communications

Frederick Engineering

Grass Valley Group

Licom, Inc.

Microtel

NEC America

NET

Newbridge Networks

Northern Telecom

Phoenix Microsystems

Porta Systems

Redcom Laboratories

Reliance

Rockwell International

Switchcraft

Telco Systems

Tellabs, Inc.

Timeplex, Inc.

T-1 Accessories (Patch Panels, Channel Service Units, etc.)

ADC Corp.
ADC Kentrox Corp.
Avanti Communications Corp.
Coastcom
Cylink
Digital Link
Larus Corp.

Phoenix Microsystems
Scitec Corp
Telecom Solutions
Teleprocessing Products
Tellabs, Inc.
Verilink Corp.

T-1 and T-3 Multiplexers

Alcatel
Amdahl Communications Systems Division
AT&T Paradyne
Avanti Communications Corp.
Aydin Monitor Systems
BBN Communications Corp.
Canoga-Perkins Corp.
Case/Datatel Inc.
Coastcom
Codex Corp.
DataProducts New England, Inc.
Digital Communications Associates, Inc.
Dowty Information Systems
DSC Communications Corp.
Equinox Systems, Inc.
Ericsson Inc., Communications Division
Fibermux Corp.
Fujitsu America, Inc.
Gandalf Data, Inc.
General Datacomm, Inc.
Granger Teleratta

Infotron Systems Corp.
Intraplex, Inc.
Micom Communications
NEC America, Inc.
Network Equipment Technologies
Newbridge Networks, Inc.
Phoenix Microsystems
Pulsecom Division, Hubbell, Inc.
Racal-Milgo
RAD Data Communications Ltd.
Raycom Systems, Inc.
Rockwell International
Spectrum Digital
StrataCom, Inc.
Telco Systems Network Access Corp.
Telecommunications Technology, Inc.
Tellabs Inc.
Teltone Corp.
Timeplex, Inc.

5

Frequency Division Multiplex

William DeForest's invention of the vacuum tube in 1906 made possible the first transcontinental telephone circuits. Those voice frequency circuits were carried on open wire, using repeaters every 300 to 350 miles to overcome loss. Vacuum tubes accelerated the development of radio and, soon after that, led to carrier telephony using frequency division multiplex (FDM). FDM is a method of deriving multiple voice frequency channels over a single analog transmission medium such as wire, coaxial cable, or microwave radio.

The first carrier systems were designed for open wire because its heavy gauge conductors had only about one-fortieth the loss of cable. Western Electric (now AT&T Technologies) C carrier, some of which remained in service past the middle of this century, added three carrier channels to the voice channel over a single open wire pair. The Western Electric J carrier system, introduced in the late 1930s, was a 12-channel system that could be applied to frequencies above C carrier, deriving a total of 15 carrier channels and one voice channel over a single pair of wires.

Open wire, which has effectively disappeared from the nation's telecommunications networks, suffers from the severe disadvantage of susceptibility to weather. In warm weather, wires sag and transmission loss increases. In cold weather, loss decreases, but icing and winds cause circuit outages, resulting in unacceptable reliability. In addition, the physical dimensions of the poles and crossarms become unwieldy when more than a few circuits are needed.

With improvements in vacuum tube technology, the closer repeater spacing required by cable carrier became feasible, and cable carrier replaced open wire carrier. Among the first, Western Electric K carrier, was a 12-channel system that operated over transmit and receive cables that were separated to prevent crosstalk. The controlled environment of K carrier cable resulted in quality superior to J carrier though they shared the same channel bank. The primary limitation of K carrier was the small number of circuits it supported. To prevent crosstalk between systems operating in the same direction, an elaborate network was required to balance every cable pair against every other pair. The size of the balancing network placed an upper limit on the number of systems that could be carried in one pair of cables.

Long Haul Carrier

The L carrier system, introduced just before World War II, is the ancestor of today's long haul carrier systems. The frequency plan is followed by all manufacturers in the United States, and with minor variations, CCITT has adopted it as an international standard. L carrier was originally designed for use on coaxial cable. As microwave radio became technically feasible in the late 1940s, L carrier was used to channelize radio using the same modulation plan used for cable. The first L carrier system, L1, developed 480 channels over a pair of coaxial tubes. This was later expanded to 600 channels. Continual improvement has resulted in the current L5E system, which supports as many as 13,200 channels over a pair of coaxial tubes.

These carrier systems, designed for transcontinental service, were either too large, as with L carrier, or too costly over short haul distances of about 100 miles or less. The increasing demand for long distance telephone service required quantities of short haul circuits that could no longer be met economically with voice frequency cables and open wire. With continuing advances in carrier telephony and new, reliable miniaturized vacuum tubes, short haul carrier was introduced in the 1950s. Western Electric N1 and Lenkurt 45BN carrier are early examples of these systems. The primary differences between short haul and long haul carrier are:

- Short haul systems use less expensive modulation techniques.
- Voice channels over short haul carriers generally have higher noise levels.
- Higher order modulation plans are available only with long haul carrier, limiting short haul systems to a capacity of approximately 24 channels.
- Long haul systems are designed to control level variations in transcontinental circuits to within 0.25 dB. Short haul regulation systems also control level variations, but not over long distances.

Both long haul and short haul carrier have undergone many advances since their introduction; however, the frequency and modulation plans remain largely unchanged. As transistors and integrated circuits became feasible, they were adopted to reduce cost and power consumption and to increase the circuit density of carrier systems. Short haul analog carrier is being rapidly replaced by digital carrier. As the changeover from analog to digital transmission systems continues, L carrier is also being phased out. Although FDM equipment is declining in importance, some of it, including carrier to channelize private analog microwave systems, remains in service.

Analog Carrier Technology

Long and short haul analog carrier use the same basic techniques of generating a carrier frequency for each channel and modulating the amplitude of the carrier with a voice signal. Amplitude modulation techniques are described in Appendix A for readers who are unfamiliar with the methods. Single sideband suppressed carrier (SSBSC) modulation is used for all long haul and most short haul carrier. To reduce costs, some versions of short haul carrier use double sideband modulation because it is less expensive and easier to synchronize.

Figure 5.1 shows a block diagram of an SSBSC channel. The voice frequency signal is limited by filters to a range of about 300 to 3300 Hz. The carrier frequency supply and the voice frequency signal are inserted into a balanced modulator, which modulates

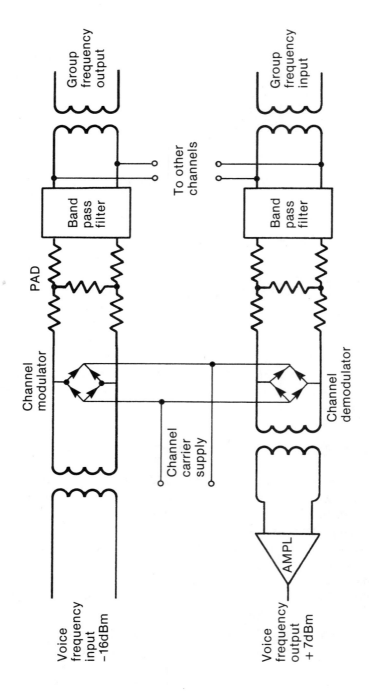

Figure 5.1   Single Sideband Suppressed Carrier (SSBSC) channel block diagram.

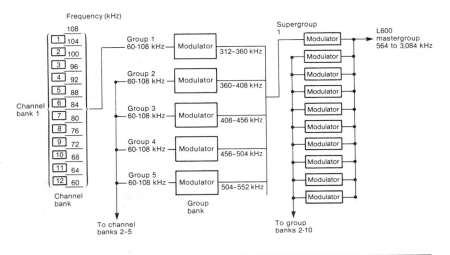

Figure 5.2 L-600 master group.

the amplitude of the carrier and suppresses the carrier in the output signal. The output of a balanced modulator has only the upper and lower sidebands. Since the two sidebands are redundant, one is filtered out, leaving a single carrier frequency modulated by the voice signal and occupying 4 KHz of bandwidth. The channel bank combines 12 channels to produce an overall band of frequencies 48 KHz wide. In long haul carriers the output of the channel bank is 60 to 108 KHz; in short haul carriers the channel output is modulated directly to the carrier line frequency.

In the receiving direction, the system injects a carrier frequency identical with the transmit frequency in one input of the demodulator. The received SSB signal is injected into the other input, and the voice frequency envelope of the carrier signal is extracted at the output.

With few exceptions, analog carrier systems require external signaling and are designed with fixed transmit and receive levels. The standard levels are -16 dBm input into the channel modulator and +7 dBm output from the demodulator; a carrier system inserts 23 dB of gain into a circuit. Unlike digital carrier systems, which have built-in signaling capability, FDM carrier provides signaling and gain transfer functions with external terminating and signaling units.

The L Multiplex System

The frequency and modulation plan of L multiplex (LMX) is shown in Figure 5.2. The 12-channel output of a channel bank is called a *group*. Five groups are combined to form a *super group* of 60 channels in a frequency range of 312 to 552 KHz. Ten supergroups are combined to form a 600-channel *master group*. Six master groups are, in turn, combined into *jumbo groups* of 3600 channels. A total of 13,200 channels can be supported on L5E coaxial cable. Some manufacturers produce a direct-to-line multiplex that modulates the voice channels directly to their final frequency.

The carrier supply is a critical element in an L carrier system. In the receiving terminal a demodulating carrier identical in frequency to the modulating frequency is injected into the demodulator. If the received carrier frequency is slightly different from the transmitted frequency, the voice signal is shifted by the difference between the frequencies, resulting in an unnatural sound. Frequency stability is essential for data transmission because any offset may make it impossible for the modem to detect the incoming data signal. In the United States, analog carrier systems connecting to the AT&T network were synchronized over a network consisting of 2.048 MHz signals transmitted over microwave radio and coaxial cable and 20.48 MHz signals transmitted over L5E coaxial cable. All carrier systems connecting to this network were phase locked to these frequencies to ensure stability.

L Coaxial Transmission Lines

The signal from an LMX system can be applied to a coaxial cable. The coaxial cable contains between 4 and 22 solid copper tubes 0.375 inches in diameter. The inner conductors are solid copper with insulating disks spaced at intervals of about one inch along the inner conductor to maintain separation from the outer tube. The spaces between the tubes are filled with twisted pair wire that can be used for short haul carrier or voice frequency circuits. Separate tubes are used in the transmit and receive directions.

Equalizers compensate for the high frequency loss of the cable. In the transmitting direction, low frequencies are attenuated and high frequencies boosted. In the receiving direction the equalization is reversed so the response curve of the signal applied to the amplifiers is flat. Repeaters are spaced at intervals ranging from one mile for L5E to 8 miles for L1. They are powered by voltages applied across the inner conductors of the transmit and receive coaxial tubes.

Pilots, which are frequencies inserted on the line and separated from the voice channels by filters, regulate amplifier gain. The purpose of pilots is to adjust the amplifier gain automatically to compensate for variations caused by temperature fluctuations and aging components. As the pilot level varies, regulating circuits detect the variation and feed back a correcting signal to the amplifiers. Because the magnitude of the variations is unequal across the frequency range of the carrier line, pilots are spaced throughout the frequency range to equalize the amplifiers and adjust their gain. Pilots also detect faults in the system. When an amplifier begins to fail, the drop in pilot level triggers an alarm and may initiate a switch to spare facilities.

Spare coaxial lines and repeaters are provided to protect working lines. When the protection equipment in the receiving terminal detects a drop in pilot level, it signals the transmitting terminal to feed its signal on the spare line. Pilots inserted on the spare line keep the gain of the amplifiers regulated so channel levels do not vary when a switch occurs.

L Carrier on Microwave Radio

Channels derived with LMX can be applied to the input of microwave radio as described in Chapter 14. The number of channels the radio supports depends on the bandwidth and modulation method used. Microwave radios with capacities as high as 5400 voice channels are available.

Short Haul Carrier Systems

The first short haul carrier used in the United States by the Bell System was Western Electric's N1, which transmits 12 voice fre-

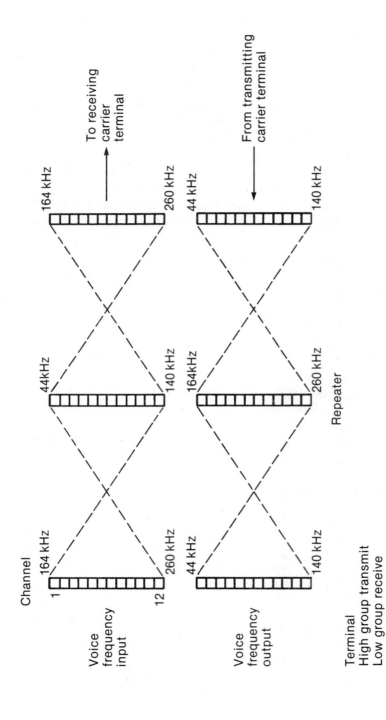

Figure 5.3   N-1 carrier modulation plan.

quency channels over separate transmit and receive pairs in a single cable. Early versions of N carrier use a double sideband transmitted carrier modulation plan. This plan has the advantages of low cost, of synchronizing the demodulator in the receiving channel from the transmitted carrier, and of regulating the gain of the line amplifiers from the carrier power without the use of pilots. The disadvantages of this technique are the additional bandwidth required and the additional load the transmitted carriers place on the amplifiers. As discussed in Chapter 2, intermodulation noise results from the additional load, which makes this type of carrier unsuitable for radio transmission. The frequency plan of N1 carrier is shown in Figure 5.3.

N carrier has undergone several improvements, resulting in the current N4 carrier system. N4 carrier, and its predecessor N3, use SSBSC modulation and transmit 24 channels in the same frequency range as N1 and N2.

N Carrier Lines

N carrier lines use separate transmit and receive frequencies, as Figure 5.3 shows, to prevent crosstalk. To improve separation, separate transmit and receive cable pairs were also required until later technology made it possible to use filters to combine the transmit and receive directions on the same cable pair. Frequency *frogging* is used to invert the transmit and receive frequencies to equalize loss at the different line frequencies. Because cable loss increases with frequency, by inverting the channels at each repeater, each channel is transmitted first at a high and then at a low frequency. This technique makes it possible to avoid the expensive equalizers used in long haul carrier systems.

Repeaters are designed for ground or pole mounting in weatherproof cabinets or in buildings. Repeaters, powered by DC voltage applied to the cable pairs at the terminals, are spaced at intervals of approximately eight miles.

Analog to Digital Connectors

During the evolution from analog to digital networks, it often becomes necessary to convert between analog and digital circuits, preferably without bringing the channels down to voice frequency. For example, when a digital switch is fed by analog facilities, some means is needed to convert from analog to digital. The devices that make this conversion generally fall into two categories, *L-to-T connectors* and *transmultiplexers*.

An L-to-T connector is a unit that contains back-to-back digital and analog channel units packaged in a single assembly. The T carrier bit stream is demultiplexed to voice frequency and is coupled to the channel input of an analog channel bank. The built-in signaling bits from the digital channel bank are converted to single frequency tones for transmission over the analog side of the connector. The costly external wiring interfaces associated with back-to-back channel banks are eliminated with this equipment, in which voice frequency and signaling interfaces are internally connected.

A second approach is the *transmultiplexer*, which digitally processes the 60 to 108 KHz signals of two analog groups into a 1.544 mb/s bit stream without reducing either the analog or the digital signals to voice frequency. All pilots, signaling, and alarm functions of both analog and digital multiplex are converted in the transmultiplexer. Also, individual controls are required to set analog channel levels. The unit must include pads to set the net loss of the circuit as discussed in Chapter 2. Transmultiplexers are packaged in groups of 24 channels that convert two analog groups to one DS-1 signal, or in groups of 120 channels, which convert two super groups to five DS-1 signals.

Time Assignment Speech Interpolation

Voice communication circuits typically have large amounts of idle time because of the nature of human conversation. Long haul circuits are inherently capable of carrying information in both directions simultaneously; however, people cannot talk and listen simultaneously, which means the typical telephone circuit is idle at least half the time. Also, when one party to a conversation is speaking, there are often pauses in which no information passes in either direction.

Time Assignment Speech Interpolation (TASI) equipment is designed to concentrate conversations from multiple input circuits over a group of output circuits to take advantage of the pauses. A user speaking over a group of TASI-equipped circuits does not have a permanently assigned circuit but has, instead, a virtual circuit that is established by the system in response to commands.

TASI was originally developed by Bell Laboratories for use in transatlantic cables where it is important to make the maximum use of high cost cable facilities. Although TASI was originally designed for overseas use, it also finds domestic use in both common carrier and private networks. The digital equivalent of TASI is Digital Speech Interpolation (DSI) equipment.

The number of circuits that speech interpolation derives depends on the number and characteristics of the messages riding on the circuit group. Unlike switching equipment, TASI is unable to tolerate delays in circuit availability. If a path is not available at the moment a talker begins, syllables are lost, which generates a repeat of the conversation and negates the benefits of the equipment. Therefore, it is essential that the system be properly engineered to prevent overloads.

Speech interpolation has two primary benefits. First, it can increase the carrying capacity of voice circuits without increasing leased circuit costs. If the cost of the equipment is less than the lease cost of the circuits, TASI results in a cost saving. Second, TASI equipment can be installed and rearranged by the user without involving the common carrier that provides the backbone circuits. This gives the network user independence from common carrier costs and delays.

Applications

Analog carrier has greatly diminished in importance as a transmission medium over the past few years as the IECs convert to fiber optic networks. Currently, it is not readily apparent to the end user whether the facility is digital or analog because the local loops remain analog. Frequency division multiplex remains in service in FDM satellite services, some overseas cables, and private and common carrier analog microwave systems.

Except for analog microwave systems, private networks rarely use FDM equipment. This low level of usage stems from two factors. First are the technical advantages of digital facilities as described in Chapter 4. Second is the nature of services available over common carrier tariffs. Although common carriers offer high speed digital facilities directly to the end user, broadband analog facilities require coaxial cable, which cannot compete with the unshielded twisted pair that digital facilities require.

Standards

Most FDM carrier standards were developed by AT&T and Bell Laboratories and have become de facto standards. The European plan for analog transmission varies from the North American plan only in minor detail. FDM standards are published by CCITT in the G series of recommendations.

Evaluating Analog Carrier Systems

The factors discussed in Chapter 4 for evaluating digital carrier systems are generally applicable to analog systems. Because special service channel units are not available with FDM carrier, these are not a consideration in evaluating systems. All the following factors should be considered in evaluating analog channel banks:

- Reliability, including redundancy of carrier and pilot supplies, power supplies, automatic protection line switching, and an adequate alarm system.

- Floor space or channel density.

- Power consumption.

- Compatibility with the system at the other end, including frequency plan, pilot frequencies and levels, and channel levels.

- Modulation plan and frequency plans must be compatible, and the same sideband, upper or lower must be used.

Manufacturers of Analog Multiplex Equipment

Analog to Digital Connectors

AT&T

Granger Teleratta

Rockwell International Collins Transmission Systems Div.

Analog Carrier Equipment

AT&T

NEC America, Inc.

Rockwell International

Direct-to-Line Multiplex

Granger Teleratta

Rockwell International

6

Outside Plant

The link between the customer's premises and the local central office is the most expensive and the least technically effective portion of the entire telecommunications system today. Wide bandwidth signals travel across the country in ribbons of fiber optic cable, are digitally routed and switched, but finally must be converted to analog and piped to the customer over a pair of wires that may cut off any frequency higher than 4 KHz. Outside plant is referred to as the "last mile," and it consists largely of twisted pair copper wire enclosed in large cables that are routed through conduit, buried in the ground, or hung on poles to reach the end user. Outside plant hasn't changed much over the years. Insulation has improved, cable sheaths have evolved from lead to non-metallic, and improved splicing techniques have increased the productivity of the LECs. Otherwise, a cable placed today is technically about the same as one placed in 1920.

Outside plant is the choke point of telecommunications, and technology has many solutions to offer, most of which are not yet economically practical. The obvious approach is to replace copper with fiber optics. The raw material is unlimited, the bandwidth it delivers is far greater than most applications need, and fiber is immune to the noise and corrosion that sometimes attack copper cables. Eventually, today's copper outside plant will undoubtedly be replaced, but now it is impractical to do so for several reasons. First is the matter of simple economics. Fiber optic cable has enormous bandwidth, but it must be multiplexed, and multiplexing equipment is expensive and must be housed somewhere.

Then there is the matter of powering station equipment. Today's copper cable carries power to the customer premises, and with the power equipment in the central office, telephone service is effectively immune to commercial power failures. Since fiber optic cable is non-conducting, other provisions for powering station equipment must be made.

A third drawback is the sheer magnitude of the task of replacing today's copper facilities. Where the type of service requires it, LECs are replacing copper plant with fiber, but extending fiber to millions of residences and small businesses is an enormous undertaking that must be justified by benefits, and the benefits are not yet great enough outside dense urban areas.

This chapter discusses how outside plant is constructed and deployed in the United States. The chapter includes a discussion on electrical protection, which is an issue that all private network managers must consider when metallic cable is used between buildings. Although this chapter primarily discusses the application of outside plant by LECs, the same fixtures are used for wire facilities in private networks. Also, because nearly every private network requires a local loop obtained from the telephone company, it is important for private network managers to understand the characteristics of the loop and how it affects the performance of the network.

Outside Plant Technology

Outside plant (OSP), diagramed in Figure 6.1, consists of the following components:

- Pole lines.
- Conduit.
- Feeder cable.
- Distribution cable.
- Terminals.
- Subscriber loop multiplex equipment.
- Aerial and drop wire.

Protection equipment and range extension devices located in the central office and on the user's premises are also included in

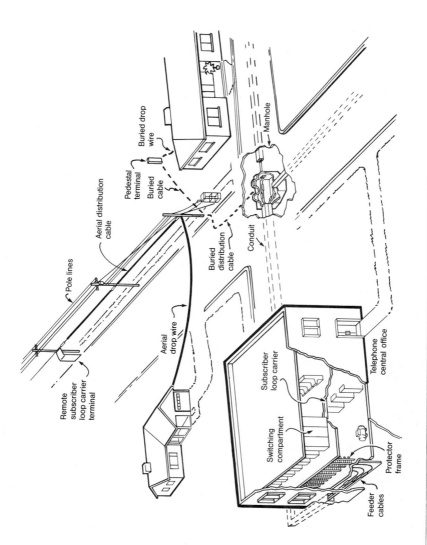

Figure 6.1   Major components of outside plant.

this discussion though the LECs do not normally considered them as part of outside plant.

Supporting Structures

Most subscriber loops are routed from the user's premises to the telephone central office over twisted pair cable, which is classified according to its supporting structure:

- *Aerial cable*, supported by pole lines.
- *Underground cable*, supported by conduit.
- *Buried cable,* placed directly in the ground without conduit.

Aerial cable is being discontinued as rapidly as economics permit because of environmental concerns and because of its vulnerability to damage. Aerial cable requires an external strength member to relieve tension on the conductors. Self-supporting aerial cable contains an internal strength member; all other cable requires an external *messenger* that is attached to poles. The messenger is a multistrand metallic supporting member to which cable is lashed with galvanized wire applied with a lashing machine. Down guys and anchors are placed at the ends and offsets in pole lines to relieve strain on the poles.

Direct burial is the preferred method for placing cable under ground because it is less expensive than conduit. Buried cable is either placed in an open trench or plowed with a special tractor-drawn plow that feeds the cable underground through a guide in the plow blade. Where the LECs place several cables simultaneously, or where future additions and rearrangements will be required, they place conduit to avoid the expense of opening streets more than once. Manholes are located in conduit runs at intervals corresponding to the maximum length of cable that can be handled physically and at 6000-foot intervals to house T carrier repeaters and load coils.

Cable Characteristics

Twisted pair cables are classified by their sheath material, their protective outer jacketing, the number of pairs contained within the sheath, and the wire gauge. Sizes available range from one- or two-pair drop wire to 3600-pair cable used for central office building entrance. The upper limit of cable size, which depends on wire gauge and the number of pairs, is dictated by the outside diameter of the sheath. Sheath diameter, in turn, is limited by the size that can be pulled through 4-inch conduit. Cables of larger sizes, such as 2400 and 3600 pairs, are used primarily for entrance into telephone central offices, which are fed by conduit in urban locations. Wire gauges of 26, 24, 22, and 19 AWG are used in loop plant. Cost considerations dictate the use of the smallest wire gauge possible, consistent with technical considerations. Therefore, the finer gauges are used close to the central office to feed the largest concentrations of users. Coarser gauges are used at greater distances from the central office to reduce loop resistance.

Cable sheath materials are predominantly high durability plastics such as polyethylene and polyvinyl chloride. Cable sheaths guard against damage from lightning, moisture, induction, corrosion, rocks, and rodents. In addition to the sheath material, coverings of jute and steel armor protect submarine cables. Besides the outer sheath, a layer of metallic tape shields the cables from induced voltages.

The twist of cable pairs is controlled to preserve the electrical balance of the pair. As Chapter 2 discusses, unbalanced pairs are vulnerable to noise induced from external sources, so the twist is designed to ensure that the amount of coupling between cable pairs is minimized. This is done by constructing cable in units of 12 to 100 pairs, depending on the size of the cable. Each unit is composed of several layers of pairs twisted around a common axis, with each pair in a unit given a different twist length.

Cable pairs are color coded within 50-pair complements. Each complement is identified by a color coded string binder that is wrapped around the pairs. At splicing points, the corresponding pairs and binder groups are spliced together to ensure end-to-end pair identity and continuity. Cables can be manually spliced with compression sleeves or ordered from the factory cut to the required length and equipped with connectors.

Splicing quality is an important factor in preserving cable pair balance. Many older cables are insulated with paper and have been spliced by twisting the wires together. These older splices are often a source of imbalance and noise because of insulation

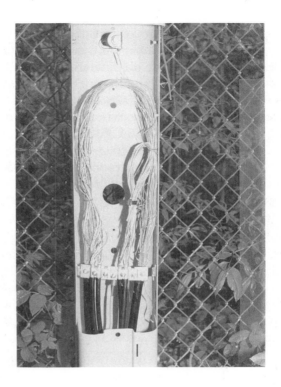

Figure 6.2   Pedestal-mounted splice case.
Courtesy, Preformed Line Products Company

breakdown and splice deterioration. To prevent crosstalk, it is also important to avoid splitting cable pairs. A split occurs when a wire from one pair is spliced to a corresponding wire in another pair. Although electrical continuity exists between the two cable ends, an imbalance between pairs exists, and crosstalk may result.

Cable splices are stored in above-ground closures in splice cases such as the ones shown in Figure 6.2. Cables must be manufactured and spliced to prevent water from entering the sheath because moisture inside the cable is the most frequent cause of noise and crosstalk. In a later section we will discuss methods of keeping cables impervious to moisture.

Loop Resistance Design

Outside plant engineers select the wire gauge to achieve an objective loop resistance. All telephone switching systems, PBXs, and key telephone systems are limited in the loop resistance range they can tolerate. The loop resistance a system can support is specified in ohms and includes the following elements:

- Battery feed resistance of the switching system (usually 400 ohms).

- Central office wiring (nominally 10 ohms).

- Cable pair resistance (variable to achieve the design objective of the central office or PBX).

- Drop wire resistance (nominally 25 ohms).

- Station set resistance (nominally 400 ohms).

The cable gauge is selected to provide the desired resistance at the maximum temperature under which the system will operate. This method of design is called resistance design. Telephone central offices have total loop resistance ranges from 1300 to 1500 ohms or more; most PBXs have less, with many supporting ranges of 400 to 800 ohms. The range can be extended with subscriber carrier or range extension devices, which are described later. The range limitation of subscriber loops depends on the current required to operate PBX trunk circuits, DTMF dials, and the telephone transmitter. Range is also limited by the supervisory range of the central office, the range over which ringing can be supplied and tripped on answer (ring trip range), and the transmission loss of the talking path. Depending on the type of switching system, one of these factors becomes limiting and determines the loop design range.

A further consideration in selecting cable is the capacitance of the pair, expressed in microfarads (mf) per mile. Ordinary subscriber loop cable has a high capacitance of 0.083 mf per mile. Low capacitance cable, used for trunks because of its improved frequency response, has a capacitance of 0.062 mf per mile. Special 25-gauge cable used for T carrier has a capacitance of 0.039 mf per mile.

Special types of cable are used for cable television, closed circuit video, local area networks, and other applications. Some types of cable are constructed with internal screens to isolate the transmitting and receiving pairs of a T carrier system. These types of cable are beyond the scope of this book; however, the reader should be aware that they exist and may be required for certain telecommunications applications such as high capacity T carrier systems.

Feeder and Distribution Cable

Cable plant is divided into two categories—*feeder* and *distribution*. Feeder cables route cable pairs directly to a serving area without intervening branches to end users. Feeder cable is of two types, main and branch feeders. Main feeders are large backbone cables that exit the central office and are routed, usually through conduit, to intermediate branching points. Branch feeders are smaller cables that route pairs from the main feeders to a serving area. Distribution cable extends from a serving area interface to the user's premises. Figure 6.3 shows the plan of a typical serving area.

Where enough pairs are needed in a single building to justify wiring an entire complement into the building, the interface between feeder and distribution plant is a direct splice. Otherwise, the interface may be a crossconnect cabinet where provision is made to connect cable pairs flexibly between feeder and distribution plant.

Distribution cable is terminated in *terminals* similar to the ones shown in Figure 6.4 to provide access to cable pairs. Terminals may be mounted on the ground in pedestals, in buildings, on aerial cable messenger, or underground. Aerial or buried *drop wire* connects from the terminal to the protector at the user's premises.

To the greatest degree possible feeder cables and distribution cables are designed to avoid *bridged tap*, an impairment shown in Figure 6.5. Bridged tap is any portion of the cable pair that is not in the direct path between the user and the central office. It has the electrical effect of a capacitor across the pair and impairs the high frequency response of the circuit. Bridged tap can render DTMF dials and data modems inoperative because of amplitude distortion, primarily at high frequencies. It can be detected by measuring the frequency response of a metallic circuit.

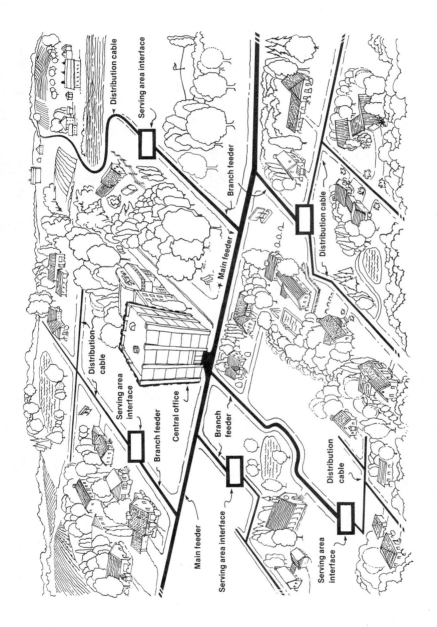

Figure 6.3   Feeder and distribution service areas.

Figure 6.4   Aerial cable showing splice cases, distribution terminals, and load coil cases mounted on pole.
Courtesy, Preformed Line Products Company

The frequency response of long subscriber loops is improved by loading as discussed in Chapter 2. Load coils are small inductors wound on a powdered iron core as shown in Figure 6.6. They are normally placed at 6000-foot intervals on loops longer than 18,000 feet. Load coils are contained in weatherproof cases that are mounted on poles or in manholes.

Electrical Protection

Whenever communications conductors enter a building from an environment that can be exposed to a foreign source of electricity, it is essential that electrical protection be considered. Protection is required for two purposes—to prevent injury or death to personnel and to prevent damage to equipment. Of the two, the overriding consideration is, of course, prevention of harm to personnel.

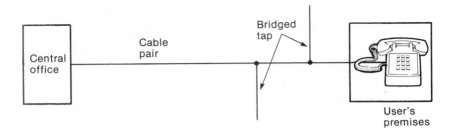

Figure 6.5   Bridge tap mounted in pairs.

Common carriers are responsible for protecting cables between their central offices and the user's premises. The type of protection provided is sufficient to prevent injury or death, but may not be sufficient to prevent damage to delicate telecommunications and computer equipment. Also, interbuilding cables may require protection, and the carrier may not be responsible for them.

Protection requirements are based on the National Electrical Safety Code. Much of the information in this section is based on AT&T practices, which often are more stringent than the Code.

Determining Exposure

The first question that must be answered in determining electrical protection requirements is whether the cable is considered *ex-*

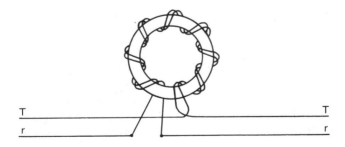

Figure 6.6   Toroidal load coil.

posed. An exposed cable is one that is subject to any of the following hazards:

- Contact with any power circuit operating at 300 volts rms (root mean square) or more from ground.

- Contact by lightning.

- Induction from a 60 Hz source that results in a potential of 300 volts rms or more.

- Power faults that cause the ground potential to rise above 300 volts rms.

Bearing in mind that safety considerations must not be compromised in designing a protection plan, it is natural to wonder why 300 volts rms is chosen as the apparent threshold of danger. Actually, any shock that results in more than about 10 milliamps of current flowing through the body is painful. More than 20 ma is dangerous, and more than 50 ma of current flow through the heart is likely to result in ventricular fibrillation, a condition that usually results in death.

The amount of current that flows through the human body in contact with electricity is unpredictable. It depends on the skin resistance (damp skin has a much lower resistance than dry skin), on the body parts in contact (current flow between two fingers of the same hand is less dangerous than current flow between the two hands), and several other factors that circuit designers cannot control. Despite the danger that contact with less than 300 volts can be fatal, this value is chosen because it is the value from which terminal equipment is designed to insulate the user.

All cables with aerial sections should be considered exposed. Even though a short section of aerial cable may not be in proximity to power at the time it is constructed, aerial power may be added later and expose the cable. Therefore it is advisable to protect all aerial cables, which include any cable that contains any pairs that may be exposed. For example, a 600-pair cable, only 25 pairs of which are connected to aerial cable, is considered exposed in its entirety. Buried and underground cables should be considered exposed unless one or more of the following conditions exist:

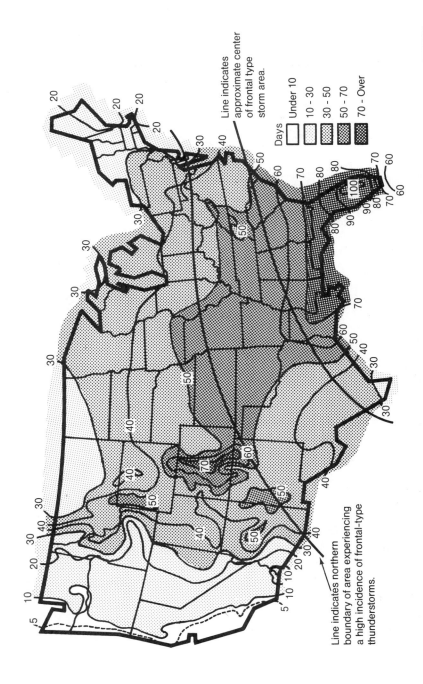

Line indicates approximate center of frontal type storm area.

Days
Under 10
10 - 30
30 - 50
50 - 70
70 - Over

Line indicates northern boundary of area experiencing a high incidence of frontal-type thunderstorms.

Figure 6.7   Average annual number of days with thunderstorms. *Courtesy, AT&T Corporation*

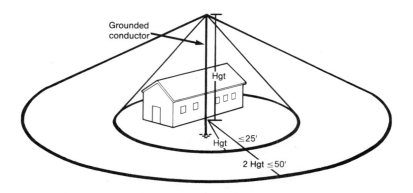

Figure 6.8   Cone of protection provided by vertical grounded conductors.
Courtesy, AT&T Corporation

- There are five or fewer thunderstorm days per year and the earth resistivity is less than 100 meter-ohms. (See Figure 6.7 for thunderstorm activity and earth resistivity in the United States.)
- A buried interbuilding cable is shorter than 140 feet and has a shield that is grounded on both ends.
- A cable is totally within a cone of protection because of its proximity to buildings or other structures that are grounded (see Figure 6.8).

In metropolitan areas, cables may be considered to exist under a *zone of protection* that diverts lightning strikes and shields the cable from damage. As Figure 6.8 shows, if a shielding mast is 25 or fewer feet high, a high degree of protection is afforded to objects within a radius equal to the height of the mast. A satisfactory degree of protection is also afforded to objects within a radius equal to twice the height of the mast if the mast is 50 or fewer feet high. To illustrate, assume that a cable runs between two buildings, each of which is 50 feet high. Each building extends a zone of protection of 100 feet, which means that a cable 200 feet long would not be considered exposed to lightning. For structures higher than 50 feet, the zone of protec-

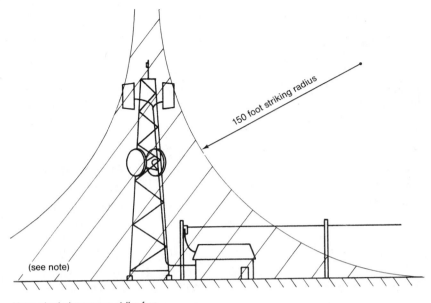

Note: shaded areas are strike-free,
      protected zones.

**Figure 6.9   Lightning strike radius of 150 feet using "rolling ball"
model for structures greater than 50 feet tall.**
Courtesy, AT&T Corporation

tion concept does not apply on the same basis as for lower structures. To visualize the protection zone that surrounds higher objects, visualize a ball 300 feet in diameter rolled up against the side of the structure as in Figure 6.9. The zone of protection is shown as the shaded area in Figure 6.9. Note that the zone of protection applies only to lightning, not to power exposures.

A cable also should be considered exposed to lightning, even though it is in an area that would otherwise be excluded by the earth resistivity and lightning requirements, if it rises above the elevation of surrounding terrain—on hilltop, on a tower, etc.

Normally, ground is considered to be at zero potential, or the potential of the earth. In practice, ground has some resistance, and when current flows through it, the ground potential can rise.

The hazard of a ground potential rise from commercial power is most severe near a power substation, but ground potential rise can occur anywhere from a lightning strike.

Induction occurs when power lines and telephone cables operate over parallel routes. Under normal conditions the magnitude of the induction is not so great as to constitute a hazard, but when telecommunications lines are unbalanced or when a fault occurs in the power line, the amount of induced voltage can rise to hazardous levels. This is not a concern in most private networks, but designers should be alert to the possibility of induction whenever power and telecommunications circuits share the same route, though they may not share a pole line.

Even though a circuit is protected to eliminate hazard to users, the equipment attached to it may be sensitive to foreign voltages. Since the equipment provider is in the best position to know of this sensitivity, all requests for proposal and purchase orders should require the vendor to specify the level of protection required.

Protection Methods

Personnel and equipment can be protected from the hazards of unexpected contact with a foreign source of electrical potential by the following methods:

- Insulating telecommunications apparatus.
- Shielding communications cables.
- Grounding equipment.
- Opening affected circuits.
- Separating electrical and telecommunications circuits.

This section discusses how each preventive measure is applied to telecommunications circuits.

Insulating Telecommunications Apparatus

Nearly all telecommunications circuits installed today are insulated with some kind of protective coating that serves as the first line of defense against accidental cross with foreign voltage. Polyethylene, which is the insulation used with most copper cables, has a conductor-to-conductor breakdown value of from 1000 to 4000 volts. Although this is enough to guard against a high value of foreign voltage, it is possible that the insulation will be damaged by the fault. A lightning strike or power cross may cause a burning effect that will destroy the insulation even if the voltage itself does not pierce the insulation.

Not only are the conductors insulated, but most apparatus is constructed to insulate the user from foreign voltage. If the magnitude of the voltage is great enough to arc from the supply conductors to the chassis, however, the inherent insulation of the equipment may not be enough to protect the user from dangerous shock, and the equipment will be destroyed or heavily damaged.

Although insulation is the first line of defense against the invasion of foreign potential, it alone is not enough to solve electrical protection problems.

Shielding Communications Cables

Cables can be shielded from lightning strikes by placing a grounded conductor above the cable so it intercepts the lightning strike. A grounded shield wire can be placed above aerial cable to serve the same function as a lightning rod serves on a building—it attracts the lightning strike to itself. Shield wires also can be buried above a communications cable. If there is enough separation to prevent arcing between the shield and the cable, this method is effective.

Grounding Equipment

An important principle of electrical protection is to provide a low impedance path to ground for foreign voltage. Both carbon and gas tube protectors, which are illustrated in Figure 6.10 operate on the principle of draining the foreign voltage to ground.

The simplest form of protector is the *carbon block*. One side of the carbon block is connected to a common path to ground. It is essential that the ground path be a known earth ground. In most buildings the grounding point for the power entrance is a suitable grounding point. A metallic cold water pipe may be a satisfactory ground, but if the water system has any non-metallic elements in it, the effectiveness of the ground may be lost. To ensure an

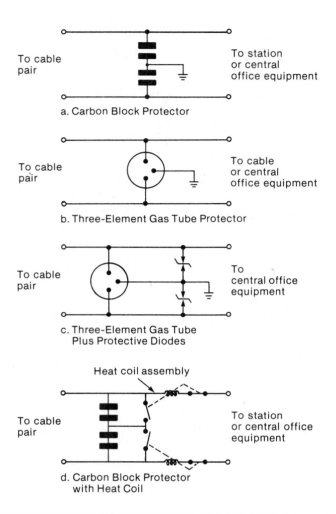

a. Carbon Block Protector

b. Three-Element Gas Tube Protector

c. Three-Element Gas Tube
   Plus Protective Diodes

d. Carbon Block Protector
   with Heat Coil

Figure 6.10   Station and central office protection equipment.

effective water pipe ground, the pipe should be bonded to the power ground with a copper wire of at least 6-gauge.

The other side of the carbon block protector is open, with a mating block separated from ground by a narrow gap. The communications conductors are connected to the mating block. When voltage rises to a high enough level to arc across the gap, current flows, the block fuses, and the communications conductors are permanently connected to ground. When a carbon block protector is activated, it is destroyed and must be replaced.

A *gas tube protector* is connected between the communications conductors and ground. Like the carbon block protector, its purpose is to provide a low impedance path to ground for foreign voltage. The electrodes of the gas tube are farther apart than the carbon block electrodes, however, and they are contained in a glass envelope that is filled with an inert gas. When the breakdown voltage is reached, the gas ionizes and current flows until the voltage is removed. When the voltage is removed, the tube restores itself. Although gas tubes are more expensive than carbon blocks, the self-restoring effect may repay the additional cost. They may be particularly effective in sensitive apparatus that is easily damaged by relatively low voltages.

Another type of grounding protector is the *heat coil*. A heat coil is a spring-loaded device that, when released, connects the communications conductors to ground. Heat coils protect against *sneak currents*, which are currents that flow from voltages that are too low to activate a carbon block or gas tube protector. The heating effect of the sneak current is sufficient to melt a low melting point metal that keeps the electrodes separated. When the metal is melted, the spring forces the electrodes together and the circuit is grounded until the heat coil is replaced.

Protectors cannot operate effectively unless they are connected to a good ground. It is essential that all protector frames and apparatus such as PBXs and key telephone systems be connected to a good ground, and that the ground be bonded to the power system ground or other known low-impedance ground.

Opening Affected Circuits

Everyone is familiar with the next method of protecting circuits and equipment, the *fuse* or *circuit breaker*. If the communications conductors are opened before they enter the building or before they reach the protected equipment, current cannot flow and damage the equipment or reach the operator. The LEC often installs a *fuse cable* between its distribution cable and the building entrance. A fuse cable is a short length of fine gauge cable, usually 26-gauge. If the distribution cable is of coarser gauge, the fuse cable will open before the protected cable opens. To restore the circuits, a new fuse cable is spliced in. Although this is an inexpensive method of protection, it can be detrimental to good service because of the length of time required to replace the fuse cable.

A fuse, by its nature, takes time to operate. Current flows during lightning strikes tend to be very short, lasting less time than the duration of most lighting strikes. Therefore, fuse cables are effective against power crosses, but not against lightning.

Separating Electrical And Telecommunications Circuits

Another method of protecting from accidental cross with electrical power is adequate spacing. Many buildings are served by buried power and telecommunications cables that share a joint trench. (Although joint trenches offer adequate spacing, joint power and telecommunications conduits are never acceptable.) The minimum acceptable separation between power and telecommunications circuits in a joint trench is one foot; more separation gives an additional measure of protection. The sharing of a joint trench with at least the minimum separation does not, of itself, create an exposure condition.

Each cable pair in a central office is protected in a frame, as described in Chapter 12. At the user's end of the circuit, protectors range from a simple single-pair device to multiple-pair protected terminals. Although station protectors are adequate to prevent injury to users, they are often inadequate to prevent damage to delicate electronic equipment. The owners of all devices connecting to the network, including modems, PBXs, key telephone systems, and answering recorders must be aware of the degree of protection offered by the telephone line and the ability of their equipment to withstand external voltage and current.

Subscriber Loop Carrier

Subscriber loop carriers are increasingly used to deliver multi-channel service to large concentrations of users. Analog subscriber carriers provide from one to eight subscriber circuits on a single cable pair. Single channel carrier derives one carrier channel in the frequency range above the voice channel. Because of the high frequency cutoff of load coils, single channel subscriber carrier cannot be used on loaded cable. Therefore, single channel carrier must be used within 18,000 feet of nonloaded cable to obtain satisfactory transmission from the voice channel.

Multiple channel analog carriers sacrifice the voice channel to gain as many as eight carrier channels on a cable pair, depending on the manufacturer. Multiple channel analog subscriber carriers are similar in concept to the trunk carriers described in Chapter 5, except they use double sideband modulation to reduce costs.

Digital subscriber carriers such as the AT&T SLC 96, which is shown in Figure 6.11, operate over T-1 lines using either PCM or delta modulation techniques. These modulation methods, as described in Chapter 4, derive from 24 to 40 voice channels over two cable pairs. T-1 repeaters are placed at 6000-foot intervals to provide a line equivalent to that used for trunk carrier. Digital carrier is replacing analog carrier in the subscriber loop as it is in trunks, and for the same reasons. Digital carrier operates effectively over either fiber optics or copper cable and provides excellent transmission quality.

Some subscriber carriers use concentration to increase the number of voice channels that can be transmitted over a T-1 line. Concentration operates on the probability that not all users will require service simultaneously. Users are not permanently assigned to digital time slots in concentrated systems. Instead, when the user requests service, the system selects an idle time slot and identifies the line to the distant terminal with a data message. Concentrated carriers allow the termination of 48 subscribers on a 24 channel T-1 line.

A line concentrator, diagramed in Figure 6.12, is similar to subscriber carrier except that it is specifically designed for concentrated service and terminates multiple T carrier trunks to a larger number of subscriber lines to reduce the probability of a trunk being unavailable when a user requests service. Contrasted to concentrated subscriber carrier with a 2:1 concentration ratio, a remote line concentrator may assign, say, 250 users to five T-1 lines, a concentration ratio of 5:1. Concentrators are equipped

Figure 6.11   AT&T SLC 96 digital loop carrier in a ground-mounted cabinet.
Courtesy, AT&T Corporation

with circuits to collect usage information that an administrator can use to avoid overloads. They must be engineered and monitored in the same manner as central office switching equipment, administration of which is described in Chapter 31.

Concentrators also may include circuitry known as *intracalling*, which enables users within the concentrator to connect to one another without using channels to the central office and back. Intracalling features require only one channel for the central office to supervise the connection. With intracalling, a concentrator may provide service between the users it serves even though the carrier line is inoperative. Without this feature a carrier line failure disrupts all service to its users.

The term *pair gain* describes the degree to which subscriber carriers and concentrators increase the channel-carrying capacity of a cable pair. The pair gain figure of a carrier or concentrator is the number of voice circuits that are added above the single voice circuit that a cable pair supports. For example, a 24-channel digital subscriber carrier requiring separate transmit and receive pairs has a pair gain of 22. The families of single and multiple channel subscriber carriers and concentrators are called *pair gain devices*. A pair gain device has a central office terminal and a matching remote terminal with intermediate repeaters if required. The remote terminal is contained in a pole-mounted cabinet or a ground-mounted enclosure.

Pair gain devices provide better transmission quality than cable facilities. The transmission loss is fixed, normally at 5 dB, regardless of the length of the system. Pair gain devices also provide quieter channels than the cable pairs they replace. An advantage of digital subscriber carrier is its ability to use special service channel units to provide the range of special services listed in Table 4.1. Pair gain devices must be powered from an external source, so backup battery power is required to maintain telephone service during power outages.

Range Extenders

Another family of loop electronic devices is classified as *range extension*. Although these devices are normally mounted only in the

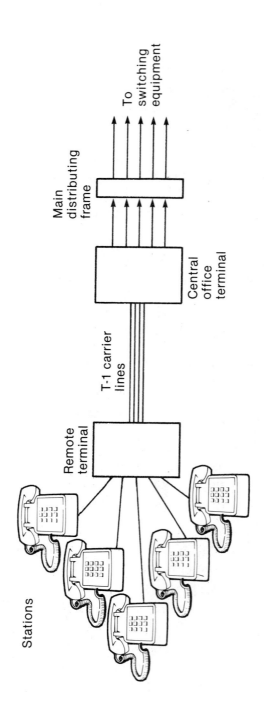

Figure 6.12   Block diagram of remote line concentrator.

central office, they are discussed here because they improve subscriber loop performance. Range extenders are single-pair devices that boost the line voltage and may include voice frequency gain. Battery boost range extenders overcome the DC loop limitations of the switching system and station equipment. Range extenders increase the sensitivity of the switching system line circuits in detecting dial pulses and the on-hook/off-hook state of the line.

A second type of range extender increases the central office sensitivity and feeds higher voltage to the station. This latter type boosts the normal -48 volt central office battery to -72 volts, which increases the line current when the station is off hook, supporting greater DTMF dial range and providing greater line current to the telephone transmitter. If the voice frequency transmission range of the cable pair is limiting, range extenders with built-in amplification to boost the voice level can be used. These devices either contain a fixed amount of gain or adjust gain automatically in proportion to the line current.

Cable Pressurization

Cable pressurization is used by LECs to keep moisture out of the cable and should be considered in private networks when cable is exposed to moisture for long distances. In a cable pressurization system, a compressor pumps dehydrated air into the cable. At terminals where pairs are exposed, the cable sheath is plugged with a watertight dam and air bypasses the dam through plastic tubing. A flow meter at the source shows the amount of leakage. When leakage exceeds a specified amount, it indicates sheath damage, which must be located and repaired to ensure water-tight integrity. When a cable run is long with multiple branches, low air pressure alarms help locate trouble.

Applications

Loop plant is part of every network application. Even in private networks that bypass the local telephone company by routing circuits directly to an interexchange carrier, a connection is made from the network terminal to the station over metallic cable facilities that must be designed as part of the total network. This section includes only electrical considerations. The evaluation of supporting structures involves mechanical considerations that are beyond the scope of this book.

Standards

With the exception of wire, which meets American Wire Gauge standards, outside plant is not manufactured to the standards of an independent agency. Manufacturers' specifications determine cable size, construction, and sheath characteristics. Outside plant is selected according to its specifications to meet the requirements of the application.

Evaluating Subscriber Loop Equipment

This section includes the principal considerations for both LECs and private network users for selecting metallic outside plant facilities.

Cable Structural Quality

Cable is selected to match the pair size and gauge required by the network design. The sheath must be impervious to the elements if it is mounted outside. Crosstalk and balance characteristics are of paramount concern. When cables support special applications such as local area networks and high speed data transmission, the cable must meet the specifications of the equipment manufacturer.

Insulation resistance and DC continuity measurements should be made on all new cables. On loaded cables, structural return loss, gain frequency response, and noise measurements, as described in Chapter 32, should be made to ensure the electrical integrity of the cable. When cable facilities are obtained from a common carrier, these measurements also should be made when trouble is experienced.

Air Pressurization

Air pressurization should be considered on long cables and on any cable that carries essential services and is exposed to weather. The system should be equipped with a dehydrator, a compressor, a flow meter, and a monitoring and alarm system to detect leakage.

Protection

All metallic circuits, both common carrier and privately owned, are subject to lighting strikes and crosses with external voltage. It is not safe to assume that the protection provided by the telephone company is enough to prevent damage to interconnected equipment. Private network users should determine the characteristics of the input circuits of their equipment and obtain external protection if needed.

Manufacturers of Outside Plant Products

Cable Air Pressurization Equipment

Chatlos Systems, Inc.   General Cable Co.

Concentrators and Digital Loop Carrier Equipment

Alcatel Network Systems

AT&T Network Systems

Broadband Technologies

Ericsson, Inc. Communications Div.

Hubbel, Pulsecom Div.

NEC America

Northern Telecom, Inc

Optilink

Reliance Comm/Tec

Terminals and Crossconnect Boxes

AT&T Network Systems

General Cable Co.

3M Co. Telcomm Products Div.

Northern Telecom, Inc.

Reliance Comm/Tec

Siecor Corporation

Protectors

See Chapter 12

Voice and Data Compression

Pulse code modulation uses an efficient encoding algorithm that provides excellent fidelity and clarity for a voice signal. Its use of bandwidth, however, is inefficient, and other coding methods can compress several voice channels into the same 64 kb/s bandwidth that a single PCM channel requires. Bandwidth costs are dropping with the arrival of nationwide fiber optic networks, but transmission costs remain high enough that decreased circuit costs often repay the cost of the hardware to compress voice and combine it with data.

Of the coding methods on the market, most are proprietary, which means that both ends of the circuit must use equipment provided by the same manufacturer. One algorithm, adaptive differential pulse code modulation (ADPCM), is a CCITT standard, but it provides only 2:1 compression, which is considerably less than that provided by other methods.

All compression technologies have a common characteristic: they cannot carry analog data at speeds supported by PCM. Some algorithms have problems with data at speeds as low as 2400 b/s. This limitation is a concern to almost every company, because Group 3 facsimile operates at 9600 b/s. There are several methods of coping with the data limitation problem. Some systems recognize modem tones, convert the data from analog to digital, transport it directly as a digital signal, and convert it back at the receiving end. Other systems packetize facsimile and data signals and interleave them with packetized voice. Still other systems can set up a dedicated non-compressed PCM channel.

The saving in bandwidth is not without cost. Some of the naturalness of the voice is sacrificed. Generally, the greater the amount of compression, the less natural the voice sounds. The loss of clarity is not severe, but because of it and the data limitation, voice compression systems are not suitable for the public network, where it is difficult to allocate traffic to appropriate circuits. Compression systems are satisfactory for private networks where some sacrifice in quality is a reasonable tradeoff for savings in transmission costs. The cost of bandwidth on shorter circuits is low enough that compression hardware cannot be justified, but on longer spans hardware costs may quickly be repaid in reduced transmission costs.

Voice compression equipment is available in four families of equipment. T-1 multiplexers, which Chapter 4 discusses, are available with various kinds of voice compression options, including ADPCM. As stand-alone devices, ADPCM transcoders are available to combine two T-1 sources into one channel. Several products, which are discussed later in this chapter, can be collectively called voice/data multiplexers. These devices divide the 64 kb/s bandwidth into a combination of voice and data channels. The fourth family of equipment is fast packet switching. Although fast packet systems do not necessarily compress the voice signal, they obtain the equivalent of voice compression by eliminating pauses and taking advantage of the half duplex nature of voice transmissions. Most commercial fast packet products also use voice compression to gain even more transmission efficiency.

Adaptive Differential Pulse Code Modulation

ADPCM equipment compresses two PCM bit streams into a single bit stream that can be transmitted over T-1 carrier lines or applied to M1-3 multiplexers and transmitted over fiber optic or radio facilities. An ADPCM transcoder encodes a digital signal at 32 kb/s rather than 64 kb/s, enabling transmission of 48 channels over a 1544 mb/s line.

ADPCM uses the same 8000 times per second sampling rate as PCM, but instead of quantizing the entire voice signal, it

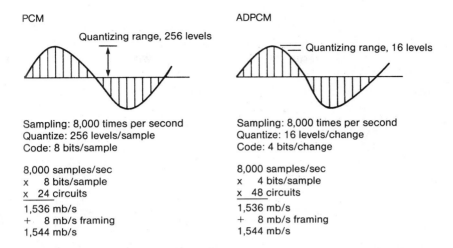

Sampling: 8,000 times per second
Quantize: 256 levels/sample
Code: 8 bits/sample

8,000 samples/sec
x   8 bits/sample
x 24 circuits
1,536 mb/s
+   8 mb/s framing
1,544 mb/s

Sampling: 8,000 times per second
Quantize: 16 levels/change
Code: 4 bits/change

8,000 samples/sec
x   4 bits/sample
x 48 circuits
1,536 mb/s
+   8 mb/s framing
1,544 mb/s

Figure 7.1   Comparison of pulse code modulation and adaptive differential pulse code modulation.

quantizes only the changes between samples. A circuit known as an *adaptive predictor* examines the incoming bit stream and predicts the value of the next sample. ADPCM quantizes the difference between the actual sample and the predicted sample into 16 levels, which can be coded with four bits. The encoder adapts to the speed of change in the difference signal—fast for speech-like signals and slow for data signals. Figure 7.1 compares PCM and ADPCM, both of which result in a 1.544 mb/s line signal. Like other compression methods, ADPCM cannot carry 9600 b/s data, but it can carry data at 4800 b/s.

ADPCM can use the bit-robbing signaling methods of PCM, but to do so presents two problems. First, the voice compression techniques of ADPCM make it necessary to rob a bit from every fourth rather than every sixth frame. This makes ADPCM incompatible with the DS-1 signal format. Second, the robbed bit can degrade 4800 b/s data on a voice channel. To address this problem, the standard offers an optional 44-channel format, in which one channel of every 12 is devoted to signaling. Some manufacturers provide either 44- or 48-channel operation as an option.

Although there are many systems on the market for compressing voice signals, ADPCM is the only one that CCITT recommends.

The standard status is important when voice compression is used as an external device because standardization can enable equipment from two manufacturers to work end-to-end. In a device such as a T-1 multiplexer, which has a proprietary line protocol anyway, the use of a nonstandard encoding system for the voice channels is of little consequence.

The primary disadvantages of ADPCM are the extra expense of the transcoder, which is required in addition to PCM channel banks; the inability of ADPCM to handle data above 4800 b/s; and the loss of two voice channels per digroup for signaling. The data speed restriction is apt to be most critical for companies that need to send Group 3 facsimile or V.32 data over ADPCM circuits. The facsimile machines will automatically downshift to compensate for the lack of bandwidth, and transmission will take approximately twice as long. Several ADPCM products on the market provide 64 kb/s clear channel capability by using two voice channels for high speed data transmission.

Other Compression Methods

Some compression methods are used commonly enough that they have become virtual standards. Others are proprietary and may carry such names as Vector Quantization Coding, High Capacity Voice, and Code-Excited Linear Prediction (CELP).

Delta Modulation

Delta modulation is a less sophisticated method of signal compression than ADPCM. Delta modulation, also called Continuously Variable Slope Delta (CVSD), uses a one-bit code to represent the voice frequency waveshape. If a sample is greater in amplitude than the previous sample, it transmits a 1. If the sample is less, it sends a 0. These signals result in a code that represents the instantaneous slope of the voice frequency waveshape as Figure 7.2 shows.

The primary advantage of delta modulation is its ability to compress more voice channels into a bit stream at a lower cost than PCM, ADPCM, or other adaptive low bit-rate systems. A reasonably good quality signal can be obtained at 16 kb/s per

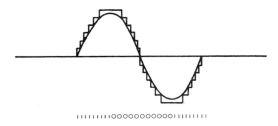

IIIIIIIIIOOOOOOOOOOOOOOOIIIIIIIII

Figure 7.2   Delta modulation.

channel. It is a simple and inexpensive method that several manufacturers support, although their products are not necessarily compatible.

The main weakness of delta modulation is its inability to follow rapid changes in the voice signal. Fortunately, however, voice signals are predictable in their behavior, so the effect is not noticeable in most conversations. A second weakness of delta modulation is the inability of the system to handle direct data transmission through data port channel units or to transport high speed data using modems.

Time Domain Harmonic Scaling

Several companies that make voice/data integration equipment use the *time domain harmonic scaling* (TDHS) algorithm. Voice is digitized and compressed by algorithms that remove redundancy and compress silent periods in a voice session. Most products that use this technology provide a combination of voice and data services over one or more 56 kb/s lines. Some products packetize the voice signal, which causes delay. A limited amount of delay can be tolerated by most users, so the quality approaches that of a toll grade circuit.

Voice/Data Multiplexers

Voice/data multiplexers, also called *line expanders* and *bandwidth managers*, are devices that enable a private line circuit to carry a combination of digitized voice and data signals. A sampling and compression algorithm such as CVSD digitizes the

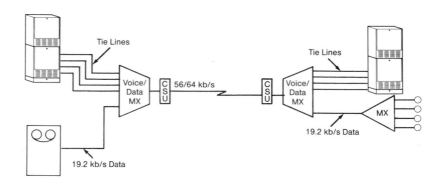

Figure 7.3   Connection of a voice/data multiplexer.

voice signals. The algorithms used in the products on the market are proprietary, so the devices on both ends of the circuit must be furnished by the same manufacturer.

With fractional T-1 prices dropping to the point that the cost of a 56 kb/s channel is little more than the price of an analog data circuit, these devices are becoming increasingly popular. For a modest capital investment, from two to five voice channels can ride with data for no additional cost. A voice/data multiplexer is connected as shown in Figure 7.3. The data channel connects to a data multiplexer to subdivide the bandwidth, and voice channels connect to a PBX as tie lines.

Currently available products compress voice signals into bandwidths as narrow as 9600 b/s, with some manufacturers suggesting that 4800 b/s systems are technically feasible. Some products vary the amount of data bandwidth available, expanding it when voice does not need it, and contracting it when the channel fills with voice signals. This strategy can slow data down when there is heavy voice traffic, but it keeps the bandwidth fully occupied when the demand exists. At night, when there is little voice traffic, the multiplexer can expand the data channel to occupy the entire bandwidth for high-speed data transfer.

There are two basic families of products on the market. One type dedicates a certain amount of bandwidth to each channel and

Figure 7.4   Newbridge 3600 MainStreet Bandwidth Manager.
Courtesy, Newbridge Neworks, Inc.

allocates it on a fixed basis, much the way a time division multiplexer operates on data. The other type statistically multiplexes
the voice. These systems, which often are used with circuit switching systems, are sometimes called Digital Speech Interpolation
(DSI). Chapter 5 discusses DSI.

The most effective multiplexers operate over 56 or 64 kb/s
digital circuits. Currently available products combine as many as
eight voice signals, or five voice and one 9.6 kb/s data signal, over
one 56 kb/s circuit. Figure 7.4 shows the Newbridge 3600

Mainstreet Bandwidth Manager, which compresses voice with ADPCM or Newbridge proprietary schemes at 32 kb/s, 16 kb/s, or 8 kb/s.

The compression algorithm used by voice/data multiplexers will not handle high-speed modem data. Some systems provide automatic recognition of modem signals, a feature that also permits the multiplexer to pass facsimile traffic. Other products have integrated facsimile capability, which permits them to recognize a fax signal and allocate it the necessary bandwidth.

Fast Packet Switching

Fast packet switching is a new technology that eventually may replace conventional packet switching and circuit switching. The characteristics of today's digital circuits, which are supplied over low error rate fiber optics, make fast packet feasible. Bandwidths of 1.544 mb/s and more are readily available, and error rates are several orders of magnitude lower than the error rates of the analog circuits of the past. This means that link-by-link flow control and error correction can be eliminated in favor of end-to-end flow control and error correction. Fixed routes can be used, and as a result, packet resequencing is unnecessary. Fast packet handles a stream of packets, delivering them without error correction to higher level protocols. The nodes use an address in the packet header to route packets to their destinations.

Unlike packet switched data networks, which carry only data, fast packet supports data, digitized voice, and compressed video. Voice and data have much different characteristics, which a fast packet network must recognize and offset. For example, while data signals can tolerate a moderate amount of absolute delay, telephone users are sensitive to excessive delay. Fast packet networks strive to maintain delay at 80 milliseconds or less. They also maintain the delay at a constant value, which may require padding out some voice packets to obtain constant delay.

The interface circuits to fast packet switches are broadband ISDN (see Chapter 26), IEEE 802.6 (see Chapter 29), frame relay, and asynchronous transfer mode (ATM). Frame relay, which is discussed later in this section, is a Level 2 protocol for sending

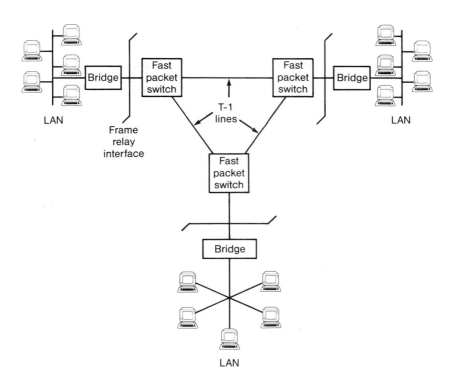

Figure 7.5   Using fast packet and frame relay to bridge local area networks.

frames across a physical network with minimum delay. Figure 7.5 illustrates how three local area networks might be connected using frame relay interfaces and a fast packet network as the transmission medium.

Fast packet has several advantages compared to a device such as a T-1 multiplexer, which has fixed bandwidth allocation.

- More efficient use of bandwidth for both voice and data.
- Faster alternate routing around congestion or failures.
- Clocking and synchronism are not a problem.
- Voice compression is integral to the system.
- Statistical multiplexing of data is integral to the system.

- The true volume of traffic can be measured by counting packets.

Fast packet has the following disadvantages:

- End-to-end delays are greater than point-to-point circuits.
- Peak voice traffic may disrupt data channels.

Unlike voice compression equipment, which obtains compression only by digitizing the voice at a lower rate, voice compression in fast packet results from two characteristics of voice sessions. First, voice is inherently half duplex since one party normally listens when the other is talking. Statistically, this means half the channel is available for sharing by other channels. Second, there are often pauses in talking, which result in silent periods that can be used by other channels. The compressor evaluates the analog waveform, removes pauses and repetition, and digitizes and packetizes the basic waveform. The receiving switch, recognizing the absence of voice packets, may insert noise to assure the listener that the circuit is still active, but it uses no circuit capacity. Repetitive data patterns such as synchronizing and framing characters are suppressed at the transmitting end and recreated at the receiving end without being transmitted in their entirety.

Packets are short—128-byte packets are common—so many packets can be interleaved during a slight pause. Packets are generated only when there is information to send, not just because a connection is established. This is in contrast to digital speech interpolation, which sets up a physical channel through a circuit switch.

In addition to the inherent compression that results from monitoring silent intervals, some fast packet switches also use ADPCM voice compression to further increase the number of voice sessions a channel can carry. If the network has the appropriate connectivity, fast packet also provides automatic alternate routing in case of circuit failure. The network shown in Figure 7.5 has two circuits to each node, which provides connectivity for alternate routing.

Fast packet overcomes the primary disadvantage of fixed circuits. When no information is flowing in a conventional circuit, bandwidth goes to waste. A voice call typically uses 40% or less of circuit capacity because of the half duplex nature of voice and the natural pauses that occur in a conversation. Data sessions often use an even smaller percentage of circuit capacity because capacity is wasted with overheads, polling messages, and other non-information characters. High bandwidth services, such as imaging and LAN interconnection, require high bandwidths for short intervals, then may require little or none for long periods. Also, these services are intolerant of long delays.

Fast packet offers these advantages compared to conventional data transmission methods:

- High throughput.
- Low delay.
- Bandwidth allocated on demand.
- Usable for all types of traffic .
- Protocol transparency.
- High circuit utilization.

Facsimile and modem tones can disrupt a fast packet network, because compression relies on pauses that do not occur with these services. It is important that the system turn compression off when a facsimile or modem tone is detected.

Frame Relay

Frame relay is an access protocol that relates to a fast packet network as X.25 relates to a packet switched data network: it is a standard access protocol to a network that may use proprietary switching methods. Frame relay is a Level 2 protocol that uses ISDN's LAPD standard, and compared to the Level 3 functions of X.25 it is much simpler and therefore much faster.

Frame relay standards are planned in two versions. FR-1 is a permanent virtual circuit that is useful for such functions as bridging local area and metropolitan area networks. FR-2 is a switched virtual circuit that is useful when bandwidth requirements vary, such as in voice and bursty data connections. Several products are on the market under the name of frame relay, but as of this writing the standard had not been approved. Therefore, such implementations are proprietary and subject to modification.

Frame relay is an abbreviated connection-oriented protocol that provides no flow control and no error correction. It simply discards errored frames. Higher layers detect the missing frames and arrange for retransmission. Higher level protocols handle queuing for access to the network.

Frame relay statistically multiplexes user data in streams called data link connections (DLC). Frame relay offers the following benefits:

- High throughput.
- Protocol transparency.
- Low delay through the network.
- Reliability because of the self-healing effect of the network.
- Improved circuit utilization.
- Full connectivity for all attached devices.

Applications

As technology advances, it becomes possible to squeeze more information into narrower bandwidths. With the price of bandwidth dropping, applications that once were prohibitively expensive are now commonplace. It is difficult to predict where the future will lead us. Standards are not yet well defined for many high compression technologies, but clearly voice and data compression will be important elements in the network of the future.

Standards

Data compression standards and ADPCM voice compression standards are currently defined and accepted for commercial applications. As with other standards, however, the speed of the standards-setting process is slow enough that many companies cannot wait for it, so they put products on the market with proprietary protocols. For the time being, and into the foreseeable future, end users should consider proprietary voice compression products if the payback time is short, say two or three years.

Proprietary products offer more compression and satisfactory quality and are constantly improving.

Although compression equipment may use proprietary standards on the line, they must interface transmission facilities and connecting terminal equipment over international standards. Equipment must, therefore, be compatible with such standards as T-1, E-1 (the European T-1 standard), V.24, V.35, and other interfaces to DTE.

Evaluation Considerations

The primary issues that any prospective user of voice compression equipment must address are voice quality and the restriction in data transmission speeds. Even companies that do not use dial-up data almost invariably use facsimile, which requires 9600 b/s for full-speed page transmission. Therefore, a fundamental consideration is how the product handles data and facsimile. If the product works on a backbone network that is accessed through tandem switches, it is particularly important that facsimile and data be handled transparently to the user.

Another issue is standards. As mentioned above, much available equipment uses proprietary standards and must therefore operate end-to-end with equipment of the same manufacture. If the equipment is used between North America and Europe, the problem of compatibility with CEPT standards may arise. For example, conversion from A-law to Mu-law companding may be required. Also, in terms of standards, compatibility with 64 kb/s clear channel also should be considered. The bandwidth increase compared to 56 kb/s may support an additional voice channel.

Signaling and interface compatibility also must be considered. Depending on the type of equipment that the voice channels must interface, signaling may be loop start, ground start, or E & M. The physical interface may be two-wire or four-wire. Foreign exchange channels also may be required. The data channel may interface EIA-232, V.35, or another physical interface such as ISDN.

The number of analog-to-digital conversions and compression and decompression steps in the total network should be considered. Each conversion increases quantizing noise and increases distortion as it decreases voice signal clarity. The manufacturer's specifications should be evaluated before any attempt is made to connect devices back-to-back through the voice frequency interface. Connections through a digital interface may be acceptable.

Synchronization requirements should be evaluated. If the multiplexer interfaces a DDS circuit, it may be necessary to derive clocking from the DDS network. If so, the multiplexer must be capable of being synchronized from an external source.

Selected Manufacturers of Voice and Data Compression Equipment

Low Bit Rate Voice and Fast Packet Equipment

Advanced Compression Technology

AT&T Network Systems

Avanti Communications

Aydin Monitor System Digital Communications Group

BBN

Case/Datatel

Coastcom

Codex

DCA/Cohesive

Doelz

General DataComm

Infotron

Micom Systems

Network Equipment Technologies Inc.

Newbridge Networks

Republic Telecom

Spectrum Digital

Stratacom

Tellabs Inc.

Timeplex

Wescom, Telephone Products Div. Rockwell Telecommunications, Inc.

T-1 Multiplexers with Low Bit-Rate Voice Options

Amdahl

AT&T Paradyne

Avanti

Aydin

Case/DataTel

Coastcom

Codex

Cohesive/DCA

Dynatech

General DataComm

Infotron

Network Equipment Technologies, Inc.

Newbridge Networks

StrataCom

Tellabs

Timeplex

Switching Systems

Switching has evolved through six generations since the birth of the telephone industry, and many people still active in the industry have experienced all six in their careers. The last manual switches were disappearing about the time electronic analog switching was inaugurated. In between were panel, step-by-step, and crossbar—all electromechanical systems. Panel has been relegated to the museums. Crossbar and step-by-step comprise an ever-decreasing share of the market, but many such systems are still in service today. The current generation, processor-controlled digital switching, probably will outlive most of us, but we haven't reached the end of telecommunications history by any means.

In this era of inexpensive multimegabyte memory and fast processors-on-a-chip, it is difficult to remember how primitive the first electronic switching systems were. Introduced in 1965, the Western Electric No. 1 ESS used twistor cards for memory and measured the size of its processor in bays of floor space. The age of microelectronics was just dawning. These switching systems were built from discrete components, and circuitry that today is compressed into a chip occupied several circuit cards.

Primitive as they were by today's standards, these systems were remarkably durable, and most of them survive, upgraded to the 1A-ESS. The processors and memory have been replaced with updated components, but the basic architecture and much of the switching and input/output circuitry will remain until analog switches finally give way to newer digital switches.

The objectives of switching technology are clear: new technology should be faster, smaller, more reliable, and cheaper and have more features. Microelectronics has delivered all this, and we are far from reaching the limits.

This part of the book discusses switching systems. Chapter 8 begins with a discussion of circuit switching technology. The following chapters describe specific applications in local and tandem switching. The final chapters in this part deal with signaling, the means by which switching systems communicate, and common equipment, which supports all types of apparatus. A discussion of customer premises switching equipment, such as voice and data PBXs, is reserved for Part 4.

8

Circuit Switched Network Systems

In telephone parlance, a *circuit* is any path that connects two or more users. In the first few years of the telephone's existence, circuits ran from point to point, and they were always connected over a physical facility, such as a pair of wires. It is obvious that running a circuit between each pair of users that wishes to communicate is impractical, so circuit switching was born. A *circuit switch* is a device that connects the output of one circuit to the input of another so information can be passed. Circuits can be switched in tandem so users can reach the desired destination over a series of built-up connections.

In the early days of telephony, subscriber loops terminated in jacks, and operators used long patch cords to connect circuits. As the number of telephones grew, the size of the jack panels increased until it became impractical to switch circuits with plug-equipped patch cords.

The next stage in the evolution of circuit switching brought manual cord boards like the one pictured in Figure 8.1. Circuits still terminated on jacks, but they were brought within reach of an operator, who sat at a fixed position that were equipped with several pairs of cords; key switches to control talking, monitoring, and ringing; and lamps to show the on-hook/off-hook status of the circuits. Circuits connected in *multiple*, which is to say that each circuit appeared in front of several operator positions. As antiquated as manual circuit switching seems, it survived in the public telephone network well beyond the middle of the 20th century and exists today in some small businesses.

**Figure 8.1   A manual switchboard of the Pennsylvania Bell Tele-
phone Company at Easton, PA, circa 1890.**
Courtesy, AT&T Archives

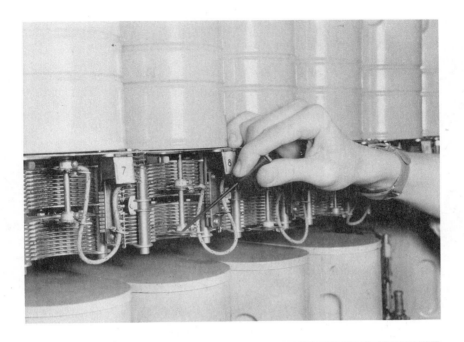

Figure 8.2   A bank of step-by-step, or Strowger, switches.
Courtesy, AT&T Archives

Manual switching was fine when labor was cheap and the telephone was a rarity, but it was an obvious candidate for mechanization. In 1891, a Kansas city undertaker named Almon Strowger became convinced that telephone operators were reporting false busy signals on his line and connecting callers to wrong numbers, depriving him of business. He designed an electromechanical replacement for the operator and invented the switch that today bears his name. Figure 8.2 is a photograph of a bank of Strowger switches, which still have not disappeared from the scene despite the many advantages that computer control brings to circuit switching. With Strowger's invention, the automatic circuit switch, which is the subject of this chapter, was born.

The nature of telecommunications requires that subscriber stations be accessible to one another. Accessibility is achieved by using switching to control routing choices and to provide a point of entry to the network. An effective telecommunications network possesses these attributes:

- Accessibility. Any station can be connected to any other station if they are compatible with the network's protocols.

- Ease of addressing. Stations are accessed by sending a simple address code. Using that address, the network does the translation and code conversions to route the call to the destination.

- Interconnectability. Network ownership rarely crosses national borders, and in the United States multiple ownership is the rule. For greatest utility, interconnection across sovereign or proprietary boundaries is required.

- Robustness. Networks must contain sufficient capacity and redundancy to be relatively invulnerable to overloads and failures and to recover automatically from failures that do occur. They must offer some form of flow control to prevent users from accessing the network when overloads occur.

- Capacity. Networks must support enough users to meet service demands.

Some type of switching is required to fill all the above demands. Networks employ three forms of switching: packet switching, in which traffic is divided into small segments and routed to the destination by nodes that are interconnected by circuits; message switching, in which traffic is stored and forwarded when a path to the destination is available; and circuit switching in which users are interconnected directly by a path that lasts for the duration of the session. Message switching is practical only for data communications. Packet switched voice is technically feasible and, as Chapter 7 discusses, some systems do use packet switching for voice traffic. Now, however, circuit switching is the only feasible form for public voice networks. Circuit switching is also feasible for data traffic, and a significant portion of the traffic carried by the public switched telephone network (PSTN) is data and facsimile.

Network Terminology

Network terminology is often confusing because of the ambiguity of the vocabulary. In this discussion of networks the following terms are used:

- A node is a network element that provides a point at which stations can access the network; it is the terminating point for internodal trunks. In circuit switched networks, nodes are always switching systems. In packet and message switched networks, they may be computers. This chapter discusses the differences between switching systems and computers.
- *Trunks* are the circuits or links that interconnect nodes. In switching systems the equipment that interfaces the internodal trunks to the switching system is also called trunks, or sometimes trunk relay equipment.
- Stations are the terminal points in a network. Telephone instruments, key telephone equipment, data terminals, and computers all fall under the station definition for this discussion.
- Lines are the circuits or paths that connect stations to the nodes.

Network Architecture

Chapter 3 discusses five basic network topologies—ring, bus, branching tree, mesh, and star. Circuit switched networks use the star and mesh topologies almost exclusively. Lines radiate from the central office to stations in a star topology, and the nodes are interconnected as a mesh.

The fundamental network design problem is determining how to assemble the most economical configuration of circuits and equipment based on peak and average traffic load, grade of service required, and switching, circuit, and administrative costs. It is practical to connect a few nodes with direct trunks between nodes, as Figure 8.3 shows. Direct connection is feasible up to a point, but as the number of nodes increases, the number of circuit groups increases as the square of the number of nodes, and the

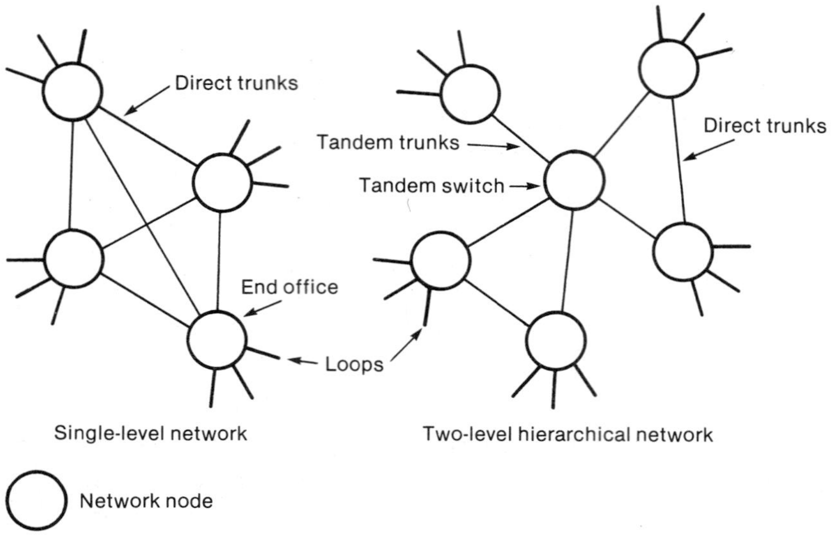

Figure 8.3   Direct and tandem trunks in single-level and hierarchical networks.

number of trunks soon becomes unwieldy. To control costs, a hierarchical network can be formed using tandem switches to interconnect the nodes.

The number of levels in a network hierarchy is determined by the network's owner and is based on a cost/service balance as explained in Chapter 31. In the past, the AT&T and Bell Operating Company network was connected in a five-level hierarchical structure. With divestiture and the increasing power and intelligence of switching systems, the hierarchical structure is giving way to a flat network structure.

The Changing Network Environment

Telecommunications networks exist in an environment that is continually changing. Service demands are not constant—they vary by time of the day, day of the week, and season of the year. Demand is continually evolving in response to changing calling habits and business conditions. Competition and new technology have a substantial effect on cost and demand. Also, network

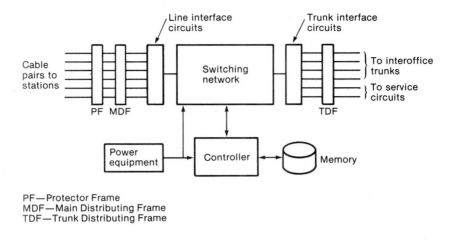

PF—Protector Frame
MDF—Main Distributing Frame
TDF—Trunk Distributing Frame

Figure 8.4   Block diagram of a switching system.

design is always a compromise that seeks to use existing equipment while providing satisfactory service. Because of these diverse forces, any network is a complex composite of modern and obsolescent equipment that is continually being shrunk or expanded to match demand. Even a new private network assembled with the latest technology is soon made partially obsolete by technical advances.

The remainder of this chapter explains the characteristics of the switching equipment that serves North American telecommunications users. This technology is common to the three major classes of switching systems—local central offices, tandem switches, and PBXs, which Chapters 9, 10, and 20 discuss. The distinctions between these three types of switching systems are not absolute. A single system can serve any or all functions.

Switching System Architecture

All switching systems include the following elements as shown in Figure 8.4:

- A *switching network,* or matrix, that connects paths between input and output ports.

- A *controller* that directs the connection of paths through the switching network. Direct control switching systems, which we will discuss later, do not employ a separate controller. The user controls the switch by dialing digits.

- A *data base* that stores the system configuration and addresses and features of lines and trunks. In direct control systems the data base is not a separate element.

- *Line ports* that interface outside plant for connection to users. All local and PBX switching systems include line ports; tandem switches may have only a few specialized line ports.

- *Trunk ports* that interface interoffice trunks, service circuits, and testing equipment.

- *Service circuits* that provide call progress signals such as ringing and busy tones.

- *Common equipment* such as battery plants, power supplies, testing equipment, and distributing frames.

Switching System Control

When a user signals a switching system with a service request, the switch determines the terminating station's address from the telephone number dialed and translates the number to determine call routing. Translation tables specify the trunk group that serves the destination, an alternate route if the first choice route is blocked, the number of digits to dial, any digit conversions needed, and the type of signaling to use on the trunk. Some switches lack translation capability. These systems, called *direct control* systems, route calls only in direct response to dialed digits. *Common control* systems include circuitry that enables them to make alternate routing choices; that is, when one group of trunks is blocked, another group can be selected. Electromechanical common controlled switching systems use wired relay logic. Modern electronic switching systems use stored program control (SPC) controllers to do all call processing functions. In central offices the controller is a special purpose computer. In many PBXs, a commercial processor is the heart of the controller.

Switching Networks

Switching systems can be classified by type of switching network. Direct controlled switching systems have inflexible networks that are directed by dial pulses to a single destination. Most common control and stored program control systems use one of four types of switching network:

- Crossbar analog.
- Reed relay analog.
- Pulse amplitude modulated (PAM) analog.
- Pulse code modulated (PCM) digital.

The basic function of the switching network is to provide paths between the inputs and outputs. Like all other design tasks, the network design objective is to provide enough paths to avoid blocking users while keeping costs to a level users are willing to pay. The first two network types use electromechanical relays for the switching medium and are more expensive than the last two types, which employ digital logic circuits to provide and control the network paths. Electromechanical networks have some restrictions on the number of users that can be served at once. A network that contains fewer paths than terminations is called a *blocking network* because not all users can be served simultaneously.

A nonblocking network enables a connection to be made between any two ports independently of the amount of traffic. Nonblocking networks are not economically feasible with electro-mechanical switching systems because the cost of the network increases directly with the number of switch points. With digital networks where the switching medium is entirely solid state, nonblocking networks are not only economically feasible, they are common in PBXs; vendors frequently stress non-blockage as a selling point.

It is easy to exaggerate the importance of a nonblocking network, which can deliver a full 36 CCS of capacity to every station. (CCS is a measure of traffic intensity. It is discussed in Chapter 31.) Not only is the need for this kind of capacity rare, it must be remembered that the switching network is but one element of the switching system; another element invariably arises to limit capacity. The phrase *virtually nonblocking* has evolved in the industry to describe a network that is not designed to be totally nonblocking but provides enough paths that users rarely find themselves blocked by the network. In switching terminology, the situation in which an incoming call cannot be connected to a port because of blockage in the switching network, is called *incoming matching loss* (IML). The percentage of IML is a useful factor in evaluating the health of the system. In a nonblocking switch, the IML should always be zero. In a virtually nonblocking network the IML should rarely be anything but zero. In a switch with concentration and a satisfactory degree of load balance, IML should be a fraction of 1%.

A nonblocking switch network does not ensure that users will not encounter blockage. Trunking is always designed to some level of blockage as discussed in Chapter 31. If the switching system is configured without enough common equipment, users will encounter delays that they will interpret as blockage. For example, not enough digit receivers results in slow dial tone. Switches are also subject to processor overloads, which can result in a variety of call processing delays. Switches are rated by the number of busy hour call attempts (BHCA), which is the factor that describes the number of calls the system can handle during the peak hour of the day. The term *call attempt* may bear little relationship to the actual number of calls handled by the system. Not only are call originations counted as call attempts, but accesses to features such as call pick up, call transfer, and call waiting, which require attention by the central processor, count as call attempts in most switches.

Modern switching networks are wired in grids as Figure 8.5 shows. Each stage of the grid consists of a switching matrix that connects input links to output links. Links, which are often called *junctors*, are wired between switching stages to provide a possible path from any input port to any output port. The network shown in Figure 8.5 is nonblocking because it has an equal number of input and output ports, and the number of possible paths equals the number of ports.

Many switching networks use concentration to reduce network cost. If the primary switch on the input side of the network

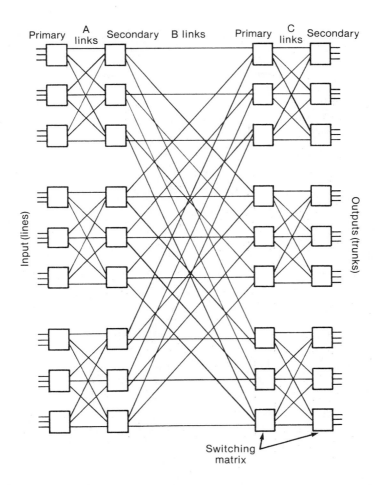

Figure 8.5   Nonblocking switching network.

has six input ports as in Figure 8.6, the network would have a two-to-one concentration ratio because only three of the six inputs could be serviced simultaneously. Local central offices and PBXs that use electromechanical networks typically use a line switch concentration ratio of 4:1 or 6:1. It should be understood that even though a switch may have a nonblocking network, it can still be blocked in the line switch networks if these use concentration. Trunk switches usually use no concentration.

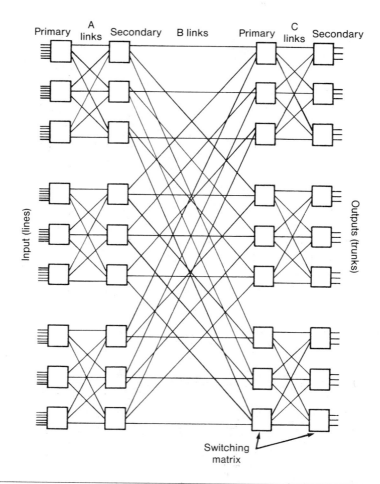

Figure 8.6   A switching network with two-to-one concentration.

The capacity of a switching network relates directly to the number of switching stages it has. The switching matrix is physically limited by the number of terminations it can support. To avoid blocking, the controller must have multiple choices of paths through the network. These paths are obtained by providing multiple switching stages so that each stage has enough choices that the probability of blocking is reduced to a level consistent with grade of service objectives.

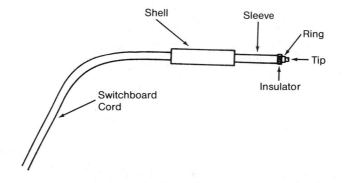

Figure 8.7 **Derivation of terms tip, ring, and sleeve from the operator's switchboard plug.**

Direct Control Switching Systems

The earliest type of switching system was a manual switchboard similar to the one shown in Figure 8.1. Manual switchboards employed operators to make connections. An incoming signal, actuated by taking the receiver off hook or turning a crank, operated a signal on the switchboard to notify the operator of an incoming call. The operator answered the call by inserting a cord in a jack, obtaining the terminating number, and inserting the matching cord in the jack of the called line or of a trunk to a distant office. Disregarding the cost of the manual switchboard, it was efficient because the operator could make alternate routing decisions.

Many terms in common use today originated with the manual switchboard. Incoming calls to some switchboards were signaled by a hinged cap that covered the jack and dropped down when a ring arrived. The term *drop* has survived to signify the equipment toward the central office from the line. The operator's cord had three connections as Figure 8.7 shows—the tip, the ring, and the sleeve. The *tip* and the *ring* connected to the two sides of the subscriber's line, and this terminology survives today. The operator detected the busy or idle status of the line by touching the tip of the plug to the sleeve of the jack. If the line was busy at another position in the lineup, a click could be heard in the headset from the battery on the sleeve, which supervised the connection. The operator's reach imposed a practical limit on the

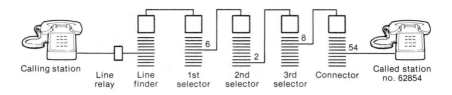

Figure 8.8   Direct control switching system step-by-step.

number of lines that a single switchboard could serve. Switchboard positions were connected in multiple, another term that remains today to describe the parallel connection of several devices.

The operator monitored a connection by observing lamps on the switchboard console. A lighted lamp meant the line was on hook; when the telephone was off hook the lamp was extinguished. The operator *supervised* the connection by watching the lamps. The term survives today to describe the process, now entirely electronic, of determining when a party answers or terminates a call. Supervision today not only directs the equipment to establish and take down a connection but also determines when to start and terminate billing for the call.

As the telephone system expanded, it exceeded the practical limitations of manual operation. Mechanical switching systems were necessary to keep the costs under control and to contain the equipment in a reasonably sized area. The Strowger, or step-by-step, switch is an electromechanical device that operates through two axes; it steps vertically to one of 10 levels and rotates horizontally to one of 10 terminals. It is actuated by pulls on the telephone dial or by an internal operation, depending on the function of the switch. Figure 8.8 is a block diagram of a simple step-by-step central office.

Subscriber lines connect to line relays that operate when the user lifts the receiver. Line relays connect to line finders that are wired in line groups to serve as many as 200 lines with up to 20 switches per group, depending on the traffic volume. When all switches in a line group are busy, new users cannot get dial tone until someone hangs up. Line finders automatically step vertically and rotate horizontally to locate a calling telephone line. A first selector switch, permanently wired to the line finder, furnishes dial tone to the user. As digits are pulsed, selector switches step upward to a level corresponding to the digits dialed and automatically rotate horizontally to find the first path to the next selector.

The final two digits in the train actuate a connector switch, which connects to the user's line. The next-to-last digit drives the connector to the appropriate level; the last rotates the connector to the correct terminal. If the terminal is busy, the connector returns a busy signal. If it is idle, the connector attaches a ringing signal, which remains attached until the called party answers or the calling party hangs up.

The step-by-step office has a theoretical concentration ratio of 10:1, which is established by 200 subscribers assigned to a line group of 20 switches. In practice, it is important that line groups contain a mix of heavy and light users to maintain a reasonable grade of service. Network administrators vary the concentration ratio by changing the number of switches in the line group or the number of subscribers assigned. Step-by-step offices require considerable administrative attention to ensure that they provide a reasonable grade of service. If all line finders are busy when a user goes off hook, dial tone is delayed; dial tone speed systems connected to line groups measure the delay. To deload an overloaded line group, it may be necessary to find who the heavy users are and move enough of them to another line group to relieve the congestion.

Two other problems, *permanent signals* and *calling party hold,* also plague step-by-step offices. A permanent signal results when a user takes the receiver off-hook and leaves it off without dialing. A line finder-first selector combination is seized and cannot be released except by manual intervention. A calling party hold condition occurs when the calling party fails to hang up. The switch train remains connected through to the called party, who cannot use the telephone until the caller releases the path. In some later step-by-step offices, anti-CPH connectors time out to release the called party's line.

A step-by-step central office can be visualized as a concentrator in which many originating stations route over fewer paths through the selector train. The selector switches find vacant paths to the expansion side of the office, which contains all the telephone numbers terminating in the central office. A step-by-step office lacks translation capability. It routes to lines and trunks directly based on the dialed digits. Different selector levels are wired to internal switches or to trunks to distant offices. The initial digit 1 is reserved for dialing to service circuits such as long distance, directory assistance, and repair service.

Incoming calls from distant offices appear on incoming selectors, which have access to the selector switch train. The dial pulses drive the selector train exactly like an intraoffice call except for the smaller number of digits needed to drive the selector train and connector to the destination.

Most step-by-step offices have no automatic message accounting (AMA) capability. A serving toll office equipped with centralized AMA (CAMA) records long distance call details.

Many telephone switches in the United States use the step-by-step system today, but they are being replaced by stored program systems. Although step-by-step comprises a significant number of offices, the remaining systems are small and serve only a fraction of the total telephone users in the country. Several pertinent points should be understood about directly controlled central offices.

- Step-by-step switches are incapable of making routing decisions. When a caller encounters blockage, the switch can return only a reorder or a busy signal. The user must hang up and try again.

- The switch can be driven only by dial pulses. To provide DTMF service, a separate converter is wired to the first selector to convert DTMF signals to dial pulses.

- The switching speed is regulated by the speed of the telephone dial and depends on the number of digits in the dialed number and the dialing speed of the user.

- All equipment used for a call remains connected for the duration of the call; the system cannot release equipment to another user.

- Each call causes wear on the mechanical equipment. Unless periodic adjustments and replacements are made, service deteriorates.

- The switches and relays in a step-by-step office cause noise that couples into other circuits. Therefore, data transmission is likely to be impaired by errors in a step-by-step office, particularly when the equipment is improperly maintained.

■ A step-by-step office is robust with no common circuits other than power and ringing supplies, that can interrupt all lines from a single failure. Redundancy is unnecessary, except in ringing systems.

■ A step-by-step office lacks a data base of subscriber connections. Each valid user is wired to a line group, which establishes the originating equipment number, and to a connector, which establishes the telephone number.

■ Step-by-step central offices have few defenses against misuse of the telephone by subscribers who take their instruments off-hook without dialing or who fail to hang up after a session. These actions cause service difficulties for other users, and the central office cannot correct them without manual intervention by a technician.

Common Control Central Offices

Common control switching systems employ electromechanical logic circuits to drive the switching network. These logic circuits are brought into a connection long enough to establish a path through the switching network, then release to attend to other calls. Figure 8.9 is a block diagram of a crossbar common control switching system.

Several types of switching networks are used with common control systems, but the most common is the crossbar switch shown in Figure 8.10. The crossbar switch is a matrix consisting of horizontal and vertical connections. Switches are manufactured in several different sizes, but for illustration, a 10 x 20 switch will be considered. With this type of switch, 20 input paths assigned to the vertical portion of the matrix can be connected to 10 output paths assigned to the horizontal side of the matrix, providing a 2:1 concentration ratio.

A set of cross points is wired to the horizontal and vertical paths at each matrix intersection as Figure 8.11 shows. The common control equipment operates and releases the crosspoints. For exam-

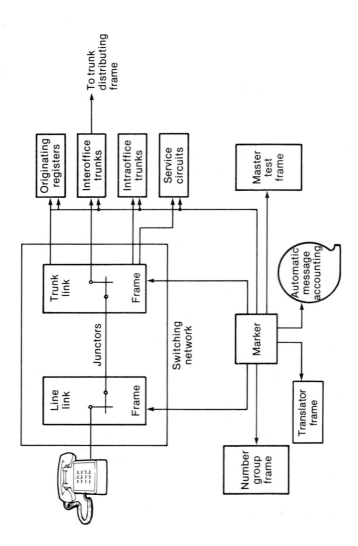

Figure 8.9 Block diagram of a crossbar switching system.

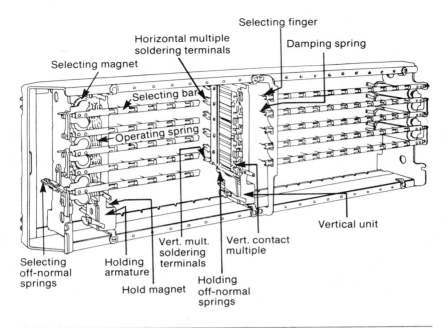

Figure 8.10   Crossbar switch.

ple, to make the connection between vertical 3 and horizontal 5 as the figure shows, an impulse from the common control operates a horizontal select magnet. This magnet moves a finger against an actuating card on the switch contacts, where the vertical hold magnet clamps it. The select magnet is then released. The hold magnet keeps the contacts in operation until the common control equipment releases it when the call ends. The function of the common control equipment is to select an idle path through the switching network and to operate crosspoints in all switches simultaneously to establish path continuity.

Crossbar switches have two-wire contacts for local central office and PBX applications and four-wire contacts for toll tandem operation. Some two-wire toll tandem systems are used for local tandem offices and lower classes of toll switching systems, but these are obsolescent and are being replaced because of the transmission deficiencies inherent in a two-wire switch as described in Chapter 2.

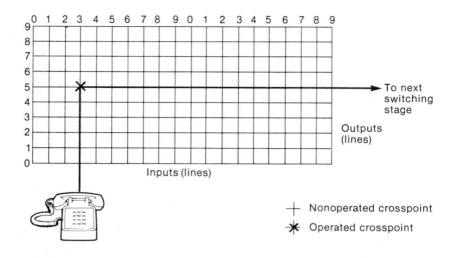

Figure 8.11   Crossbar switch schematic diagram.

The brain of a crossbar switch is the *marker,* an electrome-chanical device that performs functions analogous to those of the central processor in a computer. Instructions from the marker drive the switching network and auxiliary equipment in a crossbar office. Markers are provided in a quantity sufficient to serve the traffic load in the office. A minimum of two is provided for redundancy.

When a line goes off-hook the marker detects the change of state and connects the line to an originating register trunk. The register provides dial tone and receives the dialed digits. Registers are of two classes, dial pulse and DTMF. Dial pulse registers can detect only dial pulses; DTMF registers can detect either type of signal. The register stores dialed digits in a relay circuit and signals the marker when dialing is complete. If dialing has not been completed in a specified interval, the register times out and the marker connects the line to a reorder trunk.

After dialing is complete the marker calls a *translator,* a device that stores routing and signaling information. If the translator informs the marker that the call is to a chargeable destination, the marker calls in AMA equipment and records the initial entry. If the number is within the same office, the marker tests the status of the terminating number, and if busy, attaches the calling line to a busy signal trunk. If the called line is idle the marker reserves a path through the network, connects the called number to a 20 Hz ringing trunk, and connects the calling number to an audible ringing trunk. When the called party answers, the marker removes audible and 20 Hz ringing and connects a path through the network. When the first party hangs up, the marker takes down all the connections.

When a call comes in from a distant office, the marker recognizes the trunk seizure from the change in status of the signaling leads and attaches an incoming register to receive the digits. Based on the trunk classification, the marker tells the register how many digits to expect. When dialing is complete, the register signals the marker, which connects a path from the trunk to the terminating number. Figure 8.12 is a photograph of one switch lineup of a crossbar central office.

The most significant advantage of common control offices compared to direct control offices is the flexibility of common control. If, for example, an office has direct trunks to another office but they are all busy, it can attach an outgoing call to an alternate route to a tandem office. This capability is designed into most networks. Direct circuit groups, called high usage (HU) groups, are established to terminating offices if the traffic volume is sufficient to justify the cost. The capacity of HU groups is engineered to keep the circuits fully occupied during heavy calling periods. Overflow traffic routes over tandem trunks that are more liberally engineered to support the overflow. Chapter 31 discusses alternate routing concepts in more detail.

Crossbar offices take considerably less manual attention than step-by-step offices. The switches do not have the wiping action that wears down contacts. When troubles occur, the marker calls a trouble recorder into action and punches a card to show the state of the various leads when the trouble occurred. Crossbar offices solve the problems of permanent signals and calling party hold. If a customer remains off-hook without dialing, the register times out, and the marker connects the line to a permanent signal holding trunk, which applies tones to alert the customer to hang up the telephone. If a calling party fails to disconnect at the

Figure 8.12   A lineup of crossbar central office equipment.
Courtesy, AT&T Archives

completion of a call, the marker recognizes the termination from the called party and takes down the connection.

Crossbar offices are not bound by a fixed numbering plan that relies on the digits dialed to route the call. They can insert and translate digits, choose alternate routes to the destination, and offer *Centrex* service, which is a PBX-like service provided from the central office. Chapter 23 discusses Centrex.

The following characteristics are significant in common control switching systems:

- Alternate routing capability offers flexibility in handling overloads.

- Crossbar offices require less maintenance than step-by-step because their internal circuitry has no wiping action to generate wear. Also, trouble indications are detected by the marker and recorded in a trouble recorder for analysis.

- Although crossbar offices are not as electrically noisy as step-by-step offices, relay and switch operations cause noise that can cause errors in switched data circuits.

- The structure of crossbar switches makes four-wire tandem operation feasible to improve transmission performance.

- Common control switches are vulnerable to total central office failure. When markers are all occupied or out of service, no further users can be served, even though idle paths are available.

- Common control offices are much faster than step-by-step offices. Dial pulses are registered in shared circuits to avoid tying up equipment with slow users or long dial pulse strings.

Stored Program Control

Stored program control (SPC) central offices have been in operation in the United States since 1965 and before long will have replaced their electromechanical counterparts. The primary economies of SPC offices lie in their lower maintenance cost and their ability to provide enhanced features that are impractical with electromechanical central offices. Analog SPC systems, diagrammed in Figure 8.13, use concepts similar to common control

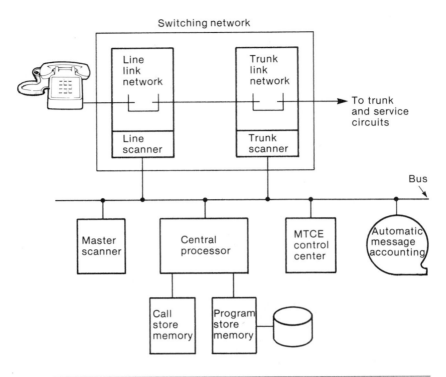

Figure 8.13   Block diagram of a stored program switching machine.

electromechanical offices except that electronic logic replaces wired relay logic.

The central processor controls call processing. When service circuits detect an off-hook signal, the processor attaches a dial pulse or DTMF receiver to the originating line. The receiver supplies dial tone and registers the incoming digits. The processor stores the details of the call in a temporary *call store* memory. Translation tables are stored in semi-permanent memory. The processor establishes a path through the switching network, attaches 20 Hz ringing to the called party and an audible ringing trunk to the calling party. When the called party answers, the processor marks completion of the connection.

The central processor in SPC central offices is similar to that used in mainframe computers, but with some important differences. First, the SPC processor is not only fault tolerant; it is almost fail-safe.

Although SPC central offices do fail, their design objective is no more than one hour's outage in 20 years, which is an outage tolerance several orders of magnitude better than that of most mainframe computers. A second difference is in the nature of the processing task. Call processing is highly input/output intensive, with little requirement for arithmetic operations compared to other data processing tasks. Where a mainframe computer is overseeing several dozen peripherals, a central office processor is managing tens of thousands of individual terminals, any of which can spring to life at any time and demand service within a second or less.

Although call processing is similar to that in a common control electromechanical office, the SPC processor offers much greater flexibility. The processor operates under the direction of a *generic program*, which contains the call processing details. Features can be added by replacing the generic program with a new issue. Because of this factor, SPC systems are far more flexible than their electromechanical counterparts. The generic program contains special features that Chapters 9, 10, and 20 discuss. These can be activated, deactivated, or assigned to a limited group of users by making translation changes. SPC systems also can collect statistical information and diagnose circuit and system irregularities to a much greater degree than electromechanical systems.

Electronic Switching Networks

Over the past two decades many changes, which can be broadly classed as analog or digital, have been made in SPC switching networks. Some systems use processor-driven crossbar switching networks, but most analog systems use reed relay networks. A reed relay has contacts enclosed in a sealed glass tube and surrounded by a coil of wire. The contacts are closed by a short pulse of current and remain closed until opened by a second pulse. The switches are wired in a matrix of horizontal and vertical paths to establish a DC circuit through the network.

Most electronic switching systems in use in the United States today are analog switches using reed relay networks; however, this technology is obsolescent and is rapidly being replaced by digital switching. Reed switches are more expensive to manufac-

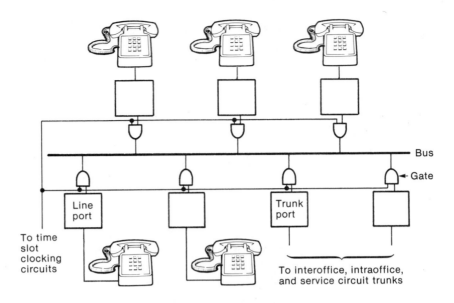

Figure 8.14   Time multiplexed bus system.

ture and require more maintenance than the digital networks that are replacing them.

Pulse Amplitude Switching

The earliest all-electronic switching networks used pulse amplitude modulation (PAM) a concept that Chapter 4 discusses. At the heart of the network is a high speed time-multiplexed bus that provides talking paths for all connected conversations. The bus is divided into time slots. Stations are interconnected by assigning them to the same time slot, during which they are allocated the full bandwidth of the bus long enough to send a single pulse. Line circuits sample the voice signal 8000 times per second and generate a PAM signal. Line and trunk ports connect to the bus through gating circuits as Figure 8.14 shows. At the proper time slot instant the gate opens to connect the parties to the bus for the duration of one pulse. By allowing a port to send during one time slot and receive during another, full duplex operation occurs.

PAM networks have the advantage of being electronic and therefore less costly to manufacture than reed networks. Western Electric Dimension PBXs manufactured during the 1970s and early 1980s use PAM switching networks. This type of network has the disadvantage of passing only analog signals and has been replaced by switching systems that use PCM networks.

Pulse Code Modulated Networks

The latest generation of switching systems uses PCM switching networks. PCM networks are similar in concept to the analog matrix shown in Figure 8.5 with some important exceptions.

First, PCM networks connect the encoded signal over parallel paths. The incoming serial bit stream from the line or trunk circuits is converted to a parallel signal and assigned to a *time slot*. At the proper time slot instant, all eight bits of the input PCM signal gate to the output port in parallel. The output circuits convert them to serial for application to trunk and line circuits.

The second exception is in the mode of switching employed in PCM networks. Analog networks use *space division* switching exclusively. That is, input paths are physically connected to output links. Digital networks use a combination of space division and time division switching. Although the term space division implies a relay operation, the switches used in digital networks contain no moving parts. Integrated logic gates form the switching element to direct the PCM pulses from one path to another.

Consider the diagram in Figure 8.15. The switching element is an *and gate*, which is a device with two inputs and a single output. If a pulse appears on both inputs simultaneously, the pulse is gated to the output. If either input is 0, which means no pulse, the pulse is blocked. The logic of a gate is shown in its truth table in the lower part of the figure. The central processor controls the opening and closing of the many gates that comprise a space division switch.

The other form of electronic switching is time division switching, which is implemented in a *time slot interchange* element (see Figure 8.16). A TSI receives digital pulses during one increment of time, stores them for one processor cycle, and releases them during the proper time slot in the next cycle. Two stations can

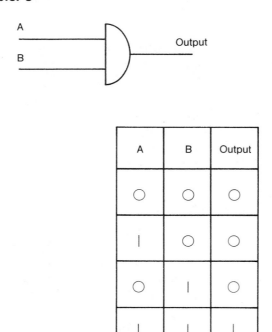

Figure 8.15   And gate truth table.

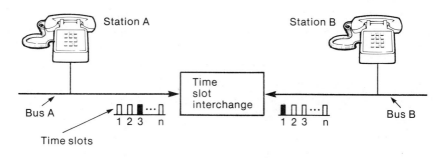

Figure 8.16   Time slot interchange.

talk to one another if they are connected to the same time slot. Time slot assignments are made by the processor and released when the call terminates. The time slot interchange process introduces an absolute delay of one processor cycle for each time division switching stage.

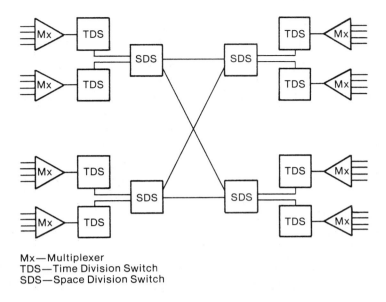

Mx—Multiplexer
TDS—Time Division Switch
SDS—Space Division Switch

Figure 8.17   Time-space-space-time digital switching network.

Practical digital switching networks contain a combination of space and time division switches. For example, Figure 8.17 shows a time-space-space-time (TSST) network. This is a four-stage network that is the functional equivalent of the space division networks of older analog switching systems.

Control Systems

Electronic switching systems are designed as *central control, multiprocessing,* or *distributed control.* In a central control system, all the call processing is concentrated in a single location. A multiprocessing system has two or more central processors that share call processing functions. The sharing takes the form of dividing the call processing load or assigning one set of functions to one processor and another to its mate. For example, one processor could handle call processing and the other maintenance. If either failed, the other could assume the entire load. The third method of control, distributed, uses multiple processors, each of which handles a designated part of the switch. There might, for example, be a separate processor for each shelf or each frame.

Electronic switching systems have four kinds of software. Although not all manufacturers use the same terminology, and there may be architectural differences between systems, the functions are contained in every SPC switch.

The *operating system* is the system that keeps the switch alive even though it is not processing calls. The operating system ties the elements of the switch together, takes care of input and output functions, and supervises the general health of the system. Closely tied to the operating system is the call processing software, which in many systems is called the *generic program*. This software contains all the features of the switch and maps the connections through the switching network.

The third type of software is the *parameters*. These are a data base that contains the types, quantities, and addresses of the major hardware components. By maintaining records of the busy/idle status of components, the processor sets up a path through the network, assigns it while a call is in process, and releases it when the call ends.

The fourth type of software is the *translations*, which are a data base of how ports are assigned and what feature is assigned to each port. Each trunk and each station in a switching system is assigned through the translation tables, and the features associated with that port are defined within the table. For example, the trunks are translated as to location, signalling, type, etc. Stations are translated as to location, restrictions, and features.

Synchronization

Networks of digital switches must be closely synchronized to prevent transmission errors. If two interconnected systems do not have a common synchronizing source, their clocks will run at slightly different rates. This means that occasionally the receiving end will miss a bit or will sample the same bit twice, either of which results in a bit error in data transmission. These momentary losses of framing are known as *slips*. Slips have little effect on voice transmission, but their effect can be serious on data or facsimile, both of which ride switched circuits.

Circuit switched networks are kept in synchronization by slaving switches on a master clock known as the *Basic Standard Reference Frequency* (BSRF). Each office has its own clock that can run freely with a certain degree of stability. The highest level clock below the BSRF is a Stratum 1 clock, which has an accuracy of at least 1×10^{-11}. There are three lower levels of clocking, which offer progressively less accuracy and lower cost. Timing passes down from each higher class office to the offices that home on it. This type of synchronization is called *plesiochronous*. When clocking is lost from a higher level office, lower level devices run freely. The greater the differences in clocking between two such devices, the higher the number of slips that will occur.

Other Switching Networks

Some PBXs use one of two other types of digital switching network—delta and pulse width-modulated networks. Like the more common PAM network, these are technically digital switches but are incapable of directly interfacing digital lines.

Comparison of Digital and Analog Switching Networks

Digital switches have several advantages over their analog counterparts:

- The switching networks are less expensive to manufacture because of the ability to use low cost integrated components.

- T-1 circuits can interface the switching system directly without using a channel bank to bring the circuits down to voice frequency.

- High speed data can be switched without the use of modems if digital line interface circuits are provided.

Compared to analog networks, digital switches have offsetting disadvantages that should be considered in small PBXs where the advantages of digital switching are not compelling:

- Their line circuits are more complex and expensive than analog line circuits. In analog switches the costs are concentrated in the switching network; in digital switches costs are concentrated in the line circuits.

- Digital switches consume more power than analog switches because the switching network is operating and drawing current continually although it is handling little or no traffic load.

Line, Trunk, and Service Circuits

All switching systems are equipped with circuits to interface the switching network to stations, trunks, and service circuits such as tone and ringing supplies. In some systems, these circuits are external devices. In other cases, they are integral to the switching equipment. For example, some digital central offices develop tones internally by generating the digital equivalent of the tone, so when it is applied to the decoder in a line or trunk circuit it is converted to an analog tone.

Line Circuit Functions

In a digital central office, line circuits have seven basic functions that can be remembered with the acronym BORSCHT. Analog central office line circuits require five of the seven functions; because they have two-wire switching networks, the hybrid and coding functions are omitted. The BORSCHT functions are:

Battery feeds from the office to the line to operate station transmitters and DTMF dials.

Overvoltage protection is provided to protect the line circuit from damaging external voltages that can occur during the time it takes the line protector to operate.

Ringing connects from a central ringing supply to operate the telephone bell.

Supervision refers to monitoring the on-hook/off-hook status of the line.

Coding converts the analog signal to a PCM bit stream in digital line circuits.

Hybrids are required in digital line circuits to convert between the four-wire switching network and the two-wire cable pair.

Testing access is provided so an external test system can obtain access to the cable pair for trouble isolation.

In PBXs and digital central offices, line circuits reside on plug-in cards. Because much of the cost of the system is embedded in the line circuits, shelves are installed, but to defer the investment, line cards are added only as needed. In analog central offices, line circuits are less expensive because they omit the analog-to-PCM conversion and the two-to four-wire conversion. Analog line circuits are permanently wired in frames that are connected to a distributing frame for crossconnection to the cable pairs.

Trunk Circuits

Trunk circuits interface the signaling protocols of interoffice trunks to the internal protocols of the switching system. For example, in an SPC office a trunk is seized by an order from the central control to a trunk distributing circuit in the trunk frame. This seizure causes the trunk circuit to connect battery to the M lead toward the carrier system. When a trunk is seized incoming, the ground on the E lead passes from the trunk circuit to a scanner that informs the controller of the seizure. See Chapter 11 for an explanation of E & M signaling.

Digital central offices interface analog trunks using external trunk circuits just as analog offices do. Digital trunks interface without the use of trunk circuits. Digital offices have interface circuitry that allows the 1.544 mb/s bit stream direct access to the switching network.

Service Circuits

All types of switching systems require circuits that are used momentarily in routing and establishing connections. These applications are briefly discussed so readers will understand how the services are obtained and applied in all types of switching systems.

Ringing and Call Progress Tone Supplies

All switching systems that interface end users require 20 Hz ringing supplies generating approximately 90 volts to ring telephone bells. In addition, switching systems require audible ringing supplies, busy tones operating at 60 interruptions per minute (IPM), and reorder tones operating at 120 IPM. In digital switching systems, these tones are generally created in software.

Recorded Announcements

Recorded announcements provide explicit information to the user when calls cannot be completed and tone signals are insufficient to explain the cause. For example, calls to disconnected numbers are connected to recorded announcements. When a transfer of calls is required, the system routes the incoming call to an intercept operator; otherwise, calls to nonworking numbers route to a recorder. Announcements are also used on long distance circuits to indicate temporary circuit or equipment overloads. Often these are preceded by a three-tone code called *special identification tones* (SIT) so automatic service observing equipment can collect statistics on ineffective dialing attempts.

Permanent Signal Tones

A *permanent signal* occurs when a line circuit is off-hook because of trouble or because the user has left the receiver off-hook. Permanent signals in trunk circuits occur because of equipment malfunctions or maintenance actions. Combinations of loud tones and recorded announcements are used on most line switching systems to alert the user to hang up the phone. Permanent trunk signals are indicated by interrupting the supervisory signal at 120 IPM, which flashes the supervision lights attached to E & M leads in some signaling apparatus.

Testing Circuits

All end offices and some PBXs contain circuits that provide testing access to subscriber lines. These circuits connect the tip and ring of the line to a test trunk to allow a test position access to both the cable facility and, to a limited degree, the central office equipment.

All tandem switching systems, most end offices, and some PBXs also include trunk testing circuitry to make transmission and supervision measurements on central office trunks. These circuits vary from 1004 Hz tone supplies that can be dialed from telephones served by the switching system to trunk testing circuits that enable two-way transmission and supervision measurements on trunks. Chapter 10 discusses trunk testing methods, and Chapter 32 discusses testing equipment.

Access to the Local Network

Until AT&T's divestiture of its Bell Operating Companies (BOCs) on January 1, 1984, the telephone network was designed for single ownership. Divestiture, which intended among other objectives to open long distance telephone service to competition, has far-reaching effects that should be understood by telecommunications managers. This section discusses the architectures of local and long distance telephone networks, how the interexchange carriers (IECs) obtain local access, and the way IECs sometimes bypass the local networks to provide service directly to end users.

Predivestiture Network Architecture

Until the mid-1970s, AT&T had a monopoly on switched long distance telephone service. The 22 BOCs and some 1500 independent telephone companies (ICs) owned the local network up to that time. The local exchange companies (LECs) furnished all local telephone service, most intrastate long distance service, and a limited amount of interstate long distance service. AT&T's Long Lines Division, which was renamed AT&T Communications after divestiture, furnished most interstate service.

The network was divided into five classes of switching systems and their interconnecting trunks. Class 5 central offices, the lowest class in the hierarchy, were owned and operated by the LECs, a situation that remains unchanged. Ownership of Class 4 and higher offices was established by agreement between the parties; many of these systems were owned jointly before divestiture, reflecting their use for both intrastate and long haul traffic.

The Class 5 offices connected to higher class offices by toll connecting trunks, now called *interLATA connecting trunks*. The higher class offices are interconnected by intertoll trunks. The LECs and the independent telephone companies, as negotiated by the parties, own interLATA connecting trunks; AT&T other IECs own the intertoll trunks. The FCC and the courts regulate the regional Bell holding companies. Among the IECs, the FCC regulates only AT&T.

Beginnings of Competition in the Toll Network

In 1978, the FCC decided to permit other common carriers to offer switched long distance telephone service in competition with AT&T. A key issue in the decision was how the carriers would obtain access to local telephone subscribers through Class 5 offices. Because the network was designed for single ownership, it was impossible to give other carriers access similar to AT&T's without extensive redesign of the local central offices. The AT&T Long Lines circuits terminated on trunk ports in the central offices as did circuits to independent telephone companies. This trunk-side access was not suitable for multiple common carriers, however, because local central offices were not designed for customer-directed access to a carrier. Switching systems route calls based only on destination, not by customer-selected access code.

The BOCs filed tariffs to provide IECs other than AT&T access to the local network through line side terminations in the central office. These tariffs were called the Exchange Network Facilities Interconnecting Arrangement (ENFIA) and were subsequently replaced by Feature Group tariffs that are discussed in a later section.

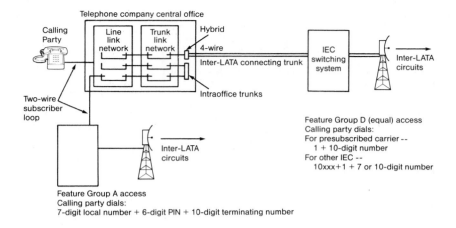

Figure 8.18   Feature groups A and D access to the local exchange network.

The line-side access to the local switching systems offered under ENFIA A tariffs allowed customers of the IECs to access the network by the arrangement shown in Figure 8.18. Compared to the trunk-side access offered to AT&T, line-side access has the following disadvantages:

- Callers obtained access to the IEC's network by dialing a seven-digit local telephone number. The IEC provided second dial tone to indicate attachment of its switching and recording equipment. Access to AT&T's network was by dialing 1.

- Automatic number identification, a feature that Chapter 9 discusses, is possible only over trunk-side connections. IEC users dial a personal identification number (PIN) for calling party billing identification. Rotary dials cannot be used for dialing PIN numbers; only DTMF dial pulses can pass through the Class 5 office to the IEC's switching equipment.

- Line-side connections are inherently two-wire and provide inferior echo performance compared to the four-wire terminations of trunk side access.

- Answer and disconnect supervision are not provided over line side connections. Call timing can be determined only by monitoring the originating party's holding time, a technique the IECs call *software answer supervision*.

- Multifrequency signaling, standard on trunks, is not available on line-side connections.

The BOCs filed two more ENFIA tariffs before divestiture to improve access. These tariffs, ENFIA B and C (now combined as Feature Group B), offer trunk-side access to the local switching system and most of the features of AT&T's access. The most notable exception to equal access under Feature Group B is that single-digit access is provided only to AT&T's network. Feature Group B uses the code 950-10XX, where XX is a two-digit code identifying the IEC, for access to the IEC's network. Although most IECs have now converted to equal access, Feature Group B continues to be used for terminating calls within a LATA and for access to the IEC for some services.

Equal Access

AT&T's agreement with the Department of Justice required the BOCs to provide access substantially equal to that given to AT&T by September, 1986, except where it was technically and economically infeasible to do so. Equal access, called *Feature Group D,* gives all IECs access to the trunk side of local switching systems. Users presubscribe to service from a preferred IEC and obtain access to that IEC by dialing 1. Callers reach other IECs by dialing 10XXX where XXX is a nationwide access code to the particular carrier. IECs choosing equal access receive automatic number identification, eliminating the need to dial a personal identification number.

Equal access requires intelligence in the Class 5 office to route the call to the required IEC trunk group. This requires changes in the generic programs in SPC offices. Electromechanical offices require extensive redesign to provide equal access; usually they are replaced instead of being converted.

Many LECs provide equal access through a tandem switching system as Figure 8.19 shows. An equal access tandem registers the dialed digits from the end office and, based on originating telephone number, routes the call to the selected IEC. Where the LEC provides equal access tandems, IEC trunks interfacing electromechanical central offices terminate on the tandem rather than the end office. The access tandem introduces some delay in call setup time, so it is advantageous for IECs to use direct trunks to the end

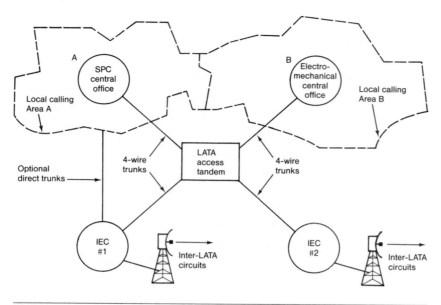

Figure 8.19   Exchange access through LEC LATA tandem.

office where practical. The equal access dialing plan is listed in Table 8.1.

Local Access Transport Areas

The terms of the agreement between AT&T and the Department of Justice prohibit the LECs from transporting long distance traffic outside geographical boundaries called *Local Access Transport Areas* (LATAs). LATA boundaries correspond roughly to Standard Metropolitan Statistical Areas defined by the Office of Management and Budget. Traffic crossing LATA boundaries cannot be transported by the LECs. State utilities commissions regulate traffic within LATA boundaries. Some states assign intraLATA traffic exclusively to the LECs; others permit IECs to carry intra-LATA traffic, but where this is permitted, users must dial 10XXX to access the IEC.

Applications

Switching system applications and standards are covered separately by type of system in Chapters 9, 10, and 20. Also, refer to

Table 8.1   Dialing Plan Under Equal Access

ACCESS	DIALING PLAN	TOTAL DIGITS
Local	NNX-XXXX	7
FGD Toll Intra NPA (presubscribed)	1-NNX-XXXX	8
FGD Toll Intra NPA (other carrier)	10XXX 1-NNX-XXXX	13
FGD Toll Inter NPA (presubscribed)	1-N0/1X NNX-XXXX	11
FGD Toll Inter NPA (other carrier)	10XXX 1-N0/1X NNX-XXXX	16
FGA Toll Intra NPA	NNX-XXXX (DT) XXXXXX NNX-XXXX	20
FGA Toll Inter NPA	NNX-XXXX (DT) XXXXXX N0/1X NNX-XXXX	23

Legend:

FGA = Feature group A
FGD = Feature group D
0/1 = Digit 0 or 1
N = Any digit from 2 to 9 or 0
10XXX = Carrier access number
XXXXXX = Personal indentification number (PIN)
(DT) = Dial tone

the Standards section of Chapter 2 for standards on the transmission performance of networks.

9

Local Switching Systems

The telephone companies are the primary users of the switching systems discussed in this chapter, although some large organizations use modified local central office systems for PBXs and tandem switching applications. The key to the application of a local switch lies in the features provided in its generic program. Hardware differences between local switches, PBXs, and tandem switches are not significant. Some manufacturers produce systems that can handle all three applications, with software changes and minor hardware variations determining whether the switch is a central office, tandem, or a PBX.

This chapter focuses primarily on digital central offices (DCOs) because they are the technology that will last into the future. Where substantial differences exist between DCOs and their analog electronic counterparts, the differences are mentioned, but the future of analog switching is predominantly one of growth additions to existing systems, so these are not covered in depth. The features covered in this chapter are available in most DCOs. Some features may be available in electromechanical offices also, but because of the obsolescence of this technology, the differences are not discussed in this chapter.

Central office switching systems are occasionally used as PBXs or tandem switches. With the right software, a local central office can function in any of the three applications. The primary differences between these applications are:

- *Line Circuits.* Tandem switches have few or no line circuits. PBX line circuits often omit some BORSCHT functions, have less loop range, and use less expensive technology than central office line circuits.

- *Trunk Circuits.* Central office and tandem switch trunk interfaces must meet identical requirements. PBX trunk interfaces are built for private network applications, have a narrower range of features than central office trunks, and are frequently two-wire compared to central office trunks, which are invariably four-wire.

- *Maintenance Features.* Local central offices include features for subscriber line testing and maintenance. These features are usually omitted from PBXs and tandem switching systems. Trunk maintenance features are usually more sophisticated in tandem switches than in either local central offices or PBXs. Both tandem and local switching systems have administrative, self-diagnostic, and internal maintenance features that exceed the capability of all but the most sophisticated PBXs.

- *Capacity.* With some exceptions, local central offices have greater capacity than all but the largest PBXs. The switching network capacity of local and tandem switches is generally equivalent.

Digital Central Office Technology

DCOs fall into two categories: community dial offices (CDOs) that support unattended operation serving up to about 10,000 lines, and central offices designed for urban applications of up to about 60,000 lines. The distinction between these categories is not absolute. Both use similar technology, but CDOs use an architecture that limits their line size. When the system exceeds this capacity, it must be replaced. The size of urban central offices, on the other hand, is limited primarily by the calling rate of the users. If the calling rate is low, some DCOs can terminate as many as 100,000 lines. With a high calling rate, the central processor or the switching network limits the capacity to fewer lines.

Switching systems are enclosed in cabinets or mounted in relay racks. CDOs tend to reside in cabinets, and larger central offices are usually rack mounted. A small system can be installed with little labor, although skilled personnel and special equipment are required to install and test the system. The interconnecting circuits in cabinet systems are prewired, and installation involves cabling the system to protector and distributing frames and to power and alarm equipment. Large central offices are installed in floor-mounted relay racks that are interconnected with plug-ended or wire-wrapped cables. Figure 9.1 shows the major components of a DCO.

Distributed Processing

The earliest SPC switches used a central processor for all call processing functions. With the advent of microprocessors, many SPC systems now use distributed processing, in which a central processor links to distributed microprocessors over a data bus. The central processor controls the primary call processing functions, such as marking a path through the switching network. Processors or service circuits located in the line switch units control such functions as line scanning, digit reception, ringing, and supervision, which require no access to the system's data base.

SPC Central Office Memory Units

DCOs require three types of memory. The *generic program* provided by the manufacturer is common to all switching systems of the same type. It resides in *program store memory* and directs call processing. *Parameters* also reside in a program store data base and are unique to the particular central office. The generic program uses parameters to find the quantities and addresses of peripheral equipment. Parameters are developed when the office is engineered and remain constant until the office is re-engineered.

Translations, which reside in the second type of memory, *data store*, are unique to the office and are created by the user or the manufacturer to enable the generic program to identify working lines and trunks, to determine the features associated with lines and trunks, and to provide trunk routing information for

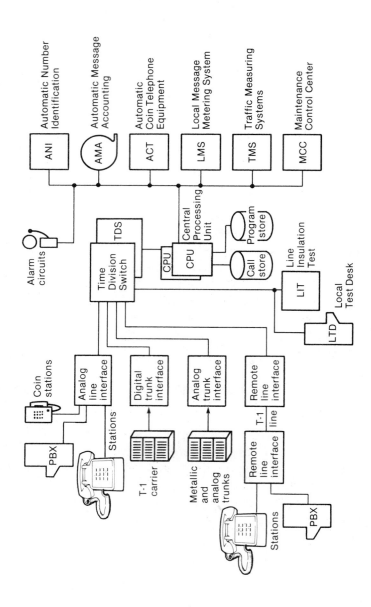

Figure 9.1   Major components of a digital central office.

interoffice calls. Translations are also stored in the program's semi-permanent data base.

Each line is assigned a record in the line translation memory. The line translation includes information about each user such as:

- Class of service—one-party, two-party, or four-party.
- Telephone number associated with the line.
- Optional features such as call waiting, call forwarding, three way calling, and DTMF.
- Status of the line—working, temporarily disconnected, out of service, etc.

Trunk translations identify signaling and terminating characteristics of the trunk such as:

- Method of pulsing—dial pulse or multifrequency.
- Terminating office identity.
- Type of signaling on trunk—loop, E & M.
- Use of trunk—local, toll, service circuit, etc.

The third type of memory is the *call store*, which is a temporary memory that the program uses to store details of calls in progress. Temporary memory is also used to store *recent change* information, which is line and trunk translations that have been added to the system but have not yet been merged with the semi-permanent data base.

Redundancy

Local DCOs provide reliability in the order of one hour's outage in 20 years of operation. This is not to imply that individual users experience that degree of reliability, because individual component failures can disrupt individual lines without failure of the entire switching system. Redundancy of critical circuit elements provides this degree of reliability.

All local DCOs have duplicate central processors. In addition, other circuit elements that can cause significant outage, such as scanners and signal distributors, are duplicated. Redundant switching networks are economically feasible and usually provided in digital systems. In analog systems, the high cost and low probability of total network failure make redundant switching networks unnecessary. Other than network redundancy, the degree of duplication is similar in digital and analog systems.

Redundancy is provided on one of three bases:

- *Shared load* redundancy provides identical elements that divide the total load. When one element fails, the others can support service to all users, but during heavy loads a poorer grade of service is provided.

- With *synchronous* redundancy, both regular and duplicate elements perform the same functions in synchronism with each other, but only one element is on line. If the on-line element fails, the standby unit accepts the load with no loss of service. Either unit can carry the entire office load alone.

- With *hot standby* redundancy, one unit is on line with the other waiting with power applied, but in an idle condition. When the regular unit fails, the standby unit switches on line with a momentary loss of service.

The critical service considerations in choosing a type of redundancy are the degree to which the system diagnoses its own problems and initiates a transfer to standby and the degree to which a transfer results in loss of service. With the first two forms of redundancy, little or no detriment to in-progress calls should be experienced. With the third form of redundancy, calls in progress are usually unaffected by a failure, but calls being established are often lost and must be redialed. When calls in progress are lost, many immediate reattempts can be expected with the possibility of temporary processor overload.

Maintenance and Administrative Features

DCOs include many features to monitor the system's health from a local maintenance control center (MCC) or from a remote location. These features enable the system to respond automatically to abnormal conditions. These features can be classified as fault detection and correction, essential service and overload control, trunk and line maintenance features, and data base integrity checks.

Fault Detection and Correction

The central processor continually monitors all peripheral equipment to detect irregularities. When a peripheral fails to respond correctly, the processor signals an alarm condition to the MCC and switches to a duplicated element if one is provided. The MCC interfaces the fault detecting routines of the generic program to maintenance personnel. At the MCC, the central processor communicates its actions with messages on a CRT, a printer, or both. Depending on the degree of sophistication in the program, the system may register the fault indication or may narrow the source of the fault down to a list of suspected circuit cards. For unattended operation the MCC transmits fault information to a control center over a data link.

The processor also monitors its own operation through built-in diagnostic routines. If it detects irregularities, the on-line processor calls in the standby and goes off-line. All such actions to obtain a working configuration of equipment can be initiated manually from the MCC or from a remote center. The ultimate maintenance action, which can be caused by an inadvertently damaged data base or a program loop, is a restart or initialization. Initialization of the system is usually done only manually because it involves total loss of calls in progress and loss of recent change information.

Essential Service and Overload Control

Switching systems are designed for traffic loads that occur on the busiest normal business days of the year. Occasionally, peaks higher than normal yearly peaks occur. Heavy calling loads can occur during unusual storms, political disorders, and other catastrophes. During these peaks, the switching system may be overloaded to the point that service is delayed or denied to large numbers of users. Central offices include *line load control* circuitry that makes it possible to deny service to nonessential users so that essential users such as public safety and government employees can continue to place calls. Nonessential users are assigned to two groups. When line load control operates, one group is denied service while the other group is permitted to dial. The two groups are periodically reversed to give equal access to both groups.

Central offices also may be equipped with features that control overloads in the trunk network. These features are discussed in Chapter 10.

Trunk Maintenance Features

Local central offices have varying degrees of trunk maintenance capability. The system monitors trunk connections in progress to detect momentary interruptions or failures to connect. For example, if a trunk fails during outpulsing, the unexpected off-hook from the far end causes dialing to abort. The system registers the failure and enters it on a trunk irregularity report, which technicians use to locate trunk trouble. The system marks defective trunks out of service and lists them on a trunk out-of-service list. When all trunks in a carrier system fail, the system detects a carrier group alarm, marks the trunks out of service in memory, and through its alarm system reports the failure to the MCC.

DCOs also include apparatus for off-line trunk diagnosis. Trunk test systems, which Chapter 10 discusses, interface with distant central offices to measure transmission performance and to check trunk supervision.

Line Maintenance Features

Switching systems contain circuits to detect irregularities in station equipment and outside plant. Like trunk tests, these are made on a routine or per call basis. On each call, many systems monitor the line for excessive external voltage (foreign EMF), which suggests cable trouble.

Line insulation tests (LIT) are made routinely during low usage periods to detect incipient trouble. The LIT progresses through lines in the office on a pre-programmed basis and measures them for foreign voltage or low insulation resistance, which is low resistance between tip and ring or from each side of the pair to ground. These tests detect outside plant troubles such as wet cable, and terminal, drop wire, and protector problems.

Most local switching systems can deal with permanent signals, which are caused by a telephone off hook, cable trouble, or a defective station protector. Any of these irregularities places a short circuit on the line, and the line circuit attaches the line to a register, which furnishes dial tone and prepares to accept digits. If the central office could not protect itself, all its common equipment could become tied up with a single case of cable trouble, and other users would be blocked. Common control and SPS offices, therefore, have the capability of dealing with permanent signals. First, the line is disconnected from the register and connected to a permanent signal holding trunk. Then the line is connected to a series of tones and recordings. It may be connected to a recording that asks the caller to hang up the line. Then it may be connected to a progressively louder series of tones to attract the caller's attention. These are of no value during cable trouble, but identifying the lines connected to permanent signal holding trunks helps maintenance forces find which cable count is defective. Then the heat coils (See Chapter 6) can be removed to disconnect the cable from the central office until the fault is corrected.

Data Base Integrity

Changes to a switching system's data base of line, trunk, and parameter translations are made only after checks to ensure the accuracy of the input record and to assure that existing records will not be damaged. Update of the data base may be allowed only from authorized input devices, and then with password control to ensure that only qualified personnel may access the files. A copy of the data base also may be kept off line in disk storage so it can be reinserted if the primary file is damaged or destroyed. The manner of assuring data base integrity varies with the manufacturer and is an important consideration in evaluating local switching systems.

Line Equipment Features

Line switch frames in DCOs are constructed modularly with several line cards concentrated into a smaller number of links to the switching network. The ratio of lines to links is the *concentration ratio* of the office. Two different architectures are employed in the line interface as Figure 9.2 shows. In the coder/decoder (*codec*) per line architecture, each line card contains a separate analog-to-digital converter. The 64 kb/s bit streams from multiple cards combine in a multiplexer into a high speed bit stream and route to the switching matrix. In the shared codec architecture, the output of the analog line circuits is switched to a group of

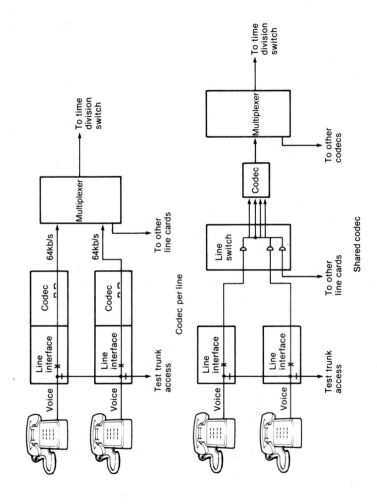

Figure 9.2   Digital central office line cirucit architecture.

shared codecs. The former method, while more expensive, reduces the service impact of a single codec failure. The line card also provides testing access to the local test desk through a relay that transfers the cable pair to a testing circuit.

The integrated circuits used in DCO line cards are highly sensitive to foreign voltage and may be damaged if not protected with gas tubes and clamping diodes as discussed in Chapter 6. The manufacturer's protection recommendations should be followed.

Transmission Performance

Because every line circuit in a digital switching system contains a hybrid circuit, line circuit balance is of particular importance in a DCO. The variability of outside cable plant makes it difficult to design an economical line circuit to balance a wide range of cable pairs. Some manufacturers compensate by designing loss into the line circuit hybrid. The addition of loss to the line circuit is undesirable because it degrades transmission performance.

Distributed Switching

Most DCOs can distribute switching to a remote location close to a cluster of users. As most line switches have a concentration ratio of four or more to one, distributed switching reduces the number of circuits needed between the central office and the users. Use of a remote line switch reduces the need for range extension and gain devices because the line circuit is moved close to the user and linked to the central office with low or zero loss trunks.

Remote line equipment comes in two general forms as illustrated in Figure 9.3. The first, a remote line switch, contains a switching matrix. Calls within the module are switched through an *intracalling* link. A single circuit to the central office supervises the connection. The second form, a remote line module, contains no intracalling features. A call between two stations within the module requires two central office links. If the *umbilical*, or data link, to the central office fails, calling within a line switch is still possible. A remote line module can neither place nor receive calls when the umbilical is inoperative.

Subscriber carrier, as described in Chapter 6, also can interface digital central offices. Subscriber carrier differs from a remote line module in that carrier usually does not include concentration.

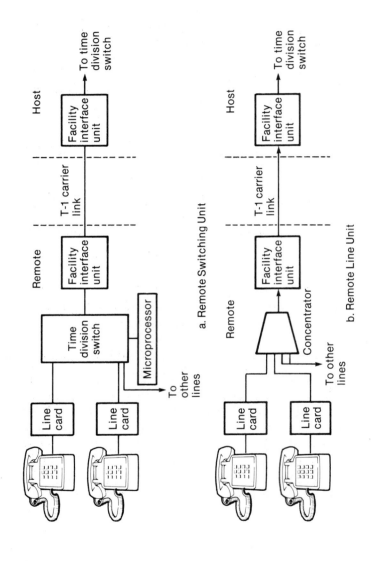

Figure 9.3   Digital remote line equipment.

The number of lines served at the remote location is equal to the number of trunks from the remote to the central office. Digital central offices can interface directly to digital subscriber carrier without using a central office terminal.

Trunk Equipment Features

DCOs are compatible with all kinds of pulsing and signaling employed in the trunk side of the network. Both analog and digital trunk interfaces are available. Analog trunk interfaces, used with trunks derived over FDM carrier and metallic facilities, mount in shelves similar to line interface mountings. Digital trunks interface the switching network in groups of 24 trunks through a digital trunk interface circuit that requires no channel banks. Special trunks interface service circuits such as directory assistance, repair service, local test desk, and disconnected number intercept.

Local Central Office Equipment Features

Local central offices contain peripheral equipment units that facilitate maintenance and special software features. The most significant of these features are listed below.

Alarm and Trouble Indicating Systems

As central offices have progressed, alarm systems have evolved from simple visual and audible alarms to systems that include internal diagnostics. In early switching systems. technicians located trouble by alarm lights on the ends of equipment frames and on the individual equipment shelf. Crossbar offices punch alarm indications into trouble cards that provide information on the status of the circuits in use when an alarm occurs.

SPC offices have internal diagnostic capability; the degree of sophistication varies with the manufacturer. Trouble indications register on the maintenance console and can be printed. The console operator sends orders to the system to transfer to backup equipment, make circuits busy, and perform other actions designed to diagnose trouble or obtain a working configuration of equipment. Some systems carry the diagnostic capability to the level of directing which circuit card should be replaced to clear the trouble.

Automatic Number Identification (ANI)

ANI automatically identifies the calling party for billing purposes. Single party lines are identified from their line circuit or telephone number equipment. In electronic offices this is a table lookup function. In electromechanical offices, separate equipment translates the billed telephone number from the line equipment. On two-party lines the ANI equipment determines which party to bill by determining whether the station ringer is wired from the tip or the ring of the line to ground.

Automatic message accounting (AMA) equipment interrogates ANI equipment to determine the identity of the calling party. Where automatic identification is not provided, as with most four-party lines, the switching system bridges an operator on the line to receive the calling party's number and key it into the AMA equipment.

Automatic Message Accounting (AMA)

AMA equipment records call details at each stage of a connection. The calling and called party numbers are registered initially. An answer entry registers the time of connection, and the terminating entry registers the time of disconnect. These entries are linked by a common identifying number to distinguish them from other calls on the storage medium.

The storage medium is paper tape (now obsolete), magnetic tape, magnetic disk, or solid state memory. Tapes are sent to distant data processing centers where the entries are assembled into completed messages. AMA systems using disk or solid state storage transmit the call details to the processing center over a data link. Fragments of incomplete calls are analyzed for administrative purposes and fraud detection. AMA equipment also registers local measured service billing details.

Coin Telephone Interface

As described in Chapter 18, private organizations now may own coin telephones in most states, in which case the telephone itself must provide all coin functions. In LEC-owned coin telephones, however, central office equipment is required to control the flow of coins. Three classes of coin operation are in use in the United States today:

- *Dial Tone First.* This class offers dial tone to the user without a coin so calls can be placed to operators and emergency numbers. When a call is placed to a chargeable number without coin deposit the central office signals the user that coins are required to complete the call.

- *Prepay or Coin First.* This class requires a coin deposit before dial tone is supplied. Calls to the operator and emergency numbers require a coin, which returns after the call is completed.

- *Postpay.* The central office supplies dial tone to the phone, and a call can be placed to any number without a coin. However, the coin must be deposited before the parties can talk. This system, which is disappearing in the United States, is widely used in Europe.

Coin telephones are assigned to a separate class of service that provides access to special coin trunks. The coin trunk supports one of three classes of coin operation. Its function is to send coin collect and return signals to operate relays in the telephone to route the coin to the collection box or to the return chute. In an SPC office, the processor controls the coin trunk; in an electro-mechanical office, the coin trunk contains the logic to supply dial tone and to collect and return coins.

For long distance calls the coin interacts with the operator or automatic coin equipment to forward tones corresponding to the value of the coins deposited. The operator controls the collecting and refunding of coins with switchboard keys that control the coin trunk. This gives the operator the ability to collect coins before the call is placed and to refund them if the call is not completed. This is done by holding the coins in the coin phone and collecting them only when the called party answers.

Common Equipment

Chapter 12 discusses equipment common to all types of central office equipment. This section describes how common equipment items provide external interfaces for the central office.

Power equipment has a commercial AC entrance facility, a backup emergency generator, a -48 volt DC storage battery string, and battery charging equipment. Emergency generators are provided in all metropolitan central offices. CDOs may be wired with an external plug to couple to a portable generator. In either case, the battery string has sufficient capacity to operate the office until emergency power can assume the load during a power failure.

The switching system connects to the battery plant with heavy copper or aluminum bus bars. Where higher voltages are required, separate battery strings are provided in some offices, but in most applications DC converters raise the battery voltage to the higher voltage required by the equipment.

Trunks, subscriber lines, loop electronic equipment, and other central office equipment are wired to terminal strips mounted on protection and distributing frames. Distributing frames provide access points to the transmission and signaling leads and are used for flexible assignment of equipment to user services and to trunks. Equipment is interconnected by running crossconnect wire or *jumpers* between terminals.

Local Measured Service (LMS)

Many telephone companies base their local service rates on usage. Flat rate calling is often available, with LMS as an optional service class. With the LMS class of service, calls inside the local calling area are billed by number of calls, time of day, duration of call, and distance between parties. The method is similar to long distance billing except that calls are usually bulk-billed with no individual call detail.

In electronic and crossbar offices equipped with AMA equipment, LMS calls are usually registered on the AMA record, separated from long distance calls by an identifying mark. In offices lacking AMA equipment, auxiliary registers are wired to subscriber lines.

Traffic Measuring Equipment

All central offices are sized based on usage. For example, in step-by-step offices the number of switches in a line group and the number of users that can be assigned to a group are determined by collecting statistical information. In common control and SPC offices, the concentration ratio and number of trunks and service circuits are also based on usage.

Usage information is based on the number of times a trunk or circuit is seized (attempts) and the average holding time of each attempt. This information is collected by attaching two registers to the equipment—one that measures the number of times the circuit is seized and one that measures elapsed time the circuit is busy. Chapter 31 discusses the method of evaluating this information. Electromechanical offices require external traffic usage registers; SPC offices use software registers. The registers are periodically unloaded to a processing center for summary and analysis.

Most electromechanical central offices also provide dial tone speed registers, which are devices that attach to line circuits, periodically go off-hook, and measure the number of times dial tone is delayed more than three seconds. Dial tone speed is an important measure of the quality of local switching service.

Traffic measuring equipment can provide a variety of other data for administering the central office. For example, data base statistical information is provided to update the availability of vacant lines and trunks. Point-to-point data collection enables the system administrator to detect the calling pattern of various subscriber lines to improve the utilization of the network by reassigning lines to different network terminations. Subscriber line usage (SLU) measurements enable the administrator to distribute heavy usage lines among different terminations on the line switch frame to avoid overloading the line switch with several heavy users. The system makes service measurements to determine key indicators such as *incoming matching loss* (IML), which is the failure of an incoming call to obtain an idle path through the network to the terminating location.

Network Management

Many local offices have network management provisions to prevent overloads. For example, *dynamic overload control* automatically changes routing tables to reroute traffic when the primary route is overloaded. *Code conversion* allows the system to block traffic temporarily to a congested central office code. This feature enables the blocked system to take recovery action without being overwhelmed by ineffective attempts from a distant central office.

Local Central Office Service Features

Local central offices provide a variety of service features that enhance call processing. In SPC offices, these are provided primarily by software. In electromechanical central offices, they are sometimes provided by hardware, sometimes by auxiliary equipment, and in some cases not provided at all. The following is a brief description of the principal features provided by most electronic end offices:

Call Processing Features

Call processing features allow the customer to recall the central office equipment by a momentary on-hook flash. The system responds with "stutter" dial tone to show that it is ready to receive the information. Each of these features is optional to the user, generally at extra cost.

Three-way calling is a feature that allows the user to add a third party to the conversation by momentarily holding the first party while a third number is dialed. *Call transfer* is a similar feature that is available only on Centrex-equipped lines. The operation is exactly like three-way calling except one party can hang up, leaving the other two parties in conversation.

If a line equipped with *call waiting* is busy, the switching system sends a tone to signal that another call is waiting. The user can place the original call on hold and talk to the waiting call by pressing the switch hook. Some LECs offer a *cancel call waiting* feature that enables users to disable the service temporarily. This feature is important to anyone who uses a dial-up modem and wants to avoid having a modem call interrupted by call waiting. *Speed calling* is different from the other features in that a switch hook flash is not used. This feature gives the user the ability to dial other numbers with a one- or two-digit number.

Call forwarding enables the user to forward incoming calls to another telephone number. While this feature is activated, calls to the user's number route automatically to an alternative telephone number. When the user of a forwarded line picks up the telephone, the system sends stutter dial tone to show the forwarded status of the line. *Call forward remote access* enables the user to activate or deactivate call forwarding from a remote location.

Equal access enables the user to choose a primary interexchange carrier (PIC) to which all long distance calls will route unless the user dials another carrier's access code.

Gab line is a feature that enables callers to dial a number to which multiple callers can be simultaneously connected. Some LECs use the gab line, which is popular with teenagers, as a revenue-generating feature.

Custom Local Area Signaling Services (CLASS)

LECs have begun to define a suite of services known as Custom Local Area Signaling Services (CLASS). CLASS services bring to residence and small business users features that are available in most PBXs. These additional features improve the service for the users and, in turn, generate more revenue for the LECs. Most CLASS features depend on Signaling System No. 7 (See Chapter 11) for communication between central offices, and others will become available only through the Integrated Services Digital Network (See Chapter 26). The LECs have just begun to deploy SS7, so CLASS features will not be widely available for several years. Many of these features are available now over 911 trunks, but are not extended to ordinary subscriber lines. The following discussion explains the principal CLASS features that are defined to date. Additional services will undoubtedly be defined in the future.

Automatic Callback. When activated by a caller, the central office automatically redials the called number for a specified period or until canceled by the caller.

Automatic Recall. This feature enables a called party to initiate a call to the number from which the last call arrived. The central office announces the call before completion of call setup so the called party can decide whether to continue with the call or drop it.

Calling Number Identification.   This feature delivers the calling number to the called party. The number can be displayed on a special telephone set, or it can be linked to a data base in a computer to give the call certain treatment before it is delivered to the called telephone. For example, the calling number could be used to retrieve a customer record from the data base before sending the call to an agent position behind an automatic call distributor. This feature is conditionally offered by some LECs now and is being subjected to court challenge based on the contention that it is an invasion of privacy. Also under debate is the issue of whether the LEC can legally deliver a nonpublished number to the called party. This feature is sometimes called Automatic Number Identification (ANI). Although this designation is technically correct, ANI is more accurately limited to the delivery of calling party identification to a common carrier for billing purposes.

Calling Number Identification Blocking.   This feature enables a calling party to block transmission of calling party identification.

Customer-Originated Trace.   With this feature the called party can initiate a trace on the last call placed. The calling number is not delivered to the customer, but is entered on a log at the LEC or a law enforcement agency.

Distinctive Ringing/Call Waiting.   This feature enables a user to enter a list of numbers, calls from which are to be announced with a special ringing tone. If the user subscribes to call waiting, the call waiting tone is also distinctive.

Ring Again.   This service allows station users who encounter a busy signal to request the network to alert them when the busy station becomes idle and to place the call automatically. When callers encounter a busy, if they flash the switch hook, the central office returns a special dial tone. The caller dials the ring again code and can then use the telephone normally. When the called party hangs up, the central office signals the caller with a ring again signal. If the caller picks up the handset, the central office places the call. This feature is not only a convenience to the user, it also reduces the load on the central office from users who repeatedly dial against a busy number.

Selective Call Acceptance.   This feature enables users to enter a list of numbers from which calls will be accepted. Calls from numbers not on the list route to an announcement and are rejected.

Selective Call Forwarding.   This feature enables users to enter a call screening list in the central office. Only calls from stations on the list are forwarded. Calls from stations not on the list ring at the dialed number.

Selective Call Rejection.   Users of this feature can enter directory numbers into a screening list. Calls from these stations will be routed to an announcement that shows that the called party is not accepting calls. Calls from other stations will be routed through normally.

Centrex Features

Centrex is a PBX-like service furnished by telephone companies through equipment located in the central office. Usually the switching equipment is a partition in the end office. Centrex features allow direct inward dialing (DID) to a telephone number and direct outward dialing (DOD) from a number without operator intervention. For calls into the Centrex, the service is equivalent to individual line service. Outgoing calls differ from individual line service only in the requirement that an outgoing access code—usually 9—be dialed. Calls between stations in the Centrex group require four or five digits instead of the seven digits required for ordinary calls.

An attendant position located on the customer's premises is linked to the central office over a separate circuit. Centrex service provides PBX features without locating a switching system on the user's premises. Centrex features are discussed in more detail in Chapter 23.

Emergency Reporting

In the United States the code 911 is dedicated to fire, police, ambulance, and other emergency numbers. The local central office switches a 911 call to a dedicated group of trunks to a Public

Safety Answering Point (PASP). Calls can be routed over the switched network to the PASP, but there is always a risk that calls will be blocked by normal telephone traffic, so dedicated lines are normally used. The PASP is staffed with personnel who have been trained in emergency call handling procedures. Emergency centers can be classified as Basic 911 (B-911) or Enhanced 911 (E-911). Electromechanical offices can route calls to the PASP, but most 911 features require SPC central offices.

The telecommunications equipment in a B-911 center can be as simple as key telephone service, or calls can be delivered to an automatic call distributor (ACD). Emergency operators can be given features that enable them to trace calls and hold up a circuit to re-ring the calling party to obtain more information, but they cannot identify the caller. Almost all exchanges equipped for 911 provide coin-free dialing, which enables a caller to dial from a pay phone without a coin. The B-911 center also can force a disconnect on a 911 trunk that a caller is holding.

To provide calling party identification, the LEC or other bureau maintains a data base of calling party information that is furnished to the PASP if E-911 service is used. Besides the originating telephone number, the data base furnishes name and address, the address of the nearest emergency facility, and identification of which facility has emergency jurisdiction. Besides automatic number and location identification, E-911 provides selective routing, which, for overlapping jurisdictions, routes the call to the appropriate PASP.

Routing to Service Facilities

All central offices provide access to certain service facilities such as operator services and repair service bureau. All local switching systems also provide access to call progress tones—busy, reorder, vacant number tone, etc.—and recorded announcements for intercepted numbers and permanent signals. Some systems also provide access to local testing facilities.

Multiline Hunt

This feature, often called *rotary line group,* connects incoming calls to an idle line from a group of lines allocated to a user. In older central offices the numbers had to be in sequence; in electronic offices any group of numbers can be linked by software into a multiline hunt group.

Call Processing

Most DCOs use similar techniques for processing calls. The following is a short description of how calls typically are processed. The discussion assumes that the call originates and terminates in the same central office. The principal processing elements are:

- *Scanners*, which are circuits that detect changes in states of lines and trunks.
- *Signal distributors*, which transmit signals from scanners to call processing programs.
- *Receivers*, which are circuits that furnish dial tone and accept and register dialed digits. Registers are normally dial pulse (rotary dial) or DTMF.
- *Generic program*, which is the call processing instructions contained in the program store.
- *Call store*, which is the temporary scratch pad memory used to store the details of calls in progress.
- *Data store*, which stores the line translations.
- *Time slots*, which, in a digital switch, are units of time reserved for the parties to share during a session
- *Network*, which contains the time slots to make connections between lines and trunks.

A call is initiated by the calling party's removing the receiver from the switch hook. A line scanner detects the change in the state of the line and sends a signal to the generic program, which marks the line busy in call store memory and consults the data store about features and options available to the line. The processor marks a path through the network and reserves a time slot to a receiver.

The processor connects the line to a receiver and sends dial tone toward the line. The receiver registers tones or dial pulses and stores them in a call store register. The processor consults the data store about the address of the called number. It marks

the called line and reserves two time slots through the network—
one for the originating party and one for the terminating party.

The called number connects to a ringing source. The calling
number is connected to an audible ringing source. The terminating line is monitored for ring trip.

When the called party answers, the ringing and audible ring
signals are removed, and the two time slots that were previously
reserved are linked through the network. The connection is
supervised for an indication that either party has gone on-hook.

When either party hangs up, the processor restores the circuits, marks the time slots idle, and restores the call store registers.
The line status is changed from busy to idle in memory, and the
call is terminated.

Calls outside the same central office are handled similarly,
except that two switching systems are involved. Chapter 11 explains how signals are exchanged between two central offices.
During call processing, many events other than those described
above may occur. One party may flash the switch hook, which
recalls the processor to send second dial tone and to be prepared
for another process such as conferencing to occur.

Applications

Digital central offices are used almost exclusively by telephone
companies, although a few have found their way into service as
large PBXs. The selection of a digital switch is a complex process
that depends on the maintenance strategies, service offerings, and
cost objectives of the LECs. This section briefly describes the
primary criteria used in selecting a DCO.

Standards

Few local switching system standards have been set by standards
agencies. Subscriber line and trunk interface standards are published by EIA; the bulk of DCO performance criteria is a matter of
matching the manufacturer's specifications to the user's requirements. Bell Communications Research (Bellcore) publishes a
comprehensive list of requirements on behalf of the seven Bell
regional operating companies. This publication, *Local Switching*

System General Requirements (LSSGR), defines the features and technical specifications required of local central offices used by the Bell regions. LSSGR is not a standard; compliance by manufacturers is voluntary, but it is the most comprehensive publication available for local central office operation.

Evaluating Digital Switching Systems

The primary criteria in evaluating a DCO are cost, features, compatibility, maintenance features, and the ability of the office to provide the desired grade of service. The complexity of a DCO makes the provision of maintenance features particularly important. The following is a list of the primary DCO evaluation criteria:

Maintenance Features and Reliability

DCOs should be designed to provide a high degree of reliability with duplicated critical circuit elements and high grade components. All processors should be duplicated, preferably on a synchronous basis. The processor should be capable of full self-diagnosis. In case of overload, automatic recovery, including discontinuing nonessential call processing operations if necessary, is essential.

The system should be operable from a remote location except for changing defective circuit cards and running crossconnects. Manufacturers should provide an on-line technical assistance center to aid in solving unusual maintenance conditions.

The system should be fully documented with maintenance practices, trouble locating manuals, software operation manuals, office wiring diagrams, and a complete listing of data base information.

The system should provide an interface to a local test desk for diagnosing subscriber line troubles. It also should have a complete suite of trunk tests to aid maintenance forces in diagnosing and correcting trunk faults.

Training

The manufacturer must provide a full line of courses designed to train the using organization in designing, engineering, maintaining, and administering the system.

Transmission Performance

The central office should insert no more than 1 dB of loss into a line-to-line and 0.5 dB into a line-to-trunk or trunk-to-trunk connection.

Line Concentration

The system should be capable of providing line concentration ratios to match the expected usage. Line concentration ratios as low as two-to-one may be required in heavy usage systems, with ratios as high as eight-to-one acceptable in low usage systems. Local switching systems are rarely designed to be nonblocking.

Environment

The system should operate under the temperature extremes that could occur with power, heating, or air conditioning failure. The normal operating temperature range of most central office equipment is 0° to 50° C (32° to 120° F).

Multiclass Operation

A DCO should contain the software needed for all end office functions. In addition, some applications require tandem software. If the DCO is used as a PBX, it must include the PBX features described in Chapter 20. Of major significance in PBX use is the ability to interface a local end office through the line side rather than the trunk side of the system.

Remote Line Capability

A DCO should include remote line capability to minimize range extension and subscriber loop costs. The remote should contain intracalling capability if the owner requires this feature. The user will notice no difference in operation if a system lacks intracalling capability unless the link to the central office is severed. This capacity is important when the remote switch is placed in a locale with a strong community of interest. The DCO should also be capable of interfacing subscriber carrier at the T-1 level.

Capacity

The system should have the capacity to handle the traffic load for the expected life of the system. The system should also be capable of terminating the required number of lines and trunks. All central offices must have the capability of measuring and recording usage, whether with built-in or external equipment.

Manufacturers of Local Switching Systems

AT&T

CIT-Alcatel Inc.

Ericsson, Inc. Communications Div.

GTE Communications Systems

NEC America, Inc.

Northern Telecom, Inc.

Stromberg Carlson Corporation

10

Tandem Switching Systems

Common carriers and many private companies use tandem switching systems to build up connections by switching trunks together. Both local central offices and PBXs can be equipped to serve as tandem switches. If trunking requirements are light, the most economical way to switch trunks is through an existing end office switch or PBX, but the market offers switching systems designed specifically for trunk switching applications. These are the subject of this chapter.

The primary users of tandem trunk switching systems are:

- LECs that use tandem switches for switching local interoffice trunks and for interexchange carrier access.

- Interexchange carriers that use tandem switches for access to their networks.

- Large government and business organizations that use tandem switches for private message and data networks.

The technologies used in these systems are similar; however, the size varies considerably from a few dozen trunks to systems equipped with more than 100,000 trunk terminations.

Long haul trunk facilities are owned primarily by private carriers and furnished to end users as individual circuits, as bulk groups of circuits, or as bandwidth that can be channelized at the user's discretion. Some large organizations own private facilities, but the majority of users obtain long haul facilities through common carrier tariffs.

Tandem Switch Technology

Tandem switch architecture is similar to local digital switch architecture except that a tandem switch has few, if any, line terminations. Systems have a nonblocking network controlled by central or distributed processors. Digital trunks terminate in a digital interface frame that couples incoming T-1 or T-3 bit streams directly to the switching network. The central processor detects signaling and sets up a path through the switching network from the incoming time slot to an outgoing time slot that it assigns to an outgoing digital channel. Calls that cannot be completed because of trunk congestion route to a tone or recorded announcement trunk. The digital switch acts as a large time slot interchange device that is transparent to the bit stream in the terminated circuits.

Most digital switches designed for the public telephone network are equipped for common channel signaling (CCS). See Chapter 11 for a discussion of common channel signaling. The CCS interface is a circuit that interprets incoming data messages and communicates them to the call processor. This outboard signaling method replaces the bit-robbed signaling contained in T carrier.

Wideband Switching Capability

Some tandem switches intended for private use can switch T-1 bit streams, a capability that can prove useful in private networks for high speed data transfer and video teleconferencing. With this capability, mainframe computers can be linked during off-peak hours to transfer data over backbone digital circuits that are used for voice during peak load periods. In this kind of application, the digital switch replaces a manual patch that would otherwise be required to set up the video circuit.

With current technology, a video signal can be compressed into bandwidths of 64 kb/s to 1.544 mb/s as described in Chapter 17. A tandem switch can therefore route video signals over a backbone network as Figure 10.1 illustrates. Because a video signal requires the use of contiguous channels in a T-1 bit stream, a preempting capability may be required to force users off voice transmissions when a video conference is initiated. Some switches

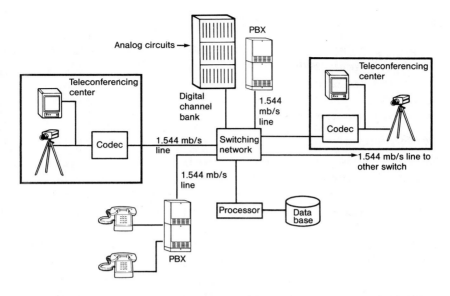

Figure 10.1   Use of a digital tandem switch for alternate voice and video service.

preempt by overriding busy channels, sending a warning tone, and cutting off the channel so it can be occupied by a video signal.

The sharing of a T-1 bit stream by voice and video offers an economical solution for occasional video conferencing. For the duration of the conference, overflow voice calls can be denied or completed over a public network, depending on the restrictions in the originator's class of service. Overflowing calls onto a public voice network is usually less expensive than establishing a separate video conferencing channel.

Tandem Switch Features

Most tandem switching system features are implemented in software. Therefore, systems can be used in either public or private networks by changing the generic program. Although the architecture for private and public tandem switches is similar, feature differences between the two applications are significant.

Public Tandem Switch Features

Tandem switches for public telephone networks terminate large numbers of both analog and digital trunks. The primary features employed are discussed in the following sections. Private networks use some of these same features in private tandem switches as noted under the feature descriptions.

Testing Access

Because of their heavy reliance on trunk quality, all tandem switches require trunk test positions. Trunks are switched through the switching network to the test position for making continuity, transmission, and supervision tests. In a network of multiple tandem switches, technicians communicate between test positions by dialing a special access code, usually 101. This connects the two test positions so technicians can talk and test over the trunk. Several different codes are employed in the long distance trunks of the IECs, LECs, and some private networks for testing as Table 10.1 shows. These test lines can be used for both manual and automatic tests.

To test direct trunks between two offices automatically, computer-controlled test equipment dials a *remote office test line* (ROTL) over an ordinary telephone circuit as Figure 10.2 shows. The ROTL seizes an outgoing trunk and dials the test line number over the trunk. A *responder* at the distant office interacts with the ROTL and the responder at the near-end office to make two-way transmission, noise, and supervision measurements. The test system registers the test results, automatically takes defective trunks out of service at the switching system, and marks them for maintenance action.

Signaling

Common channel switching is the rule for public toll tandem switching systems and is increasingly being employed on private systems. A common channel interface circuit connects between the processor and the data circuits that comprise the CCS network. The switching systems select an idle path by exchanging data messages, test the path for continuity, and assign a path through all switches that are part of the connection.

Table 10.1 Trunk Maintenance Test Lines

TYPE	FUNCTION	PURPOSE
100	Balance	Provides off-hook supervision and terminates trunk in its characteristic impedance for balance and noise testing.
101	Communications	Provides talking path to a test position for communications and transmission tests.
102	Milliwatt	Provides a 1004 Hz signal at 0 dBm for one-way loss measurements.
103	Supervision	Provides connection to signaling test circuit for testing trunk supervision.
104	Transmission	Provides termination and circuitry for two-way loss and one-way noise tests.
105	Automatic Transmission	Provides access to a responder to allow two-way loss and noise tests from an office equipped with an ROTL and responder.
107	Data Transmission	Provides access to a test circuit for one-way voice and data testing. Enables measurement of P/AR, gain/slope, C-notched noise, jitter, impulse noise, and various other circuit quality tests. See Chapter 32 for description of tests.

Operator Service Positions

Local exchange and interexchange carriers require operator service positions (OSPs) with their tandem switches. Operator service functions include intercept, directory assistance, and toll and assistance, which helps callers complete collect, third number, and credit card calls. Intercept is the function of assisting customers with calls to disconnected numbers. Directory assistance provides telephone number lookup for callers.

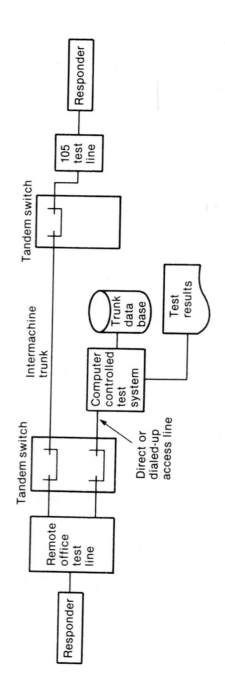

Figure 10.2   Automatic remote testing system.

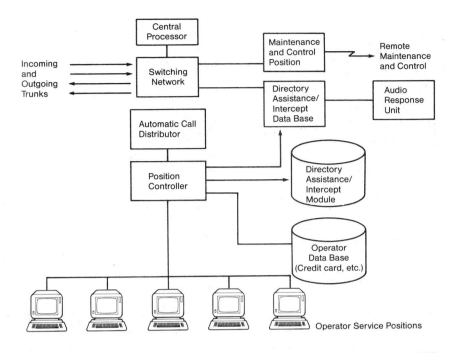

Figure 10.3 **Components of a tandem switch and operator service system.**

The objective of intercept systems is to complete as many calls as possible with a voice response unit (VRU). Some calls, such as those to numbers not yet in the data base or where the caller remains on the line, must be completed manually. In these cases the system connects the call to an OSP.

Local and interexchange carriers increasingly are centralizing operator assistance. Therefore, an essential feature is the ability to support remote terminals. Figure 10.3 shows the components of an OSP and a tandem switch system. Incoming and outgoing trunks terminate directly on the switching network or on analog trunk interfaces through channel banks. A central processor controls call processing. The system directly switches calls that do not require operator assistance. Where the caller dials an assistance code, the processor routes the call through the switching network to the front end of the OSP, which is an automatic call distributor (ACD). See Chapter 21 for further information on the functions and method of operation of an ACD.

The ACD delivers calls to the appropriate position. The position controller receives calls from the ACD and supplies the circuitry to enable the operator to communicate with the various subsystems. Within limits, the larger the work group, the more efficiently positions can be staffed. The ACD delivers calls to operators in segregated groups that are called *splits*. During normal load conditions, the three types of calls—toll and assistance, intercept, and directory assistance—might comprise three splits. The ACD would overflow calls between splits when overloads occurred. During light load periods, the splits might be combined, with the ACD routing calls to a single set of OSPs.

User-Dialed Billing Arrangements

Special networks that register and verify charging information handle most coin and credit card calls. Credit card calls are verified over a data link to a centralized data base. The customer dials a called number, then when signaled by the system, dials a credit card number. The system sends a message to the data base to verify the validity of the card number, after which it switches the call.

Coin calls are connected to a circuit that computes the rate, informs the user of the charge with a voice announcement circuit, registers the values of the coins deposited, and connects the call. The equipment monitors the conversation time and reconnects the voice announcement circuit when the caller must make an additional coin deposit.

Private Tandem Switching System Features

With the exception of the need for coin and operator services, private tandem switches require much the same feature set as public switches. Also, tandem switches provide other features unique to a private network. Many of these are the same as the PBX features described in Chapter 20. Circuit costs tend to control the total network costs in a private system; therefore tandem switches make efficient use of circuit capacity. This section covers features that are generally included in switches that use a significant part of their capacity for tandem switching.

Personal Identification Data Base

Tandem switches may provide personal identification number (PIN) access to the network. The system's data base contains a file of authorized users and their restrictions. Users access the system by dialing a seven-digit number for Feature Group A access through the public telephone network or by dialing an access code in a PBX that is directly trunked to the tandem switch. If the PBX and tandem switch are equipped for automatic number identification, PIN dialing is not required.

The user file lists the restrictions of each PIN. Most systems offer a full restriction range such as limiting calls to tie lines only or blocking calls to selected area codes, central office codes, or even station numbers. For example, a company could allow its accounting personnel to call the accounting department in another branch, but calls to all other numbers could be blocked. In addition to the PIN, most systems support accounting code information, which requires the user to dial in an account code. Many companies use this feature for distributing costs to clients or among departments.

Most systems optionally provide other methods of controlling costs. Some users may be permitted to access a tie line network, but when a call is about to advance to a high cost facility because lower cost routes are full, a call warning tone sounds. The call will not route to the higher cost facility until the user dials a positive action digit to instruct the system to proceed. When the call duration exceeds a threshold set in the user's file, a time warning signal can sound. These and other similar features are normally not available in public networks because the network owner has no interest in limiting usage.

Other features that are available for certain line classes include security blanking, which blanks the called telephone number on the billing record if the user wants to avoid leaving a record of calls to certain numbers. Some line classifications are given queuing priority to enable them to jump to the head of the queue when all circuits are busy. Most of these features are implemented in software and can therefore be provided for little or no cost, enabling an organization to customize a network to meet its individual needs.

Remote Access

The remote access feature allows a user to dial a local telephone call to the tandem switch to complete long distance calls over the private network. PIN identification is required to control unauthorized usage. Even with PIN control, security is apt to be a problem with remote access. Many systems raise an alarm when they detect repeated attempts to dial with invalid PINs.

Transmission is also a potential problem with remote access. As Figure 10.4 shows, the transmission loss of a remote access connection includes one or two additional subscriber loops, which increases loss by as much as 16 dB. If access to the tandem switch is through a PBX that inserts loss in the connection, poor transmission on many calls can be expected. If the call uses a Feature Group A trunk to an IEC, another subscriber loop is inserted in the connection. A digital tandem switch in a remote access arrangement inserts little or no loss, but requires two two-wire to four-wire conversions, which may result in poor echo performance or hollowness.

Queuing

Public networks are designed so that blockage occurs on 0.1% or fewer of the calls placed. When blockage occurs the call routes to a reorder trunk, and if the user wants to complete the call, he or she must redial. In a private network environment, circuit usage can be increased and costs controlled by queuing users for access to outgoing trunks. If a few calls always are backed up in the queue, trunk utilization can approach 100%, with the only idle time that of disconnecting and reconnecting a call.

User dissatisfaction and lost productive time always result from queuing, so public networks, where the user can easily dial a competitor, rarely use this technique. In private networks, however, the organization has control over the network and its users and may choose to pay the price of lost productive time by using queuing. An audible indication signals when the caller

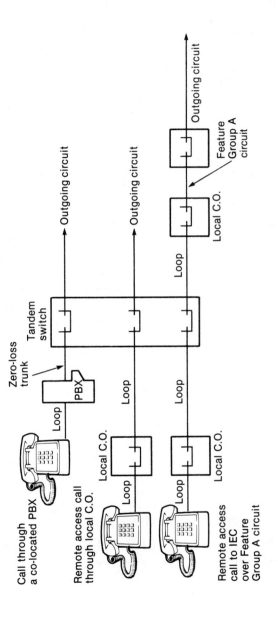

Figure 10.4 Sources of transmission problems with remote access to a tandem switch.

places a call in queue. Some systems use a tone, others a recorded announcement, and others use music in queue. Any network that employs queuing should collect statistical information to show the average length of queue, the number of calls abandoned from queue, and the average holding time in queue. This information indicates the number of productive hours lost because of queuing.

Routing

Private tandem switches include least cost routing features identical in concept to the LCR feature in PBXs, as Chapter 20 discusses. Other routing features are also available with most tandem switches and some PBXs. Code blocking prevents dialing certain digit combinations. With this feature an organization can block access to a given geographical area by blocking the area codes. This can be carried down to blocking individual terminating telephone numbers. For example, some organizations use this feature to block calls to 900 telephone numbers, the cost of which is billed to the caller. The accounting information described in a later section can be sorted by called telephone number to identify heavily used numbers that might suggest abuse of communication services. Where abuse is found, the unauthorized number is blocked.

Another feature, code conversion, limits the number of digits a user must dial to make a connection. For example, a frequently used number could be dialed with seven digits. If the system completes the call over a tie line, only the seven digits are required. If the number completes over an IEC network, the switch appends the area code before forwarding the call. Calls off-net to an IEC over a Feature Group A connection may require dialing a PIN that differs from the user's on-net PIN. The user can dial the PIN, but the switch dials the PIN required by the IEC.

Network Statistical Information

Network administrators need considerable information about calling patterns and habits to manage a network. They use information on the disposition of originating calls to size circuit groups and switching equipment. Most systems provide the following types of information:

- *Queuing statistics*, including average and peak number of calls in queue, duration of calls in queue, and abandoned calls.

- *Trunk information* for each trunk group on the network, including peak and average number of calls, holding time of calls, and number of ineffective attempts because of blockage, cutoff, or equipment trouble.

- *Service circuit statistics,* including number of attempts, holding time, and overflow to service circuits such as reorder, busy, and multifrequency receivers and senders.

The amount of statistical information collected from a system is apt to be overwhelming unless the system provides some form of analysis. Some tandem switches are controlled by commercial processors that also can analyze usage information. Otherwise, external processors are usually needed to digest the information and determine corrective action.

Accounting Information

Tandem switches provide message accounting information to allocate communications costs to the users. This information is either provided in machine readable format for separate processing or processed by the switching system's processor to assemble completed message detail. Charges can be summarized by individual user, department, and accounting code. For most effective communications cost control, machine readable information should be provided so calling habits can be analyzed and so destinations can be evaluated to determine whether additional private trunks should be added to reduce overflow to more expensive common carrier circuits.

Network Management Control

Many switching systems provide a network management control center (NMCC) to administer service and performance on private networks. The center collects all network management information in a single location. Typical NMCC functions include:

- Manual and automatic testing of trunks using apparatus and techniques similar to those used in public networks.

- Compilation and analysis of statistical information to determine loads and service levels and to determine when circuit types and quantities should be changed.
- System performance monitoring, including diagnostics and maintenance control of all system features and circuits.
- Alarm surveillance to detect and diagnose troubles and determine status of switching and trunking equipment.
- Performance and status logging to monitor and log system history, including records of trouble and out-of-service conditions.

Applications

Tandem switches find their primary applications in public networks. Large companies, which formerly used private tandem switches at the hubs of their private line networks are finding the virtual network offerings of the IECs more attractive than their networks. Also, the tandem function can be embedded in PBXs at major switching points of all but the largest users.

Standards

As with other types of switching systems, few standards are published with respect to tandem switching. Trunk interfaces in private network switches require FCC registration and must meet the standard technical interface information for compatibility. Most trunk connections are T-1 or T-3, standards for which CCITT publishes. Operator service positions, if they are provided at all, follow proprietary standards.

Tandem Switch Evaluation Considerations

Most factors that are important for other switching systems are also important for tandem switches including reliability, capacity, compatibility of external interfaces, operational features, and internal diagnostic capability. This section covers the features that tandem switches include, primarily to control private network costs.

Queuing

Tandem switch manufacturers emphasize queue efficiency as an important way of improving circuit occupancy and controlling circuit costs. The method of handling calls during blocked circuit conditions is an important factor to evaluate in comparing tandem switches. Queuing can definitely increase circuit occupancy during busy periods, but the increase in efficiency must be evaluated. The time spent in queue is generally nonproductive and can easily outweigh the cost of the alternatives. Users may lose productivity while waiting in queue for calls to be completed. Also, the time required to administer the system is an expense that must be considered. Even if users have speaker telephones so they can continue to work while waiting, which is not always practical, busy station lines tend to aggravate the "telephone tag" problem.

Three approaches can be used to avoid queuing. The first is to return the call to reorder and force redialing. With a telephone that includes a last number redial feature, this approach is tolerable. The second approach is to increase the number of circuits. With adequate data from the queuing and circuit usage statistics, the cost of this option can easily be calculated. The third approach is to overflow to a higher cost facility. IECs design their networks to a low blocking probability. Overflow to a common carrier is usually an effective way for network managers to limit delays.

Despite its hazards, queuing is an effective tool to use in managing a network. To be effective, a system should provide for variable queuing by class of service and time of day. The length of queue should be administratively variable. When a reasonable queue length is reached, additional callers should be turned back to avoid long queue holding times. The system should provide near real-time information about queue length so system administrators can take corrective action.

Network Management Control

An effective tandem switch should provide the tools needed to manage and control the network. The system should be equipped for unattended operation from a remote location. It should have complete flexibility in changing line classifications, restriction levels, trunk classifications, queuing parameters, and other features that affect line and trunk administration. The system should provide real-time information about trunk status. Defective trunks should be removed from service and referred to the control center for corrective action.

The system should diagnose trunk performance automatically during light load periods. It should be equipped for transmission and supervision tests to distant tandem switches and, if permitted, to IEC and local telephone company responders. Direct access to individual circuits should be permitted for making transmission measurements and supervision.

A full range of statistical information should be available for evaluating service and for determining when trunk quantities should be adjusted. A method of automatically analyzing the raw statistical information should be included. The information should be formatted so the corrective action to be taken is apparent.

The system should diagnose its own troubles and direct technicians on what action to take, ideally to the point of specifying the circuit card to change. The manufacturer should provide remote diagnostic and technical assistance along with a method of keeping both hardware and software current with updates.

Network Modeling

Networks are sized, as discussed in Chapter 31, by simulation or modeling techniques. If the vendor provides a simulation or modeling service to determine equipment and trunk quantities and to predict the effects of changes in load, tandem switch administration will be simplified. An effective tool should accept usage information from system-produced statistics and summaries of originating and terminating traffic to determine the most efficient use of equipment and facilities. The system also should accept cost information to find the best balance between options such as WATS lines, tie lines, and public switched networks.

Routing, Blocking, and Translations

A tandem switch should provide fully flexible routing to trunk groups based on class of service. It should have the capability of blocking area codes, central office codes, and line numbers. It also should filter calls so some users can complete calls only to selected codes. The system should block access to circuit groups to prevent unsuccessful attempts to access distant systems that are temporarily experiencing service difficulties. This capability allows the distant system to recover without being inundated with excessive call attempts. The system also should translate codes so users dial the same code to reach a destination despite the routing.

Common Channel Signaling

In a multitandem network, common channel signaling should be considered to achieve more effective circuit utilization. The cost of CCS equipment and the separate data network should be weighed against the improved circuit utilization from eliminating in-band signaling.

Remote Access

The value of remote access from a separate location should be considered. Security and transmission performance must be weighed against the benefits of remote access. A switch should provide an effective screen against unauthorized access and should alert the network administrator to unauthorized attempts. The transmission characteristics of the access circuits should be evaluated to predict whether service will be satisfactory.

High Speed Switching Capability

If video conferencing, closed circuit TV, or high speed data transfer is anticipated, the system should be evaluated for its capability to allocate the bandwidth dynamically. The system should be capable of reserving any segment of capacity required and should preempt occupied circuits when necessary to vacate the required bandwidth.

Operator Service Position Evaluation Considerations

A fundamental objective of operator service units is to reduce the average work time (AWT) per call to a minimum. A reduction in AWT is achieved by having automated equipment handle as much of the call as possible. For example, directory assistance positions almost universally use a VRU to read out the telephone number. The operator's function is to key in the name. The more effective the search algorithm, the fewer the keystrokes the operator must make before the system finds a match. Work time is also reduced by enabling the operator to access the most frequently used functions with a single key. Less frequently encountered conditions may require menu access. For new operators, a help key is important.

Signaling System Compatibility

Another important feature is compatibility with the signaling format of the central offices served. Signaling System No. 7 compatibility, as discussed in Chapter 11, is usually required. Compatibility with the Exchange Access Operator Service Signaling (EAOSS) protocol also may be required. The system must interface to or provide a data base for intercepted calls.

Force Management Capability

An important feature of operator service systems is force management software. The force management system provides productivity statistics such as the number of calls and the average work time per operator. It provides managers with service statistics such as the number of calls exceeding the waiting time objective and the number of calls abandoned without being served. The system provides service observing capability and enables operators to call a supervisor into the connection if necessary.

Selected Tandem Switching System Manufacturers

AT&T Network Systems

Datapoint Corporation

DSC Communications Corporation

Northern Telecom, Inc.

Rockwell International Switching Systems Division

11

Signaling Systems

The objectives of any network are to establish a communication path between end users, to monitor the path while it is in use, and to disconnect it when the users finish. Users need to know nothing of how the network establishes the path; they supply only the destination address and let the system select the route. Processor-driven controllers, which are the brains of the network, determine the route over the signal paths that are the nerve system. Signals travel between controllers either over the talking path or over separate data networks. In whatever manner the controllers exchange signals, the signals are ultimately converted to analog form at the user interface. Within the network, signals are converted to many different forms to accommodate differences in transmission facilities and equipment vintages.

These multiple signaling state conversions are the principal complicating factors in network signaling. Signals can be grouped into three functions:

- *Supervising* is monitoring the status of a line or circuit to determine if it is busy, idle, or requesting service. Supervision is a term derived from the function telephone operators performed in monitoring manual circuits on a switchboard. Switchboards display supervisory signals in the form of an illuminated lamp that shows a request for service on an incoming line or an on-hook condition of a switchboard cord circuit. In the network, the supervisory signals are voltage level on signaling leads or the on-hook/off-hook status of signaling tones or bits.

- *Alerting* indicates to the addressee the arrival of an incoming call. Alerting signals are audible bells and tones or visible lights.

- *Addressing* is transmitting routing and destination signals over the network. Addressing signals include dial pulses, tone pulses, and data pulses over loops, trunks, and signaling networks.

Signaling Technology

With few exceptions, switched connections over the telecommunications network today involve analog signaling; even if most of the facility is digital, the subscriber loop remains analog and requires analog signals. Digital signaling equipment is simple and inexpensive. As indicated in Chapter 4, it involves little more than robbing the lowest order bit from every sixth frame and using the binary status of this bit to drive signaling leads in the channel units. Analog signaling is considerably more complex. Most analog carrier systems require separate signaling units, which add to the cost and complexity of the circuit.

When networks are completely converted to ISDN, analog signaling will be eliminated. Signals will be passed from the IEC to the LEC and on to the user as a data message. With today's signaling systems, when a station is busy, the signal stops at the end office (unless the user has chosen the call waiting feature, which interrupts the call in progress). ISDN provides a separate signaling channel that allows the network to send alerting messages to the user, where they can appear on a readout on the telephone. The user can decide how to handle the call without terminating or interrupting the original session.

Signaling System Overview

Signaling systems can be classified as *in-band* or *out-of-band*, depending on whether the signals are carried over the talking path or over a separate channel. Presently, most interLATA connections use out-of-band signals that travel over a separate packet-switched

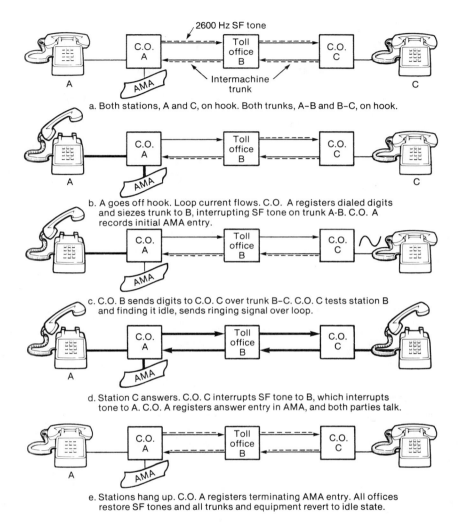

Figure 11.1   Signaling functions on an interoffice connection.

data network. Connections between the IECs and the LECs, however, are still made primarily with in-band signaling and, until ISDN arrives, connections over the local loop remain in-band.

Figure 11.1 illustrates the signaling functions in the telecommunications network, showing the signals exchanged when one user calls another over a long distance trunk using in-band signaling over an analog trunk. This diagram omits the switching connections, but switching occurs at each circuit interface. In the idle state, subscriber loops have battery on the ring side of the line and an open circuit on the tip. No loop current flows in this state. Signaling equipment attached to the trunks between the local offices and the toll office furnishes a 2600 Hz signaling tone, indicating idle circuit status. If the interoffice trunks are digital, signaling bits indicate the circuit status. In analog trunks the tone operates auxiliary single-frequency (SF) signaling sets that show the line status by changing the status of DC voltages on their signaling leads.

The switching system continually scans the subscriber line and trunk circuits to detect any change in their busy/idle status. When station A lifts its receiver off hook, current flows in the subscriber loop, signaling the local central office of A's intention to place a call. The central office responds by marking the calling line busy (another status indication) and returns dial tone to the calling party. Dial tone is one of several *call progress signals* that telephone equipment uses to communicate with the calling party. It shows the readiness of the central office to receive *addressing* signals.

Station A transmits digits to the central office using either DTMF or dial pulses. The system registers the digits and translates them into the address of the terminating station C. Included in the switching system's address translation is a routing table that tells it the destination of the call. From the address, the system determines that the call must be passed to the toll office B. System A checks the busy/idle status of trunks to office B and seizes an idle trunk. If no trunks are idle, central office A returns a *reorder,* or fast busy, call progress tone to station A. When the switch seizes an idle trunk, A hears nothing except, perhaps, the clicking of operating relays. If office A has automatic message accounting (AMA) equipment, it registers an initial entry to identify the calling and called number and to prepare the AMA equipment to record the details of the call when C answers.

The trunk seizure removes the 2600 Hz SF tone from the channel to show the change in status. Toll office B, detecting the change in status, returns a signal, usually a momentary interruption in the signaling tone toward A. This signal, called a *wink,* signifies that B is ready to receive digits. Detecting the wink, central office A sends its addressing pulses toward B. These pulses are either dial pulses, conveyed by interrupting the SF tone or, usually, *multifrequency* pulses, conveyed by coding digits with combinations of two out of five frequencies. Office B continues to send an on-hook tone toward office A and will do so until station C answers. At this point, office A has completed the originating functions and awaits the completion of the call.

Central office B translates the incoming digits to find the address of the destination, selects an idle trunk to office C, and seizes it. Office C, detecting the seizure, sends a start signal to Office B and prepares to receive digits. B detects the start signal and sends the digits forward. Office C tests the called station for its busy/idle status and, if busy, returns a busy tone over the voice channel. The calling party, recognizing the call progress tone, hangs up; the switches take the connection down. The originating switch adds no completion entry to the AMA record. If station C is idle, office C sends a 20 Hz alerting signal to ring the bell in C's telephone. It also returns an *audible ring* (another call progress tone) over the transmission path to the originating party. The line continues to ring until C answers, A hangs up, or the equipment times out.

When station C answers, central office C detects the change in status as line current begins to flow. This trips the ringing signal and stops audible ringing. Office C changes the status of its signaling set toward B from on-hook to off-hook by interrupting the SF tone. B transmits the on-hook signal to A. The AMA equipment registers call completion, indicating the time of day that charging begins.

When either party hangs up, the change in line current indicates a status change to its central office, which forwards the change to the other end by restoring the SF tone. Office A registers a terminating entry in the AMA equipment to stop charging. The SF tones are restored to all circuits to show idle circuit status. All equipment then is prepared to accept another call.

This system, with minor variations that we will discuss later, is used for signaling over both dedicated and switched circuits. Not all circuits use SF signaling, however. T-carrier and common channel signaling are making SF signaling obsolete. SF signaling can be transmitted over a digital circuit and often is when a digital link connects to an analog link. SF and MF signaling have several drawbacks that are leading to their replacement in toll circuits. First, the signaling functions consume circuit time that produces no revenue. Approximately 40% of all toll calls are not completed because the called party does not answer or is busy or because of blockage or equipment irregularities, and the circuit time consumed in signaling is substantial. The second drawback is the vulnerability of this type of signaling to fraud. Hackers have devices that defeat the operation of AMA equipment by inserting signaling tones on the circuit at the appropriate time.

To avoid these problems, the major IECs use *common channel signaling*, which will be discussed in a later section. Common channel signaling uses a separate data communications network to exchange signals, establishing the connection after routing is complete. Common channel signaling was initially not extended to local central offices, but most LECs are currently planning the conversion of their end offices to common channel signaling.

E & M Signaling

By long-standing convention, signaling on interoffice circuits uses two leads designated as the E or recEive and the M or transMit leads for conveying signals. External signaling sets and the built-in signaling of T carrier channels use E & M signaling to communicate status to attached central office equipment. Signaling equipment converts the binary state of line signals—tone on or off for analog and 0 or 1 for digital equipment—to actuate the E & M leads.

There are five types of E & M signaling interfaces, but in the most common type the M lead is grounded when on-hook. An off-hook seizure is indicated by applying -48 volt battery to the M lead. The E lead is open when on-hook; the signaling set applies ground to the E lead when it receives an off-hook signal from the distant end. Figure 11.2 illustrates the most common types of E & M signaling.

Signaling Irregularities

Signaling systems must be designed to transmit both status and addressing signals reliably enough to avoid errors. Errors are rare with multifrequency signaling and the internal signaling of digital

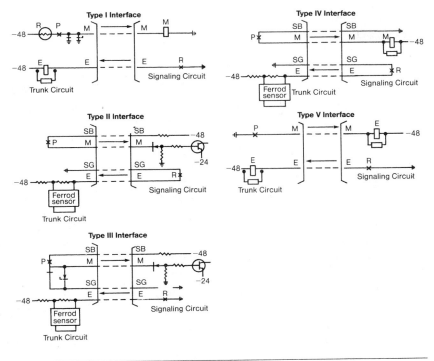

Figure 11.2   E&M signaling types.

carrier systems, but dial pulses transmitted over metallic facilities can be distorted by the line characteristics or by excessive noise.

Another irregularity occurs when both ends of a circuit are simultaneously seized. This condition, known as *glare*, can be prevented by using one-way signaling on trunks. On small trunk groups the use of one-way trunks is uneconomical for reasons explained in Chapter 31. Therefore, to accommodate two-way trunks, signaling and switching systems must prevent glare or resolve it when it occurs. In the worst case, when glare occurs the equipment is unable to complete the connection, the circuit times out, and the user receives reorder.

Direct Current Signaling Systems

DC signaling can be employed on metallic facilities, which include most subscriber loops and voice frequency interoffice trunks. The use of DC signaling over metallic facilities is not mandatory. In many applications it is desirable to use SF signaling from end to end.

The simplest status signal on the local loop occurs when the caller takes the telephone receiver off-hook, closing a DC path between tip and ring and allowing loop current to flow. This system is called *loop start*. All subscriber loops that terminate in station sets use loop start signaling.

Most PBXs connect to the central office over trunks equipped with two-way signaling and are thus subject to glare. Glare is a particular problem for loop start PBX trunks because the only indication the PBX has of a call incoming from the central office is the ringing signal, which occurs at 6-second intervals. For up to 6 seconds, the PBX is blinded to the possibility of an incoming trunk seizure and may seize a circuit for outgoing traffic when the trunk is carrying an incoming call that the PBX has not yet detected. To provide an immediate trunk seizure signal toward the PBX, central office line circuits are optionally wired for *ground start* operation. With this option the central office grounds the tip side of the line immediately upon seizure by an incoming call. By detecting the tip ground, the PBX is alerted to the line seizure before ringing begins. PBX users must specify to the LEC when ground start operation is required.

Metallic trunks and many special services use *duplex* (DX) signaling. DX signaling uses relays or electronic circuits that are sensitive to line status beyond the range of loop signaling. DX signaling equipment has separate signaling sets, circuitry built into carrier channel units as discussed in Chapter 4, or network channel terminating equipment (NCTE) as discussed in Chapter 18. An older system, composite (CX) signaling, is similar to DX signaling, except that it includes filters to separate the voice frequency path from the signaling path. Figure 11.3 is a diagram of a DX signaling set.

Trunk Signaling Systems

Trunk signaling requires the built-in signaling of digital carrier, a separate SF set, or, in some types of analog carrier, out-of-band

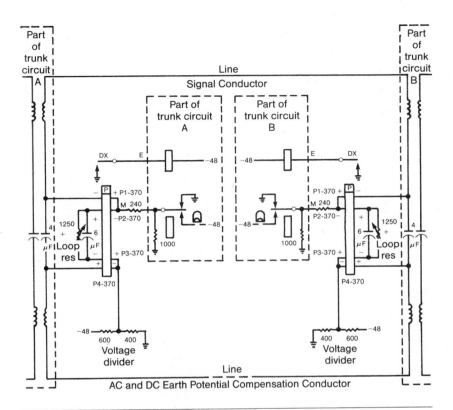

Figure 11.3   **Schematic of a DX signaling set.**
Courtesy of AT&T Corporation

tone signaling. Out-of-band tone signaling, rarely used in North America, passes a 3700 Hz signaling tone over the channel. Narrow band filters separate the signaling tone from the voice frequency passband.

Single-Frequency Signaling

The most common analog trunk signaling system is 2600 Hz single-frequency (SF) illustrated in Figure 11.4. The voice frequency leads from a carrier channel connect directly to the SF set. The SF set contains circuitry to change the state of the E & M leads in response to the presence or absence of the SF tone and to turn the signaling tone on and off when the switching system or other

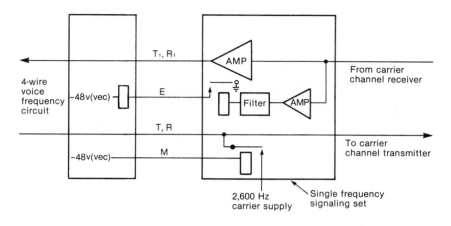

Figure 11.4   Single-frequency signaling simplified block diagram.

central office equipment changes the status of its leads. The SF set blocks the voice frequency path toward the switching system while the signaling tone is on the channel. The user does not hear the tone, although short tone bursts are occasionally audible when one party hangs up.

One hazard of SF signaling is *talk-off*, which can occur when the user's voice contains enough 2600 Hz energy to actuate the tone-detecting circuits in the SF set. Voice filters minimize the potential of talk-off, but the problem may occur, particularly to people with high pitched voices.

Addressing Signals

Addressing signals between station and central office equipment use either dial pulse or DTMF signals as described in Chapter 18. DTMF pulses require a DTMF receiver in the central office to convert the tones to the addressing signals. Because DTMF pulses travel over the voice path, they can be passed through the switching system after the connection is established. This capability is required to send addressing and identification information to interexchange carriers that use exchange access Feature Group A. It is also useful for converting the telephone to a simple data entry device. All modern electronic central offices can receive DTMF

Table 11.1   Single-Frequency Signaling Tone Frequencies

FREQUENCIES IN HZ	DIGIT
700 + 900	1
700 + 1100	2
900 + 1100	3
700 + 1300	4
900 + 1300	5
1100 + 1300	6
700 + 1500	7
900 + 1500	8
1100 + 1500	9
1300 + 1500	0

dialing. Electromechanical central offices require externally mounted DTMF receivers to convert the tones to dial pulses.

Addressing signals are transmitted over trunks as dial pulse or multifrequency (MF) signals or over a common channel as a data signal. MF signals are more reliable and considerably faster than dial pulse signals but require a *sender* to transmit the pulses. Most modern central offices support MF signaling, but older electromechanical central offices can receive only dial pulses. Dial pulse or DTMF signals are also used between PBXs and their serving central office.

MF senders use a two-out-of-five tone method to encode digits as Table 11.1 shows. Digits are sent at the rate of about seven digits per second, compared to the 10 pulses per second of dial pulsing. Since a dial-pulsed digit requires from one to 10 pulses plus an interdigital interval, MF pulsing requires substantially less time to set up a call than dial pulsing.

Common Channel Signaling

In-band signaling systems have four major drawbacks in interexchange networks. First, they are vulnerable to fraud. In the 1970s, the loss of revenue to users with devices that simulated in-band signaling tones was considerable and was a prime motivating factor in developing common channel signaling. Second, in-band call setup takes several seconds, and third, call setup consumes circuit time. A separate signaling network reduces call setup overhead. Not only is reduced call setup time important to the IECs' competitive positions, it also represents a direct expense in the access charges paid to the LECs. The fourth drawback is important to the market strategies of the IECs: in-band systems are limited to transferring call setup and supervision information and are therefore incapable of supporting virtual networks, which Chapter 30 discusses.

Common channel signaling uses a separate packet switched network to pass call setup, charging, and supervision information. It also can access the carrier's data base to obtain account information such as features and points served on a virtual network. The first implementation on a major network was Common Channel Inter-office Signaling (CCIS), which AT&T introduced in the mid-1970s and largely had in place by 1980. This network uses a protocol similar to CCITT's Signaling System No. 6 (SS6). CCITT first released the specification for Signaling System No. 7 in 1980 and subsequently modified it in 1984 and 1988. The major IECs now deploy SS7 almost exclusively.

SS7 retains the advantages of earlier CCS implementations and supports ISDN. It operates on both terrestrial and satellite networks and works with both analog and digital switching systems. Its functions are:

- Call management, which includes call setup, supervision, routing, and billing.
- Transferring account information between nodes.
- Network management.
- Network maintenance.

The next step in SS7 implementation is to extend signaling out to the end offices. This conversion will be expensive, but it is at the heart of the LECs' plans for offering new services. The LECs do not have the same motivations that drive the IECs to install common channel signaling. Fraud prevention and call setup time are not serious problems in the local network, but SS7 is the key

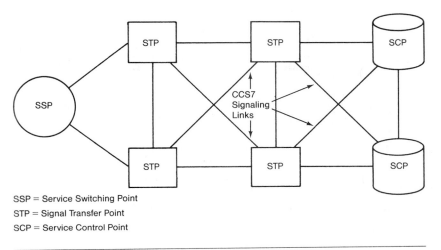

SSP = Service Switching Point
STP = Signal Transfer Point
SCP = Service Control Point

Figure 11.5   Signaling System No. 7 architecture.

to providing custom local area signaling services (CLASS), which Chapter 9 discusses. It is also the key to transporting 800 numbers between IECs.

With in-band signaling, the process of setting up the talking path determines whether the path is operative, because audible signals are passed over the channel that will be used for talking. With common channel signaling, this test is not possible; therefore the equipment makes a separate path assurance test before establishing the call.

Signaling System No. 7 Architecture

Figure 11.5 shows the architecture of SS7. The same architecture applies to earlier implementations of common channel signaling including AT&T's CCIS. The system has three major components, the *service switching point* (SSP), the *signaling transfer point* (STP), and the *service control point* (SCP). When the local exchange network connects via SS7 to the IECs' networks, it will have its own STP and SCP connecting to end offices and the IECs.

The SSP is a tandem switch in the interexchange network or an end office in the LEC network. The STPs are packet switching

nodes, and the SCPs are databases of circuit, routing, and customer information.

When the SSP receives a service request from a local end office
or a user attached on a direct access line, it formats a service
request for the SCP and suspends call processing until it receives
a reply. The SSP forwards the request to the STP over the packet
network.

The STPs are interconnected over a high speed packet network that is heavily protected from failure by alternative paths.
STPs are deployed in pairs so that the failure of one system will
not affect call processing. STPs pass the call setup request to an
SCP over direct circuits or by relaying it to another STP.

The SCP is a high speed database engine that is also deployed
in pairs with duplicates of the database. The database has circuit
and routing information, and for customers that are connected
through a virtual network, the database contains customer information such as class of service, restrictions, and whether the
access line is switched or dedicated. The SCP accepts the query
from the STP, retrieves the information from the database, and
returns the response on the network. The response generally
takes the same route as the original inquiry.

Signaling System No. 7 Protocol

SS7 uses a layered protocol that resembles the OSI model, but has
four layers instead of seven. The first three layers are called the
message transfer part (MTP). The MTP is a datagram service, which
means that it relays unacknowledged packets. The MTP has three
layers, which form a network similar to CCITT X.25.

The first layer, the Signaling Data Link, is the physical layer. It
is a full duplex connection that provides physical STP to STP, SCP
to SCP, and STP to SCP links.

The Signaling Link Layer is a data link that has three functions:
flow control, error correction, and delivery of packets in the
proper sequence.

The Signaling Network Layer routes messages from source to
destination, and from the lower levels to the user part of the
protocol. Its routing tables enable it to handle link failures and to
route messages based on their logical address.

Figure 11.6 Tellabs 334 SST Selective Signaling system.
Courtesy, Tellabs, Inc.

The fourth layer is called the Signaling Connection Control Part (SCCP). It is responsible for addressing requests to the appropriate application and for determining the status of the application. An application, for example, might be an 800 service request. The ISDN Service User Part (ISUP) relays messages to ISDN users. The user in this context refers to the interface with the end user's equipment and not to the user itself. The ISUP handles call setup, accounting and charging, and circuit supervision for ISDN connections.

Private Line Signaling

Private or dedicated lines use all types of in-band signaling discussed so far plus *selective signaling*, an in-band system for operation of certain private line switching systems. Figure 11.6

shows the Tellabs 334 SST system, which permits dial-selectable connections over a multipoint network.

Some dedicated circuits use signaling identical with that used by the telephone network. PBX tie trunks and large private switched networks require all the signaling capabilities of the telephone network. Some private networks use SS7 between tandem switches. Special dedicated circuits require signaling arrangements that use the same techniques and equipment as the telephone network but have no direct counterparts in switched systems. Examples are:

No Signaling.   Some private lines require no signaling. Examples are data circuits that include signaling in the DTE and circuits that use microphones and speakers for alerting. Other examples of circuits requiring no signaling are program and wired music circuits.

Ringdown Circuits.   In ringdown circuits a 20 Hz generator signal rings the bell of a distant station. The 300 Hz cut-off frequency of carrier channels prevents 20 Hz ringing signals from passing over the channel. Ringdown circuits require equipment to convert the 20 Hz ringing supply to SF or E & M signals and vice versa. A similar circuit actuates ringing when the receiver goes off-hook. This type of circuit requires a loop-to-SF converter. The signal at the far end may activate a light instead of a bell by using additional converter circuits.

Selective Signaling.   Some private line networks use a four-wire selective signaling system to route calls without the use of switching systems. Dial pulses generate in-band tones to drive a simple switch to build up a connection to the desired terminating point.

Coin Telephone Signaling

Coin telephones owned by the LECs use the dialing and ringing signals of ordinary telephones plus DC signals that operate apparatus within the telephone to collect and return coins. Coin tones are also generated in the telephone to enable the operator to distinguish between nickels, dimes, and quarters. Privately owned coin telephones are not connected to coin control circuits in the central office, and since supervisory signals are not repeated over the local loop, they must rely on internal circuitry for coin control as discussed in Chapter 18.

Applications

All public and private networks, except some data communications networks that supply their own signals, use signaling systems and equipment. Equipment used in these networks is identical and performs the same functions of alerting, addressing, supervising, and indicating status in both private and common carrier networks.

All major PBXs provide methods of network signaling to connect permit features such as voice mail, automatic callback, and message lamp illumination to work across the network. The methods are proprietary, and although some vendors use signals that resemble international standards, signaling is not carried through to the LECs or IECs. As the LECs deploy ISDN, PBXs will be integrated into the international signaling system.

Standards

Few published standards on the conventional single-frequency signaling system used in North America exist. Most standards have evolved through practice and are followed by signaling equipment manufacturers. Internationally, most carriers use the CCITT No. 6 and 7 standards for common channel signaling and CCITT No. 4 and 5 line signaling systems. These standards are of little concern to users because the IECs administer them. In North America, carriers have adopted similar systems for SF and MF signals.

Evaluating Signaling Equipment

The same criteria recommended for evaluating digital carrier equipment apply to signaling equipment. Reliability is the primary concern, with power consumption, circuit density, and cost being other factors to consider.

A circuit design must exist before selection of signaling equipment can begin. So many alternatives exist for interconnecting signaling equipment that it is necessary to determine the most economical design to minimize signaling costs. The most

Table 11.2   Voice Frequency Terminating and Signaling Units

Two-wire repeater
Four-wire repeater
Four-wire terminating set
Automatic ringdown unit
Conference bridge
DX signaling module
Data channel interface
Dial long line unit
Dial pulse correcting unit
Echo supressor
Line transfer relay
Loop extender
Loop signaling repeater
Program amplifier
Pulse link repeater
Repeat coil
Signaling converter, 20 Hz to E & M
Signaling range extender
Single-frequncy signaling unit
Toll diversion unit
Voice frequency equalizer

economical configuration in digital systems is the use of the built-in equipment in the T carrier channel. With the wide range of special channel units listed in Table 4.1, it is feasible to provide nearly any conceivable combination of signaling services to operate station signaling equipment.

Where built-in signaling is not included as part of the channel unit, external signaling converters are required. Table 11.2 lists the most common converters. These units are often available with amplifiers contained in the same package and are built into plug-in units that mount in a special shelf. The voice frequency

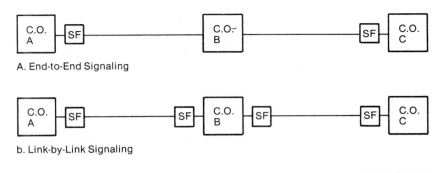

A. End-to-End Signaling

b. Link-by-Link Signaling

Figure 11.7   End-to-end versus link-by-link signaling.

and signaling leads are cabled to distributing frames as discussed in Chapter 12 for connection to carrier and subscriber loop equipment.

Signaling compatibility is also an important consideration in acquiring signaling equipment. Compatibility is rarely a problem with respect to signaling equipment of different manufacturers. Single frequencies, ringing frequencies, and E & M lead connections are universal with all manufacturers. The timing of signals, which is controlled by switching and transmission equipment connected to signaling sets, is a frequent cause of incompatibility, but this has little to do with the signaling equipment itself.

Plug compatibility is an issue that must be addressed by the manufacturer. Several types of plug-in shelves exist on the market; all are designed to manufacturer's specifications, and no standards exist. Some manufacturers make equipment that is designed to be plug-compatible with shelves of others.

Another important consideration in evaluating signaling equipment is testing capability. Circuits have either end-to-end signaling or link-by-link signaling, illustrated in Figure 11.7. End-to-end signaling is the easiest to test. If SF tones are used between both ends of a circuit, signaling status can be determined by listening to the tone over the voice channel or monitoring the signaling leads of a T carrier channel. The operation of the SF set is determined by measuring the electrical state of the E & M leads. With link-by-link signaling, the signals are extracted at intermediate points and connected by a pulse link repeater, which interconnects the E & M leads. In most private networks with station, PBX, and NCTE equipment furnished by the user, the local loop by the LEC, and the intercity circuits by an interexchange carrier, link-by-link signaling is the rule. For the user to diagnose signaling problems, testing capability is required to evaluate signaling in the station and NCTE.

Selected Signaling Equipment Manufacturers

ADC Telecommunications

AT&T Network Systems

Lear Siegler, Inc.

Northern Telecom, Inc.

Pulsecom Div., Harvey Hubbel, Inc.

Telco Systems, Inc.

Tellabs, Inc.

Transcom Electronics, Inc.

Wescom, Inc.

Common Equipment

There are several families of equipment that are not complex enough to warrant treatment in a separate chapter but serve various classes of telecommunications equipment. This equipment, which includes such diverse apparatus as power supplies, battery plants, racking and framing apparatus, distributing frames, and protection devices, is the subject of this chapter. Most such equipment is not particularly exotic though it may contain some high technology apparatus. Its lack of technical sophistication does not, however, diminish its importance.

Common equipment includes:

- Interbay cabling and wiring.
- Central office alarm equipment.
- Distributing frames.
- Power equipment.
- Relay racks, cabinets, and supporting structures.
- Protection equipment.

PBXs and tandem switches designed for private use are self-contained, with common equipment included within switching cabinets. Central office techniques are usually employed to borrow power for auxiliary equipment and to interconnect lines and trunks through distributing frames.

Cable Racking and Interbay Wiring

Central office equipment mounts in either cabinets or open relay racks, with the latter the most common for all systems except PBXs and small tandem switches. For equipment in cabinets, the interbay cabling is sometimes included in the cabinet. In relay rack mounted equipment, the cabling is external and is supported by overhead cable troughs or run through raceways in the floor. Because of the quantity of cable involved and the need for physical separation in some cables, overhead racking is common in both central offices and large PBXs.

To control noise and crosstalk in central offices, the manufacturer's specifications for the type and layout of cabling must be followed. As with outside plant cable, the twist in central office cable controls crosstalk and prevents unwanted coupling between circuits. Also, cables often must be run in separate troughs that are segregated by signal level and kept physically separated by enough distance that signals from high level cables cannot crosstalk into low level cables. For some types of cable, shielding is required to further reduce the possibility of crosstalk.

In central offices and PBXs alike, many critical leads have maximum lengths that cannot be exceeded. If lead lengths are exceeded, there may be excessive signal loss between components, signals may be distorted, or in high speed buses, timing may be affected by propagation delay. Manufacturers' specifications with respect to lead length must be followed rigorously.

Distributing Frames

Temporary connections and those requiring rearrangement terminate on crossconnect blocks mounted in distributing frames. Distributing frames also provide an access point for testing cable and equipment. The size and structure of a distributing frame are dictated by the number of circuits to be connected. Cabling to the central office equipment routes through openings at the top of the frame, fastens to vertical members, and turns under a metal shelf or mounting bracket that supports the crossconnect blocks. The crossconnect blocks are multiple metallic terminals mounted in an insulating material and fastened to the distributing frame. Equipment and lead identity are stenciled on the blocks.

Technicians make crossconnects by running *jumper* wire between blocks in a supporting wire trough. Connections are made at the block by one of three methods. In the oldest method, rarely used in modern equipment, the wire is stripped and soldered to the block. The second type uses wire-wrapped connections in which the wire is stripped and tightly wrapped around a post with a wire-wrap tool. The third type uses a split quick clip terminal that clamps the wire and pierces the insulation as a special tool inserts it in the terminal. The quick clip method has several variations that operate on the same principle of piercing the insulation and gripping the wire against a metallic connection.

Some installations use modular distributing frames, which keep the length of crossconnects to a minimum and are often administered by a computer. In small installations, distributing frame administration is usually not a problem. In large centers where thousands of subscriber lines and trunks terminate in the office, however, distributing frame congestion becomes a significant problem as large quantities of crossconnect wires are piled in troughs. In large installations, it is important that the distributing frame be carefully designed and administered to keep the wire length to a minimum.

Large PBXs may use the same hardware as central offices, or they may use a wall-mounted backboard that holds 66-type blocks or the newer condensed blocks offered by some manufacturers. Wall-mounted frames are satisfactory in small installations, but in PBXs with more than about 1000 stations, the frame becomes too large to be administered efficiently; jumpers must be long, and wiring trough congestion becomes a problem. To relieve jumper congestion, hardware that mounts wiring blocks on double-sided frames can be used.

Protector Frames

Incoming circuits that are exposed to power or lightning are terminated on protector frames. The protector module forms the connection between the cable pair and the attached equipment. As described in Chapter 6, if excessive current flows in the line,

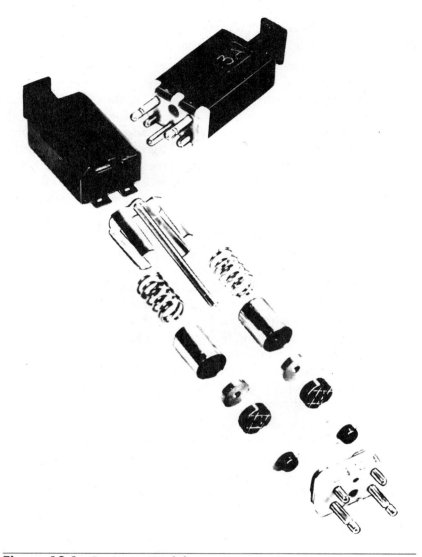

Figure 12.1   Protector module.
Courtesy, Cook *Electric Division of Northern Telecom, Inc.*

the protector opens the circuit to the central office equipment
and grounds the conductors. If excessive voltage strikes the line,
carbon blocks inside the protector module arc across to ground
the circuit. Figure 12.1 shows an exploded view of a protector

module. Modules with gas tubes are used where needed to protect vulnerable central office equipment such as digital switches.

Combined and Miscellaneous Distributing Frames

Small installations use combined protector and distributing frames. The incoming cable pairs terminate on the protector frame, where they are crossconnected to equipment that terminates on the distributing frame. In large central offices, the size of the frame may dictate separate protector and distributing frames. One or more distributing frames terminate trunks, switching machine line terminations, and miscellaneous equipment such as repeaters, range extenders, and signaling equipment. In offices large enough to need multiple frames, tie cables permit crossconnecting between cable and equipment terminated on different frames. Buildings with multiple floors almost invariably require several distributing frames linked with tie cable.

Ringing and Tone Supplies

Common equipment includes ringing, dial tone, call progress tone, and recorded announcement apparatus. In digital central offices, many of these tones are generated in software, so no external equipment is needed. Electromechanical and analog electronic central offices require external supplies.

Ringing machines are usually solid state supplies that generate 20 Hz ringing current at about 90 volts. Older ringing machines also generate dial tone. Older dial tone supplies are not compatible with DTMF dialing because they generate harmonics that fall inside the band pass of DTMF receivers. To prevent this, dial tone supplies with precisely generated tones are required. Busy tones and reorder supply tones are generated in the same manner as dial tones—either with solid state generators or with a branch circuit from the ringing machine.

Recorded announcements are stored in digital form in solid state memory or in analog form on magnetic tapes or drums. Most recorders contain multiple tracks for the several types of messages used in central offices.

Alarm and Control Equipment

Most telecommunications equipment has integral alarms in any circuit that can affect service. The extent and type of alarming varies with the manufacturer, but generally alarms draw attention to equipment that has failed or is about to fail, and direct the technician to the defective equipment.

Equipment alarms light an alarm lamp on the equipment chassis and operate external contacts that are used for remoting the alarm and for operating external audible and visual alarms. Most central offices contain an office alarm system to aid in locating failed equipment. Alarms are segregated into major and minor categories to show the seriousness of the trouble; different tones alert maintenance personnel to the alarm class and location. Aisle pilots and bay alarm lamps guide maintenance personnel to the room, equipment row, bay, and specific equipment in trouble.

In offices designed for unattended operation, telemetering equipment transmits alarms to a distant center over telephone circuits. The alarm remote is generally a slave that reports only the identity of the alarm point. The central alarm unit typically is equipped with a processor and data base that pinpoint the trouble and may also diagnose the cause. Some equipment, including most electronic switching systems, communicates with a remote that provides the equivalent of the local switching machine console. Other remote alarms report building status such as open door, temperature, smoke, and fire alarms.

Central offices designed for unattended operation frequently include control apparatus for sending orders from a distant location over a data circuit. For example, microwave and fiber optic equipment usually have control systems that enable technicians to transfer working equipment to a backup channel. Offices equipped with emergency generators frequently are arranged for engine start and shut down and transfer to and from commercial power.

The more extensive private telecommunications networks use central office techniques for reporting alarms and diagnosing trouble. Most PBX manufacturers support their systems with remote maintenance and testing systems that enable technicians to diagnose trouble remotely and, sometimes, switch around failed apparatus. Alarm systems range from those that simply report a contact opening or closure over a circuit to more elaborate systems that report values to a remote center, support remote diagnostics, and maintain a trouble clearance data base.

Power Equipment

Most central office equipment operates from direct current—usually -48 volts, which is the typical voltage supplied by central office charging and battery plants. Figure 12.2 shows a battery plant and charging equipment in an AT&T toll office. Microwave equipment usually works on -24 volts DC in radio stations and -48 volts DC in central offices. Some central office equipment operates from alternating current (AC) and requires a DC-to-AC converter known as an *inverter* to provide an uninterrupted power source during power failures. AC-operated equipment includes tape and disk drives, computers, and other equipment that is not normally designed for DC operation. Commercial uninterruptable power source (UPS) equipment, which we will discuss later, is an alternative family of equipment that contains a built-in battery supply.

Most central offices have emergency generators to carry the load and keep the batteries charged during prolonged power outages. The emergency generator connects to the charging equipment through a power transfer circuit that cuts off commercial power while the generator is on line. Offices lacking emergency power equipment usually have circuitry for connecting an external generator.

Storage batteries use technology similar to that used in automobile batteries. Lead acid and nickel cadmium cells are common, and some equipment uses batteries with solid electrolyte called *gel cells*. Power is distributed from the battery plant to the central office equipment over *bus bars*, which must be large enough to carry current for the total equipment load. The bus bars connecting the batteries are visible in the foreground of Figure 12.2. To

Figure 12.2   A central office power plant.
Courtesy, AT&T Corporation

minimize voltage drop, batteries are installed as close to the equipment as possible.

Some types of central office equipment require voltage higher or lower than the nominal -48 or -24 volts used by most equipment. These voltages are supplied either by a separate charging and battery plant or by solid state power converters. Except for very high current loads, power converters are the preferred method of supplying other voltages.

Uninterruptable Power Supplies (UPS)

Any telecommunications apparatus powered by commercial alternating current (AC) power is vulnerable to failure due to irregularities that cannot be predicted or controlled. The following are the principal types of commercial power irregularities:

- *Blackouts*, which are total failures of commercial power.
- *Brownouts*, which are reductions in voltage.
- *Surges*, which are momentary voltage changes.
- *Transients*, which are momentary open circuit conditions.
- *Spikes*, which are sharp pulses of high voltage that rapidly rise and decay.
- *Frequency variations*, which are momentary or prolonged deviations from the nominal 60 Hz power line frequency.

Many power line irregularities have no effect, but others can damage equipment, interrupt service, or both. The severity of the problem varies with locale and season. In some parts of the United States, outages occur so infrequently that protective measures are unnecessary. In other parts of the country, outages are regular occurrences, particularly in bad weather.

Power line conditioning equipment removes spikes, transients, and surges. Blackouts and brownouts require some form of backup power. Computers, tape and disk drives, many PBXs, and most key telephone systems are powered by commercial AC. These devices can be protected from failure by *uninterruptable power supplies* (UPS).

UPS devices come in a many sizes and capacities. Capacities range from enough to enable a small shared device such as a file server to shut down gracefully to enough to operate a mainframe computer, a PBX, and auxiliary equipment such as modems, multiplexers, and voice mail through a prolonged power outage.

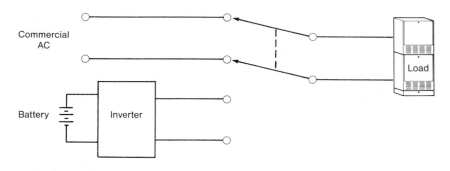

Figure 12.3   An off-line uninterruptable power supply.

UPSs are available in three general types: *off-line*, or *standby power source*, *hybrid*, and *on-line*. These UPSs are listed in order of increasing cost for a given amount of capacity.

Off-Line UPS

An off-line supply, sometimes known as a standby power source or standby UPS, is the least effective of the three types. Figure 12.3 shows schematically how this type of supply works. The inverter converts DC to AC. It connects permanently to a storage battery that charges from the AC source. The AC source carries the load, and on failure the load switches to the output of the inverter. A short break in power occurs when the load transfers. The break lasts from 5 to 20 milliseconds, which is short enough to keep most apparatus working. During brownout conditions, however, the switching time may be longer. This type of UPS lacks line conditioning, frequency regulation, and surge and spike protection.

Hybrid UPS

A hybrid UPS is similar to an off-line supply except it provides surge suppression and line conditioning as Figure 12.4 shows. The capacitance in the line conditioner tends to carry the load while the inverter switches. This type of supply still may not provide full service continuity during brownout conditions.

On-Line UPS

An on-line UPS, which Figure 12.5 shows, is the most effective and costly of the three methods. The inverter operates continuously and furnishes power directly to the protected apparatus. The

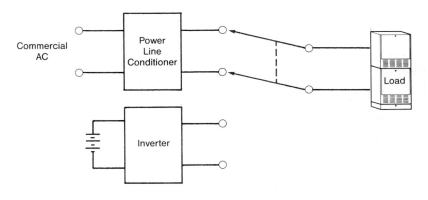

Figure 12.4 **A hybrid uninterruptable power supply.**

commercial power source keeps the UPS battery charged. When the power fails, the inverter continues to function without a break in power. The charging apparatus keeps the equipment completely isolated from power line irregularities.

Backup Battery Supplies

Apparatus that operates from direct current connects to a -48 volt bus as Figure 12.6 shows. A string of batteries connects the bus and ground. Charging equipment keeps the batteries charged and furnishes DC power to the equipment. When commercial power is on-line the charging equipment carries the central office load;

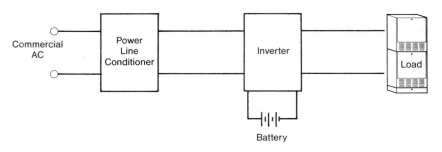

Figure 12.5 **An on-line uninterruptable power supply.**

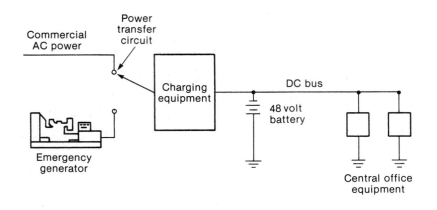

Figure 12.6   Central office power plant.

the batteries draw only enough power to compensate for internal leakage and to filter noise on the power bus.

When commercial power fails, the equipment is unaffected because it draws its operating current from the battery supply. As the batteries discharge, the bus voltage drops. Equipment is designed with a tolerance for a variance in supply voltage. Under normal operation the -48 volt bus is actually *floated* from the charger at approximately -52 volts. Most central office equipment can tolerate a drop to 44 volts or less without affecting equipment operation.

The length of time equipment can operate under power failure conditions depends on the current drain and the capacity of the batteries. For example, if equipment draws 10 amperes and the battery string can supply 100 ampere-hours, the equipment can operate for 10 hours under power failure conditions. As a practical matter, it may operate for fewer than 10 hours because of reduced battery capacity, which is described later. The operating time under power failure conditions can be extended by three methods: paralleling battery strings, end cells, and emergency generators.

Paralleling Battery Strings

Battery capacity can be extended by connecting a paralleling battery string. Each string contributes its capacity to the load. For example, if three 100 ampere-hour strings are connected in parallel, the total string will furnish approximately 300 ampere-hours.

End Cells

As battery voltage begins to deteriorate, it can be boosted by switching in auxiliary cells known as *end cells*. Switching apparatus, which is either manual or automatic, connects the end cells in series with the existing battery string so they contribute their voltage to the overall bus voltage. When end cells are not in use, an auxiliary charger keeps them charged.

Emergency Engine Generator

Organizations, such as hospitals and public safety organizations, that require continuity of telecommunications service must use an auxiliary engine generator to furnish power. The generator connects through a transfer switch to the charging equipment. If a generator is available, less battery capacity is needed because the battery must furnish power only until the generator starts.

Battery Capacity

A storage battery has three principal elements—positive and negative plates, electrolyte, and case. The plates, which are made of a metallic substance such as lead or nickel-cadmium, are suspended in electrolyte by the case, which is made of an insulating material. In contrast to automobile batteries, in which the negative pole is normally grounded, in telecommunications equipment the positive pole is grounded to aid in preventing electrolysis. Older central office batteries have open cells, which require periodic maintenance such as measuring specific gravity and adding water. Newer telecommunications applications use sealed batteries. These batteries normally have a jelly-like electrolyte that requires no maintenance.

Temperature has a significant effect on battery life and capacity. Battery capacity is highest in warm temperatures, but as temperature increases, battery life is shortened. Conversely, cooler temperatures extend battery life, but below freezing, battery capacity is greatly reduced.

To maintain the best balance between capacity and life, batteries should operate at approximately room temperature. Obviously, this is impractical in remote locations, such as repeater sites, that may lack heat and air conditioning. In such locations, batteries should be placed to minimize their exposure to temperature extremes. For example, they should be placed on the shady side of a building to reduce heat.

Applications

Common equipment is separately engineered in central offices. In private networks, the switching equipment supplier will usually engineer and furnish common equipment. This section discusses the primary considerations in evaluating common equipment in a local private network environment.

Standards

Common equipment is generally built to manufacturer's standards. The principal voltages used in central offices, -48 and -24 volts, are accepted by convention, but are not regulated by telecommunications standards. The National Electrical Safety Code and local codes apply to wiring commercial power to charging equipment, but the voltages used on central office equipment are too low to be considered hazardous.

Most manufacturers in the United States follow the Bell New Equipment-Building System (NEBS) guidelines in their bay dimensions. Relay racks are standardized at 7, 9, and 11.5 feet in height and support equipment with 19- or 23-inch wide mounting panels. The mounting screw holes are also spaced at standard intervals. In other countries metric dimensions must be supported.

Evaluating Common Equipment

Evaluation considerations discussed in previous chapters are equally applicable to common equipment. As with all telecommunications equipment, high reliability is imperative. Compatibility is important with alarm and control systems, but with power, distributing frame, and cabling, compatibility is generally not a problem if the equipment meets the specifications of the manufacturer of the interfacing equipment.

Environmental Considerations

An early consideration in establishing a system is to provide the floor space and environment required for its operation. The manufacturer's recommendations should be followed with respect to heating, air conditioning, air circulation, cabling, and mounting. The primary considerations are provision of:

- Sufficient floor space for expansion.
- Sufficient air conditioning and heating capacity.
- Ducts and raceways where required.
- Separate power equipment room where recommended by the manufacturer.
- Adequate security.

Work Space

Equipment areas should provide a physical working environment with adequate space and lighting for equipment maintenance. The manufacturer should install equipment to its standards and should specify aisle space between equipment lineups, lighting standards, and commercial AC outlets for powering test equipment.

Protection and Distributing Frames

Frame terminations should be provided for all equipment that requires rearrangement or reassignment. The primary considerations are the density of frame blocks and the amount of trough space provided for jumper wire. Block density is a tradeoff between the amount of floor space consumed by the distributing frames and the difficulty of running multiple wires to small or congested blocks.

All cable pairs exposed to lightning strikes or power cross should be protected. This includes all pairs furnished by the local telephone company unless protection is included with the service. The manufacturer's recommendations should be followed with respect to gas tube protection.

Distributing frames should always conform to a plan that is designed to eliminate congestion and support productivity in placing and removing crossconnects.

UPS Equipment

The primary criterion in evaluating UPS equipment is whether the supply is on-line, off-line, or hybrid. This can usually be determined by evaluating the manufacturer specifications. If the supply has any transition time before it assumes the load, it is not an on-line supply. If it lacks any kind of power line conditioning equipment, it is most likely an off-line supply.

A second important evaluation criterion is the *crest factor ratio*. This factor evaluates the capability of the supply to handle load peaks. Technically, it is the ratio between the non-repetitive peak load the supply can provide and the linear RMS (root mean square) load it supplies. The ratio should be at least 2.5; the higher, the better.

The output wave shape is another evaluation factor. Commercial AC is a pure sine wave, and the more effective UPS supplies also furnish sine wave output. Less expensive supplies provide square wave output, which can affect the operation of the power supply in the supported equipment. If the vendor is unable to provide photos of the output wave, this factor is easy to evaluate by examining at the wave under load with an oscilloscope.

The amount of voltage regulation and the backup time are two more important factors in evaluating a UPS. The supply should maintain voltage within +3 percent. The amount of backup time required is determined by comparing the power drain of the protected equipment to the power furnished by the UPS, and how long the equipment is to be protected. A key telephone system or PBX normally is protected through the longest expected power outage. It may be necessary to power a file server or computer only long enough to allow a graceful shut down.

Batteries and Charging Equipment

Storage batteries are evaluated by their capacity, usually stated in ampere-hours, type of plate material, and electrolyte. Central office batteries are usually strings of individual cells, each having a nominal voltage of 2.17 volts. The cells must be in leak-proof and crack-proof cases, preferably with a sealed electrolyte. Private telecommunication equipment batteries are usually purchased in 12 volt increments. Four such batteries comprise a 48 volt string.

Manufacturers also specify batteries by their expected service life. Long life central office batteries have sufficient plate material to last for up to 20 years with proper maintenance.

If a plant powers a switching system, it is important to ensure that it has enough spare capacity to power external transmission and signaling equipment. In a private network, the provision of batteries depends on whether the network must remain in operation during power failures or whether it will be allowed to fail until the power is restored. The decision to provide an emergency generator depends on whether the battery reserve is sufficient to survive a long power outage.

Cabling

The number of leads to cable to distributing frames is an important consideration in installing equipment. Apparatus such as T-1 carrier and NCTE usually has many wiring options designed to fit special services. If not all leads are cabled to the distributing frame, the use of certain options may be precluded in the future unless the equipment is recabled. If unneeded leads are cabled to the distributing frame, however, extra costs will be incurred in cabling, frame blocks, and installation labor, and more frame space will be consumed by the extra terminations.

Also of importance is proper segregation of cables. For example, cables carrying low level carrier signals usually are separated from high level cables, or the cables are shielded to prevent crosstalk. Data bus cables in many SPC switching systems must be isolated from other cables to prevent errors. The manufacturer's specifications must be rigidly adhered to in designing cable racks and troughs.

The manufacturer usually specifies maximum cable length. Most telecommunications equipment has critical lead lengths that must not be exceeded.

Selected Common Equipment Manufacturers

Alarm and Control Equipment

AT&T Network Systems
Badger/TTI
Communication Manufacturing Co.
NEC America

Rockwell International
Sanbar
SNC Manufacturing Co.

Cable and Central Office Structural Components

AT&T Network Systems
Amphenol
Anaconda-Ericsson Inc.
Brand-Rex Co.
General Cable Co.

3M Co. Telcomm Products Div.
Newton Instrument Co. Inc.
Siecor Corporation
Standard Wire and Cable Co.

Distributing and Protector Frames and Equipment

AT&T Network Systems
3M Co. Telcomm Products Div.
Northern Telecom Inc., Cook Electric Div.

Porta Systems Corp.
Reliance Comm/Tec

Power Systems and Storage Batteries

American Power Conversion
AT&T Network Systems
Cylix
Durant Technologies
EFI Electronics
Energy Control Systems
Exide Corporation
Fiskars
Gates Energy Products
General Semiconductor
IRC

ITT PowerSystems Corp.
Kohler Co.
Lorain Products
LorTec Power Systems
Northern Telecom, Inc.
Para Systems, Inc.
Power Battery
Power Conversion Products, Inc.
Reliance Comm/Tec
Sola Electric
Superior Electric

Part

3

Transmission Systems

If the evolution of switching systems has been spectacular, the advances in transmission technology over the past few years have been nothing short of astounding. A generation ago, who could have dreamed that our voices would be scanned, turned into the 0s and 1s of a binary signal, combined with the bits of thousands of other voices, used to modulate a laser no larger than a grain of salt, and accelerated halfway around the world over a tiny glass pipe no larger than a hair? Or who could have predicted that events on another continent could be beamed by radio to a satellite orbiting thousands of miles above the equator and re-layed back to earth stations so we could witness events on our own televisions even as they were happening?

The technology that makes intercontinental communication possible is beyond the comprehension of most users and if you simply use circuits provided by common carriers, there is no need to understand the underlying principles. The devices used for long haul transmission, however, are finding their way into private networks. Fiber optics and lightwave are used increasingly for private networks. Fiber optics will increase significantly in local area networks, and will someday bring high speed data directly to the desktop. Microwave radio is giving way to lightwave as the dominant long haul medium, but frequencies that not long ago were experimental are now used regularly for communication over short distances.

The best news for end users is that transmission technology is driving prices down. Digital private lines were once three times the price of analog; now they are on a par and will eventually replace analog circuits altogether.

Cellular radio systems, once so rare as to be status symbols, have become commonplace with the price of the units themselves dropping to only a few hundred dollars. Air time remains costly, however, and the limited amount of frequency spectrum now available will retard somewhat the growth of cellular systems. Meanwhile, it remains a technology with considerable promise and high demand.

Video technology, once so expensive that it was confined to public networks and CATV systems, is increasingly finding its way into corporate networks. When AT&T introduced the Picture Phone, it inspired little interest except as a curiosity. Now, with economical video compression equipment and low cost transmission facilities, we are on the verge of expanded use of video conferencing.

Part 3 begins with three chapters that explain the principal technologies—lightwave, microwave, and satellite—more or less in the order of their importance. The part concludes with a discussion of cellular and conventional mobile radio systems and video systems.

13

Lightwave Communications

Few technologies have advanced as rapidly or been accepted as enthusiastically as fiber optics. The first Bell System lightwave field trials in 1977 were not even completed when the Bell Operating Companies, driven by the compelling economics of fiber optics, began applying the technology. Just a little more than a decade later, scores of companies had laced the nation with fiber optic networks. What is truly amazing about the speed of development is not the technology so much as the billions of dollars that companies rushed to invest in right-of-way and construction costs, displacing microwave networks that were still providing satisfactory service. This willingness to invest testifies to the confidence the nation's carriers have in lightwave as the premier transmission technology of the future.

Fiber optics is one of the most remarkable developments in telecommunications, a field that has given the world such developments as satellite communication, digital switching, microwave radio, and the telephone itself. Fiber optics arrived at an opportune time in telecommunications history. It provides unlimited bandwidth in a world that is rapidly exhausting microwave frequencies. It provides interference-free communication of a quality that makes it difficult to tell whether the parties to a session are next door or half a world apart. The cable is constructed of silicon, the most abundant substance on earth, and in terms of energy consumption, the electronics are far more efficient than the technologies they it replace.

A fiber optic system is similar in concept to a microwave radio system in many ways. The primary exceptions are that the transmission medium for lightwave is a tiny glass waveguide rather than free space and that transmission takes place at lightwave frequencies, which have much shorter wavelengths than microwave. Microwave operates with a steady carrier wave that a digital or analog signal modulates, where fiber is modulated by interrupting the light beam at the speed of the modulating signal. Where microwave is generally designated by its frequency band, lightwave is designated by wavelength. At light frequencies, the wavelength is so short that its unit of measurement is the nanometer (nm.), which is one-billionth of a meter. With present technology, the usable lightwave communications spectrum extends from approximately 800 to 1600 nm.

The cost and difficulty of obtaining public right-of-way limits fiber optic ownership for private networks. Many LECs and an increasing number of private carriers, known as alternate access vendors (AAVs), offer lightwave capacity, however, so private network users can lease fiber optic pairs and multiplex them in any way they choose. The industry refers to this method of leasing fibers as obtaining dark fiber. The same carriers also lease multiplexed bandwidth, typically DS-1 or DS-3, over their fiber optic systems. Many local network applications also use fiber optic cable. Low cost optical transceivers are coupled to the ends of the fiber cable for high speed transmission within a building or campus for either a local area network, as described in Chapter 27, or point-to-point digital communications.

One reason fiber optics is so effective is that once the cable is in place, it can be expanded by further developments in electronics without adding cable. Every year the development laboratories announce new speed and distance records, and soon the manufacturers translate experimental devices into commercial products. The frenetic advances of the past will not continue indefinitely without a major technical breakthrough, however, because fiber optics is now approaching its theoretical limits. This does not mean that further developments will not occur. Considerable work remains to be done in the area of optical switches, optical amplifiers, and linear lasers.

Fiber optic cable is an important replacement for twisted pair cable in local trunking applications because of its greater capacity and smaller physical diameter. Diameter is important when conduits are congested and must be augmented to contain more voice frequency or T carrier cables. Replacing a single copper cable with fiber optics can usually increase capacity enough to forestall conduit additions for many years. Also, because the medium does not radiate into free space, the FCC does not require licensing. Its primary disadvantage is the expense of right-of-way and of keeping it free of damage. Like copper cables, fiber optics can be damaged by excavations, slides, vandalism, and accidents.

As we enter the last decade of the 20th century, most of the cross country fiber optics networks are in place, and manufacturers are looking to other applications to increase demand. The potential demand in the local loop far outweighs the scope of the long haul projects that were completed in the 1980s, but as we will discuss later in this chapter, significant technical and economic barriers prevent this demand from materializing immediately. Local area networks and campus cabling comprise another market that will gradually develop, aided by the Fiber Distributed Data Interface (FDDI) standards that we will discuss in Chapter 29.

Lightwave communication is not without its drawbacks. Where the application needs enormous amounts of bandwidth, it is without equal, but where only a few circuits are needed, it cannot compete economically with copper cable. Also, its enormous bandwidth makes it vulnerable. The natural enemy of fiber optics is the backhoe; a single cable cut can disrupt traffic to a large portion of the country. It is not enough, therefore, for a common carrier to have a lightwave system. The network must offer diversity and automatic protection of cable routes to prevent a service disaster when a fiber route is lost.

As with other telecommunications technologies, there is a constant debate on standards. The digital input side of lightwave has standards that are derived from the digital signal hierarchy discussed in Chapter 4. On the line side, however, standards are proprietary. A light signal from one manufacturer will not work with a signal from another manufacturer unless they are designed for compatibility.

Not only electronic standards but cable standards are being debated. Most manufacturers accept the dimensions of single-mode fiber, but the world has not yet agreed on the aperture and outer diameter dimensions of multimode fiber.

Lightwave Technology

The use of light for communication is an idea that has been around for more than a century but has become feasible only within the past few years. Alexander Graham Bell, in the first known light-wave application, received a patent for his Photophone in 1880. The Photophone was a device that modulated a light beam, focused from the sun, and radiated in free space to a nearby receiver. The system reportedly worked well, but free space radiation of light has several disadvantages that the devices available at the time could not overcome. Like many other ideas, this one was merely ahead of its time. Free space light communication is now technically feasible if the application can tolerate occasional outages caused by fog, dust, atmospheric turbulence, and other path disruptions. Free space light communication is covered in a later section.

Two developments raised lightwave communication from the theoretical to the practical. The first development was the laser in 1960. A laser produces an intense beam of highly collimated light; that is, its rays travel in parallel paths. The second event that advanced lightwave was the development of glass fiber of such purity that only a minute portion of a light signal emitted into the fiber is attenuated. With a laser source that is triggered on and off at high speed, the 0s and 1s of a digital communication channel can be transmitted to a detector, usually an avalanche photo diode (APD) or a PIN diode. The detector converts the received signal pulses from light back to electrical pulses and couples them to the multiplex equipment. Figure 13.1 shows the elements of a lightwave communication system. Repeaters, or regenerators, are spaced at regular intervals with the spacing dependent on the transmission loss of the fiber and the *system gain* at the transmission wavelength. System

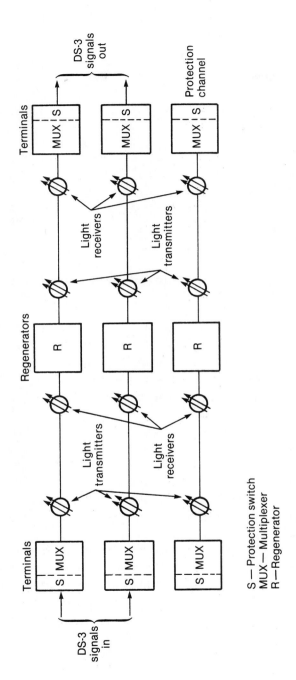

Figure 13.1   Block diagram of a typical fiber optic system.

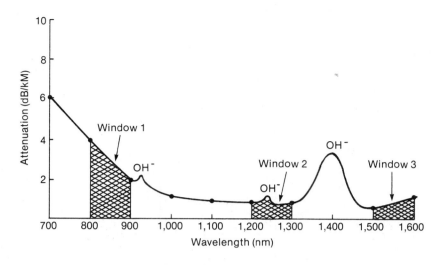

Figure 13.2   Spectral loss for a typical optical fiber; loss disturbances labeled OH⁻ result from hydroxyl ion absorbtion.

gain in fiber optics is a concept similar to system gain in a microwave radio system and is discussed in a later section.

As with microwave, a standby channel, which assumes the load when the regular channel fails, protects most lightwave systems. The two directions of transmission are normally protected separately between the digital signal input and output points. If a failure occurs, the protection equipment switches the signal to a new combination of cable, terminal equipment, and repeaters.

The advantages of lightwave accrue from the protected transmission medium of the glass fiber. These tiny waveguides isolate the digital signal from the fading and interference characteristics of free space. The optical fiber attenuates the light signal, however, and unlike microwave, the transmission medium loss is not linear across the spectrum. Figure 13.2 shows the spectral loss typical of modern glass fiber. As the figure shows, there are three regions, or *windows,* that lightwave communication can use.

The earliest fiber optic systems used the 850 nm. window because suitable lasers were first commercially available at that wavelength. As lasers became available at 1300 nm., applications

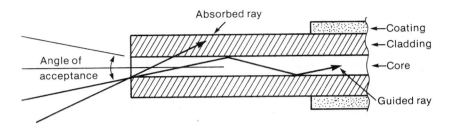

Figure 13.3   Light ray paths through a step index optical fiber.

shifted to this wavelength because of its lower loss. Glass fiber exhibits slightly lower losses in its third window at about 1550 nm.

The first commercial fiber optics system, installed in 1977, operated at 45 mb/s with repeaters required at 4-mile (6.4 km.) intervals. Current systems operate at bit rates up to about 1.7 gb/s (1700 mb/s), with developmental systems operating at bit rates greater than 2 gb/s. At 2 gb/s, a pair of fibers—one for transmit and one for receive—can carry about 30,000 voice frequency channels. At 1 gb/s, repeaters can be spaced as far apart as 30 miles (50 km.) and can transport more than 24,000 voice channels.

Lightguide Cables

A digital signal is applied to a lightguide by pulsing the light source on and off at the bit rate of the modulating signal, and the signal propagates to the receiver at slightly less than the speed of light. The lightguide has three parts, the inner core, the outer *cladding*, and a protective coating around the cladding. Both the core and the cladding are of glass composition; the cladding has a greater *refractive index* so that most of the incoming light waves are contained within the core. Light entering an optical fiber propagates through the core in *modes*, which are the different possible paths a lightwave can follow. Optical fiber is grouped into two categories, *single-mode* and *multimode*. In single-mode, fiber light can take only a single path through a core that measures about 10 microns in diameter. (A micron is one one-millionth of a meter.) The core of a single-mode fiber is about the size of a bacterium. Multimode fibers have cores 50 to 200 microns in

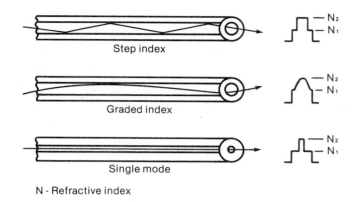

Figure 13.4 **Wave propagation through different types of optical fibers.**

diameter. Single-mode fiber is more efficient at long distances for reasons that we discuss below, but the small core diameter requires a high degree of precision in manufacturing, splicing, and terminating the fiber.

Lightwaves must enter the fiber at a critical angle known as the *angle of acceptance*. Any waves entering at a greater angle escape through the cladding as Figure 13.3 shows. The reflected waves take a longer path to the detector than those that propagate directly. The multipath reflections arriving out of phase with the main signal attenuate the signal and round and broaden the shoulders of the light pulses. This pulse rounding is known as *dispersion*. It can be corrected only by regenerating the signal. The greater the core diameter, the greater the amount of dispersion. The small core diameter of single-mode fiber reduces the amount of dispersion and supports wider repeater spacing.

Fiber also is classified by its refractive index into two general types, *step index* and *graded index*. With step index fiber, the refractive index is uniform throughout the core diameter. In graded index fiber, the refractive index is lower near the cladding than at the core. Lightwaves propagate at slightly lower speeds near the core than near the cladding. As a result, dispersion is lower and the distance between regenerators can be lengthened. Figure 13.4 shows wave propagation through the three types of fiber. Single mode fiber minimizes the effects of dispersion. Although single-mode fiber is immune to the pulse rounding caused by modal dispersion, it is subject to another type known as material dispersion. Material dispersion results from the broad range of wavelengths contained in a pulse. Because the refractive index varies with wavelength, some wavelengths are attenuated more than others. Material dispersion rounds a single-mode pulse, but the effects are far less severe than with modal dispersion, permitting greater regenerator spacing than with multimode fiber optics. Material dispersion is the primary factor inhibiting the use of bit rates in the 1 to 2 gb/s range. To get speeds this high, a laser that emits a narrow band of frequencies is required.

Besides the effects of dispersion, loss limits fiber optic regenerator spacing. Loss is caused by two factors, absorption and scattering. Absorption results from impurities in the glass core, imperfections in the core diameter, and the presence of hydroxyl ions or "water" in the core. The water losses occur most significantly at wavelengths of 1400, 1250, and 950 nm. as Figure 13.2 shows. Scattering results from variations in the density and composition of the glass material. These variations are an inherent by-product of the manufacturing process.

Manufacturing Processes

Glass fibers are made with a process known as modified chemical vapor deposition (MCVD) or an alternative process called outside vapor deposition. The MCVD process starts with a pure glass tube about 6 feet long and 1.5 inches in diameter. The tube is rotated over a flame of controlled temperature while a chemical vapor is introduced in one end as Figure 13.5 shows. The vapor is a carrier for chemicals that heat from the flame deposits on the interior of the glass. The deposited chemicals form a tube composed of many layers of glass inside the original tube. The OVD process deposits high purity glass on the outside of a ceramic rod, which is removed. When the deposition process is complete, the tube is collapsed under heat into a solid glass rod known as a preform. The preform is placed at the top of a drawing tower where the fiber is heated to the melting point and drawn through a die into a hair-thin glass strand as shown in Figure 13.6.

Figure 13.5   The modified chemical vapor deposition process.
Courtesy, AT&T Corporation

Multiple fiber strands are wound together around a strength member and enclosed in a sheath as Figure 13.7 shows. Like copper cable, fiber cable sheaths are made of polyethylene and can be enclosed in armor to protect against damage. Fiber optic cable is suitable for direct burial, pulling through conduit, suspension from an aerial strand, or submersion in water.

Fiber cables are spliced by adhesion or fusion. In the adhesion process, a technician places fibers in an alignment fixture and joins them with epoxy. The fusion method employs a splicing fixture of the type shown in Figure 13.8. The splicer precisely aligns the two ends of the fiber under a microscope and fuses them with a short electric pulse. After splicing, the loss is measured to ensure that splice loss is acceptable. Splices are made with enough slack in the cable that they can be repeated, if necessary, until the objective loss is achieved.

Cable Connectors

In midspan, fiber cables are joined by splicing, but at terminal locations connectors are added for coupling to terminal devices

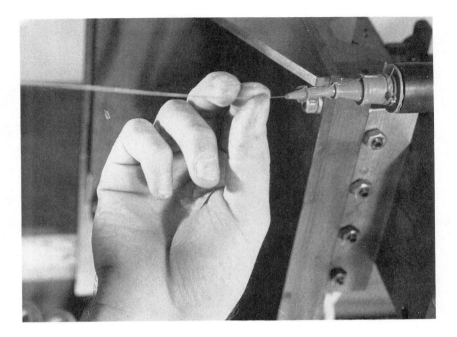

Figure 13.6   Fiber is pulled through a die into a single strand.
Courtesy, AT&T Corporation

and for ease in rearrangement. The physical structure of connectors is of utmost importance because of the exceedingly close tolerances that are required to match cable to transmission device. Connectors must be made from thermally stable materials and have tightly locking keyed parts and highly polished mating surfaces. They also must be field installable while maintaining factory level performance.

Connector performance is rated on two criteria—the amount of insertion loss and the amount of reflection attenuation. A reflection is light that travels down the lightguide, strikes a discontinuity, and reflects toward the source, causing instability or errors. A suitable connector for most applications should have an insertion loss of 0.5 dB or less and a reflection attenuation of at least 35 dB.

The dominant connector types today for LAN and premises applications are the SMA and the ST, which is a trademark of

Figure 13.7   Fiber optic cable.
Courtesy, Siecor Corporation

AT&T. The SMA connector has a screw-type connection, which makes it sensitive to misalignment if not installed properly. The ST connector is spring-loaded and keyed so that it does not exhibit rotational sensitivity. As FDDI products come on the market, the specialized duplex connector required for that application will also become a heavily used product.

Fiber Optic Terminal Equipment

A fiber optic system has separate transmit and receive fibers, the opposite ends of which terminate in light transmitters and receivers. The light transmitter employs either a light emitting diode (LED) or a laser as its output element. Lasers have a greater system gain than LEDs because their output is higher and because a greater portion of the light signal can be coupled into the fiber

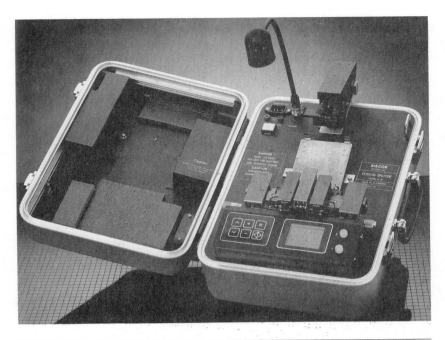

Figure 13.8   **Wave propagation through different types of optical fibers.**

without loss. The primary advantage of an LED transmitter is its lower cost. In applications such as local area networks, which do not need high system gain, the cost saving can easily justify the use of LED transmitters.

The multiplex equipment connects to the input of the transmitter, and the fiber optic cable couples to the output through a precision connector. Most fiber optic systems use digital modulation, but analog transmitters vary the intensity of the light signal or modulate the pulse rate or pulse width. Although analog modulation is normally not linear enough for transmitting analog multiplex, it is suitable for transmitting a video signal and is used in cable television systems.

The light receiver is an APD or PIN diode that couples to the optical fiber on the input end and to the multiplex equipment on the output end. The diode converts the light pulses to electrical pulses, which the receiver reshapes into square wave pulses. A

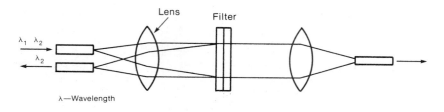

Figure 13.9   Wave division multiplex.

lightwave regenerator has back-to-back receiver and transmitter pairs that connect through a pulse reshaping circuit.

Fiber optic systems accept standard digital signals at the input, but each manufacturer develops its own output signal rate. Error checking and zero suppression bits are inserted to maintain synchronization and to monitor the bit error rate to determine when to switch to the protection channel. Because of differences in the line signals, lightwave systems are usually not end-to-end compatible between manufacturers.

Wavelength Division Multiplexing

The capacity of a fiber pair can be multiplied by using *wavelength division multiplexing* (WDM). WDM assigns services to different light wavelengths in much the same manner as frequency division multiplexing applies multiple carriers to a coaxial cable. Different wavelengths, or *colors*, of light are selected by using light sensitive filters to combine light wavelengths at the sending end and separate them at the receiving end as Figure 13.9 shows. Because the filter introduces loss, WDM reduces the distance between regenerators and limits the path length by the wavelength with the highest loss. When engineers design lightwave systems, they normally provide enough system gain to compensate for future wave division multiplexing even if it is not used initially.

Star Couplers

One limitation of fiber optics is that it is usable only for point-to-point service. It is difficult to tap optical fiber, which limits its use in multipoint applications. This disadvantage is of no concern in applications such as long haul and metropolitan trunks because these services are point-to-point by nature. However, local networks characterized by multiple terminals needing rapid access to one another require multiple access. To accomplish this, *star couplers* connect multiple terminals to a central point. The star coupler radiates the light wave equally into all branches through a reflector or an active device to boost the signal before it is transmitted. The primary application for a star coupler is in local area networks.

Lightwave System Design Criteria

Fiber optic systems are designed by balancing capacity requirements with the cost of cable, cable placement, terminal equipment, and regenerators. In most systems, a prime objective is to eliminate midspan regenerator points so regenerators are placed only in buildings housing other telecommunications equipment. This objective may require reducing bit rates, providing higher quality cable, and stretching the system design to preclude future WDM. The three primary criteria for evaluating a system are:

- Information transfer rate.
- System attenuation and losses.
- Cutoff wavelength.

Information Transfer Rate

The information transfer rate of a fiber optic system depends on the bandwidth, which in turn depends on the dispersion rate and the distance between terminal or repeater points. Manufacturers quote bandwidth in graded index fiber as a product of length and frequency. For example, a fiber specification of 1500 MHz-km could be deployed as a 150 MHz system at 10 km or a 30 MHz system at 50 km. Fiber optic transmission systems are quoted according to the number of DS-3 systems they can support, with current commercial products ranging from fewer than one to more than 36 DS-3 systems per pair. Typical values are 1, 2, 3, 6, 9, 12, 18, 24, and 36 DS-3s. Special purpose fiber optic systems intended for short range private data transmission have much lower bit rates and typically use cables with considerably more bandwidth than the application requires.

System Attenuation and Losses

In any fiber system, a key objective is to avoid placing repeaters between terminals, if possible, because of the expense of right-of-way and maintenance. Therefore the system loss and attenuation, together with available bandwidth, are key factors in determining usable range. As with microwave systems, in fiber optics system gain is the difference between transmitter output power and receiver sensitivity. For example, a system with a transmitter output of -5 dBm and a receiver sensitivity of -40 dBm has a system gain of 35 dB.

From the system gain, designers compute a *loss budget*, which is the amount of cable loss that can be tolerated within the available system gain. Besides cable loss, allowances must be made for:

- Loss of initial splices, plus an allowance for future maintenance splices.
- Loss of connectors used to couple fibers and terminal equipment.
- Temperature variations.
- Measurement inaccuracies.
- Future WDM.
- Safety margin.
- Aging of electronic components.

These additional losses typically subtract about 10 to 12 dB from the span between terminal points, which leaves a loss budget of about 25 dB for cable. Cable cost depends on loss, so system designers choose a cable grade to match the loss budget.

Cutoff Wavelength

The cutoff wavelength is the longest wavelength that can be transmitted within allowable loss limits and is based on future plans for WDM. With present technology, products under development are expected to support wavelengths of 1500 nm. or more.

Fiber Optics in the Local Loop

Now that a substantial portion of the interexchange network is converted to fiber optics, the telephone companies are turning to the next potential application, the local loop. Most major LECs are conducting trials on local loop fiber optics, but the results at this point are inconclusive. Lightwave does not find the natural match in the loop that it does in interexchange plant for a simple reason: residences do not have the bandwidth requirements. Future services, such as high definition television (HDTV), will require bandwidths that are ideally supported on fiber optics, but the cost of placing the cable remains a barrier to rapid development.

Local loop fiber will likely assume one of two architectures. The easiest approach is to replace feeder cable (see Chapter 6) with fiber. Fiber extends from the central office to a serving area interface point where it connects to digital loop carrier (DLC). The loop from the serving area interface to the customer's premises is copper cable, which greatly simplifies the interface problem and overcomes the problem of feeding power to the customer's station. The second form of local loop fiber optic provides fiber direct to the customer's premises. In some trials, two fibers are installed, one for voice and data communication and the other for video.

The rationale behind the fiber-to-the-residence architecture is the assumption that television-on-demand will eventually require fiber. When this service develops, the user will select from a menu of educational and entertainment programs and have the program delivered to the premises over the loop. This facility could be particularly advantageous when HDTV standards are established. Chapter 17 discusses video services in more detail.

The state of development of HDTV is not far enough advanced that it has any effect on demand for fiber-to-the-premises. Video compression equipment is prohibitively expensive for an entertainment medium today, although the cost of codecs will drop as demand increases. It is technically feasible to transmit a standard analog television signal over fiber, but to do so offers little advantage over signals transmitted over the coaxial cables that are in place in most neighborhoods today.

The real demand for fiber in the local loop is for business. The two driving factors are an increase in DS-3 services, which cannot be transmitted for long distances over twisted pair wire, and an increase in the demand for broadband services. Many LECs already provide fiber optic capacity in metropolitan areas to serve business, so this form of growth does not greatly affect local loop technology. Fiber optics will eventually become a dominant local loop medium, but before that happens it must become cost competitive with copper, and bandwidth requirements must grow to a level that cannot be economically served with alternative media. Meanwhile, several issues must be resolved. One is how to solve the problem of furnishing power to customer premises. It cannot be done over fiber optic cable, so if the customer is left to supply power, telephone outages will follow power outages, which will result in a reduction of telephone service. The second issue is whether multimode or single-mode fiber is the preferred medium. Most of the LEC field trials are using single-mode fiber; however, multimode offers sufficient range for most loops, reduced cost, and greater ease of splicing.

Undersea Fiber Optic Cables

Intercontinental communications services, which have, until recently, been the province of satellite and conventional voice cables, are rapidly shifting to fiber optics. The first transoceanic fiber optic cable, the TAT-8, became operational in 1988. TAT-8 can carry 40,000 simultaneous conversations. By comparison, the first undersea cable between Europe and the United States, TAT-1, could carry 36 simultaneous calls. During its 22-year life span, TAT-1 carried 10 million calls, a number that TAT-8 can handle in two days. TAT-8 has six fibers; two pairs in use and a third pair for backup, with regenerators placed at 79 km. intervals. The cable is buried one meter below the ocean floor where the water is less than one km. deep. Figure 13.10 shows TAT-8 beside its much larger predecessor, TAT-7, which is a coaxial cable.

Figure 13.10 **TAT-8 transatlantic fiber optic cable shown with the larger TAT-7 coaxial cable.**
Courtesyt, AT&T Corporation

Since TAT-8, as Table 13.1 shows, large numbers of fiber cables have been placed and are planned in both the Atlantic and Pacific regions.

The rapid growth of undersea cable will inevitably bring down the price of intercontinental circuits and switched services, just as it has domestically. The availability of satellite and fiber optic circuits between continents makes route diversity feasible for those services that must have a high degree of availability.

Free Space Lightwave Transmission

Free space lightwave communication devices operate on principles similar to those that govern fiber optics, except that the signal

Table 13.1   Existing and Planned Transoceanic Fiber Optic Cables

CABLE NAME	TERMINAL POINTS	IN SERVICE
B-M-P	Brunei, Malasia, Phillipines	1991
G-P-T	Guam, Phillipines, Taiwan	1989
H-J-K	Hong Kong, Japan, South Korea	1990
HAW 4	California, Hawaii	1988
HKG-Phil	Hong Kong, Phillipines	1990
HONTAI 2	Hong Kong, Taiwan	1990
NPC	California, Alaska, Japan	1990
PAC RIM East	Honolulu, New Zealand	1993
PAC RIM West	Australia, Guam	1996
PTAT 1	US, Bermuda, United Kingdom, Ireland	1989
PTAT 2	US, United Kingdom	1992
SINHON 2	Singapore, Hong Kong	1992
TASMAN 2	New Zealand, Australia	1991
TAT 8	US, United Kingdom, France	1988
TAT 9	US, United Kingdom, France, Spain	1991
TPC 3	Honolulu, Guam, Japan	1988
TPC 4	US, Canada, Japan	1992

radiates directly from a light transmitter to a receiver mounted a mile or less away. Free space lightwave communication is subject to the same effects that cause microwave fading, only to a more significant degree. Free space lightwave has the advantage of spanning short distances without the need for securing licenses or the cost of obtaining right-of-way. It is used for short range communications, such as between buildings, or over longer ranges when path reliability is not vital.

Because of the short wavelengths involved, fog and dust particles attenuate infrared light transmission. It is also subject to fading because of differences in the refractive index of the atmosphere, which is the effect that causes shimmering mirages to appear over flat surfaces on hot days. Scattering attenuates the signal when the optical wavelength is shorter than the size of particles suspended in the atmosphere. Free space light is subject to interference from other light sources including sunlight. Even with these drawbacks, however, for many applications the low cost of this transmission medium makes it a feasible alternative compared to other media. It is particularly adaptable to short spans such as between buildings across public right-of-ways such as streets.

The cost of short range microwave radio has dropped to the point that there is little economic advantage of light transmission compared to microwave. It is faster to get a lightwave transmission system operational, however, because there is no FCC licensing requirement.

Applications

Lightwave communications systems have applications in both private and public communications systems. The primary applications are:

- Long haul transmission systems.
- Local trunking.
- Metropolitan area backbone systems.
- Digital loop carrier feeder systems.
- Local area networks.
- Cable television backbone transmission systems.
- Private network backbone systems.
- Short haul data transmission systems through noisy environments.

Standards

Except for special applications, the digital signal input of fiber optic systems interfaces Bell or CCITT digital signals. The manufacturer determines the output signal with no accepted standards. Therefore, fiber optic systems are not end-to-end compatible between manufacturers. EIA issues physical standards on fiber and connectors. A new set of standards known as Synchronous Optical Network (Sonet) are currently under development.

Synchronous Optical Network (Sonet)

Sonet is a new hierarchy of optical standards that will eventually replace the present digital signal hierarchy such as DS-1 and DS-3. Internationally, Sonet is known as the Synchronous Digital Hierarchy (SDH). At this writing, Sonet standards are not complete, but they should be published early in the 1990s. The initial standards, which were adopted in November, 1988, are commonly referred to as Sonet Phase 1 (ANSI T1.105 and ANSI T1.106). Phase 1 standards enable different manufacturers to build equipment that can transport data from one point to another. Phase 2 standards define the functions and message sets to be used over the Sonet channels.

Sonet standards are defined in 48 increments. OC-1 (Office Channel 1), the lowest level on the hierarchy, is the basic Sonet building block. OC-1 can carry and becomes the envelope for a DS-3 (45 mb/s) signal. In the Sonet design, OC-1 is known as Synchronous Transport Signal-Level 1 (STS-1), which has a synchronous frame structure and a speed of 51.840 mb/s. The synchronous frame structure makes it possible to extract DS-1 signals without disassembling the entire frame. At OC-3, which is 155.520 mb/s, the North American and European standards converge. Within Sonet are *virtual tributaries*, which enable transmission of non-standard bandwidths through Sonet frames. The top level of the Sonet hierarchy, OC-48, is 2488.320 mb/s. Table 13.2 lists the line rates of the principal Sonet levels. The standard supports up to 2.5 gb/s now, but it can be extended to more than 13 gb/s if necessary.

Sonet begins with an eight-bit byte repeated every 125 microseconds, the same as the European and North American basic voice channel of 64 kb/s. Sets of 810 bytes form a 51.840 mb/s OC-1 signal, which is known as STS-1. Multiple STS-1 signals interleave to form the higher levels. The STS-1 signals comprise two elements, a synchronous payload envelope (SPE) and data communication channels (DCC). The DCCs are overhead used for maintenance, monitoring, control, and alarm functions. The SPE carries the actual traffic.

Sonet will be used widely by LECs to deliver clear channel DS-1 and DS-3 digital services between offices and directly to end users.

**Table 13.2 North American Sonet
OCC Levels and Line Rates**

OC LEVEL	LINE RATE MB/S
OC-1	51.840
OC-3	155.520
OC-9	466.560
OC-12	622.080
OC-18	933.120
OC-24	1244.160
OC-36	1866.240
OC-48	2488.320

As bandwidth demand increases, Sonet will probably be the physical layer technology that the LECs use to carry services from the customer's premises to the central office, where they can access a variety of services including broadband ISDN (see Chapter 26). B-ISDN standards are not part of Sonet, but the two standards will be compatible. OC-3 will be used as the primary transport for the B-ISDN signal.

Application Criteria

The high cost of right-of-way often stands in the way of companies' installing fiber optic systems, but the advantages of this medium will undoubtedly result in more private applications. The following are ways companies can apply fiber optics.

Campus and Building Backbone Networks. Fiber optics is an excellent medium for a campus or building backbone. Many systems, such as IBM's token ring, employ a fiber backbone. Fiber optics not only provides bandwidth but also offers security and noise immunity that no other medium can match. Any campus or riser cable system should at least consider the potential future need for fiber optics. Either fiber pairs should be installed for future expansion or empty conduit should be installed to support future fiber.

Fiber to the Desktop.   The experts are in agreement about using fiber as a backbone in a building or campus network, but the question of carrying it all the way to the desktop is still open. Unshielded twisted pair (UTP) is still much cheaper than fiber optic cable. UTP has enough bandwidth for most applications and must be installed anyway, since fiber is not an alternative for voice. Fiber optics is an ideal transmission medium for LANs, but the cost of terminating equipment is at least an order of magnitude higher for fiber than for UTP. In today's environment, fiber to the desktop can be justified only if the application has a genuine need for high bandwidth or if there is an overriding consideration, such as security, that mandates the use of fiber.

If fiber is not feasible today, should it be installed today and left dark to support a future application? The answer to this question depends on economics. Many buildings are difficult to wire, and placing a composite fiber and UTP cable to desktops may make economic sense because so much of the cost is in installation labor. The chief question to evaluate here is whether the location of future applications can be foreseen reliably enough to justify the expense of fiber optics.

Video Systems.   Until the last few years, the lack of reasonably priced linear modulators has limited the use of fiber optics for video. Fiber is an ideal medium for digitized video, but the high cost of compression equipment has made video prohibitive for many non-commercial applications. Now, the transmission of analog television signals over fiber is technically feasible, although fiber is more expensive than coaxial cable.

Environmental Concerns.   Fiber optics has a far greater ability to survive in hostile environments than copper cable. The fiber itself is essentially immune to damage from water, caustic chemicals, and a corrosive atmosphere. However, care should be taken to ensure that the outer sheath is equally immune to the environment.

Fiber is also immune to electromagnetic interference, which may impair UTP or even coaxial cables. This makes fiber ideal in industrial environments where heavy equipment may radiate interference. The elevator shaft, for example, is an acceptable housing for riser cables in some buildings, but the motors and controls may cause noise in twisted pair. This is not a problem with fiber.

Security Concerns.   Fiber optic systems offer a high degree of security. They are almost impossible to tap undetected, and if properly constructed they can meet TEMPEST standards. TEMPEST is a Department of Defense specification that stands for Transient Electromagnetic Pulse Emanation Standard. Equipment that meets TEMPEST standards must restrict the radiation of energy that could be picked up by nearby devices. Organizations that have sensitive information that could be compromised will find that fiber optics offers security that is unequaled by other media.

Evaluation Criteria

Fiber optic equipment is purchased either as an integrated package of terminal equipment and cable for specialized private applications or as separate components assembled into a system for trunking between switching nodes. For the former applications, which include local area, point-to-point voice, data, and video networks, the evaluation criteria discussed below are not critical. In such systems, the main question is whether the total system fits the application. In all fiber optic systems the questions of reliability, technical support, cost, and compatibility are important. Fiber optic systems do not vary widely in their power consumption or space requirements, so these criteria may usually be safely ignored. In longer range trunking applications, the following criteria should be considered in evaluating a system.

System Gain

In selecting lightwave terminating equipment, the higher the system gain, the more gain is available to overcome cable and other losses. The cost of a lightwave system relates directly to the amount of system gain. High output lasers and high sensitivity diodes are more expensive than devices that produce less system gain. The least expensive transmitters use light emitting diodes for output and have less system gain than lasers. When the limits of lightwave range are being approached, obtaining equipment with maximum system gain is important. For applications with ample design margin, low system gain is acceptable.

Cable Characteristics

Cable is graded according to its loss and bandwidth. The cable grade should be selected to provide the loss and bandwidth needed to support the ultimate circuit requirement. If the cable can support the ultimate requirements, there is little reason to spend extra money to purchase a higher grade. Unless some compelling reason exists for purchasing multimode cable, single-mode cable should be purchased for all applications. The price of single-mode fiber is approximately the same as the price of multimode, and its greater bandwidth makes it considerably more valuable for future expansion. The cable composition should be selected with inner strength members sufficient to prevent damage when the cable is pulled through conduits or plowed in the ground. Armoring should be considered where sheath damage hazards exist.

In private applications, the core size of multimode cable is an important consideration. There are no universally accepted standards, but the trend is toward 62.5/125 micron cable. This designation means that the cable has a core diameter of 62.5 microns and an external diameter of 125 microns. Cable with cores of 50, 85, and 100 microns and outer diameters of 140 microns or more is also available. IBM specifies 100/140 micron fiber for its backbone networks. It is important to match the cable to the application. A company that uses IBM computers and token ring networks should follow IBM's specifications and use 100/140 micron fiber. If the application has not been selected, and cable is being placed for future applications, the safest choice is 62.5/125 micron cable.

Wavelength

With present technology, the most practical wavelength to choose is 1300 nm. FDDI specifications call for 1300 nm. cable with a bandwidth of at least 500 MHz-km. Cable should be purchased with a 1550 nm. window if circuit requirements will ultimately justify the use of WDM. For most applications, 850 nm. should be avoided because of its greater loss. Exceptions are in local networks and private networks implemented by using leased fibers. With leased fibers, the 850 nm. window can be used with WDM as a way of increasing capacity without leasing more fiber, providing the distance between terminals supports the use of 850 nm. and WDM. In other applications, such as local networks, the wavelength may be predetermined by the manufacturer. If the total system has enough gain and bandwidth to support the application, the wavelength is of little or no concern to the user.

Light Source

The two choices for light source are laser and LED. Both are semiconductor devices that emit light when an external voltage is applied. A laser has much higher power output than a LED and can operate at higher bit rates. An LED costs less and lasts longer, but it produces a wider beam of light and has a wider spectral width, which means that its light wavelength is broader than that of a laser.

LEDs are typically used where the distance between terminals is short—normally 10 km. or less—and the bandwidth of the signal is lower than about 150 mb/s. An LED is generally satisfactory for local networks. In long haul networks where long repeater spacing and high bandwidth are important, a laser is the device of choice.

System Integration

In some applications, such as local networks, fiber cable and terminal equipment are purchased as part of a total system designed and furnished by one vendor. In most applications, however, terminal equipment and cable are purchased from separate vendors. Because fiber optic equipment is not standardized, it is advisable to purchase cable through the terminal equipment vendor or to the equipment vendor's specifications so the equipment vendor can assume responsibility for total system operation.

Wavelength Division Multiplexing

Deciding whether to plan a fiber optics system with future WDM designed into the transmission plan requires the manager to balance future capacity requirements and current costs. WDM can double or triple the capacity of a fiber pair for little additional cost, or it can enable a single optical fiber to perform full duplex operation by transmitting in both directions on the same fiber. It accomplishes this by reducing regenerator spacing, however, which is important in long systems but unimportant in systems that do not require intermediate regenerators. In very short systems, the cost of the WDM equipment may be greater than the cost of extra fibers.

Selected Lightwave Product Manufacturers

Lightguide Cable

AMP, Inc.

Alcatel Cable Systems

Alcoa Fujikura Ltd.

AT&T Network Systems

Belden Wire and Cable

Corning Glass Works, Telecommunications Products Div.

Northern Telecom Inc., Optical Systems Division

Siecor Corporation

Sumitomo Electric Fiber Optics Corp.

Superior Optics

US Fiber Optics, Inc.

Lightwave Transmission Products

Alcatel Network Systems Corp.

AT&T Network Systems

Fujitsu America

GTE Communication Systems

Harris Corporation Fiber Optic Systems

Jerrold Communications

LDC Inc. Fiber Optics Communications

Licom

NEC America Inc., Radio & Transmission Div.

Northern Telecom Inc., Optical Systems Division

PCO Inc.

Rockwell International Network Transmission Systems

Stromberg Carlson Corp.

Telco Systems Fiber Optics Corp.

Fiber Optic Test Equipment

Advantest America, Inc.

Alcoa Fujikura Ltd.

American Laser Systems, Inc.

Ando Corporation

Anritsu America Corp.

AT&T Network Systems

Broadband Communications Products

GTE Fiber Optic Products

Industrial Technology, Inc.

Photon Kinetics

Siecor Corporation

Infrared Transmission Equipment

Light Communications
Corporation

NEC America Inc., Radio &
Transmission Div.

Opto-Electronics, Inc.

Optical Switches

AMP

APA Optics

BT&D Technologies

Crystal Technology, Inc.

DiCon Fiberoptics

Splicing Equipment and Connectors

3M Fiber Optic Products, Inc.

Alcatel Cable Systems

Alcoa Fujikura

AMP NETCON Division

American Lightwave Systems

Amphenol Corporation

AT&T Network Systems

Corning Telecommunications
Products Div.

Ensign-Bickford Optics Co.

Ericsson

Gould Inc. Fiber Optics
Operation

Kaptron, Inc.

Light Control Systems, Inc.

Northern Telecom

OFTI

Opto Electronics, Inc.

Power Technology, Inc.

Preformed Line Products Co.

Siecor Corporation

Sumitomo Electric Fiber Optics

US Fiber Optics, Inc.

14

Microwave Radio Systems

From the end of World War II until the mid-1980s, microwave radio increased in importance as a long haul transmission medium. The major interexchange carriers used backbone microwave routes to haul large quantities of circuits across the United States. With the introduction of fiber optic transmission facilities, the use of microwave by the IECs has declined, but microwave is far from an obsolete medium. For private organizations that have limited ability to acquire the right-of-way that fiber routes demand, microwave is the only practical method of bridging obstructions such as highways, lakes, and rivers. Short haul microwave in the 18 GHz and 23 GHz bands has assumed increasing importance in metropolitan areas, and satellites remain important users of microwave frequency spectrum. (GHz is the abbreviation for gigaHertz, which is one billion Hertz.)

Short haul microwave is a logical choice as a bypass technology for private networks. The equipment is reliable and inexpensive, licensing procedures and installation are uncomplicated, and ample frequency spectrum is available. In the 18 GHZ and 23 GHz bands, a total of 4.4 GHz of bandwidth is available. This bandwidth is more than four times the *entire* radio frequency spectrum below the microwave region. For private networks, the emphasis in microwave is shifting toward these higher frequency systems because of the ease of applying them.

The primary drawback of microwave results from its free space radiation. Although the available bandwidth is enormous, it is still a limited resource, and users must coordinate microwave paths to prevent interference. Because of congestion in metropolitan areas, it is often impossible to obtain frequency assignments in the lower end of the band. Table 14.1 lists the microwave common carrier and industrial, or operational fixed, frequency band assignments in the United States.

Table 14.1 Common Carrier and Operational Fixed (industrial) Microwave Frequency Allocations in the United States

COMMON CARRIER	OPERATIONAL FIXED
2.110 2.130 GHz	1.850 1.990 GHz
2.160 2.180 GHz	2.130 2.150 GHz
3.700 4.200 GHz	2.180 2.200 GHz
5.925 6.425 GHz	2.500 2.690 GHz (television)
10.7 11.700 GHz	6.575 6.875 GHz
	12.2 12.700 GHz*

* Based on noninterference with direct broadcast satellite service.

Microwave Characteristics

The general principles of microwave radio are the same as those of lower frequency radio. A radio frequency (rf) signal is generated, modulated, amplified, and coupled to a transmitting antenna. It travels through free space to a receiving antenna where a receiver captures a portion of the radiated energy and amplifies and demodulates it. The primary differences between microwave and lower frequency radio are the wavelength and behavior of the radio waves. For example, VHF television channel 2 has a wavelength of about 20 feet. To gain the maximum efficiency, a half-wave antenna receiving element is about 10 feet long. A 4 GHz microwave signal has a wavelength of about 3 inches, so an effective antenna at microwave frequencies is small compared to those at lower frequencies.

At microwave frequencies, radio waves behave similarly to light waves. They can be focused with large parabolic, or horn, antennas similar to the Gabriel UHR-6 antennas shown in Figure 14.1, or they can be reflected with large, flat, passive reflectors, such as the one shown in Figure 14.2, to redirect the path around obstructions.

A second significant feature of microwave is the amount of bandwidth available in the microwave spectrum. To put this bandwidth in perspective, assume that the effective microwave frequencies extend from 2 GHz to 24 GHz (higher frequency bands are usable, but at short repeater spacing). This 22 GHz of bandwidth is 11 times the total frequency spectrum, ranging from very low frequency to the bottom of the microwave band. The essential point is that, although bandwidth is limited, a significant amount is available for point-to-point communication in the microwave bands, and competition for it is intense.

A third essential characteristic of microwave also relates to its lightwave-like behavior. Because microwaves follow line-of-sight paths, it is possible to operate stations in physical proximity without interference. On lower frequencies, radio waves cannot be focused narrowly enough to prevent them from radiating in all directions and interfering with other services on the same frequency.

On the minus side of the ledger, microwaves have some of the undesirable characteristics of light waves, particularly at the higher frequencies. The primary problem is fading. Microwave fading is caused by multipath reflections and attenuation by heavy rain. Multipath reflections occur when the main radio wave travels a straight path between antennas, but a portion of it reflects over a second path as Figure 14.3 shows. The reflected path is caused by some changing condition such as a temperature inversion, a heavy cloud layer, or reflection off a layer of ground fog. The reflected wave, taking a longer path, arrives at the receiving antenna slightly out of phase with the transmitted wave. The two waves added out of phase cause a drop in the received signal level. A second cause of fading is heavy rain, which absorbs part of the transmitted power at frequencies higher than about 10 GHz. The two primary causes of microwave path disruption, fading and equipment failures, are partially alleviated by diversity as described in a later section.

Figure 14.1   Gabriel UHR-6 microwave antennas.
Courtesy, Gabriel Electronics, Inc.

Figure 14.2   A billboard microwave reflector.
Courtesy, Gabriel Electronics, Inc.

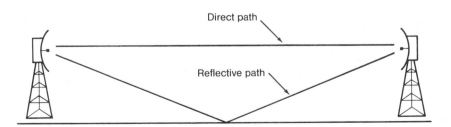

Figure 14.3   Directed and reflected microwave paths between antennas.

Microwave Technology

Microwave routes are established by connecting a series of independent radio paths with repeater stations. Line of sight is required between the transmitting antenna and the receiving antenna for all microwave systems except those that use forward scatter techniques to transmit beyond the horizon. Repeater spacing varies with frequency, transmitter output power, antenna gain, antenna height, receiver sensitivity, number of voice frequency channels carried, free space loss of the radio path, and depth of expected fading. At the high end of the band, repeaters are spaced as close as 1 mile. At the low end of the band repeater spacings of up to 100 miles are possible.

Modulation Methods

Microwave systems are broadly classed as digital or analog, depending on the modulation method. When the primary use of microwave was for long haul telephone service, most microwave was analog. Now, with the growth of digital services, demand has shifted to digital radio.

Analog Modulation Methods

Analog radio is either amplitude or frequency modulated, with the latter comprising the bulk of analog equipment in service today. Recent developments have proven the suitability of single sideband (SSB) modulation for long haul analog microwave. The primary advantage of SSB is that it uses bandwidth more efficiently than FM does. In the 30 MHz bandwidth of the 6 GHz common carrier band, 2400 voice channels is the theoretical limit that current FM technology can support while meeting channel noise objectives. This is an efficiency of 12.5 KHz of microwave bandwidth per voice frequency channel. With SSB AM, modern equipment can carry up to 6000 channels for an efficiency of 5 KHz per voice frequency channel.

Digital Modulation

Direct modulation of an rf carrier with a digital signal has been commercially feasible since about 1975. The principal limit before that time was the FCC requirement that digital radio use the spectrum as efficiently as analog radio. The problem with digital radio lies in the 64 kb/s coding of the voice channels. With a coding scheme that yields one bit per Hz of bandwidth, a digital channel would occupy 64 KHz, compared to the 12.5 KHz bandwidth efficiency of an FM analog radio. This excessive consumption of frequency spectrum impeded the use of digital radio until more efficient modulation methods could be developed. The earliest systems used phase shift modulation. Two radio channels were applied to the same frequency on cross-polarized antennas. Cross polarization means that one radio operates with vertically polarized waves and the other radio with horizontally polarized waves. When the system works properly, the cross-polarization discrimination is enough to prevent interference between channels on the same frequency.

Later modulation systems employ more efficient phase shift keying (PSK) or quadrature amplitude modulation (QAM) systems. QAM, which is the system used in the latest microwave generation, is a simultaneous amplitude modulation phase shift system. The earliest are 16 QAM systems, which support 1344 voice channels (two DS-3s) on a 30 MHz radio channel at 90 mb/s for an efficiency of 3 bits per Hz. The latest technology, 64 QAM, supports 2014 channels (three DS-3s) at 135 mb/s for a spectral efficiency of 4.5 bits per Hz.

The major advantage of digital radio results from regeneration of the signal at each repeater point. If the incoming signal is sufficiently free of interference to allow the demodulator to distinguish between 0s and 1s, digital radio provides the same high quality, low noise channel that T carrier provides. Unlike analog radio, which becomes progressively noisy during fades, however, digital radio remains quiet until it fades to a failure threshold, at which point the bit error rate (BER) becomes excessive and the radio "crashes."

Although each repeater regenerates the signal, errors are cumulative from station to station and cannot be corrected unless the radio employs forward error correction. Therefore the errors that occur in one section repeat in the next section where additional errors may occur, until finally the signal becomes unsuitable for data transmission. For voice, however, the errors have relatively little effect.

Besides the advantage of higher quality, digital microwave offers the advantage of directly interfacing T-1 carrier circuits without use of channel banks. This is particularly advantageous for transporting circuits between digital switching systems.

Bit Error Rate

The most important measure of digital microwave radio performance is the bit error rate (BER). BER is expressed as the number of errored bits per transmitted bit, and usually is abbreviated as an exponential fraction. For example, one error per billion transmitted bits is expressed as 10^{-9}. In a 90 mb/s system this would result in an average of one error in 11.1 seconds for the entire radio. The error rate in an individual channel would, of course, be much less. A BER of 10^{-6} is generally accepted as the highest that can be tolerated for digital data transmission over microwave. At a BER of 10^{-3} a radio is considered failed, although voice transmission can still take place at this error rate.

Diversity

To guard against the effects of equipment and path failure, microwave systems use protection or diversity. Engineers provide *space diversity* by spacing receiving antennas several feet apart on the same tower. This system protects against multipath fading because the wavelength of the signal is so short that the phase cancellation that occurs at one location will have little effect on an antenna located a few feet away.

Another protection system, permitted on common carrier bands, is *frequency diversity*. This system uses a separate radio channel operating at a different frequency to assume the load of a failed channel. When fades occur they tend to affect only one frequency at a time, so frequency diversity provides a high degree of path reliability. The primary disadvantages of this system are the use of the extra frequency spectrum and the cost of the additional radio equipment.

FCC rules do not permit frequency diversity in most non-common carrier frequency bands. Therefore, many microwave systems use *hot standby* diversity. In a hot standby system, two transmitter and receiver pairs connect to the antenna, but only one system is working at a time. When the working system fails, the hot standby unit automatically assumes the circuit load. Hot standby protection is effective only against equipment failure. Hot standby cannot protect against fading and absorption, which affect the microwave path between stations.

Transfer to a protection system is initiated by the received noise level in an analog radio or by BER in a digital radio. When the noise or BER becomes excessive on a protected channel, the diversity switch initiator sends an order to the transmitting end to switch the entire input signal to the protection channel. Technicians can initiate switches manually to clear a channel for maintenance. In any protection system, some loss of signal is experienced before the protection channel assumes the load. Many systems can perform a *hitless* switch when a channel is manually transferred, but if equipment fails or fades, degradation will be experienced in the form of noise, excessive data errors, or both.

Protection systems protect working channels on a one-by-one or one-by-N basis with N being the number of working channels on the route. The FCC does not permit one-by-one protection where the application requires more than one radio channel because this method is wasteful of frequency spectrum. Figure 14.4 illustrates the three applications of protection—frequency diversity, space diversity, and hot standby.

Microwave Impairments

Microwave signals are subject to impairments from these sources:

- Equipment, antenna, and waveguide failures.
- Fading and distortion from multipath reflections.
- Absorption from rain, fog, and other atmospheric conditions.
- Interference from other signals.

Microwave reliability is expressed as percent availability, or uptime, which is the percentage of the time communications circuits on a channel are usable. The starting point on a microwave path calculation is to determine the number of hours of path downtime that can be tolerated in a year. For example, eight hours per year of path outage would equate to 99.91% availability from the following formula:

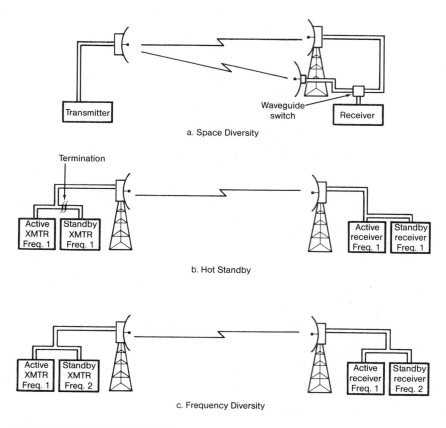

a. Space Diversity

b. Hot Standby

c. Frequency Diversity

Figure 14.4   Microwave diversity systems.

$$\text{Percent Availability} = 1 - \frac{\text{outage hours}}{8760 \text{ hours per year}}$$

Because of path uncertainties, a satisfactory reliability level is attainable only with highly reliable equipment. Fortunately, equipment reliability has progressed to the point that equipment failures cause little downtime, and those failures that do occur can be protected by diversity. Most private microwave systems require at least 99.99% availability. Bear in mind that microwave path failures do not usually last long. An hour per year of outage caused by rain fades is more likely to occur as 60 outages of 1 minute each than as one failure of 60 minutes.

Microwave Path Analysis

Microwave path reliability is less predictable and controllable than equipment performance. The first factor to consider in laying out a microwave system is obtaining a properly analyzed and engineered path. The path designer selects repeater sites for availability of real estate, lack of interference with existing services, accessibility for maintenance, and sufficient elevation to overcome obstacles in the path.

The first step in microwave path analysis is to prepare a balance sheet of gains and losses of the radio signal between transmitter and receiver. Gains and losses are measured in decibels or dB, a concept that Appendix A explains. The dB is a measure of relative power gains and losses. Absolute measures of signal level are measured in decibels compared to one milliwatt (0 dBm). One milliwatt is equal to 1×10^{-3} watts of power. A signal of +30 dBm is equal to one watt, a signal output that is typical of many microwave transmitters.

The spreadsheet in Figure 14.5 shows a sample microwave path calculation. The following explains the elements that comprise the calculation and provide information from which a similar spreadsheet can be constructed.

The *transmitter output power* is obtained from the manufacturer's specifications. For systems in the lower end of the microwave band, power is often 5 watts or more; for systems in the higher end of the spectrum power is a fraction of a watt. Power outputs of +12 to +20 dBm are common at 18 and 23 GHz. Remember that one watt is +30 dBm, so with the logarithmic nature of the decibel scale, a reduction of 10 dB is a reduction factor of 10. Therefore, +20 dBm is 0.1 watt.

Antenna gain can overcome the low powers in the 18 GHz to 23 GHz band. Although the industry commonly uses the term antenna gain, it is somewhat of a misnomer because an antenna is a passive device that is incapable of amplifying the signal. Gain

SITE NAME	Mt. Baldy	Three Peaks
Path length (miles)	5.2	
Frequency (GHz)	23	
Gains		
Transmitter output power (dBm)	20.5	20.5
Antenna gain	46.0	38.0
Total gains	66.5	58.5
Losses		
Free space	-138.2	-138.2
Atmospheric	-0.8	-0.8
Antenna alignment	-0.5	-0.5
Safety factor	-0.5	-0.5
Total losses	-140.0	-140.0
Unfaded receive signal level	73.5	81.5
Receiver sensitivity	74.5	74.5
Fade margin	39.0	31.0

Figure 14.5   Worksheet for analyzing a microwave path.

is a relative term compared to the performance of a free space mounted dipole, or *isotropic* antenna. Figure 14.6 illustrates this concept, which shows the difference between a dipole radiating equally in all directions and a microwave antenna that focuses the signal to provide a narrower beam consisting of a major center lobe and side lobes of lesser intensity. The amount of gain is proportional to the physical characteristics of the antenna, primarily its diameter. Generally, the greater the diameter of the antenna, the greater its gain. Also, for a given diameter of antenna, the gain increases as frequency increases and wavelength decreases. Because the wavelength is very short at these frequencies (1 centimeter, or slightly less than 0.5 inch, at 30 GHz), antennas with gains in the order of 40 dB or more are readily available without the high cost of both antennas and tower structures required by large diameter antennas.

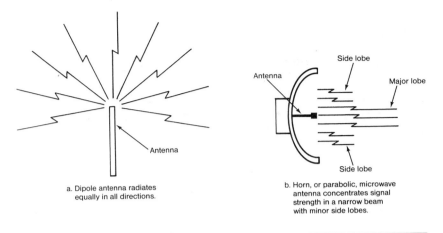

a. Dipole antenna radiates equally in all directions.

b. Horn, or parabolic, microwave antenna concentrates signal strength in a narrow beam with minor side lobes.

Figure 14.6   Antenna radiation patterns.

Antenna gain is obtained from manufacturers' specifications. The size of the antenna is one variable that is reasonably easy to change to improve path reliability. Note that antenna gain operates in both transmitting and receiving directions. It is not necessary to choose the same antenna gain for both ends of a microwave path.

The factor that has the most influence on path loss is *free space attenuation*, which can be calculated by the formula:

$$A = 96.6 + 20 \log P_L + 20 \log F$$

Where:

A = free space attenuation in dB
P_L = path length in miles
F = frequency in GHz

In addition to free space attenuation, *atmospheric losses* are caused by absorption of the signal by oxygen molecules and water vapor in the atmosphere. This factor should not be confused with rain attenuation, which is covered later. Generally, atmospheric losses can be estimated at 0.12 dB per mile at 18 GHz and 0.16 dB per mile at 23 GHz.

The *antenna alignment factor*—usually about 0.5 dB—is a factor that designers choose to reflect the imperfect alignment of antennas. When antennas are installed, they are aligned on major radiation lobes. With time, temperature changes and tower shifting because of wind stress may cause the signal to drift slightly. This factor is added to provide a margin of safety. Besides the antenna alignment factor, other safety factors should be added to account for other imperfections. Usually another 0.5 dB of loss is added to be conservative.

Gains and losses are algebraically added to find the *unfaded received signal level*. This is the signal level that should be received at the input to the receiver in the absence of conditions such as rain that cause fade. The manufacturer supplies the *receiver sensitivity* figure as the minimum signal level that will provide a bit error rate of 10^{-6} or better. If the unfaded received signal level is added algebraically to the receiver sensitivity, the result is the *fade margin*, which is the amount of fading the signal can tolerate.

If fading did not occur, it would be easy to calculate a reliable microwave path using the above formulas. Fading occurs, however, and the major cause at frequencies above about 10 GHz is rain. At these frequencies the raindrop size is a significant fraction of the signal wavelength (wavelength is about one inch at 10 GHz). The rain rate that will attenuate the microwave signal by an amount equal to the fade margin is called the *critical rain rate*. The most important factor is not so much the amount of rain that falls, but the nature of the rain. The larger the raindrops and the more intense the rainfall, the greater the attenuation and the higher the probability of outage.

Absorption is a most significant impairment in areas of heavy rainfall with large drop size such as the Gulf Coast and southeastern United States. Conventional diversity is not effective against rain absorption because rain fading is not frequency selective. The most effective defenses are frequency diversity using a lower band such as 6 GHz, if permitted by the FCC, use of large antennas, and closely spaced repeater stations. The easiest method of obtaining rainfall data is from the microwave manufacturers, who usually can estimate the number of minutes and frequency of outage that will be caused by rain in your part of the country.

Fresnel Zone Clearance

In microwave path engineering, it is not enough to have line-of-sight communication between stations; it is also necessary to have a minimum clearance over obstacles. If insufficient clearance exists over buildings, terrain, or large bodies of water, the path will be unreliable because of reflection, or path bending.

The amount of clearance required over an obstruction is expressed in terms of *Fresnel zones*. A Fresnel zone is an imaginary elliptical zone surrounding the direct microwave beam. The first Fresnel zone is calculated by the formula:

$$FZ_1 = 72.2 \sqrt{\frac{D1 \times D2}{F \times D}}$$

Where:

F1 = the radius of the first Fresnel zone in feet

D1 = the distance from the transmitter to the reflection point in miles

D2 = the distance from the reflection point to the receiver in miles

F= the frequency in GHz

D = the length of the signal path in miles

To illustrate the principle of Fresnel zone calculations, refer to Figure 14.7, in which a signal is beamed between two buildings 5.2 miles apart with an obstruction 2.1 miles from one transmitter. The first Fresnel zone is calculated to be 16.8 feet. For best results, the clearance over the obstacle should be one Fresnel zone, but satisfactory results will usually be obtained if the clearance is at least 0.6 Fresnel zone, which in this case is 10 feet. If the clearance is insufficient, multipath fading will result.

Multipath Fading

Multipath fading is a source of impairment in both analog and digital microwave. It is caused by conditions that reflect a portion of the signal so both the main wave and the reflected wave arrive at the receiving antenna slightly out of phase. The phase differences between the two signals cause a reduction in the received

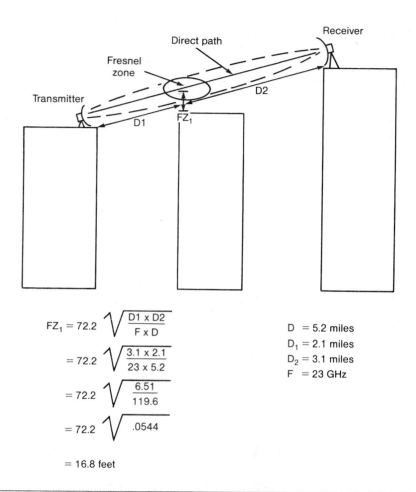

$$FZ_1 = 72.2 \sqrt{\frac{D1 \times D2}{F \times D}}$$

$$= 72.2 \sqrt{\frac{3.1 \times 2.1}{23 \times 5.2}}$$

$$= 72.2 \sqrt{\frac{6.51}{119.6}}$$

$$= 72.2 \sqrt{.0544}$$

$$= 16.8 \text{ feet}$$

D = 5.2 miles
D_1 = 2.1 miles
D_2 = 3.1 miles
F = 23 GHz

Figure 14.7   Fresnel zone clearance over an obstruction.

signal level. Multipath reflections usually do not affect all frequencies within a band equally, which results in signal distortion within the received pass band. Distortion is of particular concern with digital microwave, which is susceptible to a higher BER under multipath fading conditions. One way of minimizing the effects of distortion is to use an *adaptive equalizer*, a device inserted in the receiver to cancel the effects of distortion within the passband. Digital radio specifications usually include the *dispersive fade margin*, which states the tolerance of the radio for the frequency selective fades that cause received signal distortion.

Both frequency and space diversity are effective defenses against multipath distortion. With a second receiving antenna mounted a few feet below the first on the same tower, the main and reflected paths do not affect the signal received in both antennas equally. The system selects the best of the two signals. Frequency diversity is also an effective defense against multipath distortion because of the frequency-selective nature of signal reflections. Frequency diversity is not, however, permitted for all types of service.

Other defenses against multipath distortion include an effective path profile study with proper site selection and sufficient tower height to provide adequate clearance over obstacles. Also, the use of large antennas focuses the transmitted signal more narrowly and increases the received signal level at the receiver.

Interference

Adjacent channel and overreach interference are other microwave impairments. Overreach is caused by a signal feeding past a repeater to the receiving antenna at the next station in the route. It is eliminated by selecting a zigzag path or by using alternative frequencies between adjacent stations.

Adjacent channel interference is another potential source of trouble in a microwave system. Digital radios, particularly those using QAM modulation, are less susceptible to adjacent channel interference than PSK and FM analog radios because of the bandpass filtering used to keep the transmitter's emissions within narrow limits. Multichannel radio installations usually employ cross polarization to prevent adjacent channel interference. In this technique, channel combining networks are used to cross-polarize the waves of adjacent channels. Cross-polarization discrimination adds 20 to 30 dB of selectivity to adjacent channels.

Heterodyning vs. Baseband Repeaters

Analog microwave repeaters use one of two techniques to amplify the received signal for retransmission—*heterodyning* or *baseband*. In a baseband repeater, the signal is demodulated to the multiplex (or video) signal at every repeater point. In a

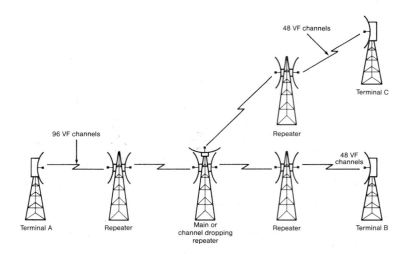

Figure 14.8   Channel dropping at main microwave repeater stations.

heterodyne repeater, the signal is demodulated to an intermediate frequency, usually 70 MHz, and modulated or heterodyned to the transmitter output frequency. Heterodyne radio is reduced to baseband only at main repeater stations, where the baseband signal is required to drop off voice channels.

The primary advantage of baseband radio is that some carrier channel groups can be dropped off at repeater stations. For example, in Figure 14.8, at the point where the microwave route branches, FM terminal equipment would be required in a heterodyne radio to split the baseband. Heterodyne radio has the advantage of avoiding the distortions caused by repeated modulation, demodulation, and amplification of a baseband signal. Therefore, heterodyne radio is employed for transcontinental use with drop-off points only at major junctions.

Multiplex Interface

Digital microwave interfaces to multiplex equipment through either a standard or a special digital interface. Most long haul systems marketed in the United States provide a standard DSX

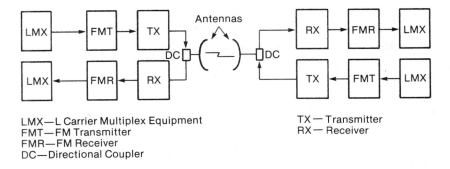

LMX—L Carrier Multiplex Equipment
FMT—FM Transmitter
FMR—FM Receiver
DC—Directional Coupler

TX — Transmitter
RX — Receiver

Figure 14.9   General model of an analog microwave system.

interface to one, two, or three DS-3 signals or to one DS-2 signal. Some radios designed for light route application have sub-DS-3 interfaces consisting of 12 or 14 DS-1s and requiring special multiplexers to interface DS-1 signals to the radio. Short haul microwave generally supports two or three DS-1 signals. These systems usually support only standard DSX-1 interfaces directly into a channel bank or PBX.

Analog microwave connects to analog multiplex through frequency modulated transmitter (FMT) and frequency modulated receiver (FMR) equipment. The multiplex baseband signal connects to the input of an FMT, which generates a frequency modulated intermediate frequency, usually 70 MHz. This signal is applied to the input of the radio, as Figure 14.9 shows, and is modulated to the final rf output frequency. At the receiver, rf and if amplifiers boost the incoming signal and connect it to the input of the FMR. The output of the FMR is a baseband signal that is coupled to the multiplex equipment.

Microwave Antennas, Waveguides, and Towers

Microwave antennas are manufactured as either parabolic dishes or horns, and range in diameter from 1 or 2 feet for short, high frequency hops to 100 feet for earth station satellite service.

At lower frequencies, microwave antennas are fed with coaxial cable. Coaxial cable loss increases with frequency; therefore most microwave systems use waveguide for the transmission line to the antenna. Waveguide is circular or rectangular, with dimensions designed for the frequency range. At 18 to 23 GHz, and sometimes in lower frequency bands, the radio frequency equipment mounts directly on the antenna, which eliminates the need for waveguide.

Multiple transmitters and receivers can be coupled to the same waveguide and antenna system by *branching filters. Directional couplers* are waveguide hybrids that allow coupling of a transmitter and receiver to the same antenna. This technique often is used in repeater stations to permit using one antenna for both directions of transmission.

Antennas are mounted on rooftops, if possible. If more elevation is needed, they can be mounted on towers as shown in Figure 14.10. Antennas must be precisely aligned. They are first oriented by eye or calculated azimuth and then adjusted to maximum received signal level. In orienting antennas, it is important to know the calculated received signal level and to ensure that the received signal is within 1 or 2 dB of that level. Otherwise, it is possible that the antenna will be oriented on a minor signal lobe instead of the main lobe.

Manufacturers supply microwave towers in guyed and self-supporting configurations. Self-supporting towers require less space and must be designed more rigidly to support the antenna against the effects of weather. If enough land is available to accommodate down guys, a less expensive guyed tower can be used. The larger the antenna diameter, the more rigid the tower must be to prevent flexing in the wind. Tower rigidity is important because excessive flexing can disorient the antennas.

Entrance Links

The facility used to connect the final radio station in a route to the terminal equipment is the *entrance link*. The preferred way to terminate a microwave route is by mounting the radio and multiplex equipment in the same building. However, frequency congestion and path obstructions in metropolitan areas often make it necessary to terminate the radio some distance from the

Figure 14.10   Tower supporting microwave antennas.
Courtesy, Gabriel Electronics, Inc.

multiplex terminal. The entrance link links the multiplex to the radio. Entrance links operate at baseband or, for short distances, at intermediate frequencies. Either coaxial cable or lightwave can be used for digital radio entrance links.

Digital Termination System

In 1981, the FCC opened the frequency band of 10.55 to 10.68 GHz for Digital Termination System (DTS), a short range microwave service designed for metropolitan digital communications. DTS is implemented in sectors similar to the way cellular radio is implemented. A central node broadcasts a digital signal through a sector of 90° to 120°. A combination of different frequencies and cross polarization of antennas prevents interference between sectors. The central node broadcasts to one or more remotes in a sector at data speeds up to 1.544 mb/s. As many as 24 devices can be connected to the DTS equipment. The remote-to-central link has one or more transmitters, all operating on a single frequency. Remote units use a time division multiple access (TDMA) system, which allows each unit to transmit in an allotted time slot to prevent interference.

DTS has a range of 7 to 10 miles from the central node to the remotes. Range depends on the amount of rain absorption and on multipath reflections, which can be significant because of buildings and other obstructions. In the Southwest, the longer range is possible, while in heavy rain areas of the Southeast 7 miles is generally the maximum achievable.

Short Haul Digital Microwave

As microwave technology advances, frequencies that once were considered experimental have come into common use. The FCC authorizes two bands of frequencies in the 18 and 23 GHz range for point-to-point use in both the common carrier and operational fixed services. These systems support operation over distances of 2 to 14 miles, with the range depending on terrain, polarization, and rainfall. Transmission over flat, reflective terrain with horizontal polarization in high rainfall areas yields the shorter ranges, while transmission over rugged terrain with vertical polarization in low rainfall areas allows greater range.

The radio is easy to install. It can be mounted on a rooftop or, in some applications, aimed out a window. Units are available for from DS-1 (24 voice channels) to DS-3 (672 voice channels) operation. The primary use is for linking local area networks and voice and data transmission between locations where broadband common carrier facilities are unavailable or prohibitively expensive. The equipment is relatively inexpensive, easy to install, and not difficult to license. Its primary drawback is the occasional outage that occurs when the received signal level fades, usually because of rain.

Short haul equipment is available with a variety of non-voice interfaces as well. It can be used for video and local area network extensions (both token ring and Ethernet), or it can extend cluster controllers in an IBM SNA network.

Applications

Following World War II, when microwave was used on a limited basis, the technology evolved from an experimental medium with limited reliability to the point where it now is used routinely. This section lists the most important factors to evaluate in applying microwave.

Microwave finds its most important applications in private networks in the following:

- Running T-1 circuits to IECs, bypassing the local exchange carriers.
- Connecting PBXs in a metropolitan network.
- Interconnecting local area networks.
- Providing diverse routing to protect against failure of the primary circuit route.
- Crossing obstacles such as highways and rivers.
- Implementing local data communications networks.

With the advent of low cost short haul equipment, microwave technology has come within the reach of many companies and can quickly pay back the initial investment in savings of common carrier facilities.

In applying short haul digital microwave, it is necessary to consider the following factors:

- What alternatives are available? Is microwave more cost-effective than common carrier alternatives such as fiber optics and leased T-1 facilities?

- How much bandwidth is required now and for the future? Systems that support bandwidth of up to DS-3 are available. The greater the amount of bandwidth, the more expensive the systems, although it is generally less expensive to purchase spare capacity with a new system than it is to add capacity later.

- What kind of availability is needed to make the system feasible? With the spacing between terminals and the rainfall factor, is it possible to obtain the required availability factor with short haul microwave?

- Is there line of sight between the terminal locations with sufficient clearance over intervening obstacles? If not, repeaters may be required. If repeaters are required, is the necessary real estate available?

- Where will the equipment be located? The most desirable location is on rooftops. If necessary, small towers can be constructed on the rooftops. Separate, ground-mounted towers are expensive and should be avoided if possible.

- What kind of specialized technical assistance will be required? Most companies require assistance with path surveys, license applications, and frequency coordination. Often, this can be supplied by the equipment vendor.

Standards

Microwave standards and specifications are set by the Federal Communications Commission in the United States and by the Consultative Committee on International Radio (CCIR) internationally. The FCC licenses transmitters only after the equipment is type accepted. FCC rules and regulations list the operating rules for radio equipment within the United States. The EIA has established wind loading zones in the United States for use in radio, tower, and antenna design, and several electrical and mechanical criteria for antenna and waveguide design. The Federal Aviation Administration (FAA) specifies tower lighting requirements.

Microwave equipment made by different manufacturers usually cannot be connected at the radio frequency level. Although the frequencies and number of channels are the same, proprietary alarm and maintenance signals prevent interconnection. At a repeater station, it is usually possible to interconnect signals from different manufacturers at baseband because at this level they conform to standard digital signal (DS) specifications.

Evaluation Considerations

The factors of reliability, power consumption, availability, floor space, and the ability to operate under a variety of environmental conditions are important with microwave as with other telecommunications equipment. Besides these considerations, which are covered in previous chapters, the following factors also must be evaluated.

System Gain

When a microwave signal radiates into free space it is attenuated by losses that are a function of the frequency, elevation, distance between terminals, and atmospheric conditions such as rain, fog, and temperature inversions. The amount of free space loss that a system can overcome is known as the *system gain*. System gain is expressed in decibels and is a function of the output power of the transmitter and the sensitivity of the receiver. Receiver sensitivity is a measure of how low the signal level into the receiver can be while still meeting noise objectives in an analog system or BER objectives in a digital system. For example, if a microwave transmitter has an output power of +30 dBm (1 watt) and a receiver sensitivity of -70 dBm, the system gain is 100 dB.

With other factors being equal, the greater the system gain, the more valuable the system because repeaters can be spaced farther apart. Given the same repeater spacing, a microwave radio with higher system gain has a greater fade margin than one with lower system gain. System gain can be improved in some microwave systems by the addition of optional higher power transmitters, low noise receiver amplifiers, or both.

Spectral Efficiency

Microwave radio can be evaluated based on its efficiency in using limited radio spectrum. The FCC prescribes minimum channel loadings for a microwave before it is type accepted. Within the frequency band, the license granted by the FCC limits the maximum bandwidth. Where growth in voice frequency channels is planned, the ability to increase the channel loading is of considerable interest to avoid adding more radio channels. Spectral efficiency in both analog and digital radios is a function of the modulation method. The controlling factor is noise in analog radio and BER in digital radios.

Fade Margin

The *fade margin* refers to the amount of fading of the received signal level that can be tolerated before the system crashes. A crash in an analog radio is defined as the maximum noise level that the application can tolerate. In a digital microwave, fade margin is the difference between the signal level that yields a maximum permissible BER (usually 10^{-6}) and the crash level (usually 10^{-3}). Analog radios fade more gracefully than digital radios. As the received signal diminishes, the channel noise level increases in analog radio, but communication may still be usable over a margin of about 20 dB. The fade margin of a digital radio is narrow—on the order of 3 dB. Either a digital signal is very good or it is totally unusable, and the distance between the two points is short.

Protection System

The user's availability objective determines the need for protection in a microwave system. Availability is affected by equipment failures and fades. Equipment availability can be calculated from the formula:

$$\text{Percent Availability} = \frac{\text{MTBF}-\text{MTT}\ (100)}{\text{MTBF}}$$

Availability as affected by fades can be determined by a microwave path engineering study. It is possible to calculate percent availability within a reasonable degree of accuracy for both fades and failures, but it is impossible to predict when failures will occur. Therefore, protection may be necessary to guard against the unpredictability of failures even though the computed availability is satisfactory.

Another factor weighing in the decision to provide diversity is the accessibility of equipment for maintenance. In a service such as DTS, the equipment normally mounts in an office building where it can be accessed within a few minutes. On that basis it may be reasonable to provide spares and to forego diversity to save money. In a system with remote repeaters, diversity usually is needed because of difficulty in reaching the site in time to meet availability objectives.

Alarm and Control Systems

All microwave radios should be equipped with alarm systems that provide both local and remote failure indications. An alarm system is evaluated based on how accurately the alarm is identified. Primitive systems indicate only that trouble exists, but not what it is. Sophisticated systems provide a complete remote diagnosis of radio performance. A microwave system equipped with protection and emergency power also requires a control system to switch equipment and operate the emergency engine.

Standard Interfaces

Most digital microwave systems should be designed to connect to a standard digital signal interface such as DSX-1, DSX-2, or DSX-3. Systems designed for the operational fixed band sometimes use nonstandard interfaces such as 12 or 14 DS-1 signals. Special multiplexers are required to implement these interfaces.

Frequency Band

Frequency availability often dictates the choice of microwave frequency band. Where choices are available, the primary criteria are the number of voice frequency channels required, the availability of repeater locations, and the required path reliability. As stated earlier, path reliability decreases with increasing radio frequency because of rain absorption. Reliability can be improved by decreasing the repeater spacing or increasing the antenna size.

Path Engineering

A microwave path should not be attempted without an expert path survey. Several companies specialize in frequency coordination studies and path profile studies and should be consulted about a proposed route. Sites should be chosen for accessibility and availability of real estate and a reliable power source. Engineers choose tower heights to obtain the elevation dictated by the path survey. The antenna structure must support the size of antenna in a wind of predicted velocity. Wind velocities for various parts of the country are specified by EIA.

Environmental Factors

Frequency stability is a consideration in evaluating microwave equipment. FCC rules specify the stability required for a microwave system, but environmental treatment may be needed to keep the system within its specifications. Air conditioning usually is not required, but air circulation may be necessary. Heating may be required to keep the equipment above 0° C. Battery plants lose their capacity with decreasing temperature. Therefore in determining the need for heating, designers should remember that battery capacity is lowest during abnormal weather conditions when power failures are most apt to occur.

Test Equipment

All microwave systems require test equipment to measure frequency, bandwidth, output power, and receiver sensitivity. This equipment, which should be specified by the manufacturer, is required in addition to the test equipment needed to maintain multiplex equipment.

Selected Microwave Radio Equipment Manufacturers

Long Haul Microwave Transmitters and Receivers

AT&T Network Systems

Aydin Microwave Division

California Microwave

Digital Microwave Co.

Ericsson, Inc.

Microwave Antennas, Waveguides, and Towers

Gabriel Electronics Inc.

NEC America, Inc.

Rockwell International Collins
Transmission Systems Division

Scientific-Atlanta, Inc.

Short Haul Microwave Transmitters and Receivers

Digital Microwave Co.

Ericsson, Inc.

Farinon Division, Harris Corporation

M/A-Com

Microwave Networks Corp.

NEC America, Inc.

Rockwell International Network Transmission Group

Telesciences Transmission Systems

Terracom Division, Loral Corporation

15

Satellite Communications

Like other telecommunications technologies, communications satellites have advanced dramatically in the last three decades, evolving from an experimental technique to the stage that they are now commonplace. Telstar 1, the first communications satellite launched by AT&T in 1962, carried only 12 voice circuits. By contrast, the first Telstar 4 satellite, which is a new generation of satellites, will be launched in 1992. Telstar 401 and 402 will be hybrid vehicles operating in two bands, C and Ku. Each will each carry 24 *transponders*, which are the radio relay portion of the satellite, in each band. Telstar 4 will be equipped to carry high definition television (HDTV) and direct broadcast satellite (DBS) television to all 50 states, Puerto Rico, and the Virgin Islands.

Telstar 1 was launched in a low elliptical orbit, circling the earth in about two hours. A ground station tracked it for the short time it was visible, often less than half an hour. AT&T chose Telstar 1's low orbit because it minimized the length of the radio signal's round trip from earth to satellite and back. The low orbit proved impractical, however, because a chain of several satellites was needed to provide continuous service, and the satellite antennas required constant re-aiming. Present-day communications satellites orbit the equator at a *geosynchronous* altitude of 22,300 miles. The equatorial orbit has the advantage of covering both the northern and southern hemispheres. Except the extreme polar regions, about one third of the earth's longitudinal surface can be covered by a single equatorial satellite.

Table 15.1   Communications Satellite Frequency Bands

BAND	UPLINK	DOWNLINK
C	5925 6425 MHz	3700 4200 MHz
Ku	14.0 14.5 GHz	11.7 12.2 GHz
Ka	27.5 31.0 GHz	17.7 21.2 GHz

At geosynchronous orbit, the satellite travels at the same speed as the earth's rate of spin, and it remains at a fixed position with relation to a point on the earth. From this distance, three satellites can theoretically cover the entire earth's surface, with each satellite subtending a radio beam 17° wide. The portion of the earth's surface that a satellite illuminates is called its *footprint*.

Satellites fall into three general categories—domestic, regional, and international. Domestic satellites carry traffic within one country. Regional satellites span a geographical area, such as Europe, and international satellites are intended for traffic that is largely intercontinental. Although undersea fiber optic systems are taking much of the international voice traffic because of their lower propagation delay, international television is still a large and growing market for satellites. New technologies, which will be discussed in a later section, are expected to further increase the amount of international satellite traffic.

International satellite communications are controlled by the International Telecommunications Satellite Organization (INTELSAT), which is an international satellite monopoly operating under treaty among 115 member nations and serving more than 171 countries and territories. INTELSAT operates 13 satellites. The United States partner in this venture is COMSAT World Systems, which owns 26% of INTELSAT. Domestic satellites are owned and operated by COMSAT, AT&T, Satellite Business Services (SBS), Western Union, RCA, American Satellite, and GTE.

As Table 15.1 shows, the frequencies available for communication satellites are limited. The 4 and 6 GHz C band frequencies are the most desirable from a transmission standpoint because they are the least susceptible to rain absorption. Satellites share

Figure 15.1   Satellites are positioned in equatorial orbit 22,300 miles above the Earth's surface.
Courtesy, AT&T Corporation

the C band frequencies with common carrier terrestrial microwave, requiring close coordination of spacing and antenna positioning to prevent interference. Interference between satellites and between terrestrial microwave and satellites is prevented by using highly directional antennas. Currently, satellites are spaced about the equator at 2° intervals. At geosynchronous orbit each degree is equal to 450 miles, which means that satellites are spaced at 900-mile intervals. Figure 15.1 shows conceptually how a satellite is positioned in equatorial orbit.

The Ku band of frequencies is coming into more general use as the C band becomes congested. K band frequencies are exclusive to satellites, allowing users to construct earth stations almost anywhere, even in metropolitan areas where congestion precludes placing C band earth stations. The primary disadvantage of the Ku band is rain attenuation, which results in lower reliability. With identical 2° spacing for both C and Ku bands, the hybrid satellite is becoming feasible. A hybrid satellite carries transponders for both bands.

Ka band satellites are on the verge of becoming feasible. Ka band operates with an uplink of 27.5 to 31 GHz and a downlink of 17.7 to 21.2 GHz. Although the higher frequency of Ka band subjects the signal to a higher probability of fading, it is possible to construct satellites with smaller antennas and to use less expensive earth stations, which makes the band attractive. The Ka band frequencies are even more susceptible to attenuation. Although considerable bandwidth is available, further development is needed before these frequencies come into general use. An experimental system planned by the National Aeronautics and Space Administration (NASA) will make use of the Ka band as discussed later.

The terms *uplink* and *downlink* used in Table 15.1 refer to the earth-to-satellite and the satellite-to-earth paths respectively. The lower frequency always is used from the satellite to the ground because earth station transmitting power can overcome the greater path loss of the higher frequency, but solar battery capacity limits satellite output power.

Satellites have several advantages over terrestrial communications. These include:

- Costs of satellite circuits are independent of distance within the coverage range of a single satellite.

- Impairments that accumulate on a per hop basis on terrestrial microwave circuits are avoided with satellites because the earth-station-to-earth-station path is a single hop through a satellite repeater.

- Sparsely populated or inaccessible areas can be covered by a satellite signal, providing high quality communications service to areas that are otherwise difficult or impossible to reach. The coverage is also independent of terrain and other obstacles that may block terrestrial communications.

- Earth stations can verify their own data transmission accuracy by listening to the return signal from the satellite.

- Because satellites broadcast a signal, they can reach wide areas simultaneously.

- Large amounts of bandwidth are available over satellite circuits, making high speed voice, data, and video circuits available without using an expensive link to a telephone central office.

- The satellite signal can be brought directly to the end user, bypassing the local telephone facilities that are expensive and limit bandwidth.

- The multipath reflections that impair terrestrial microwave communications have little effect on satellite radio paths.

Satellites are not without limitations, however. The greatest drawback is the lack of frequencies. If higher frequencies can be developed with reliable paths, plenty of frequency spectrum is available, but atmospheric limitations may prevent their use for commercial grade telecommunications service. Other limitations include:

- The delay from earth station to satellite and back is about one-quarter second, or about one-half second for an echo signal. This delay is tolerable for voice when echo cancelers are used, but is detrimental to block-mode data protocols and polled data circuits.

- Multihop satellite connections impose delay that is detrimental to voice communications and is generally avoided. Because direct satellite-to-satellite transmission is not yet feasible, multiple hops are required when the distance between earth stations exceeds the satellite's footprint.

- Path loss is high (about 200 dB) from earth to satellite.

- Rain absorption affects path loss, particularly at higher microwave frequencies.

- Frequency crowding in the C band is high with potential for interference between satellites and terrestrial microwave operating on the same frequency.

The satellite-to-satellite radio link is one solution to the multi-hop limitation, but it still lies in the realm of future technology. The delay is greater than with a single hop, but intercontinental satellite communications will be improved when this technology becomes feasible.

The rapid growth of fiber optic systems will have an adverse effect on satellites' share of the telecommunications market, but the technology shows no signs of dying. Though the satellites' market share may be dropping, the traffic carried by communications satellites continues to increase and will do so into the future. The growth in underseas fiber optic cables is the primary factor limiting the use of satellites for voice. Also, in the near term there is a glut of satellite capacity, but an expected increase in the type of traffic that uses the unique capabilities of satellites will probably absorb any excess capacity.

Satellite Technology

Satellite positions are measured by their relative longitudes east of the Greenwich meridian. For example, the Telstar 4 satellites will be positioned at 271° and 263° (89° and 97° west latitude), which centers them approximately at the same longitude as New Orleans and Dallas.

A satellite circuit has five elements—two terrestrial links, an uplink, a downlink, and a satellite repeater—as shown in Figure 15.2. If the earth station mounts on the user's premises, the terrestrial links are eliminated. The satellite itself has six subsystems described below:

- Physical structure.
- Transponder.
- Attitude control apparatus.
- Power supply.
- Telemetry equipment.
- Station keeping apparatus.

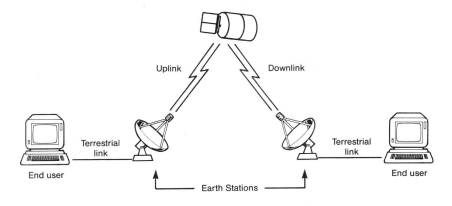

Figure 15.2 A satellite system.

Physical Structure

The size of communications satellites has been steadily increasing since the launch of Early Bird, the first commercial satellite, in 1965. Size is limited by the capacity of launch vehicles and by the need to carry enough solar batteries and fuel to keep the system alive for its design life of five to ten years. Advances in space science are making larger satellites technically feasible. Launch vehicles can carry greater payloads, and the demonstrated ability of the space shuttle to service a satellite in flight or return it to earth for maintenance is changing design considerations that previously limited satellite size.

A large physical size is desirable. Not only must the satellite carry the radio and support equipment, but it also must provide a platform for large antennas to obtain the high gain needed to overcome the path loss between the earth station and the satellite.

Transponders

A transponder is a radio relay station on board the satellite. Transponders are technically complex, but their functions are identical with those of terrestrial microwave radio relay stations. The diagram in Figure 15.3 shows the major elements. The receiving antenna picks up the incoming signal from the earth station and amplifies it with a low noise amplifier (LNA), which

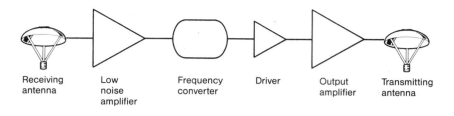

Receiving antenna · Low noise amplifier · Frequency converter · Driver · Output amplifier · Transmitting antenna

Figure 15.3   Components of a transponder.

boosts the received signal without adding noise. The LNA output is amplified and applied to a mixer that reduces the incoming signal to the downlink frequency. The downlink signal is applied to a high power amplifier, using a traveling wave tube (TWT) or solid state amplifier (SSA) as the output amplifier. The output signal couples to the downlink antenna. Traveling wave tubes provide up to 10 watts of power. Solid state amplifiers are becoming increasingly popular because of their high reliability. Most satellites carry multiple transponders, each with a bandwidth of 36 to 72 MHz. For example, AT&T's Telstar 4 contains 48 transponders—24 in the C band and 24 in the Ku band. The output power of Telstar 4 is much higher than that of previous generations—20 watts for the C band transponders and 120 watts in the Ku band.

Both satellite and earth station antennas are cross polarized to double the capacity of a single frequency. In some satellites, beam focusing techniques concentrate radio frequency energy on a small spot of earth. For example, some satellites illuminate the continental United States with spots focused on Alaska, Hawaii, and Puerto Rico. The NASA Advanced Communications Technology Satellite (ACTS), which is discussed later, uses on-board switching of spot beams to minimize interference.

Attitude Control Apparatus

Satellites must be stabilized to prevent them from tumbling through space and to keep antennas precisely aligned toward earth. With current equipment, alignment can be maintained within 0.1. Satellite stabilization is achieved by two methods. A *spin stabilized* satellite rotates on its axis at about 100 RPM. The antenna is despun at the same speed to provide constant positioning and polarization toward earth. The second method is *three-axis stabilization*, which consists of a gyroscopic stabilizer inside the vehicle. Accelerometers sense any change in position in all axes, and fire positioning rockets to keep the satellite at a constant attitude.

Power Supply

Satellites are powered by solar batteries. Power is conserved by turning off unused equipment with signals from the earth. On spin stabilized satellites, the cells mount outside the unit so that one-third of the cells always face the sun. Three-axis stabilized satellites have cells mounted on solar panels that extend like wings from the satellite body. Solar cell life is a major factor that limits the working life of a satellite. Solar bombardment gradually weakens the cell output until the power supply can no longer power the on-board equipment.

A nickel-cadmium battery supply is also kept on board most satellites to power the equipment during solar eclipses, which occur during two 45-day periods for about an hour per day. The eclipses also cause wide temperature changes that the on-board equipment must withstand.

Telemetry Equipment

A satellite contains telemetry equipment to monitor its position and attitude and to initiate correction of any deviation from its assigned station. Through telemetry equipment, the earth control station initiates changes to keep the satellite at its assigned longitude and inclination toward earth. Telemetry also monitors the received signal strength and adjusts the receiver gain to keep the uplink and downlink paths balanced.

Station Keeping Equipment

Small rockets are installed on the vehicle to keep it on station. When the satellite drifts from position, rockets fire to return it. The activities that keep the satellite on position are called *station keeping* activities. The fuel required for station keeping is the other factor, with solar cell life, that limits the design life of the satellite. With future satellites, refueling from the space shuttle may become feasible, extending the design life accordingly.

Earth Station Technology

Earth stations vary from simple, inexpensive, receive-only stations that can be purchased by individual consumers to elaborate two-way communications stations that offer commercial access to the satellite's capacity. An earth station includes microwave radio relay equipment, terminating multiplex equipment, and a satellite communications controller.

Radio Relay Equipment

The radio relay equipment used in an earth station is similar to the terrestrial microwave equipment described in Chapter 14 except that the transmitter output power is considerably higher than that of terrestrial microwave. Also, antennas up to 30 meters in diameter provide the narrow beam width required to concentrate power on the targeted satellite. Figure 15.4 is a photograph of a Scientific Atlanta earth station.

Because the earth station's characteristics are more easily controllable than the satellite's and because power is not the problem on earth that it is in space, the earth station plays the major role in overcoming the path loss between the satellite and earth. Path loss ranges from about 197 dB at 4 GHz to about 210 dB at 12 GHz. Also, the higher the frequency, the greater the loss from rainfall absorption. Therefore the uplink always operates at the higher frequency where higher transmitter output power can overcome absorption, while the lower frequency is reserved for the downlink where large antennas and high power amplifiers are not feasible.

Antennas are adjustable to compensate for slight deviations in satellite positioning. Antennas at commercial stations are normally automatically adjusted by motor drives, while inexpensive antennas are adjusted manually as needed. Thirty-meter antennas provide an extremely narrow beam width, with half-power points 0.1° wide.

Figure 15.4   An earth station in Jakarta, Indonesia.
Courtesy, Scientific Atlanta

Satellite Communications Control

A satellite communications controller (SCC) apportions the satellite's bandwidth, processes signals for satellite transmission, and interconnects the earth station microwave equipment to terrestrial circuits. The SCC formats the received signals into a single integrated bit stream in a digital satellite system or combines FDM signals into a frequency modulated analog signal in an analog system.

Multiplexing

The multiplex interface of an earth station is conventional. Satellite circuits use either analog or digital modulation, with interfaces to time division and frequency division terrestrial circuits of the types described in Chapters 4 and 5.

Access Control

Satellites employ several techniques to increase the traffic carrying capacity and to provide access to that capacity. *Frequency Division Multiple Access* (FDMA) divides the transponder capacity into multiple frequency segments between end points. One disadvantage of this system is that users are assigned a fixed amount of bandwidth that cannot be adjusted rapidly or easily assigned to other users when it is idle. Also, the guard bands between channels use part of the capacity.

Time Division Multiple Access (TDMA) uses the concept of time sharing the total transponder capacity described under Digital Termination Systems in Chapter 14. Earth stations transmit only when permitted to do so by the access protocol. When the earth station receives permission to transmit, it is allotted the total bandwidth of the transponder, typically 50 mb/s, for the duration of the station's assigned time slot. Access is controlled by a master station or by the earth station's listening to which station transmitted last and sending its burst in a preassigned sequence. Each earth station receives all transmissions but decodes only those addressed to it. TDMA provides priority to stations with more traffic to transmit by assigning those stations more time slots than it assigns to low priority stations. Therefore, a station with a growing amount of traffic can be allotted a greater share of total transmission time.

Demand Assigned Multiple Access (DAMA) is an alternative to preassigned multiple access. DAMA equipment keeps a record of idle radio channels or time slots. Channels are assigned on demand by one of three methods—polling, random access with central control, and random access with distributed control. Control messages are sent over a separate terrestrial channel or contained in a control field in the transmitted frame from a TDMA station.

Another method of assigning capacity is *Spacecraft Switched Time Division Multiple Access* (SSTDMA). Under this system the satellite aims its power at a single station based on instructions from the earth. The NASA ACTS uses this method as discussed in a later section.

Signal Processing

The SCC conditions signals between the terrestrial and satellite links for transmission. The type of signal conditioning depends on the vendor and may include compression of digital voice signals, echo cancellation, forward error correction, and digital speech interpolation to avoid transmitting the silent periods of a voice signal.

Satellite Transmission

Much of the previous discussion is of only academic interest to those who use satellite services. However, satellite circuits and terrestrial circuits have different transmission characteristics. Users should be aware of the differences so satellite circuits can be applied where they are both technically and economically feasible.

Satellite Delay

The quarter-second delay between two earth stations is noticeable in voice communications circuits, but most people become accustomed to it and accept it as normal if the circuit is confined to one satellite hop. Data communications circuits are another matter. Throughput on circuits using a block transmission protocol such as IBM's Binary Synchronous (BSC) drops to an unacceptably low level through a satellite because a station can transmit a block only after the receiver acknowledges the preceding block. Since the

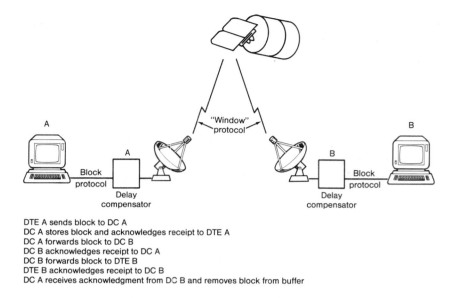

DTE A sends block to DC A
DC A stores block and acknowledges receipt to DTE A
DC A forwards block to DC B
DC B acknowledges receipt to DC A
DC B forwards block to DTE B
DTE B acknowledges receipt to DC B
DC A receives acknowledgment from DC B and removes block from buffer

Figure 15.5   Data transmission through satellite delay compensators.

transmission and acknowledgement sequence requires two round trips, each block takes a half-second. At this rate, a maximum of only two blocks per second can be transmitted, assuming other data transmission delays such as the CPU processing time are zero. Throughput on polling circuits likewise drops because a complete poll from a host computer is an inquiry and a response, requiring two earth-station-to-earth-station links, and a half-second of propagation delay.

A satellite delay compensator can mitigate the effects of delay in data circuits as Figure 15.5 shows. Delay compensation cannot, by itself, resolve the deficiencies of a satellite in a polling network because acknowledgements must come from the terminals themselves. In a delay compensator, the DTE communicates in its native protocol, but communication is with the delay compensator instead of the DTE at the other end of the circuit. The delay compensator buffers the transmitted block, awaiting acknowledgement from the distant end. If it receives a negative acknowledge message, indicating an errored block, the delay compensator retransmits either the errored block and all succeeding blocks (go back N) or only the errored block (selective retransmission). Figure 15.5 lists the steps the DTEs and the delay compensator use. Throughput is somewhat lower than a terrestrial circuit because the delay compensator interrupts transmission until an error is corrected. Throughput depends on error rate as it does on terrestrial circuits, although satellite circuits react more severely to a high error rate because of delays during error correction. The alternative to using a delay compensator is to change to a protocol such as HDLC or SDLC that permits multiple unacknowledged blocks. Extensive changes needed in the host computer system may make this alternative economically unfeasible.

Rain Absorption

Rain absorption has a dual effect on satellite communications: heavy rains increase the path loss significantly, and they may change the signal polarization enough to impair the cross-polarization discrimination ability of the receiving antennas. (See Chapter 14 for an explanation of cross polarization.) Unfortunately, the greatest impairment exists at the higher frequencies where interference is less and greater bandwidths are available. Rain absorption can be countered by these methods:

- Choosing earth station locations where heavy rain is less likely.
- Designing sufficient received signal margin into the path to enable the circuits to tolerate the effects of rain.
- Locating a diversity earth station far enough from the main station with the expectation that heavy rain storms will be localized.

Technical considerations limit the first two options. Transmit power and antenna gain from the satellite can be increased only within limits dictated by the size of the satellite and the transmit power available. Locations with low precipitation cannot always deliver service where required. These considerations mandate the use of earth station diversity at higher frequencies, which suffers the disadvantage of being costly.

Sun Transit Outage

During the spring and fall equinoxes for periods of about 10 minutes per day for six days, the sun is positioned directly behind the satellite and focuses a considerable amount of high energy radiation directly on the earth station antenna. This solar radiation causes a high noise level that renders the circuits unusable during this time. Solutions are to route traffic through a backup satellite or to tolerate the outage.

Interference

Interference from other satellites and from terrestrial microwave stations is always a potential problem with satellite circuits. The FCC requires all proposed licensees to conduct interference studies before it grants either a satellite or a terrestrial license. The FCC permits some licenses in the 12 GHz operational fixed microwave band to exist only if they do not interfere with direct broadcast satellite (DBS) services.

Carrier-to-Noise Ratio

Satellite transmission quality is based on carrier-to-noise ratio, which is analogous to signal-to-noise ratio measurements on terrestrial circuits. The ratio is relatively easy to improve on the uplink portion of the satellite circuit because transmitter output power and antenna gain can be increased to offset noise. On the downlink portion of a circuit, the effective isotropic radiated power (EIRP), which is a measurement of the transmitter output power that is concentrated into the downlink footprint, can be increased only within the size and power limits of the satellite or by using spot beams to concentrate signal strength.

Representative Satellite Services

In this section, four different types of satellite services are discussed to illustrate the versatility of communications satellites. Two of the services, maritime and direct broadcast television, are not feasible except through communications satellites. The third service, very small aperture terminal (VSAT), replaces conventional terrestrial communications and offers the advantage of bringing signals directly to the user without requiring the last link in a communications path—the local telephone loop—that is often expensive and bandwidth limiting. The fourth service, ACTS, is experimental and may pave the way for a new suite of satellite services in the future.

International Maritime Satellite Service (INMARSAT)

INMARSAT is an international maritime satellite service operating under the auspices of the International Maritime Organization (IMO), a United Nations agency. The INMARSAT system has a network of 17 existing and planned coastal earth stations. These stations form one terminal of a circuit; the other terminal is the ship earth station. The ship earth station mounts above decks and automatically stays in position with satellite tracking equipment. INMARSAT type-accepts and regulates shipboard equipment.

INMARSAT provides the same kinds of communications services for ships at sea that land stations can access through satellite or terrestrial circuits. In the past, the principal methods of record communication from ships were telex and Morse code over high frequency radio, which were unreliable and expensive. Now data circuits are replacing those modes of communication. Voice circuits replace the high frequency ship-to-shore radio that often suffered from poor signal propagation reliability. In addition, services such as video and facsimile can be carried over INMARSAT. Other services that do not generally apply to land stations also can be accessed through INMARSAT. Ship locations can be monitored precisely through polling equipment. Distress calls can be received and rebroadcast to ships in the vicinity but out of radio range. Broadcasts such as storm warnings can be made to all ships in an area.

Direct Broadcast Satellite (DBS)

The services discussed to this point have been two-way communications between earth stations. A substantial demand exists for receive-only satellite services. Such services have existed for several years to transmit television signals to cable TV services such as Home Box Office, Movie Channel, and Cinemax. Many of these services are picked up by privately owned earth stations for

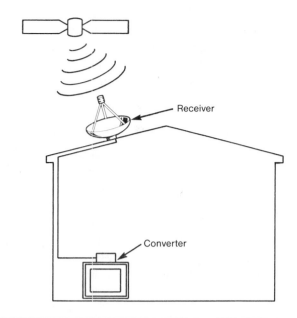

Figure 15.6   Direct broadcast satellite television.

personal use. These services are not intended for personal use, but a 1984 court ruling declared such reception to be legal, leading to a decision by many services to scramble their signals.

Unlike other satellite video services, DBS service is commercial television intended for individual reception. The 200 watts of power—considerably more than that used in most communications satellites—is needed to limit the size of receiving antennas to about 1 meter in diameter. The viewer receives TV channels through a personal earth station consisting of the components shown in Figure 15.6. A frequency down-converter mounts on the antenna to reduce the 12 GHz downlink signal to approximately 1 GHz. This signal is down-converted to a TV channel by a multiple channel selector at the TV set. Signals are usually encoded, requiring a descrambler in the TV receiver. DBS is expected to have a wide impact on TV broadcasting in the United States because of the ability of broadcasters to reach a nationwide market from a single source. DBS also is intended for reception by broadcast, master antenna, and cable television operators as well as individual users. In many cases, DBS will supplement rather than replace existing services.

DBS has been expected to take off in this country for several years. Since 1982, the FCC has granted construction permits to nine DBS companies, but to date no DBS satellites have been launched. One consortium, consisting of Hughes Communications, National Broadcasting Co., News Corporation, and Cablevision Systems, has announced plans to launch a DBS service called Sky Cable in 1993. Another company, K Prime Partners, is expected to begin service in the early part of the decade. DBS offers greater bandwidths than most cable systems, but the uncertainty about its future lies in whether users will pay the price of receiving apparatus plus a monthly fee for service.

Very Small Aperture Terminal (VSAT)

When VSATs first entered the market, they were viewed as a solution in search of a problem, but in the past few years applications have begun to emerge, and users have become comfortable with VSAT technology. VSATs are named for the size of the transmitting antennas, which are much smaller than those used in conventional earth stations. VSAT antennas are normally 1.8 meters (6 feet) in diameter, which makes them easy to conceal on rooftops and in areas with zoning restrictions.

A VSAT network is star-connected with a hub at the center and dedicated lines running to the host computer as shown conceptually in Figure 15.7. The hub has a larger antenna, often 4 to 11 meters in diameter aimed at the satellite. Hubs cost from $1 million to $1.5 million to construct, so only the largest organizations can justify a privately owned hub. Usually, the VSAT vendor owns the hub, or one organization owns it and shares it with others. Not only is a shared hub more cost-effective for most companies, it also relieves the company of the necessity of managing the hub, which may require one or two people per 100 nodes. Generally, a privately owned hub is feasible when there are about 200 remote stations.

The hub controls demand assignment to the satellite and monitors and diagnoses network performance. Demand is allocated in one of four ways—pure aloha, slotted aloha, time division

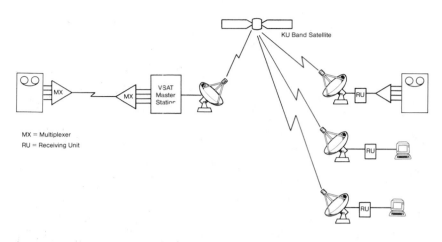

MX = Multiplexer
RU = Receiving Unit

Figure 15.7   A typical VSAT network.

multiple access (TDMA), or spread spectrum. The first three methods generally are used on Ku band, and the last on C band. Pure aloha is an inefficient method of regulating access. Stations transmit on a free-for-all basis and when their transmissions collide, they must retransmit. Slotted aloha is somewhat more efficient in that stations can transmit only during allotted time slots. TDMA and spread spectrum are the most effective ways of allocating access. A VSAT network is effectively a packet switched network. The master station accepts data from the host and packetizes it, using X.25.

The remote station has an antenna and a receiving unit, which is about the size of a personal computer base unit. Figure 15.8 is a photograph of a Scientific Atlanta VSAT master station with a 7-meter antenna and a remote with a 1.8-meter antenna. The receiving unit contains a modulator/demodulator, a packet assembler/disassembler, and a communication controller. The remote transmitter operates with an output power of about 1 watt. The receiver uses a low noise amplifier.

The primary application for VSAT is data, although it also can carry voice and video. Typically, C band VSATs carry 9.6 kb/s data, and Ku band VSATs carry 56 kb/s data; some systems carry a full

Figure 15.8   A very small aperture (VSAT) master station with a 7-meter antenna and a remote station with a 1.8-meter antenna terminal.
Courtesy, *Scientific Atlanta*

or fractional T-1. Most applications are two-way interactive. The primary advantage of VSAT is its ability to support multiple locations. For a few locations, the terrestrial link from the host computer to the hub plus the investment in remote stations may make VSAT prohibitively expensive. As the number of remote sites increases, however, VSAT becomes more attractive.

Advanced Communications Technology Satellite (ACTS)

The National Aeronautics and Space Administration is launching an Advanced Communications Technology Satellite (ACTS) to serve as a platform for technologies that are now experimental but hold promise for dramatically improving satellite capacity. ACTS, which operates in the Ka band, provides a changing amount of bandwidth where needed. The satellite contains an on-board processor (OBP) that directs hopping spot beams. The earth station accepts data from the source and directs a burst to the satellite using TDMA. The OBP demodulates and stores the burst and routes it to an output memory module. The OBP aims the antenna at the receiving station, generates the signal, and transmits it on the downlink. Compared to a conventional satellite, which subtends a footprint that covers as much as the entire continent, the ACTS footprint is only 135 miles in diameter. Not only does this improve security, it also provides 20 dB of gain. Coverage is increased further with cross-polled antennas. With cross polarization, frequencies can be reused without interference.

ACTS is an immature technology. The satellite is expected to live from two to four years, during which time organizations can apply to use its capabilities to advance the technology.

Applications

In one sense, satellite applications will diminish as terrestrial and underseas fiber optic circuits become more plentiful and economical. Satellite services are still uniquely suited for many applications, however, and the heavy investments the major providers are making shows that they expect satellites to survive well into the future.

Standards

The FCC in the United States and CCITT and CCIR internationally regulate satellite communication. Satellite carriers are free to design systems to proprietary standards and objectives, but the radio frequency spectrum and satellite positioning must conform to standards set by the FCC. Most users obtain their services from a satellite carrier and therefore are not concerned with the performance of the satellite and earth station equipment, but they are concerned with circuit performance. The carrier establishes circuit performance criteria. CCITT recommends circuit performance objectives, but compliance is voluntary.

Satellite Service Evaluation Considerations

Satellite space vehicle evaluation criteria are complex, technical, and of interest only to designers, owners, and manufacturers of satellites and on-board equipment. Therefore, this discussion omits these criteria. Likewise, common carrier earth station equipment evaluations are omitted from this discussion. Evaluation criteria discussed in Chapter 14 on microwave equipment generally apply to satellite services except that multipath fading is not a significant problem in satellite services. Also, alarm and control systems in terrestrial microwave are different from those used in satellite systems.

The following factors should be considered in evaluating satellite services and privately owned earth station equipment:

Availability

Circuit availability is a function of path and equipment reliability. To the user of capacity over a carrier-owned earth station, equipment reliability is a secondary consideration. The important issue is circuit reliability measured as percent error-free seconds in digital services and percent availability within specified noise limits for analog services.

These same availability criteria apply with privately owned earth stations, but the carrier can quote availability based only on path reliability. Equipment availability depends on MTBF and MTTR as discussed in Chapter 14 and must be included in the reliability calculation. The frequency and duration of any expected outages because of solar radiation or solar eclipse should be evaluated.

Access Method

Satellite carriers employ several techniques to increase the information-carrying capacity of the space vehicle. Techniques such as DAMA can result in congestion during peak load periods and the possibility that earth station buffer capacity can be exceeded, or access to the system blocked. Some carriers employ delta modulation or adaptive differential pulse code modulation to increase the voice circuit carrying capacity of the satellite and may thereby limit data transmission speeds. Users should determine what methods the carrier uses to apportion access, whether blockage is possible, and whether transmission performance will meet objectives.

Transmission Performance

The carrier's loss, noise, echo, envelope delay, and absolute delay objectives should be evaluated. Except for absolute delay, which cannot be reduced except by using terrestrial facilities to limit the number of satellite hops, satellite transmission evaluation should be similar to the criteria discussed in Chapter 2.

Earth Station Equipment

Earth station equipment is evaluated against the following criteria:

- Equipment reliability.
- Technical criteria, such as antenna gain, transmitter power, and receiver sensitivity, that provides a sufficiently reliable path to meet availability objectives.
- Antenna positioning and tracking equipment that is automatically or manually adjustable to compensate for positional variation in the satellite.
- Physical structure that can withstand the wind velocity and ice loading effects for the locale.
- The availability of radome or deicing equipment to ensure operation during snow and icing conditions.

Network Management Capability

Network management is important in VSAT networks where many earth stations are under the control of a single hub. The service provider should be able to reconfigure the network rapidly from a central location. Monitoring and control equipment should be able to diagnose problems and detect degradations before hard faults occur. The network management package should collect statistics on network use and provide information for predicting when growth additions will be require

Selected Satellite Equipment Manufacturers and Service Vendors

Earth Station Equipment

Aydin Microwave Division

Equatorial Communications Co.

M/A-COM DCC Inc.

NEC America Inc., Radio & Transmission Division

Rockwell International Collins Transmission Systems Div.

Satellite Transmission Systems, Inc.

Scientific Atlanta

Satellite Transmission Services

AT&T Tridom

American Satellite Corporation

Contel ASC

GTE Satellite Corporation

RCA Americom

Satellite Business Systems

Western Union Telegraph Co.

VSAT Equipment

AT&T Tridom

Contel ASC

GTE SpaceNet

Hughes Network Systems

Scientific Atlanta

16

Mobile Radio Systems

Compared to most telecommunications technologies, mobile telephone has been only moderately applied and, until recently, has undergone relatively little advancement. The first recorded use of mobile radio was in 1921 by the Detroit Police Department. Mobile telephone was introduced in 1946, about 25 years after the first mobile radio system went into operation. The term *mobile radio* often is used synonymously with mobile telephone. Although the two services use technology and equipment that are essentially the same, they differ in these ways:

- Mobile telephone uses separate transmit and receive frequencies, making full duplex operation possible. Mobile radios operate either on the same frequency in a simplex mode or on different frequencies in a half duplex mode.

- Mobile telephones are connected directly to the telephone network and can be used to originate and terminate telephone calls with billing rendered directly to the mobile telephone number. Mobile radio, if connected to the telephone network, connects through a coupler to a telephone line. Billing, if any, is to the wireline telephone.

- Mobile telephones signal on a 10-digit dialing plan. Mobile radios use loudspeaker paging or selective signaling that does not fit into the nationwide dialing plan.

Conventional mobile telephone service suffers from several drawbacks as a communications medium. First, demand greatly outstrips capacity in the limited frequency spectrum, resulting in long waiting lists for service in many parts of the country. Also, a mobile telephone channel is a large party line with the disadvantages of limited access and lack of privacy. Some parts of most serving areas have only limited coverage. When a vehicle leaves a coverage area, transmission is poor and the conversation often must be ended and reestablished on a different channel or deferred until signal strength improves. Within the coverage area, communication is apt to be sporadic or impossible.

In 1974, the FCC designated part of the UHF television spectrum between 800 and 900 MHz for a new cellular radio service. The concept of cellular radio had been studied for more than two decades, but the lack of FCC approval, a sufficiently large block of clear frequencies, and a suitable control technology impeded its advancement. Although the FCC allocated frequencies in 1974, they delayed approval of the service pending a lengthy hearing process, which included a solicitation of proposals for demonstration systems. Advanced Mobile Phone System (AMPS), an AT&T subsidiary, installed the first cellular radio demonstration system in the United States in Chicago in 1978.

In 1981, the FCC authorized 666 cellular radio channels in two bands of frequencies—825 to 845 MHz and 870 to 890 MHz. The lower half of each band, called the A band, is designated for *wireline* carriers, which are defined roughly as operating telephone companies. The upper half, or B band, is designated for *nonwireline* carriers, which are all non-telephone company common carriers. The FCC grants licenses in both bands to serve a Cellular Geographic Serving Area (CGSA). A CGSA corresponds to a Standard Metropolitan Statistical Area (SMSA), which is a major metropolitan area defined by the Office of Management and Budget. The FCC requires that license applicants cover 75% of the CGSA's surface area within two years of the date of operation.

The demand for cellular service grew rapidly, to the point that the carriers returned to the FCC for additional frequencies. The FCC reluctantly granted an additional 10 MHz—5 MHz in each band. With the prospect of again running out of frequency spectrum, the FCC is evaluating alternative methods of compressing more channels into the existing frequencies. The most probable method involves a shift to digital modulation, which raises the problem of how to make the cellular system compatible with existing analog radios.

Cellular demand has exceeded the most optimistic projections. Industry estimates are that cellular will have grown to 20 million users by 1995 and will serve approximately 10% of the population in the United States by the year 2000. To accommodate this kind of demand, the industry must develop and adopt methods for compressing more information into the available frequency space. Later in this chapter we will discuss the methods proposed for bandwidth compression.

Conventional Mobile Telephone Technology

As an aid to understanding cellular radio, it is instructive to review the operation of conventional mobile telephone service. The FCC assigns 44 channels to Public Mobile Service in three ranges—35 to 44 MHz, 152 to 158 MHz, and 454 to 512 MHz. Coverage in all three bands is essentially line-of-sight with the lower frequencies providing the widest coverage. Under some propagation conditions in the 35 MHz band, coverage is so broad that mobile units frequently communicate with unintended base stations. To prevent interference, channels can be reused only with a geographical buffer of 50 to 100 miles between base stations.

A metropolitan mobile telephone service area has transmitters centrally located and operating with 100 to 250 watts of output. Because of the difference between mobile and base station transmitter output power, common carriers often install receivers in more than one site to improve coverage, as Figure 16.1 shows. These receivers are called *voting receivers* because a central unit measures the relative signal-to-noise ratio of each receiver and selects the one with the best signal. This improves the power balance between the mobile, which has relatively low output and a low gain antenna, and the base station unit. Most coverage areas have several radio channels. Transceivers can shift between channels within the same band,

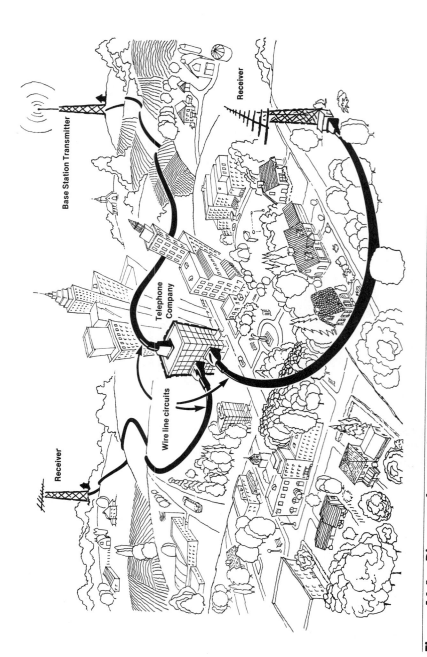

Figure 16.1   Diagram of conventional mobile telephone service.

but not between bands. Modern mobile telephone sets that employ a single control head that can switch between a cellular and conventional mobile telephone are available.

For about the first 20 years of mobile telephone use, the telephone companies operated the service manually. Users placed calls by lifting the handset and keying on the mobile transmitter momentarily to signal the operator. The operator placed and timed the call to a wireline telephone or other mobile unit. With this system the operator supervised only the wireline telephone. Mobile-to-mobile calls were manually monitored to detect the start and end of the conversation. The operator signaled the mobile telephone by multifrequency dialing; a selector inside the mobile transceiver responded to a five-digit number. Because of frequency congestion, many users purchased multiple channel sets. The greater number of channels improved the chances of finding an idle channel for outgoing service, but more channels did not improve incoming service to the mobile unit because users could be called only on the channel they monitored.

In 1964, AT&T introduced Improved Mobile Telephone Service (IMTS) to align mobile telephone service more closely with ordinary telephone service. The IMTS mobile receiver automatically seeks an idle channel and tunes the transceiver to that channel. When the user lifts the handset, the system returns dial tone, and the user dials the call like a conventional telephone. Calls from wireline to mobile units are dialed directly without operator intervention. The base station automatically selects the first idle channel and signals the mobile unit over that channel. IMTS, with its idle channel seeking capability, improved service for users by eliminating the need for manual channel changes and by making more channels available to reduce congestion.

With both manual and IMTS systems, the base station configuration presents several disadvantages. The coverage area is more or less circular; the actual coverage area depends on the directivity of the antenna system and on the terrain. Obstructions are a particular problem with ordinary mobile telephone service. A hill some distance from the base station typically creates a radio signal shadow on the side away from the transmitter. Even within the range of the primary coverage area, transmission is impaired.

Roamers—users who travel between serving areas—present a particular problem for mobile telephone service providers. Mobile users have a designated home channel and can be called only while they tune that channel. When they leave their home areas, they must inform potential callers of their location, or they cannot be called.

Private Mobile Radio Service

Mobile radio operates in one of three modes—single-frequency simplex, two-frequency simplex, and duplex. Both of the simplex modes use push-to-talk operation. When the transmitter button is in the talk position, the receiver cuts off. In a single-frequency mode, the mobile units and base unit send and receive on the same frequency. In a two-frequency operation, the base transmits on one frequency and receives on another; the mobile units reverse the transmit and receive frequencies.

In a duplex mode, the carriers of both the mobile and the base are on for the duration of the session. Normally the base station will use separate transmit and receive antennas. Most mobile units use the same antenna to transmit and receive. A filter separates the transmitter's rf energy from the receiving transmission line. The transmit and receive frequencies must be separated sufficiently to prevent the transmitter from desensitizing the receiver. Duplex operation provides two mobile radio units with the equivalent of a land line telephone conversation.

To improve mobile radio coverage, which is apt to be spotty in mountainous terrain, repeaters are often employed. If the session between a mobile and a base station is set up through a repeater, two sets of frequencies are used—one between the mobile and the repeater and the other between the repeater and the base station.

The base station often is mounted at a remote location to improve coverage and therefore must be remotely controlled. Control functions, including keying the transmitter, selectively calling the mobile unit, and linking the audio path between the base station and the control unit, may be carried on over land line or point-to-point radio. The siting of the base station is a complex process. Because obstructions adversely affect mobile signals, it is advantageous to mount the antenna as high as possible. To overcome the effects of fading, it is desirable to use high transmitter power. Both of these, however, must be balanced with the objective of frequency reuse. On crowded frequencies, interference from distant stations becomes a problem.

Mobile-to-mobile communication is easy to administer in a single- frequency simplex operation because the mobiles can hear each other. In a duplex operation, the mobiles can hear only the base station unless the base station retransmits the signal from mobile units. The retransmission of the mobile signal, which is called *talk-through*, permits mobiles to communicate with one another. It is necessary for the base station to monitor a mobile-to-mobile conversation and to disconnect the path when the session ends.

Mobile Unit Signaling

The simplest form of signaling a mobile unit is voice calling. The base station calls the mobile unit's identification, and the mobile unit responds if the operator is within earshot. On a crowded radio frequency, the constant squawking of the speaker can be annoying, which leads to the need for some form of selective calling.

The simplest form of selective calling relies on the receiver's squelch circuit. The squelch is the circuitry that deactivates the receiver's audio in the absence of a received carrier. Several receivers can operate on the same frequency by assigning sub-audio tones to break the squelch of the desired receiver.

For a few stations, the tone activated squelch is satisfactory, but it does not permit many users to share the same channel. In channels with more users, a selective calling system similar to that used in mobile telephone can be employed. The receivers has a selector that responds to a series of audio tones. When the user's unit is signaled, the selector rings a bell, which also can activate an external signal such as honking a horn or turning on a flashing light.

Trunking Radio

As discussed in Chapter 31, if many people are contending for a single communication channel, the channel occupancy will be high, but service will be poor. As channels are added to a radio system, the number of calls that can be carried for a given grade of service increases dramatically. *Trunking* radio employs multiple channels to improve service to a group of users. The best example of trunking radio is a cellular system, but many private and public safety radio systems also use trunking to improve service.

A trunking system designates one channel as the calling or control channel, and all idle receivers tune to that channel. The control channel can be the next idle channel in a sequence, or it may be a channel that is designated as the control. Some loss of efficiency occurs when units must switch signaling channels, so high usage systems, such as cellular, reach a point at which it is more efficient to have a dedicated signaling channel.

Trunking systems must resolve the occasional conflict of two stations signaling simultaneously. Two methods commonly are used—polling and contention. Both systems work the same way channel sharing methods in data communications systems work. In a polling system, the base station sends a continuous stream of polling messages to all mobiles on the channels. The polling messages consume signaling channel time and are therefore inefficient. In a contention system, the mobile unit listens for an idle channel before transmitting. If two mobiles transmit simultaneously, the base station recognizes the collision and informs the mobiles of it. They then back off a random time before again attempting to transmit.

Mobile Radio Design Objectives

Private and public mobile radio and paging systems share a common set of design objectives. The design process is not precise because of the unpredictable nature of radio waves. Obstructions and fading cause the principal disturbances. Designers of point-to-point radio systems have several tools at their disposal to compensate for the effects of disturbances. They can use high power, directional antennas, and diversity to design a reliable path. The mobile radio designer is at a disadvantage because omnidirectional antennas are needed to reach roaming users. The nature of the remote unit may make it difficult to increase power because of the resulting increase in battery drain.

Also, the remote unit frequently operates in an undesirable noise environment (for example, ignition noise), and most important, the base station is attempting to communicate with a target that is constantly moving. As a result, no mobile radio system gives quality that is consistently as good as that provided by land telephones. This section discusses some techniques that designers use to generate satisfactory mobile radio service.

Wide Area Coverage

The major objective in mobile system design is to provide coverage that allows a mobile unit to move through a coverage area without loss of communication. Cellular radio, which is discussed later, is one way of accomplishing this. Another way is *quasi-synchronous* operation.

FM receivers have a tendency to be captured by the strongest signal. Quasi-synchronous, which also is called Simulcast, employs adjacent transmitters operating on frequencies that are slightly offset. The offset is small enough that the resulting beat frequency is inaudible.

A second method of achieving wide area coverage is a receiver voting system. When a mobile unit initiates or responds to a call, the receivers in the coverage area compare signal strength and "vote" on which unit has the best signal. That unit and its associated transmitter establish communication with the mobile until it moves beyond the coverage area and captures another transmitter.

Adequate Signal Strength

Mobile units live in a hostile environment of high noise, most of which is man-made with the predominant source being auto ignition and charging systems. Portable units often are carried inside buildings where the signal may be attenuated or other noise sources, such as elevators and industrial machinery, may interfere with the signal. These noise sources tend to be most disruptive at lower frequencies.

Another source of signal loss is fading. A primary cause of fading is a multipath signal: one path may arrive slightly out of phase with the other path, which causes a reduction in the received signal strength. A stationary user may experience a slow fade due to gradual changes in atmospheric reelection. A moving user on the edge of the coverage area is likely to experience a fast fade as the signal bounces off buildings, trees, and other obstructions. As the vehicle moves, the frequency of the fade changes. If the fade is fast enough, it can be tolerated and sounds much like a noisy signal. A fade of about 10 cycles per second has the greatest effect on the user and makes communication practically impossible. A user on the fringes of the coverage area often can improve communication by stopping the vehicle and edging forward to a high signal strength location. A move of only a few inches can make a great difference in received signal strength.

Fading is often a frequency selective. If a band of frequencies is transmitted, one range of frequencies may be subjected to heavy fading while the other suffers little or not at all. The range of frequencies that are subject to similar fading effects is called the *coherence bandwidth*. Because of the frequency selective nature of fading, designers can use frequency diversity to establish a reliable communication path.

Since VHF and higher frequencies have a short wave length, it is often possible to counter the effects of fading by using space diversity. In a space diversity system, antennas are mounted at a distance that reduces the probability of a similar fade striking both antennas simultaneously. In a vehicular radio, for example, one antenna might be mounted on the front fender and another on the rear.

Wave Propagation

Radio waves propagate by one of three methods—the *ground wave,* the *tropospheric wave,* and the *ionospheric,* or *sky,* wave. Each of these acts differently on different frequency ranges and has a significant effect on the propagation characteristics of the signal.

The ground wave guides radio frequencies below about 30 MHz. The signal follows the contour of the earth and diminishes with distance. Ground wave communication is effective for short distances and has little effect on VHF and higher frequencies.

The tropospheric wave is effective at VHF and higher frequencies but has little effect below 3 MHz. At microwave frequencies, the tropospheric wave can be used to communicate beyond the line of sight.

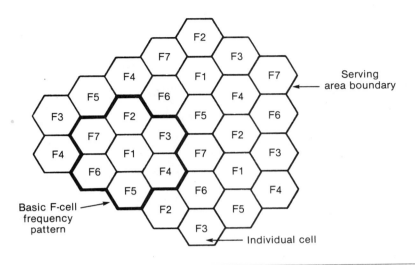

Figure 16.2   Frequency reuse in a cellular serving area.

The ionospheric wave is most effective below VHF frequencies. The ionosphere reflects high frequencies in a manner that is highly frequency selective. With ionospheric reflection, signals can travel well beyond the range of the ground wave, a condition that is called *skip*. Skip conditions can result in excellent communication capability most of the way around the world with low power, but the communication path is unreliable and difficult to predict.

Cellular Mobile Radio

Cellular mobile radio overcomes most of the disadvantages of conventional mobile telephone. A coverage area is divided into hexagonal *cells* as shown in Figure 16.2. Frequencies are not duplicated in adjacent cells, which reduces interference between base stations. It also allows the carrier to reuse frequencies within the coverage area with a buffer between cells that are operating on the same band of frequencies. This technique greatly increases the number of radio channels available compared to a conventional mobile telephone system, which uses a frequency only once in a coverage area.

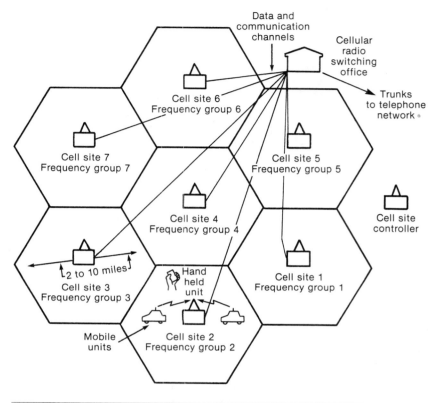

Figure 16.3   Cellular radio serving plan.

The general plan of cellular radio is shown in Figure 16.3. The carrier selects the number and size of cells to optimize coverage, cost, and total capacity within the serving area. FCC rules and regulations do not specify these design factors. The mobile units are *frequency agile*; that is, they can be shifted to any of the 416 voice channels. Mobile units are equipped with processor-driven logic units that respond to incoming calls and shift to radio channels under control of the base station. Each cell is equipped with transmitters, receivers, and control apparatus. One or more frequencies in each cell are designated for calling and control. For incoming and outgoing calls, the *cell-site controller* assigns the channel and directs a *frequency synthesizer* inside the mobile unit to shift to the appropriate frequency.

An electronic central office serves as a *mobile telephone switching office* (MTSO), and controls mobile operation within the cells. The cell-site controllers connect to the MTSO over data links. The MTSO switches calls to other mobile units and to the local telephone system, processes data from the cell-site controllers, and records billing details. It also controls *handoff* so a mobile leaving one cell switches automatically to a channel in the next cell.

Cellular radio overcomes a major drawback of conventional mobile telephone service, the lack of supervision from the mobile unit. Cellular radio uses the control channel to supervise the mobile station. Unlike conventional mobile telephone service, in which calls are timed on the basis of supervisory signals from the wireline telephone, cellular radio permits either the wireline or the mobile unit to control timing. This aids mobile-to-mobile calling, which closely approximates ordinary telephone service.

Cell-Site Operation

A cell-site has one radio transmitter and two receivers per channel, the cell-site controller, an antenna system, and data links to the MTSO. The hexagon was chosen for the cell shape because it provides a practical way of covering an area without the gaps and overlaps of circular cells. As a practical matter, cell boundaries are not precise. Directional antennas can approximate the shape, but the MTSO switches a user from one cell to another based on signal strength reports from the cell-site controllers. The handoff between cells is nearly instantaneous, and users are generally unaware that it has occurred. The handoff, which takes about 0.2 seconds, has little effect on voice transmission aside from an audible click, but data errors will result from the momentary interruption. As many as 128 channels per cell can be provided, with the number of channels based on demand; most cells operate with 70 or fewer channels.

Cell sites provide coverage with the relatively low power of the cell-site transmitters. FCC rules limit cellular transmitters to 100 watts output, with higher power used only if necessary to cover large cells. At the UHF frequencies of cellular radio, trans-

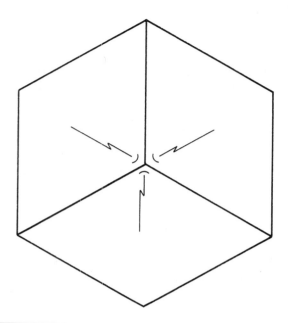

Figure 16.4 **A sectored cell.**

mission is line-of-sight, so considerable planning is needed to define the coverage area of the individual cell while minimizing the need to realign cells in the future.

A minimum of one channel per call is provided for control of the mobile units from the cell-site controller. The cell-site controller directs channel assignments, receives outgoing call data from the mobile unit, and pages mobile units over the control channel. When the load exceeds the capacity of one channel, separate paging and access channels are used.

The cell-site controller manages the radio channels within the cell. It receives instructions from the MTSO to turn transmitters and receivers on and off, and it supervises the calls, diagnoses trouble, and relays data messages to the MTSO and mobile units. The cell-site controller also monitors the mobile units' signal strength and reports it to the MTSO. It scans all active mobile units operating in adjacent cells and reports their signal strengths to the MTSO, which maps all

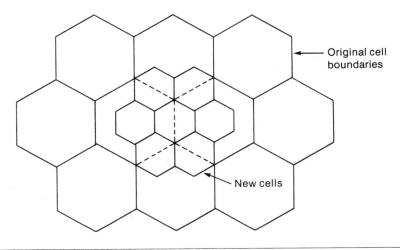

Original cell boundaries

New cells

Figure 16.5   Increasing capacity by splitting cells.

working mobile units. This map determines which cell should receive a mobile unit when handoff is required.

The number of users that a single cell can support depends on traffic. As cellular radio is introduced to an area, usage is low. As the prices of portable units and monthly service charges drop, the demand grows, necessitating increases in cell capacity. Cell capacity can be expanded by adding radio channels up to the maximum. When cells reach their channel capacity, they can be *sectored*, that is, subdivided into two to six sections with frequencies reused within the cells. Interference is avoided by providing directional antennas as Figure 16.4 shows. Sectored patterns also are used near mountains, water, and other terrain obstructions to direct radio frequency energy away from areas where it is not needed.

Cells also can be split to increase capacity. One strategy for introducing cellular radio is to begin with large cells as shown in Figure 16.5. As demand increases, a larger cell can be subdivided into smaller cells by reducing power and changing the antenna patterns. A fourth method of increasing capacity is to borrow unused channels from an adjacent cell.

Supervisory audio tones (SAT tones) prevent a mobile unit from talking on the same frequency at separate cell sites. The base station sends one of three SAT tones, and the mobile transponds it. If the SAT tone returned by a mobile unit is different from the one sent by the cell site, the MTSO will not accept the call.

Mobile Telephone Serving Office

The MTSO is essentially an end office switching system of the type described in Chapter 9 with a special purpose generic program for cellular radio operation. Not all MTSOs are local switching system; some products are designed specifically for cellular radio. In most cases, MTSOs are digital switching systems. The objective of most service providers is to offer cellular radio features that are essentially identical to wireline telephone features.

The MTSO links to the cell-site controller with data circuits for control purposes and with four-wire voice circuits for communication channels. When the cell-site controller receives a call from the mobile unit, the controller registers the dialed digits and passes them over the data link. The concept is similar to common channel signaling as described in Chapter 11, but X.25 protocol is used. The MTSO registers the dialed digits and switches the call to the telephone network over an intermachine trunk or to another cellular mobile unit within the system. When mobile-to-mobile calls or calls from the local telephone system are placed, the MTSO pages the mobile unit by sending messages to all cell-site controllers.

The MTSO receives reports from the cell-site controller on the signal strength of each mobile unit transmitting within the coverage area. Data is relayed to the MTSO to enable it to decide which cell is the appropriate serving cell for each active unit. The MTSO also collects statistical information about traffic volumes for allowing the system administrator to determine when to add channels. The MTSO stores usage records for generating bills.

Mobile Units

When cellular radio first was introduced, mobile units were expensive, with many units retailing for as much as $3000. The increasing demand for cellular has resulted in a decline in prices, and the least expensive units are currently selling for less than

Figure 16.6   The Motorola MicroTAC cellular telephone.
Courtesy, Motorola, Inc

$200. Hand held units are becoming so compact that they can be fit into a shirt pocket or purse. The Motorola MicroTAC unit, shown in Figure 16.6, folds to become one of the most compact units on the market.

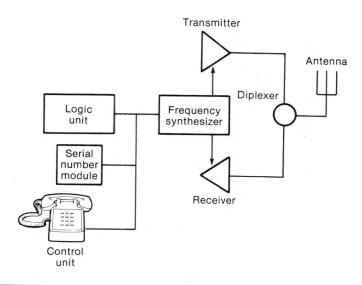

Figure 16.7   Block diagram of a cellular mobile radio transceiver.

The transceiver is a sophisticated device that can tune all channels in an area. Unlike conventional mobile transceivers that use individual crystals for setting the frequency of each channel, cellular transceivers are frequency agile. That is, they use frequency synthesizers, which are circuits that generate the end frequency by multiplying from a reference frequency. When cellular theory was first examined in 1947, the science of solid state electronics was undeveloped, and control circuitry was electromechanical and bulky and consumed considerable power. Transceivers of today are small enough to be contained in a housing the size of a telephone handset or smaller and are powered by rechargeable batteries.

The major components of a typical mobile unit are shown in the block diagram in Figure 16.7. The transmitter and receiver are coupled to the antenna through a *diplexer*, which is a device that isolates the two directions of transmission so the transmitter does not feed power into its own receiver. The frequency synthesizer generates transmit and receive frequencies under control of the logic board. The synthesizer generates a reference frequency from a highly stable oscillator and divides, filters, and multiplies it to generate the required frequency.

The most complex part of the mobile unit is the logic equipment. This system communicates with the cell-site controller over the control channel and directs the other systems in the functions of receiving and initiating calls. These functions include recognizing and responding to incoming signals, shifting the rf equipment to the working channel for establishing a call initially and during handoff, and interpreting users' service requests. The logic unit periodically scans the control channels and tunes the transceiver to the channel with the strongest signal. The user communicates with the logic unit through a control unit, which consists of the handset, dial, display unit, and other elements that approximate a conventional telephone set.

The unit also includes a power converter to supply the logic and rf equipment with the proper voltages from the battery source. FCC rules limit the transmitter to 7 watts output, but many mobile units use 3 watts or less to reduce battery drain. Battery drain is particularly important in hand-held or portable units. The FCC segregates mobile units into three power classes ranging from 0.6 watts to the maximum power permitted.

Another module electronically generates the unit's 32-bit binary serial number to prevent fraudulent or unauthorized use of a mobile unit. The serial number is communicated to the cell-site controller with each call for comparison with a data base maintained by the MTSO. The unit's 10-digit calling number and a station class mark also are built into memory and transmitted to the cell-site controller with each outgoing call. The class mark identifies the station type and power rating.

Mobile Telephone Features

A full description of mobile telephone features is beyond the scope of this book. The following is a brief description of the most popular cellular radio mobile features. Among the most important features are those that improve safety by enabling the user to operate the system while driving.

- *A/B System Selection*. Offers a choice between wireline and nonwireline carrier bands.

- *Call Timer*. Displays elapsed time of calls, displays accumulated time to aid in estimating billing costs, and provides a preset interval timer during a call.

- *Dialed Number Display*. The dialed number is displayed in a readout on the handset. Misdialed digits can be corrected before the number is outpulsed.

- *Last Number Dialed*. As in a conventional telephone, this feature stores the last number dialed so it can be recalled with a touch of a button.

- *Muting*. The handset cuts off with a button so the distant party cannot hear a private conversation within the car.

- *On-Hook Dialing*. This feature allows the user to dial a number while the unit is on-hook. If the unit has dialed number display, the number can be pulsed into a handset and reviewed before it is sent.

- *Repertory Dialing*. The unit stores a list of telephone numbers that can be selected by dialing one or two digits.

- *Scratch Pad*. This feature stores numbers entered with the keypad in a temporary memory location.

- *Security*. Because of the high price of the units, theft is a potential problem. Each unit is equipped internally to report its serial number to the cell-site controller with each call. This identifies the specific transmitter from which a call originates, and makes it difficult to change the telephone number for fraudulent reporting. Other security features include both key locks and digital locks that must be activated before the unit can be operated. Some units are easy to remove so they can be stored in the trunk or glove box.

- *Self-Diagnostics*. Internal diagnostics indicate trouble in transceiver and control unit to aid in rapid trouble shooting.

- *Speaker*. Some units include a speaker and remote microphone so conversations can be monitored by others in the car and to permit hands-free operation of the unit.

- *Special Signaling*. A "call in absence" indicator turns on a light when a call is received but not answered. Auxiliary signals can honk the horn or turn on the lights when a call arrives at an unattended unit.

Roaming

Roaming is the ability of a mobile unit to move outside its normal service area. The cellular operator must know about a roaming user to route calls to the proper service area and to know where to send the bill. There are three types of roaming. In *preregistered roaming* the user registers with the cellular company in each service area. *Automatic roaming* enables the user to drive into a service area and log in, after which cellular operation is permitted. *Follow me roaming* is a fully automatic system in which the mobile unit and base station can carry on a dialog without the need for the user to do anything except dial a three-digit code to inform the control center of his or her arrival. This roaming method is just being introduced in some metropolitan areas.

Cellular Radio Services

Cellular radio duplicates the services of wire line carriers as nearly as possible. Some carriers offer operator services to allow users to place collect, third number, and credit card calls. An attendant service is also required so roaming users can check in when they leave one carrier's service area and enter another. Although the mobile unit automatically identifies the user, the different jurisdictions require identification and registration of the user for billing purposes.

Digital Cellular Radio

Cellular radio design has alleviated the problems of poor coverage and congested frequencies, primarily in urban areas. The FCC initially allocated 40 MHz for cellular radio, which was supposed to last indefinitely. Within four years, however, the carriers were back to the FCC asking for additional frequencies because the design theories were not working as expected. The principle of cell splitting, which was supposed to reduce large cells to smaller ones as traffic increased, was not proving as technically or economically feasible as expected. The FCC granted an additional 10 MHz, which increased the size of the A and B band allocations to

25 MHz each. At the same time, they proposed that the industry develop methods of improving utilization.

The strength of the present system is that the standards are accepted industry-wide and followed by all manufacturers. Some manufacturers are proposing that the current standard be replaced by a digital cellular system. For a digital system to be feasible, efficient modulation methods must be developed to compress the voice into narrower bandwidths. Many observers believe it is possible to compress the present bandwidth by factor of three or four by using a highly efficient digital modulation algorithm and by using different access control methods.

Under the present system, a user has exclusive use of a channel in a cell site for the duration of a session. The inherent half duplex character of voice communications, plus the frequent pauses in most conversations wastes much airtime. The time division multiple access (TDMA) techniques used to increase the carrying capacity of satellites and digital termination radio hold promise for increasing the capacity of cellular radio.

The second approach to increasing capacity is through more efficient modulation. AT&T Bell Laboratories has developed two digital coding systems that promise to digitize voice at 8000 b/s with no loss in clarity. One technique, Multipulse Speech Coding, was developed in the early 1980s. The other technique, Code Excited Linear Prediction (CELP), appears to be the front runner, supported as it is by several companies, including AT&T.

While converting the present cellular system to digital is a desirable objective, difficulties arise in making the transition from the existing to the new system. Because digital and analog modulation schemes are inherently incompatible and because users have a huge investment in station equipment, some means of making the two systems coexist until obsolete equipment is phased out must be found. The two methods proposed are partitioned and non-partitioned systems. A partitioned system would have a portion of the bandwidth set aside for digital and another portion for analog. Unfortunately, the reduction in the size of the channel allocations makes this inherently an inefficient solution. A non-partitioned system would allow either a digital or an analog radio to share the same bandwidth, but the cell-site equipment would be expensive

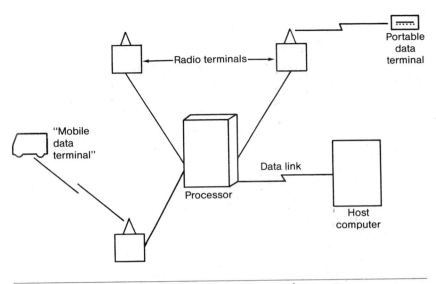

Figure 16.8   Metropolitan radio data network.

and complex. It is not clear at this writing what solution the industry and regulatory authorities will devise.

Mobile Data Transmission

Data can be transmitted over cellular mobile radio. The interruption of about 200 milliseconds when a mobile unit is handed off from one cell to another can be detrimental to data transmission, but otherwise the service is equivalent to wireline data transmission. The mobile unit is equipped with a special modem, sometimes built into the radio equipment, and a data terminal intended for vehicular operation. Private radio systems also use mobile terminals for such purposes as linkage between a law enforcement agency and a vehicular or law enforcement data base.

Hand-held mobile data equipment is also available for use in a metropolitan data network as Figure 16.8 shows. The mobile data terminal is a small hand held terminal such as Motorola's KDT 840 Data terminal, which Figure 16.9 shows. The unit operates on a single full duplex channel in the 800 MHz frequency range. Data is transmitted by keying into a small compact key-

Figure 16.9   The Motorola KDT 840 portable data terminal.
Courtesy, Motorola, Inc.

board. Messages return in a portable display. A processor controls multiple radio channels, which operate on the same frequency within the metropolitan area. The system is designed for two-way applications such as dispatching.

Personal Radio

Within the next few years, a new generation of personal two-way radio will enter the market if developers receive FCC authorization. One type of equipment uses low powered transmitters in metropolitan areas. It is intended for pedestrian, as opposed to vehicular, service and will be used in place of public telephones.

Motorola announced plans to develop a second type of service that could be used anywhere in the world. A group of 77 communications satellites would circle the globe in low orbit. Users would carry 25-ounce handsets that could communicate with the satellite on microwave frequencies. The receiving satellite would relay the signal to a second satellite, which would check a data base to verify that the call was authorized. If so, the satellite would relay the call to another satellite that could reach the destination of the call. If Motorola's plans are fulfilled, the service will be operating in the mid-1990s.

Basic Exchange Telecommunications Radio

Basic exchange telecommunications radio (BETR) is a point-to-point radio service operating in the 800 MHz frequency range. The FCC authorized the service in December, 1987 to provide telecommunications to rural subscribers. In sparsely populated areas, it is expensive to provide land line telephone service. With a network of base stations and repeaters, the BETR system can provide a grade of service and quality that approximates land line service without the outside plant costs. The BETR remote unit is similar to a cellular unit except that it uses digital modulation, higher power, and directional antennas to achieve reliable service. BETR fills a small niche in the radio market: users who are too far from the central office to be served economically with wire plant or loop carrier. Equipment has entered the market slowly, and at the time of this writing usage is confined to a few field trials.

Radio Paging

Paging is a radio application that is less sophisticated and less costly than cellular radio. Developed under the centralized transmitter and receiver plan of conventional mobile telephone service, radio paging offers dial access from a wireline telephone to a pocket receiver. Portable paging units sell for $100 to $450 plus a monthly fee. Most paging systems do not offer two-way communication. The user receives a page and either listens to the message over the portable unit or dials a number to receive the message. The number is either predetermined or displayed on the pager. Some units have a dual number system so a user can respond to one wireline telephone for one signal and a second number for another signal.

A new generation of pagers that eventually will work worldwide is just entering the market. The user wears a pager, which may be in a wrist watch. Messages are sent by satellite to a selected group of FM broadcast stations in the major metropolitan areas. Paging messages are broadcast on an FM subcarrier, which is inaudible to station listeners. If the message is undeliverable because, for example, the recipient is outside the coverage area, the message is stored in a page retrievable service until it ages out or finally is delivered.

Applications

Cellular radio is rapidly becoming a commodity, much like ordinary telephone service for those who can afford it. This section includes considerations that users of cellular radio service should evaluate, in terms of both the service itself and the mobile radio equipment.

Standards

In the United States, the FCC Rules and Regulations set forth mobile radio standards. FCC rules establish the authorized frequencies, power levels, bandwidth, frequency stability, signaling formats, and other such variables in the public mobile service. Cellular radio standards are outlined in the Cellular Mobile/Land Station Compatibility Specification issued by the FCC and EIA in 1981. Internationally, CCIR issues mobile radio recommendations.

Evaluation Criteria

Cellular mobile telephone equipment is evaluated on much the same basis as other telecommunications equipment. Reliability and the ability to obtain fast and efficient service is a paramount concern. Cost is also an important consideration. When cellular equipment was introduced, costs were high, but with the popularity of the technology, prices have dropped to the point that equipment cost is now a minor consideration. The cost of air time, however, remains high.

Security Issues

Regular mobile radio is inherently an unsecure medium. Anyone with a receiver tuned to the mobile frequency can eavesdrop on any conversation, and there is little practical means of preventing it aside from scrambling, which is impractical on public radio systems because of the need for matched scrambling devices. Cellular radio offers inherent security that may be sufficient but still is not interception-proof. If a session takes place in one cell, it is easy for someone to intercept it. If, however, the vehicle is moving, each time it is handed off to another cell, an eavesdropper may have some difficulty resuming reception of the conversation. The smaller the cells, the more frequent the handoff, and the less likely it is that the entire session can be monitored.

Coverage

A coverage area is one of the two or three primary considerations most users review in an evaluating a mobile radio system.

Coverage can best be evaluated by taking a test drive and making calls from the areas you plan to drive through, paying particular attention to the fringe areas.

Number of Cell Sites

Cellular services with large numbers of cell sites are the most likely to provide satisfactory service. Large cells are likely to be sectionalized as usage increases. Sectionalization itself does not necessarily disrupt service, but the cell is apt to become crowded before the need for sectionalization is apparent.

Selecting Cellular Radio Equipment

The first decision in selecting equipment is to determine whether you need vehicular, transportable, or portable equipment. As the name implies, vehicular equipment is mounted inside a vehicle. It usually consists of a separate radio unit and control unit. The radio equipment mounts under the seat, in the trunk, or in another out-of-the-way place. The control unit mounts within easy reach of the person who will operate it usually the driver.

Transportable equipment also comes with separate control and radio units. The radio comes in a carrying case. Portable equipment is a one-piece device with all the radio equipment, power supply, and antenna mounted in a unit that can be used in a hand set. With both portable and transportable equipment, the output power is important because it directly affects battery capacity. The greater the capacity, the heavier the unit but the better the coverage. Ruggedness is also an important consideration with equipment that can be carried because inevitably it will be dropped.

Service Quality

The FCC established the frequency allocation plan for cellular radio with the intention of encouraging competition. In areas where competition exists, differences in price may be reflected in differences in service quality. If the carriers offer coverage demonstrations, it is advisable to try the service before making a commitment to ensure that the coverage area is satisfactory and that channels are not overloaded. If the vendor does not provide demonstrations, it may be possible to rent a mobile-equipped car to evaluate service quality. If portable units will be used extensively, coverage checks should be made to ensure that the unit will deliver the needed performance.

Usage Charges

Cellular radio charges are based on duration of both originating and terminating calls. Carriers charge for total air time and add on other message charges such as long distance. Therefore, both originating and terminating calls are charged to the terminating mobile number; outgoing long distance usage is billed twice once for the air time and once for the wireline long distance service. Extra charges may be imposed for roaming between service areas.

Selected Mobile Radio Equipment Manufacturers

Cellular Central Office Equipment

AT&T Network Systems

Ericsson Inc., Communications Division

NEC America Inc. Switching Systems Division

Motorola Communications & Electronics, Inc.

Northern Telecom Inc., Digital Switching Systems

Cellular, Pagers, and IMTS Mobile Equipment

BBL Industries

CIT-Alcatel, Inc.

General Electric Mobile
Communications Division

Glenayre Electronics

Harris Corporation, RF
Communications Group

E.F. Johnson Company

NEC America Inc. Switching
Systems Division

Motorola Communications &
Electronics, Inc.

M/A-COM Land Mobile
Communications, Inc.

NEC America Inc., Radio &
Transmission Div.

Video Systems

Since the end of World War II, television has grown steadily as an entertainment medium. In addition, many businesses have employed closed circuit television (CCTV) in security surveillance systems and have used it for internal communications and training. The effectiveness of television in enhancing classroom and business meetings has long been recognized, but until recently, the cost of long haul transmission facilities has been prohibitive for all but a few large organizations. Recent developments are changing television into an economical medium for enhanced communication as travel costs continue to climb.

The first factor inducing the change is the rapid growth of community antenna television (CATV). CATV has been around since the 1950s, but its use for services other than repeating signals into areas without television service is recent. Not only is the medium useful for television alone, but CATV providers offer bandwidth for data communications in many metropolitan areas.

CATV systems have grown rapidly in major market areas that once were served exclusively by broadcasters. Companies seeking franchises have agreed to provide at little or no cost institutional channels for use by municipalities and school districts. In most cities today a broadband communications channel routes to a substantial portion of businesses and residences. CATV serves approximately 40 million households in the United States, representing nearly half the television-owning households. Of this number, about 25 million are on CATV systems with premium entertainment channels.

At first, the FCC did not regulate CATV; as recently as 1959, the FCC ruled that it had no jurisdiction over CATV systems, but in 1966 it asserted jurisdiction. The FCC issued the first rules regulating CATV in 1972, requiring Certificates of Compliance from CATV companies and establishing minimum technical standards for CATV transmissions.

CATV has had several effects on the growth of video communication systems in business. First, CATV hardware is used for CCTV and, increasingly, for local area networks in many businesses. Second, CATV is the transmission medium that connects many customers to *teleports*, which are communications centers that concentrate broadband facilities in urban areas for connection to satellite communication systems. Third, CATV offers an alternative to common carrier point-to-point communication facilities.

The second significant development is the growth of communications satellites. Many CATV programs are carried by satellite, which offers the potential of delivering service to the entire continent. Satellite broadcasts have the enormous social impact of bringing video accounts of worldwide events into millions of homes almost at the instant they occur. The effects of this are only beginning to be felt. Satellites also provide nationwide transmission facilities for multipoint video conferences and one-way broadcasts for a fraction of the cost of terrestrial facilities. The broadcast nature of satellites and the fact that rates are independent of distance makes video conferencing feasible over satellites where it would be prohibitively expensive over terrestrial facilities.

A third factor, and the one that has the greatest long range impact on video communications, is the development of video compression technology. As discussed in a later section, video compression takes analog video signals that occupy 6 MHz of bandwidth and squeezes them into narrow digital channels. The Picturephone, which AT&T introduced in 1964, failed to attract enough interest to make it a commercially successful product at the time. Like so many other product developments, however, it was merely ahead of its time. Advancements in video technology now make it technically (although not economically) feasible to compress a signal of moderately good quality into a passband that can be supported by most subscriber loops in the United States. Although the cost of compression technology is high, the limits are not yet in sight. As costs drop, businesses, and then later residences, will begin to adopt video as a normal way of communicating.

A fourth development is the availability of inexpensive video recorders and cameras. Not many years ago, VCRs were beyond the reach of all but businesses and the most wealthy individuals. In addition, trained technicians were required to operate expensive video cameras, and studio conditions were needed for lighting and sound. Now, VCRs and video cameras have become commodities well within the reach of most households. The ready availability of this equipment will cause people to adopt video as part of their natural way of conducting business.

A fifth development that is not yet as far reaching as the first four is the provision of video meeting services as a utility. Conference rooms equipped with cameras, monitors, and access to transmission facilities are available in many cities to any organization wanting to conduct a multipoint meeting. Portable equipment can bring conference facilities to the user's premises or to hotels, many of which have satellite receiving equipment. In larger organizations, these facilities are duplicated within the organization itself, but for most businesses the cost of a full studio is prohibitive. Recently developed standards, inexpensive studio equipment, and declining costs for compression and transmission facilities will bring video conferencing within the reach of many companies within the next few years.

Video Technology

At its present state of development, video is inherently an analog transmission medium because of the method of picture generation. Video signals in the United States are generated under the National Television Systems Committee (NTSC) system. A video signal is formed by scanning an image with a video camera. As the camera scans the image, it creates an analog signal that varies in voltage with variations in the degree of blackness of the image. In the NTSC system, the television *raster* has 525 horizontal scans. The raster is composed of two fields of 262.5 lines each. The two fields are interlaced to form a *frame*, as Figure 17.1 shows. The

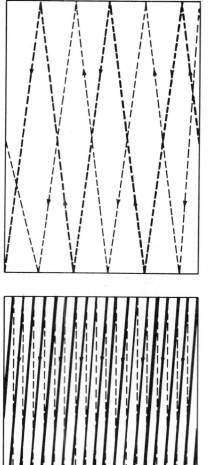

Inactive Fields
Heavy lines show retrace pattern from
bottom to top of screen during vertical
blanking interval. Heavy lines represent
first field and light lines the second.

Active Fields
Heavy lines represent first field.
Light lines represent second field.
Dotted lines represent retrace lines
that are blanked out.

Figure 17.1   Interlaced scanning frame.

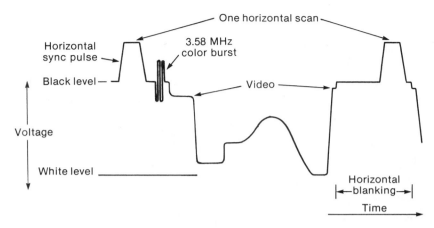

a. Voltage levels during one horizontal scan. As image is scanned, voltage varies from reference black to reference white level.

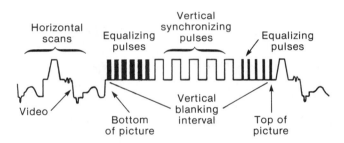

b. Vertical synchronization. Vertical blanking occurs during retrace of scanner to top of screen.

Figure 17.2   Synchronizing and blanking in a television signal.

frame repeats 30 times each second; the persistence of the human eye eliminates flicker.

On close inspection, a video screen is revealed as a matrix of tiny dots. Each dot is called a *picture element*, abbreviated *pixel*. The resolution of a television picture is a function of the number of scan lines and pixels per frame, both of which affect the amount of bandwidth required to transmit a television signal. The NTSC system requires about four MHz of bandwidth for satisfactory resolution. Because of the modulation system used and the need for guard bands between channels, the FCC assigns 6 MHz of bandwidth to television channels in the United States.

The signal resulting from each scan line varies between a black and a white voltage level as Figure 17.2a shows. A horizontal synchronizing pulse is inserted at the beginning of each line. Frames are synchronized with vertical pulses as Figure 17.2b shows. Between frames the signal is blanked during a vertical synchronizing interval to allow the scanning trace to return to the upper left corner of the screen. Teletext services transmit information during this interval, which is known as the *vertical blanking interval*.

There are two parts to a color television signal, the *luminance* signal and the *chrominance* signal. A black and white picture has only the luminance signal, which controls the brightness of the screen in step with the sweep of the horizontal trace. The chrominance signal modulates subcarriers that are transmitted with the video signal. The color demodulator in the receiver is synchronized by a *color burst* consisting of eight cycles of a 3.58 MHz signal that is applied to the horizontal synchronizing pulse as Figure 17.2a shows.

When no picture is being transmitted, the scanning voltage rests at the black level, and the television receiver's screen is black. Because the signal is amplitude modulated analog, any noise pulses that are higher in level than the black signal level appear on the screen as *snow*. A high quality transmission medium must keep the signal level above the noise to preserve satisfactory picture quality. The degree of resolution in a television picture depends on bandwidth. Signals sent through a narrow bandwidth are fuzzy with washed-out color. The channel also must be sufficiently linear. Lack of linearity results in high level signals being amplified at a different rate than low level signals, which affects picture contrast. Another critical requirement of the transmission medium is its envelope delay characteristic. If envelope delay is excessive, the chrominance signal arrives at the receiver out of phase with the luminance signal, and color distortion results.

The four primary criteria for assessing a video transmission medium, therefore, are noise, bandwidth, amplitude linearity,

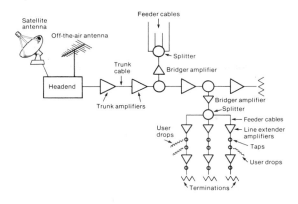

Figure 17.3   Block diagram of a CATV system.

and phase linearity. The primary media used are analog micro-wave radio, analog coaxial cable, and, for broadcasting, free space. As video signals increasingly are being digitized, digital radio and fiber optics also are feasible transmission media. Analog signals also can be transmitted over fiber optics using intensity modula-tion, or frequency modulation of a light carrier.

Cable Television Systems

Cable television systems have three major components; headend equipment, trunk cable, and feeder and user drop equipment. Figure 17.3 is a block diagram of a CATV system. A principal limitation of CATV systems is a lack of selectivity for the end user. All channels that originate at the headend are broadcast to all stations, which means the operator must either limit the number of channels carried or find a way to block premium channels for which the user is not paying. Except for various devices to prevent unauthorized reception of pay television signals, any receiver can receive all services on the network. This is in contrast to the telephone network, which routes lines in a star configuration to each user individually.

Headend Equipment

Headend equipment, as Figure 17.4 shows, receives and gener-ates video signals and, in two-way systems, repeats the signal from

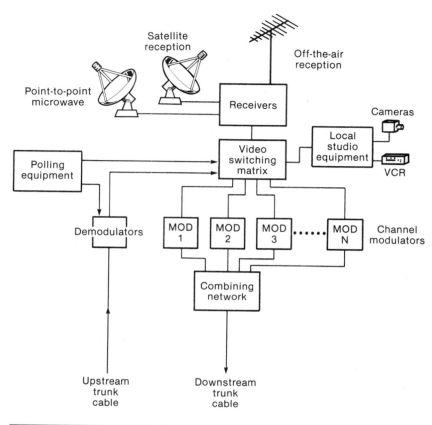

Figure 17.4 Headend equipment.

the user on the upstream channels to terminals on the down-stream channels. Signals from these sources are inserted at the headend:

- Off-the-air pickup of broadcast signals including both television and FM radio.

- Signals received over communications satellites.

- Signals received from distant locations over microwave radio relay systems.

- Locally originated signals.

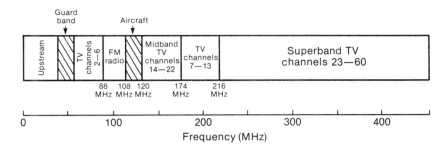

Figure 17.5   Cable television frequency bands.

The headend equipment modulates each television signal to a separate channel in the range of 50 to 450 MHz. Some companies use narrower bandwidth systems, but the present state of the art can support up to 60 channels over this frequency range as Figure 17.5 shows. UHF television, which occupies frequencies from 470 to 890 MHz, cannot be transported over a CATV system, so off-the-air UHF channels are converted into another channel within the passband. Most CATV systems use a single coaxial cable to carry signals, but some systems double their capacity by using two cables. All amplifiers and cable facilities are duplicated in a two-cable system, but the labor cost of placing dual cables, which often is a significant part of the total investment, is little more than the cost of one.

Trunk Cable Systems

Headend equipment applies the signal to a trunk to carry the signal to local distribution systems. Some systems use *hub headends* to distribute the signal. Hub headends are satellites of a master headend and have the ability to add or distribute services before sending the signal through the local feeder area. The cable between the master headend and the hubs is called a *super trunk*. Hubs may be fed by point-to-point microwave radio operating in a band designated by the FCC as Cable Television Relay Service. Increasingly, CATV companies use fiber optics for trunks.

Early CATV systems used a separate amplifier for each television channel. This technique simplified the amplifier design, but restricted the practical number of channels that could be transported. Current systems use broadband amplifiers that are equalized to carry the entire bandwidth. Amplifiers have about 20 dB of gain and are placed at intervals of approximately one-third of a mile. Amplifiers known as *bridgers* split the signal to feeder cables.

Amplifiers contain automatic gain control circuitry to adjust gain as cable loss changes with temperature variations. Power is applied to amplifiers over the coaxial center conductor, with main power feed points approximately every mile. Many subscribers use CATV systems for home security and alarm systems, so continued operation during power outage is essential. To continue essential services during power outages and amplifier failures, the cable operator provides redundant amplifiers and backup battery supplies.

Trunk cable uses a high grade of coaxial cable with diameters of 0.75 to 1 inch. The cable often shares pole lines and trenches with power and telephone. The cable and amplifiers must be free of signal leakage. Because the CATV signals operate on the same frequencies as many radio services, a leaking cable can interfere with another service or vice versa. FCC regulations curtail the use of CATV in frequency bands of 108 to 136 and 225 to 400 MHz in many localities because of the possibility of interference with aeronautical navigation and communication equipment.

As with other analog transmission media, noise and distortion are cumulative through successive amplifier stages. Noise and distortion limit the serving radius of 60-channel CATV to about 5 miles from the headend.

Feeder and Drop System

Bridger amplifiers split feeder or distribution cable from the trunk cable. Multiple feeders are coupled with *splitters* or *directional couplers*, which match the impedance of the cables. The feeder cable is smaller and less expensive and has higher loss than trunk cable. Subscriber drops connect to the feeder cable through *taps*, which are passive devices that isolate the feeder cable from the drop. The tap must have enough isolation that shorts and opens at the television set do not affect other signals on the cable.

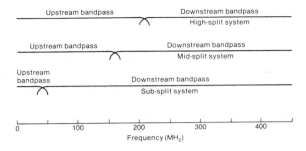

Figure 17.6   Two-way cable frequency splitting.

Pay Television Equipment

As Figure 17.5 shows, only 12 of the 60 channels in a CATV system are within the normal tuning range of a television set. Converters at the set shift the midband and superband channels to a channel that is unused in the local broadcast area. Some newer types of converters are addressable; that is they can be accessed by a signal at the headend to allow reception of only authorized channels.

Because addressable converters are expensive, cable operators often employ other systems to prevent reception of unauthorized channels by cable ready television sets and VCRs, which are capable of receiving all channels on a cable. The simplest system uses *sync suppression,* which removes synchronizing pulses from incoming channels, making it impossible to synchronize the television set without an adapter. A second system places a jamming carrier on the signal from the headend. A trap at the television set filters out the carrier. Another system uses a trap at the tap to "suck out" channels the user is not paying for. The trap is surrounded by a sleeve to make it difficult to access without a special tool. Increasingly, cable systems use scrambling to render unauthorized channels unusable without a descrambling device.

Two-Way CATV Systems

Two-way communication is available on relatively few CATV systems, but it is this that changes CATV from a medium reserved for entertainment to one that can support two-way communications.

The key to a two-way system is the bidirectional amplifier. Filters split the signal into the high band for downstream transmission and the low band for upstream transmission. Figure 17.6 shows three splitting methods. The subsplit is the most common in CATV systems with the midsplit and high split methods often used in broadband local area networks. A guard band 15 to 20 MHz wide separates the two directions of transmission. The upstream direction shares frequencies with high powered short wave transmitters operating on 5 to 30 MHz frequencies, so interference from these sources is a potential problem. Cable and amplifiers must be adequately shielded to prevent interference.

Headend equipment is considerably more complex in a two-way than in a one-way CATV system. User terminals access the upstream cable by contention, described in Chapter 27, or by being polled from the headend. The headend of a two-way system contains a computer to poll the terminals. Some systems use a transponder at the user end to receive and execute orders from the headend. For example, a polling message might instruct the transponder to read utility meters and forward the reading over the upstream channel.

Video Compression

When transmitted as analog, a video signal with full color and motion uses 6 MHz of bandwidth. Digitizing a video signal results in a 96 mb/s data signal. Depending on the modulation method, this would use the capacity of two transponders on a satellite or most of the capacity of a digital microwave radio with 30 MHz of bandwidth. As a result, digital television in uncompressed form is unable to compete economically with analog television.

Video compression equipment has entered the market in the past few years to reduce video signals to narrower bandwidths. Current equipment can compress a video signal of reasonable quality with full color and motion into a single 1.544 mb/s T-1 line. Excellent quality, suitable for all but the most demanding conference applications, can be obtained on one-third of a T-1 line, or 512 kb/s. With sacrifices in resolution and the ability to handle motion precisely, narrower bandwidths can be used. Currently, video signals can be compressed into 64 kb/s with quality that is acceptable for many conferences. Most conference video, however, uses 128 kb/s, or two digital voice channels.

Video signals contain considerable redundancy from frame to frame. Often large portions of background do not change between frames, but conventional transmission systems transmit these anyway. Video compression systems use techniques known as *interframe encoding* and *intraframe encoding* to transmit only changes between frames. An interframe coding device compares sample elements of succeeding frames and transmits only the pixels that have changed from the previous frame. Approximately every 2 seconds, the entire frame is refreshed, but in intervening frames, only the changed pixels are transmitted.

Intraframe encoding provides another element of compression. The picture is broken into blocks of 16 x 16 pixels. A block is transmitted only when pixels within that block have changed. Otherwise, the decoding equipment retains the previous block and forwards it to the receiver with each frame. By using combinations of inter- and intraframe encoding, video transmission quality is improving gradually. The equipment that encodes and decodes the video signal is called a *codec*.

At the present state of development, video compression equipment costs on the order of $35,000 to $50,000 per codec for a full color and motion system. When manufacturers recover their development costs, the prices of codecs will drop, but it will probably be several years before smaller organizations can afford them. At some sacrifice in quality, signals can be sent over narrower channels. It is currently possible to send a conference quality picture over a 128 kb/s channel. The tradeoff with bandwidth is in the lack of ability of the equipment to convey motion. Abrupt motions smear across the screen until the codec catches up. This characteristic is unsatisfactory for commercial broadcast use, but is acceptable for video conferencing in exchange for the lower cost of transmission facilities.

Video Conferencing

Some companies offer video conference facilities as a utility, with conference rooms and full video facilities available for lease. Some corporations that want to reduce travel and meeting costs own their own video conference facilities. Conferencing equipment is categorized as audio only, audio with graphics, freeze-frame video, and full motion video. Video conferencing is sometimes called *teleconferencing*, but in this book that term means audio-only conferences.

A video conference facility has the following subsystems integrated into a unit:

- Audio equipment.
- Video production and control equipment.
- Graphics equipment.
- Document hard copy equipment.
- Communications.

A full description of these systems is beyond the scope of this book. We will discuss them here briefly to describe the composition of a video conferencing facility.

Audio Equipment

Some analysts contend that audio equipment is the most important part of a video conference facility. In large video conferences it is often impossible to show all participants, but it is important that everyone hear and be heard clearly. Audio equipment comprises microphones, speakers, and amplifiers placed strategically around the room, sometimes coupled to a four-wire voice private line. Sometimes speaker telephones are used, but with generally less satisfactory results than a dedicated circuit. If the signal is transmitted by satellite, it is essential that the audio be transmitted over the same circuit to keep the sound and the speakers' lips synchronized.

Video and Control Equipment

Video equipment consists of two or three cameras and associated control equipment. The main camera usually is mounted at the front of the room and often automatically follows the voice of the speaker. Zoom, tilt, and azimuth controls are mounted on a console, where the conference participants can control them from a panel with a joystick. A second camera mounts overhead for graphic displays. The facility sometimes includes a third mobile camera that is operated independently. A switch at the console operator's position selects the camera. Monitors placed around the room can easily be seen by the participants. Usually one monitor set shows the picture from the distant end and another shows the picture at the near end.

In a video conference, the camera position largely determines the adverse effects of smearing. When the camera is positioned to encompass a passive group, smearing is generally not objectionable. It is most objectionable when there is considerable action or when the camera shows a closeup of the face of an individual who is talking.

Digitizing and encoding equipment compresses full motion video or creates freeze-frames. In addition, encryption equipment may be included for security. Other equipment can freeze a full motion display for a few seconds while the participants send a graphic image over the circuit. Sometimes digital storage equipment enables participants to transmit presentation material ahead of time so graphics transmission does not waste conference time.

Graphics Equipment

Video conference facilities may include graphics-generating equipment to construct diagrams with arrows, circles, lines, and other symbols. This type of equipment is similar to facsimile equipment, which Chapter 24 covers in more detail.

Communications

Communications facilities are audio and video circuits, the type of facility depending on the bandwidth required. They range from voice circuits to full DS-1 video facilities and satellite earth stations. When satellite communication facilities are used, the audio channel must be diplexed over the video channel to keep the audio sychronized with the picture.

Justification for Video Conferencing Equipment

Video conferencing long has been touted as a way of reducing travel costs. Several companies have undertaken expensive and unsuccessful forays into the business of providing conference room and transmission facilities. To date, the market has not developed the way its proponents had hoped, but several developments are generating a renewed interest in video conferencing.

Video conferencing is now becoming economically feasible—not just to reduce travel but as a way of doing business.

Interest in video conferencing is surging because costs are dropping dramatically. Coder/decoders (codecs) that cost more than $100,000 in the mid-1980s are now available for less than half that amount, and indications are that prices will continue to drop. Codecs can handle conference quality video over bandwidths ranging from 56 kb/s to 1.5 mb/s. Users can dial the amount of bandwidth they require, with the quality improving as bandwidth increases.

Complementing the drop in codec costs are reductions in the costs of transmission and equipping conference rooms. Many LECs and the major IECs offer switched 56/64 kb/s services. The interexchange portion of the service is only marginally more expensive than ordinary direct-dialed telephone service. It requires a dedicated loop to either the LEC or the IEC, which adds to the fixed cost of the service, but it is still only a fraction of what it cost a few years ago.

Portable conference room facilities, consisting of a camera with pan, tilt, and zoom; audio equipment; codec; and monitor can be purchased for about $50,000. Although this is still too high to be within the reach of casual users, it is less than half the price of a few years ago and will undoubtedly drop further as demand increases.

CCITT Standards

Another factor that is renewing interest in video conferencing is the newly adopted CCITT H.261 standards. Some observers expect these standards to revolutionize video conferencing the way Group 3 facsimile standards inspired rapid acceptance of that technology.

CCITT standards are known as P x 64 (pronounced P times 64). Two options are offered. The full Common Intermediate Format (CIF) offers frames of 288 lines by 352 pixels. This is approximately half the resolution of commercial television, which is 525 lines by 480 pixels. The second alternative is one-fourth CIF (QCIF), which is 144 lines by 176 pixels. The modulation method is the discrete3 cosine transform (DCT) algorithm. The amount

Figure 17.7   The Kodak SV9600 video transceiver.
Courtesy, Eastman Kodak Company

of bandwidth supplied in the transmission facilities must be in multiples of 64 kb/s. There are proprietary algorithms that yield better quality on the market, but as with many other CCITT standards, the standardization process takes so long that it is difficult for standards to keep pace with advances in technology.

The H.261 standard has other shortcomings. It lacks in-band audio and the capability of handling in-band graphics and data. The audio can be carried on a separate channel, but unless the audio and video channels take a path with the same amount of absolute delay, the picture will suffer lip-synchronization problems.

Freeze-Frame Video

Another form of video transmission known as *freeze-frame* can be used to transmit video signals over much narrower channels than compressed video. Freeze-frame equipment scans and digitizes the video signal and transmits a single frame over a digital line or over a modem-equipped analog line. Unlike compressed video, which results in a continuously varying picture, freeze-frame video presents a still picture that is refreshed periodically. The refresh rate depends on the transmission speed. For example, over a 56 kb/s line the signal is refreshed about every 15 seconds. At the receiving end the picture gradually fills the screen one line at a time from top to bottom. This waterfall effect can be eliminated by using a frame storage unit to accept the frame and relay it to the monitor after the entire frame is received. Freeze-frame video is particularly adaptable to conferences that make extensive use of graphics. The Kodak SV9600 transceiver, which Figure 17.7 shows, can be coupled to a printing device along with the CRT display for both video and hard copy output.

The main advantage of freeze-frame compared to compressed motion video is cost, and the gap between freeze-frame and motion is rapidly narrowing. There are a few applications, such as transmitting images, for which freeze-frame is superior, but for most applications, compressed motion video is the medium of choice.

High Definition Television

The present NTSC television standard was defined in 1941 when 525-line resolution was considered excellent quality and when such technologies as large scale integration were hardly imagined. Consequently, the standard was satisfactory for the time, but it is far from the present state of the art. Larger cities are running out of channel capacity. Although not all channels are filled, co-channel interference prevents the FCC from assigning all available channels.

High definition television (HDTV) has become the rallying cry for those who contend that the United States is losing dominance in electronics to the detriment of both the economy and national security. The issue isn't simply the entertainment value of HDTV; its components are expected to spawn a generation of new products. For example, the flat panel displays that form the HDTV readout will be used for improved displays on such applications as personal computers, radar, and aircraft cockpits. HDTV technology is expected to father new technologies in much the same way that the transistor revolutionized the electronics industry.

Whether the expected benefits are overstated as a way of inducing the government to relax some of its barriers is difficult to say. There is little doubt, however, that HDTV will eventually replace the current standards, which were developed when the capabilities of modern technology could not be foreseen. The 525 scan lines of broadcast television and the 4:3 width-to-height ratio of the screen, called the *aspect ratio*, place severe limitations on picture quality. With wide screen movies and the growing popularity of large screen television sets, the definition of the current scanning system is considerably less than that of the original image. Japanese HDTV experiments are using 1125 scan lines, and many proponents insist that images of motion picture quality will need at least 2000 lines.

The FCC has placed several reasonable constraints on HDTV development. The two that are most difficult to achieve are compatibility with existing NTSC receivers and living within the 6 MHz bandwidth of broadcast channels. HDTV will be a digital service, and compressing the enormous amount of bandwidth required into 6 MHz while still maintaining high picture quality is beyond today's technology.

Because of bandwidth problems, HDTV probably will be distributed over cable. As discussed in Chapter 13, the LECs are experimenting with bringing fiber optics to the household. To equip every household in the United States with fiber optic facilities will be an expensive undertaking. Because fiber cannot easily be tapped and branched as coaxial cable can, the service will cost 10 to 20 times as much per household as the current cost of serving a CATV customer with coaxial cable. The cost makes it unlikely that HDTV will serve many households over fiber optics in the immediate future. Eventually, broadband ISDN (B-ISDN), which Chapter 26 discusses, may become a distribution medium for HDTV.

CATV operators are not limited in bandwidth in the same way as are broadcasters. They can add more channels and can use twice the bandwidth per channel, but they are constrained by the state of television receivers: they do not want to force their customers to own separate receivers for broadcast and cable television. Also, there is a great deal that is not known about how

HDTV will behave on cable networks, and several years of testing will be required as the technology develops.

Testing will begin on HDTV over cable facilities in the early 1990s. It is unlikely that HDTV will be available before the middle of the decade of the 1990s, and then only in restricted markets until it is proven that customers are willing to invest in the equipment and pay the extra costs of the service.

Video Services and Applications

Entertainment is likely to remain the primary use of video into the future because it is a service used nearly everywhere in the world. The growth of the use of television for other services is predictable, however. These services are examined here.

As CATV provides a broadband information pipeline into a substantial portion of United States households, the growth of non-entertainment services is expected. The services described below are intended primarily for residences, but business applications will follow the availability of the services.

Teletext

Teletext is the transmission of information services during the vertical blanking interval of a television signal. As discussed earlier, the vertical blanking interval is the equivalent of 21 horizontal scan lines of a television signal, during which no picture information is transmitted. Teletext services transmit information such as magazines and catalogs over a television channel. An adapter decodes the information and presents it on the screen.

The British Prestel system is the first widespread application of teletext. The French have introduced teletext throughout much of the country, but it has not proved to be economically successful. The service is not used widely in the United States, but if the demand develops, it can become an inexpensive way of transmitting information for little more cost than the price of a converter.

Security

Television security applications take two forms—alarm systems and closed circuit television (CCTV) for monitoring unattended areas from a central location. Many businesses use CCTV for intrusion monitoring, and it is also widely used for intraorganizational information telecasts. Alarm services have principally relied on telephone lines to relay alarms to a center, which requires a separate line or automatic dialer. The expense of these devices can be saved by routing alarms over a CATV upstream channel, but to do so requires a terminal to interface with the alarm unit. As described earlier, a computer in the headend scans the alarm terminals and forwards alarm information to a security agency as instructed by the user.

Data Communications

Many CATV companies offer two-way data communications over their systems. A modem converts the digital data signal to analog for application to the cable. Speeds up to 1.544 mb/s are available over systems equipped for two-way operation. Broadband local area networks, as described in Chapter 27, are a growing application that uses the technology, but not necessarily the CATV facility.

Control Systems

Two-way CATV systems offer the potential of controlling many functions in households and businesses. For example, utilities can use the system to poll remote gas, electric, and water meters to save the cost of manual meter reading. Power companies can use the system for load control. During periods of high demand, electric water heaters can be turned off and restored when reduced demand permits. A variety of household services such as appliances and environmental equipment can be remotely controlled by a computer at the headend. CATV companies themselves can use the system to register channels that viewers are watching and to bill on the basis of service consumed. They also can use the equipment to control addressable converters to unscramble a premium channel at the viewers' request.

Opinion Polling

Experiments with opinion polling over CATV have been conducted. For example, CATV has been used to enable viewers to evaluate the television program they have just finished watching.

The potential of this system for allowing viewers to watch a political body in action and immediately express their opinion has great potential in a democracy, although it has not yet been used to any extent.

Image Transmission

The equipment and applications for capturing images and transmitting them over telecommunications networks are in their infancy now, but will become vital to physicians, engineers, architects and designers. The medical profession urgently needs imaging equipment to multiply the effectiveness of highly trained personnel. X-rays, magnetic resonance imaging, CAT scans, and other applications can be transmitted to the physician at high speed, providing detail as good as the original image. Teams of physicians can collaborate on diagnoses without being colocated and without the delay of transmitting documents by mail or courier.

Images can be viewed and rotated through three dimensions on powerful workstations. Engineers and designers currently create models and drive the manufacturing process from a computer, but the transmission requires large amounts of bandwidth. When the image is rotated, the screen must be refreshed several times per second. For example, a screen of 1000 lines and 1000 pixels per line requires a megabit of information for each frame. If it is refreshed 30 times per second, it is obvious that even with high compression a broadband channel will be required. New generations of powerful workstations put even more demands on telecommunications equipment.

The science of imaging falls outside the realm of telecommunications and is not covered here, but imaging is becoming one of the primary forces that drive the demand for large amounts of bandwidth. An imaging system includes image acquisition equipment, viewing stations, data management and storage equipment, peripheral devices such as high quality laser printers, and a transmission network. The bandwidths required are so great that current networks are too slow to support imaging. Networks such as Fiber Distributed Data Interface (FDDI), which Chapter 29 discusses, are needed to support imaging. Even at FDDI speeds, data compression is needed to reduce transmission times to tolerable limits.

Applications

Companies that had never considered video conferencing are beginning to investigate it more closely as the economics become more compelling. The first line of justification is generally replacement for travel, but as organizations adopt video as a way of doing business, the need for economic justification will disappear. For example, the telephone and the facsimile machine no longer need to be justified; it is unthinkable to do business without them, and neither is viewed as a replacement for doing business face-to-face.

The most obvious video application is for meetings, but other applications will develop as costs continue to decline. For example, here are some applications that show unexpected benefits of video applications.

- A food producer has farmers bring produce to a staging area and dump it on slabs for later redeployment. Video equipment shows the production department the types of produce and quantities on hand at plants located in three different cities.

- A county-wide fire and rescue system uses the CATV system to administer training to firefighting crews who must remain at their present facilities to respond to emergencies. Not only is the CATV system used for sending video, it also is used as a data communications system to provide access to the host computer and to transmit location maps from the 911 center when alarms are dispatched.

- A company has found a secondary benefit of video conferencing. Not only are travel costs reduced, but since conference participants must schedule video facilities, it forces managers to limit time, resulting in more efficient and productive meetings.

- Video conferencing makes it economical for more people to participate directly in events. Before video conferencing facilities were available, the company authorized only a

few people to travel. With video conferencing, more people can obtain information first-hand.

Standards

United States television signals are generated according to standards developed by the National Television System Committee
(NTSC). Rules and standards of the FCC regulate television broadcasts and CATV. EIA specifies electrical performance standards of
television signals and equipment. CCITT establishes standards for
international television transmission, recommends signal quality
standards, and also specifies compression standards.

Evaluation Considerations

This section discusses evaluation considerations of video conferencing and transmission equipment. Other video services,
including CATV, are provided only as and where available and are
not usually subject to choice. The exception to this is data communication over CATV facilities, which is an alternative to using
the telephone network. This alternative is evaluated on criteria
discussed in Chapter 25. Examples of the criteria are speed of
transmission, data error rate, and cost.

Type of Transmission Facilities

The initial issue to resolve is whether full motion, compressed
motion, or freeze-frame video will fulfill the objectives. The decision
largely is driven by costs, which in turn are determined by the
transmission facilities available. If private facilities with bandwidths
of 64 kb/s or greater are available, compressed or full motion video
is preferable unless the application can be fulfilled with still images.
If only dial-up facilities are available, freeze-frame is the only feasible
method of transmission because the other methods required dedicated entrance facilities to the IEC or LEC. Note, however, that
companies that have T-1 facilities to the IEC for long distance service
usually can obtain switched 56 kb/s service.

If compressed video is required, the following questions
should be evaluated:

- Is the compression algorithm proprietary or does it support CCITT standards or both?

- What level of quality is needed? Is a highly compressed signal satisfactory?
- Does the system support still graphics?
- Does audio ride on the video facility?
- Is single-point or multipoint communication required? If multipoint, can the system support both voice and video at multiple points, or is it necessary to use external bridging equipment?

Single- or MultiPoint Conferences

Video conferences are classed as point-to-point or multipoint. With terrestrial facilities, the distance and number of points served have a significant effect on transmission costs. Satellite facility costs are independent of distance and, except for earth station costs, are independent of the number of points served if the points are within the satellite footprint. If earth stations exist for other communications services, such as a company-wide voice and data network, multipoint video conferences can be obtained for costs equivalent to those of point-to-point conferences.

The type of transmission facility also is a function of the bandwidth required. Full motion, full color video requires a 6 MHz analog channel or a 1.544 mb/s digital channel. With a sacrifice in clarity during motion, digital bandwidths can be reduced to as little as 64 kb/s. Freeze-frame video can be supported over narrower bandwidths. Digital transmission is usually less economical for multipoint or one-way broadcasts because of the cost of video compression equipment.

System Integration

Video conference equipment is usually an assembly of units made by different manufacturers. To ensure compatibility, it is usually advisable to obtain equipment from a vendor who can assemble it into a complete system.

Security

The type of information being transmitted over the channel must be considered. Often, proprietary information is discussed during conferences. Both terrestrial microwave and satellite services are subject to interception; signals transmitted over fiber optics are less vulnerable. Scrambling of both video and audio signals often is warranted.

Public or Private Facilities

Private video conference facilities have a significant advantage over public access systems. Public facilities are unavailable in many localities, which may preclude holding many video conferences. The travel time to a public facility offsets some of the advantages of video conference. Unless a private facility is used frequently, however, public facilities are usually the most cost-effective option..

Future Expansion

Video conference facilities should be acquired with a view toward future expansion plans. For example, a conference facility may start with freeze-frame with plans to convert to full motion video later. The facility should be expandable to other points if growth is foreseen.

Fixed or Portable Equipment

Portable video conference equipment is available, and some applications require it. A roll-around unit about the size of a two-drawer filing cabinet can quickly be set up for an impromptu video conference. Unless there is a need for portability, however, the best results will be obtained with fixed equipment. Portable satellite equipment also is used in some video services—particularly one-way broadcasts to hotels and other meeting facilities.

Manufacturers of Video Equipment

CATV Equipment

Reliance Comm/Tec
C-COR Electronics

Jerrold Division of General Instrument Corp.

Video Conferencing Equipment

AT&T Skynet Video Conferencing
Colorado Video
Compression Labs, Inc.
Eastman Kodak
GPT Video Systems
NEC America Inc., Radio & Transmission Division

PictureTel Corporation
Satellite Transmission Systems, Inc.
Sony Corporation of America
Videoconferencing Systems, Inc.
VideoTelecom Corp.

Part

4

Customer Premises Equipment

Of telecommunications products, customer premises equipment is the most tangible to users and gains the most attention among managers. Part 4 is primarily concerned with station equipment— telephones and related apparatus—and customer premises switching equipment—data PBXs, voice PBXs and key telephone systems. Switching equipment in particular has borrowed heavily from the technologies that Part 2 discusses. The digital PBX differs from a digital central office only in size and features. Manufacturers have adapted some central office switching systems as large PBXs.

Before the large digital PBX, most organizations with more than 1000 stations used Centrex, which this part also covers. Centrex is still a feasible alternative for many companies. Because the switching equipment is not located on the customer's premises, the maintenance and administrative responsibilities that go with customer-owned apparatus stay with the LECs.

Computer technology has brought two other important families of products into the office. Automatic call distribution equipment, responding to the growth of telemarketing and 800 service, has brought a new set of theories on how to manage calls in a large pool of users that the industry calls *agents*. Voice store-and-forward, or *voice mail,* equipment is also having a significant effect on the way people work in an office. The technical capabilities of this equipment have outstripped our ability to manage it, however, and the challenge facing most telecommunications managers is how to extract the maximum return from the investment.

The final chapter in Part 4 deals with facsimile transmission. None of the telecommunications technologies has lain dormant for so long (it was invented more than 30 years before the telephone) before being accepted so vigorously. A decade ago only a few companies had facsimile machines; but now they are so pervasive that they have changed the very way we do business.

18

Station Equipment

The least exotic and technically sophisticated element of the telecommunications system is the ordinary telephone. Yet its importance in the design of the network should not be underestimated. Because of the enormous numbers of telephone instruments in service, much of the rest of the network is designed to keep the telephone simple, rugged, and economical. Over the more than 100-year history of telephony, the telephone set has been improved, but the fundamental principles that make it work have changed little since Alexander Graham Bell's original invention. The primary changes have been improvements in three areas: packaging to make telephones esthetically appealing and easy to use, signaling to improve the methods used to place and receive telephone calls, and transmission performance to improve the quality of the talking path between users.

This chapter discusses the various types of telephones, station protection equipment, network channel terminating equipment (NCTE), station wiring, and auxiliary devices such as recorders and dialers.

Telephone Set Technology

The telephone is inherently a four-wire device. Transmit and receive paths must be separate to fit the user's anatomy, but they must be electrically combined to interface the two-wire loops that serve all but a small fraction of the telephone services in the country. Figure 18.1 is a functional diagram of a telephone set.

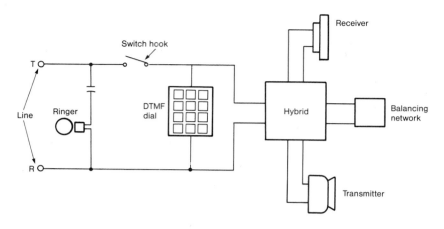

Figure 18.1   Functional diagram of a telephone set.

Elements of a Telephone Set

A <u>transmitter</u> in the telephone handset converts the user's <u>voice</u> into a <u>pulsating direct current</u>. The most common type of transmitter has a housing containing tightly packed granules of carbon that are energized by <u>DC voltage</u>. The voice waves impinging on the transmitter compact the granules, changing the amount of current that flows in proportion to the strength of the voice signal. This fluctuating current travels over telephone circuits to drive the distant telephone receiver, which has coils of fine wire wound around a magnetic core. The current causes a diaphragm to move in step with changes in the line current. The diaphragm in the receiver and the carbon microphone in the transmitter are *transducers* that <u>change fluctuations in sound pressure to fluctuations in electrical current</u>, and vice versa.

Many new telephone sets substitute electronic transmitters for the carbon units that have been used for more than a century. Most telephone sets still use the carbon transmitter, however, because it is inexpensive and rugged.

The telephone set contains a hybrid coil that performs the four-wire to two-wire conversion as described in Chapter 2; it couples the two-wire line to the four-wire telephone handset. By design, the isolation between the transmitter and receiver is less than perfect. It is desirable for a small amount of the user's voice to be coupled into the receiver as *sidetone,* the feedback effect that regulates the volume of the user's voice. Given too little sidetone, users tend to speak too loudly; given too much, they do not speak loudly enough.

The telephone set includes a switch hook, whichisolates all the elements except the ringer from the network when the telephone is idle, or on-hook. When the user lifts the receiver off-hook, the switch hook connects the line to the telephone set and furnishes the power needed to energize the transmitter. When the telephone is on-hook, the ringer is coupled to the line through a capacitor that prevents the DC talking current from flowing, but allows AC ringing voltage to actuate the bell. The telephone bell is an electromagnet that moves a clapper against a gong to alert the user to an incoming call. In many modern telephone sets an electronic tone ringer replaces the bell.

The dial circuit connects to the telephone line when the user lifts the receiver off hook. Dial circuits are of two types: rotary dials, which operate by interrupting the flow of line current, and tone dials, which operate by sending a combination of frequencies over the line. Tone dialing, known as dual tone multifrequency (DTMF), uses a 4 x 4 matrix of tones, as Figure 18.2 shows, to transmit pairs of frequencies to the tone receiver in the central office. Each button generates a unique pair of frequencies, which a DTMF receiver detects. Ordinary telephones send only three of the four columns of DTMF signals. The fourth column can be sent by special telephones or can be electronically generated by DTMF chips that are embedded in auxiliary telephone apparatus.

The two wires of a telephone circuit are designated as *tip* and *ring*, corresponding to the tip and ring of the cord plugs used by switchboard operators. The central office feeds negative polarity talking power over the ring side of the line. When the receiver is off-hook, current flows in the line. The amount of current flow is limited by the resistance of the local loop, which depends on the wire gauge and length. For adequate transmission, at least 23 milliamps of current is needed. If too

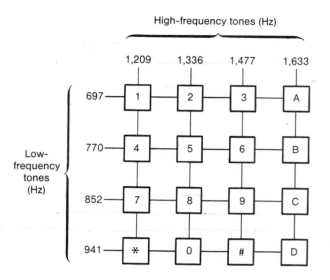

High-frequency tones (Hz)

Figure 18.2 DTMF dialing frequency combinations.

little current flows, the transmitter is insufficiently energized and the telephone set produces too little output for good transmission. If more than approximately 60 milliamps of current flows, telephone output will be uncomfortably loud for many listeners. Also, DTMF dials need at least 20 milliamps of current for reliable operation. The telephone set, the wiring on the user's premises, the local loop, and the central office equipment interact to regulate the flow of current in the line and the quality of local transmission service.

Rotary dial contacts are wired in series with the loop. When the user rotates the dial to the finger stop, a set of off-normal contacts opens the loop. When the dial is released the contacts alternately close and open to produce a string of square wave pulses. Equipment in the central office uses these pulses to operate switches that route the call.

Before the FCC opened the telephone network to connection of customer apparatus, the LECs owned all telephone sets, and because of the large numbers of sets in service, they designed the network for reliable operation with a minimum investment in station apparatus. The basic telephone set is a rugged and inexpensive device that provides satisfactory transmission over properly designed loops. If the current flowing through the loop is sufficient to provide between 23 and 60 ma. of current to the telephone set and the telephone is in good working order, satisfactory service is assured.

Telephone Sets for Party Lines

The previous discussion assumes the use of single-party telephones. In a single-party line, the ringer is bridged across the line and detects an AC ringing signal between the tip and ring of the local loop. If more than one user is connected to such a line, coded ringing is required. Early party lines used combinations of long and short rings to signal the called party. The disadvantage, of course, is the annoyance of hearing unwanted rings, but because they are inexpensive, party lines still exist in some parts of the United States. Three methods are used to prevent rings from reaching any but the intended recipient.

The first method, used on two-party lines, requires wiring the ringer from one side of the line to ground as in Figure 18.3a. The party is wired in the central office as a *tip party* or a *ring party*, and the ringer is wired from either the tip or the ring of the line to ground. The ringer wiring also actuates the automatic number identification equipment in the central office when either of the two parties places a long distance call. This method of connecting ringers may unbalance the line, as described in Chapter 2, and increase the noise level. To alleviate the noise, the LECs often install ringer isolators to disconnect the ringer except in the presence of a ringing signal.

The second method, used on four-party lines, employs a special tube or solid state device that responds to only one polarity of ringing voltage inside the telephone. The central office applies either a positive or negative DC voltage superimposed over the ringing voltage to cause the device to conduct. Bells connect from tip or ring to ground through a device that is polled positive or negative, yielding four ringing combinations as Figure 18.3 shows. Because the device conducts only in the presence of DC voltage

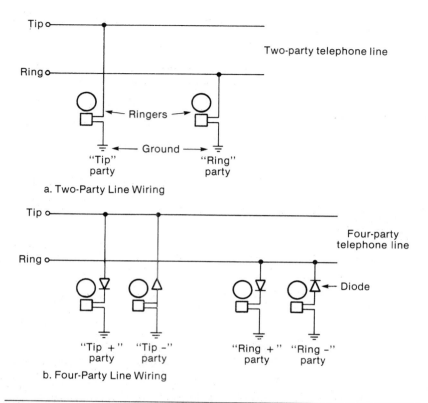

Figure 18.3   Multiparty signaling in a telephone system.

superimposed over the ringing signal, it isolates the line from ground to improve balance.

The third system is harmonic ringing. In this system, the ringers are tuned to respond to only one ringing frequency. This system is rarely used in the United States because the ringers can easily be detuned if the telephone is dropped. Number identification for toll calls is manual on four-party lines.

Station Protection

Telephone circuits are occasionally subject to high voltages that could be injurious or fatal to the user without electrical protec-

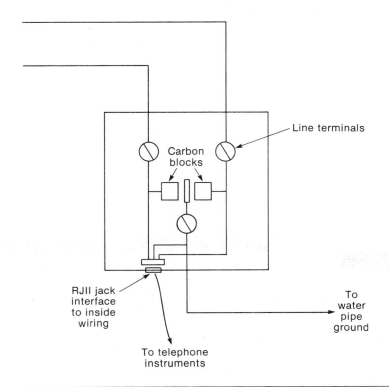

Figure 18.4 Diagram of a station protector.

tion. Lightning strikes and crosses with high voltage power lines are mitigated with a station protector, which is diagrammed in Figure 18.4. Protectors use either an air gap or a gas tube to conduct high voltage from either side of the line to ground if hazardous voltages occur. The telephone is insulated so that any voltage that gets past the protector will not injure the user. The LEC places protectors, which also may form a demarcation point with customer-owned wiring, as shown in Figure 18.4. Protectors are connected to a ground rod, metallic water pipe, or other low resistance ground.

The protector connects to the telephone set by jacketed wiring, called *inside wiring*, that is the user's responsibility to place. Inside wiring terminates on the protector on the end nearest the central office and on a connecting jack designated by the FCC as RJ-11 at the telephone end. Multiple lines terminate on a multiple-line jack such as the RJ-21X. FCC regulations require registration of telephone sets and other apparatus, including modems, PBXs, and key equipment, that connects directly to the network. Registration shows that the FCC approves apparatus for connection to the telephone network.

For more detailed information on station protection, refer to Chapter 6.

Coin Telephones

The advent of the customer-owned coin operated telephone (COCOT) is another byproduct of divestiture that is confusing to many users. In the first few years following the dissolution of the Bell System, many private companies saw COCOTs as a potentially lucrative business, which they are. The companies that ventured into this market with less-than-adequate equipment, however, quickly discovered what the LECs have long understood: the risks and administrative costs of coin telephones are high, and companies that enter the market without understanding the hazards can lose large amounts of money. The two major risks are fraud and vandalism. These can be combatted with durable instruments and by building defenses into the telephone in the ways discussed below.

COCOTs have earned the distrust of many users—partly because of the inherent design of the telephone system and partly because of operator service providers (OSPs) that often charge more for long distance calls than the major IECs. The courts have ruled that the LECs must permit COCOT owners to choose a primary interexchange carrier, which permits the owner of the host premises to invite OSPs to bid for the highest commissions.

It is not necessary for the owners of high volume coin locations to own the telephones to gain commissions on long distance calls, but for those users who do own or contemplate owning the instruments, an understanding of the features and technology is essential.

Coin Telephone Technology

A coin telephone has the following components:

- *Communication circuitry*, which is essentially identical with that of non-coin telephone sets.

- *Totalizer*, which is the device that identifies coin denominations and counts or relays the value of the money received.

- *Coin chute*, which is the physical channel that directs the coins from the coin slot through the totalizer and into the coin box.

- *Coin collect and control apparatus*, which controls whether coins are directed to the coin box or the refund chute.

- *Coin box*, which is the receptacle that receives and stores collected coins.

Besides the above, coin telephones may include a variety of intelligent features that substitute for centralized telephone control.

The coin telephones operated by the LECs were, until the last few years, devices with no local intelligence. All call rating, collect, and refund decisions and other such functions were handled centrally. Since the central office does not send answer supervision signals over the local loop, central office circuitry was, and for the LECs still is, used for coin control. When a caller deposits a coin, the coin chute holds it until the called party answers and then drops it into the coin box. If the caller hangs up before the answer supervision signal is received, the coin is refunded. An operator or automatic apparatus rates the long distance call, and a human or synthesized voice announces the charge to the caller. As the caller deposits coins, the totalizer returns to the central control tones that announce the denomination of the coins. Since COCOTs are not connected to central coin control apparatus, intelligence in the coin telephone handles the timing, collection, and return features.

The vast majority of toll calls made from coin telephones are billed to credit cards. Many coin telephones have credit card readers. Some telephones include rating apparatus and are therefore self-sufficient. Most such telephones, however, use a centralized OSP to handle the calls and collect the revenues through agreements with the credit card companies.

Coin Telephone Features

The following are typical of features of COCOTs. The LECs also are introducing many of these same features into their telephones.

Coin Box Accounting.   This feature enables the owner to determine the amount of money in the box without counting it. This helps prevent theft but is perhaps most important as a way of determining remotely when the box is ready for collection.

Alarming.   Many coin telephones have reporting systems that sound a local alarm, dial a number, or both when tampering or vandalism occurs.

Remote Diagnostics.   The ability to dial into a coin telephone from either a manual or an automatic center and determine whether it is functioning properly is an important feature for controlling maintenance costs.

Call Timing.   Most LECs measure the usage on public access lines and charge the COCOT owner accordingly. This feature times the call, calls for additional coin deposit when required, and cuts off the caller when the call exceeds the time limit. Some telephones have a readout that shows the amount of time remaining so callers can feed in more coins to keep the call in progress without interruption.

Call Restrictions.   The call restriction feature blocks certain codes. For example, the 976 prefix that information service providers use may be restricted because of the difficulty of rating and collecting for such calls.

Voice Store and Forward.   This feature enables the caller to leave a message that the coin phone will attempt to deliver at certain intervals. For example, a traveler could leave a message to be delivered to a busy telephone and resume his or her trip.

Database Access.   Intelligent coin telephones can retain a database of telephone numbers that users can speed dial. For example, the database might include taxi, hospital, hotel, and other such numbers. The COCOT owner may collect a fee from the called party for this service.

Facsimile Capabilities.   Telephones with facsimile transmission capabilities are available in many public locations. These devices can levy a charge for facsimile service in addition to the normal long distance charge, with the fee generally charged to a credit card.

Keypad Volume Control.   The receive volume of some coin telephones can be adjusted under keypad control. This facility is valuable in noisy public locations.

Dialing Instruction Display.   Given the complexity of operating some coin telephones, the need to access multiple IECs, the need for compatibility with different kinds of credit cards, and the requirement for the user to dial unfamiliar codes, a telephone with a display and help keys helps the caller use the device.

Cordless Telephones

In recent years, cordless telephones have gained wide consumer acceptance. These instruments use a low powered radio link between a base unit and the portable telephone. The units have sufficient range to enable the user to use them on an average residential lot. As with all radio systems, privacy is problematic with cordless telephones. Early units were subject to interference and could be signaled by any base unit operating on the same frequency. A more serious problem is that anyone using a telephone on the same frequency can place unauthorized long distance calls or eavesdrop on private calls. As only five frequencies in the 49 to 50 MHz range were allocated initially by the FCC, false rings and unauthorized long distance calls were a problem on early units.

Some systems operate on 49 MHz frequencies in both directions, while in others the base station transmits on a frequency between 1.7 and 1.8 MHz. These base stations use the house AC power wiring for an antenna. The frequencies are fixed, and interference with nearby units may be encountered. When interference occurs, the unit usually must be exchanged for a unit on another frequency. Because sets have a limited range, some units sound a warning when the user carries the portable unit outside the base station range.

The new generation of telephones contains safeguards against false rings and unauthorized calls. The base-to-portable link is authenticated with a code from the portable unit so the base responds only to a unit with the correct code. This prevents unauthorized calls. The ringer in the portable unit is coded to prevent false rings. Encoders affect only the signaling and do not improve privacy. Anyone who has a telephone tuned to the same frequency can listen to the call, so extended range is not necessarily an advantage.

Cordless telephones were originally available only as single-line sets. AT&T has introduced its new Merlin Cordless, however, which is the multibutton set shown in Figure 18.5. Its five buttons can be assigned to outside lines, intercom paths, or system features such as speed dial. The handset and base can talk on any of ten channels; the user can select channels for the best reception. Standard key telephone features, such as transfer and hold, can be activated from the cordless unit.

Answering Equipment

Answering equipment varies from telephone answering sets such as the Code-A-Phone Model 3780 that Figure 18.6 shows to elaborate voice mail equipment that provides service similar to electronic mail. Chapter 22 covers voice mail, or voice store-and-forward equipment. Answering sets, once provided exclusively by the LECs, are widely available, and no more difficult to install than ordinary telephones. Units like the one shown in Figure 18.6 use separate cassette tapes for recorded announcements and messages from callers. Many modern units use digitized voice for the answering function, which eliminates the moving tape and reduces wear and tear on the equipment.

Because the central office does not relay answer supervision over the local loop, answering machines must include timing circuitry to determine when the calling party has hung up. Most answering machines detect the caller's voice; when a silent period

Figure 18.5   The AT&T Merlin Cordless multi-line telephone.
Courtesy, AT&T Corporation

of more than a specified length is detected, the machine assumes the caller has hung up, and disconnects. If a caller hangs up when the answering message is first heard, the machine may hold the line busy for a time while it completes the announcement and times out.

Network Channel Terminating Equipment

Network channel terminating equipment (NCTE) is any apparatus mounted on a telephone user's premises that can amplify, match

Figure 18.6   The Code-A-Phone Model 3780 answering set.
Courtesy, Code-A-Phone Corporation

impedance, or match network signaling to the signaling of the interconnected equipment.

Modems technically meet this definition, but for this discussion, NCTE is confined to devices that process signals outside the range of ordinary telephone sets. It includes the CSU and DSU equipment that terminates digital lines as discussed in Chapter 4. It also includes the customer premises end of the signaling equipment discussed in Chapter 11 and the terminating equipment for local area data transport discussed in Chapter 25.

The FCC and CCITT disagree on the demarcation between the network and customer premises equipment. At issue in the United States is whether NCTE is part of the network provided by the telephone company or part of the customer premises equipment provided by the user. Under CCITT definition, NCTE is considered part of the network, and the LEC provides it. The FCC has ruled to the contrary. This ruling presents design and compatibility hazards that users should understand before obtaining private line services from telephone companies.

The characteristics of private line signaling are discussed in Chapter 11. In brief, private line signals travel over the voice telecommunications network and are actuated by combinations of tones inside the voice passband. At the local loop, these signals can be carried to the user's premises as tones or converted to DC signals in the telephone central office. In most cases, DC signaling is used. Often, the cable between the central office and the user's premises has too much resistance and loss to support reliable signaling. NCTE at the user's premises amplifies the voice, boosts the DC voltage on the line, or both. Sometimes the form of the signal is altered to interface with the terminal equipment. For example, a single-frequency signaling tone may be converted to 20 Hz ringing to ring a telephone on the end of a circuit. Like any other equipment connected to the telephone network, NCTE must be registered with the FCC.

NCTE is usually constructed on plug-in circuit packs that mount in shelves. The connector on the NCTE shelf is wired to a demarcation point to meet the LEC's cable pair on the input side and to the terminal equipment on the output side. Individual shelves can be wall mounted. Large concentrations of NCTE are usually mounted in racks or cabinets as Figure 18.7 shows.

Station Wiring Plans

When wiring systems were used only for voice, no one paid much attention to them. They either worked or they didn't, and when they didn't the problem was referred to technicians to solve. Buildings were laced with the 25-pair wire required by 1A-2 key telephone systems. The high cost of the cabling and the bulk, which rapidly filled conduits and raceways, led to the wiring plan shown in Figure 18.8. *Horizontal wiring* is the cabling from the station to the wiring closet. The cabling from the wiring closet to the equipment room is called *riser cable*, a term that applies both to the vertical interfloor wiring in a multistory building and the interbuilding cabling in a campus wiring system.

Figure 18.7   Bays of Tellabs network channel terminating equipment.
Courtesy, Tellabs, Inc.

Twisted pair wiring may have been largely ignored in past years, but interest has surged recently as the trend toward a data device on every desk develops. Normally, a building is wired with telephone outlets at most desk locations so a station user can move telephones by making a simple crossconnection change in a wiring closet and plugging the telephone into a new jack. *Baluns* (derived from *ba*lanced/*un*balanced) are devices that can connect terminals requiring coaxial cable to controllers or host computers over twisted pair wire.

Although 1A-2 key telephone systems are far from extinct, modern electronic key systems require only two or three pairs of wire, so 25-pair cable is unnecessary. This raises many important questions that any organization planning a new telephone or data system should address:

- Can unused conductors in 25-pair cable be used for EIA-232 and twisted pair LAN wiring?

- Should wiring be shielded or unshielded?

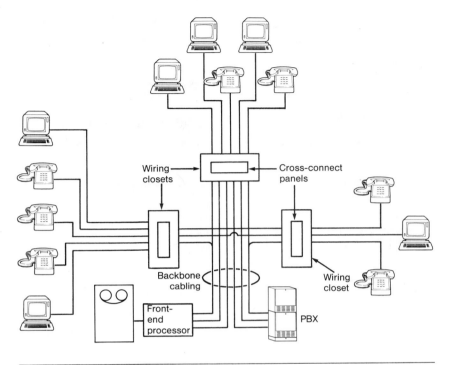

Figure 18.8   Building wiring plan.

- How many pairs should extend to the workstation?
- How should wiring terminate at the workstation?
- Is it safe to run voice and data through the same cable?
- How long can horizontal wire runs for both voice and data be?
- Is it feasible to terminate wiring and patch panels so equipment can be easily reassigned?
- Should wiring run through intermediate wiring closets or "home run" directly to the equipment room?

Anyone who seeks absolute answers to these questions will be disappointed because many conditions can cause trouble with an arrangement that has previously been used successfully. Factors such as the following have a significant impact on the usability of twisted pair wire:

workability of twisted wire :

- The nature of the signals traveling over the wire (e.g., signals traveling at higher speeds are more susceptible to interference).

- The presence or absence of external sources of electromagnetic induction (EMI).

- The quality of the manufacture and installation of the wire.

- The degree to which the wire has deteriorated since its initial installation.

- The care with which the wire is terminated.

This section explains the principles involved in designing and selecting a wiring system. This discussion will provide an understanding of the issues and enough guidelines to enable an administrator to make an intelligent selection most of the time. When there is doubt about whether a particular case will support data, you can consult an expert or try it and see if it works. The latter strategy may be risky in a new wiring plan, but when you are considering whether to run data or local area networks over existing 25-pair wire, it often pays to experiment because the fallback position is to replace the wire anyway.

A frequent issue in designing an inside wiring system is whether to use shielded or unshielded wire for local area networks. Shielding is a metallic braid or layer of foil surrounding all or some of the conductors in the cable. The purpose of the shield is to reduce electromagnetic interference (EMI). The shield reduces EMI by attenuating the electrical energy radiated from the cable and minimizing energy coupled from outside sources.

Shielding operates through one of two effects, the *field effect* or the *circuit effect*. The field effect holds that the shield reflects and absorbs the interfering waves. The circuit effect assumes that interfering signals generate a secondary field in the shield, canceling the original field. It is difficult to connect the shield to ground in some types of connectors, so most shielded cables include a drain wire, which is in direct contact with the shield throughout the cable length.

As Figure 18.9 shows, shielding affects the electrical characteristics of the wire. The effects are not significant at voice frequen-

	ATTENUATION DB/1000 FEET		CHARACTERISTIC IMPEDENCE	
KHz	1KHz	1MHz	1KHz	1MHz
Shielded	.43	9.4	500 Ohms	65 Ohms
Unshielded	.41	6.1	600 Ohms	105 Ohms

Figure 18.9   Comparison of characteristics of shielded and unshielded 4-pair solid conductor twisted-pair wire.

cies, but at the higher frequencies typical of LANs, shielding can increase loss by 50% or more.

The issue of shielded vs. unshielded wiring will be considered first. Many organizations choose shielded wire for one of two convincing reasons: the equipment manufacturer specifies it, or it seems the most conservative approach. Both are rational reasons for using shielded wiring, but there are equally convincing reasons for avoiding it if possible. Shielded wiring is significantly more expensive than unshielded. It is more difficult to install and terminate, and it has higher loss.

The first principle is to be certain that the wire meets the specifications of your application. Wiring that will be used for a 10 Base T local area network, for example, should meet the 802.3 standards. These standards are generally met by wire manufactured to the same specifications as AT&T's D Inside Wire. The Bell Operating Companies installed enormous quantities of this wire before divestiture. If there is any doubt about the type of wire, it usually can be identified by markings embossed in the sheath. Since end users became responsible for inside wiring, other types of wire have been installed in many buildings, and some of these may not meet D Inside Wire specifications. Improperly manufactured wire may disrupt the balance that is necessary to cancel interference.

Some services are inherently unbalanced, which makes them susceptible to interference. The most frequently used DTE-to-DCE connection is EIA-232-C, which uses a common signal ground path for transmit and receive. This limits the transmission distance, which the specification lists as 50 feet. Many organizations violate this limit, however, without encountering trouble. Without heavy EMI, it is probably safe to run unshielded wire for 100 meters—a distance that matches the 10 Base T limitation. Although many organizations run EIA-232 for 1000 feet or more, it is generally safer to use a balanced EIA-422 or line drivers for such long wire runs.

To sum up the shielded vs. unshielded question, most administrators should consult an expert on their particular installations before making the decision. Most users find that a properly installed unshielded twisted pair (UTP) system provides perfectly satisfactory results for 10 Base T LANS, EIA-232 wiring up to 300 feet, and 4 mb/s token ring networks. If the network manufacturer will not support the system without shielding, the administrator must decide whether support or economy is the most important consideration. For 16 mb/s token rings, shielding must meet IBM's specifications. The requirement is not simply to control errors; it also limits radio frequency radiation. Terminating equipment produced by other manufacturers permits running 16 mb/s token ring over UTP.

If the station-to-equipment room distance does not exceed 100 meters and if conduit congestion is not a problem, a point-to-point, or home run, wiring plan is the easiest to administer. The next question is how many pairs should be run to each workstation.

Bearing in mind that most of the expense in the wiring system is labor, there is little economy in limiting the number of pairs in the horizontal wiring. A good balance is achieved by providing at least two four-pair cables—one for voice and one for data. These can be terminated at the workstation in a dual RJ-45 jack or a special purpose jack. If the existing wiring terminates in connectorized 25-pair cable, adapters known as *harmonicas* can be used to bring out conductors to four-pair RJ-45 or two-pair RJ-11 jacks. Electrically, these jacks are equivalent. In any case, separate cables should be used for voice and data if new cables are being run. With existing cables, it may be feasible to combine voice and data in the same cable. Modem data is electrically equivalent to voice and should be run over the voice cable. This arrangement

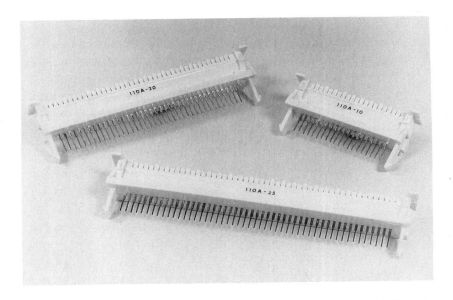

Figure 18.10   AT&T 110-type connectors.
Courtesy, AT&T Archives

provides the one or two pairs that most telephone systems require, the two to four pairs for EIA-232 or twisted pair LAN data,
and at least two spare pairs. This plan also supports future ISDN
station wiring.

At intermediate wiring closets, the horizontal wire is crossconnected to the riser cable, usually using 66-type blocks. It is
important that the wiring be thoroughly documented and designated to avoid delays in making wiring rearrangements.

The main distributing frame in the equipment room also can
be constructed of 66-type blocks on a backboard, free-standing
distributing frames of the type described in Chapter 12, or a
collection of a combination patch panel and wired cross connect
devices such as the AT&T 110 block, which Figure 18.10 shows.
This connector is compact, and crossconnects can be run with
either jumper wire or patch cords. Separate fields should be
provided for connecting to PBX ports, riser cable, horizontal
distribution cable, data devices, tie cables, and common carrier

facilities. These should be clearly labeled and documented. The cost of coaxial and EIA-232-C cables usually precludes this kind of flexibility for data terminals that are wired with other than UTP.

When it is necessary to rewire an existing building or to wire a new building initially, a carefully designed wiring plan should be created. AT&T and IBM have wiring plans that support both voice and data terminals. The primary characteristics of the plans are:

- A backbone route links outside telecommunications circuits, PBX, and computer to wiring closets that are placed strategically throughout the building as Figure 18.8 shows.
- Wire is distributed from the wiring closet to station locations and cross connected to the backbone circuit on a panel in the wiring closet
- Data terminals connect (within range limits) to twisted pair wire. In the IBM system, the wire is shielded; in the AT&T system, it is unshielded
- Wall connectors are provided for both voice and data terminals. Terminals crossconnect in the wiring closet to provide a path to the PBX, computer room, or other terminating point.

The AT&T and IBM wiring plans are similar except for the number of conductors and the shielded wire that IBM specifies. The shielding is provided for a token ring local area network as described in Chapter 27. The chief advantages of these systems are the elimination of coaxial cable for runs of less than about 300 feet, the provision of a common wall outlet for both voice and data terminals, and the flexibility of a crossconnect panel for assigning circuits. Similar wiring plans can be assembled from components made by a variety of manufacturers.

National Electrical Code (NEC)

The National Electrical Code (NEC) specifies fire resistance standards for communications cables to protect people and property from fire hazards. The code, covered by the National Bureau of Standards Handbook H43, addresses the methods of limiting the hazards of cable-initiated fires and cable-carried fires. The 1987 code requires that communications and signaling wires and cables in a building be listed as suitable for the purpose. The following summarizes the code requirements. Further information can be obtained by consulting the code itself.

Article 800 Communications

This article lists four categories of communications cables:

- CM cables for general purpose use except plenums and risers.
- CMP cables for use in plenums.
- CMR cables for use in risers.
- CMX cables for residential and restricted commercial use.

Any cable used for telephone communications must be tested and listed as meeting the fire resistance, mechanical, and electrical standards of the testing laboratory.

Article 725 Remote Control, Signaling, and Power Limited Circuits

This portion of the code lists products classed as Class 1, Class 2, and Class 3 remote control, signaling, and power limited circuits. Communications cables are permissible for Class 2 and 3 applications.

Applications

The market offers two categories of telephone sets—general purpose sets (known in the industry as 2500 sets) and special purpose telephones such as COCOTs, cordless sets, and answering sets. General purpose sets are easy to apply. They are enough of a commodity that purchase can be based on price plus special features such as speed dial, hold, and speakerphone. Users should be aware of one fundamental difference in general purpose sets with push button dials. One type of push button dial sends only dial pluses and therefore is not compatible with services that require DTMF pulses.

The price of general purpose sets is often a clue to their quality. Many inexpensive instruments provide poor transmission quality and fail when dropped. At the high end of the scale, price usually is a function of features or decorator housings.

Since the FCC began to permit users to attach any registered device to the telephone network, the market has become flooded with special purpose telephones. At the heart of answering machines, COCOTs, and cordless telephones is still the basic inner workings of the 2500 set, which can be evaluated by the criteria discussed in this section.

Standards

Telephone instruments and auxiliary equipment such as recorders and dialers are not constructed to any standards. The FCC sets registration criteria, but these criteria relate to potential harm to the network or personnel from hazardous voltages or to interference with other services from excessively high signal levels. The FCC also sets frequency requirements for cordless telephones and regulates the amount of electromagnetic radiation that processor-equipped devices can emit. FCC rules specify the amount of internal resistance of a telephone set but otherwise do not regulate technical performance.

EIA sets certain criteria for telephone equipment, and CCITT standardizes certain aspects of the telephone set and its operation. Telephone technical standards have evolved primarily from practices of AT&T that were established when it had complete network design control. Other manufacturers have adopted most of those criteria.

Evaluation Considerations

Telephone sets, key telephone equipment, answering sets, NCTE, and all other equipment connected to the network must be registered with the FCC to guard against harm to the network. Although it is unlikely that equipment offered for customer premises will be unregistered, it should be noted that it is illegal to connect such apparatus. All telephone apparatus must be protected from hazardous voltages as Chapters 6 and 12 discuss. The LECs equip their lines with carbon block protectors. These are adequate for ordinary telephone sets, but some electronic equipment may not be adequately protected. The manufacturer's recommendations should be consulted, and if necessary, gas tube protection should be provided as Chapter 6 explains.

Telephones

The primary consideration in obtaining a telephone should be the intended use of the instrument itself. The following criteria are important in evaluating a telephone instrument:

- *Durability and reliability*. Telephone sets are often dropped, and it is often difficult to have them repaired, so the ability of the telephone to withstand wear and tear is of prime importance.

- *Type of dial*. Specialized common carriers and other telephone related services require a DTMF dial to enter personal identification number and call details. Some telephones with pushbutton dials have rotary dial output and are incompatible with these services.

- *Number of telephone lines served*. The number of telephone lines has a significant effect on whether a single-line, multiline, or key telephone system is acquired.

- *Transmission performance*. Some inexpensive telephones offer inferior transmission performance and may give unsatisfactory service. They should be evaluated before purchase.

- *Additional features*. Such features as last number redial and multiple number storage are often desirable.

Special Feature Telephones

The garden variety telephone set has gone the way of Henry Ford's Model T. Now, telephone sets can be obtained with dozens of optional features and with auxiliary equipment such as clock radios that have nothing to do with the telephone itself. Special features are available as either parts of the telephone or as add-on adapters.

Dialers. These units store a list of telephone numbers that can be outpulsed by selecting a button. Dialers are particularly advantageous for accessing special common carriers who require 23-digit dialing for long distance calls. Evaluation considerations include capacity, ability to handle 23-digit numbers, and ability to pause for a second dial tone.

Speaker Telephones.   These units provide speaker and microphone for hands-free operation. The primary considerations are range of coverage—an office or a conference room—satisfactory voice quality, and the ability to cut off the transmitter for privacy during conversations.

Cordless Telephones.   These units should include circuitry to prevent false rings and to restrict call origination to authorized telephones. The range of the base station and remote should be considered. Extended range may be an advantage in some applications, but may result in loss of privacy. Multiline operation is available and may be essential for some applications.

Memory.   Telephones that store multiple digits and contain last number redial capability are often advantageous. Some telephones visually display the number dialed and allow correction of dialed digits before outpulsing begins.

Telephones for the Handicapped.   Telephones with a variety of aids for handicapped users are available. These include special dials, amplified handsets, visual ringing equipment, and other such features. Of special concern are *hearing aid compatible* telephones. Some hearing aids rely on magnetic pickup from the handset and are incompatible with some types of electronic handsets. Special telephone sets are equipped with keyboards and single- line readout for communication by the deaf. Compatibility between devices is important.

Answering Sets

Answering sets have many special features that should be considered before purchasing a unit. Among the most important features are:

- Battery backup for continued operation during power failures.
- Call counter to display the number of messages recorded.
- Call monitoring capability so incoming calls can be screened over a speaker.
- Dual tape capability so it is unnecessary to listen to the recorded message when playing back recorded calls.

- Remote control recording so the announcement can be changed from a remote location.

- Ring control so the number of rings before the line is answered can be adjusted.

- Selective call erase to allow selective erasing, saving, and repeating of incoming messages.

- Multiple line capability so one device can answer more than one line.

- Synthesized voice readout so the answering machine can announce the time and date that each call was received.

Coin Telephone Application Issues

The primary concern of most readers is how to use coin telephones, not how to evaluate them for purchase. The COCOT market is growing, however, and many companies have more than an academic interest in coin telephone applications. This section discusses the principal issues to be considered in selecting and applying COCOTs.

The first concern is physical. Coin telephone should not only have the look and feel of the traditional phones used by the LECs, they also must have the durability of traditional phones. To prevent damage by vandals and theft of coin box contents, the housing must be made of a durable material. Coin box locks must be sophisticated enough to deter lock pickers. The handset cord must be armored and the caps on the handset cemented in place so the transmitter and receiver units cannot be removed. The appearance of the telephone set also is important. The familiar shape and style of the Western Electric coin telephone that most LECs use has been widely copied because COCOT owners have found that users prefer the look and feel of the familiar instrument.

A related issue is the instrument's ability to withstand the elements. This factor is not important in interior environments, but for outdoor installation the telephone must withstand extremes of temperatures. Cold temperatures often affect mechanical apparatus, such as totalizers and coin chutes, while hot temperatures affect the electronics.

Another key consideration is the degree of intelligence contained within the telephone. "Dumb" telephones slave off the central office and are generally used by LECs. Though the LECs have access to central office coin control apparatus, they are beginning to retrofit telephones with intelligence to handle such features as alarming and diagnostics and to meter the number of coins in the box. Intelligent telephones can prompt users and are generally locally powered, compared to dumb telephones, which are powered from the line. The amount of intelligence also is important in handling coin collection. Coin phones should be capable of recognizing call progress signals, including ringing, reorder, and busy tones, and not collecting the coin even though time has elapsed. The phone also should be able to recognize the two-tone signal of a blocked call and not collect the coin.

Selected Telephone Station Equipment Manufacturers

Telephone Instruments

American Telecommunications Corporation

AT&T Information Systems

GTE Business Communications Systems, Inc.

Northern Telecom, Inc

Panasonic Co. Telephone Products Div.

Siemens Corporation

Cordless Telephones

AT&T

Cobra/Dynascan Corp.

Panasonic Co. Telephone Products Div.

Uniden

Telephone Answering Machines

Code-A-Phone Corporation

Dictaphone Corporation

Panasonic, Co. Telephone Products Div.

Phone-Mate, Inc.

Coin Telephones

AT&T Technologies
Cointel Communications
Digitech Communications
Elcotel Telecommunications
Systems, Inc.
Intellicall, Inc.

Northern Telecom, Inc.
Omniphone
Reliance Comm/Tec R-Tec
Systems
Tatung Telecom
US Telecommunications

Coin Telephone Administrative and Switching Systems

America's Business Software
Elcotel, Inc.

Ernest Telecom, Inc.
Digital Services

Coin Telephone Enclosures

Acoustics Development Corp.
AdcoAmerican Specialties, Inc.
Amfas, Inc.
AT&T Consumer Products
Benner-Nawman, Inc.
CDA Industries South, Inc.
Coin-Op-Telecommunications
Enclosures, Inc.
Fabrication Technologies Of
America, Inc.

Fortech, Inc.
JM Industries, Inc.
Modular Systems, Inc.
Phillips & Brooks, Inc.
Quality Industries
Rainbow Communications
Tele-Source Corp.
TelFab, Inc.
U.S. Teletron, Inc.

Network Channel Terminating Equipment

AT&T Network Systems
Lear Siegler, Inc.
Northern Telecom Inc.
Proctor & Associates Co., Inc.
Pulsecom Division, Harvey
Hubbell, Inc.

Telco Systems, Inc.
Tellabs Inc.
Wescom, Telephone Products
Div. Rockwell Telecommunica-
tions, Inc.

Premises Cable and Distributing Frames

AT&T

Adirondack Wire & Cable

Alcatel Cable Systems

Alpha Wire

Belden Corp.

Northern Telecom

Montrose Products Co.

Manufacturers of Station Wiring Products

AMP Corp.

AT&T

Crest Industries, Inc.

Keptel

Leviton Telecom

Nevada Western

Northern Telecom

Panduit

Suttle

19

Key Telephone Systems

Key telephone systems (KTS) are not high technology products compared to radio, satellite, and fiber optics, and they don't even have the technical appeal of a PBX, but they are the workhorses of American business. Like other customer premises products, KTSs have evolved from wired logic and electromechanical operation to stored program or firmware control. In the process, they have adopted many features that were once the exclusive province of the PBX. The line between the PBX and the key system is now indistinct enough that the industry has coined the term *hybrid* to describe one class of system that has elements of both.

Small businesses wanting to share a few lines among several users, departmental work groups behind Centrex or a PBX with analog lines, and even some residences comprise the market for key telephone systems. The demand for key systems is substantial, as evidenced by the number of manufacturers that are producing them. Like other forms of switching, key systems began with electromechanical equipment, which went through several evolutions before culminating in the ubiquitous 1A-2 system with which nearly everyone is familiar. The LECs installed these systems by the millions; many of them are still in operation and undoubtedly will remain through the end of this century.

The 1A-2 system is the design model that modern electronic systems now attempt to emulate. The system is disarmingly simple, and more than one user, faced with the complexity of its electronic replacement, has longed for its return. Lines terminate on telephone buttons that have transparent key caps. An idle line is dark, and a busy line has a steady lamp, a ringing line a slow flash, and a line on hold a fast flash.

The 1A-2 design is admirable, but it has several shortcomings that electronic key telephone systems (EKTS) overcome. The first drawback is the cabling system. Even a six-button telephone set requires a 25-pair cable, which is costly and difficult to install; congests ducts, raceways, and backboards; and weighs heavily on suspended ceilings. Electromechanical key systems lack intelligence and are therefore incapable of speed dialing, station message detail recording, do not disturb, and other features that EKTSs can provide.

An EKTS offers most of the features of a PBX, especially in the hybrid version, which is a cross between a PBX and a key system. The distinction between key telephone systems and PBXs is becoming more blurred as technology brings more intelligence to the key system. The principal characteristics that distinguish a key system from a PBX or a hybrid are:

- EKTSs have hardware or firmware control. Although the control logic may originate in software, it is usually embedded in a chip, so changing the program requires changing a chip, contrasted to the full software control stored in the volatile RAM memory of a PBX.

- Station features for EKTSs are usually not programmable. All stations that have the same type of telephone instrument have the same features.

- A key system attendant announces calls to station users over an intercom; hybrid and PBX attendants transfer calls directly to extensions.

- Outgoing trunks are directly selected by pushing a button in a KTS; PBX and hybrid users dial an access code such as 9. The direct line termination limits the number of lines that can be terminated on a telephone.

- Key system users dial other stations over a limited number of intercom paths. In a PBX the number of intercom paths can equal the number of pairs of stations.

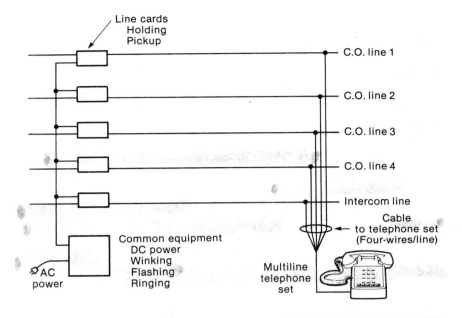

Figure 19.1 Diagram of a 1A-2 key telephone system.

- Key systems have a narrower range of features than PBXs and hybrids. Many PBX-like features, such as station message detail recording and least cost routing, are appearing in key systems, but others, such as direct inward dialing, are unavailable in most key systems.

Further blurring the distinction between key systems and PBXs is the trend of some manufacturers to make their key telephone instrument lines compatible with their PBX lines. A company can begin with a key system and grow to a PBX while retaining the same instruments. A later section further amplifies the differences between these types of systems. Chapter 20 discusses PBXs in detail.

Key Telephone System Technology

The electromechanical 1A-2 KTS, which is still in widespread use in the United States, brings central office lines to stations over multipair cable. The system uses a common bell for all lines and shows which line is ringing by flashing a lamp on the telephone button. Separate leads are used for talking and illumination. A hold button transfers the line from the telephone set to a holding relay, which terminates the line in a resistor and applies a flashing signal to the lamp on the telephone set. Figure 19.1 is a simplified diagram of how the 1A-2 KTS operates. Although this equipment is obsolescent, it shows the functions of a key telephone system clearly.

The control equipment is mounted in a cabinet and powered by commercial AC. The circuitry that supplies illumination and responds to pickup and hold signals is contained in plug-in units called *400 type* line cards. The common equipment and line cards light a steady lamp on busy lines, apply 60 flashes per minute to ringing lines, and apply 120 flashes per minute to lines on hold. The common equipment also isolates lines in the holding mode so they cannot talk to each other when on hold. The central control circuitry is known as a *key service unit* (KSU).

The 1A-2 system has a significant drawback—it requires large multipair cables that are costly to buy and time-consuming to install. The number of conductors varies with the number of lines, but most stations are wired with a minimum of 25-pair cable. The 1A-2 systems also lack many of the enhancements that more modern equipment offers. For example, special attention must be paid to 1A-2 KTS to ensure compatibility with DTMF dialing on the intercom line. Many systems use an electromechanical intercom line selector that is not compatible with DTMF dials. Auxiliary intercom line converters are required to select stations from DTMF pulses. Many other desirable features, which the next section lists, are lacking in the 1A-2 KTS. Some special features, such as speakerphone, can be obtained by adding external equipment.

The recent generations of EKTSs replace electromechanical control with processor control and greatly reduce the number of cable pairs required for operation. A typical system uses two- or three-pair cable for each station with separate paths for talking and control. EKTS uses a microprocessor to scan incoming lines. When the scanner detects an incoming ring, it signals the attendant. The attendant answers an incoming call by depressing a button—the same procedure used in electromechanical KTS. Instead of directly accessing the incoming line, however, the telephone set sends a data

Figure 19.2   TIE Businesscomm 16 key telephone system.
Courtesy, TIE/communications, Inc.

message to the controller, which connects the incoming line to the station. Calls are held by depressing the hold button, which applies a flashing lamp signal to the line button. Figure 19.2 shows the major components of the TIE Businesscomm 16, which is an electronic key telephone system.

Electronic KTS telephone sets have many features that are unavailable on electromechanical systems. For example, the TIE Exel 2 display telephone shown in Figure 19.3 includes push button access to special features that in other systems can be accessed only by dialing codes. A digital readout displays date and time, message waiting, called number, and other such messages. Effectively, EKTS is the equivalent of electromechanical KTS except that lines and trunks are switched in a central switching matrix instead of by the telephone set. KTSs that use electronic telephones are compatible only with telephones designed to

Figure 19.3   TIE Excel 2 display telephone.
Courtesy, TIE/communcations, Inc.

interface with the control equipment. In EKTSs, telephone sets are generally available only from the manufacturer.

Key systems are rated according to the number of stations and lines they support. For example, a 6 x 12 system could terminate six telephone lines and 12 stations. Unlike 1A-2, which usually has only one intercom line, most key systems have multiple intercom paths for station-to-station conversations and announcing calls. Intercom lines use either the telephone handset or a speaker/microphone for the intercom talking path.

The type and size of the switching matrix vary with the manufacturer. Manufacturers class larger systems supporting as many as 50 trunks and 100 lines as hybrids, but the difference between hybrids and small PBXs is not distinct. The provision of processor control allows KTSs to provide many features that are

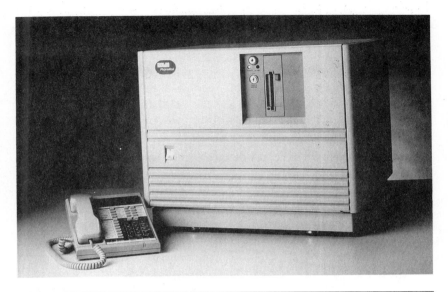

Figure 19.4   Rolm Redwood hybrid telephone system.
Courtesy, Rolm Corporation

similar to PBX features. Figure 19.4 illustrates the components of a Rolm Redwood hybrid telephone system.

Several manufacturers produce multiline systems that do not require a KSU. Most KSU-less systems require one pair of wires per line, which limits the size of the system to four lines or fewer. Some systems employ a special signaling arrangement and use two-pair wire—one pair for talking and one for signaling. The primary advantages of KSU-less systems are low cost and ease of installation. Anyone who knows how to install a single-line telephone can install KSU-less telephones, which makes them ideal for small offices and residences.

The primary drawbacks of KSU-less systems are limited expandability and lack of features. Since the systems have no KSU, the only features available are those contained in the telephone set itself. Most KSU-less systems also lack an intercom path, which means calls cannot be announced over an intercom as they are with most key systems.

Key Telephone System Features

All KTSs, including KSU-less systems, have the following features, which are the original features of 1A-2, in common:

- *Call Pickup*. The ability to access one of several lines from a telephone by pressing a line button.

- *Call Hold*. The ability to press a button to place an incoming line in a holding circuit while the telephone is used for another call.

- *Supervisory Signals*. Lamps that show when a line is ringing, in use, or on hold.

- *Common Bell*. The ringing of a single bell to indicate an incoming call.

Many EKTSs have the following additional features:

- *Automatic Hold Recall*. After a call has been left on hold for a specified period, the telephone emits a warning tone.

- *Conferencing*. The conferencing feature permits a station user to bridge two or more lines for a multiparty conversation.

- *Data Port Adapter*. A modem or facsimile machine can be connected. Without a data port adapter, data stations are unable operate through the KTS.

- *Direct Station Selection*. The DSS feature, usually combined with a busy lamp field, enables the attendant to determine if the called station is busy or idle and connects the attendant to the station at the press of a single button.

- *Do Not Disturb*. The station user can press a button that prevents intercom calls from reaching the station and silences the bell.

- *Hands-Free Answerback*. This feature permits the station user to answer the intercom or an incoming call without picking up the handset.

- *Intercom*. A shared path appears on all stations. By dialing the station intercom code or pressing a DSS button, users can announce calls and hold conversations.

- *Last Number Redial.* The last number dialed can be redialed by pressing a button.

- *Message Waiting.* Enables the attendant to signal a busy station user that another call is waiting.

- *Music on Hold.* While a call is on hold, music or a promotional announcement is played.

- *Power Fail Transfer.* When commercial power fails, the system automatically connects the central office lines to analog station sets.

- *Privacy.* This feature prevents other stations from picking up a line that is in use. In some systems privacy is automatic unless the user presses a privacy release key.

- *Remote Maintenance.* A central maintenance center can call into the system through a modem for remote trouble diagnosis.

- *Speed Dial.* Many EKTSs have both a system speed dial, which all users share, and station speed dial, which is contained in the telephone set.

- *Station Display.* Proprietary telephones are equipped with readouts that may display date and time, last number dialed, elapsed time on the call, etc.

- *Station Message Detail Recording.* A port in the key service unit puts out the details of calls for connection to a call accounting system.

- *Station Restriction.* Although most EKTSs lack station-programmable features, some systems provide different classes of service for restricting long distance calls.

- *Tie Line.* The EKTS can be connected via tie lines to another KTS or a PBX. This feature gives the key system user access to the features of the other system.

KTSs usually include one or more intercom lines. These are used for station-to-station communication—primarily for conversations between the attendant and the called party. In large systems, however, the intercom line takes on the characteristics of the intrasystem talking paths of a PBX. Most EKTSs provide multiple intercom paths so several intrasystem conversations can be held simultaneously. Most systems provide a built-in speaker so the intercom line can be answered without using the telephone handset. Optionally, the handset can be lifted for privacy. The number of intercom lines provided is a feature that distinguishes a PBX from a hybrid. Many hybrid systems provide a limited number of intercom paths, which limits their usefulness in systems that support a large amount of intrasystem calling.

While calls can be answered from any station in many systems, a special attendant's telephone often is provided. The attendant has all the features of regular stations and also may be provided a busy lamp field (BLF) to show which stations are occupied and a direct station selection (DSS) field, which allows him or her to transfer calls to stations by pushing a button instead of dialing the station number. To support the attendant, many systems include paging. The paging system is accessed by pushing a button or dialing a code and can be divided into zones if the building is large enough to warrant it. Many systems provide for "parking" a call so a paged user can go to any telephone, dial a park number, and pick up the incoming call.

KTS and Hybrids vs. PBX

Although the distinction between EKTSs, hybrids, and PBXs is not clear in the larger KTS line sizes, if an organization requires more than 100 central office line and station ports, a PBX may be required because of its range of features and greater line, trunk, and intercom capacity. The upper line size range of an EKTS is set by the size of the telephone instrument. When the organization has more than about 24 lines, it is impractical to terminate them all on the telephone, so the user must dial 9 to get an outside line, and the attendant must transfer incoming calls. When an EKTS has these pooled trunk capabilities, it is defined as a hybrid.

Because the cost of common equipment is distributed among all stations and because the common equipment for a PBX is more expensive, in smaller sizes an EKTS is definitely more economical. Between a lower range of about 30 ports and an upper range of about 100 ports, the decision as to which type of system to buy can be based on cost, features, and technical performance. For fewer than 30 ports, an EKTS generally is the most practical unless the organization expects growth.

EKTS supports a limited variety of trunks. Most EKTSs cannot support direct inward dialing, and only a few high end systems support tie lines. Direct T-1 interface is available on some hybrids but is not available for EKTS.

PBXs generally support a wider variety of telephone sets, ranging from single-line 2500 sets to multiline display sets and integrated voice and data terminals. Most EKTSs have two or three telephone sets in their product range, with hybrids somewhere between the two. Most PBXs and some hybrids have station-programmable features, compared to EKTSs, in which the telephone set buttons are usually fixed and available for only one function. PBXs and most hybrids support off-premises extensions, answering machines, modems, and facsimile transmission over standard analog station ports. EKTS supports such devices through a special OPX port or, in some systems, not at all.

EKTSs usually have limited or no capability for call distribution, so users in an incoming call center must press a button to pick up calls. This results in lost time and poor customer service because calls in progress must be interrupted to answer incoming calls, and when calls are placed on hold there is no way to tell which call arrived first. Most PBXs and some hybrids offer a uniform call distribution feature, which Chapter 21 discusses. And few EKTSs can be integrated with voice processing systems such as the automated attendant and voice mail, products that Chapter 22 discusses.

Applications

The variety of EKTSs and hybrid systems on the market is so vast that managers must carefully evaluate their requirements before selecting a system. The following are some general rules, but readers must realize that there are many exceptions, and product lines are changing constantly, which may invalidate some of these distinctions:

- If more than 24 central office trunks are required, favor a PBX or a hybrid.
- If fewer than eight central office trunks are required, favor an EKTS.

- If the system will never grow beyond three lines and about eight stations, favor a KSU-less system.

- If any form of call distribution or voice processing is required, favor a PBX or a hybrid.

- If half the total system traffic is intercom, favor a PBX or, depending on size, a hybrid.

There are many more criteria that should be considered in choosing a system. some of which are covered in the evaluation criteria section that follows.

Standards

There are few standards for key telephone systems beyond those that govern connection to the telephone network. Manufacturers are free to define their features and method of operation in any way they choose. Most, however, emulate 1A-2 operation for basic features.

Evaluation Criteria

The first issue that must be addressed is whether the application requires a PBX, a hybrid, or an EKTS. The discussion that follows assumes that an EKTS is required. See Chapter 20 for PBX evaluation criteria, which also can be applied to most hybrids.

Capacity

Key telephone systems should be purchased with a view toward long term growth in central office lines and stations. Key system capacity is specified as the line and trunk capacity of the total system. For example, a 4 x 8 system would handle four central office lines and eight stations. This figure is the capacity of the cabinet, and further expansion may be expensive or impossible. Some systems can grow by adding another cabinet, but it also may be necessary to replace the power supply and main control module. With some systems it is possible to move major components, such as line and station cards, to a larger cabinet to increase capacity.

Most EKTSs use plug-in circuit cards. These are less costly than wired systems, which must be purchased from the outset at their ultimate size. The number of internal or intercom call paths also should be considered.

Cost

The initial purchase price of a KTS is only part of the total lifetime cost of the system. As with all types of telecommunications apparatus, the failure rate and the cost of restoring failed equipment are critical and difficult to evaluate. The most effective way to evaluate them on a key telephone system is by reviewing the experience of other users.

Installation cost is another important factor. In general, the more pairs the station cables require, the more expensive the installation. Another factor is the method of programming the station options in the processor. Some systems provide such options as toll call restriction, system speed calling of a selected list of numbers, and other features that are contained in a data base. If these features require a technician to program them, costs will be higher than for a system with features that can be user-programmed.

The least costly systems allow the user to rearrange telephones easily. Rearrangement costs are likely to be a function of the wiring plan the vendor uses when the system is installed. With some EKTSs all ports are brought out to modular jacks so stations can be rearranged by moving modular cords.

Maintenance costs may be significant over the life of the system. Cost savings are possible with systems that provide internal diagnostic capability. Some systems provide remote diagnostic capability so the vendor can diagnose the system over an ordinary telephone line. These features can offer cost savings in hybrids, but are less important in EKTS.

Blocking vs. Nonblocking Switching Network

A nonblocking switching network is one that provides as many links through the network as there are input and output ports. For example, one popular key system has capacity for 24 central office trunks, 61 stations, and eight intercom lines. The system provides 32 transmission paths, which support calls to and from all 24 central office trunks. The eight intercom paths limit intrasystem conversations to eight pairs of stations. A nonblocking network provides enough paths for all line and trunk ports to be simultaneously connected. In this system, if all central office trunks are connected, of the remaining 37 stations, only eight can be in conversation over the intercom paths. Although this system is not nonblocking, it meets an important test of having sufficient paths to handle all central office trunks and intercom lines.

Power Failure Conditions

During power outages, a KTS is inoperative unless the installation includes battery backup. Some systems include emergency battery supplies, while others remain inoperative until power is restored. If no backup supply is provided, the system should at least maintain its system memory until power is restored.

The system should include a power-failure transfer system that connects incoming lines to ordinary telephone sets so calls can be handled during power outages. The method of restarting the system after a power failure is also important because the method affects cost and the amount of time required to get the system restarted. Some systems use nonvolatile memory that does not lose data when power fails. Other systems reload the data base from a backup tape or disk, which results in a delay before the system can be used following restoral of power. If the system makes no provision for backup power, it can be operated from an inexpensive UPS supply of the type designed for personal computers.

Wired vs. Programmable Logic

Most key telephone systems built after the mid-1970s use programmable logic. Older systems including 1A-2 and equivalent KTS and KSU-less systems use wired logic. The primary advantage of wired logic is simplicity. Most failures in wired logic systems are in the plug-in 400 type cards, which can be replaced by the user for minimal cost. The primary disadvantages of wired logic systems are lack of flexibility and the amount of cabling required. In stored program systems, new features can be added by changing the program, which usually is contained in a ROM. Features can be added and removed to customize stations by changing the feature data base.

The most important advantage of stored program systems is the wide range of features they offer. Wired logic systems offer essentially the features of the telephone system itself plus basic key features. Other features are added with outboard equipment. Stored program systems offer features that duplicate those of more expensive and complex PBXs.

Station Equipment Interfaces

Most key telephone systems support only a proprietary station interface. Therefore, inexpensive 2500 sets cannot be used except with an off-premises extension card. With some key systems, not even the OPX card alternative is available. The lack of a single-line interface is not a disadvantage in many applications, but some organizations prefer to have 2500 sets in areas such as lunch rooms, warehouses, and reception areas.

An important feature for many users is upward compatibility of telephone sets and line and trunk cards across the manufacturer's entire product line. This capability reduces the cost of converting from a key system to a PBX and enables users to keep their instruments, which not only reduces cost, but also minimizes retraining.

An increasingly important feature is the ability connect a modem or facsimile machine to a key system port. These analog devices are incompatible with proprietary station interfaces, but for many organizations, the cost of providing a dedicated line is excessive. It is possible to connect modems and facsimile machines ahead of the key system and use the same line for telephone calls, but some means must be provided to prevent telephone users from barging in on a facsimile or modem session. Several manufacturers offer adapters that permit telephones and facsimile machines or modems to share lines.

Alphanumeric displays are not as fully functional on a key system as they are on a PBX. Nevertheless, they may be useful. A display field shows the number dialed, time of day, and station status information, such as busy or do not disturb, and in some systems the display may prompt the user in programming special features.

Attendant and Intercom Features

One feature that distinguishes a key system from a PBX is that in the former the attendant announces calls over an intercom path, while in the latter calls are transferred directly to the extension. The number of paths provided is important; paths are used for station-to-station communication as well as announcing calls.

Most key systems provide hands-free answer capability so a station user can answer without picking up the handset. This feature does not, however, automatically mean that speaker-phone capability is available on outside calls. This often requires a special telephone set.

Many systems give the attendant the choice of announcing calls by dialing the station number or by pressing a direct station selection (DSS) key. The DSS key is usually the most effective method on small key systems and may double as a station busy lamp. If a busy lamp field is not provided, the attendant hears a busy signal or receives a busy indication on a display.

Station Features

EKTS telephone sets are a substantial improvement over 1A-2 equipment. Practically all telephone sets have station speed dial capability and a common list of system speed dial numbers. Speaker phone capability is a standard feature on many key systems, and most systems can announce through a built-in speaker.

Some systems have message-waiting capability, which enables the attendant to turn on a light to show that the user has a message. Most systems have a privacy button, which enables the user to exclude others from the line in use or to toggle the button to permit access. A do-not-disturb button prevents others from reaching the station on the intercom, while permitting the user to make outgoing calls.

Key Service Unit vs. KSU-Less Systems

Some systems provide two- or three-line capability without a KSU. For small systems these can be effective, providing the capabilities of a full key telephone system without the need for a separate central unit. KSU-less systems have disadvantages, however, which make them inappropriate for many installations. First, they have limited capacity, so they are usable only for small locations and cannot be expanded. Second, they usually lack intercom paths, on-hook voice announcing, and other features that are essential in a multiroom office.

Selected Key Telephone Equipment Manufacturers

Key Systems with KSU

Alcatel/Cortelco

AT&T Information Systems

CMX Communications

Concord

Eagle Telephonics, Inc.

Executone Information Systems

Galaxy Communications

Inter-Tel

Iwatsu America

Kanda Telecom

Lanier Voice Products

Marubeni America

Mitel

NEC America

Northern Telecom, Inc

Panasonic Communications

Sanyo Business Systems

Siemens

Tadiran

Teledial Devices

Telerad

TIE/communications, Inc.

Toshiba America

Vodavi Communications Systems

KSU-Less Systems

Alcatel/Cortelco

Comdial

Deka

Panasonic Communications

TIE/communications, Inc.

Hybrid Key/PBX

Executone (Vodavi)

Fujitsu

Harris Digital Telephone Systems

Hitachi America, LTD

IBM/Rolm

Iwatsu America

Macrotel International

Mitel, Inc.

Northern Telecom, Inc.

Siemens Information Systems

Tadiran Electronic Industries

TIE/communications, Inc.

Toshiba

20

Private Branch Exchanges

The office PBX increasingly controls private voice networks. As networks evolve toward all-digital, so does the PBX in all but low end applications of, say 100 stations or fewer, where some systems remain analog. For years, the makers of analog PBXs argued that the key issue was whether the system operated on stored program control and that the user had little interest in knowing whether the switching technology was analog or digital. That argument is no longer valid. As transmission facilities evolve toward digital and as the integrated services digital network (ISDN) emerges, PBXs will evolve to the point that they have few, if any, analog interfaces.

The advent of T-1 carrier as the preferred transmission medium is the principal force driving the evolution of the PBX. The IECs make it increasingly attractive to bypass the local central office with T-1 trunks directly to the carrier's point-of-presence. The cost of T-1 circuits for PBX tie lines is decreasing to the point that a tie line group larger than six or seven circuits should be considered for T-1 carrier, particularly where data transmission facilities parallel the route of voice. The integration of voice and data on the circuit level often increases the availability of bandwidth with a reduction of cost compared to analog services.

The telephone station interface to the PBX is also rapidly evolving toward digital. Over the past few years, telephone sets with the coder decoder (CODEC) in the station set have dropped in price to the point that they are cost-competitive with analog sets. Even the use of analog station ports for modems is disappearing as telephone sets with RS-232-C interfaces become more economical, and modem pooling becomes an essential feature of most PBXs. A few analog station ports are still required for such devices as facsimile, voice mail, and answering machines, but these too will eventually become digital.

Even the interface to local trunks will gradually evolve toward digital, even before the arrival of ISDN. Some LECs now offer two classes of digital local trunks: one class to the line side of the local central office, and the other to the trunk side. Both classes offer the advantage of significantly improved transmission service. In addition, trunk side access offers the advantage of relaying answer supervision from the central office to the PBX. If the PBX supports it, answer supervision solves the problem of inaccurate call timing that plagues call accounting systems. Most companies use call accounting systems to generate usage information for allocating long distance costs to individuals and organizational units.

The PBX is the precursor of future public network technology. ISDN, which Chapter 26 discusses, is an end-to-end digital network that supports simultaneous voice and data transmission. ISDN is evolving slowly in public networks because the costs of change are enormous and the needs are not yet developed fully, but ISDN concepts are developing rapidly in the office. Digital PBXs are the present test bed of future ISDN services in an environment where experimentation is encouraged in the quest for improved productivity.

PBXs conform to the general purposes of the voice switching systems described in Chapters 8 and 9, but their architectures are diverse and their features are different from those of switches designed for central office operation. This chapter discusses PBX features and ways that PBXs depart from conventional central office practice and concludes with a discussion of factors to be considered in evaluating PBXs. Subsequent chapters cover related products. Chapter 21 discusses automatic call distributors, which are a feature of many PBXs. Chapter 22 covers voice processing systems, including voice mail, which frequently is integrated with a PBX. Chapter 28 covers data PBXs, which are similar to voice/data PBXs except that they switch only data.

PBX Technology

PBX technology has progressed through three generations and, according to most manufacturers, is entering the fourth. There is some ambiguity about the definition of the fourth generation of PBXs, with some manufacturers labeling their products as fourth generation when they differ little from third generation systems. All generations are still currently in use, although first generation systems are no longer manufactured.

First generation systems used wired solid state, or relay logic, and space division analog switching networks. First generation telephones are nonproprietary rotary dial or DTMF analog sets. If key features are required with a first generation PBX, a separate key telephone system is necessary. The second generation introduced stored program control processors driving reed or PAM switching networks. Second generation systems use either standard analog or proprietary telephones, most of which are analog sets with separate wiring, to control a limited number of key telephone features. The third generation, which is the first to support end-to-end digital transmission, employs PCM switching technology and both digital and analog proprietary telephones.

The fourth generation of PBXs is not clearly defined. Some products that claim to be fourth generation systems employ LAN-type architecture to provide a highway for interconnecting the variety of terminals and mainframes found in the automated office as illustrated in Figure 20.1. Fourth generation systems provide an interactive user interface that supports other office automation functions besides voice. The user's terminal can be a multipurpose workstation that integrates voice, enhanced telephone features, and data applications into a single device. The fourth generation system is intended to be a total office communication system, but PBXs that are advertised as fourth generation also support standard DTMF telephones and a full line of proprietary instruments.

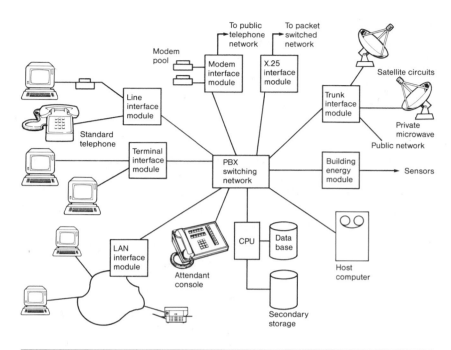

Figure 20.1   Block diagram of a fourth generation PBX.

Contrasts Between PBXs and Local Central Offices

The first three generations of PBX used technology closely resembling that of central offices. Local telephone service is a standardized product furnished by a switching system that is designed for long life and low cost operation within a carefully controlled environment of numbering plan, trunking plant, outside plant, and standard features. The modern PBX is intended for a specialized environment. Because each organization is unique, products must have the capacity to be customized to the application. A standard user interface is of less concern in a PBX than in a public environment because within an organization system operation can be taught and controlled. In a public network, features must operate uniformly because people expect telephones to work the same wherever they are.

The main differences between a PBX and a local central office are:

- A PBX is intended for private operation on the user's premises; a central office is intended for common carrier ownership in a central office.

- Because a PBX is intended for private use, it often omits service protection features that are mandatory in central offices. For example, backup battery power and processor redundancy may be omitted to save money in a PBX.

- PBXs are constructed to be economical in much smaller line sizes than central offices. Clusters of users that would be directly cabled or handled by a remote line unit in central offices are served by PBXs.

- Most PBXs have an attendant console for answering calls to the main listed telephone number. This extra equipment is unnecessary in central offices except those equipped for Centrex service.

- Central offices connect to the interexchange network with trunk-side connections to a higher class office. A PBX terminates on the line side of the local central office and therefore uses line signaling methods (loop or ground start and dial or DTMF signaling). This distinction is diminishing, however, as some LECs offer trunk-side connections to their end offices.

- PBXs have numbering plans that are more flexible than those of central offices. End offices normally enforce seven-digit dialing. PBXs employ flexible numbering systems to suit the needs of users and uniform dialing plan to support multi-PBX networks.

- PBXs increasingly are equipped with voice/data integration features. They contain data communications features such as X.25 interface, digital addressing, and high speed digital bus interface. These features are available with digital Centrex, but otherwise are not characteristic of central offices.

Figure 20.2   The Northern Telecom Meridian SL-1 Digital PBX.
Courtesy, Northern Telecom, Inc.

- PBXs can restrict stations from selected features such as off-net and tie trunk access. Central offices provide unrestricted access to other numbers.

Figure 20.2 is a photograph of the Northern Telecom Meridian SL-1, one of the newest models of digital PBX.

Interfaces

PBXs connect to three types of networks: local, interexchange, and private. Also, many systems support special services such as WATS lines and foreign exchange trunks to local calling areas in distant cities. Systems serving automated offices and data communications require interfaces to data terminals, gateway circuits, and other computer networks. The variety of interface circuits is a key distinguishing feature among PBX generations.

Line Interfaces

PBXs often include key telephone-like features in their software and may employ line interface circuits that require more than one pair of wires for the station set. Also, integral data transmission features often require one- to three-pair station wiring. The station loop resistance range of a PBX, especially one with digital telephone sets, is usually less than the 1300 to 1500 ohm range typical of a central office. Therefore, many PBXs operate within a building or campus and must either use special off-premises line circuits for longer loops or use remote line switch units to move the line circuits closer to the end users.

Voice-only PBXs have line interface circuits that resemble those used in digital central offices except that some central office features, such as line testing access, usually are omitted from PBX line circuits. Line ports mount on plug-in printed circuit cards that carry from four to 16 circuits per card. PBX digital line circuits are of three types: separate voice and data ports, combined voice and data ports, and universal ports that can be used interchangeably for voice or data. The first two types may result in unused port capacity if the PBX has the wrong ratio of data to voice stations.

PBX Trunk Interfaces

PBXs, like central offices, interface with the outside world through trunk circuits that exchange signals with other switching systems through a variety of signaling interfaces. Trunk circuits mount on cards that contain from two to eight trunks per card. Analog trunk cards support two-way central office trunks, WATS lines, and 800 lines. A separate type of trunk card is required for direct inward dial (DID) trunks in most PBXs.

Many digital PBXs can support direct T-1 line interface with a local central office, but LEC services permitting T-1 interface to the central office are unavailable in some locations. It is important to remember that a PBX interfaces with the line side of a local switching system. Therefore, ground or loop start signaling is employed; the central office furnishes dial tone to the PBX when it is prepared to receive digits, and DTMF or dial-pulse addressing is used. Many local central offices do not support signaling and supervision over a T-1 line interface to a PBX except through channel banks.

Compatibility with central office line equipment is important for proper PBX operation. The interface standard is EIA-464, which specifies technical and performance criteria for the interface between the two types of systems. The central office interfaces the PBX with the central office's own supervision; the supervision from a distant trunk is not transferred through the line circuit to the PBX. Therefore, the PBX cannot pass answer supervision through its SMDR port to an external call accounting system. Some LECs offer digital line and trunk connections to the central office, and these may provide answer supervision. Supervision is also passed from the T-1 long distance facilities of many LECs.

PBXs require an access digit, usually 9, to connect station lines to central office trunks. When the user dials 9, the PBX seizes an idle central office trunk and connects the talking path through to the station if the station is permitted off-net dialing. The station hears central office dial tone as a signal to proceed with dialing.

Automatic Call Distribution

Automatic call distribution is a feature that allows PBXs to concentrate incoming lines or trunks at a group of service positions. Typical applications are the service positions of any large organization such as airlines, utilities, catalog houses, and department stores.

Incoming calls route to an agent position based on incoming line type. For example, airlines typically screen calls by providing one number to the public and a different number to travel agents. These partitions are called *splits*. The system directs the call to the appropriate split based on the number dialed, or callers can direct their own calls via an automated attendant.

When agent positions are idle, the call routes immediately. If all positions are occupied, the ACD places calls in queue and notifies the caller by recorded announcement that the call is being held. ACDs often are designed for multiple system operation so calls can be transferred to a distant location during off-peak hours. Chapters 21 and 22 discuss ACD and automated attendant features in more detail.

Integrated Services Digital Network Interface

The first generation of digital PBX interfaces emulates a channel bank. The interfaces use bit-robbed signaling to pass numbering information and to relay on-hook and off-hook status. Therefore, the PBX can pass only 56 kb/s. Many PBXs are beginning to support ISDN interfaces, which provide two B channels (64 kb/s) and one D channel (16 kb/s signaling) as a basic interface. The ISDN primary interface provides 23 B channels plus one 64 kb/s signaling channel. Refer to Chapter 26 for a discussion of ISDN features.

Although ISDN has just begun to emerge in the last decade of the 20th century, PBX manufacturers are touting ISDN compatibility as an essential feature of their systems. At the time of this writing, ISDN standards are not complete. Most LECs are running ISDN trials, with tariffed offerings available in selected central offices. The major interexchange carriers offer primary rate interfaces to their switching systems without access through the local exchange network.

The question in the minds of most telecommunications managers is how much importance to place on ISDN compatibility, either present or future, in purchasing a PBX now. Questions such as these naturally arise:

- When will ISDN services be available in my local exchange?
- When the services are available, will they be necessary?
- When the services are available, will they be affordable?
- Will ISDN services make my PBX obsolete, or can it be upgraded?

No one knows the answers to these questions now because the suite of ISDN services is evolutionary and probably will develop as demand occurs. ISDN advancement will be no different from the existing telephone network, which has evolved in step with technology and demand for services. Eventually, almost every PBX in existence will be ISDN compatible; the question is when. While there is no easy way to assess the importance of ISDN compatibility, the Applications section of this chapter offers some guidelines.

Tie Trunks

Organizations operating multiple PBXs often link them through tie trunks, which are intermachine trunks terminating on the trunk side of the PBX. Trunk facilities may be privately owned or obtained from interexchange carriers. They may be analog or digital, with a definite trend toward digital with the introduction of fractional T-1 tariffs. Signaling compatibility is a concern with tie trunks. The trunks normally use E & M signaling, but the trunk interface in the PBX may require the use of signaling converters.

If tie trunks terminate in a single location they are accessed by dialing a digit, such as 8, which connects them to the distant PBX. Many multi-PBX organizations have a separate dialing plan for each system plus a single organization-wide dialing plan. The PBX then is programmed to provide the translations necessary to reach the distant number over the tie trunk network. This feature is called *uniform dialing plan*.

Transmission is of concern in designing a tie trunk network. Transmission loss is designed according to the via net loss or fixed loss plans as discussed in Chapter 2.

Special Trunks

Many PBXs have a variety of special trunks, such as WATS lines, foreign exchange, and 800 numbers, to provide access to lower cost long distance service. When several of these special trunks are connected to the PBX it is impractical to expect users to select which trunk to use. Most PBXs use least cost routing features, which enable the system to select the most economical route

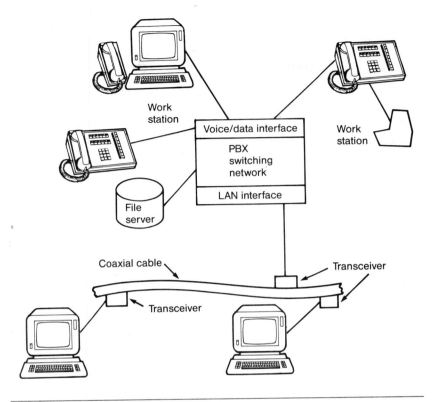

Figure 20.3   PBX to LAN interface.

based on the class of trunks terminated, their busy/idle status, and the station line class.

Gateways and External Interfaces

All PBXs provide interfaces to public voice networks. In addition, some PBXs offer gateways to public data networks such as Tymnet and SprintNet. These gateways usually are implemented with an X.25 interface (see Chapter 25) or a proprietary equivalent. This interface allows a device to address an off-net station over a digital circuit. The protocol conversions are handled between the PBX and the public data network.

Interfaces to local area networks (LANs) are also provided by some PBXs as Figure 20.3 shows. Token rings and contention bus interfaces are available with some PBXs. See Chapter 27 for a description of LAN technologies. With a LAN interface, data devices on the LAN can communicate with printers and file servers as usual. In addition, they can use the PBX as a gateway to public telephone or data networks, and terminals connected to PBX ports can address devices attached to the LAN. Through the LAN interface, the PBX emulates a node on the LAN and communicates with its protocol so a terminal on the PBX can have access to devices on the LAN.

Some PBXs also provide interfaces to mainframe computers. For example, a PBX may emulate an IBM 3270 terminal and support access by non-compatible terminals into a mainframe cluster controller.

Principal PBX Features

Features common to PBXs and central offices are not repeated in this chapter. Refer to Chapter 8 for a discussion of voice switched network features that are not discussed here. Many features that are impractical or unnecessary in a local telephone network are both feasible and desirable in the private environment of a PBX. This section discusses the main features that most PBXs support.

Direct Inward Dialing (DID)

DID offers station users the ability to receive calls from outside the system without going through the PBX attendant. The LEC's central office contains a software table with the location of the DID trunk group. When a call for a DID number arrives, the central office seizes a trunk and outpulses the extension number. The extra central office operations cause some delay on DID calls. DID is effective in reducing the load on PBX attendants. It also enables users to receive calls when the switchboard is closed. A separate group of trunks from the LEC is required. Most LECs charge a premium for DID trunks compared to normal central office trunks. Also, most LECs levy a charge for each DID number.

Voice and Data Integration in the PBX

Most organizations that are large enough to justify a T-1 line to a distant PBX have a data communications network that also can

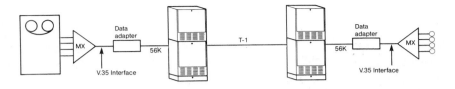

Figure 20.4   Integrating voice and data through the PBX.

ride on the same facilities. Figures 20.4 and 20.5 show two methods of integrating voice and data at the facility level. Figure 20.4 would logically be used when the PBX is digital and voice is the dominant circuit requirement. One or more channels of the T-1 are set aside for data by a "nailed up" connection through the PBX. Depending on the architecture of the PBX, the data adapter is either a plug-in circuit card or an external device that gives the data circuit access to the digital channel. Any standard transmission speed from 2.4 to 64 kb/s is available, with some variation among manufacturers. The connection through the PBX is either defined in software or dialed by the user.

An even simpler arrangement is to dial the connection through an analog circuit port. With this arrangement, the full duplex data speed is limited to 9.6 kb/s. Technically this arrangement is inferior to a direct digital connection, but if the company is already using the DCE on an analog private line, this can be a fast and inexpensive method of integrating voice and data.

The architecture shown in Figure 20.5 would logically be used if the PBX were analog or if most T-1 circuit requirements were

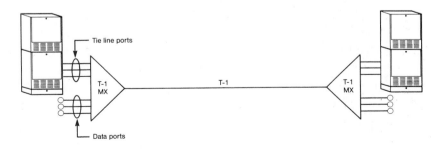

Figure 20.5   Integrating voice and data through a T-1 multiplexer.

data. This method makes effective use of low bit-rate voice channels, which Chapter 7 discusses. With the ability to digitize voice at speeds as low as 8 kb/s, the T-1 multiplexer can derive considerably more voice and data channels than the arrangement shown in Figure 20.4, which is limited to a maximum of 24 channels per T-1. Although the T-1 multiplexer is considerably more expensive than a direct connection through the PBX, it may be cost-justified because of the resulting increase in the number of circuits. A less expensive method of dropping data channels is a drop-and-insert multiplexer, which routes the T-1 line to the PBX and picks off one or more channels for data.

Least Cost Routing (LCR)

Most PBXs terminate a combination of public switched and private trunks on the system. For example, in addition to local trunks, the PBX may terminate WATS lines, foreign exchange lines, tie trunks to another PBX, and access lines connected directly to an IEC. Educating users about which service to use is a difficult task, particularly as rates vary with time of day and terminating location, and the dialing plan varies with the carrier called. It is a reasonably simple matter, however, to program route selection into the central processor of the PBX. With LCR the user dials the number; the system determines the least expensive route and dials the digits to complete the call over the appropriate trunk group.

The most sophisticated LCR systems can screen calls on six or more digits. Some less elaborate systems can screen on only three digits. Three-digit screening limits the PBX to routing by area code or prefix, but not both. The ability to screen on both area code and prefix is important to users on the edge of an area code boundary where it may be less costly to use one service for nearby prefixes and another for distant prefixes in the same area code.

A related issue is digit insertion and deletion. Some services, such as foreign exchange (FEX), may require the PBX to insert or delete an area code for correct routing. Users are the least confused if the dialing plan requires them to dial 9 + 1, then the seven- or ten-digit telephone number. For example, if the PBX has FEX trunks to another area code, the user would dial the area code, but the PBX would strip it off before passing the digits forward to the FEX trunks.

Many systems also provide a warning tone when calls are about to be routed over an expensive service so the user can hang up before the call completes. Complete flexibility in route selection is a highly desirable PBX feature that is available on most stored program controlled systems.

Networking Options

Most PBXs now provide networking options, which allow multiple systems to operate as a single system. Call processing messages pass between PBXs over a separate data channel using some form of common channel signaling. With the networking option, call processing information, such as a station's identification and class of service, travels across the network to permit features to operate in a distant PBX as they do in the local system. At the present state of development, networking is possible only between systems provided by the same manufacturer.

The objective of networking is to provide feature transparency, which is the ability of users to have the same calling features across the network as they have at their PBX. For example, users want be able to camp on a busy station, regardless of whether it is in their PBX or in a distant system, and they want to share a voice mail system across the network.

Single-Button Feature Access

Users can access several of a PBX's principal features by code dialing. For example, call pickup, call hold, and call forwarding all require distinctive codes, such as *7. Code dialing has an important drawback: users often forget the dialing codes, so they do not use the features. The solution is to assign the features to single buttons on proprietary telephone sets. If users want to pick up a call in a pickup group, for example, they need only press the call pickup button to bring the call to that telephone.

Station Message Detail Recording (SMDR)

This feature, in combination with a call accounting system, provides the equivalent of a detailed toll statement for PBX users. If the users have access to a common group of trunks to the local central office, the telephone company provides a toll statement listed by local telephone number. The calling PBX station number is not identified to the local central office, so such a toll statement will not provide the identity of the calling station. Most businesses require call detail to control long distance usage and to spread costs among the user departments. The SMDR port forwards this information to a call accounting system, which, as discussed in a later section, provides this capability. An SMDR is limited by the lack of answer supervision over a local telephone loop; the system cannot tell whether the called station answered or not. The determination of called station answer is based on the amount of time the calling station is off-hook. Because of the lack of answer supervision, the SMDR output cannot be balanced precisely with central office billing detail. However, it is accurate enough for most organizations.

Voice Store-and-Forward (Voice Mail)

Voice mail (see Chapter 22) is available as an optional integrated feature in some PBXs and can be added as a nonintegrated service to any PBX. When a station is busy or unattended, the caller can leave a message, which is stored in secondary storage, usually digitally. The station user can dial an access and identification code to retrieve the message. Voice mail is the voice equivalent of electronic mail, a service that allows a terminal-equipped station to leave a data message for another station.

Some voice mail systems include automated attendant, an option that enables callers to route their own calls within the system with a DTMF dial. Incoming calls are greeted with an announcement that invites them to dial the extension number if it is known, to dial a number for extension information, or to stay on the line for an attendant. This feature saves money by decreasing the amount of work required of the attendant.

Code, Speed, and Protocol Conversion

The greatest impediment to data communication is the lack of standard codes, speeds, and protocols. Some PBXs can interface dissimilar protocols. The system automatically adjusts to the terminal, either after a short log-on sequence or from the system's line translations. The system likewise adjusts to the requirements of the called station, enabling dissimilar terminals to communicate through the system.

Dialed Number Identification System (DNIS)

Offered by IECs along with 800 services, DNIS provides the equivalent of direct inward dialing for 800 calls. Incoming calls are preceded by a number that either is or can be converted by the PBX to the number the caller dialed. The DNIS feature in the PBX routes the call to the appropriate station number. DNIS enables an organization to have several 800 numbers and to route each call to a station, UCD or ACD hunt group, voice mail, or any other location within the PBX.

Direct Inward System Access (DISA)

The DISA feature enables callers to dial a telephone number and a password to gain access to the features of the PBX. If the DISA number is restricted, callers can dial extension numbers or tie lines to on-net locations. If the DISA feature is unrestricted, callers can gain access to long distance services. DISA helps reduce credit card calls by enabling users outside the PBX to access low cost long distance services.

Security is an obvious problem with DISA. Companies should change the password frequently and check the call accounting system for evidence of misuse. A second hazard is poor transmission as discussed in Chapter 2.

Power Failure Transfer

Unless a PBX is configured to run from batteries or from an uninterruptable power supply, a commercial power failure will cause the system to fail. The power failure transfer feature connects central office trunks to standard DTMF telephones. Since most PBXs require ground start trunks, provisions must be made to operate from loop start telephones. There are two methods of accomplishing this: use a separate loop start-to-ground start converter or equip the telephones with a ground start button. The former method is prevalent.

The power failure transfer feature is an inexpensive and effective way to obtain minimum service during power failure conditions. Even users of systems with battery backup or UPS should consider power failure transfer to retain some service if the PBX itself fails.

Trunk Queueing

The trunk queueing feature enables a user to camp on a busy trunk group. Two queueing methods are in common use: call-back queueing and hang-on queueing. With call-back queueing, the user activates the feature by dialing a code or pressing a feature button and hangs up. The system calls back when a trunk is available. With hang-on queueing, the user activates the feature but remains off-hook until the call completes. Some queueing features enable high priority users to jump to the head of the queue. The system should, however, have a maximum wait, after which even low priority users are cut through.

Restriction Features

An important feature of every PBX is its ability to restrict the calling of certain stations. Even companies with an unrestricted policy normally require restricted telephones in public locations such as waiting areas and lunch rooms. The type of restriction varies with manufacturer, but it is possible with most systems to restrict incoming, outgoing, and any type of long distance. Some systems can restrict down to a specific telephone number. All restriction systems should restrict area codes and prefixes. Prefix restriction is necessary to prevent users from dialing numbers, such as 900 numbers, for which a charge is collected.

Uniform Call Distribution

This service distributes calls evenly among a group of stations. When one or more active stations are idle, incoming calls are directed to the station that is next in line to receive a call. When all stations in the UCD group are busy, incoming calls are answered with a recording and held in queue. When a UCD station becomes idle, the call in queue the longest is directed to the station. In many UCD systems, a station user can toggle between active and inactive status by dialing a code or pressing a feature button. Compared to ACD, UCD is unsophisticated, lacking the supervisory and management features that an ACD offers. Chapter 21 discusses UCD in more detail.

Uniform Dialing Plan

Uniform dialing plan software in a network of PBXs enables the caller to dial an extension number and have the call completed over a tie line network without the caller's being concerned about where the extension is located. The PBX selects the route and takes care of station number translations. UDP software is effective only among PBXs of the same manufacture.

Universal Card Slots

The card slots in some PBXs are designated for a particular type of card. Therefore, it is possible that a shelf or cabinet may have vacant slots but not have any available for the type of card that is needed. Except processor and power supply cards, which usually require dedicated slots, PBXs with universal card slots can accept any type of line or trunk card in a vacant slot. This feature lends an important degree of flexibility to the system.

PBX Voice Features

As all PBXs are designed for voice switching service, they have features intended for the convenience and productivity of the users. Not all the features listed below are universally available, and many systems provide features not listed. This list briefly describes the most popular voice features found in PBXs.

- The PBX can be equipped with *paging* trunks that are accessed by an attendant or dialed from a station. An option is *zone paging,* which allows the attendant to page in specific locations rather than the entire building.

- *Distinctive ringing* enables a station user to tell whether a call has originated from inside or outside the system.

- *Speed dialing* enables station users to dial other numbers by using abbreviated codes. Speed dial is available from telephone set buttons or from a system speed dial list that everyone within a speed dial group shares.

- *Integrated key telephone* system features, such as those described in Chapter 19, can be integrated into the PBX software and accessed from a non-key telephone. Features such as call pickup, call hold, call forwarding, and dial-up conferencing can be provided.

- *Camp-on* is a feature that allows an attendant to queue an incoming call to a busy station. When the station becomes idle the call is automatically completed. A related feature, *automatic callback* enables station users to camp on busy lines.

- The caller's name or telephone number can be displayed on special telephones equipped with an *alphanumeric display*.

- *Special dialing features* are provided in many systems. Besides digit dialing, some systems can interface a workstation keyboard for addressing by a mnemonic or name.

- *Executive override* allows a station to interrupt a busy line or preempt a long distance trunk if the class of that station is higher than the class of the user.

- *Trunk answer any station* allows stations to answer incoming trunks when the attendant station is busy.

Attendant Features

Most PBXs have attendant consoles for incoming call answer and supervision. The following features are important for most consoles and represent only a fraction of the features available.

- *Direct station selection* (DSS) allows the attendant to call any station by pressing an illuminated button associated with the line. This feature is usually available only in small PBXs.

- *Automatic timed reminders* alert the attendant when a called line has not answered within a prescribed time. The attendant also can act as a central information source for directory and call assistance.

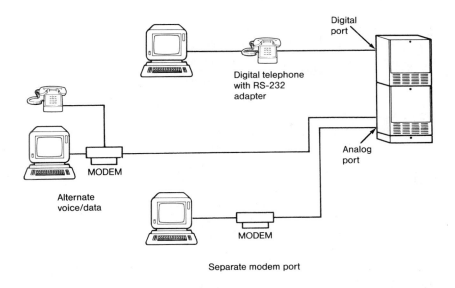

Figure 20.6   Connecting data terminal devices through a PBX.

- *Attendant controlled conferencing* is available for multi-port conference calls.
- *Centralized attendant service* (CAS) is provided on many systems to enable a central group of attendants to act as the attendants for remote PBXs.

Data Switching Capability

A highly touted capability of a digital PBX is its ability to switch voice and data with equal ease. Many companies take advantage of this capability, although data switching has limitations that this section discusses.

PBXs can interface to local area networks, host computers, and external analog and digital trunks. Data terminal devices can connect through the PBX in one of three ways as shown in Figure 20.6. The simplest way is through a modem that connects to a separate analog port. This method provides simultaneous voice and data sessions. Separate circuits are required for the voice and data devices. The advantage of this method is its flexibility. A data rate of 2.4 kb/s is common; rates up to 9.6 kb/s are available. The full range of PBX features is available with this method. The most important features for data terminal users are least cost routing and call accounting. A modem call uses the same circuits and facilities as voice and is indistinguishable from a voice call.

The second method, alternate voice and data, is often effective when the user has an analog station set and does not receive data calls. The telephone connects into a jack on the modem or the two bridge with a T adapter to the wall jack. This method is usually ineffective for receiving data calls, although some external devices that switch between voice and data are available.

Modems are cost effective for a few connections. If data usage is extensive, however, it becomes expensive because of the need for separate analog ports and modems, which together may exceed the cost of the third method, voice/data integration at the telephone set. The integrated voice and data option requires a digital telephone set. The station set is equipped with an EIA-232-C port, which is mounted either in the telephone set or in a separate data adapter. The PBX can connect data devices to computer ports or to a modem pool for placing trunk calls. A fifth method that is used less frequently is the integrated voice/data terminal such as the Rolm system that Figure 20.7 shows.

The modem pool has circuit cards or external data adapters in the PBX that interface a bank of modems. When the user initiates a data call, the PBX attaches a modem and the user can dial outside the PBX as usual. A data session can be carried simultaneously with a voice session in most PBXs. The PBX requires either one or two ports per session. If an incoming data call is directed to a DID telephone number that is identified as a data device, the PBX diverts the call through the modem pool, attaches a modem, and completes the call.

Data Switching Applications of a PBX

The voice and data requirements of the automated office can be fulfilled in any of three ways: separate PBX and LAN, a PBX that interfaces a LAN, or a PBX that integrates the total voice and data requirements in a single system. In terms of data switching capabilities, a PBX is approximately equivalent to a data PBX, which Chapter 28 covers. The telecommunications industry is unable to

Figure 20.7   Rolm Cypress integrated voice/data terminal.

agree which approach is the most effective because the needs of organizations differ so widely that no single approach meets the communications needs of all offices.

Any organization large enough to justify a PBX needs voice communications capability; data communications requirements vary greatly with the organization. Where the need for voice communication predominates, the conventional solution of a PBX with modems for occasional data traffic is the least expensive alternative. Where the organization has data terminals that require high speed access to a file server, printer, plotter, or host computer, a separate LAN or a PBX with a LAN interface will usually be most effective. If the organization has several lightly loaded terminals, the integrated voice/data PBX with digital telephones becomes an attractive means of obtaining port selection, port contention, and queuing. A principal benefit of using the PBX to switch data is that management features such as class of service restriction, call detail recording, and least cost routing can be extended to data terminals.

A PBX has limitations, however, when it comes to data switching. The following are some of the main drawbacks of using a PBX rather than a LAN for data communications:

- PBXs equipped with modems are incapable of passing data at speeds higher than 9600 b/s. Data speeds are limited to 64 kb/s on a direct digital connection.

- Call setup time in most PBXs is excessive, sometimes exceeding the transmission time of a short message.

- A PBX usually is cost-effective for only a few data connections. When the application requires many data devices, a LAN is less expensive and more effective.

- The load imposed on the switching system by data is different from the load imposed by voice. Overload of the PBX is a hazard.

As discussed in Chapter 28, the principal limitation of a voice/data PBX for data switching is the maximum speed of 64 kb/s that the PBX can accommodate. For applications such as electronic mail, where the user establishes a keyboard-to-CPU session through the PBX, the speed limitation is of little consequence. In CPU-to-CPU sessions, however, or in applications, such as computer aided design, that transfer large quantities of data, 64 kb/s is too slow.

A second limitation is inherent in the architecture of the PBX itself. Some PBXs have enough capacity to handle many simultaneous data sessions; in others, data sessions can adversely affect voice performance. Data sessions tend to be of two types. In the first type, the session is short but frequent; users dialing electronic mail boxes, for example, establish several short sessions per day. These affect the processor capacity of the PBX.

The other kind of call is typified by a host-to-printer session where the connection may be established for several hours. This type of session has little effect on the processor capacity, but each session takes a path through the switching network. If the PBX has a blocking switch network, several of these sessions can reduce capacity for voice calls. Blocking versus nonblocking networks are discussed in a later section. If the connection will be established more than a few hours per day, wire terminal equipment directly to the host.

Conversely, the PBX has advantages that makes it an ideal system for some data switching applications:

- It is unnecessary to install separate voice and data wiring as it is with a LAN or data PBX.
- For a few data devices, the PBX offers an economical alternative to installing a separate network.
- A PBX offers an effective method of port selection, port contention, and queuing for a few devices.
- A PBX extends call-processing features to data devices.

When several users share a few ports on the host computer, the PBX can be an effective way of providing port selection and port contention. Users can queue on busy ports and automatically be connected when one becomes available. The key to data transmission through a PBX lies in choosing the application intelligently, sizing the switching network and processor specifically for the data traffic load, and providing line ports designed for data transmission.

One method of PBX-to-host connection that is gaining popularity is the digital multiplexed interface. Known by various trade names, this connection is a proprietary interface between a selected PBX and host computer pair. The interconnection channel is a T-1 line, which replaces the ports in both the computer and the PBX. Other than providing the increased efficiency and lower cost of the 24-channel interface, the T-1 interface acts like separate analog circuits.

Call Accounting Systems

All PBXs, most hybrids, and many key telephone systems include a station message detail register (SMDR) port that receives call details at the conclusion of each call. The call details can be printed or passed to a call accounting system for further processing.

The SMDR output of most systems is of little value by itself because calls are presented in order of completion and usually lack rates, identification of the called number, and other such details that control of long distance costs requires. Call accounting systems add details to create management reports and a complete long distance statement for each user. The primary purposes of a call accounting system are to discourage unauthorized use and to distribute costs to users.

Most call accounting systems on the market are software programs for personal computers. Programs for minicomputers and mainframes and several stand-alone units that use custom processors are also available. Some personal computer systems include a plug-in board that collects call details and buffers them while the computer is used for other purposes. With this kind of protection, a dedicated computer is unnecessary. Some personal computer-based systems operate as a terminate-and-stay-resident program in a computer that is used for other purposes. This arrangement is hazardous because, if the user reboots the computer, call processing halts and data is lost.

In multi-PBX environments, a networked call accounting system may be required. These systems use buffers or computers to collect information at remote sites and upload it to a central processor at the end of the collection interval. If long distance calls can be placed from one PBX over trunks attached to another, a tie line reconciliation program is important. The tie line reconciliation program uses the completion time of calls to match calls that originate on one PBX and terminate on trunks connected to another.

Most PBXs can output to the SMDR port any combination of long distance, local, outgoing, and incoming calls. The amount of detail to collect is a matter of individual judgment, but remember that sufficient buffer and disk storage space must be provided to hold all the information collected.

Applications

Nearly every business that has more than 30 to 100 stations is in the market for a PBX or its central office counterpart, Centrex. PBXs are economical for some very small businesses that need features that most key system do not provide such as restriction and least cost routing. They are also economical for very large

businesses that have PBXs using central office switching systems ᴏ.
a size that rivals many metropolitan public networks. This chapter
discusses an application halfway between these two extremes.

PBX Standards

Few standards exist for PBXs. The interface between a PBX and
its serving local central office is standardized by EIA, and trunk
interfaces follow accepted industry practices for signaling and
electrical interface. The industry generally adopts the same PBX
features, but the manufacturer may use a unique method of
operating the feature. Analog telephones follow accepted industry
signaling practice, but the loop resistance range is left to the
manufacturer. Proprietary station interfaces are determined entirely by the manufacturer with little uniformity among products.
With only a few exceptions, proprietary station sets intended for
one PBX cannot be used in another manufacturer's system.

All PBXs require FCC registration of line and trunk terminations to public telephone networks.

Case History: A Steel Producer

A steel producer has four offices and plants located within a
40-mile radius. Before completing the current network, the company had four separate telephone systems, three of which were
leased, and one of which was a company-owned SL-1 model M.
Separate WATS and 800 lines served each office. Analog tie lines
linked three of the four offices, and one office was served by five
foreign exchange lines that were used for both incoming and
outgoing service. Separate analog data circuits connected three
of the offices; the fourth was served by a company-owned cable
that linked two of the plants. Figure 20.8 shows the configuration
as it previously existed. The company established the following
objectives for a new telephone system:

- All PBXs should be from the same manufacturer so a
  uniform dialing plan could be established and maintenance done by a single organization.
- Existing tie lines, foreign exchange lines, and data communication lines should be replaced with a T-1 network

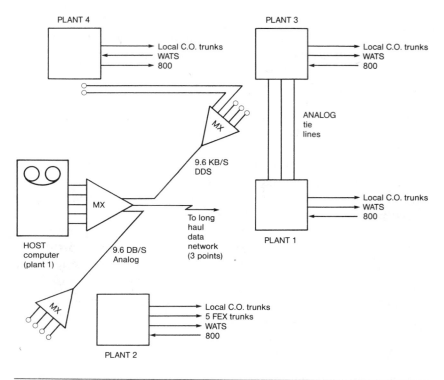

Figure 20.8   Steel Company PBX network—original configuration.

to obtain capacity at a lower cost than that provided by analog lines.

- Incoming and outgoing long distance should be routed to one IEC to gain the maximum benefit from bulk discounts.

- The network should be made as invulnerable to service interruption as economically feasible. Of particular concern was interruption of calls from customers.

- Costs should be no higher, and preferably lower, than those of the existing system.

The system shown in Figure 20.9 replaced the previous system. The company purchased three new Northern Telecom SL-1 PBXs, two of which were ST models and one of which was an NT model. The NT model with its dual processors was placed at the

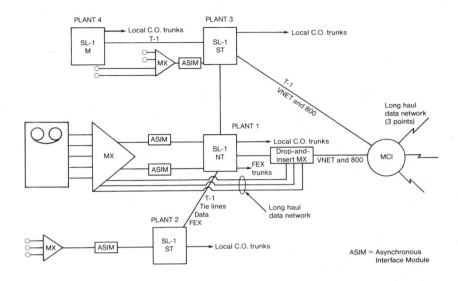

Figure 20.9   Steel Company PBX network—new configuration.

Plant 1 location, which was company headquarters and had T-1 access to MCI, which was the primary interexchange carrier. The second MCI link to Plant 3 was installed later to haul 800 traffic and provide an alternate route in case the primary T-1 fails. All outgoing long distance for Plants 1 and 2 routes through the Plant 1 PBX. Long distance for Plants 3 and 4 routes through the Plant 3 PBX. If either route fails, the LCR overflows traffic through the T-1 connecting Plants 2 and 3 and over the other T-1.

The analog data circuits were converted to digital by picking off spare channels in the T-1 through the PBXs at Plants 1, 2, and 3. Terminals at Plant 4 were extended to Plant 3 over a privately-owned cable. In a subsequent project, the long haul data circuits were routed through the T-1 from Plant 1 to MCI. Drop-and-insert multiplexers separate data from voice. All the PBXs are protected by battery backup.

All the objectives of this project have been met. The four PBXs have operated through their first three years without a major failure. A faulty repeater in one T-1 line caused an intermittent outage between Plants 1 and 2 for several days, but otherwise there have been no trunk failures. The net saving has exceeded

Chapter 20

$6000 per month, including the cost of the PBXs, which were purchased on a five-year lease-purchase plan. The T-1 configuration has proven to be effective in enabling the company to take advantage of MCI's changing tariffs. MCI's Prism 1 service initially was used for outgoing long distance; later the company changed to MCI's virtual private network service, V-NET, in which incoming and outgoing calls are handled over T-1, enabling a reduction in local trunks. As data circuits were shifted from previous carriers to MCI, it became possible to eliminate the local loops by using spare capacity on the T-1.

Evaluation Considerations

The uniqueness of every organization makes a universal PBX specification impractical. Considerations that are important in some applications will have no importance in others. Therefore, the buyer should weigh them accordingly. It is, of course, essential that the system contain the required features and that it meet the requirements for numbers of line and trunk terminations. Reliability and cost are implicit requirements in any telecommunications system and are not separately discussed.

External Interfaces

Every PBX must conform to the standard EIA-464 interface to a local telephone central office and must be registered with the FCC for network connection. In addition, interfaces such as these should be considered:

- X.25 interfaces to packet switching networks.
- EIA-232-C or EIA-449 data set or workstation interface.
- IBM 3270 or equivalent mainframe terminal interface.
- Protocol and format conversion.
- Interface to local area networks.
- 1.544 mb/s interface to external trunk groups.

Terminal Interfaces

A key consideration in evaluating a PBX is the type of terminals it supports. All PBXs have, at a minimum, a two-wire station interface to a standard analog DTMF telephone. Ordinary telephones are the least expensive terminals, and because of the quantities involved in a large PBX, inability to use standard telephones can add significantly to the cost. The standard analog telephone falls short, however, as a terminal in most offices. The most effective telephone sets are integrated devices that interact with the PBX processor to operate its features.

Integrated telephones may be the only practical way of accessing some integrated key telephone features. Some features tend to fall into disuse because of the difficulty of using them from standard telephones. A proprietary terminal may improve ease-of use for some features, such as call pickup and hold, by using buttons to replace the switch hook flashes and special codes required with standard telephones.

Consideration should be given to the different types of ports the PBX employs. Where the port type is restricted to voice or data, it may be impossible to use the full capacity of the system. The most flexible ports can handle either voice or data with no restriction on the type of terminal connected to the port. This, of course, requires that the telephone digitize the voice.

These features should be considered in evaluating a PBX terminal interface:

- Proprietary or non-proprietary telephone interface.
- Number of conductors to the station.
- Station conductor loop range.
- Number of line ports required for voice/data operation.
- Where data is encoded (i.e., in the line interface circuit or telephone set).
- Dialing interface (i.e., keyboard, telephone, mnemonic).
- Integrated key telephone system features.

Universal Shelf Architecture

Universal shelf architecture permits various types of line and trunk cards to be installed in any slot. Lacking this feature, slots are dedicated to a particular type of card. It is, therefore, possible to have plenty of spare slot capacity in the PBX but have no room for cards of the desired type.

Switch Network

First and second generation PBXs use analog switching networks. All the analog networks described in Chapter 8 were employed by early vintage systems. Third generation systems predominantly use electronic switching networks with pulse code modulation. Some PBXs may have switching networks that use pulse amplitude, pulse width, or delta modulation.

PCM switching is the most desirable in full-featured PBXs because of its compatibility with T-1 carrier. Note, however, that just because a PBX has a PCM network does not mean it supports direct T-1 carrier interface. Special digital terminal interface (DTI) cards are required. Pulse amplitude modulation, pulse width modulation, and delta modulation networks are equally satisfactory for voice. Although modemless interfaces to these non-PCM networks are possible, they are limited in data speed to 4800 b/s or less in many PBXs, whereas PCM can handle 56 or 64 kb/s data. Where modems are employed, little difference will be perceived by the user among the four types of networks, and the PBX choice can be based on other factors.

A key evaluation consideration is whether the network is blocking or nonblocking. With nonblocking networks, a further consideration is whether line concentration limits the number of simultaneous connections to fewer than the number of line and data ports on the system.

Issues in Data Switching Through a PBX

Number of PBX Ports Required

Some PBXs have true voice/data integration at the line port. One circuit is run from the PBX to a single port, which can support simultaneous voice and data communication. Other PBXs require separate data ports, or have voice/data ports with only half the density of single-purpose ports, decreasing the capacity of a cabinet.

Retrofittable Telephone Instruments

If you plan to purchase a PBX without the data feature and gradually add data capability, it is important to know whether the telephone instruments can be retrofitted with an EIA-232-C interface. Some telephones can be field upgraded as easily as removing the base and plugging in a circuit card. Others require a complete instrument changeout.

Integrated Telephone vs. Separate Data Adapter

In some systems the data adapter is built into the telephone instrument; in others a separate unit is required. The combined data adapter requires less desk space but is more apt to be a permanent arrangement than the separate adapter, which can be easily switched between users.

Voice and Data Integration Issues

If you have enough circuits to justify a T-1 carrier, whether to integrate voice and data over the T-1 is rarely an issue. In most cases, it will pay; however, there are several situations that should be avoided. Switching data through the PBX as shown in Figure 20.4 will be defined as Type I integration. The other method of connecting PBX circuits through a T-1 multiplexer as shown in Figure 20.5 will be called Type II integration.

Continuity of Service. With either integration method, if the T-1 line goes down, both voice and data service are lost. If the services are distributed across more than one T-1 line, a single failure impairs, but does not sever, service. With Type I integration, a PBX failure will disrupt not only voice communication but data communication as well. Because the data network is digital and operates at 56 kb/s, it is difficult to use traditional dial backup methods for restoring service. As switched 56 kb/s services become more common, dial backup will become feasible. Meanwhile, however, PBX failures, though they are rare, will disrupt the network. It may be necessary, therefore, to consider redundancy in the switch if it handles critical data circuits.

In Type II integration, the system is vulnerable to T-1 multiplexer failure, but PBX failure has no effect on data. T-1 multiplexers are available with redundancy to improve service protection.

Equipment Costs. Although data may ride on a T-1 network for little, if any, increase in circuit cost, there are increased equipment costs associated with its use. The PBX costs are insignificant. The interface equipment costs about the same as a V.32 modem in most manufacturers' equipment. Most of the cost is in port cards in the PBX and the T-1 multiplexer in Type II integration.

In Type I integration, the PBX is equipped with a T-1 card that connects all 24 channels of the T-1 line to the PBX switching network. In Type II integration, the cost is in analog trunk cards, 24 of which are more expensive than a single T-1 card for nearly every PBX on the market. On the average, a T-1 card is equivalent in cost to about three analog trunk cards.

The other issue is the cost of a T-1 multiplexer, which is generally three or four times as expensive as its cousin, the channel bank. The T-1 multiplexer makes unnecessary the statistical multiplexer used in Type I integration. However, Type II integration will still be significantly more expensive, although with a substantial increase in circuit capacity. The tradeoff between the two is not difficult to calculate.

ISDN Compatibility Issues

ISDN is not now available in most locations, but the LECs will gradually convert their central offices to ISDN over the next several years. IECs offer ISDN-like services now, so any company considering a new PBX must evaluate ISDN compatibility.

Interexchange Carrier ISDN Services.   Most IECs have announced services that are available through direct access to their switch. The PBX must be compatible to take advantage of the service. Generally, these services are available only over the primary rate interface. The PBX manufacturer must develop the interface compatibility. If ISDN compatibility is not developed at the time of purchase and if you foresee a need for these services, you should obtain assurance from the PBX manufacturer that compatibility will be developed, and determine how much it will cost.

Local Exchange Company ISDN Services.   Most LECs have developed plans to make tentative initial offerings of ISDN services. These offerings will likely be installed in only a few central offices in areas of heavy business concentration until the extent of demand is determined. Given this limited availability, ISDN will be of limited utility to most companies for the next few years.

Assessment of a PBX Manufacturer's Technology.   PBX manufacturers are always improving compatibility with new technology, and ISDN is no exception. Before you purchase a switch, ask
what the manufacturer's plans are:

- Will ISDN compatibility be developed for this switch?
- When will it be available?
- Can all older versions of the switch be retrofitted for ISDN?
  If the switch is not to be upgraded, will the manufacturer
  make trade-in concessions?

Company's Need for ISDN Services.   Regardless of the capabilities of the PBX, companies should look closely at their requirements for ISDN services over the life of the switch, which generally
ranges up to ten years. ISDN services should be studied, and their
implications for strategic positioning of the company's services or
products should be evaluated. If the future services are given little
value, then little importance should be placed on ISDN compatibility. Be careful, however, to not sell the future short. In the early
1980s, few companies could have predicted the impact of the
personal computer; it is likely that ISDN will have a similar impact,
although possibly over a longer period.

Environmental Considerations

Except the largest systems, PBXs are cabinet-mounted and connected to external circuits with distributing frames or wall-mounted
backboards. Power supplies are self-contained; backup battery
power may be provided or not, depending on the application.

Most PBXs can operate without air conditioning in an ordinary
office environment. The operating temperature range should be
evaluated, however, because some systems do require an air
conditioned environment. Even without air conditioning, adequate air circulation will be required.

Data Base Updates

The ease of changing classes of service and telephone numbers is
an important evaluation consideration. If the attendant console
or an easy-to-use maintenance terminal can control these, it is

possible to add, remove, and move stations and to change restrictions without using a trained technician. With a truly flexible system, station jacks are wired to line ports. A new station is added by plugging in the telephone and activating the line from an attendant or maintenance console.

Diagnostic Capability

The degree to which a PBX can diagnose its own trouble and direct a technician to the source of trouble is important in controlling maintenance expense. It also is important that a system have remote diagnostic capability so the manufacturer's technical assistance center can access the system over a dialed-up port.

Transmission

Some PBXs insert loss into line connections to improve echo performance. A line-to-line loss of 4 or 5 dB is acceptable under many conditions. If, however, the system makes extensive use of tie lines, WATS lines, and other external trunks, transmission performance may be unacceptable to some stations, particularly those with long station loops. The total network should be designed before choosing a PBX to determine whether the insertion loss of the switching system is acceptable.

Station Wiring Limits

The station loop range of both proprietary terminals and ordinary telephones must be considered in evaluating a PBX. Most proprietary terminals and those terminals requiring an EIA interface can operate only over restricted range. Range limits can be extended in some systems by using distributed switching, which moves the line circuits close to the stations.

Bandwidth Requirements

Bandwidth is of concern with systems that interface with high speed digital lines. Digital voice PBXs limit the data speed to 9600 b/s or less. With special data ports, higher speeds are supported, including, in some systems, enough bandwidth to switch a 1.544 mb/s bit stream.

Call Accounting Evaluation Issues

Most PBXs today are purchased with a call accounting system. Most systems are developed by someone other than the PBX manufacturer. The following are some criteria for selecting a call accounting system.

Stand-Alone or Computer-Based

Call accounting systems are either software packages that reside in a personal computer, minicomputer, or mainframe or are stand-alone units that operate with a proprietary processor. If the system is computer-based, evaluate what kind of computer is required—mini or micro, dedicated or shared? If the company already has a mini or a mainframe computer, determine whether the software is compatible.

If the system operates on a stand-alone computer, evaluate the computer as you would any other type of hardware. Find out who makes the processor and, most important, what support is available. For some proprietary systems, the cost of replacement parts, such as disk drives, keyboards and monitors, is much higher than for standard IBM-compatible PCs.

Reports

The main reason for buying a call accounting system is for its reports. Evaluate factors such as these:

- What kind of reports are provided? Do they meet the organization's requirements?
- Are customer-designed reports possible?
- Is is possible to link report information to an external program, such as a spreadsheet or data base management system, to produce custom reports?
- Are traffic reports produced? If so, are they accurate?
- Are management reports, such as inventories, provided?
- What kind of manual effort is needed to produce reports? Does it require a trained operator, or can clerical people perform the month-end operations with little or no formal training?
- Does the manufacturer support tie line reconciliation, or will it be necessary to match calls manually?

Vendor Support

As with most software packages, vendor support is important for installing and maintaining the system. Evaluate the vendor's experience in supporting the package. Determine whether the vendor has people who have been specifically trained. Evaluate the amount of support the package developer has available and what it costs. Some vendors sell ongoing support packages, and where these are available, the cost-effectiveness should be evaluated.

Call Rating

Most call accounting packages have call rating tables. Most are based on V & H (vertical and horizontal) tables. These divide the United States and Canada into a grid from which point-to-point mileage can be calculated. Tables must be updated regularly as rates change. Also, consider that many companies do not need absolute rate accuracy. To distribute costs among organizational units, precision is usually not required. See *The Dow Jones-Irwin Handbook of Telecommunications Management* for a detailed explanation of V & H rating. Determine facts such as these:

- What kind of rating tables does the manufacturer support?
- How frequently are tables updated?
- What do updates cost?
- What vendors' rates does the package support?
- How are intrastate rates calculated?
- Do you need to bill back with high accuracy?

Capacity

Call storage equipment is intended to maintain information on a certain number of calls. When buffer storage is full, it must be unloaded and calls processed. Usually, the system must contain at least one month's worth of calls. Evaluate questions such as these:

- How much storage space is required?
- What is the capacity in number of calls, both incoming and outgoing?
- How much growth capacity is provided?
- Is storage non-volatile so if power fails calls are not lost?

Selected Manufacturers of Digital PBXs and Related Products

PBX Manufacturers

Alcatel/Cortelco
AT&T Information Systems
Comdial
CXC
Ericsson, Inc. Communications Div.
Executone (Vodavi)
Fujitsu
Harris Digital Telephone Systems
Harris/Lanier
Hitachi America, LTD
Intecom, Inc.
Iwatsu America
Mitel, Inc.

NEC America, Inc.
National Telecom/Solid State
Northern Telecom, Inc.
Redcom Laboratories
Rolm
Siemens Information Systems
SRX
Tadiran Electronic Industries
Telenova
Telrad
TIE/communications Inc.
Toshiba
Walker Telecommunications

Call Accounting Systems

Account-A-Call Corporation
Bitek International, Inc.
Burnup & Sims
Com Dev
Compucom
Contel Information Systems
Datatel
Ericsson, Inc. Communications Div.
Infosystems
Infortext
Moscom
NEC Information Systems
Northern Telecom
Protel
Rolm Corporation

Soft-Com
Stryker Systems
Summa Four
Sykes Datatronics, Inc.
Tekno Industries, Inc.
Tel Electronics
Telco Research
Telecommunications Software
Telecorp Products
Telemon
Transaction Recording Systems
Western Telmatic
Westinghouse Communications
Xiox
Xtend

Call Storage Buffers

E-Coms, Inc.   Western Telematic

21

Automatic Call
Distribution Equipment

Several converging forces have increased the importance of incoming call management in the last few years. First is the increasing use of telemarketing. A telemarketing center typically has banks of 800-numbers with different numbers associated with different product lines or promotions, groups of agents equipped for access to the corporate database, and a call distribution system to direct incoming calls to the appropriate agent. Telemarketing centers also may use an offshoot of call distribution equipment that places outgoing calls automatically and delivers connected parties to a group of agents.

The second force involves the changing methods of delivering incoming calls. The major long distance carriers now deliver 800 calls on T-1. The fixed cost of T-1 lines has dropped to the point that T-1 is the preferred method of delivery for companies that have more than a handful of 800 lines. Once a T-1 is installed, its entire 24-channel bandwidth is available, and the Dialed Number Identification System (DNIS) option identifies the number the caller dialed.

The third force is call distribution technology itself. A call distribution system is a marriage of telephone and computer technology used to identify callers and route them to the agents best equipped by training or availability to handle their calls. The arrival of inexpensive computers and improved tools for creating software along with the decreasing cost of PBXs has resulted in greatly improved call distribution capabilities. The dramatic decreases in long distance costs that have occurred since divestiture and improvements in distributed computing have led companies to centralize operations that once, of necessity, took place in proximity to the work force. Now, it is no longer necessary to be near paper records; they can be brought to an agent over a data link.

An incoming call center can be set up with ordinary key telephone equipment, which is the way most companies handle calls to a defined work group. Calls arrive on trunk hunting lines, and an agent pushes a button to answer the call. If there are more lines than available agents, someone must interrupt a call in progress to answer it and put it on hold. If several calls are on hold, there is no easy way to know which caller has waited longest. Also, distribution of the workload depends on the action of the agents and how effectively they are supervised. Any organization with more than a few answering positions finds that the cost of some form of machine-controlled call distribution pays for itself quickly.

A uniform call distribution system (UCD), which is a standard feature of many PBXs, often significantly improves call handling. The PBX station set is the agent telephone. The UCD routes incoming calls to the first available agent. If no agent is available, the UCD routes calls to an announcement, holds them in queue, and sends the call that arrived first to the first available agent. In most UCD systems, the caller hears only the initial announcement and listens to music on hold or silence after that. UCDs relieve agents of the need to interrupt a call in progress to answer another call and put it on hold. UCDs generally lack the ability to balance workload among agents, nor do they provide sophisticated management reports.

The stand-alone counterpart of a UCD is the call sequencer. This device may work with a PBX or key telephone system, or it may be connected directly to incoming lines. Unlike the UCD, a call sequencer does not direct calls. It simply alerts agents to the presence of incoming calls by lighting keys on the telephone or lighting an external beehive lamp. It does answer the call and provide a delay announcement to the caller.

The most sophisticated device is the automatic call distributor (ACD), which is the primary focus of this chapter. ACDs can be either stand-alone or integrated with a PBX. An ACD routes calls to the least busy agent, which equalizes the work load. Agents can be grouped in identifiable answering units that are known in the industry as *splits, queues,* or *groups.* The ACD administrator typically has a video display terminal that presents call statistics in real time and has many management tools that monitor and improve service and measure the agents' effectiveness.

The differences between ACDs, UCDs, and sequencers are significant but not always apparent without analysis. Table 21.1 lists the most important differences.

Automatic Call Distributors (ACDs)

Unlike a PBX, which has more stations than trunks, an ACD has more trunks than positions. Most ACDs average from 1.2 to 1.8 trunks per agent position. Any organization that has a large number of incoming calls targeted for service positions is a potential ACD user. This includes departments that handle mail orders, literature delivery, inquiries, technical support, field service, credit, and collections.

An ACD, such as the Aspect CallCenter shown in Figure 21.1, has the following major components:

- Switching unit.
- Agent positions.
- Supervisory and monitoring equipment.
- Management software.

The functions of an ACD are to answer calls, place them in priority order, route them to the appropriate position, queue them if no agents are available, provide music and announcement while callers are in queue, overflow queued calls to an alternative queue or voice mail after a prescribed interval, and collect and process call statistics.

One feature that distinguishes an ACD from a UCD or a call sequencer is its ability to overflow calls from one queue to another. Queue overflow is based on one or more of the following variables:

- Length of time in queue.

Table 21.1 Comparison of Automatic Call Distributors (ACDs), Uniform Call Distributors (UCDs), and Call Sequencers (CSs)

	ACD	UCD	CS
BASIS FOR CALL DISTRIBUTION TO AGENTS	Based on time: usually distributed to the least busy agent	Based on sequence: usually top down or circular hunt.	Does not distribute calls. Alerts agents to incoming calls by lighting button on key set.
STATISTICAL INFORMATION	Provides real-time information on agents, groups, trunk groups, etc. External application processor provides basic sophisticated reports, including forecasting and scheduling.	Provides basic statistics, usually only line utilization reports. Reports are generally not real time.	Provides limited reports. Because it does not route calls, information is provided by station number, not by agent or group.
TELEPHONE SYSTEM INTEGRATION	Is either integrated with a PBX or functions as a stand-alone device. May function with with a key system or a PBX.	Furnished only as part of a PBX.	A stand-alone device that is designed to function with a key system.

- Position in queue. For example, the fifth caller might be overflowed to the alternative queue while the first four callers remain in the primary queue.

Figure 21.1 The Aspect CallCenter ACD.
Courtesy, Aspect Telecommunications

- The trunk group the call arrived on. Arrival on a priority trunk group might entitle the caller to different treatment than callers on non-priority groups. Calls on more expensive trunks might be afforded priority to reduce the company's expense for 800 service.

- Caller classification. Some callers may be asked to call special numbers to identify them as priority callers.

ACD Features and Operation

ACDs commonly are equipped with an automated attendant on the front end to assist in call routing and voice mail on the back end to handle overflows and give callers the option of leaving a message instead of waiting. Chapter 22 discusses these technologies. The automated attendant can be either a front end device that is not connected with the voice mail or part of the voice mail system. Commonly, an ACD is divided into several splits or queues. When calls are queued for a group of agents, they must have some common set of characteristics, which may be identified by the automated attendant or simply by the dialed number.

When a call arrives at the head of a queue, if an agent is available the ACD routes the call directly to the agent unless the caller is forced to listen to an announcement before being routed. The agent must press a button to answer the call, or, if the system is equipped for automatic routing, the agent hears a zip tone and the call is delivered automatically.

To be recognized by the system, agents must log on to a particular queue. In some systems agents can log onto more than one queue. The act of logging on may not, however, mean the agent is available to take a call. In most ACDs the agent also must press a key on the telephone set. The system identifies agents as being in one of several states. Typically, the following states are provided:

- Available. When an agent is available, the system can deliver the next call.
- Busy. The busy state indicates that the agent is currently handling a call.
- After call work or wrap-up. Most ACDs permit the agent to spend a variable or fixed amount of time after each contact completing paper work.
- Unavailable. This state is used when the agent is temporarily away from the position, typically during breaks.
- Manual. In the manual state, instead of the system delivering calls automatically, the agent must press a button to take calls.

Figure 21.2 An Aspect CallCenter Workstation.
Courtesy, Aspect Telecommunicatons

The call center supervisor usually has a terminal like the Aspect CallCenter terminal shown in Figure 21.2 to monitor the status of service and load. The terminal lists agents by name, shows their current state, and displays a summary of their production statistics. In some systems the display also shows how long agents have been in their current state, which is useful for determining when wrap-up or unavailable time is excessive. The terminal also should display information about service levels.

Most ACDs also provide supervisory monitoring capability for service observing. Call monitoring is a sensitive issue, and company policy or state law may prohibit monitoring unless the agent is notified. Monitoring may be silent or accompanied by a tone that is audible to the agent but not the caller,

The agent's position set is important to the effectiveness of the ACD. Most PBX-integrated ACDs use one or more of the manufacturer's line of telephone sets for the agent terminal. Multibutton digital sets make it possible for the agent to perform functions such as logging in and out and changing state without

Figure 21.3 **An Aspect TeleSet proprietary agent telephone set.**
Courtesy, Aspect Telecommunications

dialing the special access codes that are required with single line sets. Display sets make it possible for the system to deliver to the agent such information as the trunk group on which the call arrived, length of time the caller waited, and number of calls currently in queue. In most applications, improved agent productivity justifies the extra expense of a multiline digital display set.

High end stand-alone ACDs normally are equipped with proprietary telephones like the Aspect TeleSet shown in Figure 21.3. Some systems use a combined telephone and video display terminal as the agent position. This arrangement is common in applications such as directory assistance, which Chapter 10 discusses.

Call-Handling Strategies

One reason for using an ACD as opposed to a UCD or call sequencer is the ACD's ability to provide distinctive treatment to certain classes of callers. A company's best customers can be routed to a group of agents that have special training or equipment. Most managers want a system that enables their agents to give personalized service to callers, which means that the position has access (or the ACD is linked) to a data base of caller information. The most effective call-handling strategies enable the company to identify the caller early in the session, order calls by priority, and respond flexibly, using automated equipment to handle the transaction if appropriate. Increasingly, ACD applications link the telephone system directly to the data base so the agent receives incoming calls with a screen full of customer information.

Identify Callers

The first key to flexible call handling is to identify the caller. If a primary rate interface to the interexchange carrier is available, or if the LEC provides automatic number identification, the calling telephone number may be carried with the call. If this links to a customer database, the caller can be identified with no action on the agent's part.

A second identification strategy is to prompt callers to dial an account number or identification code while they wait in queue. The ACD may have a forced queuing feature so all callers listen to a preliminary announcement from an automated attendant. The automated attendant prompts callers through a two- or three-level menu before directing them to an agent.

A third possibility is to assign different DID or 800 numbers to a particular group of callers. For example, airlines customarily distinguish between travel agents, frequent fliers, and the general public in handling calls in queue. A company may use one 800 number for information requests and another for orders. Although this method does not identify callers as individuals, they are recognized as members of a class and as such can be routed to an appropriate queue.

Prioritize Calls

Once the caller is identified or categorized, the call can be treated appropriately. Known customers can be given priority in the queue or overflowed to a secondary queue ahead of low priority callers. Callers arriving on expensive 800 trunks can be answered ahead of other customers to minimize the company's 800 expense, and other strategies can be employed to handle calls in priority order.

Prospective ACD purchasers should inquire into the method of priority queuing used by the system. The least sophisticated systems have only one priority level. More complex systems have two or three priority levels, but may process the queues by first clearing all Priority One calls, then Priority Two calls, and so on. A low priority call may sit in queue for an excessive length of time unless the system provides some method of raising the priority of a call as its length of time in queue increases.

An effective method of call handling is to add priority *points* to a call based on certain criteria. For example, priority points might be assigned based on the following criteria:

- The trunk group on which the call arrived.
- The menu choice selected in an automated attendant.
- The caller's account number (as dialed into the system).
- The number of times the caller transfers or overflows to another queue.
- The total time in the system.

Handle Calls with Automated Equipment if Appropriate

Many calls do not require the personal attention of an agent. Requests for literature, verification of account balances, and calls to leave information are examples of transactions that voice mail, automated attendant, or interactive voice response units can handle. If these systems are applied intelligently, the callers can route themselves to the appropriate queue by pressing a button on a DTMF telephone. Refer to Chapter 22 for more information on voice processing devices.

Respond Flexibly

An effective ACD can give a caller several alternatives to waiting in queue for the next agent. If the waiting time is excessive, the caller can be offered the option of leaving a message on voice mail for call-back. Other flexible response options include overflowing to backup positions that are occupied, but which log on only at workload peaks. Another option is overflowing the call to a secondary queue where the agent may be less than fully trained, but still can satisfy the caller. The system also can mollify callers by changing the message according to how long the caller has waited and informing them of their position in queue to keep them from hanging up.

One important feature in handling overflows is the ability of the ACD to look ahead to a secondary queue and look back to the primary queue. An ACD with look-ahead queueing evaluates the amount of congestion on the secondary group and determines whether to route the call to that group. An ACD with look-back queueing monitors the load in the primary queue and sends the caller back to that queue if conditions improve. If the ACD routes the call back to the primary queue, it should not be returned to the end but should resume its original queue position or be given some form of priority treatment.

The ACD should avoid overflowing into a secondary queue unless there is evidence that the caller will be handled more quickly there. Most ACDs compare the number of calls in the primary and secondary queues and route to the secondary queue if the call has exceeded holding time objectives and the secondary queue has fewer callers than the primary. A more effective method is to evaluate the probable waiting time in the secondary queue by computing the average holding time per call and predicting whether the wait in the overflow queue will be shorter than the wait in the primary queue.

The method of programming the routing algorithm is another factor that should be considered. Some ACDs have an English-like programming language that enables the administrator to change the routing based on operators such as "and," "if then," and "if not." The routing algorithm should be easy to read so a trained administrator can diagnose routing problems. The system also should provide a way to vary the route for holidays and different times of the day and days of the week.

Equalize Agent Workload

The chief weakness of UCDs and call sequencers is their inability to route calls to the least busy agent. This means that the first agent in the hunting sequence receives the most calls and the last agent may be idle much of the time. Most ACDs analyze the workload and route the call to the least busy agent based on call handling time or the sum of call handling and wrap-up time.

Outbound Calling

Many ACDs (also specialized devices) are equipped for outbound calling. A system with outbound capability dials numbers from a database and plays a recorded message or connects the caller to an agent only after dialing is complete. Some systems have answer detection capability and connect to an agent only after the called party answers. Although answering machines and voice mail usually fool such systems, most systems detect busy and unanswered calls and store the numbers for later retry.

The primary hazard with outcalling systems is completing a call when no agents are available. Because so many lines are busy or do not answer and because it takes time to set up each call, the system is generally placing calls when there are no idle agents. If the system waits for an agent to be idle before initiating the call, the productivity of the agents will drop. Most systems use some type of predictive calling to anticipate when an agent will become available. If an agent is not available within seconds of the time the called party answers, the party perceives the call as a nuisance and hangs up.

Integrated PBX vs. Stand-Alone ACD

A key question facing an ACD owner is whether to select a stand-alone or a PBX-integrated system. Both systems have their applications and advantages, and the selection should be made with the factors in this section in mind. A third choice, which we will discuss in a later section, is the central office ACD, (CO-ACD), which is on the LEC's premises.

The first factor to consider is the status of the existing PBX, if any. If the existing PBX is unsatisfactory and must be replaced, the cost per position of an integrated ACD will be less than half the cost per position of a stand-alone ACD. If the PBX is satisfactory and can be retrofitted for an ACD package, this also will be less expensive than purchasing a stand-alone system. If, however, the PBX cannot be retrofitted, a stand-alone or CO-ACD should be considered.

Very large applications, including systems that require networking, usually require stand-alone systems. In large applications, such as airline reservations systems, the ACD requirements may outstrip the capabilities of a PBX. Generally, stand-alone ACDs offer more processing power, more sophisticated software, and better reporting capabilities than integrated PBX ACDs.

The amount of communication with non-ACD users behind a PBX is another factor that should be considered. An integrated ACD has all the features of the PBX and all the features of the ACD, which usually facilitates call transfer within the total system. If ACD and non-ACD users share central office trunks, DID trunks, and 800 lines, the PBX attendant or the DNIS feature can route calls to the ACD. If the trunks terminate directly on the ACD and there is little inter-machine communication or transfer requirement, a stand-alone ACD may respond somewhat more rapidly.

A stand-alone ACD can be connected to a PBX through station or tie line ports. Tie lines are more effective because they are faster and give ACD agents access to more of the PBX's features than the station port connection. In either case, the Achilles' heel of some stand-alone ACDs is the difficulty of transferring calls between the PBX and the ACD. A PBX user can transfer to an ACD group easily but lacks a way of reaching a specific station user unless the ACD station has a PBX station line. In some centers the ACD agent requires two telephones, one for the PBX and one for the ACD. The ACD usually can route calls to the voice mail on the PBX, but in a non-integrated system there is usually no way to turn on the ACD user's message waiting light. If it is possible to terminate a PBX extension directly on an ACD telephone, it will often be an analog station lacking direct push button access to PBX features.

Central Office ACD

Many LECs offer ACD features as a central office function. Agent sets and supervisory consoles are mounted on the user's premises and extended from the central office on local loops. The user's capital investment is reduced, and the LEC takes care of maintenance. If the CO-ACD is trunk-rated, the LEC applies a software "choke" to limit the number of incoming trunks. If the tariff is not trunk-rated, a CO-ACD can offer the advantage of reducing trunk costs for the user. This can, however, be a disadvantage because the user may lose some control. For example, one way of handling temporary overloads is to let incoming calls ring several times before answering and queueing them. This way, 800 costs are reduced and the caller may be less critical of service because the length of time in queue is reduced.

The features of a CO-ACD are similar to the features of a stand-alone unit. The advantages and disadvantages compared to customer-owned equipment are essentially the same as those of Centrex versus a PBX, as discussed in Chapter 23.

Uniform Call Distributors (UCDs)

Most PBXs offer a uniform call distribution package as a standard or optional feature. A group of agents is defined as a UCD group, and the PBX queues calls when all agents are busy, provides music or an announcement, and routes the call to the first available agent. A UCD is similar to an ACD, but it does not provide the flexible response capability of an ACD. Most UCDs route calls in sequence, starting with the agent at the head of the sequence, which means that work load is not equalized. The agent at the head of the hunt pattern receives the largest number of calls, while the agent at the end of the sequence receives calls only when all other agents are busy.

The UCD supervisory terminal is usually less sophisticated. Most UCDs use a display telephone for the supervisory terminal, so the reports and status of agents and service that an ACD provides are not available. The routing and overflowing capabilities are also less flexible with a UCD. The flexible response features discussed earlier are generally not available with a UCD. Reports are limited to what is programmed into the system and are considerably less useful than those provided by a full ACD.

On the positive side, UCDs are much less expensive than ACDs. In many PBXs the UCD software is a standard feature, and ordinary telephone sets can be used for the agent terminals. If the company does not have an extensive call center and does not require extensive reports, UCD is an inexpensive way to improve

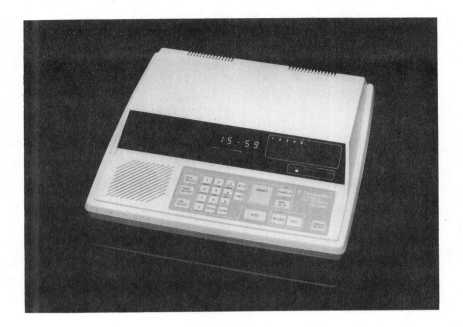

Figure 21.4   U.S. Takachiho CS-D40 automatic call sequencer.
Courtesy, U.S. Takachiho Corporation

customer service. Also, the UCD can take advantage of features, such as voice mail, that the PBX provides.

Call Sequencers

Call sequencers are the least sophisticated call distributors. Unlike ACDs and UCDs, which deliver calls to idle agents, sequencers require the agent to press a button to select the call. Most call sequencers do not force an agent to pick up a call. Different colored lights show which call has been waiting the longest. Therefore, although customer service and productivity usually are improved by answering and holding calls automatically, there is no way to ensure that the workload is evenly distributed. Figure 21.4 shows a U.S. Takachiho CS-D40 call sequencer.

Sequencers are not integrated with the telephone system, so it is difficult to take advantage of features such as voice mail. It also may be difficult to transfer calls from a call sequencer to a

PBX extension; frequently a complex sequence of switchhook flashes is required. Sequencers are most effective when the work group has other duties besides call answering. For example, a dispatch center might receive service requests from customers, make remote tests, and dispatch service people. The only portion of the job that involves answering calls is the incoming requests, which may be only a small fraction of the total process. The sequencer is valuable because it can answer calls when all agents are occupied and indicate which call has been waiting the longest.

Applications

Selecting the correct call distribution system and applying it intelligently is critical to the success of most organizations that require one. In most applications, the arriving calls are customers or potential customers, and the objective of the organization is to treat them professionally and promptly. Many companies ensure that customers are handled by a human until they are well enough established to risk handling their contacts by machine. This section discusses some aspects of selecting and evaluating a call distribution system.

Standards

There are no call distribution equipment standards as such. External interfaces are regulated by the same standards that cover PBXs, but internal operation is governed by proprietary standards.

Case History: Software Development Company

A computer hardware development company has four separate departments that deal with the public. The largest is the Customer Service Department, which is responsible for helping customers with applications of the company's products and solving problems over the telephone. Other call centers are the Telemarketing Department, which sells products directly to end users, the Finance Department, which is responsible for collection, and the Sales Department, which takes orders from an extensive network of distributors.

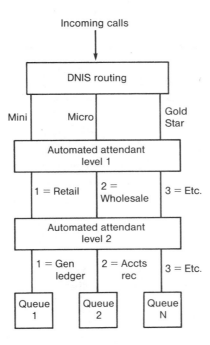

Figure 21.5   Service department call flow.

The most complex ACD application is in the Customer Service Department. Figure 21.5 shows how calls flow. The company sells personal computer products—principally hard disks and a line of special plug-in boards. A special category of customers known as Gold Star pays a premium for priority service over 800 lines. The other customers call at their own expense.

The company offers five separate product lines. The problem is complicated by specialization of the customer support representatives. No representative can handle all questions on all products; most are fully qualified on two or three products and can handle some questions on additional products. The problem the company evaluated when searching for a product was how to route calls to the appropriate representatives, while keeping all representatives occupied as efficiently as possible.

The company chose an AT&T Definity Generic 1 with integrated ACD, Audix voice mail, and front end automated attendant. Arriving calls are distributed to the proper ACD group by DNIS, direct inward dialing, or the attendant. Calls to the customer service organization arrive at the automated attendant separated into the hard disk, plug-in board, and Gold Star categories.

The first menu in the automated attendant asks for industry grouping by telling the caller to press 1 for retail, 2 for wholesale, etc. The second menu level asks for hardware type. Based on the DNIS routing and the two automated attendant selections, the call arrives at an ACD input. The treatment at this point is conventional. If an agent is available, the call is sent forward; if not, a recording answers the call and places it in queue. After 20 seconds in queue, and every 20 seconds after that, a second recording comes on to offer the caller the opportunity to either wait or leave a call-back message in voice mail.

The ACD groups are small in this application. Sometimes, only one or two representatives are assigned to a group because of specialization. Each group is defined as one or more combinations of products about which a representative is qualified to answer questions. As a call comes out of the gate, it is routed by a table that lists all the groups that have a member that could handle the call. The call goes to the first group that has an idle member and overflows to other groups in line. Representatives with strong qualifications normally are placed in the middle group. Those with weaker qualifications, which the company wants to strengthen by experience, are placed in the group at the head of the routing table. Those who have the fewest qualifications for the product but who could handle a call in a pinch are placed in the group at the end of the table.

This structure is an effective way of dealing with the problem of highly specialized representatives. The ACD's routing and overflow capabilities ensure that if a representative with some qualifications is available, the call is sent there instead of waiting for a well-qualified representative. There is a hazard, however, in this method that must be monitored to ensure that the workload is balanced. In normal ACD operation, the call is distributed within a group to the least busy member. If the group has only one or two members, the calls are routed to the group and overflowed if necessary. The routing method does not meet the least busy objective. Therefore, it is possible that some representatives could be very busy while others are idle. This problem is cured by carefully assigning the group to different positions in the queues of which it is a member.

Evaluation Criteria

Most of the criteria listed for evaluating PBXs also apply to call distribution equipment. For example, the questions of redundant processors, backup battery supply, universal port structure, cabinet capacity, and other such criteria should be evaluated. If the call distributor is part of a PBX, all the criteria discussed in Chapter 20 apply along with the criteria discussed here.

Type of Call Distributor

The first issue to resolve is whether the application requires an ACD, a UCD, or a call sequencer. If an ACD is required, a second issue is whether a stand-alone unit or one integrated with a PBX is most suitable. The following is a list of generalizations, most of which have exceptions in some product lines.

- If the office is served by a key telephone system, use a call sequencer.
- If the incoming call load is handled by a pool of people for whom answering incoming calls is only one of a list of duties, choose a call sequencer.
- If handling incoming calls is a primary duty, the office is already served by a PBX, detailed reports are not important, low cost is important, and workload equalization is unimportant, choose a UCD.
- If handling calls is a primary job, detailed reports are important, and the call center must be closely integrated with non-ACD operations in the office, choose a PBX with integrated ACD.
- If the call center is large and needs few PBX functions, choose a stand-alone ACD.

The dividing line between call distribution applications is not distinct, and product features are constantly changing. In selecting a product, it is important to match the product to the application, bearing in mind that much of the improvement achieved with a call distributor may come from changing existing procedures.

System Architecture

The architecture of most call distribution systems is similar within a particular category, but there are important differences among systems. In sequencers, the generic program is usually contained in ROM; in ACDs and UCDs it is contained in volatile memory and loaded from a disk. These criteria are important considerations in selecting the architecture:

Type of Trunk Interface.   Consider what types of trunks the system needs to interface. The most common types are loop start, ground start, T-1, E & M, DID, and DNIS. Also consider whether the system can interface two-way trunks when both in- and out-calling are required.

Port Capacity.   Consider the number of ports in the system. Port types to be included are trunk, agent, supervisory, and CRT. Also consider whether the architecture permits universal or specialized slots for ports.

Traffic Capacity.   ACDs inherently are designed for blockage, but they can be designed with nonblocking switch networks. As with other switching systems, the principal evaluation criteria are expressed in terms of call completions per hour and CCS per line.

Type of Display.   The type of display for both agents and supervisors can affect productivity. Color displays are less tiring for the operator, and the color can be used to display call criteria. For example, a call that has been on hold for a long time can be presented to the agent in red. Supervisory displays can show critical criteria such as low service levels in red. Supervisory graphs can be displayed with the evaluation criteria highlighted in different colors. Also consider whether the display is proprietary or whether a standard terminal or personal computer can be used. Split-screen displays permit the operator to view more than one call at a time and are particularly useful to a supervisor who monitors multiple queues.

Networking Capability.   Large organizations with multiple ACDs may be interested in networking, which is the ability to connect ACDs over tie lines. Networked systems should have the capability of passing call-specific information such as caller identification from one machine to another.

Queueing and Routing Algorithms.   The most flexible systems use true if-then-else operators to program the treatment a call receives as it enters the queue. It is important to know how many steps can be programmed for a call.

Switch Architecture.   The architecture of the switch is fully as important in an ACD as in any other type of switching system. Questions to be considered are:

- Is the switch expandable in modular increments?
- Does the switch have built-in maintenance features that improve reliability?
- Does the switch use open architecture to permit easy interface with another system for both reading and writing information?
- Does the switch have universal port architecture?
- How many separate queues does the system support?
- How many agents does the system support?
- How many supervisory consoles does the system support? Can more than one queue be monitored from a single terminal?

External Interfaces

Most ACDs and a few UCDs and call sequencers have interfaces to external systems. For example, consider whether the system must interface with a data base on a mainframe, minicomputer, or desktop computer. Callers are given several strategies for completing their calls if the system has interfaces to voice mail, automated attendant, or an interactive voice response unit. The system may require an interface to an outbound telemarketing unit, or the outbound unit may be included as a portion of the ACD.

Features

Many of the PBX features discussed in Chapter 20 are equally important for call distributors. The following are some features that should be considered in evaluating systems.

Agent Call Access and Display.   ACDs can automatically cut the call through to an agent, while some UCDs and call sequencers require agents to press a key to receive the next call. The most effective systems display for the agent such information as how many calls are waiting and, when the call is connected, how long the caller waited in queue.

Overflowing Capability.   Consider whether it is acceptable for callers to remain in one queue or whether they should overflow to a second queue. If overflowing is required, determine whether it should be based on length of time in queue, position in queue, trunk group over which the call arrived, caller identification, or some other criterion. Also, consider whether the system provides look-ahead and look-back capability and whether the system can dynamically reassign agents to different queues to react to changes in load.

Outbound Calling Capability.   Whether a feature of an ACD or of a stand-alone unit, outbound calling capability is important to companies that have telemarketing functions or other functions such as collections that require a volume of outgoing calls. The system should be able to interface with a user data base. Other important features include computer-controlled pacing of agents, predictive dialing, some type of reliable detection of called party answer, and rescheduling of unanswered calls.

Wrap-Up Strategy.   Many applications require time for the agent to wrap up the call after completing the transaction. For example, it may be necessary to complete an order before taking the next call. ACDs should offer one or more ways to determine the duration of wrap-up:

- *Manual.* The agent presses a key to show availability for another call.
- *Forced.* The system provides a set amount of time for wrap-up.

- *Programmable.* The ACD supervisor can create a program to vary the amount of wrap-up time.

The strategy for handling wrap-up can have a significant effect on productivity. With the manual method, an agent can extend wrap-up time and reduce productivity. With the forced system, the machine fails to recognize the variability in the amount of wrap-up time needed for different types of transactions. If the system is programmable it can vary the amount of wrap-up time allotted for each type of transaction.

Reporting Capabilities

Most companies receive as much value from the reports a call distributor creates as they do from the functionality of the unit itself. The following factors should be considered:

Record vs. Status Orientation.   A record-oriented system provides call status after completion. A status-oriented system provides calling information in real time. With a record-orientated system it is possible to determine how long a caller waited in queue after the transaction is finished, but not while it is in process.

Data Accumulation.   ACDs have different periods of time during which they can accumulate statistical information. Hourly and sub-hourly information is valuable for making immediate force adjustments or changing switch parameters such as wrap-up time. Daily and monthly information is useful for load forecasting and making long term force adjustments. Consider how the information is accumulated and displayed.

- Can it be extracted in some standard file format to analyze in a spreadsheet?
- Is information stored in a volatile medium such as random access memory, and if so, is it lost in case of power failure?
- Does the system collect information on how the call is handled in the second queue when it overflows?

Management Software.   Many systems provide software for management analysis. These programs fall into three categories:

- *Scheduler*. This software, which may be combined with forecasting software, helps the supervisor prepare schedules. The program analyzes force requirements by hour of the day and day of the week and optimizes available staff to meet the requirements.

- *Tracker*. Tracker software dynamically reviews service levels based on the number of staff logged on and the volume of calls arriving. Force requirements are calculated based on service objectives. The software keeps track of absences and number of agents required per hour and calculates predicted service levels based on work load and the available force.

- *Forecaster*. Forecasting software reviews historical data and predicts call volume, workload, and force requirements.

Transaction Audit Trail.   A transaction audit trail may be an important feature for an ACD manager. The audit trail time stamps each event in the transaction from start to finish. The system identifies the agent and position handling the call and leaves a trail of the times the call was transferred or put on hold. The amount of wrap-up time is registered, and any telephone numbers, such as supervisor or wrap-up position, dialed during the transaction are recorded. If the system is equipped with DNIS or DID, the system logs the number the caller dialed. If the call fails for such reasons as inadequate facilities, excessively long wait, or poor queue management, this feature helps the supervisor diagnose the cause.

Report Types.   The following reports are typically produced by the more sophisticated systems:

- Percent abandoned calls.
- Percent all trunks busy.
- Percent calls answered in X seconds.
- Percent all positions busy.
- Percent position occupancy.
- Longest waiting time in queue.
- Average number of calls in queue.

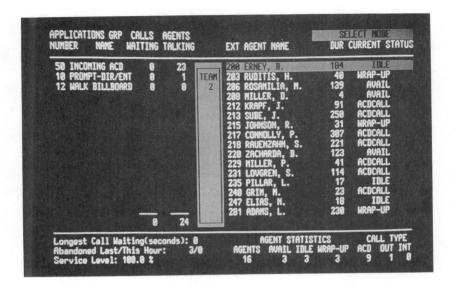

Figure 21.6   Online ACD work group results.
Courtesy, Apect Telecommunications

Consider whether the reports are produced in real time or only after the fact. Real time reports should display on the supervisor's console while calls are in progress, although they may be updated at intervals of 10 seconds or so. Figures 21.6 and 21.7 show real-time work group and individual statistics from an Aspect CallCenter ACD.

Most call distributors include basic reports as part of the system's generic program. These are usually not user-programmable and seldom satisfy all users' requirements. Many call distributors provide a port to an outboard processor, which is usually a mini or personal computer. The following questions should be considered:

- Are the fixed reports provided with the system sufficient? If not, does the call distributor provide a port to an outboard processor?

- For preparing special reports, does the system support a programming language that is widely understood?

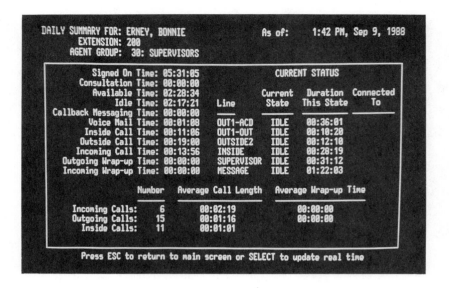

Figure 21.7   Online ACD individual agent results.
Courtesy, Apect Telecoimmunicatons

- Is statistical information stored for some period, or is it lost each time the data is refreshed?

- Can the user change the reporting period—for example, from hourly to half-hourly update?

- If agents shift between queues, do their production statistics follow them as individual agents, or do the statistics remain as part of the queue? Is it possible to track both?

Call Center Supervisor's Information

A major reason for acquiring a call distributor is to provide the call center supervisor with real-time information about workload and service. Some systems use a video display terminal for the supervisor's console. Low-end systems may use a display telephone or audible or visual signals or provide no information at all to inform the supervisor when certain thresholds are exceeded. The following criteria should be evaluated:

- What type of display is provided?

- Does the display alert the supervisor to critical situations with different colors, intensity, inverse video, or other means?

- If the display is variable, can the user change it to suit individual preference?

- Are thresholds programmable?

- How frequently is the information on the display refreshed? Can the user change the refresh interval?

- Is the information display programmable or fixed?

- Does the display show the supervisor how long each individual agent has been in the current state?

- Can the supervisor remotely force the agent from one state to another—for example, from wrap-up to available?

- Can the supervisor monitor calls without being detected?

- If the system provides an audible monitoring tone to the agent, does the caller hear it also?

Agent Terminals

Most call distributors will function with single-line telephones for the agent terminal. In some applications single-line sets are satisfactory, but the additional information that can be obtained from a display feature set is worth the extra cost for most call centers. The following are some criteria to use in evaluating agent terminals:

- What information is displayed on the agent's set? For example, does it show how long a call has waited in queue?

- If the agent set lacks a display, how is information such as incoming trunk group identity or the queue from which a call overflowed conveyed to the agent?

- How are agents informed in real time of critical service indicators such as waiting-time objectives exceeded?

- Do agent terminals support headsets? If so, is a particular brand or model required?

- How do agents perform such functions as logging on and off, holding and parking calls, and changing to and from available state?

- Do functions require the agent to dial codes or does the system provide push-button access?

- How do agents transfer calls to one another and to an attached PBX?

Queue Management

The degree of flexibility the system offers in managing the way calls are routed to particular queues and the way agents are assigned to queues is fundamental to call center management. Low end systems may have only one fixed queue and little or no ability for the administrator to reprogram the system. High end systems have some flexibility in changing routing to meet changes in workload conditions. Consider the following:

- Can call routing be changed? If so, is the programming language easy to understand?

- Is a method provided for testing the routing of incoming calls?

- Can the routing be changed in real time?

- If the system provides priority treatment for certain classes of callers, how is the priority recognized? How many priority classes are there?

- When a call is given priority treatment, how is the priority administered. For example, is the caller moved to the head of the queue, placed at the end of the first third, etc.?

- Can the system look ahead to evaluate congestion before overflowing to an alternative queue? If so, does the system predict waiting time in the next queue based on a dynamic evaluation as opposed to merely counting calls?

- After the system looks ahead to an alternative queue, can it look back to the primary queue?

- If a call returns to a previous queue, is it given priority treatment based on total waiting time?

- Can the supervisor remotely assign agents to another queue to relieve congestion?

- Can an agent log on to more than one queue?

- Can the queue routing be varied by time of day, day of week, and other such variables?

Incoming Call Handling

The least effective call distributors provide little flexibility in handling incoming calls. Calls are answered and placed in queue, and the caller may not hear anything until an agent is available. The most flexible systems offer callers a choice. These are some questions that should be evaluated:

- What does the caller hear after the initial announcement— music, promotional announcements, silence?
- Is a second announcement available?
- Can the system vary the announcement based on time in queue?
- Does the system inform callers of their position in queue?
- Can the caller choose to exit and leave a message in voice mail?

Manufacturers of Automatic Call Distribution Equipment

Stand-Alone ACDs

Aspect Telecommunications
Harris
Rockwell International

Teknekron
Telcom Technologies

Call Sequencers

Automation Electronics Corp.
Dacon Electronic, Inc.
Innings Telecom
MetroTel Corp.

Telecom Technologies
US Takachiho Corp.
Viking Electronics

PBX-Integrated ACDs

Alcatel Cortelco

AT&T

Ericsson

Fujitsu Business Communications

Harris Corp Digital Telephone Systems Division

Intecom

Mitel

National Telecom Solid State Systems, Inc.

NEC America

Northern Telecom

Redcom

Rolm

Siemens Information Systems

Shared Resource Exchange, Inc.

SRX

Tadiran Electronic Industries

TIE/communications Inc.

Uniform Call Distributors

See Chapter 20 for listing of PBX manufacturers. Most PBXs have the UCD feature.

Voice Processing Systems

The marriage of computer and telecommunications technologies has brought to the market a family of equipment collectively known as *voice processing* systems. Three classes of equipment comprise voice processing:

- Voice store and forward (usually called simply *voice mail*).
- Automated attendant.
- Voice response or *audiotex* equipment.

This equipment often is applied with a PBX, but its use is not so restricted. Some are stand-alone systems, and some are made up of services available from service bureaus.

The costs and features of voice processing equipment vary widely, and satisfaction with the equipment ranges from enthusiastic acceptance to vigorous rejection. Although a variety of features is available, the primary factor governing the acceptance of a system by employees and customers is how intelligently it is applied.

The voice processing technologies are an excellent example of engineering competence that has outstripped our ability to manage technology. It is difficult to believe that anyone would establish a voice mail or automated attendant application without thoroughly user-testing it, but the abundance of badly designed installations demonstrates that many companies do just that. Although this chapter discusses the technologies and not their administration, managers must be aware that this is one area where management must control the technicians, because the risk of irrational applications is great and the penalty for mistakes can be a loss of customers.

Even given the occasional misapplication, voice processing technologies have an enormous potential for improving customer service and cutting costs. Voice mail makes it possible to leave messages across time zones, keeping voice inflections intact and avoiding the misunderstandings that so often result from passing messages through a third party. Audiotex, or interactive voice response, makes it possible for people to receive information outside normal working hours and without enduring the delays that often occur during peak hours. The organization saves labor costs, employees are relieved of the mind-numbing task of repeatedly delivering the same information, and customers do not have to wait. The automated attendant enables callers to route their own calls quickly to the appropriate department without lengthy oral exchanges and enables the company to eliminate the cost of direct inward dialing and attendants. Everyone benefits from voice processing if the applications are chosen carefully and administered intelligently.

This section discusses the elements of the three principal voice processing technologies and describes the features available. The Applications section discusses typical uses and the precautions that must be observed in applying them. The chapter also covers digital announcers. Although these are not technically voice processing devices, they have many of the same elements and are used behind PBXs and ACDs to make announcements to callers who dial a particular number or are placed in queue waiting for a service process.

Voice Mail

Voice mail has potential for improving internal communications in most large organizations. It is no secret to anyone who has worked in an office that a large percentage of telephone calls are not completed because the called party is away from the desk or on the telephone. Thus, the frustrating game of telephone tag begins. Voice mail enables people to exchange messages and often serves as a satisfactory substitute for person-to-person communication. Calls can be exchanged across time zones, messages

Figure 22.1   The Rolm PhoneMail with the Rolm 9751 PBX in the background.
Courtesy, Rolm Corporation

can be left and retrieved quickly when only a few minutes are available between meetings or airplanes, and the group broadcast feature enables a manager to convey information to everyone in the work group with a single call.

A voice mail system is a specialized computer that stores messages in digital form on a fixed disk. Figure 22.1 shows the Rolm PhoneMail, which is fully integrated with the Rolm 9751 PBX, shown in the background. Analog voice mail systems also exist, but these are being replaced by digital systems and are not covered in this book. In most systems, the voice is digitized—usually at a much slower rate than the 64 kb/s signal the PBX uses in its switching network. The digitized voice is compressed and stored on a hard disk that maintains the voice mail operating system, system prompts and greetings, and the messages themselves. A processor controls the compressing, storing, retrieving, forwarding, and purging of files. Voice mail systems connect to a PBX through station ports, as shown in Figure 22.2.

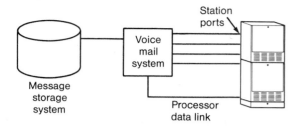

Figure 22.2   Voice mail integration with a PBX.

Voice mail systems are grouped into three categories:

- Stand-alone.
- Non-integrated.
- PBX-integrated.

All three types share the same basic architecture, but different manufacturers design systems for different applications. Furthermore, virtually no standards for the voice mail user interface exist, and few serious attempts have been made to develop them. Therefore, the transfer of experience from system to system on the part of both users and callers is minimal.

Stand-Alone Voice Mail

In a stand-alone configuration, a PBX is unnecessary. The voice mail system can be connected directly to central office trunks and even used as a service bureau that offers voice mail services to outside callers. Service bureau voice mail systems normally have large capacity. They are accessed through the public telephone network, and the system operator charges a flat fee plus usage. Since the incoming ports are shared by all users, there must be some way to route the incoming call to the appropriate mailbox. The most effective method makes use of direct inward dialing or, over 800 lines, the Dialed Number Identification System (DNIS). Chapter 20 explains DID and DNIS. These methods of called party identification are not always available, however. For example, calls may be trunked over private lines to a voice mail system in a distant city. In such cases, the caller is prompted to enter a code, which may be the last four digits of the telephone number or a mailbox number that the user has printed on a business card.

Service bureau voice mail systems are excellent for users who need a few mailboxes and cannot justify the purchase of a private system. They are also effective for users who are out of the office a great deal and have no need of message waiting lights to indicate the arrival of a call. The lack of message waiting lights is one of the chief drawbacks of stand-alone systems for people who are regularly in the office. A second drawback may be the lack of station identification, which requires callers to know and enter the mailbox number. A third drawback is the dead end nature of the medium. When a call enters the mailbox, the caller's only options are to leave a message or hang up.

Non-Integrated Voice Mail

Non-integrated voice mail has most of the same characteristics as a service bureau. The system is connected behind a PBX as shown in Figure 22.2. A shared group of PBX ports is connected to the voice mail system. Users can forward their calls to voice mail, but the system cannot identify the forwarding station, so the user must be prompted to enter a mailbox number, which is usually the last three or four digits the caller dialed. A caller who dials the company's main listed number, asks for a user by name, and reaches an extension that has been forwarded to voice mail is usually confused by a prompt asking for the extension number to be entered. Therefore, non-integrated systems are not widely accepted.

Integrated Voice Mail

PBX-integrated systems integrate with a specific PBX to provide features that enhance the value of the voice mail system. Integration is difficult or impossible behind an older PBX for which voice mail has not been developed, and it may not be economically feasible behind newer PBXs where only a few mailboxes are required. In this case, an inexpensive PC-based voice mail or service bureau is the most effective solution.

A fully integrated voice mail system has three features that require direct communication with the PBX:

- *Return To Attendant.* A caller, upon being transferred by the system into voice mail, can transfer (escape) from voice mail to a message center or switchboard operator by dialing digits on a DTMF telephone.

- *Called Party Recognition.* Calls can be transferred directly into voice mail when the called PBX extension is busy or does not answer.

- *Message Waiting Indication.* When a message arrives in a user's mailbox the voice mail system and PBX activate a message waiting light or apply stutter dial tone to remind users to retrieve messages.

The first of these features allows the caller to escape from the voice mail system and leave a message with an attendant. Lacking this feature, a caller can reach an attendant only by hanging up and redialing a number that is not forwarded to voice mail. Without the return-to-attendant feature, a voice mail system is, to the caller, no more useful than an answering machine.

The second feature, station number recognition, is equally important to the caller. Without it, the called party can transfer calls to the voice mail system, but the system cannot tell what extension the caller dialed. Therefore, the voice mail system asks the caller to enter the called party's extension, which may or may not be known. Most people who have had bad experiences with voice mail have encountered one of these two conditions.

The third feature, message waiting light illumination, is of no concern to the caller, but greatly affects voice mail's utility to the called party. This feature turns on a message waiting light when a message reaches the mailbox. With an electronic telephone that displays the light on a feature button, the user may have only to press the button to retrieve messages. Without the feature, the user must periodically call voice mail to check for waiting messages. This often results in delays in returning calls. For users who are rarely in the office, message waiting light illumination is of little or no value, but for users who are frequently in the office, it is an essential feature. Some systems substitute a short burst of stutter dial tone as an alternative, which is useful if telephone sets lack the message waiting lamp.

There are two principal methods of achieving integration. The first is through a direct data link from the voice mail processor to the PBX processor, and the second is through emulation of a display telephone. The first method is faster and more efficient, but it is usually available only to the PBX manufacturer or other manufacturers who pay a license fee. Anyone can reverse engineer a display set to integrate voice mail with another system, but the switch hook flashes are slower than the data link method. Furthermore, if the PBX uses a called party name data base, it may be necessary to enter both the extension number and the name in the voice mail system to identify the called party. And some features are available only through processor integration. For example, if a user has forwarded calls to a second position and that position is forwarded to voice mail, the second party's greeting may answer the call.

In addition to the above, some voice mail systems have enhancements that are known as *adaptive integration*. The following features are available on some voice mail systems:

- *Personal Assistance.* The system transfers calls to the called party's personal assistant rather than to the PBX attendant.

- *Time of Day Control.* The called party can vary call coverage and personal assistance options by time of day.

- *Internal Caller Identification.* The name of a person calling from within the system is inserted into the message header.

- *Busy/No Ring Status:* The voice mail message indicates to the caller whether the called party is on the telephone or did not answer the call.

- *Trunk Group Routing:* This feature causes the caller to be routed to the correct greeting depending on the trunk group on which the call arrived.

To achieve integration, the PBX and voice mail system must be a matched pair. Many PBX manufacturers offer proprietary voice mail systems, but their systems are not the only ones to achieve full integration. Most voice mail service bureaus provide only non-integrated service. It is, however, possible for the PBX and the service bureau voice mail system to be integrated over private lines, which can provide the same features as a directly attached system.

Voice Mail Capacity

Voice mail systems are sized by number of ports and hours of storage. The number of ports limits the number of callers that can be connected simultaneously. Ports are occupied while callers are listening to prompts, leaving messages, and retrieving messages. The number of ports required is calculated from the number of accesses and the holding time per access during the busy hour. (See Chapter 31 for an explanation of how to calculate voice mail port and storage requirements.) Long-winded prompts, the inability to bypass prompts, and verbose greeting messages not only irritate callers but consume port and hard disk capacity. Designing the system with the correct number of ports is important. Having too many ports increases the cost of the voice mail system. Having too few restricts the ability of callers to reach voice mail and blocks users when they attempt to retrieve messages. Ports normally are added in increments of four at a cost of, perhaps, 10 to 20% of the original cost of the system.

The type of integration often affects the efficiency with which the voice mail system uses ports. A popular feature on many systems is *outcalling*, which is the ability of the voice mail system to dial the user's pager or cellular phone. This feature requires ports to handle both incoming and outgoing calls, and a problem may arise when a port is seized from both directions at the same time. This condition, which is called *glare* (see Chapter 11), causes the port to lock until both ends hang up. In a system in which the processors are linked together, glare is resolved by the processors without affecting the users. In a system integrated by emulating a display telephone, it is usually necessary to provide separate incoming and outgoing ports, which increases the number of ports required.

The amount of storage required is highly variable and depends on the number of users and the number of stored messages per user. It also depends on whether disk storage capacity varies with the announcement messages and how efficiently the manufacturer packs the disk. Efficient packing algorithms compress the silent intervals so disk space is not wasted. As a rule of thumb in sizing voice mail systems, the average user takes about 3 minutes of storage for greetings and messages. A system serving 100 users, therefore, would require five hours of storage.

The voice mail system's purging algorithm also improves storage efficiency. The more effective systems inform the administrator when the disk is reaching capacity. Over-age messages are manually or automatically purged after a specified time.

Networked Voice Mail

A large multisite operation can often bring its employees closer together with networked voice mail. There are three ways of accomplishing the objective of permitting users in one location to use voice mail in other locations.

The simplest way of networking voice mail is to use guest mailboxes, which are boxes assigned to people outside the system. Guest mailboxes have the drawbacks of stand-alone voice mail systems, and sometimes a long distance charge is incurred in placing and retrieving messages. For organizations that need only a few mailboxes, the cost of maintaining guest mailboxes is often less than the cost of a service bureau and is almost invariably less than the cost of a separate voice mail system. The advent of PC-based voice mail, however, is making smaller systems more economically attractive.

A more effective method of networking voice mail is to terminate the voice mail on one PBX and connect other PBXs to the central PBX with networking software. This software, which Chapter 20 discusses, is an additional cost item that permits feature transparency across the network. All voice mail functions are available to users outside the main PBX just as if the voice mail system were attached to their PBX. The advantages of this method extend beyond voice mail because it permits automatic callback, extension-to-extension dialing without access codes, and other features that are lost in a tie line network.

A third method is networking the voice mail systems themselves as shown in Figure 22.3. This method is effective when there are many users at each site. Messages are stored on the local

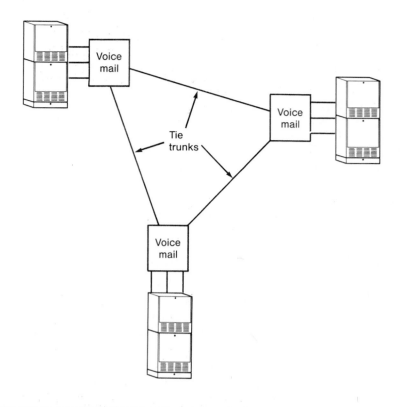

Figure 22.3   Networked voice mail systems.

voice mail system, which reduces the tie line traffic. Networked voice mail permits a user to have a mailbox in a distant PBX and have the message delivered to his or her own voice mailbox. For example, a sales manager could provide local telephone numbers for key clients in several different cities. Managers with staffs in more than one location can maintain distribution lists and forward calls across the network.

Currently, voice mail systems must be of the same manufacture to be networked because there are no standards for communication between systems. Work is underway, however, to develop a set of standards known as Audio Message Interchange

Service (AMIS). When AMIS standards are approved, they will form a common language that networked voice mail systems can support so voice mail of different manufacture can communicate.

Automated Attendant

The automated attendant is the most misused and maligned of the voice processing technologies. The system answers the telephone and offers the caller a menu of choices such as "dial 1 for sales, 2 for service, 3 for engineering." A properly designed system can save time for callers, but systems with lengthy prompts and endless menus can be a source of great frustration to callers and may cause a loss of business. The automated attendant is usually a feature of a voice mail system, but the two are not inseparable.

Many companies prefer not to have their customer calls answered by an automated attendant, in which case, it is a simple matter to establish separate trunk groups for customer and employee calls. The employee calls are answered by the automated attendant, and the customer calls by an operator. In most systems, pressing 0 returns the caller to the attendant. And usually callers do not have to wait for the prompting menu but can dial directly through the menus to the desired function.

The simplest form of automated attendant is a substitute for direct inward dialing. The system prompts the caller to enter the extension number, if known, or to wait for an operator. This an effective tool that may reduce the extra cost of DID trunks if there is a high probability that the caller will know the extension number. When the callers are the public, however, they are less likely to know the extension number, and the automated attendant may lengthen the average time it takes to process a call.

The second use of automated attendant is to enable callers to route their own calls to an answering position by dialing a code from a menu of choices. The system manager must take great care in creating the menu, because it is here that callers most frequently experience frustration. If there are too many choices at a menu level, callers will fail to remember them and have to start over or return to the attendant. If there are too many levels to the menu, callers become impatient with the delay, particularly if they are paying for a long distance call. A good policy is to permit no more than four or five choices (plus return to the operator) at each menu level, and no more than two or, rarely, three menu levels. The system should be set up to allow callers who know the menu to dial the code immediately without waiting for the prompt. Also, if a numbering conflict does not occur, callers may be permitted to dial an extension number.

Deserving of special attention is the name-dialing feature offered by many automated attendants. This system encourages callers to dial by last name if the extension number is unknown. The automated attendants' algorithm compares the three-letter combinations of the digits dialed and presents the caller with a menu of choices. These systems are accurate and may cut operator costs, but they are time-consuming for the caller and a source of frustration if the called party's name is not in the database.

Interactive Voice Response (Audiotex)

Interactive voice response (IVR) is a system that prompts the user to enter information such as an account number via DTMF dialing. This information is passed to a host computer for processing, and a voice synthesizer reads the information back to the caller. Banks and credit unions use the technology to enable customers to obtain their account balances without waiting for an agent.

Applications of IVR are not limited to financial institutions, however. With custom programming, they can be used in many applications where a customer calls an agent who reads back information from a data base. For example, IVR could be used in the following applications:

- An airline could allow frequent fliers to query the number of miles credited to their accounts.

- An automotive service agency could ask callers to enter a license number to determine the status of repairs.

- A gas company could ask customers to enter their account numbers to enter orders to relight pilot lights at the start of a heating season.

■ A wholesaler could accept orders outside normal working hours for delivery the following morning.

There are many other electronic methods of obtaining the same results, but IVR is uniquely suited for applications where the caller's primary means of communication is a DTMF telephone and voice is adequate for response or confirmation of the input message.

Digital Announcers

Digital announcers are the devices that play announcements over ACDs and UCDs and provide information announcements and announcements-on-hold. Unlike analog announcers that record messages on a tape or drum, digital announcers store messages in digitized form on a chip. They are, therefore, not practical for long announcements because the cost of the device increases with the length of the message.

It is important to evaluate the application carefully before buying an announcement system. As with voice mail, the primary criteria in selecting a system are the amount of message storage and the number of channels required. It is also important to decide how the message will be changed. A permanent message such as an informational message about a company's product line probably would be recorded professionally and might change infrequently. The message might even be encoded on a chip before it leaves the factory. Conversely, a school using an announcement system to distribute announcements about closures due to weather will want to record messages locally and, perhaps, from a remote location.

The control circuitry should determine when to connect the caller to the announcement. Some messages play only from the beginning; in other cases the listener can barge in on the message wherever it happens to be in a cycle. For example, if a promotional or informational message is being played, it would be appropriate to break in at only certain spots, and the message would play only once. Messages on hold might play repeatedly while the caller is on hold, or the system might vary the message depending on how long the caller waits.

Voice quality is another important consideration. As with voice mail, the higher the degree of compression, the lower the storage cost and the lower the voice quality. The best way to evaluate quality is to listen to a sample.

Applications

Voice mail often is perceived as simply an expensive answering machine. It can be used as an answering machine, but a properly chosen and applied system can improve the effectiveness of the company's staff. The features, the most important of which are listed in Table 22.1, lend voice mail a flexibility that cannot be achieved without processor-driven or human intelligence. Its applications are too numerous to list and, in most cases, are self evident. Some creative uses that are not so obvious are:

- A hospital offers voice mail for its patient rooms, allowing patients to receive messages while they are asleep, in surgery, etc. and play them back at their leisure. In addition to being good for patient morale, such a system is a source of revenue for the hospital.

- A public telephone service provider allows a caller who reaches an unanswered or busy telephone the option of leaving a voice mail message for later delivery. This is a valuable service for callers who can't afford to wait.

- A food processing plant provides guest mailboxes for its growers to inform them of recommended planting schedules and the availability of seed and fertilizer. During the harvest season, daily tonnage quotas are left in voice mail. Not only does this system eliminate calls to farmers who are away from the telephone, it also makes it possible for the processing plant to verify that the message has been retrieved.

To gain maximum benefit from voice mail, an organization must ensure that its employees do not abuse the service. The most frequent abuse is the tendency of some users to hide behind voice mail, using it to answer all calls, which they can return at their

Table 22.1   Voice Mail: Principal Features and Their Definitions

ACCOUNT BILLING	System provides for user chargeback based on variables that are established by the system administrator.
AUDIOTEXT	A voice bulletin board° feature that permits the caller to choose from a menu of announcements. Caller can interrupt the announcement by pressing a key and is returned to the next higher menu level.
AUTOMATIC PURGE ADMINISTRATOR INITIATED	The system administrator can set a date threshold, and the system will purge all messages that are older than the threshold.
AUTOMATIC PURGE SYSTEM CONTROLLED	When the remaining storage drops to a preset threshold, the system automatically purges over-age messages to recover storage space.
COMMENT ANNOTATION	A voice mail user can add comments to a message and forward it to another user's mailbox.
DELIVERY CONFIRMATION	System permits the original caller after confirmation to determine whether a voice mail message has been retrieved.
DISTRIBUTED LISTS	System permits users to establish lists of mailbox holders who receive messages when the appropriate code is dialed. Message is stored once by the system. System provides confirmation of delivery.
EXTENDED ABSENCE GREETING	Informs callers that the mailbox holder is unavailable during a prolonged period and prevents messages from going undelivered.
GROUP ANNOUNCE	A voice mail message, which is stored only once, is routed to the voice mailbox of a closed user group. System provides confirmation of delivery.
GUEST MAILBOX	The voice mail system permits the system administrator to establish mailboxes for customers and temporary users.
MESSAGE NON-DELIVERY	If a voice mail message has not been picked up after a specified time, the system initiates a call to the voice mailbox of the caller and informs him or her that the message was not delivered.

Table 22.1   Voice Mail: Principal Features and Their Definitions (cont'd)

MESSAGE WAITING	System alerts caller that a voice mail message is waiting by turning on a message waiting lamp on the telephone, stutter dial tone, or equivalent method.
NETWORKING	Multiple voice mail systems of the same manufacturer can be linked with a network of private lines. Users can send and receive messages from any station on the network.
OUTCALLING	The system can call subscribers at a predetermined telephone number, cellular telephone, or pager to notify them that they have received a message.
PERSONAL GREETING	System permits user to greet callers who arrive at voice mail in his or her own voice with a customized message.
PROMPT BYPASS	Callers can bypass system prompts by dialing codes.
REPLACE/SAVE/DELETE	The system requires the user to dispose of a message after it has been read by replaying it, saving it, or deleting it. When messages are replayed, the system announces which are previously saved messages.
RETURN TO OPERATOR	Allows a caller who has arrived in voice mail or automated attendant to return to a live answering position by pressing the 0° key on a DTMF phone or remaning off-hook.
SYSTEM GREETING	System provides a standard greeting, which may be changed by the administrator, for callers who arrive at a voice mailbox when no personal greeting has been provided.
TIME/DATE STAMP	When user retrieves messages, the system announces the time and date each message was filed.

convenience. When used this way, voice mail aggravates, instead of alleviates the problem of telephone tag.

A second form of abuse is the verbose greeting message. Callers are annoyed by the constant repetition of a message and detailed instructions on how to use a system that should be self explanatory. Also, verbose greetings waste ports and disk storage.

Improperly designed and applied voice mail and automated attendant systems have led to the creation of the term *voice mail jail*, which refers to the situation in which a caller is locked in the voice mail system and cannot escape to get personalized assistance. A well designed system should be brief and clear in its instructions and should give callers a choice.

Many companies are reluctant to use voice mail with their customers because of the impersonality of the service. The first contact a company has with a new customer should not be over voice mail, but when the relationship is firmly cemented, voice mail can be as advantageous to a customer as it is to another employee. The key is to leave the caller in control. Many companies answer outside calls in person but give the caller the option of leaving a message in voice mail. Even if messages are taken manually, the receptionist can read them into voice mail, which is usually a more effective means of distributing messages than writing them on message slips.

Evaluation Criteria

Evaluations of voice mail, automated attendant, and audiotex systems should be based on the features outlined in Table 22.1 and on the criteria listed below, which include the most important features.

Integration with a PBX

The most important consideration in evaluating and using a voice mail system is the degree to which it integrates with the PBX. This is not to say that integration is always necessary; often, a stand-alone voice mail system is perfectly satisfactory. For most office workers, however, an integrated system provides essential features.

Compression Algorithm

All digital voice mail systems use some form of compressed voice technology to digitize and store messages and announcements. Part of the compression is gained by pause compression and expansion, in which the duration of a pause is coded instead of the pause itself. Voice mail systems use pause compression to speed or retard playback. If a listener wants a faster playback , the system shortens pauses; for a slower playback, it lengthens them. Also, the specific technology used for digitizing the voice affects the efficiency of the system. The more the voice is compressed, the less natural it sounds and the less storage space it occupies. Manufacturers have a choice between a natural sounding system that takes more storage space and a more efficient system that sacrifices some intelligibility. The best way to evaluate this feature is to listen to the voice quality of several different systems and decide whether the lower cost of a highly compressed system is worth the decrease in quality.

Cost Per Hour of Storage

The cost per hour of message storage is the most effective way of comparing costs of voice mail systems. The cost per hour of storage is the total time on the disk less overhead for such things as system greetings and user prompts. Cost is not, however, the only criterion for evaluating systems. It is possible to reduce the amount of overhead and increase the amount of available storage by providing only a system greeting instead of personal greetings. The personal greeting greatly improves the usability of the system because it permits users to leave messages that tell callers where they are and when they plan to return.

Port Utilization

The number of ports determines how many users can leave and retrieve messages simultaneously. Not all ports are necessarily available for full voice mail use. Some systems require dedicated ports for automated attendant. Some systems require separate ports for outgoing messages such as calls the voice mail system places to a paging or cellular radio system. Systems that integrate through display set emulation generally cannot resolve the glare situation that arises when users seize a circuit simultaneously from both ends. Therefore, such systems may require separate incoming and outgoing ports.

System Reports

System reports can be used to determine how efficiently the system is being utilized. Reports should provide information such as the following:

- Number of messages sent and received by a specific system user.
- Average length of messages by specific user or group.
- Percentage of disk space used.
- Busy hour traffic for various ports.
- Number of times all access ports are busy.
- Message aging by individual mailbox.
- Number of messages not deleted after specified time.

Personal Greeting

The personal greeting feature permits users to leave messages in their mailboxes. Although this feature uses more storage space than the system greeting, it improves user satisfaction. With a personal greeting, users can state where they are and when they will return and give callers any special routing instructions. If the user chooses not to use a personal greeting, the system should automatically provide one.

Electronic Mail Integration

One form of electronic mail integration permits transfer of an e-mail message from a computer into the user's voice mailbox by synthesized voice. The primary advantage is that users can retrieve e-mail messages from a telephone; there is no need to have a data device to retrieve messages. This form of integration is available only from a specific computer and voice mail pair.

Although technology to convert between text and voice is not available, electronic mail also can notify the user of a voice mail message or vice versa. This feature can replace a message waiting light on the telephone and can be advantageous to users who are away from the office and are using a data terminal that is part of an electronic mail network.

Networking Capability

This feature permits multiple voice mail systems to act as an integrated unit. From the system administrator's standpoint, an important issue is how to maintain distribution lists across the network. Some systems exchange messages that automatically update the other machines on the network.

Another important function of networked voice mail is how systems exchange messages. In some systems, the voice mail system can dial-up during low cost hours to exchange messages.

Evaluating Automated Attendant

In applying an automated attendant system, administrators should carefully consider its effect on callers. Although the number of people who lack DTMF dialing capability is dropping continuously, there are those who still have rotary dials and must wait through the entire menu to reach an operator. Other callers will resent the automated attendant and may refuse to do business with an organization that uses one. Some automated attendants offer a confusing array of menu choices and levels. Frequent callers usually have no problem navigating the menus, but a first-time caller may be baffled by the variety of choices. Any company considering an automated attendant, will be well advised to study the applications carefully, design it intelligently, and listen to the comments of callers.

The disadvantages of automated attendant notwithstanding, there are many applications where it makes good business sense. First, it is a good substitute for DID in a system where DID is not available. Second, an automated attendant is often an excellent way to enable callers on 800 lines to reach an appropriate destination without an attendant. Although dialed number identification system (DNIS) is available in 800 service, not all PBXs can handle it, nor does the numbering plan allow dialing every station on a PBX.

A third application where the automated attendant is effective is with an overloaded switchboard. Instead of installing a second attendant console, the company may find that the automated attendant offers a quick solution to customer complaints of delays in answering. Remember that it isn't necessary to require callers to listen to a voice message to get the value from an automated attendant. Employees and frequent callers can be told that when the telephone is answered they can immediately dial an extension number. Other callers simply hear a short greeting and are queued to the human attendant, whose load is reduced by the callers who dial extensions directly.

Evaluating Audiotex

The audiotext feature of voice mail is a useful means of distributing information. Callers receive a menu of choices. They can select two or three levels of menu before reaching the desired information. For example, a university might disseminate class information via audiotext by listing the major courses of study—science, liberal arts, engineering—on the first menu, the field of study—biology, botany, chemistry—on the second menu level, and class—freshman, sophomore—on a third. If the menu choices are no more than the caller can easily remember, this can be an effective way of delivering information. The system should be designed to enable callers to interrupt the menu by pressing a special key such as # to repeat.

The most important criteria in evaluating audiotex are the types of host interfaces, applications development tools, and local databases supported.

Evaluating Digital Announcers

Digital announcers are available as stand-alone devices that can interface to any PBX or public access line and as integrated devices that fit into a card slot in a PBX. The primary criteria in evaluating digital announcement systems are:

- Voice quality.
- Storage capacity.
- Number of ports.
- Method of integration with the PBX—through the bus or through a port.
- Method of storing the announcement. Is it on RAM or PROM? How is it protected against power outage?
- Method of updating the announcement—locally, remotely, or through a professional service.

Selected Voice Processing Equipment Manufacturers

Voice Processing Equipment

ABS Systems

Active Voice

Advanced Voice Technologies

AEC

American Digital Voice Corp.

American Telesystems Corp.

Applied Voice Technology

AT&T

BBL Industries, Inc.

Boston Technology

Brooktrout Technology

Centigram Corp.

Cobotyx Corp.

Dictaphone

Digital Speech Systems

Digitcom

Dytel Corp.

Ericsson Information Systems

Executone

Expert Systems

Fujitsu Business Communications

Genesis Electronics

Innovative Technology

Lanier Voice Products

MacroTel International

Miami Voice

Microlog

NEC Technologies, Inc.

Northern Telecom, Inc.

Octel Communications

Omnivoice

Rolm Corporation

Siemens

SDI

Summa Four, Inc.

Tadiran Electronic Industries

Telescan

TIE/communications, Inc.

Toshiba America

Unisys

VMX/Opcom

Voicemail International

Wang Laboratories

Xerox

Digital Announcer Manufacturers

Adtech

AEC

ATIS

Audichron

Audiocom

Com Dev

Dacon

Electronic Tele-Communications

Eltrex

Interalia

MacKenzie Laboratories

Metro Tel

Northern Telecom, Cook Division

Racom

Teac America, Inc.

US Takachiho

Viking

23

Centrex Systems

Before the arrival of micro electronics and stored program control PBXs, large companies were reluctant to place switching systems on their premises to provide PBX service. An electromechanical PBX required considerable floor space to house it and a large electrical supply to power it. In effect, these large PBXs were the equivalent of small central offices. The technology they used—crossbar or step-by-step—was nearly identical with that used in a central office, and the maintenance requirements were high. To meet this demand for complex switching systems, the LECs offered a service called *Centrex.*

Centrex blends the features of a PBX with those of ordinary business lines. A partition is established in the central office, and individual lines are run to the customer's premises. Within the partition, an array of PBX-like features is defined. Early Centrex systems operating on crossbar switches had few features; call transfer and four-digit dialing between extensions were the most popular. As electronic central offices came into operation, features requiring intelligence in the switch were added. With electronic offices, it was possible to establish call pickup groups and provide features such as call forwarding and speed dialing that required a database and a processor.

The FCC's Computer Inquiry II, which required the LECs to offer customer premises equipment only through a fully separated subsidiary, dealt Centrex a near-fatal blow. Centrex was a central office-based service, and the LECs could no longer offer it, because the subsidiary could not provide service from the central office. The LECs were, however, permitted to grandfather existing services.

The divestiture decree rejuvenated Centrex because it again permitted the LECs to offer central office-based services in competition with PBXs. The decree prevented the LECs from offering customer premises equipment, but their subsidiaries could, or the customer could purchase the CPE from another source. Many LECs filed new tariffs to provide Centrex, including small office Centrex services, which many LECs today offer with as few as two or three lines. Most of these services no longer bear the name Centrex but go by a variety of trade names, some of which are recognizable by their inclusion of the letters *cent* somewhere in the name.

With the coming of digital central offices, many LECs began offering digital Centrex services, which more closely approximate the features offered by digital PBXs. Digital Centrex extends a signal from the digital central office to the user's premises. The digital loop permits Centrex, with a proprietary feature set, to offer single-button feature access on lines. By contrast, analog Centrex features are accessed by depressing the switchhook to get a second dial tone and dialing a code or pressing a speed dial button. In both PBX and Centrex service, features that are accessible only through code dialing tend to fall into disuse.

It is possible to assign the codes to speed dial buttons on an analog set, but the features can be reprogrammed by users, so it is difficult to keep consistency in the feature pattern among stations on the system. Digital Centrex allows the administrator to assign buttons that cannot be changed by users.

The once moribund Centrex has been reborn, and it appears that it will be a contender for switching services for some time to come. As ISDN services come on line, the LECs see their Centrex customers as the most logical users of the service, which may lend further impetus to Centrex development. In this chapter we will discuss the differences between Centrex and PBX and explore the applications for which each is most appropriate.

Centrex Features

In the United States, Centrex is offered almost exclusively on analog and digital electronic switching systems. Some residual Centrex systems may still be provided on crossbar switches, and the characteristics described in this section do not apply to them because crossbar systems do not have the flexibility or speed necessary to satisfy most users.

Most features of digital Centrex are identical with analog Centrex except those provided by integrating the telephone set with the central office line circuit. Stations equipped with single line telephone DTMF sets have essentially the same features regardless of whether they are served by an analog or a digital central office. Digital telephone sets can access more features, but their range is limited compared to an analog station.

Special features, including WATS lines, tie lines, and 800 lines, can be terminated on Centrex in essentially the same manner as on a PBX. T-1 lines to IECs for bulk-rated long distance also can be installed. Also, Centrex switches can serve as an electronic tandem switch for a company's private network.

Advantages of Centrex

Centrex service provides each user the equivalent of a personal business line. A Centrex group is defined in the central office so that members of the group have a variety of PBX-like features. The following are the primary advantages of Centrex service compared to a PBX.

Reliability

Since Centrex service is furnished from a central office, the reliability is high. Central office switching systems are inherently protected against the failure of a processor or major common control equipment item. The Centrex subscriber does not have to worry about providing battery backup, duplicate processors, duplicate power supplies, or spare equipment for service restoration. The most likely cause of Centrex failure is cable trouble, which should be rare. Local central office switching systems average one hour's outage per 40 years in service, and even if these objectives are not met, the reliability is still higher than that of most PBXs.

Integration of Multiple Locations

To link multiple small locations with a PBX, customers must use off premises extensions, tie lines, or a combination of both. For example, most school districts have a large central administration office and a combination of large, intermediate, and small schools. Centrex is often a less costly system for tying diverse locations together than one or more PBXs. Also, when some locations are too small to justify a PBX, they lose the features of a fully integrated system. Centrex provides uniform services to all locations, integrating them into a single system. It should be noted, however, that the range limitations of digital Centrex may preclude using feature sets in all locations.

Reduced Capital Investment

Station equipment for a PBX costs about the same as it does with Centrex. Since the LEC owns and maintains the switching equipment, the initial capital investment required for Centrex is about half that required for a PBX. The monthly costs, however, are greater for Centrex.

Reduced Maintenance and Administrative Responsibility

The Centrex customer is relieved of maintenance and administrative responsibility except that associated with the station equipment. The LEC delivers a service and takes care of repair, record-keeping, and system management. This factor is frequently overlooked by companies that underestimate the administrative work associated with owning a PBX.

Freedom from Obsolescence

PBXs have evolved through at least three and, by some counts, four generations, following similar evolutions in central offices, which have tended to lead PBX technology. Centrex users have ridden through the evolution without feeling the impact of the technological change except insofar as it brought new features. In the future, Centrex may provide a relatively painless method of evolving into ISDN.

Virtually Unlimited Growth

PBXs grow in smooth increments right up to existing shelf, cabinet, or system capacity. Growth beyond the capacity of one of these elements requires an investment that is sometimes substantial and sometimes impossible. Centrex capacity is not unlimited, but if the LEC has sufficient notice, most growth requirements can be met without a major investment by the user.

Reduced Floor Space

Centrex service requires almost no floor space other than the space required for the distributing frames. This can be important in companies that have several thousand lines. In very large PBXs, the vehicle used for switching is usually a central office switch, such as the AT&T 5ESS or the Northern Telecom SL-100, which is the PBX version of the DMS-100. Besides requiring floor space, these switches require a full-time trained staff to administer.

Short Term Commitment

Although some LECs contract Centrex services, others offer them month-to-month. This can be important if future growth is uncertain or if the customer needs service for a short time while awaiting a more permanent type of service.

Centrex Drawbacks

Offsetting the advantages of Centrex are disadvantages that many organizations find outweigh the advantages.

Life Cycle Cost

The life cycle cost of a system is a composite of initial capital investment and recurring costs over the life of the investment. The cost of PBX service generally drops after the initial lease/purchase period of the equipment is over. Centrex costs continue for the life of the service and may increase with inflation. Subscriber line access charges are levied per line in a Centrex compared to a PBX where they are levied per trunk. Centrex is usually less expensive at the outset than a PBX, but many organizations find a PBX to be less costly over the long term. The key factor in determining the break-even point between a PBX and Centrex is usually the length of time it is expected to be in service.

Features

Digital Centrex has most of the features available in a PBX; analog Centrex has most of the important features, but they must be activated by code dialing. With either system it is difficult and costly to integrate a customer-owned voice mail or call accounting system. An integrated automatic call distributor (ACD) may be more costly or less effective in a Centrex system. Application program interfaces, which are available on some PBXs are generally not available on Centrex, which may limit the ability of a company to use services such as dialed number identification service (DNIS) and automatic number identification service when it becomes available.

Feature Costs

Though features equivalent to those in a PBX may be available with Centrex, there is often an extra monthly charge for each feature. Often the additional cost makes Centrex service non-competitive with a PBX.

Add, Move, and Change Flexibility

Customer-controlled adds, moves, and changes are an important feature of PBXs that may be unavailable or available only on a reduced level with Centrex. With Centrex, if a terminal for making customer-controlled rearrangements is provided, the LEC often posts the changes on a batch basis. Batched changes are not posted immediately, so the changes are not effective until the next working day. With a PBX, the changes can be made instantaneously.

Applications

This section discusses the principal factors to be considered in selecting between Centrex services and in choosing between Centrex and a PBX.

Analog vs. Digital Centrex

Most LECs provide a choice of analog or digital Centrex, although in a particular exchange only one or two wire centers may be equipped for digital Centrex. For most customers, the question whether an analog or a digital switching machine provides the service is not relevant. The quality of service will be equivalent, and the use of Centrex to carry directly connected digital data will be rare. There will usually be differences in telephone sets, however, that favor digital Centrex.

Analog Centrex is generally incapable of furnishing integrated key telephone service. The switch itself can provide functions such as call transfer, call pickup, and call hold, but the users must dial codes to activate the features. Attempts to train users to dial feature codes are rarely successful, so either the features fall into disuse or the enterprise installs key telephone equipment to provide the features.

Digital Centrex can support integrated key system features on proprietary telephone sets. This feature is the principal advantage of digital Centrex over its analog counterpart.

Trunking Issues

In the past, one advantage of Centrex was the low probability of call blockage. LECs furnished enough Centrex trunks to provide the same grade of service that the central office as a whole received. Compared to a PBX where the number of trunks was an economic issue determined by the customer, Centrex often provided better service.

Recently, many LECs have begun providing Centrex as a trunk-rated service. In a trunk-rated service, the LEC interposes a software block that permits only the contracted number of incoming and outgoing calls to be connected. Therefore, the number and cost of trunks required may be identical for both Centrex and a PBX.

Multiple Location Issues

Centrex allows an organization that spans an entire metropolitan area to function as if it were a single system. The differences between Centrex and a PBX in this respect are slight. Both require off premises extensions, the cost of which may be identical, and in neither case is it possible to operate feature sets from remote locations.

Ancillary Equipment Issues

Nearly half the PBXs installed today are equipped with voice mail, automated attendant, and call accounting systems. These features are all available with Centrex, but they may be provided as an extra cost option. Ancillary features may be charged per use by the LEC, which often makes them more costly than privately owned systems. Call accounting information may be connected back to the customer over a remote line, or it may be provided from the LEC's automatic message accounting system and not be available on as short notice as privately owned call accounting information.

Centrex CPE Equipment Manufacturers

Automatic Call Distribution and Call Sequencing Equipment

Automation Electronics Corp.   Perimeter Technology

Centrex Attendant Consoles

Comdial   Telescan
Conveyant Systems   Tone Commander

Telephone and Key Telephone Systems

Alcatel/Cortelco   Siemens
David Systems   Solitare
Harris/Lanier   Tadiran
Marubeni   Teledial/Deka
Multimil   Telerad
Northern Telecom
Panasonic   Teltone
Premier   TIE/communications, Inc.
Sanbar   WIN Communications

Call Storage Buffers

E-Coms, Inc.   Western Telematic

Voice Mail and Automated Attendant Equipment

Active Voice   Metro Tel
Automation Electronics Corp. Octel
David Systems   Tel Electronics
Dictaphone   Viking

Call Accounting Systems

Account-A-Call Corporation

Bitek International, Inc.

Burnup & Sims

Com Dev

Compucom

Contel Information Systems

Datatel

Ericsson, Inc. Communications Div.

Infosystems

Infortext

Moscom

NEC Information Systems

Northern Telecom

Protel

Rolm Corporation

Soft-Com

Stryker Systems

Summa Four

Sykes Datatronics, Inc.

Tekno Industries, Inc.

Tel Electronics

Telco Research

Telecommunications Software

Telecorp Products

Telemon

Transaction Recording Systems

Western Telmatic

Westinghouse Communications

Xiox

Xtend

Facsimile Transmission

Is facsimile transmission the technology that sounds the death knell of the Postal Service? A former Postmaster General said, "The facsimile systems and the countless other applications of electricity to the transmission of intelligence yet to be made must eventually interfere with the transportation of letters by the slower means of post." Countless facsimile users agree. No longer is it necessary to wait several days for delivery of a letter. A facsimile machine can send it in a fraction of a minute and for approximately the same cost—less if the transmission is in the local telephone calling area. Facsimile quality isn't quite as good as the original letter, but recipients are often more than willing to sacrifice quality for speed.

If we were to project the growth in facsimile transmission linearly into the future, it would eventually surpass the volume of first class mail. For now, mail has a formidable edge: 83 billion first class mail pieces delivered in 1988 versus an estimated 3 billion facsimile messages. It is safe to predict that the Postal Service is secure for at least a little while and that facsimile transmission will continue to enjoy the phenomenal growth it has experienced during the past few years. The Postmaster General who made the prediction quoted in the paragraph above was Jonathan Creswell, and he was speaking in 1872, some 30 years after the invention of facsimile transmission.

Facsimile transmission was invented in 1843, six decades before the invention of the teletypewriter. Despite this early start, the technology found little application for several decades. It first came into use in the 1920s for transmitting wirephotos and weather maps, and for years law enforcement agencies used it extensively for sending mug shots and fingerprints, but only in the last decade has it become an indispensable business machine. No longer is a facsimile machine considered merely a useful tool; it is now essential to most businesses.

To transmit a page of information over a data circuit, two methods can be employed. In the first, the characters are encoded in an eight-bit alphanumeric code and transmitted to a terminal that displays the characters on a screen or prints them on paper. The second alternative is to scan the printed page, encode it, and transmit a facsimile of the image in shades of black and white without identifying individual characters. Facsimile has several significant advantages over alphanumeric data communication: it conveys both graphic and textual information, source documents can be transmitted without rekeying, and facsimile transmission is less affected by transmission errors than data communications. A noise burst that would obliterate several characters in ordinary data transmission may damage a facsimile scan line, but unless perfect reproduction is required, the document will be readable. Facsimile is also fast. Graphic information can be transmitted anywhere there is a telephone at the rate of about 20 seconds to 6 minutes per page, with only older obsolescent machines taking more than a minute per page. Compared to the alternative of overnight courier services, facsimile is markedly faster. The comparison is not entirely valid, however, because facsimile costs are directly proportionate to the quantity of information transmitted, whereas courier services usually transmit several pages for a fixed fee. Also, facsimile transmissions are practically instantaneous, and the best an express service can do is overnight delivery.

The primary drawback of data terminals compared to facsimile is their inability to transmit graphics. Signatures, logos, and illustrations cannot be sent from a data terminal. Also, if the source document is not machine readable, information must be rekeyed from the source or converted with an optical character reader before it can be transmitted. Both of these alternatives are slow and costly. Offsetting the advantages of facsimile transmission are two drawbacks. First, the terminal equipment is costly. Facsimile transceiver costs range from less than $1000 for a basic machine to more than $5000 for a full-featured system. Second, facsimile requires about ten times the transmission time to send a standard 8 1/2 x 11-inch page of text compared to sending it from a data terminal. Though facsimile vendors advertise 20 seconds-per-page transmission time, this speed is achieved only for pages with considerable white space. A full page of single-spaced text contains 550 to 600 words, or approximately 3500 characters. At 9.6 kb/s such a page can be transmitted in less than four seconds; to transmit a facsimile of the same page requires nearly 1 minute.

Facsimile technology can be used to implement one form of electronic mail. The primary differences between computer-based electronic mail and facsimile are the type of output and the storage method. Facsimile transmission is inherently a hard-copy system in contrast to electronic mail, which can be left entirely in a soft-copy state (that is, information is displayed on a screen but not printed). Although facsimile messages can be stored on electronic media, computer-based electronic mail messages can be stored in one-tenth or less of the storage space and can be retrieved with any asynchronous terminal. Facsimile and electronic mail can be used interchangeably with low message volumes, but if the volume is high the inherent advantages of each system tend to dictate which is the most feasible for a given application.

Facsimile technology has other applications that will become more important as the technology matures. Currently, some facsimile machines can double as printers. From this application it is a short but complex leap to linking a facsimile machine with a communicating word processor for printing documents remotely. The CCITT X.400 standards make it easy to send documents from a computer to a facsimile machine. As discussed later, many electronic mail services now offer the capability of sending a document from a computer to a facsimile machine.

Although facsimile got off to a slow start compared to other telecommunications technologies, its use is expanding to the point that it now is indispensable for many forms of record communication. This has happened because CCITT standards are now universally accepted and machine prices have dropped to the point that most businesses can afford them.

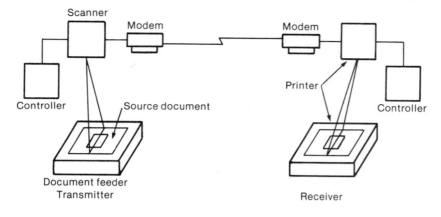

Figure 24.1 **Block diagram of a facsimile system.**

Facsimile Technology

A facsimile machine has four major elements as diagrammed in Figure 24.1—scanner, printer, controller, and communications facilities. The scanner sweeps across a page, segmenting it into multiple lines in much the same way that a television camera scans an image. The scanner output can be either a continuous analog signal that varies between white and black level or a digital output that converts the image to a binary code. Analog scanner output modulates an analog carrier. Digital scanner output is compressed and applied directly to a digital circuit or through a modem to an analog circuit. Control equipment directs the scanning rate and, in digital facsimile, processes the signal to compress solid expanses of black or white. At the receiving end, the incoming signal is demodulated and drives a print mechanism that reproduces the incoming image on paper.

Facsimile Machine Characteristics

Facsimile equipment is categorized by modulation method, speed, resolution, and transmission rate. Both frequency and amplitude modulation are applied directly to telephone circuits. Digital machines produce a binary signal that is applied to the circuit through a modem. The digital transmission speed varies from 1200 b/s to 64 kb/s; the speed of sending a page varies from 6 minutes down to less than 1 minute. Resolution is measured in lines per inch (lpi) and varies from slightly less than 100 lpi to 400 lpi.

CCITT divides facsimile standards into four groups:

- *Group 1.* Frequency modulated analog, 6 minutes per page transmission time, 100 lpi resolution, 1500 Hz white frequency and 2400 Hz black frequency. (These are U. S. conventions. The CCITT standard is 1300 Hz white and 3100 Hz black).

- *Group 2.* Amplitude modulated analog, 2 to 3 minutes per page transmission time, 100 lpi resolution, 2100 Hz carrier frequency using amplitude, phase, or vestigial sideband modulation.

- *Group 3.* Compressed digital, 1 minute or less per page transmission time, 200 lpi resolution, 4800 to 9600 b/s data rate.

- *Group 4.* Compressed digital, less than 1 minute per page transmission speed, 200 to 400 lpi resolution, data rates up to 64 kb/s.

CCITT sets standards for protocol, scanning rate, phasing, scans per millimeter, synchronization, and modulation method. Facsimile machines must be both phased and synchronized. Phasing is the process of starting the printer and the scanner at the same position on the page at the beginning of a transmission. Synchronization keeps the scanner and printer aligned for the duration of the transmission. Many machines are compatible with more than one CCITT group; for example, machines compatible with both Group 2 and 3 are common. Compatibility between Groups 2 and 3 should always be verified between machines of unlike manufacture because subtle differences may yield less than satisfactory results. Group 3 facsimile machines are essentially a commodity and only rarely incompatible.

Group 1 machines transmit a signal by shifting a carrier frequency between white and black levels. As with FM radio transmission, the constant amplitude of an FM facsimile signal is less susceptible to noise and amplitude variations than an AM signal. Group 2 machines modulate an analog carrier with a signal that varies in level or phase from white to black. This more efficient modulation system enables transmission of a page in half the time or less compared to a Group 1 machine. These analog machines can reproduce a full range of gray signal levels between the black and white limits.

Digital machines break a signal into dots, or picture elements, which are analogous to the pixels in a video signal. Unlike a video signal, which varies in intensity, digital facsimile produces a binary signal that is either on (black) or off (white) for each picture element. The number of picture elements per square inch determines the resolution of a digital facsimile and the transmission time.

Transmission times of all digital and some analog machines vary with the density of the information on a page. It is customary, therefore, to specify transmission time using a standard ISO test page called A4, which includes images, to help in making a subjective evaluation of quality and speed. Compared to Group 1 and 2 machines, transmission time is reduced in Group 3 facsimile by increasing the speed of the modem and compressing the data signal. Modem speeds of 9600 b/s are standard with most digital machines, with some lower priced machines capable of only 4800 b/s. As with other data signals, 9600 b/s cannot always be transmitted reliably over the switched telephone network, which sometimes results in the transmission slowing to 4800 b/s or less. As discussed in Chapter 7, low bit rate voice modulation systems are incapable of carrying 9600 b/s data signals. If a carrier uses ADPCM or another low bit rate method, facsimile transmission will be slow or impossible.

Group 3 facsimile uses data compression to reduce transmission time. Many documents have expanses of white or black that are compressed by a process called *run-length encoding*. Instead of transmitting a string of zeros or ones corresponding to a long stretch of white or black, the length of the run is encoded to mark its limits. Run-length encoding is either limited to horizontal runs or encodes both horizontal and vertical runs. By using run-length encoding, a digital facsimile machine compresses data into approximately one-eighth of the number of non-encoded bits.

Even with data compression, facsimile is a less efficient way to send text than ASCII encoding. For example, the standard pica type pitch is 10 characters per inch horizontally and 6 lines per inch

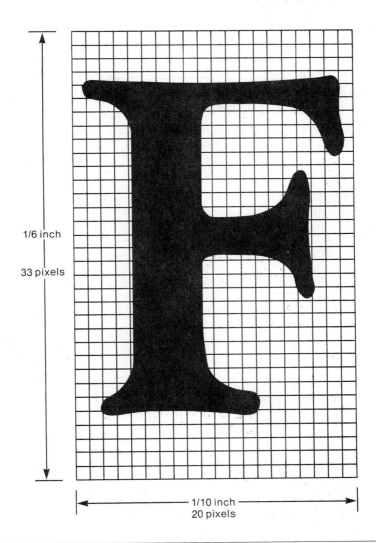

Figure 24.2 **Encoding a character with facsimile.**

vertically. To encode a character over facsimile with 200 pixels per inch resolution requires 660 bits, as Figure 24.2 shows. Assuming an 8:1 compression ratio, a character can be transmitted in about 80 bits. Compared to the 8 bits required to send a character in ASCII, facsimile requires ten times the transmission time. Because of this difference, it is more economical of circuit time to transmit data in alphanumeric coded form than by facsimile.

The lower resolution of Group 1 and 2 facsimile machines is acceptable for most forms of text where there is little ambiguity between characters, but analog modulation methods require considerably more transmission time than digital. As a result, Group 1 and 2 machines have all but disappeared from the market. Labor costs must be considered when deciding whether to pay for features such as automatic feed, document storage, and document routing for unattended operation.

Scanners

Document scanning produces either analog or digital output. Although many scanning techniques are used, a description of two representative techniques will illustrate how documents are converted to a signal for transmission over telephone lines. In the analog system illustrated in Figure 24.3a, a point source of light sweeps across the document. A photocell detects the reflection, which varies in intensity with shading on the source document. The photocell output produces a continuously varying analog signal that modulates the amplitude or frequency of a carrier within an audio passband. The digital modulation system illustrated in Figure 24.3b uses a row of photocells, consisting of one cell per picture element and corresponding to one scan line. The photocells detect light from the source and emit a 1 or 0 pulse, depending on whether the reflected light is above or below the threshold between black and white.

Printing

A facsimile machine uses one of several techniques for printing documents. The first two methods described below have stationary and movable styluses mounted above and below the paper. An electric current passing between the styluses through the paper changes the contrast of the paper in synchronism with the original image. The following printing methods are used:

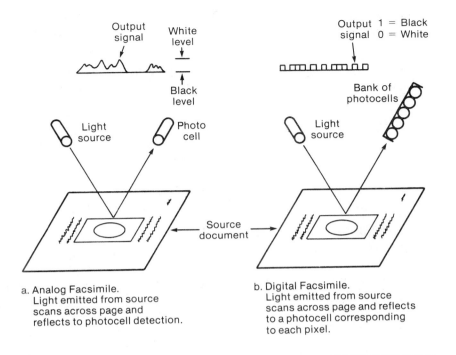

Figure 24.3   Analog and digital facsimile scanning process.

- *Electrosensitive.* This method uses paper with a special coating that burns off as current varies in proportion to image contrast.
- *Electrolytic.* Similar to the electrosensitive process, this process uses a paper with a special electrolytic coating. The paper changes contrast in response to changes in current.
- *Electrostatic.* This process is similar to that used by electrostatic copiers. The incoming signal impresses a charge proportional to the image on a drum. Toner is applied to the drum and then transferred under heat to untreated paper.
- *Dielectric.* This process is similar to electrostatic, except that a charge proportional to the image is applied to

treated paper. Toner is applied to the paper and fixed with heat.

- *Photographic.* The received image exposes light-sensitive paper, which is then chemically processed through a photographic stabilization processor.

- *Percussive.* Several techniques are used to apply an image directly to paper. In the ink jet method, the received signal drives a mechanism that applies droplets of ink directly to the paper in proportion to the signal. Other methods drive a hammer that strikes a ribbon to impress dots on the paper.

Facsimile printers vary in their ability to reproduce gray shades or halftones. Analog facsimile machines can reproduce a full range of gray tones, but digital facsimile machines can send only a black or white signal in each picture element. The degree of black intensity is regulated by the amount of resolution in the picture. Machines with greater resolution are more capable of reproducing halftones than machines with less resolution. The photographic process produces the best halftone quality.

Most machines today use treated paper, which has the dual drawbacks of impermanence and a tendency to curl. The image can easily be transferred to plain paper with a copy machine, but plain paper facsimile machines are also available. These are high end machines that include other telecommunications features.

Special Telecommunications Features

Some facsimile machines have features that make them complete document-communications centers, designed for attended or unattended operation. For example, stations can be equipped with polling features so a master can interrogate slave stations and retrieve messages from queue. In some machines the master polls the remote, after which the remote redials the master to send the document. Other machines have a feature called *reverse polling*, which enables the receiving machine to transmit a document on the initial poll. Some machines have automatic digital terminal identification capability and apply a time and date stamp to transmitted and received documents. Machines can be equipped with document feeders and stackers to enable them to send and receive documents while unattended and cutters to cut the document after each page. Some digital facsimile machines contain memory to store digitized messages and route them to designated addressees on either a selective or a broadcast basis. Most facsimile machines handle only standard letter or legal size paper, but some machines have a larger bed for handling oversized paper.

Organizations that have spare capacity on a data network may be interested in facsimile machines with private line capabilities. The digital signal is brought out to an EIA interface, where it can be connected to a multiplexer input like any other data device. This is particularly useful to companies that have data networks that are idle outside normal business hours. Facsimile traffic can be stored and transmitted at little or no cost. Private line facsimile machines often have dual port capability so they can double as a dial-up machines.

Alternatives to Facsimile Machines

Personal computer users do not have to have facsimile machines to communicate by facsimile, particularly to transmit documents that are stored in a personal computer. Two developments, PC facsimile boards and facsimile transmission over electronic mail networks, make it possible, with some limitations, to exchange documents between a personal computer and a facsimile machine.

Personal Computer Facsimile Boards

A board plugged into a vacant slot in any IBM-compatible personal computer makes the computer emulate a facsimile machine. Terminate-and-stay-resident (TSR) software enables the user to pop up a facsimile menu and send a document over an ordinary telephone line. Facsimile boards are Group 3 compatible and offer several advantages and some drawbacks compared to facsimile machines. If the personal computer has a scanner, graphics can be transmitted. Otherwise the facsimile board transmits only ASCII files.

The programmability of a personal computer offers features that are available only on expensive facsimile machines. Since the file to be transmitted is retrieved from a disk, a personal computer facsimile board can transmit a document or a list of documents to a list of different telephone numbers. With a conventional facsimile machine this is possible only with memory, which is an expensive option. The multiple document feature requires a document feeder, which also raises the price of a conventional facsimile machine. Signatures, logos, and other graphics may be integrated from a separate file. PC facsimile is also useful as a relay device. With conventional facsimile, each time a received document is rescanned and transmitted, it loses clarity. Since a PC facsimile is received and sent from a file, it can be relayed indefinitely without loss of detail.

Having a facsimile machine in a personal computer is either an advantage or a disadvantage, depending on how the system is used. For a single operator, a personal facsimile device is a convenience. If the facsimile must be shared by several people, the work in progress on the personal computer must be interrupted to send a document. If the facsimile is used primarily for text, a personal computer is highly satisfactory for sending. If the documents to be sent are a combination of text and graphics, it takes time to integrate the graphics, and if a scanner must be purchased to use the system, the total cost will be prohibitive.

Although a personal computer board is a satisfactory means of transmitting facsimiles, receiving is another matter. Not all facsimile boards operate in background mode, and those that do tend to slow down the personal computer while a document is being received. Received documents can be displayed on either the screen or printer. Since a personal computer screen is incapable of displaying an entire page in readable form, it is necessary to scroll the document. Some standard personal computers reformat the screen very slowly, and the resolution may be too low to read the document reliably. When a personal computer document is downloaded to a printer, the quality will be good, but the speed may be less than satisfactory. The built-in printer on a facsimile machine can print at about the speed at which the document is received. Even a laser printer attached to a personal computer may take several times longer to print a document than a facsimile machine.

Although the personal computer facsimile board has many applications, it should not be considered a substitute for a facsimile machine. Although the cost is lower than that of a full-featured facsimile machine, a facsimile board is less convenient for users to share, more time consuming for transmitting graphics, and less than adequate for receiving documents. The strength of the personal computer facsimile is in network applications. It makes it easy to send multiple documents to multiple recipients. The personal computer can receive a document, store it on a disk, and retransmit it without the loss of clarity that results from receiving and retransmitting a paper facsimile document.

Delivering Facsimile Via Electronic Mail

Most public electronic mail services offer facsimile delivery service. The user dials the electronic mail number, usually a local telephone number in larger metropolitan areas, identifies the addressee, and transmits the document. The electronic mail service delivers the document to the recipient's facsimile machine and returns a notice of delivery to the sender. The service tries several times to deliver to a busy or no-answer station before reporting non-delivery to the sender. Electronic mail is usable only for outgoing facsimiles, but it can be used to relay a message to the sender's own facsimile machine. Although receiving software was not available at this writing, software that will display a received facsimile on a personal computer screen or print it to a printer will undoubtedly be developed soon, in which case the electronic mail services will offer service almost identical with that offered by personal computer facsimile boards.

Electronic mail services can transmit documents with embedded graphics stored in their library. For example, a sender can furnish a logo and signature block, have them scanned and stored by the electronic mail service, and call them from storage with the transmitted document.

Group 4 Facsimile

CCITT has developed standards for Group 4 facsimile, which is a high speed, high resolution digital system operating at speeds up to 64 kb/s. Most IECs now offer a switched 56 kb/s service, which is an ideal medium for Group 4 facsimile. Resolution is from 200 to 400 lpi using high compression. The standard for Group 4 separates facsimile machines into three classes. All three classes

Table 24.1   CCITT Group 4 Facsimile Terminal Characteristics

SERVICE	CLASS		
	1	2	3
FACSIMILE	Transmit/-receive	Transmit/-receive	Transmit/-receive
TELETEX		Receive	Create/transmit/receive
MIXED MODE		Receive	Create/transmit/receive
RESOLUTION:			
STANDARD	200	200/300	200/300
OPTIONAL	240/300/400	240/400	240/400
PAGE MEMORY	No	Yes	Yes

support 100 picture element per inch resolution. Classes 2 and 3 have 300 picture element per inch resolution with options of 240 and 400 picture elements per inch. Table 24.1 lists the characteristics of the three classes of Group 4 machines.

In addition to offering the advantages of high speed and improved resolution, Group 4 standards can ease communications between word processors. Currently, memory-to-memory data transfers are a feature of communicating word processors. This feature is known as *teletex* (not to be confused with teletext, which is the transmission of information during the vertical blanking interval of a video signal). Most manufacturers now use proprietary protocols that are incompatible with the protocols of other equipment. Also, like other data terminals, word processors lack the ability to transmit graphic information. Group 4 facsimile standards make it possible to integrate facsimile and communicating word processors. To overcome the inherent disadvantages of each type of system, Class 2 and 3 machines send textual information in alphanumeric form and graphic information in facsimile form. Terminals capable of this form of communication are called *mixed mode*. Page memory is required for memory-to-memory transmission.

Group 4 facsimile standards are developed around the ISO Open Systems Interconnection model for data communications. See Chapter 3 for a description of the OSI model. Currently, Group 4 facsimile is not widely used for several reasons:

- Dial-up 56 kb/s circuits are not available to most companies.

- Group 4 machines cost several times as much as Group 3 machines.

- Many documents now transmitted by facsimile do not need the higher resolution of Group 4. Business culture will change to adopt Group 4 quality, which approaches that of a laser printer, when machines are more widely used.

Facsimile Line Sharing Devices

It is awkward to receive facsimile messages if the machine is not connected to a dedicated telephone line. Without a dedicated line, someone must answer the telephone and on hearing facsimile tones, manually initiate the handshake sequence with the sending machine. Several devices on the market enable the facsimile machine to share the telephone line with voice. Some devices answer the telephone with synthesized voice that instructs the caller to press a DTMF key to direct the call to a person. Otherwise, the device connects to the facsimile machine to initiate a facsimile session.

Some line sharing devices monitor the line for a voice signal from the calling end. If no voice is heard, the incoming line switches to the facsimile port. If no tones are heard, it transmits a voice message and monitors for voice. If a voice response is heard, it switches the call to the voice port. Other devices monitor the line for facsimile tones, and switch the line to voice if no tones are heard from the sending end. For residences and smaller businesses, a line sharing device can save money on dedicated telephone lines.

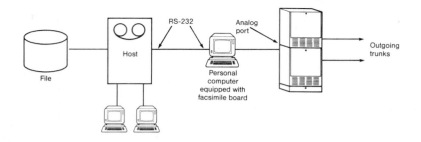

Figure 24.4   Using a personal computer equipped with a facsimile board to transmit documents from file.

Applications

The business application for facsimile equipment is in organizations that need rapid transmission of combined text and graphic information. Figure 24.4 shows an interesting application for personal computer facsimile boards used by one company that transmits many documents to a widespread group of recipients. Personal computers equipped with facsimile boards connect to ports on the host computer. Software in the host automatically downloads ASCII files to the personal computers with instructions to send them to a fixed address list. The personal computers automatically dial out when the rates are low and transmit documents to the recipients' facsimile machines. The personal computer software reports any irregularities in delivering the messages.

Standards

The principal source of facsimile standards is CCITT, which sets the standards to which most facsimile machines adhere. As with many other telecommunications technologies, equipment was produced and marketed well in advance of standards, resulting in some equipment that does not meet all CCITT specifications. Also, CCITT standards deal only with the protocols and line signals exchanged between machines. Manufacturers' specifications control other features intended to integrate facsimile into a network. Differences in storage, polling, machine identification, and other features may result in incompatibility with some machine functions, even among machines conforming to the standards of one CCITT group. Fortunately, incompatibility between facsimile machines is becoming increasingly rare.

Evaluation Criteria

The criteria discussed below apply primarily to the telecommunications aspects of facsimile. A discussion of the technical requirements and features of facsimile machines is beyond the scope of this book. Refer to the bibliography for further information on terminal equipment and operational considerations.

Transmission Facilities

Facsimile transmission facilities should be evaluated and selected on the same bases as voice and data circuits are evaluated. Group 1 and 2 facsimile machines use voice frequency facilities that should conform to the loss, noise, and echo criteria of a telephone circuit. Digital facsimile can be transmitted over either analog or digital circuits. These circuits should meet the same requirements as any other data communication service applied to the telephone network or to a public data network.

Some facsimile machines support either half or full duplex operation, but four-wire leased circuits are required for full duplex. Most facsimile applications do not require full duplex transmission, although if many documents are sent in both directions, savings in circuit costs may be possible by using full duplex. If transmission is in only one direction, it is possible to save money by acquiring receive-only and transmit-only machines instead of transceivers.

Compatibility

CCITT Group 3 standards were completed in 1980, so most digital machines manufactured before 1981 are incompatible with Group 3 unless they have been converted. Many machines can operate in two or three groups; if communication is planned with machines controlled by other organizations, this feature should be investigated. If possible, test transmissions should be made to determine the degree of compatibility with dissimilar machines.

Circuit Transmission Capabilities

If the circuit cannot support transmission at 9600 b/s, a facsimile session automatically downshifts to a slower speed. Some IECs may use voice compression techniques that will not support high speed facsimile, or lines may be so noisy that documents are consistently sent at slower speeds. The best way to evaluate this factor is to set up test transmissions. A benchmark can be established at 9600 b/s by sending over local circuits to another machine of known capabilities. The same document can be tested to IECs by dialing their carrier access codes.

Document Characteristics

The primary factors in determining which group of facsimile equipment to select are the document volume and resolution required. Digital machines are available at 4800 and 9600 b/s. The higher speed machines are more costly, but they save both labor and circuit costs.

Many machines offer a high resolution mode, which produces quality close to that of a letter quality printer. If copy quality is important, a high resolution machine should be selected. The need for halftones in documents also should be considered. Facsimile machines vary widely in their ability to handle halftones, with the level of gray scale varying from 0 to 64 shades of gray.

Labor saving features such as automatic document feed, paper cutter, automatic dial and answer, document storage, and document routing should be considered. If confidential information is being transmitted, encryption should be considered.

Document Memory

Many high end facsimile machines offer memory for document storage. This feature is useful for unattended operation. If the machine runs out of paper, received documents can be stored in memory. Multipage documents can be sent without fear of paper jams. Documents can be sent to address lists.

Selected Facsimile Equipment Manufacturers

Adler-Royal Business Machines

AEG Olympia

AT&T Information Systems

Brother International

Canon USA

Citifax Corp.

Fujitsu Imaging Systems of America

Harris/3M Document Products

Hitachi America

Iwatsu America

Konica Business Machines, USA

Medbar

Minolta Business Equipment Division

Mita Copystar America

Mitsubishi Electric Sales America

Monroe Systems for Business

Murata Business Systems

NEC America Inc.

Olivetti USA

Panasonic Communications and Systems

Pitney Bowes Facsimile Systems

Ricoh Corp.

Sanyo Business Systems

Savin

Sharp Electronics

Telautograph

Toshiba America Information Systems

Xerox Corporation Information Products Div.

Manufacturers of Personal Computer Facsimile Boards

American Data Technology, Inc.

Apple Computer, Inc.

AT&T Data Systems Group

Brooktrout Technology, Inc.

Brother International Corp.

Complete PC

Data Race, Inc.

Datavue Corp.

GammaLink, Inc.

Hayes Microcomputer Products

Hybrid Fax, Inc.

Intel Personal Computer Enhanced Operations

Microtek Lab, Inc.

OAZ Communications, Inc.

Omnium Corp.

Pacific Image Communications, Inc.

Quadram Corp.

Ricoh Corp.

SpectraFAX Corp.

Xerox Imaging Systems

Manufacturers of Line Sharing Devices

Tecom Northwest

Viking

Telecommunications Networks

The preceding four parts have discussed the building blocks: the switching systems, transmission equipment, and customer premise equipment. This part ties the elements together into private and public networks. Chapter 25 leads off with a discussion of how private voice and data networks are implemented. Most private networks contain elements of public networks, which this and the following chapter discuss.

Like all aspects of telecommunications, networks are continually evolving. Although the shape of the network at the threshold of the next century is not entirely clear, voice communications will undoubtedly be carried over a network that bears a strong resemblance to the integrated services digital network (ISDN), which is the subject of Chapter 26. Recognizing that the old principles of single-purpose analog subscriber loops and circuit switching are not sufficient to carry us into the future, CCITT has taken the lead in the development of standards for a new network architecture in ISDN.

Private networks convey the impression of large customers with many users of voice and data communications, and in the past, those did comprise the market for networks, but that is no longer the case. Local networks offer many companies, including small businesses, the ability to communicate over short distances. The personal computer has generated a need for local area networks to enable as few as three or four people to share files, printers, and disk space. There are so many options and such an abundance of equipment that two chapters are devoted to LANs. Another chapter discusses metropolitan area networks, which use many of the same techniques but permit high speed voice, video, and data communications over a metropolitan area.

Telecommunications managers must find the most economical balance between cost and service. Chapter 31, which discusses network design principles, explains how to make the tradeoffs between the amount of capacity provided and the amount of blockage users can tolerate.

Two chapters are devoted to an overview of network management and testing. Although these are largely outside the scope of this book, network management and testing systems are part of the technology, and understanding what they do and how they function is essential for understanding how networks operate.

The book concludes with a look at the future. We make no attempt to theorize on what might happen over the next 10 or 20 years. Instead, the final chapter discusses current developments that will have a significant effect on telecommunications in the future.

25

Data Communications Networks

The objective of a data communications network is easy to state, but difficult to realize in practice. The objective is to enable remote devices to function with their host as if they were locally attached. This means that response is nearly instantaneous, errors are practically nonexistent, and the resources of the host are available to the remote device. All this assumes that the host has sufficient processing power, because the network can do nothing to compensate for an overloaded host computer.

It is difficult to make sense out of data communications networks because there are so many options, none of which seems to fulfill all the requirements. For the past two or three decades, as data communications has gradually evolved to its present state, vendors have been years ahead of standard-setting agencies, and the result has been a helter-skelter procession of products, many of which are mutually incompatible. Even a single company's protocols may be incompatible with one another. The world leader in data communications is IBM, and by one count it had more than 35 telecommunications access methods before its introduction of Systems Network Architecture (SNA) in 1974.

More devices communicate over SNA networks than over any other single architecture, but considerable incompatibility remains, even within IBM's product lines. Most other manufacturers offer products that emulate SNA at some level but use proprietary protocols for communication with their devices.

Meanwhile, the International Standards Organization is putting the finishing touches on the first parade of standards for its

Open Systems Interconnect (OSI) model. Although most manufacturers have made gestures toward adoption of individual OSI standards, no major manufacturer has announced that its present architecture will be abandoned in favor of OSI. Many experts contend that OSI introduces too much overhead to meet the throughput requirements of future applications. Competing standards, such as the Transport Control Protocol/Internet Protocol (TCP/IP), have meanwhile carved a niche from territory OSI might claim, which impedes the introduction of OSI.

The world is on the threshold of significant changes in data communications. The hierarchical networks of the past are evolving into nonhierarchical or flat networks driven by the following trends:

- Applications such as imaging and CAD/CAM that demand greater bandwidths.

- Workstations that have processing power greater than mainframe computers had a few years ago.

- Replacement of dumb terminals by personal computers.

- Local area networking of personal computers, with a requirement to link LANs with an internet.

- Reductions in transmission costs that result from an oversupply of low error rate high speed digital fiber optic facilities.

- Emerging standards such as IEEE 802.6, Fiber Distributed Data Interface, frame relay, and cell relay.

- Evolution from centralized to distributed processing facilities.

- Compression technology that squeezes voice, video, and data in ever smaller bandwidths.

- Transition from single-vendor to multivendor networks.

One factor that the above list omits is the Integrated Services Digital Network that Chapter 26 discusses. Although the LECs will undoubtedly deploy ISDN, it will emerge slowly and have little immediate effect on most private line data communications applications. IBM's SNA and its companion product Systems Applications

Architecture (SAA) will continue to influence data communications networks heavily as they adapt to the changing environment.

This chapter discusses some important issues in selecting network equipment and facilities. Sections are devoted to SNA and SAA, to de facto standards such as TCP/IP, and to some emerging applications, such as electronic mail and electronic data interchange (EDI), that will propel future network architectures.

Data Network Facilities

The data communication user has several key decisions to make in selecting network facilities. This section discusses the primary network choices the user must make in implementing a data communication network. Decision points such as these must be considered:

- Will facilities be privately owned, leased, or a combination of both?
- If facilities are leased, will a single vendor furnish the circuits?
- Will facilities be terrestrial, satellite, or a combination?
- Does the application require switched or dedicated facilities?
- Is the application inherently point-to-point or multipoint?
- Is line conditioning required?
- Are digital or analog facilities required?
- Is there an opportunity to support other applications such as compressed voice and video on the network?

Private vs. Public Ownership

Private ownership is the rule with local area data networks, but in metropolitan networks the cost of right of way often precludes private ownership. Wide area networks are feasible for private ownership by only the largest companies. Most networks today are evolving toward a combination of private and public ownership. Such networks are one form of the *hybrid networks* discussed in Chapter 30.

Digital vs. Analog

Digital versus analog decisions are gradually being resolved in favor of digital circuits. New tariff offerings such as fractional T-1 are driving the network from analog to digital, so designers who choose analog facilities should do so with the knowledge that it is probably only an interim step toward an all-digital network.

Common Carrier or Value Added Carrier

A common carrier delivers data communications circuits to an interface point on the user's premises. The carrier transports the signal but does not process the data.

A *value added carrier* not only transports data but also may process it or add other services such as store-and-forward, error correction, and authentication. The carrier also may provide other message processing services such as electronic mail, filing, and message logging and receipting. The value added carrier furnishes the user a dial-up or dedicated interface and provides the equivalent of a private network over shared facilities.

Switched or Dedicated Facilities

The nature of the application determines whether it requires a switched or dedicated network service. With terrestrial services, the cost of a channel relates to length and duration of the connection. If multiple users communicate over distances greater than a few miles and send a few short messages, switched services tend to be most effective. If messages are long and the number of points limited, dedicated or private line services are most economical. Three types of switched services can be obtained.

Circuit switching is the connection of channels through a centralized switching system. The telephone network is an example of a circuit switched network. Its primary advantage is world-wide access to any location with telephone service. Another advantage is that messages cannot arrive out of sequence because the circuit is intact from end to end. Its disadvantages are cost, lack of error detection and correction capability, and limited bandwidth. As the LECs deploy ISDN, bandwidths will increase, and as the network evolves toward fiber optic facilities, errors will decrease.

Message switching, or store-and-forward switching, is a service that accepts a message from a user, stores it, and forwards it to its destination later. The storage time may be so short that forwarding is almost instantaneous, or messages may be stored for longer periods while a receiving terminal is temporarily unavailable or while awaiting more favorable rates.

The primary advantage of store-and-forward switching is that the sender and receiver do not need to be on line simultaneously. If the receiving terminal is unavailable, the network can queue messages and release the originating terminal. If instantaneous delivery is not important, the store-and-forward technique can make maximum use of circuit capacity. Its primary disadvantages are the added cost of storage facilities in the switching device and the longer response time compared to circuit or packet switching.

Packet switching, as described later, controls the flow of packets of information through a network by routing algorithms contained in each node. Stations interface with the packet nodes on a dedicated or dial-up basis and deliver preaddressed packets to the node, which routes them through the network to the destination.

Packet switching is flexible. During temporary overloads or circuit outages, service can be maintained by the dynamic routing capability of the network. Packet switching is also good for overseas applications because many network vendors have interconnection agreements that permit delivering packets world-wide. Its primary disadvantages are its cost and the delay that packet nodes introduce.

Terrestrial or Satellite Circuits

Communications satellites offer a cost-effective alternative to terrestrial circuits for distances of 1000 miles or more and to multiple destinations over shorter distances. Because the tariff rates of terrestrial circuits are distance-based, terrestrial circuits are less expensive over shorter routes unless the network has many terminal locations. Beyond a break-even point, satellite circuits are less expensive because their cost is independent of distance within the coverage field of a single satellite.

With all else equal, terrestrial circuits are more effective for data than satellite circuits. At longer distances, however, the greater cost of terrestrial circuits often offsets the disadvantages of a satellite. The primary disadvantage of a satellite circuit is the round trip propagation delay, which is approximately 0.5 seconds. Some protocols will not operate with this much delay. Other protocols function with reduced throughput because of error retransmission time. Satellite delay compensators, which Chapter 15 discusses, can alleviate some protocol problems, but they introduce additional end-to-end delay.

Another disadvantage of satellites is the lack of coverage by an earth station in some locations. If a common carrier owns the earth station, the cost of terrestrial links from the user to the earth station may offset any cost saving. If the end user owns the earth station, the cost of the station itself increases the cost of the data circuits.

Line Conditioning

As Chapter 2 discusses, ordinary voice channels have limitations that prevent the transmission of full duplex data above 9600 b/s. With line conditioning, voice channels can transport half duplex data up to 19.2 kb/s. Two types of line conditioning, designated as types C and D, are available from telephone companies.

Type C conditioning minimizes the effects of amplitude distortion and envelope delay distortion. See Chapter 2 for a description of these impairments. Conditioning levels are designated as C1, C2, C3, C4, and C5 in increasing order of control over distortion. Type D conditioning controls the amount of harmonic distortion on a data channel and controls noise to tighter limits than C conditioning.

Analog circuits generally need conditioning when the transmission speed is greater than 9600 b/s. Most modems contain adaptive equalizers that compensate for circuit impairments without conditioning at or below 9600 b/s.

Point-To-Point Network Technology

The first data communications networks consisted of teletypewriters wired to a common circuit. All machines printed all the traffic on the network; the operator removed messages from the machine, discarded those intended for other stations, and delivered messages to the addressee. Security in such a system obviously left a great deal to be desired, and the operation was labor intensive.

Addressing

To improve security and reduce the time wasted in screening unwanted messages, teletypewriter networks began to use addressing to select the receiving station. Using an electromechanical selector, the sender preceded messages with a call directing code that blinded all machines but the addressee. Many modern data networks precede messages with the recipient's address. This system is common in local area networks where all stations except the addressee electronically discard messages. Addressing has several advantages. First, it is simple to design and administer. Also, it is inexpensive because all machines share the transmission medium. Because the network has the characteristics of a large telephone party line, interference between stations may be a problem.

LANs use various methods to minimize interference. These are discussed in Chapter 27. Although stations are programmed to respond only to their addresses, it is not difficult to program a terminal to respond to all messages. It is even simple to connect a protocol analyzer to the network to copy all traffic. Therefore, if the application requires absolute security, encryption may be necessary.

Point-to-Point Digital Facilities

Most point-to-point and multipoint data networks use analog facilities and modems, but with the introduction of fractional T-1 services, networks are rapidly converting to digital. Very large users can justify communication over a digital satellite with earth stations mounted on their premises. Very small aperture terminals (VSAT) are reducing earth station costs to the point that private stations can be justified by many larger organizations. Satellite communication has certain drawbacks—primarily absolute delay—for some types of data protocols. Chapter 15 discusses these problems in more detail.

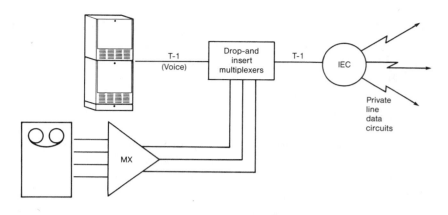

Figure 25.1   Sharing a T-1 to the interexchange carrier to support voice and data.

Private microwave and lightwave systems offer another alternative for digital communication. Facilities are privately owned or leased from common carriers. Digital microwave is covered in Chapter 14, and lightwave in Chapter 13.

Digital facilities are available in a variety of configurations from common carriers. AT&T has offered Dataphone Digital Service (DDS) for many years. Similar types of service are available from other carriers. Digital circuit speeds of 2.4, 4.8, 9.6, 19.2, 56, and 64 kb/s are common. The user can multiplex signals to lower speeds if desired. DDS service objectives are 99.5% error-free seconds and 99.96% availability. The carriers transport most digital circuits on lightwave and extend service to the end user over four-wire non-loaded cable facilities furnished by the LECs. Increasingly, the IECs deliver digital facilities over T-1 facilities that the customer obtains for both voice and data services. Figure 25.1 shows how a T-1 can provide entrance facilities for both voice and digital data.

DDS uses a bipolar signaling format that requires the user's data signal to be converted from the usual unipolar output of terminal equipment. A data service unit (DSU) located on the user's premises does the conversion. If the user's equipment can accept a bipolar signal and provide and timing recovery, the data signal is coupled to a channel service unit (CSU). Both units provide loopback facilities, so the local cable can be tested by looping the transmit and receive pairs together. The signal is fully synchronized from end to end. A DDS hub office concentrates data signals from multiple users and connects them to the long haul network. The hub is also a testing point.

Most IECs and LECs offer bulk digital T-1 transmission facilities at prices that are more attractive than those of multiple analog lines. The major interexchange carriers also offer the fractional T-1 services that Chapter 4 discusses in more detail. AT&T offers 56 kb/s and 64 kb/s channels in quantities of one, two, four, eight, or 12 channels. Other carriers may offer the service in different multiples. Unlike DDS, submultiples of the basic 64 kb/s channel are not offered, but users can further divide the channels with multiplexers.

Multidrop Networks

Point-to-point circuits are cost-effective only when there is enough traffic on the network to justify the cost of a dedicated circuit between two devices. Where the traffic flows in bursts or short transmissions, some method of sharing the circuit among multiple devices is needed. Such a method, typical of IBM's SNA network is *polling*.

Polling

A multipoint or multidrop network, as Figure 25.2 shows, uses polling to apportion access. A host computer connects to a circuit through a *front end processor*, which is a computer equipped for telecommunications. The front end processor's role is to relieve the host computer of teleprocessing chores. Each station is assigned an address code. The host polls the stations by sending short polling messages to the controller. If the station has no traffic, it responds with a negative acknowledgement message. If it has traffic, it responds by sending a block of data, which the host acknowledges. Before sending data to the distant devices, which are usually terminals or printers, the host sends a short message to determine whether the device is ready to receive. If it is ready, the host then sends a block of data.

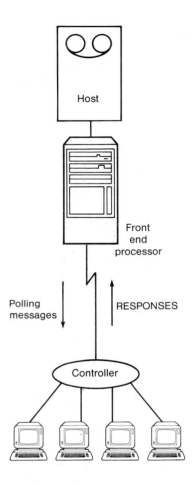

Figure 25.2   A multidrop network.

Multidrop networks are designed as full duplex or half duplex. In half duplex networks, the modem reverses after a poll or response. In full duplex networks, the devices can send data in both directions simultaneously. Polling is an efficient way of sharing a common data circuit, but it has drawbacks that limit its applications. First, the overhead of sending polling messages, returning negative acknowledgements, and reversing the modems consumes a substantial portion of the circuit time.

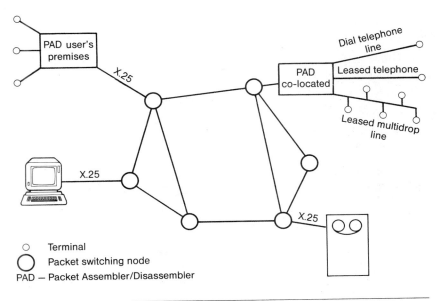

Figure 25.3 **A packet network showing access options.**

Throughput can be improved by using *hub polling*. In hub polling, when a station receives a poll, it passes its traffic to the host and passes the polling message to the next station in line. Hub polling is more complex than *roll call* polling and is not as widely used. Security is also a problem in polling networks. Any time stations share a common circuit, messages can be intercepted if the transmission medium can be tapped.

Packet Switching

Unlike circuit switched networks, which provide a circuit between end points for the exclusive use of two or more stations, packet networks provide *virtual circuits*, which share many characteristics with switched circuits. The difference is that the circuits are time-shared rather than dedicated to the connection. As Figure 25.3 shows, a packet network has multiple nodes that are accessed through dedicated or dialed connections from the end user, using one of several access options that are described later. The nodes control access to the network and route packets to their destinations over a backbone of high speed data circuits.

The packet assembler/disassembler (PAD) creates a packet when one of three things occurs:

- A predetermined number of bytes is received.
- A specified time elapses.
- A particular bit sequence occurs.

Packet networks are effective in both public and private implementations. The primary advantages of packet switching are:

- *Ready Availability*. Most computer manufacturers support the X.25 protocol.
- *Reliability*. Alternative paths can be built between packet switches, minimizing the effect of a switch or circuit failure.
- *Ease of Crossing International Boundaries*. Public data networks cover the major countries in the world. Time-consuming circuit setups are not required to begin sending data.
- *Economy of Multiple Sites*. Since costs are usage-based, small sites that often cannot justify fixed private lines can justify a connection to the nearest node.

Disadvantages are:

- *Delays*. Packet switches are subject to both packetizing and switching delays; the more nodes, the longer the delay.
- *Packet Overhead*. The X.25 protocol adds headers that reduce throughput.
- *Probabalistic Performance*. The response time of a packet network depends on load. During heavy load periods, response time deteriorates.

Packet Switching Nodes

The packet switching nodes are processors interconnected by backbone circuits. High speed analog or digital facilities operating at 9.6 or 56 kb/s are usually employed between nodes.

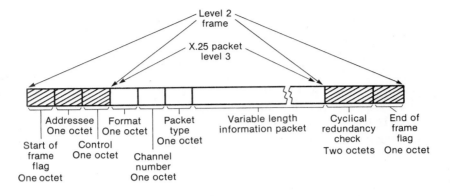

Figure 25.4   Level 2 frame enclosing X.25 packet.

Data flows through the network in packets consisting of an information field sandwiched between header and trailer records. Figure 25.4 shows the packet used by CCITT's X.25 protocol. Note in the figure that *octet* is the CCITT word for an eight-bit byte. The X.25 packet is enclosed in a frame consisting of a one-octet flag having a distinctive pattern that is not repeated in the data field. The second octet is an address code that permits up to 2555 addresses on a data link. The third field is a control octet that sequences messages and sends supervisory commands. The X.25 packet has three format and control octets and an information field that contains the user data. The final three octets of the trailer are a 16-bit cyclical redundancy check field (see Chapter 3) and an end-of-frame flag.

Packet Assembly and Disassembly

A packet assembler/disassembler slices the message into packets. The PAD communicates with the packet network using a packet network protocol, X.25, which a later section discusses. X.25 is a CCITT protocol recommendation that most public and private data networks use. The packet network uses the address field of the packet to route it to the next node on the way to the destination. Each node hands off the packet following the network's routing algorithm until it reaches the final node. At the terminating node, the switch sequences the packets and passes them off to the PAD. The PAD strips the data from the header and trailer records and reassembles it into a completed message.

Error checking takes place in each link in the network. If a block is received in error, the node rejects it and requests a replacement block. Because errors require resending blocks and because blocks can take different paths to their destinations, it is possible for blocks to arrive at the destination out of sequence. The receiving node buffers the message so the PAD receives the blocks in the proper sequence.

In many ways packet networks are similar to the message switching or store-and-forward networks discussed in Chapter 3. There are, however, there are several differences:

- Packet switching networks are intended for real-time operation. Message switching networks store messages for later delivery. Although the time is often short, it may be a substantial fraction of a minute.

- Message networks typically retain file copies of messages for a given period. Packet networks deliver the messages and clear them from their buffer.

- Message networks transport the message as a unit. Packet networks slice the message into shorter blocks and reassemble them at the receiving end.

A special type of message known as a *datagram* is available in some packet networks. A datagram is a single packet that flows through the network to its destination without acknowledgement. Although a market for this type of message exists, the X.25 protocol and the major packet networks do not support datagrams. An alternative to the datagram is the *fast select* message, which is a single packet and response. A typical application for fast select messages is the credit checking terminal that transmits the details of a transaction from a point-of-sale terminal and receives an acknowledgement from a credit agency's data base.

The network designer specifies packet size to optimize throughput. Because each packet has a fixed length header and trailer record, short packets reduce throughput because time must be spent transmitting overhead bits in the header and trailer. On the other hand, long packets reduce throughput because the switching node cannot forward the packet until it receives all bits, which increases buffer requirements at the node. Also, the time spent in retransmitting errored packets is greater if the packet length is longer. Most packet networks operate with a packet length of 128 to 256 bytes.

Virtual Circuits

Packet networks establish two kinds of virtual circuits, switched and permanent. *Permanent virtual circuits* are the packet network equivalent of a dedicated voice circuit. A path between users is established, and all packets take the same route through the network. With a *switched virtual circuit,* the network path is established with each session.

Packets consist of two types, data and control. *Control packets,* which contain information to show the status of the session, are analogous to signaling in a circuit switched network. For example, a call setup packet would be used to establish the initial connection to the terminating machine. An answer packet would be returned by the terminating machine. The network uses control packets to interrupt calls in progress, disconnect, show acceptance of reversed charges, and other functions that operators and supervisory signals control on telephone networks. Switched virtual circuit operations use these control packets to establish a session. In permanent virtual circuit operation, the path is pre-established and no separate packets are needed to connect and disconnect the circuit.

Public Data Network Access Methods

Access to public data networks is provided by one of three methods as Figure 25.5 shows:

- A dedicated X.25 link between the user's host computer and the data network.
- A dedicated link between the data network and a PAD on the user's premises.
- Dedicated or dial-up access over the telephone network into a PAD provided by the network vendor.

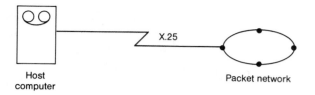

Host
computer

Packet network

a. User supplied computer and software on user's premises with
certified interface.

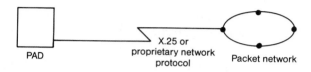

PAD

Packet network

b. User or network supplied PAD on user's premises.

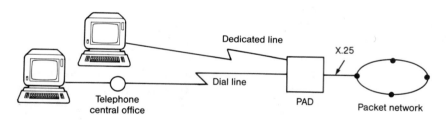

Telephone
central office

PAD

Packet network

c. Network supplied PAD on network vendor's premises with dedicated or
dial access, typically from asynchronous terminals.

Figure 25.5 **Alternatives for access to packet switched networks.**

In the first option, the user's host computer performs the PAD
functions. The second option requires either a PAD provided by
the vendor on the user's premises or a user-owned PAD that the
vendor certifies is compatible with the network.

The third option, dial-up access, is the least complex and is
the only method economically feasible for small users. It does,

however, have several disadvantages. The first problem is the loss of end-to-end error checking. Most networks and telecommunications programs support several asynchronous error checking protocols (for example, X Modem, Y Modem, and Kermit), but none is accepted as a universal standard. Those that personal computer telecommunications programs support substantially reduce the effective throughput of the data circuit. Modems with a built-in error correcting protocol such as MNP are a more effective method of error correction if they are available at both ends of the circuit.

Besides the error checking problem, the telephone network has other deficiencies for data communications. Data calls may progress through several switching machines, some of which may be electromechanical machines that introduce impulse noise. Also, local telephone service costs may not be effective for data communications, particularly where the LECs measure local service usage. Intermachine communication also requires code and speed compatibility, and unless the two devices are using identical protocols, they will be unable to communicate.

CCITT X.25 Protocol

CCITT's X.25 is an example of an important protocol that the OSI model uses. X.25 describes the interface between DTE and a packet switched network. It forms a network from the physical, link and network layers of the OSI model. The physical layer interface is the X.21 standard, a new digital interface that is not yet widely available. Another version of the standard, X.21 *bis*, is nearly identical with RS-232-C and is more commonly used.

The link layer uses a derivation of HDLC called Link Access Protocol-B (LAP-B) to control packet transfer, to control errors, and to establish the data link. CCITT recommends a similar version of this protocol, LAP-D, for ISDN. The third, or network, layer establishes logical channels and virtual circuits between the PAD and the network. The X.75 protocol recommends the interface for gateway circuits between packet networks.

X.25 is far from static. It has undergone several major revisions since its provisional introduction by CCITT in 1974. Little commercial use was made of the first issue, but it was revised again in

1980 to add many options that earlier versions omitted, and it has since gradually become accepted.

Although most data networks accept X.25 as a standard interface, its acceptance does not assure universal compatibility. The CCITT recommendations include many options, of which about two-thirds are discretionary. Therefore, public data networks accept X.25 connection from users only after the equipment vendor certifies the equipment as compatible.

Value Added Networks

Public data networks, also known as *value added networks*, provide an alternative to the telephone network for long haul data communications. The term "value added" derives from processing functions that are added to the usual network functions of data transport and switching. The value added services include such features as error checking and correction, code conversion, speed conversion, and storage.

Public Packet Switched Data Networks

Two nationwide networks, British Telecom's Tymnet and U.S. Sprint's Telenet have provided packet switching services in the United States since the 1970s. Several other networks offer packet switching service, and many LECs now provide packet switching within their LATAs. Because of the nature of the applications, most users require interLATA connections. These can be provided by the user as private lines, or the user can obtain a connection to a long haul packet network for the interLATA connection.

Public packet switching networks have developed more rapidly in Europe where it is more difficult to obtain private network facilities from the postal telephone and telegraph agencies. Public data networks in the United States can often transport data overseas by interconnecting through a gateway to a data network in another country.

Switched 56 kb/s Service

Several IECs and LECs offer switched 56 kb/s services, which allow users to set up 56 kb/s connections between locations equipped for the service. Switched 56 is intended for applications that need a digital connection for a time too short to justify the use of a dedicated channel—generally three or fewer hours per day. Examples are video conferences, high speed facsimile transmission, graphics, and part-time extensions to existing digital networks. As with other switched services, switched 56 charges are based on usage time and carry a rate slightly higher than an ordinary voice connection.

Transport Control Protocol/Internet Protocol (TCP/IP)

TCP/IP is a combination of two coordinated protocols, Transport Control Protocol and Internet Protocol. The protocols emerged from research that spanned three decades under the auspices of Advanced Research Projects Agency (ARPA). The agency is now called Defense Advanced Research Projects Agency (DARPA). ARPANET was a loosely confederated collection of networks operated by colleges, universities, and defense-related companies and agencies. In late 1989,the original ARPANET gave way to a network that now is known as the *Internet*.

The Internet is a series of independent packet switched networks that are interconnected to act as a coordinated unit. Each connected network agrees to carry transit traffic in exchange for the right to send its traffic through the Internet. Governmental agencies, military branches, educational institutions, and commercial companies operate the networks. The protocols compensate for the unreliability of the underlying networks and insulate users from the need to understand the network's architecture and addressing scheme. Internet has three primary purposes:

- To provide electronic mail service to the users.
- To support file transfer between hosts.
- To permit users to log on to remote computers.

The TCP/IP protocol has evolved over the years to become increasingly sophisticated. Although no standard-setting agencies sponsor TCP/IP, it is so widely used that most computer manufacturers support the protocol. It has achieved the status of a com-

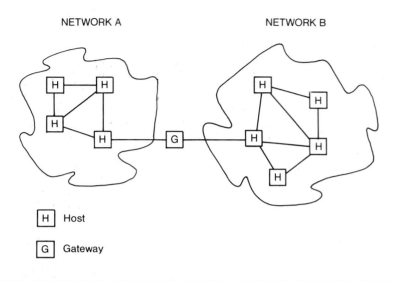

Figure 25.6   Architecture of a TCP/IP internet.

mon language between otherwise incompatible computers and will remain a de facto standard until OSI protocols are more universally accepted. TCP/IP is designed for operation on the Internet, but it is equally adaptable to communication within a closed network.

How TCP/IP Functions

Figure 25.6 shows the architectural structure of a TCP/IP network. The primary elements are hosts, gateways, and circuits. An individual network such as network A is called an *autonomous system*. An autonomous system is controlled by a single authority and linked to the Internet through a gateway. The members of the network have access to their *interior neighbors* by direct or indirect circuit connections. They have access to their *exterior neighbors*, which are the members of another autonomous system, only through a gateway.

Gateways are of two types—core gateways and non-core gateways. Core gateways have, through routing tables, information about the structure of the network. Non-core gateways have incomplete routing information; they know the route to a core gateway but have no knowledge of packet routing beyond the core. From their routing tables, core gateways boost each packet toward its ultimate destination, handing it from gateway to gateway until the packet reaches a gateway that has direct connection to the addressee. A stream of packets can travel over different routes to the destination and can arrive out of sequence, mangled, or not at all.

IP is roughly analogous to the OSI network layer, but it has some important differences. First, it is a connectionless protocol. Its basic transmission unit is the datagram, which, as discussed earlier, is a unit of information carried through the network without assurance of delivery. Unlike OSI's data link protocol, which ensures message integrity from link to link, IP lacks end-to-end error checking and acknowledgement. TCP takes care of those functions.

TCP is analogous to OSI's transport layer. Its function is to discipline an otherwise chaotic path through the Internet. TCP performs end-to-end error checking, correction, and acknowledgement. It resequences packets that arrive out of sequence and communicates directly with the application program in the host. Some host operating systems even include a TCP module.

TCP/IP Addressing

TCP/IP uses 32-bit addresses to identify hosts and networks. The addressing system was developed when 32 bits seemed more than enough, but it has subsequently become one of TCP/IP's limitations. There are three categories of addresses. Category A addresses have 24 bits for hosts and 8 bits for networks. Category B addresses have 16 bits for hosts and networks, and Category C addresses have 8 bits for hosts and 24 bits for networks. The 32-bit address makes it difficult to connect Ethernets, which have 48-bit addresses embedded in hardware. A special address resolution protocol (ARP) enables a host to find its target given its Internet address.

Gateways

Gateways are the key to a host's finding its way through the Internet. The host does not have to know the route to the destination; it needs only the route to the nearest gateway.

Gateways contain routing tables that the programmer enters or that the gateway builds by querying neighboring gateways. A gateway has detailed routing information for all directly attached networks and knowledge of where to send traffic for remote networks. If a gateway is unable to handle an address, it broadcasts an ARP message, which causes other gateways to aid in resolving the dilemma. Ultimately, if traffic cannot be delivered because there is no valid route to the destination, the network returns a delivery failure message to the originator.

Internet Protocol

IP is a laissez-faire protocol. The Internet lacks flow control and has no way of detecting duplicate, out-of-sequence, or lost packets. The gateways attempt to send messages over the shortest distance to the destination, but there is no assurance that a packet is always heading toward its destination. Every packet, therefore, contains a time-to-live field that has a maximum value of 255 seconds. If the time-to-live timer expires before delivery, the network discards the packet. This process prevents undelivered packets from traveling the Internet forever.

An Internet Control Message Protocol (ICMP) enables gateways and hosts to send messages over the Internet to other gateways and hosts to do functions that lower levels handle in the OSI model. For example, flow control is achieved by sending a Source Quench message to throttle back a host that is outstripping the recipient's ability to handle traffic. A Destination Unreachable message is returned when a route to the destination does not exist, and a Time Exceeded message is returned when a packet is killed because its time to live has expired.

Transport Control Protocol

TCP can be used with a variety of networks, not just IP. Its function is to receive messages from the applications program and break them into packets, which may be further fragmented for transmission on the Internet. Datagrams are received at the destination and reassembled into the original message. TCP hosts, therefore, must contain adequate buffering to resequence packets. TCP provides positive acknowledgement of the receipt of packets from

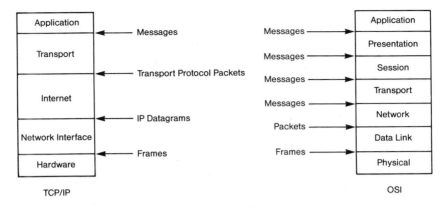

Figure 25.7   Comparison of the layered structure of TCP/IP and OSI.

the distant end. The sender waits for the acknowledgement, and if it fails to arrive before a transmission timer has expired, it retransmits the packet. This may result in duplicate packets, so the receiving TCP host must be prepared to discard them.

TCP uses a sliding window protocol to control the session between two hosts. The receiving machine acknowledges the number of correctly sequenced bits it has received and the number it is prepared to accept. If its buffers have plenty of space, it opens the window further, and when they begin to overflow, it reduces the size of the window in its next acknowledgement.

TCP/IP vs. OSI

The above discussion shows that there are significant differences between TCP/IP and OSI. TCP/IP's primary advantage is that it is an existing protocol that is widely supported, whereas OSI is not a protocol, but an architectural model against which protocols can be designed. The designers of TCP/IP intended that it would be used only until the arrival of suitable international standards, and then it would evolve to be compatible with a standard. Figure 25.7 shows how TCP/IP and OSI compare. Although both use a layered architecture, the functions of the layers are different and the functions of the protocols within the layers are dissimilar, particularly in the network layer.

The primary difference between the two is that TCP/IP lacks link-by-link error correction and flow control. These exist only in the transport layer. By contrast, in OSI, which also has end-to-end error correction in the transport layer, the data link and network layers present a more disciplined architecture. OSI has additional overhead, however, that may prove unacceptable for applications that need greater throughput. Also, the amount of error checking may be unnecessary with the lower error rate of today's fiber optic circuits. For example, fast packet, which Chapter 7 discusses, does away with link-by-link error correction in favor of the greater speed of end-to-end error correction.

Communicating between incompatible networks has been, and remains, a problem that the OSI model is expected to solve sometime in the future. Meanwhile, enough computers and other devices support TCP/IP that it has achieved the status of a de facto internetworking standard. Some observers believe that TCP/IP will disappear when OSI becomes more widely accepted. Meanwhile, applications developers are faced with the dilemma of which standard to support. TCP/IP has several benefits:

- It is a well-defined and widely accepted protocol.
- It carries less overhead than OSI and may provide better performance.
- There are plenty of experienced programmers who can implement TCP/IP.

OSI offers several advantages that will probably cause it to supplant TCP/IP in the future:

- It is an international standard.
- It probably has greater longevity than TCP/IP applications.
- It provides for accounting chargeback.
- It offers an expanded list of addresses compared to the 32-bit limit of TCP/IP.

IBM Systems Network Architecture

SNA is a tree-structured hierarchical architecture, in which a mainframe host computer acts as the network control center. The

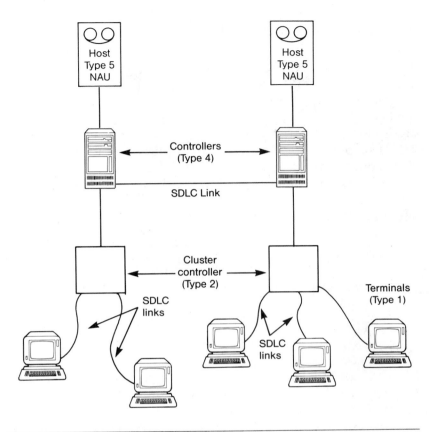

Figure 25.8   IBM Systems Network Architecture.

boundaries described by the host computer, front end processors, and cluster controllers and terminals are called the network's *domain*. Figure 25.8 is a diagram of two such domains linked by a communication path between two front end processors. Unlike the switched telephone network that establishes physical paths between terminals for the duration of a session, SNA establishes a logical path between network nodes and routes each message with addressing information contained in the protocol. The network is therefore incompatible with other protocols. SNA uses the SDLC data link protocol exclusively. Devices using asynchronous or binary synchronous can access SNA only through protocol converters.

The access method provides access to applications in the host computer. The most common access methods are Advanced Communications Function/Virtual Telecommunications Access Method (ACF/VTAM) and ACF/Telecom Communication Access Method (ACF/TCAM). These are normally abbreviated VTAM and TCAM respectively. VTAM gives an application more direct network control than does TCAM, which isolates the application from the network environment.

Network Addressable Units

The major components in the network are called Network Addressable Units (NAUs). SNA defines four types:

- Type 1—Terminals.
- Type 2—Controllers.
- Type 4—Front End Processors.
- Type 5—Hosts.

The host NAU is categorized as a System Service Control Point (SSCP). Each network contains at least one SSCP, which resides in an IBM mainframe computer. The SSCP exercises network control, establishing routes and interconnections between logical units. The end user interfaces the network through a Logical Unit (LU). The LU, generally a terminal or a PC, is the user's link to the network. The next higher unit in the hierarchy is a Physical Unit (PU). Although its name implies that it is a piece of hardware, a PU is a control program executed in software or firmware.

SNA's Layered Architecture

SNA is defined in layers roughly analogous to the layers in ISO's OSI model. Unlike OSI, however, SNA is fully defined at each level. SNA was first announced in 1974 and is the basis for much of the OSI model, but it differs from OSI in several significant respects.

Level 1, Physical, is not included as part of the SNA architecture. The physical interface for analog voice grade circuits is CCITT V.24 and V.25. The digital interface is X.21.

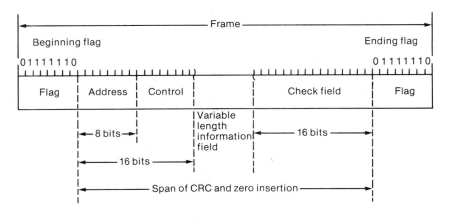

Figure 25.9   Synchronous Data Transmission (IBM SDLC frame).

Level 2, Data Link Control, uses the Synchronous Data Link Control (SDLC) protocol. Figure 25.9 shows the SDLC frame, which has six octets or bytes of overhead. The first octet is a flag to establish the start of the frame. This is followed by a one-octet address and a one-octet control field. Next is a variable length data field followed by a two-octet cyclical redundancy check field and an ending flag. The control field contains the number of packets received to allow SDLC to acknowledge multiple packets simultaneously. SDLC permits up to 128 unacknowledged packets, which makes it suitable for satellite transmission. This layer corresponds closely to ISO's data link layer and the LAPB protocol used in X.25 networks.

Level 3, Path Control, is responsible for establishing data paths through the network. It carries addressing, mapping, and message sequencing information. At the start of a session, the path control layer establishes a virtual route, which is the sequence of nodes forming a path between the terminating points. The circuits between the nodes are formed into transmission groups, which are groups of circuits having identical characteristics—speed, delay, error rate, etc. The path control layer is also responsible for address translation. Through this layer, LUs can address other LUs by terminating address without being concerned with the entire detailed address of the other terminal. This layer is also responsible for flow control, protecting the network's resources by delaying traffic that would cause congestion. The path control layer also *segments* and *blocks* messages. Segmenting is the process of breaking long messages into manageable size pieces so errors do not cause excessive retransmission. Blocking is the reverse—combining short messages so the network's resources are not consumed by small messages of uneconomical size.

Level 4, Transmission Control, is responsible for pacing. At the beginning of a session the LUs exchange information about factors, such as transmission speed and buffer size, that affect their ability to receive information. The pacing function prevents an LU from sending more data than the receiving LU can accept. Through this layer, SNA also provides other functions such as encryption, message sequencing, and flow control.

Level 5, Data Flow Control, conditions messages for transmission by *chaining* and *bracketing*. Chaining is the process of grouping messages with one-way transmission requirements, and bracketing is grouping messages for two-way transmission.

Layer 6, Function Management Data Services, has three primary purposes. Configuration Service activates and deactivates internodal links. Network Operator Services is the interface through which the network operator sends commands and receives responses. The Management Services function is used in testing and troubleshooting the network.

Layer 7, NAU Services, is responsible for formatting data between display devices such as printers and CRTs. It performs some functions of the ISO presentation layer, including data compression and compaction. It also synchronizes transmissions.

SNA lacks an applications layer as such, but IBM has defined standards that allow for document interchange and display between SNA devices. Document Interchange Architecture (DIA) can be thought of as the envelope in which documents travel. DIA standards cover editing, printing, and displaying documents. The document itself is defined by Document Content Architecture (DCA), which is analogous to the letter within the envelope. The purpose of the DIA/DCA combination is to make it possible for business machines to transmit documents with formatting commands such as tabs, indents, margins, and other format information intact. Documents containing graphic information are defined by Graphic Codepoint Definition (GCD), which defines the placement of graphic symbols on printers and screens.

Peer-to-Peer Communications

A drawback of SNA in the past has been the requirement that all data flow through the host. This condition was reasonable when terminals lacked intelligence, but as the terminal of choice evolved from dumb to intelligent, it became undesirable to have the host control every session between intelligent devices. PU Type 2 cluster controllers could support only one SDLC link and could not communicate among themselves.

IBM developed a cluster controller modification known as PU 2.1, which enabled two controllers to be linked across an SDLC or dial-up connection without requiring a path through the PU type 4 communications controller. Although PU 2.1 supports the physical connection, it does not provide all the logical functions necessary for peer-to-peer communications exclusive of the host computer. To enable device-to-device communications, IBM introduced the LU 6.2 Advanced Program-to-Program Communications (APPC) protocol. LU 6.2 does away with the SNA master/slave relationship between devices and, instead, permits communication between peers. Either device can manage the session, establishing and terminating communications and initiating session error recovery procedures without the involvement of an SSCP.

SNA Usage Considerations

SNA is not the only choice IBM users have for data communications between devices. Other options include the use of public data networks or private networks using packet switching, circuit switching, or other architectures. SNA can be connected to X.25 to permit intermixing of the two network architectures. SNA by itself, however, offers several advantages:

- It is mature. Developed in 1974, the architecture has undergone several evolutions and is reliable. The architecture is not static, however. IBM is constantly adapting it to changing conditions.

- The architecture is flexible. It can accommodate simple or complex networks and can communicate between networks.

- Because SNA is the most widely used data network architecture in the world, it enjoys a wide base of support.

- IBM can supply many office products under a single SNA umbrella, and offers a single source of support for many customers.

- The network has the power of IBM behind it, therefore assuring users of continuing support and compatibility with IBM's future enhancements.

Despite these advantages, SNA also has several limitations:

- It is not supported by all other vendors' products. Although IBM has taken steps to open the network to other vendors, many manufacturers have developed proprietary architectures instead.

- Installation and change procedures and protocols are cumbersome to administer.

- The network is not readily adaptable to dynamic alternate routing if failure or congestion occurs.

- The cost per device is high compared to other alternatives.

- SNA is suited only for data, not for voice communications. This limits the use of SNA in integrated voice/data communications.

Systems Application Architecture (SAA)

As we have seen throughout this book, voice and data networks are increasingly inseparable and are, in many companies administered under common management. A network manager's objective is to develop a design consisting of architectures and standards that facilitate control of the network. An effective network manager reviews higher management's policies, strategies, and objectives and develops an initial design to carry them out. The problem, however, is that management policies and strategies are easier to change than networks. Acquisitions and divestitures can change the organization's complexity overnight. A decision to open the company's data base to its customers and suppliers may be a strategic move that will improve the company's market position, but it increases the complexity of the network. In addition, the advent of the personal computer means the information systems manager no longer "owns" the network. Departmental networks and applications can spring up overnight, and higher management calls on the information systems manager to support them.

These trends, which are increasingly common in the 1990s, mean that information is dispersed throughout the network. Instead of a single corporate data base residing on a mammoth mainframe computer, an organization is likely to have multiple data bases. Without some unifying architecture, users find themselves with multiple passwords and ID numbers or, worse, with multiple special purpose terminals. The user's objective is simple to state, but complex to realize: ideally, users should merely state what information they need, and the network should retrieve it without the users knowing where the resource resides or what form it takes. Business needs, not technology, should drive the decision on where to place a resource.

IBM's Systems Application Architecture (SAA) offers a method that network and software developers can follow to ensure that the end user always sees the same thing when addressing a request to the network. SAA is a book of specifications that comprises three elements:

- Common programming interfaces.
- Common user interfaces.
- Common communications support.

When a user addresses a request to the local operating system, it is unnecessary to know whether the resource resides on the local host. If the requested resource is elsewhere, the local operating system sends a request to the network operating system, which locates the resource, and executes the request.

The logical engine that executes the request within SNA is Advanced Program-to-Program Communications (APPC), or LU 6.2, which was discussed in the previous section. An application program talks to the network operating system as shown in Figure

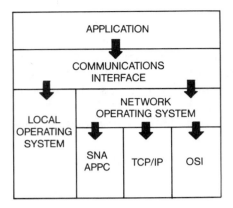

Figure 25.10   **In Systems Application Architecture, applications are independent of the network architecture.**

25.10. The network operating system talks to the network through its interface, which, in this illustration, could be APPC, OSI, or TCP/IP. The application program is not concerned with whether the network itself is SNA, OSI, TCP/IP, or another architecture.

The resource is located through a process known as Advanced Peer-to-Peer Networking (APPN), which is a standard feature of the IBM AS/400. To illustrate the principles of APPN, assume an eight-node network as shown in Figure 25.11. The user attached to Node A wants information that is in Node G, but neither the user nor the operating system in A knows where the information is. The user knows the name of the information, which we will assume is I, but knows nothing about the configuration of the network, the addresses of the various attached devices, or the line protocols that interconnect the nodes.

This network has two types of nodes. Nodes A and F are known as *end nodes*. They provide the attached users only with access to the network. The remaining nodes are called *network nodes*. They not only provide services to the users but also handle routing requests to other systems. Network nodes can perform the following functions:

- Determine the topology of the network.

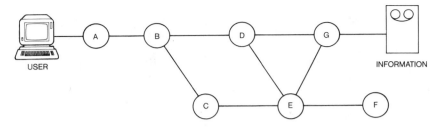

Figure 25.11 **Advanced peer-to-peer networking scenario.**

- Locate requested resources (directory function).
- Determine the optimum route for a session.
- Establish and supervise the session—control data flow, pacing, etc.
- Communicate with other nodes.

Each network node maintains a data base that is dynamically updated to reflect the status of the links. As a node encounters congestion in its links to an adjacent node, it updates its data base and passes the information to other nodes so they can update their data bases. The link information stored by the network enables a node to establish a route for a session, considering such requirements as bandwidth, security, encryption, and whether facilities are on a private or public network.

When a user requests a resource from a network node, the node searches its data base to see if it knows about the resource. If the resource is in its directory, the node establishes a session; if not, it initiates a broadcast search to each node in turn. Network nodes have information about their own resources and the resources of attached end nodes. When the node finds the resource, it updates its directory. With this update method, a node's directory never contains information that its users do not need. The node stores only information its users request.

The best route is determined from a combination of factors based on the user's requirements. A class of service is established to express such variables as priority, need for security, and whether the session is batch or online. The network evaluates the links and establishes a weighting value for each link. It selects the route with the lowest score from the weighting process. Following route selection, the nodes negotiate a set of rules for the session to optimize the use of network resources. The rules are for the duration of the session only and are established without the user's being aware that the process is going on. When the session is established, the nodes communicate the data and terminate the session when it is finished.

SAA is an emerging adjunct to SNA that is currently more theory than implementation. It expresses a direction in which IBM intends to take the network, however, and as such deserves careful consideration by network designers.

Electronic Mail

Pundits have observed, not altogether facetiously, that the mail today is delivered at about the same speed as the Pony Express. We've grown so accustomed to communicating at electronic speeds that moving a letter from sender to recipient in three or four days is unacceptable. The desire for instantaneous document communication has led to the rapid acceptance of facsimile transmission and the not-so-rapid acceptance of electronic mail. Much of facsimile's growth can be attributed to standards. A sender can purchase a Group 3 compatible machine and confidently expect that the receiving machine will produce a reasonable replica of the original with a minimum of difficulty.

Electronic mail has theoretical advantages over facsimile; for example, a page in ASCII form can be transmitted in less time and with superior quality than the equivalent page can be transmitted via facsimile machine. Documents can be transmitted to a list of addresses, with the user needing to establish only one connection to the e-mail host. The recipients of the documents can be in different time zones or different parts of the world and can receive on either a facsimile machine or a terminal. Also, the document can be manipulated in a word processor and retransmitted endlessly via electronic mail. The theory of e-mail is compelling, but the practice has been less than ideal for two primary reasons: the lack of standards and the difficulty an untrained person has in using the system.

The purpose of electronic mail has changed over the two decades or so of its existence. Initially, it was conceived as a medium for communicating textual information between individuals. Now, it is equally applicable to forwarding any type of electronic information including forms, graphics, and text. Information is communicated not only among individuals but among application programs as well.

Within a closed system, such as a local area network or a minicomputer, electronic mail is simple to use and readily accepted. It may even be implemented for little or no cost. For example, electronic mail is a standard feature of the Unix operating system that many computer vendors support. Unix-based computers can be linked electronically with UUCP, a Unix electronic mail system that enables diverse systems to operate as a unit. The major drawback of every private electronic mail system has been, however, the inability to move messages across multiple networks as easily as they can be sent in the user's own network. These difficulties are being overcome by second generation e-mail systems that support the X.400 protocol and provide the untrained user with an interface that is somewhat instinctive to use.

Second Generation Electronic Mail Systems

In electronic systems such as PBXs and computers the generations are rarely distinct, and vendors fail to agree on what constitutes a leap from one generation to another. Electronic mail systems are no different in that respect. First generation systems require the user to produce an ASCII file, which may require a file conversion. The user calls the electronic mail service, often over a dial-up line, using a separate telecommunications program. The file may be a message, or it may be separately stored with a message sent to the recipient to retrieve the file. The recipient complies with the message, responds, and retrieves the file, often conditioning it by removing hard carriage returns and restoring lost formatting.

There are many variations in first generation electronic mail systems, but generally they have these characteristics in common:

- The mail is transmitted through a different application program than the one in which it was created.
- The sender must know the recipient's address.

- The sender usually has to enter routing instructions to send the message to someone on a different network.

- Where multiple networks are involved, the sender normally must belong to (i.e., have a user identification for) all networks involved in the exchange.

The process is easy enough for anyone who has done it a few times, but learning the log-on procedures of a new network is bound to be intimidating to a new user and discourages the use of electronic mail. The process is a little like learning to use the telephone system in a foreign country (or trying to relearn how to use pay telephones in the United States); it takes time, but it is easy after you master the procedures. Many vendors of first generation systems have embedded the procedures in personal computer software, making the computer substitute for a trained operator.

Second generation systems are attempting to make electronic mail more transparent to the user. Software includes application program interfaces (APIs) that enable an electronic mail program to interface directly with the user's application program so that e-mail becomes an extension of an application such as a spreadsheet or word processor. Some vendors already offer the ability to send electronic messages directly from an application program; the API enables vendors to connect with applications programmed by others.

Second generation systems make it easier for users to exchange messages across networks. The networks themselves exchange directories so that all a sender needs to know is the address of the recipient; the network takes care of routing and delivery. The user's computer may not be connected permanently to the network, which would ordinarily present a problem in both message origination and receipt. Second generation electronic mail systems repeatedly attempt to deliver the message and notify the sender whether they failed or succeeded. The network takes care of any translation between machine languages and protocols. Effectively, the user says, "Here is my message and here is where I want it to go. You (the network) take care of the rest." Sending an electronic mail message should be as easy as making a telephone call, in which the caller needs to know only the identity of the called party. The caller is unconcerned with the route, the transmission medium, or the identity of any of the local exchange carriers that may transport part of the call.

X.400 Protocol

The ideal electronic mail system is being made possible by the X.400 message handling protocol. X.400 is the first application level (layer 7) protocol standardized by ISO and CCITT. X.400 establishes a standardized addressing and directory structure that makes it possible to exchange messages among devices produced by different vendors. The protocol is transparent to the type of computer and even the type of receiving machine. For example, it is possible to create a message on a personal computer, transport it over an X.400 network, and deliver it to a Group 3 compatible facsimile machine or a Telex machine.

The X.400 protocol has two major parts, the *user agent* and the *message transfer agent*. Although the user agent is nominally in contact with the user, the standard does not prescribe the method of user interface or message presentation; that is left up to the program developer. Messages are accepted from the user's application program and are posted to the message transfer agent for delivery.

The message transfer agent is concerned with delivery of messages not with their content. It forwards addresses to lower levels in the protocol stack for delivery through the network to the corresponding X.400 application at the distant end.

Currently, the primary application for the X.400 protocol is transferring personal messages. In the future, however, an increasing portion of electronic mail traffic will be machine-to-machine. Electronic document interchange, which is described later in this chapter, is a principal application of electronic mail. Also, electronic funds transfer will use the X.400 system.

X.500 Directory Service Standards

X.500 is a sister protocol to X.400, providing the "directory assistance" function. X.500 provides the structure with which users can search the listings of the network. It enables users to find subscriber names, locations, and lists of companies and users within the companies.

The X.500 protocol contains a Directory Access Protocol (DAP) and a Directory System Protocol (DSP). The DAP function is used between two X.500 systems, the user agent and the service agent. The DSP handles requests between directory service agents.

Now that the world has agreed on an electronic mail standard, it is predictable that an increasing volume of documents will be handled electronically. Anyone today can access one of the many electronic mail services to deliver messages to other subscribers of the same service. As the X.400 and X.500 protocols begin to be supported by public mail services, it will be easier to send messages anywhere in the world with assured, receipted, and immediate delivery.

Electronic Document Interchange (EDI)

Global markets are changing the way we do business. To remain competitive, businesses must know their customers and respond to their needs. In international trade it takes an average of 46 documents to move products across boundaries. EDI assists in standardizing the format and moving documents more expeditiously.

EDI was conceived more than 20 years ago, but its acceptance has been slow. Recent technical developments and emerging standards make it more important than ever that American businesses adopt EDI in international trade. Domestically, companies use EDI to shorten delivery time, simplify paperwork, and adopt a common language that trading partners can use in moving products.

EDI has received a boost by the Department of Defense's announcement that it will begin paying bills electronically. Defense is using the Corporate Trade Exchange (CTX) format to handle its bill paying. CTX is one of many formats that comply with ANSI's X.12 standard.

The government is taking steps to force companies and individuals with which it does business to use electronic communications. The Government OSI Profile (GOSIP) directed governmental agencies, including the Department of Defense, to adopt OSI or internetworking beginning in 1990. Since TCP/IP networks carry much of the Department of Defense's communication, the GOSIP regulations should hasten the transition from TCP/IP to OSI. Office of Management and Budget officials predict that 75% of all private transactions with the government will be handled electronically by the year 2000.

Telephone companies are considering the use of EDI for service ordering. Currently, most service orders are handled by telephone. And for the small business and residence customers, service ordering will probably be handled by telephone for many years to come. The major customers of the telephone companies such as the IECs represent a large portion of their business, and handling documents by EDI would improve both timeliness and accuracy.

Adopting EDI is not a technological hurdle; it is a business hurdle. The technology is simple to set up, but it requires companies to adopt new ways of doing business.

EDI Standards

There are four types of EDI standards:

- Proprietary.
- Non-compliant and industry-specific.
- National, such as ANSI X.12.
- International, such as EDIFACT (EDI for Administration, Commerce, and Transport).

EDIFACT is a set of EDI standards developed under the auspices of the United Nations. As with many other standards, it is a compromise—an amalgamation of the desires of many agencies. Nor is it yet a fully formed standard. At the time of this writing, the EDI data dictionary and syntax are approved as ISO 9370 and 8735 respectively, but the implementations are not yet developed for the full set of documents. At present, the following documents have been adopted:

- Invoice.

- Purchase Order.
- Quality Data Message.
- International Forwarding and Transport Message.
- Customs Declaration.
- Customs Response.

Currently, EDIFACT is too immature to be integrated into domestic applications. Unless international trading partners demand adherence to EDIFACT documents, it is better to stay with present ANSI standards and be prepared to adapt as the need develops. Eventually, ANSI X.12 and EDIFACT will probably reach a common ground. Meanwhile, companies must be prepared to support multiple standards.

Applications

Data network applications can be separated into the following general types:

- *Inquiry/response.* This is typical of information services where a short inquiry generates a lengthy response from the host. Because the data flow is much greater in one direction than in the other, half duplex facilities generally offer the greatest throughput. Either dedicated or dial-up facilities can be used depending on two primary factors, cost and setup time. If sessions are held occasionally, setup time is not a significant factor, but if many sessions are established each day, the time required to dial the connection may mandate a dedicated line.
  Applications that are typical of inquiry/response are airline reservations and rental car checkout. The operator keys a few characters into the terminal, and the host computer responds with a lengthy message that might be confirmation of a reservation, a printed ticket, or an automobile rental agreement. Many remote queries into a central data base are also typical inquiry/response applications. A user may log on to a remote data base, construct a query, and receive a lengthy response.

- *Conversational.* This mode, typical of terminal-to-terminal communication, is characterized by short messages that are of approximately equal length in both directions. Throughput is improved by using full duplex operation.

  A typical inquiry/response session is credit card verification, in which calls are made to a central data base. The query consists of the credit card number and amount of purchase. The response consists of a confirmation number. Low usage establishments dial the nearest node, often via 800 number. High usage establishments use a dedicated line.

  Conversational mode is typical of many data circuits that link LANs via remote bridges. Users log on to remote file servers and, in an application such as word processing, send approximately equal amounts of data in each direction when files are retrieved and periodically saved.

- *Bulk data transfer.* This is typical of applications such as mainframe-to-mainframe communications where large files are passed, often at high speed, in only one direction. This method is often used when a local processor collects information during the day and makes daily updates of a master file such as an inventory on the host. Bulk data transfer is usually a half duplex operation because large amounts of data flow in one direction with the line reversed periodically to return an acknowledgement.

- *Remote job entry.* This is typical of applications in which terminals send information to a host. The bulk of the transmission is from the terminal with a short acknowledgement from the host. Half duplex circuits may be the most effective form of transmission because the bulk of the information flows from remote to host.

Dedicated lines are almost invariably needed for this kind of application. Many remote terminals, each of which is used only occasionally, share a higher speed line to the host. Multiple terminals make dial-up too costly to be feasible.

Standards

CCITT sets international data network standards, with supporting U.S. standards set by ANSI, EIA, and major equipment vendors whose products take on the character of de facto standards. For example, in data communications, IBM's Systems Network Architecture (SNA) is so widely used as to constitute a de facto standard. The primary CCITT and EIA standards that affect data communications networks are included in Appendix B.

Evaluation Considerations

The criteria used to evaluate data networks differ significantly from those used to evaluate voice networks. For example, the short length of many data messages makes setup time, which is of little concern in voice networks, an important factor. Also, error considerations are important in data networks. Circuit noise that is merely annoying in a voice network may render the channel unusable for data. Also, because many data networks' billing is not distance sensitive and because billing is based on volume rather than connect time, cost evaluations are significantly different for the two types of network.

Digital or Analog Facilities

Although most data circuits are analog today because of the analog local loops, the IEC facilities are largely digital. Increasingly, the local loop facilities are also becoming digital, and as analog circuit prices increase and digital prices drop, facilities will evolve to the point that the majority are digital.

Digital circuits do not require a modem; instead, DTE connects through a CSU/DSU which often is built into the DTE device. Common carrier network services such as AT&T's Dataphone Digital Service (DDS) provide the equipment to multiplex circuits from the base speed of 2.4 to 56 kb/s up to the backbone transmission speed of 1.544 mb/s. At the distant end, the speed is demultiplexed to the base speed. Chapter 4 discusses this method of deriving digital circuits. Bulk digital circuits operating at 1.544 mb/s (T-1) are also widely available. To apply these services, the user supplies the multiplexers to subdivide the wideband channel into narrow data or voice channels.

Digital facilities have the additional advantage of providing improved performance. The carrier can monitor the bit error rate performance of backbone circuits and take corrective action when it exceeds the advertised limits. Also, as such circuits are inherently full duplex four-wire circuits and have no modems, the time consumed in modem reversals and modem failures is eliminated.

The trend in both metropolitan and long haul circuits is toward the use of digital facilities. Although these circuits are more expensive than analog facilities, several developments, including the construction of long haul fiber optic facilities and fractional T-1 tariffs, are reducing the cost of using them.

Reliability and Availability

Data circuit reliability is the frequency of circuit failure expressed as mean time between failures (MTBF). A related factor is circuit availability, which is the percentage of time the circuit is available to the user. Availability depends on how frequently the circuit fails and how long it takes to repair it. The average length of time to repair a circuit is expressed as mean time to repair (MTTR). The formula for determining availability is:

$$(MTBF{-}MTT) \; x \; \frac{100}{MTBF}$$

For example, a circuit with an MTBF of 1000 hours and an MTTR of 2 hours would have an availability of:

$$(1000 - 2) \; x \; \frac{100}{1000} = 99.8\%$$

It is important to reach with the supplier an understanding of the conditions under which a circuit is considered failed. When the circuit is totally inoperative, a failure condition clearly exists, but when a high error rate impairs the circuit, it is less clear whether the service is usable. The error rate in a data circuit is usually expressed as a ratio of error bits to transmitted bits. For example, a data circuit with an error rate of 1×10^{-5} will have one bit in error for every 100,000 bits transmitted. Reliability and error rate have a significant effect on throughput. Most error correction systems initiate retransmission of a block, and retransmission of blocks reduces throughput.

Costs

Cost comparisons between public data networks are difficult to make because of differences in the way data is handled. Cost depends on how the network handles messages and renders bills for usage. To compare a network that bills on a character basis with one that bills on a packet basis, the administrator should determine whether the costs of partially filled packets tend to outweigh slightly higher per-character transmission costs. The geographic area to be covered has a significant effect on the cost of public data network services. Costs are higher in low density areas. With dial access, the cost of measured local telephone service or long distance charges to the node when none is available in the locality must be considered.

Network Setup Time

Setup time is critical to most data applications. When using dial access over a public data network, setup time is significant—often longer than message transmission time. Whether data communication is conducted over a public data network or the telephone network, however, call setup time is apt to be equivalent. Dedicated access to a public data network eliminates the dialing, answer, and authentication routines, greatly reducing call setup time. The time it takes to establish a session through the network to the terminating station remains a significant factor and is comparable whether dial or dedicated access to the public data network is used. This time can be reduced by using a permanent virtual circuit, if offered by the network, which establishes a preassigned and dedicated path between terminals.

Response Time

Response time in a data communications network is evaluated by analyzing the time required for each step of the process shown in Figure 25.12. Response time definitions vary, but the most generally accepted definition and the one used here, is the interval between the time the terminal operator sends the last character of a message and the time the first character of the response from the host arrives at the terminal.

Note that modem reversal time applies only to half duplex circuits. In public data networks the, model shown can be simplified to eliminate the waiting times on input and output. The transit time of a public data network can be substituted for the

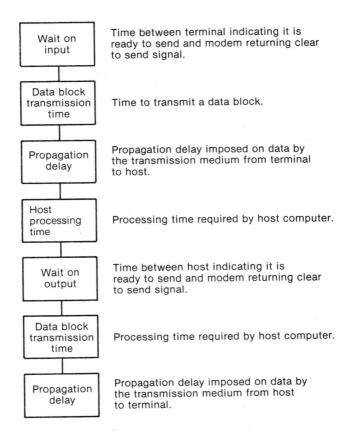

Figure 25.12   Generalized data network response time model.

medium propagation delay. Response time is affected by packet size and the process the network uses in handling packets and assembling messages. The considerations in evaluating response time are:

- *Type of Protocol.* A full duplex protocol eliminates modem turnaround time. Block protocols are more sensitive to absolute delay. Error recovery methods affect response time.

- *Modem Reversal Time* varies with modem design in circuits using half duplex protocol. The shorter the reversal time, the more rapid the response time.

- *CPU Response Time* is independent of the telecommunications network and has no effect on the choice of data communications facilities.

- *Absolute Delay* varies with the type of transmission medium and the choice of network alternative. Satellite services interpose a minimum delay that cannot be reduced except by operating one direction of transmission over terrestrial facilities. Packet networks introduce delays that may vary with load.

- *Error Rate* affects the number of rejected messages that must be retransmitted and thus increases response time.

For additional information on evaluating response time, refer to *The Dow Jones-Irwin Handbook of Telecommunications Management* or one of the books on data network design listed in the bibliography.

Type of Interface

Value added networks provide three general types of interface as shown in Figure 25.5. Small users are usually limited to dial access. Large users requiring end-to-end error checking will select an interface using a PAD or host computer on the user's premises. The primary considerations are:

- Certification of compatibility with the network.
- Lease versus ownership cost comparisons for interface equipment.
- Transmission speed supported by the interface.
- Type of terminals and protocols supported by the PAD.
- Number of devices supported.

Features

Data communications features required by the user should be examined and compared to the services available from the different data communications network alternatives. Features to be considered include:

- *Virtual circuit or datagram service.* Users with very short messages may require a datagram or fast select service.

- *Type of message delivery*. Consider whether message delivery is to be automatic or delayed awaiting a busy or unattended terminal.

- *Message storage or electronic mail services* may be offered by the network or a value added service on the network.

- *Multidestination message service*. Consider whether it is important to broadcast messages to many stations simultaneously.

- *Billing service*. Consider whether detailed call accounting is required or whether message charges are bulked to a user number.

- *Security*. Networks should offer password security and also should offer encryption and a private storage facility that can be unlocked only with an additional private code.

- *Closed user groups*. These are private networks within the network that are designated for the exclusive use of users who gain access only with proper authentication. They are used either for terminal-to-terminal communication or for privately accessed store-and-forward service.

- *Protocol conversion*. Communication between terminals using unlike protocols may be supported by the network.

- *Disconnect of idle stations* should be provided.

- *Abbreviated or mnemonic addressing* may be provided, with the system generating the data network number from a simplified address.

Line Conditioning

High speed analog private line data transmission facilities may require conditioning. Type C conditioning improves the attenuation distortion and envelope delay distortion in the facility. Type D conditioning also improves noise performance and harmonic distortion of the circuit. Some types of modems equipped with adaptive equalization may not require conditioning, but other modems will require conditioned lines at 9600 b/s. Now that fiber optic circuits comprise most of the interexchange network, an analog circuit may be completely digital except the local loops. In such circuits, conditioning may be unnecessary.

Availability

Data networks are evaluated by their availability, which measures the percentage of time the network is available for service and the number of error-free seconds provided by the network. Availability should run as close to 100% as possible—typically at least 99.9%. It is affected by the failure rate and redundancy in network paths and switching equipment. The error-free second criterion applies only to facilities. If the network provides an end-to-end error checking process, transmission can be presumed to be error free.

Selected Vendors Of Data Network Services

Packet Switched Network and Value Added Services

ADP Autonet

AT&T

British Telecom Tymnet

CompuServe, Inc.

Computer Sciences Corporation

Grafnet, Inc.

MCI Telecommunications Corporation

RCA Cylix Communications Network

Other Data Communications Network Services

AT&T

MCI Telecommunications Corporation

ITT Worldcom

RCA Americom

RCA Global Communications

Uninet, Inc.

U. S. Sprint

Williams Telecommunications

26

The Integrated Services Digital Network

It is commonly acknowledged that the weak point in today's telecommunications networks is the local loop. Loops are expensive, required on virtually every service, and can be used for only one service at a time. Also, they tend to be noisy, and cause data transmission errors. The best thing that can be said for today's loop plant is that it is already in place and works reasonably well. Billions of dollars are invested in copper wire, conduit, pole lines, buried cables, and all the other elements that comprise loop plant. There is not a great groundswell of demand that it be replaced, and the cost to do so would be enormous.

It is also commonly conceded that if we were to start all over again to design a telecommunications system, it would be designed differently. The network would not be partially analog and partially digital; it would be all-digital with a consequent reduction in error rates, increase in bandwidth, and improvement in transmission quality. Loops would not only be digital, they would be multiplexed so they could carry more than one type of service. The same loop would transport voice, data, graphics, video—whatever form the information took..

Today's telecommunications networks give users little control over their options. Networks are either circuit switched, packet switched, or private. Separate local loops are provided for every service; telephone circuits have two-wire loops, data circuits usually have four-wire loops, other special services such as alarm circuits have either two- or four-wire loops, and all services can be rearranged only with the participation of the telephone company. Although the internal networks of the LECs and IECs are largely digital, users do not realize the benefits of end-to-end digital connectivity because of the analog local loops and analog switching systems.

Both voice and data circuits can have either a digital or an analog interface, but the interface and terminating equipment are far from uniform. Public data networks have different interfaces from those of the telephone network, and video networks such as CATV have yet another type of interface. Furthermore, the networks are incapable of handling information interchangeably. Analog voice networks are slow and inefficient at handling data, and low speed data networks are ineffective for voice transmission.

Integrated Services Digital Network Technology

The next step in the evolution of telecommunications services is the Integrated Services Digital Network (ISDN). A network architecture based on standards set by CCITT, ISDN supports any combination of voice, data, and video services over a unified network. ISDN standards are based on the ISO Open Systems Interconnect model. They specify physical, data link, and network layer protocols for the physical interface and electrical characteristics for the network. The standards specify how information is encoded and how supplementary services such as calling features are provided. As with present telecommunications networks, ISDN has a local and an interexchange element. An LEC usually provides the local element, and an IEC furnishes the interexchange element. When ISDN is fully deployed, users in the United States will be served by a single LEC and will have a choice of multiple IECs, just as they have today.

ISDN improves telecommunications services and potentially reduces cost in several ways:

- End-to-end digital connectivity results in improved transmission quality.

- The need for special DCE apparatus such as modems and CSUs will be eliminated.

- Local loops will carry multiple communications channels.

- Users will reassign channels from one communications service to another without involving the LEC.

- Much greater bandwidth will be available from the local loop than with analog technologies; the bandwidth increase is 15-fold.

Whether an actual cost reduction will result from ISDN is open to question. To implement the service, LECs must invest enormous sums in improving local loops and replacing or upgrading switching systems. Furthermore, not all users need the services ISDN can provide. Residential customers can profit from having only one circuit to carry a second telephone line, but they rarely need end-to-end digital service or the ability to reassign services between channels. Many new services that ISDN makes possible are desirable, but it is questionable how many residential customers will be willing to pay for them. In the future, most experts predict that video service will be compressed to 64 kb/s, which will open the way for video telephones. Until technical limitations are overcome, ISDN probably will be primarily a business service.

Future network intelligence will allow the user to instruct the network to respond differently according to time of day, day of week, or identity of the calling party. Incoming calls will be treated with the same kind of discrimination the caller himself would receive if he arrived in person. For example, nuisance calls can be turned away, priority callers can be shunted to trained specialists, and callers can leave voice or data messages when it is unnecessary to speak in person with someone at the receiving end. Dedicated services will be rearranged by users without the need for intervention by the carrier.

ISDN enables the LECs to introduce to their customers a range of services that generally are covered under the umbrella of Custom Local Area Signaling Services (CLASS), which will generate more revenue. The suite of services that will be offered under CLASS is not yet fully defined, and some of those services are still subject to challenge. Chapter 9 discusses CLASS services in more detail.

It is likely that most CLASS services will be offered by some LECs, and it is certain that additional services will be developed. These services will be spotty at first because their full implementation depends on the end offices being linked by Signaling System No. 7 (SS7), which Chapter 11 discusses. Many CLASS services can be delivered from existing central offices, so these services are not necessarily the features that will drive the transition to ISDN.

Since the calling party's identification is transmitted with the signaling message, the user has the opportunity to handle the call in a variety of ways, either manually or under processor control. The call could be selectively forwarded, rejected, sent to an answering point, or asked to hold. The central office could deliver a distinctive ring to the called party's premises. This feature has tremendous potential for eliminating annoyance calls and for selectively handling important calls, but groups such as the American Civil Liberties Union have challenged calling party identification as a violation of privacy. Before these services are universally authorized, they will undoubtedly be subjected to further court challenge.

Another potential CLASS service is wide area Centrex. Centrex services now must be switched in the same wire center, which makes them expensive across a multiwire center city. With SS7, lines furnished from several central offices can be made to appear as if they were served from a single office.

ISDN implementation will not occur spontaneously. Instead, it will gradually evolve as LECs provide the switching and local loop facilities and service providers offer services based on ISDN standards. At this writing the major LECs are completing or have completed ISDN trials that test the equipment and services, and many are offering a limited introduction of ISDN—usually in the core business regions of major metropolitan areas. The pace of ISDN development will be driven by two primary factors: the availability of services and the schedule under which the LECs will replace or modify their central offices.

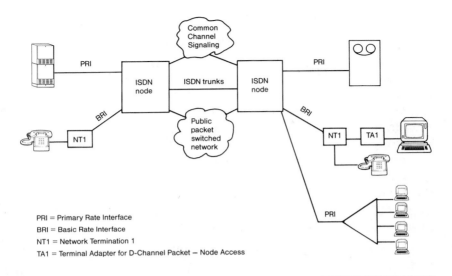

PRI = Primary Rate Interface
BRI = Basic Rate Interface
NT1 = Network Termination 1
TA1 = Terminal Adapter for D-Channel Packet — Node Access

Figure 26.1   ISDN architecture.

ISDN Architecture

The architecture of ISDN, as shown in Figure 26.1, was approved by a 1984 plenary assembly of CCITT and updated by the 1988 session, providing the foundation for cooperating nations to build upon. The objectives of ISDN are:

- To provide end-to-end digital connectivity.

- To gain the economies of digital transmission, switching, and signaling.

- To provide users with direct control over their telecommunications services.

- To provide a universal network interface for voice and data.

The basic building block of ISDN is a *bearer* or B channel. A B channel is a 64 kb/s clear channel, which means that no bits are robbed for signaling. Signaling takes place over a 16 kb/s D channel, which carries call-control information. When the D channel is not being used for signaling, it can be used for carrying X.25 packets, which makes it useful for electronic mail and signaling.

Customer services are delivered over two standard interfaces, the Basic Rate Interface (BRI) and the Primary Rate Interface (PRI). The BRI consists of one D and two B channels (2B +D) for an aggregate line speed of 144 kb/s. The BRI directly terminates customer premises equipment such as ISDN telephones and data terminating equipment. A PRI in North America consists of 23 B channels and one 64 kb/s D channel for an aggregate line speed of 1.536 mb/s. A 31-channel standard is used in Europe and in countries that use the 2.048 mb/s T-1 standard. Most often the PRI is connected to a digital PBX, but it also can be connected to a multiplexer or any other device that supports directly connected T-1.

An ISDN node is a digital switching system that includes terminations for handling both circuit switched and packet switched traffic. ISDN nodes are interconnected by SS7 data links. ISDN nodes can also be connected to non-ISDN central offices over SS7-supported trunks and links.

ISDN Standards

ISDN standards are based on OSI. Figure 26.2 shows the major CCITT standards that have been set and how they relate to the OSI model. The physical layer specifies the movement of bits over the physical medium. The data link layer comprises the Link Access Protocol D (LAPD), which permits multiple terminal devices to communicate with higher level devices in ISDN. The Level 3 protocol, Q.931, is the signaling protocol that provides for call setup, supervision, and disconnection. The first two layers are well defined, and have been implemented in chip sets. The Level 3 protocols are not yet stable; for example, many fundamental features are not covered by Q.931. Supplementary services, which will be covered by Q.932, are not standardized yet. They will be submitted for ratification at the 1992 plenary session of the CCITT.

Network Terminations

Equipment connects to ISDN over network termination equipment designated as NT1 and NT2. NT1 provides functions dealing

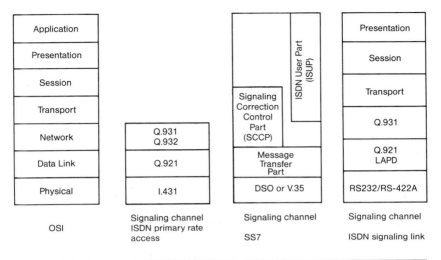

Figure 26.2   CCITT standards related to the OSI model.

with physical and electrical termination of the network, corresponding to the physical layer of the OSI reference model. Devices that combine the services of both NT1 and NT2 are called NT12. The NT1 functions are:

- Termination of the two-wire transmission line and conversion to four-wire.

- Monitoring performance and maintenance functions.

- Timing the loop.

- Termination of the four-wire user interface and conversion to two-wire.

NT2 terminations, which may be built into a PBX, multiplexer, local area network, or terminal controller, perform the data link and network layer functions of the OSI model.

The basic rate service permits as many as eight terminal devices to be connected to a passive bus as Figure 26.3 shows. The passive bus is a four-wire circuit—one pair for transmit and one for receive. Since the basic rate is limited to two B channels, only two of the devices connected to the passive bus can be active simultaneously, but the D channel could be used for data communications from other devices on the bus.

Non-ISDN devices connect to the network through a terminal adapter (TA). Terminal adapters will be required for the major non-ISDN devices such as EIA-232-D, EIA-449, X.21, V.35, and voice terminals. Figure 26.4 shows an AT&T 7507 ISDN telephone.

ISDN Interfaces

Five points of demarcation have been defined in ISDN standards as Figure 26.5 shows.

- The R interface is a link between non-ISDN equipment and an ISDN terminal adapter.
- The S interface connects ISDN terminals to NT2 and NT12 devices.
- The T interface connects NT2 and NT1 devices.
- The U interface connects NT1 and NT12 devices to the public network.
- The V interface, located in the ISDN node, separates the line termination equipment from the exchange termination equipment.

The U-V connection is the ISDN access line and replaces the local loop of pre-ISDN services. It is a single twisted pair metallic line with a maximum length of 6500 meters. NT1 and the ISDN node obtain a full duplex connection by using a technique called *echo cancellation*. The transmitting power of the four-wire input to the NT1 splits between the line and an equalizing network in the NT1. An electronic filter determines whether a line signal is original data or an echo caused by a mismatch between the line and the network. Echoes are canceled out so only the original signal remains.

ISDN Issues

Telecommunications managers are in an ambivalent position with respect to ISDN. On the one hand are equipment manufacturers and LECs touting the importance of ISDN as if its services were a

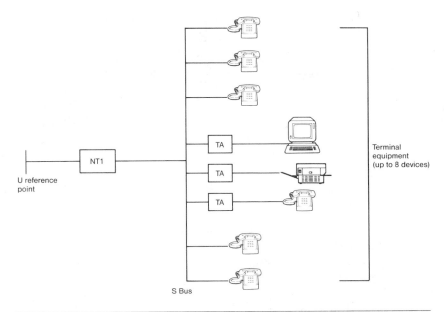

Figure 26.3   Connection of devices to the ISDN basic rate service bus.

Figure 26.4   The AT&T 7505 ISDN telephone.
Courtesy, AT&T Corporation

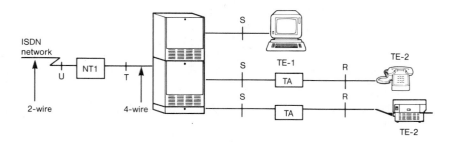

Figure 26.5   ISDN demarcation points.

real and immediate alternative. On the other hand are many detractors who question whether ISDN is needed at all by one class of users and suggest that another class will find its bandwidth insufficient.

It would be a mistake to assume that ISDN is trivial because it is the architecture under which telephone services will be offered in the future. It isn't necessarily the exclusive architecture; ISDN and non-ISDN services can coexist and will undoubtedly do so for many years to come. The key issues are when the applications that justify ISDN will emerge and whether the cost will be affordable, particularly for residential users.

Many LECs have conducted ISDN field trials, but so far the "golden application" has not emerged. It seems likely that ISDN will continue to be a slow revolution, adopted first by companies that need video conferencing, Group 4 facsimile, and data transfer capability to support part time applications such as image transfer and CPU-to-CPU file transfer. If LECs begin to supply PRI services at a price competitive with non-ISDN local trunks, the service could develop more rapidly.

This section discusses the primary factors that should be considered in evaluating the importance of ISDN in an organization.

LEC Deployment Strategies

ISDN has always been touted as providing end-to-end digital connectivity. If one end of a session is analog, ISDN offers little advantage compared to the capabilities of a non-ISDN digital central office. As the LECs equip existing offices with SS7, they can deliver most of the CLASS services without ISDN. To justify replacing the analog central offices that still comprise the backbone of their switching networks, the LECs must derive increased revenues, replace equipment that has reached the end of its service life, or simply take the risk that ubiquitous availability of ISDN will ensure its success.

A combination of all three motivators will undoubtedly occur, but the question of cost remains. As regulated entities, the LECs cannot drive up the cost of local telephone service without the participation of regulatory authorities. Most regulators will prefer that ISDN service be financed as a value-added layer above existing non-ISDN service.

The question of ISDN development is particularly interesting in non-metropolitan areas. Ironically, these are more likely to be equipped with digital switches because they were the last to be converted to electronic switching. Many rural central offices, including independent telephone companies, have only recently been converted to electronic switching with systems that can be ISDN-equipped. Usually, however, rural offices are the last to offer ISDN services because they are heavily residential.

Standards and Compatibility

Another issue affecting ISDN is standards development. ISDN standards have been under development for more than a decade and some will not be solidified until the 1992 CCITT plenary session. Meanwhile, manufacturers offer proprietary standards, but these do not necessarily conform to ISDN, nor are they compatible with each other.

The major IECs offer PRI interfaces that are advertised as ISDN but which lack features such as clear channel capability. North American countries have adopted the 2B1Q line coding technique for ISDN, but most PRI services are delivered using alternate mark inversion. Central office equipment manufacturers offer ISDN capability, but the switches do not necessarily interconnect. Also, there is no assurance that an ISDN telephone set made by one manufacturer will work on the line interface of another.

A further question is whether ISDN will be truly compatible across international boundaries. No one is yet certain whether international gateways will be required between some countries to make ISDN functional from end-to-end.

Calling Number Suppression

As discussed in Chapter 9, local switching systems automatically identify callers' line numbers and deliver them to the billing equipment. The circuitry that performs this function is called Automatic Number Identification (ANI). ANI information has been retained within the network of operating telephone companies and IECs. With the advent of Open Network Architecture (ONA), the LECs arrange to deliver the calling number over the line on which the call terminates. ISDN delivers the calling number over the separate D channel.

Calling party identification is a highly desirable service for many applications. For example, by linking incoming lines with a company's automatic call distributor and computer data base, it would be possible for an incoming call to arrive on the voice terminal and customer information from the data base to arrive on the data terminal simultaneously. Here are examples of other services that ANI makes possible:

- *Single Number Service.* A company can advertise a single number throughout a calling area; the network routes the call to the nearest service location based on the calling number.

- *Call Trace.* This feature provides the user with a record of incoming calls, including the calling number and time. It is particularly effective in reducing annoyance calls.

- *Selective Call Rejection.* Based on the calling number, the user can accept or reject a call. Rejected calls are routed to an announcement; other calls are routed to an answering position.

- *Executive Screening.* Calls from a selected list are sent to the user; calls from other numbers can go to an alternate destination such as a secretary.

	155 mb/s	620 mb/s
DS-0 voice channels (64 kb/s)	2100	8000
ISDN Basic Rate (2B + D)	940	3760
DS-1 (1.544 mb/s)	56	224
DS-3 (45 mb/s)	2	8
HDTV channels	1	4

Figure 26.6 How services fit into B-ISDN.

The display of ANI information raises important privacy issues. With ANI delivered to the called party, no longer is it possible for callers to remain anonymous. Few people will deplore the loss of privacy for nuisance and annoyance callers, but in other cases telephone users claim a right to privacy. For example, LECs protect non-published telephone numbers, which users obtain for a variety of legitimate purposes.

On the one hand, the provision of the calling number enhances the utility of ISDN. On the other hand it raises privacy issues that have not, as of this writing, been settled.

Broadband ISDN

One objection to ISDN is that its bandwidth is insufficient for many service requirements. To meet the requirements of services that need wide bandwidth on demand, ISDN study committees are developing broadband ISDN (B-ISDN) standards, with a future wideband ISDN (W-ISDN) even further from deployment. CCITT defines B-ISDN as "a service requiring transmission channels capable of supporting rates greater than the primary rate." The B-ISDN data rate has tentatively been set at 155 mb/s and 620 mb/s in multiples of 51.84 mb/s. B-ISDN will be a new network structure using SONET-based fiber transport and a new high speed switching method. Figure 26.6 shows how services fit into the B-ISDN framework.

Assuming high speed channels can be provided at an economical price over fiber optics, B-ISDN will become a medium for

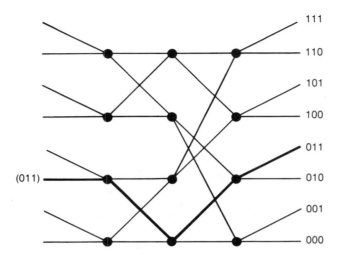

111
110
101
100
011
(011)
010
001
000

Figure 26.7 A banyan switch.

carrying services that require large amounts of bandwidth. High quality television on demand—probably eventually high definition television (see Chapter 17)—can be delivered over a broadband circuit. High speed data interconnecting LANs with no reduction in throughput between widely separate networks would be feasible with a high speed medium. Teleconferencing and computer aided design over wide distances become feasible with B-ISDN. CCITT defines B-ISDN services in two parts: Interactive Services, which require a two-way exchange of information, and Distribution Services, which are essentially one-way. Video conferencing and video telephone are expected to be the most important interactive services, and broadcast video is expected to be the primary distribution service.

At the heart of B-ISDN is an ingenious switching system known as the *banyan* switch, or *asynchronous transfer mode* (ATM) switch. Illustrated in Figure 26.7, the banyan switch is a two-stage device that takes its name from the many branches of the banyan tree. The banyan system switches packetized information a full packet at a time. The packet header finds a path through the switch, and the path remains intact for the duration of the packet, after which it is torn down and reused.

ATM data packets are typically short—128 bytes or less. The header directs the packet through each of the bidirectional switching stages. A 1 in the header causes the switch to operate to the upper path, and a 0 to the lower. The remainder of the packet follows the header through the path. If the headers are sorted by destination address, the switch is non-blocking. If two packets converge on the same output, one is rejected and sent through the switch again, causing a delay. This delay characteristic is the reason the process is called asynchronous transfer mode.

A banyan switch is fast and therefore ideally suited to switching the high speeds of B-ISDN. It is also inexpensive and easily can be implemented in large scale integration.

B-ISDN is currently only in the conceptual stages and will probably not be implemented before the 1995 to 1998 time frame. The protocols are formative, and the services are just beginning to emerge.

Switched Multimegabit Data Service (SMDS)

Currently, the only medium available for linking LANs is a private point-to-point facility. This alternative can be expensive, considering the fact that the network of bridges, routers, and gateways interconnecting LANs becomes increasingly complex as the number of nodes grows. Furthermore, the amount of traffic flowing over any single link may vary from none during idle periods to enormous bandwidth demands for short periods.

The LECs' answer to the need for bandwidth on demand is Switched Multimegabit Data Service (SMDS), which will be the first broadband ISDN service to be offered. SMDS permits high speed LAN-like performance over metropolitan networks. Initially, SMDS will offer connection speeds of 1.544 and 45 mb/s, but the speeds are expected to go much higher. SMDS provides access to the transport medium through a dedicated DS-1 or DS-3 link using 802.6 standards. Users have no access to other data carried by the transport medium, so the service is secure.

SMDS, which currently is undergoing field trials, will likely be billed on a usage-sensitive basis. The service will be most attractive to users who have too little data flowing between points to justify a full time high speed circuit.

Applications

ISDN service providers are in a chicken-and-egg situation. ISDN will not develop widely without demand, and demand will not develop without applications. So far, despite ISDN trials held by most of the major LECs, applications have not emerged, partially because of its limited geographical coverage. As services become available, however, applications will develop, and ISDN will probably become demand-driven instead of technology-driven as it is today. Initially, ISDN applications are expected to be these:

- High speed image applications such as Group 4 facsimile.
- Second line-in-the-home applications driven by the development of telecommuting.
- High speed file transfer.
- Video conferencing.

The initial ISDN applications will be voice for the practical reason that ISDN-compatible central offices are needed at both ends of the connection to make data and video services work. The first large scale ISDN users will probably be Centrex customers, because their switching is done in the central office now.

Many LECs are beginning to offer ISDN services under tariff where facilities permit. The major IECs are providing or have announced PRIs as an alternative to the T-1 connections over which they offer bulk outgoing and incoming WATS services. For example, AT&T's PRI offers the user connection to Megacom, Megacom 800, Accunet Switched 56, Accunet Spectrum of Digital Services, and Software Defined Network (SDN). With the PRI, the user can reallocate channels to any of the above services on demand. At present, however, the major carriers' PRI services do not offer clear channel service.

ISDN services are divided into three categories:

- *Teleservices.* These services, which are not used in the United States, apply to a specific application such as teletext.
- *Supplementary services.* These services, examples of which are call forwarding, call transfer, and call waiting, are used in conjunction with bearer services or teleservices.
- *Bearer services.* These are the basic services offered to telephone subscribers, including both circuit-mode and packet-mode services.

Standards

Most of the important ISDN standards have been completed and accepted by CCITT. National differences, however, leave the objective of a universal standard in doubt. In the United States, for example, the FCC has decreed that the NT1 interface is furnished by the customer, whereas in the rest of the world it is part of the network. In Germany, line power is furnished from the network, where in most other countries it is furnished by the customer. In the United States, ISDN standardization work is handled by ANSI's T1S1 subcommittee.

ISDN standards promulgated by CCITT are grouped into the following categories:

- *I.100 series.* ISDN general concepts, methods, structure, and terminology.
- *I.200 series.* ISDN service aspects.
- *I.300 series.* ISDN network aspects.
- *I.400 series.* ISDN user-network interface aspects.
- *I.500 series* Internetwork interfaces.
- *I.600 series.* Maintenance principles.

The 1988 recommendations contain 77 separate standards plus another 100 recommendations that are relevant to ISDN. Appendix B lists the primary ISDN standards.

Selected ISDN Equipment Manufacturers

Customer Premises Equipment

AT&T

Datagraf, Inc.

Develcon Electronics

Ericsson Network Systems, Inc.

Fujitsu

Harris Corp.

Hayes Microcomputer Products, Inc.

Hewlett-Packard Corp.

Hitachi America

IBM

Idacom

Meridian Networx

Newbridge Networks

Northern Telecom

Siemens Information Systems, Inc.

SRX

Teleos Communications, Inc.

Universal Data Systems

Tekelec

Central Office Equipment

AT&T

Develcon Electronics

Ericsson

Fujitsu Network Switching

Microcom, Inc.

NEC

Northern Telecom

Siemens Public Switching Systems

Tekelec

27

Local Area Network Principles

In the late 1970s and early 1980s, local area network (LAN) protocols were proposed by several companies that foresaw the need for short range data communications. Before then, data communication had been largely long haul. Data networks connected remote terminals to a host or enabled a host to send files to remote printers, but there was little need for data communication within the office. The gradual introduction of office automation equipment, however, began to change the complexion of office communications. Analysts learned that a large percentage of information travels by paper over a short distance. In most organizations, as much as 80% of the information produced stays within a room, a building, or a campus. As office workers increasingly accepted personal computers, the need grew to share files and peripherals such as printers and plotters.

Communication has become an essential part of most computing systems; in some functions such as electronic mail, it is the essence of the application. Declining computer costs have made it economical to distribute many operations that previously were centralized, but related costs have remained high. The prices of printers, high speed disk drives, and, most important, program development have not followed the rapid decline of processor prices. Consequently, the need has arisen for a low cost, high speed network to allow many small computers to share files and resources and to communicate with one another via electronic mail.

Limited range messages require a different form of network than traditional networks such as the telephone system. Local networks must meet the demand for high speed, short range communication at a cost low enough to justify an appearance on nearly every desk. The most economical solution for many offices and industrial applications is the *local area network* (LAN). A LAN is a network dedicated to a single organization, limited in range, and connected by a common communication technology. This definition has important implications. Because the network is private, it can be specialized for a function. Security may be less critical than in wide area networks, and because range is limited, a LAN can operate at high speeds without incurring the high costs of broadband transmission.

As with other data communication technologies, local area networks got their start with proprietary protocols. Proprietary standards meant that one manufacturer's equipment would not communicate with that of another manufacturer, which diminished the value of the equipment and impeded local area network advancement.

In 1980, the Institute of Electrical and Electronic Engineers (IEEE) formed the 802 committee, which was charged with developing LAN standards. A few years earlier, Digital Equipment Coorporation, Intel, and Xerox had collaborated to produce Ethernet, a LAN that enables devices to share a common bus through a listen-before-transmitting protocol. Ethernet was offered to the 802 committee as a potential standard. Several companies objected to Ethernet as the sole standard, however, so eventually IEEE settled on the three standards that will be discussed in this chapter.

The lack of standards was not the only problem LANs had in gaining acceptance. Not only are there three official standards that CCITT has since adopted, but there are also variations in speed, transmission media, and network options, so communication between dissimilar devices is still far from assured. Furthermore, standardization is no guarantee of success for a network, nor is lack of standardization a fatal defect. In terms of numbers of devices served, the most widely used network in the United States at this time is Arcnet, which does not conform to any of the IEEE standards.

LANs would still be a product in search of a market if not for the rapid acceptance of personal computers that followed IBM's introduction of the original PC in 1981. Until that time, office workers had one of two types of terminals on their desks: a dumb terminal working against a mainframe or mini computer, or a word processing terminal on a centralized or standalone word processing system. Although personal computers existed before that time, they were handicapped by a lack of software and an inability to communicate, except in a terminal emulation mode. The IBM Personal Computer offered two significant advantages to would-be office communicators. First, it provided an open bus architecture for which developers could obtain the specifications to interface hardware and write software. Second, IBM's market penetration made it feasible for programmers to develop software applications with some degree of assurance of a market.

The IBM Personal Computer gave LANs the boost they needed. Office workers soon had on their desk processing power that exceeded the power of earlier mainframe computers, and they used it to create files that other workers needed to share. Also, the simultaneous development of high quality peripherals, such as laser printers and plotters, led to the need to share these devices as well as files. Although the personal computer network was hardly conceived of in the early days of LANs, it soon became the essence of the office communication system, with mainframes and minicomputers added almost as an afterthought. In today's networks large computers meet the objective of obtaining lower cost storage and permitting personal computer users to download files to manipulate in their word processors and spreadsheets. Processing power, however, is concentrated in the personal computer.

Today, the LAN has cleared its initial hurdles, but the technology still has a long way to go. The vast majority of organizations still lack networks, and most have no immediate plans to develop them. Although the networks in operation number in the tens of thousands, LANs are still far from being a commodity, and although they alleviate the problems of sharing files and peripherals, LANs introduce problems of their own that this chapter discusses. Just as a large leap in knowledge and ability is required to move a worker from a pencil to a typewriter and calculator to a personal computer, a similar leap is required to make personal computer users comfortable with LANs.

American workers have advanced dramatically in the last decade with respect to their ability to handle computer technology, but there is little evidence that improved productivity has resulted. LANs have an important role to play in correcting the problem of lagging office productivity and in linking production apparatus on the factory floor. The next decade will see large advances in LANs as the technology matures.

Local Area Network Technology

Many products marketed under the local area network banner do not meet the true test of a LAN. These products, including data PBXs and voice/data PBXs, can properly be called *local networks*, but not local *area* networks. A LAN is a form of local network that has the following characteristics:

- High speed that permits users to transfer data at speeds approaching or exceeding the rate of transfer from a directly attached hard disk.
- A restricted range—usually one mile or less.
- An access protocol that permits stations to share a common transmission medium and address file and print servers as if they were directly attached.

LANs can be classified according to five criteria, which this section discusses:

- Topology.
- Access method.
- Modulation method.
- Transmission medium.
- Interface method.

Devices access LANs through circuitry that goes by several names, but which we shall call a *network access unit* (NAU). The form of the NAU is determined by the designer. Often it takes the form of an interface card that plugs in a computer bus or a personal computer expansion slot. In other hardware, the NAU may be built into the device itself. Although various manufacturers call the NAU by other names, its functions are common to all LANS:

- Provides a physical interface to the transmission medium.
- Monitors the busy/idle status of the network.
- Buffers the speed of the attached device to the speed of the network.
- Converts the protocol of the attached device to the network protocol.
- Monitors for and corrects errors.
- Assembles the transmitted data stream into packets for transmission on the network and restores the data stream at the receiving end.
- Recovers from *collisions* that may result from simultaneous transmissions.

Topology

Network topology is the pattern of interconnection of the network nodes. LANs use the same topologies as global and metropolitan networks: star, bus, ring, and branching tree, but rarely mesh.

The most common topology is the bus, in which devices connect to a single circuit, as in Figure 27.1a. Messages or packets are broadcast simultaneously to all devices on a bus. Either access is allocated by a control node, or the nodes contend for access.

Star networks, which are illustrated in Figure 27.1b, are the preferred topology in virtually all LANs that use twisted pair wire or fiber optics as the transmission medium. The wire from the device is connected to a hub at a central branching point. Multiple hubs often are interconnected to form a network of multiple stars. Electrically, the star network is identical to the bus. Note, however, that a ring network that is configured as a star is not electrically identical to a bus.

Branching tree networks, illustrated in Figure 27.1c, are often used in broadband LANs that employ cable television technology. The branching tree is electrically identical to the bus except that its branches are connected only through properly designed impedance-matching devices. Otherwise, data signal reflections will cause the network to malfunction.

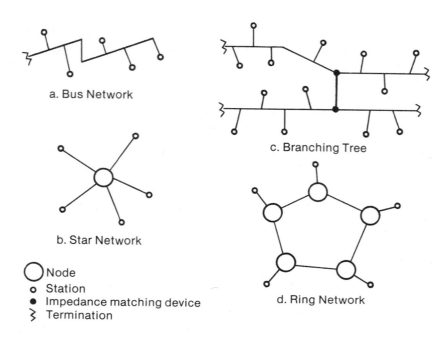

a. Bus Network

b. Star Network

c. Branching Tree

d. Ring Network

○ Node
o Station
● Impedance matching device
⌇ Termination

Figure 27.1   Local area network topologies.

The star, branching tree, and bus topologies function identically in a LAN: a station with a message to send gains access to or *acquires* the network and broadcasts a signal that all stations receive. The addressee retains the message; all other stations discard it.

In a ring topology, illustrated in Figure 27.1d, all stations are connected in series, and the signal is transmitted one bit at a time. Each station receives the signal, regenerates it, and transmits it to the next station in the ring. Bits flow in only one direction. The addressee copies the message, but it continues to circulate until it returns to the sending station, which is the only station entitled to remove it from the ring. Other stations act as repeaters that pass the message but do not retain it.

Access Method

A key distinguishing feature of LANs is the method of providing the stations access to the network. In a switched network, stations gain access by signaling over the network and transmitting an address to the controller. The controller determines the destination and sets up a path or circuit between the sender and receiver. Because the network has multiple paths, stations cannot interfere with one another if the capacity of the network is not exceeded.

By contrast, a LAN has only one path to handle high speed data. The total capacity of the path, however, far exceeds the transmission speed of any station. Stations are given exclusive access to the entire network for long enough periods of time to send a packet of data or a message. LAN access methods are classified as contention or non-contention.

Contention Access

A contention network can be visualized as a large party line with all stations vying for access. In contention networks, control is distributed among all stations. When a station has a message to send, it listens to the network and, if it is idle, sends a packet of data.

It is not always possible, however, for a station to determine when the network is idle. As Figure 27.2 shows, two stations may begin to transmit simultaneously. Because of the delay between the time a data pulse is transmitted and the time it is received at the distant end, neither station is aware that the other is sending. When simultaneous transmissions occur, the two signals *collide*.

During the time it takes a pulse to travel from the sending terminal to the furthest terminals on the network, known as the *collision window,* stations are blinded to potential collisions. In one kilometer of coaxial cable the collision window is approximately 5 microseconds wide. Because of potential collisions, contention networks are restricted in diameter; the wider the network the longer the collision window. The practical limitation in contention LANs operating at a data rate of 10 mb/s is about two kilometers.

The most common system for managing access and collisions in a contention network is known as *Carrier Sense Multiple Access With Collision Detection* (CSMA/CD). CSMA/CD, which is used in Ethernet, is a listen-before-transmit protocol. A station wishing to transmit monitors the network to determine whether any traffic is present. If the network is idle, it begins to transmit. If two stations transmit simultaneously, their packets collide. The first

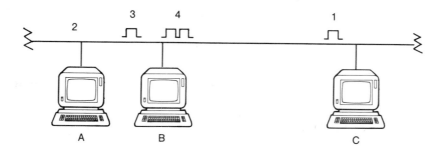

1. Station C begins to transmit.
2. Station A listens to network but signal from C has not arrived.
3. Station A transmits and collides with signal from C.
4. Station B detects collision and transmits jamming signal.
5. Both A and C stop transmitting and wait random time before retransmitting.

Figure 27.2   **Collisions in a contention network.**

station hearing the collision transmits a jamming signal, and when the two transmitting stations hear it they immediately cease to transmit. If an entire packet was transmitted before a collision was detected, the collision would mutilate both signals and valuable network time would be wasted in retransmission.

The procedures that stations follow when a collision occurs is called their *backoff algorithm*. If stations attempted to reacquire the network immediately following collision, repeated collisions between the same two stations would occur. To prevent repeated collisions, stations must wait a random time before the next attempt.

A variation of CSMA/CD is CSMA/CA (collision avoidance). In the most common variation of this method, each station is assigned a time slot in which to transmit data. If the station has no traffic to send, the time slot remains unused. Therefore, this system is capable of less throughput than CSMA/CD.

Non-Contention Access

CSMA/CD is known as a *statistical* access method, relying on the probability that its stations will get enough share of the network to send their traffic. Although unlikely, it is possible for a station to be excluded from network access during periods of heavy load.

A non-contention system called *token passing* introduces a form of control that overcomes the drawbacks of the free-for-all system used by CSMA/CD. A token is a unique combination of bits that circulates through the network following a predetermined route. When a station has data to send, it captures the token, transmits its message and replaces the token on the network. Token passing is a *deterministic* system. If a station has traffic equal to or higher in priority than other traffic on the network, the control mechanism will allocate it a portion of the network's capacity.

The advantages of control are purchased at the price of greater complexity. One of the stations in a token network must be equipped to initiate recovery action if the token is lost or mutilated, which can occur if a station fails or loses power at the time it possesses the token. Other functions required of the control station include the removal of persistently circulating packets, removal of duplicate tokens, control of priority, and addition and removal of stations. Further complicating the process is the need for a recovery routine if the control station fails. All stations are equipped with the logic to assume control if necessary. Because of this greater complexity, token passing systems are generally more expensive than contention systems. Moreover, additions and deletions are more complex because all stations must be programmed with the route of the token.

Ring and bus topologies predominate in token networks. In a token ring, (Figure 27.3), each station receives each message and repeats it to the next station in turn. Sequencing is automatic; it always follows the same route in the same direction around the ring.

In a token bus network, messages are broadcast to all stations simultaneously, but control follows a logical ring sequence as illustrated in Figure 27.4. When a station acquires the token, it is permitted to broadcast a message, but the token can be passed to any other station without regard to its position on the network.

Modulation Methods

LANs use one of two methods of pulsing a data signal on the transmission medium. In the first, known as *baseband*, the signal

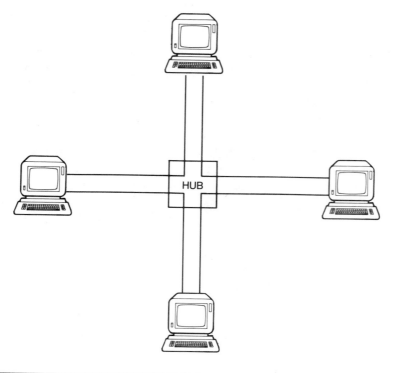

Figure 27.3   **Token ring network.**

is transmitted directly in the form of high speed, square wave pulses of DC voltage. *Broadband* systems use cable television (CATV) technology to divide the transmission medium into frequency bands or channels. Each broadband channel can be multiplexed to carry data, voice, or video.

Baseband and broadband networks accept identical data streams from the terminal, but they differ in the network access unit. In a baseband system, the NAU is coupled to a *transceiver*, which is a simple cable driver that matches the impedance of the cable and transmits pulses at the data transfer rate. In many systems, the transceiver and NAU are contained in a single element such as a personal computer card. In a broadband network,

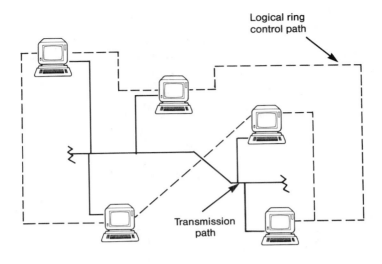

Figure 27.4   Token bus network.

the NAU contains a *radio frequency modem* to modulate the data to an assigned channel.

Baseband

The primary advantage of baseband is its simplicity. No tuned circuits or radio frequency apparatus is required. A baseband system has no active components aside from the NAUs and transceivers. Only the cable is common to the network, making baseband less vulnerable to failure than broadband, which contains amplifiers and other active components.

A baseband network is composed of transceivers, the transmission medium, and data devices, which usually house the NAU in an expansion slot. Some types of network do not have a separate transceiver; the transmission medium is brought directly to the NAU. The devices send a data stream to the NAU, where it is formed into packets that are pulsed directly on the transmission medium. The transmission medium, discussed in a later section, can be ribbon or paired copper wire, coaxial cable, or fiber optic cable. In fiber optic cable, data pulses drive a light transmitter,

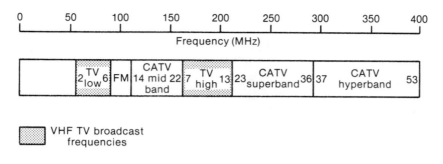

Figure 27.5   CATV frequency allocations.

which turns a laser or light emitting diode on and off corresponding to the 0s and 1s of the data signal.

Broadband

Broadband networks use a coaxial cable and amplifier system capable of passing frequencies from about 5 Mhz to 400 Mhz as shown in Figure 27.5. Television channels each occupy 6 Mhz, with the total cable supporting more than 60 one-way channels, which can be used for a LAN, video, or voice. The primary advantage of broadband over baseband LANs is their greater capacity. The equivalent of several baseband networks is derived by using multiple subcarriers for increased LAN channels, video, or in some cases, voice.

Unlike baseband, where signals are broadcast in both directions simultaneously, broadband is inherently a one-way system because of its amplifiers. Bidirectional amplifiers are available, but the transmitting and receiving signals must be separated to obtain bidirectional transmission. The reverse direction is handled either by sending on one cable and receiving on another or by splitting the sending and receiving signals into two different frequencies. The first method is called a *dual cable* system, and the second a *single cable* system. *Head end equipment* is used to couple the transmit cable to the receive cable in a dual cable system and to shift the transmit frequency to the receive frequency in a single cable system. Head end equipment in a single cable system and amplifiers in all broadband systems are active elements; a failure can interrupt the network.

Devices in a broadband network connect to the transmission medium through radio frequency (rf) modems that contain a transceiver tuned to the network transmit and receive frequencies. There are two types of rf modems. *Fixed frequency modems* are tuned to a single frequency; *frequency agile* modems can be shifted. Frequency shifts are directed by a central controller that connects stations by selecting an idle channel, directing the two modems to the channel, and dropping out of the connection.

Baseband and broadband LANs are similar in most respects except for the frequency separation in a broadband network and differing methods of collision detection. With some products it is possible to start at baseband and later convert to broadband by replacing the transceiver in the NAU with an rf modem. Collisions are detected on a direct current basis in a baseband network, but because broadband networks are incapable of passing DC, they employ a different method of collision detection. A common technique is for the station to listen for transmissions mutilated by collision. This reduces network throughput compared with baseband. Another system of collision detection is the bit comparison method in which a series of bits is transmitted to acquire the network. If a collision occurs, the first section detecting the collision transmits a jamming signal on a separate channel. Throughput is reduced by the added length of the doubled cable. These two factors plus higher cost are the primary drawbacks of broadband.

Transmission Media

All of the transmission media used in other networks—twisted pair wire, coaxial cable, fiber optics, radio, and light—are employed in LANs. Radio and light are used for special applications; the other three for general LAN application. The choice of transmission medium is usually dictated by the vendor. Because of differing characteristics, therefore, the choice of vendor may be driven by the transmission medium required. The principal factors to consider are:

- Presence of electromagnetic interference (EMI).

- Network throughput.
- Bandwidth required.
- Network diameter.
- Multiple terminal access.
- Cost.
- Security.

Twisted Pair Wire or Ribbon Cable

The primary advantages of twisted pair wire are cost, ease of installation, and the availability of spare pairs that are installed for the telephone system. Wire is readily available from many vendors and can be installed by relatively unskilled personnel with simple and inexpensive hand tools. It has enough bandwidth to handle data speeds of 1 mb/s for distances of about one mile, although LAN standards support higher speeds over shorter distances. Many manufacturers are offering 10 mb/s LANs that permit stations to operate at a distance of 100 meters (330 feet) from the hub. Wire is available in multiple twisted pair cable, both shielded and unshielded, and in flat ribbons that can be installed under carpet. It is durable and capable of withstanding considerable abuse without damage, and with its sheath intact, it is impervious to weather.

When LANs first entered the market, twisted pair wire was rarely the medium of choice, but recent advances have made it the preferred medium when the distance between devices is short enough that wire can be used. AT&T was the primary force behind the development of twisted pair LANs; its experience with twisted pair in building wiring and outside plant led it to conclude that the advantages of using preexisting wire were too great to disregard. Their StarLANan network became the predominant product using twisted pair at 1 mb/s. In 1988 AT&T introduced StarLan at 10 mb/s, a few months after other companies such as Synoptics introduced 10 mb/s twisted pair LANs.

IBM, which was the primary force behind token ring networks, recommends shielding to protect the network from interference and to prevent radiation in excess of that permitted by FCC regulations. If the wire is designed to IBM specifications, they support the use of unshielded wire with reduced station capacity and shorter distances over its 4 mb/s token ring network. Many users have successfully applied token ring over unshielded wire that does not comply with IBM specifications.

When IBM announced its 16 mb/s token ring network, it recommended against the use of unshielded wire under any circumstances. Several companies have, however, announced token ring products that work at 16 mb/s over unshielded wire.

Despite its advantages, wire has limitations that preclude its use in some applications. Its bandwidth is too narrow for the speeds required by many systems. Also, unless cable is shielded, EMI from such sources as elevators and industrial equipment can cause errors, or the network's radiation can interfere with other devices. Where security is important, wire is a poor choice, for it is easily tapped. For further information on the characteristics of wire, refer to Chapter 6.

Coaxial Cable

Coaxial cable, or "coax," is an excellent transmission medium for many LANs. It is inexpensive, has wide bandwidth, and can be installed by moderately skilled workers. Coax can support both high speed data and video, and because it is widely used for cable television (CATV), it is readily available at moderate cost.

Coaxial cable has one or more center conductors surrounded by a shield of flexible braid or semi-rigid copper or aluminum tube, with an outer jacket of PVC or Teflon. When properly installed, the conductor is shielded from EMI and is reasonably impervious to weather. Special precautions are required to avoid unwanted effects in installing coaxial cables. In baseband networks, cables must be grounded in only one place; precautions are required to insulate connectors from ground at unwanted places. Branching points in broadband coax must be equipped with splitters and directional couplers to avoid impedance irregularities. The bend radius of coax must be sufficiently wide to prevent kinking, which can either short the cable or cause an impedance irregularity.

Coax can be tapped with little difficulty, which is advantageous when adding stations to a LAN without interrupting service. This means, however, that communications on the network are not entirely secure from unauthorized access, although compared to wire, coax is less susceptible to unauthorized taps. Refer to Chapter 17 for further discussion of CATV components.

Fiber Optics

Fiber optic cable with its wide bandwidth can support data speeds far higher than those needed by most LANs. It can be used in either baseband or broadband systems when equipped with lightwave transceivers. Perhaps more important in LANs, lightwave is immune to EMI, which is advantageous in many industrial applications.

Offsetting its advantages, lightwave has disadvantages that limit its applications in LANs. First, a lightwave system employs a combination of electronic and light technology that is more costly than coaxial cable drivers. Optical cable requires special tools and techniques for installation. The fibers must be carefully aligned into fixtures on the light transceivers, and they can be spliced only with special apparatus. Furthermore, glass fibers are difficult to tap. Although this is advantageous for security, it renders fiber optics almost unusable in a bus topology except when fibers are linked at a central point through a star adapter, creating the equivalent of a bus. Fiber optics also can be used in a ring configuration, with each node regenerating the light signal. In networks such as IBM's token ring, it is used for a backbone linking media access units in distant wiring closets.

Although fiber optic cable and its associated light drivers are more expensive than coax, in terms of capacity, lightwave may be less expensive. Furthermore, the technology is advancing rapidly, resulting in both technical and cost improvements. Fiber optics is the transmission medium that is used with the new Fiber Distributed Data Interface (FDDI) covered in Chapter 29. Refer to Chapter 13 for additional information on lightwave.

Microwave Radio

Microwave radio is inherently a point-to-point medium. Microwaves travel in a straight line, so intermediate stations can be linked only if they are on the path of the radio beam. Radio is useful where right-of-way is a problem, as in crossing obstructions and spanning moderate distances. It is also useful in connecting

LANs and for linking a LAN with distant terminals. Some companies have announced plans to develop wireless LANs, using microwave radio as the transmission medium.

Among its limitations, radio is not easily secured. It is impossible to prevent unauthorized detection of data signals over a microwave path, so when security is important, encryption is required. Frequency allocations are coordinated by the Federal Communications Commission and may be difficult to obtain. Also, microwave is expensive to purchase, requires trained technicians to install and maintain, and is susceptible to interference from outside sources. Refer to Chapter 14 for additional information on microwave.

Light

Optical transceivers are available for the same kinds of applications as described above for radio. These systems use light transceivers operating over short line-of-sight distances such as crossing a street between two buildings. Distances are limited, and transmission is not completely reliable because light beams can be interrupted by influences such as fog and dust. Its application is limited to short distances where other alternatives are prohibitively expensive. Some products entering the market use infrared light to communicate between devices on a LAN. Light is transmitted from the workstation to a centrally located infrared transceiver mounted on the ceiling.

Local Area Network Standards

Local area network standards originated in much the same way that other communications standards have been set. Manufacturers experimented with communications and access methods, developed proprietary techniques, and gradually demonstrated their feasibility. Most protocols were proprietary, limiting the compatibility between the network and existing equipment and that of other manufacturers. Ethernet is a case in point. Developed in the early 1970s by Xerox Corporation in its Palo Alto Research Center, Ethernet was offered for licensing at a nominal cost. However, rarely do proprietary systems become adopted as standards without modification. Ethernet was no exception.

The IEEE 802 Committee

In 1980, the IEEE Computer Society appointed a committee to work on project 802, the development of LAN standards. The 802 committee's objectives were to establish standards for the physical and data link connections between devices. The following requirements were established:

- Existing data communications standards were to be incorporated into the IEEE standard as much as possible.
- The network was intended for light industrial and commercial use.
- The maximum network diameter was set at two kilometers.
- The data speed on the network was to be between 1 mb/s and 20 mb/s.
- The network standard was to be independent of the transmission medium.
- The failure of any device on the network was not to disrupt the entire network.
- There was to be no more than one undetected error per year on the network.

The committee concluded that Ethernet would not suffice as a single standard because of the potential of blockage under heavy load conditions. Therefore, the committee set two incompatible standards. For light duty, a bus contention network similar but not identical to Ethernet was selected. For applications where assurance of network access is needed, token passing bus and ring standards were selected.

The 802 standards, which are changing as the technology progresses, include these first six parts:

- 802.1 Overview document containing the reference model, tutorial, and glossary.
- 802.2 Link Layer Protocol Standard.
- 802.3 Contention Bus Standard.
- 802.4 Token Bus Standard.
- 802.5 Token Ring Standard.

- 802.6 Metropolitan Area Network.

The 802 standards are developed around layers 1 and 2 of the OSI protocols (see Chapter 3) and do not include all the functions of a complete network. Each manufacturer applies its own design to the network; as a result, though a network complies with an 802 standard, apparatus is not necessarily interchangeable between networks. Also, many products on the market do not conform to the IEEE standards. Therefore, it is important to understand that the 802 standard does not imply universal compatibility.

The CSMA/CD LAN IEEE 802.3

The 802.3 standard is a CSMA/CD network intended for commercial or light industrial use. The specification supports Network Access Units (NAUs) for baseband and broadband coaxial cable and baseband fiber cable. The standard is not a complete network; for example, although the protocol detects errors, it does not include an error recovery process, so this and other high level functions must be provided by the network operating system.

Although the terms 802.3 and Ethernet sometimes are used interchangeably, there are differences between the two protocols. Both use CSMA/CD, but the frame structure is different, and the transmission media they support are not identical. Ethernet specifies only a 50 ohm coaxial cable medium; 802.3 supports 50 ohm coax, 72 ohm coax, twisted pair, and fiber optics.

The 802.3 standards are identified by a three-part designation that specifies the data rate, modulation method, and, except for twisted pair wire, the maximum segment length. The following standards are supported or in draft stages:

- 10 BASE 5: 10 mb/s baseband, 500-meter segments (also known as *thick net*).

- 10 BASE 2: 10 mb/s baseband, 200-meter segments (also known as *thin net*).

- 10 BROAD 36: 10 mb/s broadband, 3600-meter segments.

- 10 BASE T: 10 mb/s baseband twisted pair, 100-meter segments.

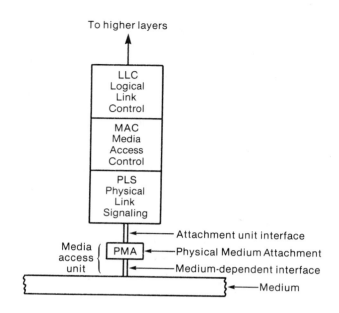

Figure 27.6   IEEE 802 standard.

- 1 BASE 5: 1 mb/s baseband twisted pair, 500-meter segments (also known as StarLAN).

Both the Ethernet and IEEE standards call for a maximum bus length of two kilometers and a maximum of 1024 workstations supported on the network. Ethernet permits a maximum of two repeaters between any two workstations; 802.3 permits as many as five segments and four repeaters between workstations.

Figure 27.6 illustrates the elements of 802.3. The link layer is divided into two sublayers—the Logical Link Control (LLC) and the Media Access Control (MAC)—which together correspond to the data link layer in the OSI model. The 802.3 standard interacts with higher layers for error recovery and network control. The interface between the media access sublayer and the LLC transmits and receives frames and provides status information to forward to higher levels for error recovery. The interface between the media access and the physical layers includes signals for framing,

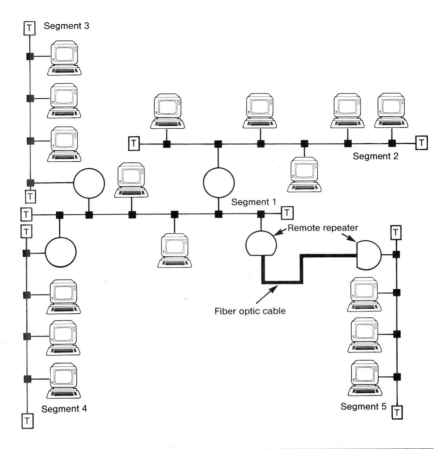

Figure 27.7   A five-segment Ethernet.

detecting and recovering from collisions, and passing serial bit streams between the two layers.

The network is composed of cable segments a maximum of 500 meters (1640 feet) long—the greatest distance that can be spanned at the maximum signaling rate of 20 mb/s. As many as five segments can be interconnected through a maximum of four repeaters as Figure 27.7 shows. The repeaters sense carriers from both cable segments to which they are connected and also detect and avoid collisions. When a repeater detects a collision in one segment, it transmits a jamming signal to both segments. The

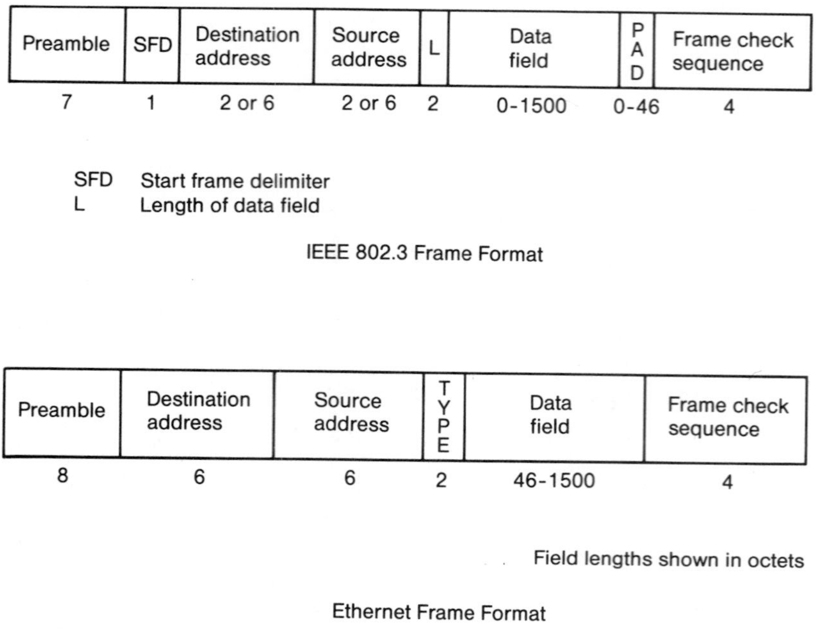

Preamble	SFD	Destination address	Source address	L	Data field	P A D	Frame check sequence
7	1	2 or 6	2 or 6	2	0-1500	0-46	4

SFD   Start frame delimiter
L   Length of data field

IEEE 802.3 Frame Format

Preamble	Destination address	Source address	T Y P E	Data field	Frame check sequence
8	6	6	2	46-1500	4

Field lengths shown in octets

Ethernet Frame Format

Figure 27.8   802.3 and Ethernet data link frames.

design of the NAU is simple, consisting of a high impedance bridge on the transmission medium.

The 802.3 and Ethernet datalink frames, which Figure 27.8 shows, require the data field to have a minimum length of 46 octets. This minimum frame length makes it risky to connect asynchronous devices directly to the network because of the potential of overloading. Since asynchronous characters are individually synchronized, every character from an asynchronous terminal generates a frame. If the characters are going to a host computer that uses echoplexing, a return character also is generated and transmitted on the network, which means that every keystroke generates two frames that are at least 72 octets or 576 bits long. A lightly loaded Ethernet can handle this kind of load, but in heavily loaded networks there is a definite risk of overload. The solution is to use a terminal server, which is a device that buffers asynchronous characters and creates a frame of an appropriate size.

The Token Bus LAN IEEE 802.4

A token bus LAN, illustrated in Figure 27.4, uses the same topology as CSMA/CD, but control flows in a logical ring. Although messages are broadcast as with CSMA/CD, control passes in sequence from station to station. Each station is programmed with the address of the preceding and succeeding stations.

Token passing allows a wider physical network diameter than CSMA/CD. The diameter can range from 1280 meters (4200 feet) to 7600 meters (25,000 feet) depending on cable grade. Although the network diameter can be increased by repeaters, for most LANs the range will be sufficient to make their use unnecessary.

The MAC in a token bus performs many of the same functions that it does in CSMA/CD, such as address recognition and frame encapsulation, but several functions are added to accomplish the more complex control. The primary functions of the MAC are to determine when its station has the right to access the medium, to recognize the presence of a token, and to determine when and how to pass the token to the next station. The MAC must be capable of initializing or resetting the network. It must be able to recognize when a token has been lost and to regenerate it when necessary. It also must be able to control the addition of a new station to the network and to recognize when a succeeding station has failed.

On the surface, token passing does not appear complicated, and if all goes well, the protocol has little work to do. Each MAC is programmed with the address of its successor and predecessor stations. When it passes the token to its successor, it listens for the successor's transmission. If the successor fails to transmit, the MAC sends a second token and again listens for a response. If it hears no response, it assumes the next station has failed and transmits a message asking which station follows. Each MAC on the network compares its predecessor station number with the number contained in the "who follows" message. The station that follows the failed station responds to the message, and the failed station is bypassed. A similar process is required for a station to reinsert itself in the network.

The Token Ring LAN, IEEE 802.5

The token ring, illustrated in Figure 27.4, is both a logical and a topological ring. Each station is a repeater, enabling greater diameter than bus networks. Because each node repeats the data stream, failure of a node could disrupt the network. Therefore, nodes are equipped with trunk coupling units to bypass a failed station automatically.

Tokens contain a priority indicator. When a token circulates through a station that has traffic of a priority equal to or greater than the priority designator, that station can seize the token and send priority traffic until a timer within its MAC, known as the *token holding timer*, expires. In this manner, the network ensures that traffic always is transmitted up to the capacity of the system and that low priority traffic is deferred.

One station on the ring is designated as the active monitor (AM) to supervise the network. The AM controls error recovery, detects the absence of a token or valid frames of data, and detects a persistently circulating token or frame. Although only one station is designated as the AM, all stations contain its logic. If the AM fails, the station first detecting the failure assumes the role.

A token ring network is wired as a ring in a star topology, with a hub known as a media access unit (MAU) at its center. MAUs are either passive or active devices that couple the twisted pair wire of the side legs to the central ring. MAUs can be chained to broaden the scope of the ring. If the ring becomes overloaded, it is split by breaking the tie between MAUs and segmenting a single ring into two or more rings.

The 802.6 Metropolitan Area Network

The limited speed and range capabilities of LANs spawned the need for a standard network that can transmit data at speeds of 100 mb/s or more over a range approximating the size of a metropolitan area. The 802.6 metropolitan area network, which Chapter 29 discusses, fulfills this requirement. Unlike LANs, which are intended for private use, the 802.6 network is intended for shared use over public rights of way.

Ethernet on Other Transmission Media

Since the original LAN standards were published, the 802 committees have been requested to produce more standards—usually variations on proprietary networking protocols. A major drawback to the 802.3 standard was its requirement for RG-8 coaxial cable, which is expensive, somewhat difficult to install, and too bulky to be concealed easily. A major difficulty with Ethernet is its required 2.5-meter minimum spacing between transceivers and its maximum of 50 meters of cable from transceiver to station. The cable can be easily routed through open office areas, but retrofitting Ethernet into an existing building with fixed partitions usually requires a compromise between a desire to conceal unsightly cables and the need to place the major components where they are accessible for maintenance.

One of the first requests for deviation from the original 802.3 standard was a proposal to use RG-58 cable, which is about the thickness of a pencil and much lighter and easier to install. The specification that evolved, called 10 BASE 2, has the same carrying capacity as thick coax, but has a segment length limited to 200 meters. Thin net, as this specification is called, uses a network interface card that has the transceiver and controller contained in a unit that mounts in a personal computer expansion slot. The cable is brought directly to the personal computer and coupled with a T connector.

Thin net brings a new set of limitations to 802.3. Although the cable is easier to install, it must be routed directly past each workstation. If it is concealed in walls, it must be looped down the wall and back up again, the result being a longer cable than with thick net, which connects devices to the transceiver through a tail cable. In some installations it is easy to reach the maximum segment length with only a few workstations. Also, since the stations connect in series, the network must be taken down to add or remove a station. Some manufacturers solve this problem with a wall-mount adapter that taps the transmission medium.

One solution to the cabling problem is to use twisted pair wire, a commodity that is inexpensive and plentiful in many buildings. Twisted pair does not lend itself readily to tapping because of difficulty in controlling impedance irregularities, so a

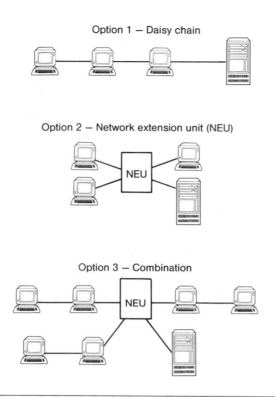

Figure 27.9 **StarLAN configuration and components.**

twisted pair network cannot easily be deployed in the standard Ethernet bus topology. Instead, most products, typified by AT&T's StarLAN, are configured as a physical star that radiates from a central hub, which AT&T calls a Network Extension Unit (NEU). Figure 27.9 shows the major components and configuration of StarLAN. Stations may be connected directly to an NEU, or as many as ten stations may be connected in a daisy chain with standard modular telephone cord. The daisy chain arrangement is electrically equivalent to thin net and has the same disadvantages when it comes to adding and removing stations.

The StarLAN specification, which is the 1 BASE 2 network under 802.3, requires two twisted pairs a maximum of 185 meters long. NEUs can be interconnected to form a single segment of as many as 240 stations. As with any contention network, the actual number of stations the network supports depends on the load and may be much less than the theoretical maximum.

In 1987 Synoptics, a spin-off from Xerox, the original developer of Ethernet, introduced a product called Lattisnet that operates on twisted pair at 10 mb/s. The following year, AT&T announced a 10 mb/s StarLAN product that complements its 1 mb/s product. The IEEE began considering a standard for a 10 mb/s network on unshielded twisted pair (UTP) which, at the time of this writing, has not been finalized.

Running a network at 10 mb/s over UTP overcomes the drawback of slow speed encountered on earlier twisted pair products and the difficulty of installation of coaxial products. Most offices are wired as a physical star so networks can be constructed with a combination of coaxial backbone between wiring closets and twisted pair from the closets to the stations.

Designing products and networks at this speed is not without its challenges. The attenuation of the wire is higher at 10 mb/s, and without shielding the wire is susceptible to electromagnetic interference and may itself radiate interfering signals in excess of FCC standards. Current practices call for a maximum of 100 meters from the station to the wiring hub. AT&T's practice calls for the use of D inside wire, which is plentiful in many buildings. The LAN must co-exist with a variety of other services that may be sharing the wire, which could be a problem if its condition has deteriorated.

Synoptics handles the design problems by connecting stations to the UTP medium via an attachment unit interface (AUI) that couples the workstation to a transceiver over a 15-wire cable that may be up to 50 meters long. Transceivers are connected to an active hub or Lattisnet concentrator. The concentrators regenerate the data packets, detect collisions, and retransmit the signals over the star-wired logical bus.

Other LAN Issues

The foregoing factors are the principal issues involved in selecting and applying LAN technology. Several lesser issues must be considered, however, when deciding which product to purchase. These issues are:

- Interface method.
- Dedicated vs. non-dedicated file servers.
- Throughput.
- Network size or diameter.
- Interconnection with other networks.
- Fault tolerance.

Interface Method

Personal computers are attached to a LAN either through a specialized adapter card or through the computer's serial port. The latter are called RS-232 LANs or zero slot LANs. Although the speed of the LAN is not restricted to the 19.2 kb/s EIA-232 speed, the data rate is considerably less than LANs that use interface cards. Typically, speeds are approximately 150 kb/s per second compared to the data rate of 10 mb/s or more that is typical of LAN interface cards. RS-232 LANs are relatively inexpensive and are suitable only for small offices that have few workstations.

Dedicated vs. Non-Dedicated File Server

The purpose of a file server in a LAN is to act as a central shared resource that users can access to store and retrieve files if they are authorized. The network operating system regulates access to the file server, permitting users to offer the various levels of restrictions that are discussed in the section on network operating systems in Chapter 28. Some types of operating systems require a dedicated file server. Others permit any workstation to offer its hard disk as a shared resource.

The idea of a non-dedicated file server has superficial appeal. Instead of concentrating shared files on one or more servers, the server is distributed throughout the network. The crash of one hard disk under a fully distributed arrangement may be serious, but it does not destroy all the files in the organization. The loss of data problem, however, is a major reason for using a dedicated server. The tendency of users to fail to backup their disks regularly is legendary. A dedicated server is more likely to have one person assigned the responsibility of backing it up.

A non-dedicated server has several disadvantages. If users turn their personal computers off, the files on those machines cannot be shared. If a user reboots or hangs up his or her personal computer at a time that a file is being accessed by another user, the effect will be unpredictable and may result in loss of the file. A personal computer being used as both a file server and a workstation may slow down noticeably when it is being used for a heavy print job or to access a large file.

A dedicated server is also used in most networks to drive printers. Within the limits of the available expansion slots and the capability of the operating system to address printers, the file server can serve as host for multiple printers. Physical considerations become an important factor in locating file servers and determining whether it is necessary to have multiple servers. Parallel cables are limited to approximately 50 feet in length, and attaching printers within that diameter may be inconvenient for users. Serial printers can be located at much larger distances by using line drivers, but they require more administrative effort.

The need to place printers near users may generate a requirement for multiple file servers or for software that enables users to offer their printers as a shared resource. The same drawbacks that apply to sharing files apply to sharing printers, but it may be an economical alternative to multiple file servers.

Throughput

Throughput, or rate of transmission of information between stations, is an important issue with LANs as with any other network. LANs have high data transmission speeds, generally ranging between 1 and 20 mb/s, with newer FDDI networks operating at 100 mb/s. Transmission speed should not be confused with throughput, however, which may be a fraction of the transmission speed. Throughput is limited by several factors in a LAN:

- Data transmission speed of the network.

- Overhead bits used by the network because of the coding system and the protocol.

- Time spent in collision and error recovery.

- Bandwidth of the transmission medium.

- Diameter of the network.

- Load imposed on the network.

Throughput is predictable in token ring networks but is difficult to predict in contention LANs. In contention networks, throughput can be determined by a computer simulation or experimentally by loading the network to see how response time is affected.

Although the network itself may have a high throughput, communication may be slowed because of characteristics of the file server, which is the principal device other stations wish to communicate with. Factors affecting file server efficiency are discussed in Chapter 28.

Interconnecting LANs

With the exception of closed loop manufacturing processes, many LANs require interconnection to other LANs, to public telephone or data networks, or to private networks. There are two methods of interconnecting networks. A *gateway* communicates between two dissimilar networks, using each network's protocol. A gateway is needed for each pair of networks. The second method is by use of a *bridge*. Contrasted to a gateway, which communicates by using each network's own protocol, the bridge allows the protocols to coordinate, accommodating any difference between the two, and making the protocols appear as if they were compatible. Bridges and gateways also expand the diameter of LANs as discussed in the next section. A third device, known as a *router*, performs the same functions as a bridge, plus the additional function of routing signals between networks over alternate paths. Routers either use fixed routing tables or support *source routing*.

Source routing charges the originating station with the responsibility for finding a route through the network to the destination. The procedure ensures that frames do not loop between segments connected by multiple bridges. The originator sends a route discovery frame, a copy of which is sent to every ring on the network. The target station returns the discovery frame to the originator. Each ring along the path back to the originator marks the discovery frame with the route. The originator reviews all the returning frames and picks the optimum route.

Network Size or Diameter

All LANs have a limited diameter, which can be overcome with ancillary devices such as bridges, routers, and gateways. Network designers must be careful not to exceed the maximum diameter. Remember that the limiting factor is measured in cable feet, not in point-to-point distance. Designers must take into account routing that may add to network diameter.

Fault Tolerance

A fault tolerant LAN is one that can handle irregularities in network operation while allowing users to continue processing or, at worst, to terminate their operation without losing data. Network irregularities fall into three categories, each of which may require a different recovery strategy: *faults*, which are software or hardware defects; *errors*, which are incorrect data; and *failures*, which are breakdowns of network components. End users do not distinguish between these three categories; their concern is the continued operation of the network.

Fault tolerant LANs employ a combination of hardware and software, usually consisting of the following elements:

- An uninterruptable power supply to protect against AC power failure or at least permit a graceful shutdown.
- A duplicate file allocation table (FAT) kept on the disk.
- Software that logs what users were doing at the time of a crash and saves their files. For example, Novell fault tolerant software provides a transaction log that helps bring a failed system back to the starting point.
- Redundant hardware, such as multiple disk drives that mirror each other so the second drive takes over when the

first fails, mirroring servers, duplicated bridges, and redundant cabling.

- Applications software that stores information between saves.
- Careful backup procedures.

A key to fault tolerance is a network management system that alerts the administrator to impending problems by detecting minor faults before they grow into major problems. All the systems comprising fault tolerance come at a price, so the degree of fault tolerance a network is likely to have is a function of the willingness of management to pay for it.

Applications

The data communications industry is learning to apply LANs, and their growth is expected to accelerate over the next few years. An organization that requires a LAN will have one or more of these characteristics:

- Widespread use of terminals or personal computers.
- Use of automated office features such as electronic mail, computer messaging, computer graphics, and electronic filing.
- Sharing of common files and data bases.
- Sharing of high cost peripherals such as hard disks and printers.
- Use of computer-controlled manufacturing processes.
- Use of alternate forms of communication such as video for security and training.

As the use of personal computers and automated office features grows, nearly every business that has more than a handful of employees will be a potential user of LANs.

Standards

As mentioned earlier in this chapter, LAN standards are promulgated by the IEEE in the United States and by CCITT world wide.
Although the present 802.3 and 802.5 standards predominate,

nonstandard networks such as Arcnet are widely used because of their simplicity and low cost.

Above the 802 standards, which comprise the first two layers of the OSI model, network operating systems are proprietary. The primary network operating system vendors, Novell, 3Com, IBM, Microsoft, and Banyan, provide incompatible operating systems, which means that networks can interconnect only through protocol converters.

Application Criteria

This chapter has discussed the primary criteria that users consider in selecting a network. The following are the most important considerations in deciding among the many alternatives on the market.

Preferred Vendor.   Companies who use IBM equipment and software should consider the token ring network because it is directly supported by IBM. Companies who use Digital Equipment computers will favor Ethernet or 802.3. Other computer manufacturers may support either or both networks, but the predominant network for most manufacturers is Ethernet.

In-Place Wiring.   Many buildings are wired with 25-pair UTP wiring, which once was used for 1A2 key telephone systems and is now vacant except for one or two pairs that are used for voice. This wiring becomes a valuable resource if it is capable of supporting a LAN. The most important considerations are length of wire run and type of wire. AT&T D Inside Wire or equivalent is suitable; other wire of unknown ancestry may be unsuitable. The wire length must not exceed the distance limits for the network being installed. The wire must terminate in connecting blocks of suitable quality, such as 66-type blocks or, preferably, 110-type connectors.

Environmental Concerns.   The environment should be carefully inspected for EMI, corrosive atmosphere, and other such elements that could interfere with the LAN.

Applications.   The principal LAN applications tend to fall into two categories, regular and broadband. Broadband in this sense refers to the amount of bandwidth required and is not used in the same sense as the broadband modulation method. Broadband applications include imaging, CAD/CAM, and other systems that require transmission of large amounts of data over the network. If the throughput requirements are high enough, FDDI should be considered.

It is also important to determine whether the network should support video transmission. If a coaxial cable must be installed for video anyway, it can potentially support one or more local area networks.

Access Protocol.   When LANs were first introduced, there was a common belief that contention protocols would not provide enough throughput to support applications that required guarantees of data delivery. Experience has shown, however, that CSMA/CD networks are as effective in most applications as token passing. The access protocol argument has largely disappeared. The most important reason for using token passing is that the application or manufacturer supports it.

Local Area Network Equipment

The local area network industry endured several years of uncertainty through the early and middle 1980s. As each year opened, the pundits proclaimed it the year of the LAN—the year that users would embrace the technology and business would boom. Office productivity would climb and manufacturers would finally turn a profit. Somehow, the customers failed to get the message, and many of the weaker manufacturers fell by the wayside or were swallowed by stronger companies.

The viability of LANs is no longer in question. Although a significant percentage of personal computers are not yet networked, the benefits of networking are undisputed. The path from a collection of standalone personal computers to a fully integrated network is not yet crystal clear. The principal issues were discussed in Chapter 27. Standards have aided immensely in narrowing the options, but there are still so many standards that prospective purchasers are often bewildered by the choices. The fundamental difficulty that plagues LANs is no different from the issue that plagues mainframes and minicomputers: proprietary operating systems.

There is an important difference between LANs and mainframes, however. The latter are designed for centralization of processing power and administration, while the former distributes that power. Computing power and, incidentally, computing budgets, are moving from the MIS department to end users, and users are not unanimous when it comes to selecting operating systems and software. The battle began with the Macintosh vs. IBM question; now most network managers must support both. The problem was tangled further by IBM's introduction of Microchannel Architecture and the splinter group led by Compaq, which elected to improve the original IBM bus with the Extended Industry System Architecture (EISA) bus.

These issues affect only the first two layers of OSI—the 802 standards. Between the computer's operating system and 802 is an amorphous structure that comprises the many network operating system options. As it turns out, the arguments of the 1980s were largely irrelevant. From a performance standpoint, it makes little difference whether an Ethernet or token ring protocol is used. It also makes little difference whether thick net, thin net, or twisted pair is used; that issue is structural, having to do with existing plant and the network's environment. The broadband/baseband argument has also resolved itself in favor of baseband except in those applications where a broadband cable is in place or needed for video.

Now attention has shifted to higher layers in the protocol stack, which raises issues such as these:

- Performance of the network operating system.
- Performance of the file server.
- Extension of the network limits.
- Sectionalization of the network to improve performance.
- Alternatives to the LAN such as the data PBX and central office LAN.

The industry uses the term *system integration* to describe the process of bringing together software and devices from multiple sources and causing them to operate as a unit. Network managers have three choices in the matter: turn the project over to the mainframe vendor, who usually can furnish all the components; contract with an independent system integrator; or become their own system integrator. This chapter is an overview of the major equipment-related issues that must be addressed no matter which path is chosen.

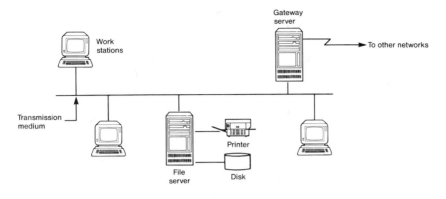

Figure 28.1 **Major components of a LAN.**

LAN Components

Figure 28.1 is a conceptual view of a LAN showing its major components. This section discusses all components except the transmission medium, which is discussed in Chapter 27, and workstations, which usually are standard personal computers.

File Servers

The file server is the king-pin of any local network. It serves these major functions:

- Provides storage facilities for user files.
- Provides storage facilities for application programs.
- Provides facilities for sharing common resources such as disk space and printers.
- Provides, in most LANs, a residence for the network operating system.

Peripherals are not attached to the network only through the file server. As Figure 28.2 shows, peripherals may be attached in three ways: through the file server, through a workstation, or directly to the network itself. Workstation attachments have a place in smaller networks where the administrator can ensure that the station user makes the peripheral available for sharing, but in

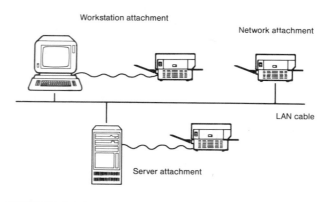

Figure 28.2   How peripherals attach to a LAN.

larger networks workstation attachments may create administrative problems. Direct attachment is completely satisfactory but is not available with most printers and plotters. The alternative of server attachment is feasible with most networks.

Servers can be personal computer-based or host computer-based. For a host computer to act as a file server, it must run file server software. Generally, a host computer will serve more users and provide more disk space at lower cost than a personal computer-based file server.

The file server in a LAN is treated as a virtual drive on the user's personal computer. A virtual drive is one that appears to be directly attached but is shared with other users. The network operating system maps the drive to the user's personal computer, intercepts calls from the personal computer's operating system, and directs them to the file server.

Factors Affecting File Server Performance

The file server is the most vulnerable part of a local area network, from the standpoint of both failures that can result in potentially disastrous file loss and efficiency problems that affect the user's ability to access disks and printers. Techniques for guarding against data loss are discussed in the Chapter 27 discussion of fault tolerant networks. This section discusses the design and administrative factors that affect file server efficiency.

Network Data Rate.   The data rate of the network has a significant effect on efficiency. The data rate is not the same as the data transfer rate or throughput; the latter is often no more than one-third of the data rate because of overhead and collision recovery time. In every network, some factor limits throughput. Usually it is a factor other than the data rate of the network, but with other factors equal, a faster network will provide better response time to the users.

Number and Activity of Users.   With other factors equal, the greater the number of users and the greater their activity, the slower the network's response time will be. The effect is more pronounced in a contention network, but file servers attached to deterministic networks will experience greater demand with more users and respond less efficiently to service requests.

Hard Drive Access Time.   Access time is a function of how rapidly the disk moves to the sectors where data is stored. The access time of a hard disk is composed of two factors: seek time, which is the time it takes for the read head to move to the proper track, and rotation time, which is the time it takes for the disk to rotate to the appropriate sector. Also, the design of the hard disk controller affects access time. The shorter the access time, the more efficient the file server will be. Generally, access times greater than about 22 milliseconds should be avoided in LANs with more than a few users.

File Server Memory.   In addition to housing operating system and application software, file servers use memory to execute read and write commands and to buffer print data. It is better to err on the side of providing too much RAM than too little because a shortage of memory will adversely affect file server efficiency.

The network operating system uses caching to improve network efficiency. When a user issues a read instruction to the disk, the operating system reads more data than necessary on the probability that the next read operation can be served from memory rather than from the disk. Caching, which requires RAM, reduces the frequency of disk access, and therefore improves response time.

Network Software Efficiency. Network operating system vendors are quick to point out differences in efficiency between their products and those of their competitors. This factor, which the next section discusses, is probably the most difficult for a LAN owner to evaluate because it is difficult to construct tests that match reality and because organizations use networks in so many different ways.

Network Operating Systems

As discussed in Chapter 27, the IEEE 802 standards cover only the first two layers of the OSI model. The DOS and NETBIOS functions of the computer's operating software comprise the Applications (seventh) and part of the Presentation (sixth) layers of the model. Between is the network operating system. Like computer operating systems, network operating systems contain utilities and executable programs that perform basic functions. The basic programs perform the following functions:

- Capture calls to DOS from the application program and convert them to network operating system calls.

- Manage the hard disk in the server to maximize the efficiency of information transfer between the network and the server.

- Manage security on the network, permitting users to offer their files for shared access and restrict them from unauthorized access.

- Designate shared resources as if they were directly attached to the users' personal computers.

- Provide tools with which the network administrator can manage the network.

These functions are described briefly in this chapter. For a more detailed description, readers should refer to books on local area networks, several of which are listed in the bibliography.

Choosing the network operating system is the most crucial decision most companies make in selecting a network. Network interface cards for popular systems such as Ethernet, token ring, StarLAN, and Arcnet are becoming a commodity. Although all four protocols began as proprietary products of individual manufacturers, standardization and cross licensing have effectively brought them into general use. File servers too are virtually a commodity, with the 80286 and 80386 computers filling the function in most networks, and 486-based servers becoming the standard for future networks. The lower protocol levels and the transmission medium move data around the network, but they require an operating system to control matters such as these:

- Who is authorized to access what files and with what level of rights.

- What shared resources are available and to what group of users.

- How security is managed to prevent unauthorized access and damage to files.

- What administrative tools are available to evaluate network performance, control access to the network, and add, move, and change stations.

- What other networks are accessible and how access is controlled.

- What maintenance, statistical, and trouble-shooting tools are available to alert managers to impending problems and assist in restoral when they occur.

- What utility programs are made available to the users and administrator.

Many of the same matters apply to a multiuser computer operating system but with an essential difference: in a multiuser computer the users share the processor; in a LAN each station has its own processor.

The central concept of a network operating system is *redirection*. The operating system intercepts calls to peripherals and redirects them to another resource, such as the file server, without the user's changing operating procedures except to log on the network and comply with its security provisions.

Administrative Tools

Many local area network users underestimate the amount of administrative effort it takes to keep a network operating. The network administrator is defined in software as the person who has the right to modify and control the rights of other users. In most networks, the rights approximate the following list, which is ordered by the degree of control the right provides, with the highest rights listed first. Each right has the rights of succeeding but not of preceding levels of authority:

- *Hidden:* the presence of the file or directory is itself concealed from unauthorized users.
- *Parental:* has full control over any file in the directory
- *Private:* only users with parental rights can read files.
- *Modify:* can change any file in the directory
- *Read/write:* can read any file or write any file in the directory but cannot modify existing files.
- *Read only:* can read files in the directory but cannot add a file.

The operating system permits managers to create a directory structure similar or identical to the tree-structured directory in MS-DOS. Files are contained in directories and subdirectories; the network administrator can regulate rights at any level from a file up to the entire directory.

The operating system also should provide statistical information that should allow the administrator to isolate trouble and reconfigure the network as necessary. For example, the administrator needs to know the volume of traffic on the network and the frequency with which users encounter delays. Contention networks should show the frequency of collision. The operating system should inform the administrator of the operating efficiency of the file server.

Utility Programs

Most network operating systems also provide a set of utilities for performing the same sorts of functions that a user expects on a single-user operating system. Utility programs enable users to list directories, copy files, and perform other DOS-like functions. The network administrator has utilities to add and remove users, establish rights, change the classifications of files, and oversee the activities of the users. In most networks, administrators have

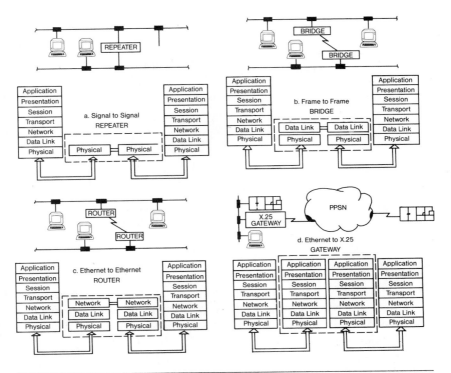

Figure 28.3   Repeaters, bridges, routers, and gateways related to the OSI model.

utilities that allow them to create menus to insulate users from the operating system's command language.

Network Linking and Segmentation

Four classes of devices—*repeaters, bridges, routers, and gateways*—are used to segment networks and link together like or disparate networks. Figure 28.3 shows the relationship of each type of device to the OSI model.

Repeaters

A repeater operates at the physical level. It has no processing ability. The only function of the repeater is to regenerate the bit stream. Its purpose is to extend the diameter of the network by linking segments.

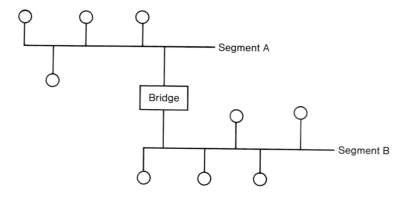

Figure 28.4   Isolating LAN segments with a bridge.

Bridges

A bridge operates at the data link level and can read packet addresses to determine whether the packets should be routed to another segment. A major function of a bridge is to divide a network to relieve traffic congestion. If two segments are linked, as in Figure 28.4, the bridge blocks traffic originating in segment A and destined for a station in segment A, from segment B. If the traffic is intended for a station in segment B, the bridge allows it to cross. The bridge provides a repeater function as well as segmenting the network. Bridges also can change from one type of transmission medium to another. For example, bridges are available to access twisted pair on one side and fiber optics or coax on the other.

The *learning bridge* or *adaptive bridge* is a special type of bridge that stores station addresses in a table. The table is initialized by sending broadcast packets to all stations on the network and registering the location of each address. This feature enables the bridge to learn automatically which segment contains which addresses, and relieves the network administrator of reinitializing the bridge when stations change.

Another special type of bridge is the *remote bridge,* which links LANs over a distance outside the normal range limitation as Figure 28.5 shows. Remote bridges operate in pairs with one side of each element connecting to the LAN and the other side to a lower speed data link. Since the speed of the data link between

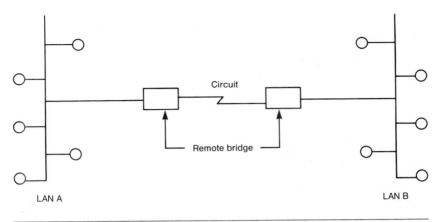

Figure 28.5   Linking two LANs with a remote bridge.

the two halves of the bridge is considerably slower than the speed of the LANs, a remote bridge can become a point of congestion. Figure 28.6 is a photograph of a Vitalink remote bridge.

A bridge is also a potential failure point that can disrupt a network that lacks backup protection. Local area network protocols do not provide for alternate routing, but it is possible to run two bridges in parallel. One bridge is designated as primary and carries all traffic unless it fails, in which case the secondary bridge takes over.

The industry tendency is to build more intelligence into bridges. Some products that are sold as bridges provide functions of higher level devices such as a routers and gateways. A bridge equipped for alternate routing is called a *brouter*. Also available are bridges that support multiple links and prioritize traffic. For example, some devices can block longer packets, such as file transfer, during periods of heavy traffic.

Routers

A router performs the functions of a bridge, plus routing. Routing is important when multiple segments are connected in such a way that there is more than one possible path by which a station can reach another station on the network. Figure 28.7 shows three token ring networks interconnected by routers. Station A can

Figure 28.6   Vitalink TransLAN 350 remote bridge.
Courtesy, Vitalink Communications, Inc.

reach station B by the direct route or via the third ring, which both A's and B's network have in common. *Source routing* is a technique that enables the source to specify the route that a packet should follow to its destination. Source routing requires the originating station to map the network with the location of addressees and routers. Packets originated by the source are transmitted with routing information to the destination.

Gateways

The fourth device for linking networks is the gateway, which spans all seven layers of the OSI protocol model. A gateway is designed to link incompatible networks. For example, a gateway could link Ethernet to an SNA network. A gateway is a protocol converter that must be specific to the network pairs it is intended to link. For example, SNA gateways are available for most LANs. These

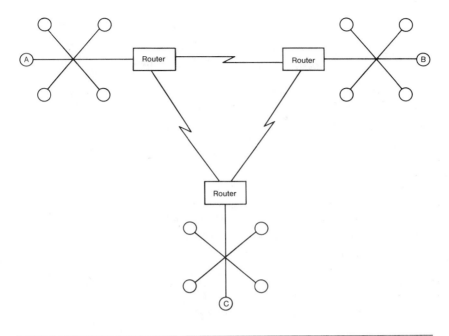

Figure 28.7 Token ring networks linked by routers.

permit stations on the LAN to function as if they were terminals behind a cluster controller.

Network Interface Cards

The network interface card (NIC) plugs into an expansion slot or connector on the station. The functions of the interface card are:

- *Buffering* the speed of the network to the speed of the device
- *Packetizing and depacketizing* the information. The NIC accepts a data stream from the device and converts it to a network packet. Incoming data packets are converted to a continuous data stream to present to the device.
- *Parallel/serial conversion.* The NIC plugs into a parallel slot in the personal computer and converts data into the serial form required by the network.

- *Encoding and decoding.* Many LANS use a scheme such as Manchester coding for pulsing the data on the network. The NIC makes the conversion from the coding on the computer bus to that required by the network.

- *Access to the transmission medium.* The NIC checks the busy/idle status of a contention network or checks for the token in a token network.

- *Address detection.* The NIC checks incoming packets to determine if it is the addressee.

Network interface cards are specific to the type of network, but they are standardized to such a degree that cards from one vendor can be used on the networks of other vendors. The speed of the network card is affected by its access to the personal computer bus. Cards with 16-bit connectors are faster and more expensive than 8-bit cards. Computers with 286 and higher processors can use 16-bit cards.

Terminal Servers

As discussed in Chapter 27, connecting an asynchronous device directly to a contention network is risky because each character is individually packetized. If a host echoes the character, each key stroke generates two packets that must be padded to the minimum length. An Ethernet can support several users manually keyboarding, but the safest course is to use a terminal server as shown in Figure 28.8. The figure also shows that the terminal server can connect asynchronous ports from a host computer to a LAN.

A terminal server accepts characters from asynchronous terminals or ports, buffers them, packetizes them, and inserts them on the network in an Ethernet frame. It recognizes the addresses of its attached ports, breaks down the packets, and distributes a data stream to the appropriate port. The concept of a terminal server is similar to that of a statistical multiplexer, using Ethernet as the transmission medium.

Data PBXs

The data PBX has many of the same attributes as the voice/data PBXs discussed in Chapter 20 except it is incapable of switching

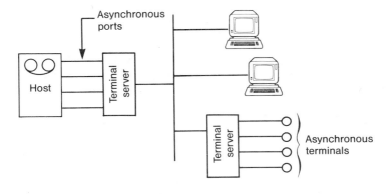

Figure 28.8   Connecting asynchronous terminals through a terminal server.

voice and is less expensive per port. Conceptually, the data PBX does the same thing as an electromechanical A/B switch; it switches ports together but under software control.

A data switch and a local area network have ranges of applications that overlap to some degree. Both the data PBX and the LAN, however, have shortcomings that are filled by the other. A data PBX is ideally suited for switching asynchronous terminals to multiple hosts or for concentrating a large number of terminals to a smaller number of ports on a single host, an application that a LAN handles with some difficulty through terminal servers. On the other hand, most data PBXs lack the ability to connect a personal computer to a file server operating as a virtual disk on the user's PC. File transfers on a data PBX are restricted by the port speed of the system—usually 19.2 kb/s.

The distinction between a LAN and a data PBX is blurred by the tendency of some manufacturers to call their switching products LANs. For example, many LECs offer products they call central office LANs. As we will discuss later in this chapter, CO LANs are circuit switches and technically resemble data PBXs more closely than LANs. Although the technology used by some manufactures makes it difficult to generalize about what constitutes a data PBX, data PBXs generally have the following characteristics:

- The DTE interface is an EIA-232-C or other DTE/DCE equivalent interface.

- Connections are circuit switched, not packet switched.

- Port-to-port transmission speed is limited to 19.2 kb/s, with some products going as high 64 kb/s.

- Connections are controlled by one or more central processors as opposed to LANs, which have distributed control.

- Data PBX software does not interact directly with the operating system of an attached device.

As the requirement for local area networks grew, some observers predicted the demise of the data PBX, but the technology is very much alive and shows signs that it will continue to fill a particular niche in the local networking market. The strength of the data PBX lies in its support of asynchronous terminals, but as the price of personal computers drops, the use of PCs to replace terminals is increasing. The data PBX has the advantage of lower cost and lower administrative requirements than the LAN alternative, and in some applications it may neatly supplement a local area network. This chapter discusses products that deviate from one or more of the above criteria but which are still classified as data PBXs or, using the more general term, data switches.

Data PBX Technology

The architecture of most data PBXs closely resembles that of a voice/data PBX. A switching matrix makes connections between ports. The line ports usually have an EIA-232-C or equivalent interface. Typically, the terminal-to-PBX connection is made over twisted pair wire. Most systems require at least four wires. Connections through the switch are controlled by a processor that has access to a database containing information about the port such as terminal parameters, features, and restrictions.

A data PBX provides three primary functions: port selection, port contention, and port queuing. *Port Selection* is the process of connecting a device to one of several ports. The ports can be located on more than one host, or port selection can be used to share peripherals such as printers and modems. This feature also permits users to select between different classes of ports on the same host if, for example, some ports have speed or feature restrictions. Some systems allow a high priority user to jump to the head of the queue.

When multiple terminals share a limited number of ports, the function of *port contention* comes into play. The data PBX connects the originating terminal to an available port on a first-come-first-served basis. If no ports are available, *port queuing* holds the originating terminal in queue and connects it to the first available port.

When users signal their desire to connect to a host, the data PBX presents a menu of choices. Most data PBXs have a security feature that prevents users from accessing unauthorized hosts. The menu may be customized to blind users to the existence of hosts they are not permitted to access. When the connection to the host is made, the user conducts the session as usual. Many data PBXs can set parameters automatically, matching, for example, the originator's terminal to the host's parity, speed, and number of data bits. Within limits, the data PBX also may allow dissimilar devices to communicate. Some systems have the capability of protocol conversion so, for example, a user could communicate with either an IBM synchronous or an ASCII host from the same asynchronous terminal.

When the session is finished, the user logs off and the computer port is available for others to use. If the user fails to log off or is idle for a prescribed period, the data PBX may be able to log the user off automatically. If so, it is important that the PBX send a log-off string. If the computer has not been informed by a proper log-off procedure that the user has terminated, the port may be held in limbo and the next user may be unable to establish a session. Equally hazardous, if the computer is not aware that the session has not been terminated, the next user may be connected to an active port and be given access to the array of services or permissions for which the previous user was authorized.

Data PBXs offer the advantage of being almost transparent to the user. Users who know how to access the host computer can be prompted by the PBX. There is no need to address the device the user is connecting to; the user connects by making a menu selection. There is no need for the user to be computer literate as is frequently the case with local area networks, and the simplicity of the data switch makes it easier to administer than a LAN. It is necessary, however, for the administrator to monitor traffic volumes to ensure that the proper number of ports has been provided.

Many data PBXs provide networking capability, with systems interconnected over high speed trunk facilities. In a campus environment switches can be distributed to reduce the length of EIA-232-C connections. Depending on the manufacturer, the inter-switch trunks could be fiber optics, coaxial cable, T-1 carrier, or twisted pair wire. Data PBXs that are T-1 compatible can be networked over much greater distances. A data PBX network provides users with access to remote host computers using the same techniques as they use to access a local system.

Central Office LAN

Despite the misleading terminology, a central office LAN (CO LAN) belongs to the data switch family. Data rides over voice lines on a data/voice multiplexer (DVM). Voice operates at the baseband (unmodulated) frequency. A full duplex data signal operating at 19.2 kb/s is derived by modulating a carrier in each direction with the data signal. The signal travels over a non-loaded local loop to the central office, where a matching DVM separates the voice and data signals, sending them to separate circuit switches. The data switch may offer access to other services, such as a public data network.

The limiting factor in the application of a CO LAN is the need for a local loop to connect each data terminal. The number of trunks to an organization using a key telephone system or PBX would limit the number of devices that could be attached to the CO LAN. The most obvious application, therefore, is in an organization served by Centrex. The economics of a CO LAN application are evaluated in the same way Centrex is evaluated; the lower capital cost of CO LAN is compared with higher monthly charges.

Applications

The applications for local area networks are as varied as the organizations they serve. This section discusses some of the criteria used in selecting LAN equipment and presents two case histories that illustrate the variety of configurations that LAN equipment can assume.

Case History: Local School District

A school district consisting of a central administration building, two high schools, four middle schools, and 22 elementary schools was faced with a communications problem. A study showed that money could be saved and service improved by replacing their Centrex system with one or more district-owned PBXs. Also, their data processing capability, which was furnished by an outside service bureau, was insufficient to meet the needs of most users. Although the district intended to retain the outside service for student records, payroll, and accounts payable and receivable, they wanted the capability of downloading information from the service bureau's master file to process in their computer for producing more detailed reports.

A project was implemented in two phases, which spread over two academic years. The first phase was replacement of the analog Centrex system with a network of PBXs and key telephone systems. AT&T System 75 PBXs were installed in the administration building and the high schools and were linked with T-1. AT&T Spirit key systems were installed in the middle and elementary schools and connected to the administration PBX by off-premises extensions. Separate DID trunks were installed in all three PBXs.

The second phase of the project was to overlay data communications capability on the voice network. The data network shown in Figure 28.9 was developed. An AT&T 3B-2/1000 Model 80 computer was installed in the administration building and connected via SNA emulation to the IBM AS/400 used by the service bureau. StarLAN networks operating over twisted pair at 10 mb/s were installed—one in Administration to serve approximately 60 stations and one in each of the high schools to serve 30 stations each. The administration LANs were linked directly to the 3B-2. The LANs in the high school were linked to the 3B-2 via remote bridges over 56 kb/s circuits that were derived from spare capacity on the T-1. In the high schools, 386

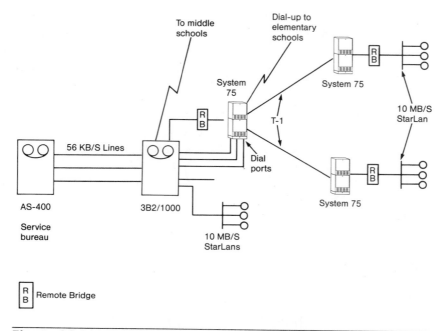

Figure 28.9   Local school district LAN and host computer network.

file servers were installed to store application programs and shared files and to host the shared printers.

The 56 kb/s circuits were derived from the T-1s by using Processor Data Modules, which are devices that directly interface the PBXs to 56 kb/s circuits through digital station cards. The middle schools were connected to the 3B-2 through multiplexers and asynchronous ports. The elementary schools, which had light data processing requirements, were connected over the off premises extensions.

The 3B-2 acts as a file server for all stations on the network. With this architecture, any station on the network can log on to the service bureau's AS/400 through the 3B-2. All the district's dumb terminals were replaced with personal computers, about half of which are IBM-compatible and the remainder Apple Macintosh. Terminal operators can toggle between terminal emulation mode, in which they perform regular data entry work, and the personal computer mode, which makes their computers active stations on the StarLAN network.

This architecture has several advantages compared to the traditional host/dumb terminal architecture of unconnected LANs. The district is easily able to transfer files from the service bureau computer. Previously, only a limited number of operators who had direct access to terminals connected to the service bureau computer could access the service bureau and then only to enter information and print reports. Now, any authorized employee in the district can access the service bureau, with security handled through passwords. Because the elementary schools are on off-premises extensions, the network is not subject to the same security risks that a dial-up network connected to the PSTN would be.

All users on the network enjoy the ability to share files and printers. The network is well positioned for future expansion should the district decide to do its own data processing.

Case History: Data Switching and LAN Combined in a Community College

The following case history describes an interesting application involving a combination of terminals—both directly wired and switched—and personal computers using an AT&T Information Systems Network (ISN) in a community college.

ISN is a hybrid that has many of the characteristics of a data PBX and other characteristics of a LAN. Internally, it uses a packet switching protocol on separate transmit and receive buses. The data buses are short, which, as explained in Chapter 27, reduces the probability of collision. Collisions are entirely eliminated with ISN, however, by using a separate contention bus that controls which port has access to the network. The buses and control mechanism are contained in a module known as the Packet Controller. ISN connects to external devices through Interface Modules. Modules are provided for asynchronous terminals, Ethernet, and StarLAN.

Terminals connect through the ISN at speeds up to 19.2 kb/s, which gives the system the characteristics of a data PBX. ISN performs all the data PBX functions, such as port selection,

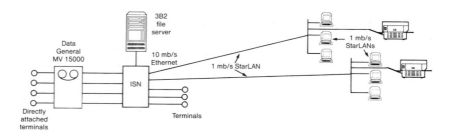

Figure 28.10 **A community college LAN and data switching application.**

contention, and queuing, in which it acts as an effective (and expensive) data PBX. With its ability to bridge StarLAN and Ethernet, it also performs some LAN functions.

Figure 28.10 shows the case study application in which ISN was applied. The principal computer on campus was a Data General MV 15000, which was overloaded and running short of ports. The college planned to supplement the existing array of approximately 70 terminals with an additional 150 personal computers. All personal computers are equipped with fixed disks, which limits the need for storage space on a file server. All users need to share a limited number of printers, and all users need access to the Data General computer, in some cases acting in terminal emulation mode and in other cases using the Data General as a virtual drive.

To improve response time on the Data General and to enhance security, the college downloads a portion of the database from the Data General to the file server each evening. Users who need access to the database download portions of it to complementary database management systems in their personal computers or perform file searches on the file server. Word processing and spreadsheet applications were moved from the file server to individual personal computers, which, in conjunction with other measures, reduced the load on the Data General.

Figure 28.10 shows how ISN and a combination of other products were integrated to solve the college's problem. Terminals with a full-time need for access to the Data General were left permanently wired. Terminals with occasional or part-time use are wired through asynchronous ports on the ISN. Personal computers are connected to departmental StarLAN networks, which are attached to StarLAN Interface Modules on the ISN. AT&T 3B-2 computers are used as file servers and connect to the ISN over StarLAN connections and to the Data General host over a 10 mb/s Ethernet running TCP/IP. Personal computers having a need for both terminal access to the Data General and LAN access to the file server are dual ported. StarLAN cards provide access to the file server, and EIA-232-C wiring provides access to the Data General through the ISN. All wiring is twisted pair except the 10 mb/s Ethernet connection, which is coaxial cable.

Evaluation Criteria: Local Area Networks

Each LAN application is unique enough that the list of requirements should be custom designed to fit the organization. This section briefly discusses the primary factors to consider in evaluating LANs and selecting the best product.

Vendor Support

The choice of LAN will frequently be dictated by the degree of support offered by the vendor. Unless someone in the organization is equipped to become the systems integrator, it is usually necessary to have assurance of continued local support from the vendor. The following support features should be evaluated:

- *Implementation and Installation Assistance.* The design and engineering of LANs is specialized enough that vendor support will usually be required to implement a system. For some types of transmission medium it will be feasible to obtain installation labor from the open market, but in CATV and fiber optics systems, the vendor will normally be required to install the network. In most cases the vendor should have the resources to turn the network up and debug the software.

- *Maintenance Support.* When a LAN fails, immediate and competent support is needed. Most failures will be of the transmission medium. Difficulties with the network operating system will be the next most frequent. The vendor should employ enough technicians to cover absences and resignations. The vendor also should have the necessary test equipment to diagnose troubles with the transmission medium and the operating system. The vendor should be an authorized dealer who offers warranty support on both hardware and software.

- *System Integration Capabilities.* Most networks do not come out of the box ready to install. It may be necessary to apply cable from one vendor, network interface cards from another vendor, and personal computers from a third. Also, most LANs require integration with existing applications programs and interfacing with hardware of diverse manufacture. Unless an organization has internal capabilities for integrating the network, it will be necessary to obtain the service from the vendor or a contractor.

Costs

LAN costs vary widely and change frequently enough that it is risky to generalize. Costs ranging from $200 for network interface cards to more than $5000 per device for FDDI are quoted, but it is essential to determine total costs before acquiring a network. The following cost factors should be considered:

- Design and engineering of the network, including the cost of collecting usage data for sizing it.
- Purchase price of the equipment, including spare parts, delivery, and taxes.
- Purchase price of new devices required because of incompatibilities.
- Installation costs, including labor, building and conduit rearrangements, and special permits and licenses.
- Software right-to-use fees, including both the operating system and upgrading applications software to operate on a network.
- Cost of growth when the system exceeds its capacity.
- Transition costs, including cutover from the old network, if any, training of users and operators, and preparation of new forms and passwords.

- Purchase of special test equipment, such as protocol analyzers, necessary to maintain the network (unless the vendor maintains the network).

- Documentation of the network, so repairs will not be delayed by lack of information.

- Maintenance costs, including the cost of finding and repairing trouble and lost production time during outages.

- Costs of periodic hardware and software upgrades.

- Administration costs, including usage monitoring, service monitoring, and interpretation of network statistics.

Traffic Characteristics

The volume, character, and growth rate of data traffic are important factors to consider in selecting a network. Bulk data transfer can usually be handled most economically on a point-to-point basis. The ultimate size of the network must be considered so it can be segmented as it approaches capacity.

When predicting future requirements, it is valuable to have a network that includes the ability to gather statistics on current usage. Some network operating systems provide usage information, which is used to expand the network and assess its health.

Bridges, routers, and gateways are potential bottlenecks in networks. It is important to understand the volume of traffic crossing these devices and to pick the device that handles the required traffic. Capacities are usually stated in packets per second. The load they are called upon to carry will depend on the demands of the application.

Reliability

The initial cost of a network often pales in significance compared to the cost of outages. The cost of lost production time can mount rapidly when people are depending on the network for their productivity. Networks should be invulnerable to the failure of a single element. Where common equipment such as amplifiers, repeaters, and head end equipment exists, spares and duplicates should be retained. Most important, qualified repair forces must be available within a short time of failure.

When a network element or the total network fails, the more rapidly it can be restored to service, the more valuable the network. Some systems have internal diagnostics that aid in rapid trouble isolation and restoral. The network also should be designed for fault isolation. For example, a ring network should be designed to identify which node has failed. It should be designed for bypass of a failed node, and the media access controller or network control center should provide alarms indicating a loss of received signal to aid in rapid fault isolation.

Off-Net Communications

LANs differ widely in their ability to handle off-net communications. Gateways or bridges are required to interconnect networks using different protocols. Where the protocols are identical, repeaters will normally be required. For access to public data networks, local networks require gateways—usually using X.25 protocols toward the public network.

It is important to anticipate what other networks will be communicated with, what their protocols are, and what the speed and volume of traffic will be. A network under consideration should support these external interfaces.

Compatibility with Existing Equipment

A company having a large investment in existing terminals and computers will find it essential to select a network that is compatible with the existing equipment. This may dictate a standard interface such as EIA-232-C or EIA-449 between the network and its terminals. Some networks can interface only through controllers that plug into specific apparatus and will, for that reason, be unsatisfactory for some applications.

Compatibility with Other Vendors' Equipment

When proprietary networks are purchased, it may be difficult to obtain equipment from other than the network supplier, though existing equipment is initially compatible. Network integration, or conversion of equipment to be compatible with the network, is likely to be costly and, in the worst case, may be impossible.

Need for Voice and Video Communications

In selecting between baseband and broadband equipment, the choice often will depend upon the need for other forms of communication. Where video is required, a LAN can ride for a small additional investment. An extensive voice communication requirement may mandate the use of a PBX in addition to or instead of a LAN.

Security

Both contention and token networks allow access to all traffic by all stations on the network. Although the stations are programmed to reject messages that are not addressed to them, the potential of unauthorized reception exists. For example, a protocol analyzer can see all messages. Where security is important, it may be necessary to select a network with additional security provisions such as encryption. The transmission medium is also an important element of security. Twisted pair wire is easy to tap. Radio transmissions can be easily intercepted. Fiber optic cable is difficult to tap, and coaxial cable lies somewhere between fiber optics and twisted pair wire on the ease-of-tapping spectrum.

Throughput and Response Time

Ideally, a LAN should not impose response delays on the attached devices. The choice of operating system and the characteristics of the file server are the most important variables affecting throughput. For minimum delay, the file server must have a 386 or 486 processor, running at high speed, say 25 MHz or higher. The file server should have plenty of RAM for print buffering and disk caching. The speed of the network will also affect throughput.

Network Diameter

Distance limitations may dictate the choice of a LAN. When the network diameter exceeds the design limitations of the network, it must be segregated through a repeater or a bridge. To obtain the maximum diameter, a high speed medium such as fiber optics may be used.

Connectivity

The most effective LANs are designed so all devices on the network can be interconnected with simple addressing. The systems that are easiest to use offer complete flexibility to the operator, using, for example, initials for addresses and allowing the LAN to convert them to the address needed by the network.

Evaluation Criteria: Data PBXs

The first step in evaluating a data PBX should be to review the user requirements carefully to ensure that a data PBX is the proper vehicle for fulfilling them. If so, the next step is to determine how sophisticated the system needs to be. If the requirement is simply for single-node data switching, the data PBX can be an unsophisticated model. If, however, the requirement is for multiple nodes and interface to LANs, a more complex system will be required. The following are some selection criteria.

- *Concentration ratio.* A data PBX with concentration has more ports than it has paths through the switching network. For example, if a PBX had 200 ports and 100 switching paths, the ports would not experience blockage because there would be a path available for each pair of ports. A machine with 100 paths and 400 ports would have a 2:1 concentration ratio. The degree of concentration acceptable depends on the number of call attempts and average holding time per attempt. Chapter 31 explains how to make the calculations.

- *Off-net calling.* Some data PBXs offer modem pooling and can connect to local central office trunks so users can call outside the system. The availability of an interface to a public data network may be a related consideration.

- *Port speed.* Most data PBXs can support 19.2 kb/s transmission speed. A few machines are equipped to handle 38.4 kb/s, and fewer still can accommodate up to 64 kb/s. For most keystroking and printing applications, 19.2 kb/s is more than adequate. For large CPU-to-CPU file transfers, the higher the speed, the less time the transfer requires.

- *Need for protocol conversion.* When it is necessary to communicate with hosts that use different protocols, the data switch may replace a protocol converter that would otherwise be required.

- *Interface to a LAN.* Some data PBXs have a local area network interface that enables them to be accessed by devices on the LAN, to bridge LAN segments together, and to provide public network access to devices on the LAN.

- *Security.* In some applications the host computer may provide all the security that is needed; in others, it may be important that the data switch provide a second level of security.

Selected Manufacturers of Local Area Network Equipment

Coaxial, Twisted Pair, and Fiber Optic Cables

Alpha Wire Corp.

Anaconda Ericsson Inc. Wire and Cable Div.

Belden Corp.

Brand-Rex Co.

General Cable Co.

Panduit

Siecor Corporation

Standard Wire and Cable Co.

LAN Equipment

AT&T Information Systems

Bridge Communications

Concord Data Systems

Contel Information Systems

Complexx Systems, Inc.

Corvus Systems, Inc.

Data General

Datapoint Corporation

Digital Equipment Corp.

Fibermux Corp.

IBM Corp.

Interlan

Novell, Inc.

Optical Data Systems

Retix

Siecor Fiberlan

Sytek, Inc.

Ungermann Bass Inc.

Wang Laboratories, Inc.

Western Telematic, Inc.

Xerox Corporation Information Products Div.

Bridges, Routers, and Gateways

Advanced Computer Communications

Allen Bradley Co. Communications Div.

Andrew Corp.

Applitek Corp

Artel Communications Corp.

Chipcom Corp.

Cross Comm Corp.

Cryptall

Digital Equipment Corp.

Fibercom, Inc.

Fibermux Corp.

Gateway Communications, Inc.

Cabletron Systems, Inc.

Hewlett-Packard Co.

Hughes LAN Systems

IBM Corp.

Infotron Systems Corp.

Isolan

Lanex Corp.

Microcom

Netronix, Inc.

Performance Technology, Inc.

Proteon, Inc.

Racal InterLan

Rad Data Communications, Inc.

Raycom Systems, Inc.

Retix

Synoptics Inc.

3Com Corp.

TRW Inc. Information Networks Division

Ungermann-Bass, Inc.

Vitalink Communications Corp.

Wellfleet Communications, Inc.

RS-232 LANs

Applied Knowledge Groups

Axon Computers

Computer Pathways

Digital Products

Equinox

Data PBX Manufacturers

Applied Innovation

Commtex

Develcon Electronics

Equinox

Fujitsu Business Communication Systems

Gandalf Data

Infotron

Micom

Microscience

Newbridge

Quasitronics

TDS

Western Telematic

Ethernet over Unshielded Twisted Pair Wire

AT&T Information Systems

Cabletron

David Systems

Digital Equipment Corp.

Hewlett-Packard Roseville Networks Division

NetWorth, Inc.

Synoptics Communications

3Com

Ungermann-Bass

29

Metropolitan and Campus Networks

Local area networks have fulfilled many of the expectations users held for them. With bridges and routers, they have overcome the distance limitations that confine the LAN to a building or campus, but where the reach of the LAN exceeds its natural boundaries, it is usually at the price of reduced bandwidth.

Many new applications that require bandwidths greater than T-1 are entering the market, and as speeds increase, power users are requiring an ever-increasing amount of bandwidth. T-1 is available from most LECs, and T-3 is available where LECs and independent fiber optic carriers have extended their facilities. These facilities are point-to-point, however, and do not meet the requirements of a company that needs bandwidth on demand and connectivity over an entire metropolitan or campus area.

New products just entering the market fill the need for high speed connectivity over a campus or metropolitan area. Several newly developed products support Fiber Distributed Data Interface (FDDI), which is a 100 mb/s network that extends for some 50 kilometers—enough to cover all but the largest industrial campus but not enough for an entire metropolitan area.

The telephone industry supports the IEEE 802.6 Metropolitan Area Network (MAN), which eventually will support speeds of 600 mb/s or more. MANs operate as a public facility and, as such, must ensure that users cannot intercept or damage one another's data. MANs fill the gap between the circuit switched telephone network that is excellent for voice but has shortcomings for data, and packet switched networks that are excellent for bursty data but unsuitable for voice.

Besides FDDI and MANs, many companies choose to implement their MANs over dedicated facilities, using bridges and routers or fast packet switches to get the necessary connectivity. Private and public MANs are designed to carry digitized voice and video. Metropolitan and campus networks are designed to support high bandwidth applications including:

- High speed graphics such as CAD/CAM and imaging.
- Backbone that supports interconnection of LANs.
- CPU-to-CPU high speed data transfer.
- Digitized voice.
- Compressed video.

This chapter discusses the protocols of FDDI and the 802.6 MAN. Previous chapters on pulse code modulation and local area networks cover the bridges, routers, and T-1 transmission facilities of LANs.

Fiber Distributed Data Interface (FDDI)

The 10 mb/s speed of Ethernet and the 16 mb/s speed of the latest version of token ring provide ample speed for most present office applications, but the emerging technologies of imaging and graphics require moving massive amounts of data. These applications and the back end connections to high speed disk drives, require higher speeds than LAN protocols support. Fiber Distributed Data Interface (FDDI), developed by the ANSI X3T9.5 Committee, is a new standard for a 100 mb/s network that operates on 62.5/125 micron multimode fiber over the 1300 nanometer wavelength window. The FDDI specification also can be met by 50/125 micron fiber. The network has counter-rotating token rings; one ring is designated as primary, and the other as secondary.

The ANSI standard specifies two classes of stations. Class A stations connect to both rings, while Class B stations connect only to the primary ring through a wiring concentrator. The dual ring appearance of Class A stations permits double the throughput

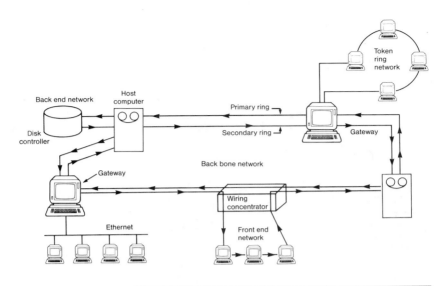

Figure 29.1   Fiber distributed data interface.

since the station can send on both rings simultaneously. The FDDI network supports three types of networks (Figure 29.1):

- *Front end networks.* These are networks connecting workstations to a host computer or other peripherals over the FDDI network.

- *Back end networks.* These allow connections from a host computer to peripherals such as high speed disks and printers to be connected over FDDI to replace the present parallel bus connections.

- *Backbone networks.* These are connections between the main nodes on the network.

The FDDI specification permits a maximum of 500 nodes with no more than two kilometers between attachments. The total end-to-end diameter of the network cannot exceed 200 kilometers, which is too narrow to serve many metropolitan area network applications. Figure 29.2 illustrates the method of wiring Class A and B stations to the ring.

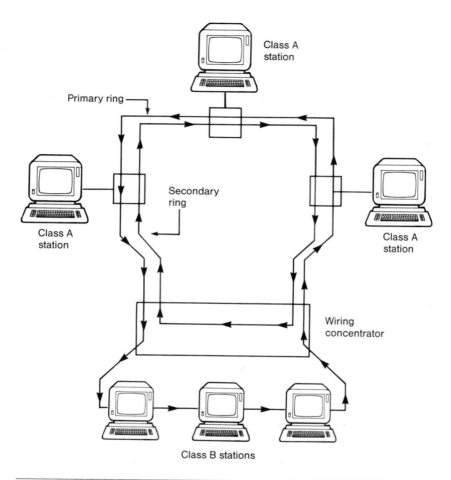

Figure 29.2   Class A and B stations on an FDDI network.

The dual ring architecture provides an effective measure of protection. As illustrated in Figure 29.3, if a link or a station fails, the stations go into an automatic bypass mode to route around the failure. The possibility of a failed station or link must be considered when designing the network to stay within the interstation and total length limitations.

FDDI operates much like the 802.5 token ring with some important exceptions in addition to the obvious difference in

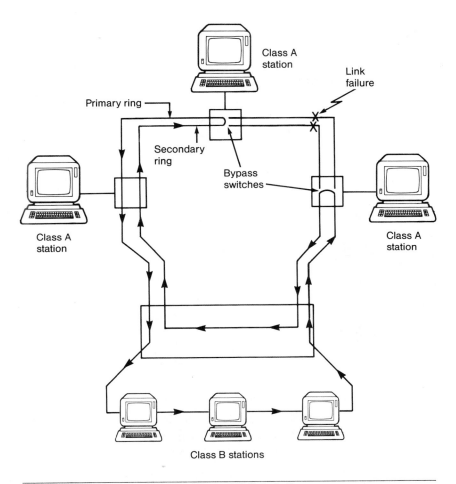

Figure 29.3   FDDI bypass around a link failure.

speed. First, multiple frames can circulate simultaneously on an FDDI network. When a station completes sending a frame, it reinserts the token on the network. A second station on the ring can seize the token and send a frame while the first frame is still making the trip back to the originating station. As the frames circulate, each station checks for errors and if it detects one, sets an error indicator. The network protocol does not, however, attempt to correct errors. It sends an error indication to higher level protocols to resolve.

Other differences include the transmission medium. Token ring uses twisted pair wire and fiber optics, while FDDI supports only fiber. Token ring supports only a single ring, while FDDI supports dual rings. Another difference is in the line coding format. Token ring uses Manchester coding, while FDDI supports a five-bit encoding system discussed later.

The FDDI Protocol

The FDDI protocol fits into the OSI model in a manner closely paralleling the 802 protocols. Figure 29.4 shows the two-layer protocol with its sublayers that connect the physical ring to the higher protocol layers.

The physical layer uses a four-bit out of five-bit (4B/5B) coding scheme. The code, shown in Figure 29.5, is encoded on the ring using a nonreturn to zero inverted (NRZI) signal, in which a transition in the light wave represents a 1, and no transition represents a 0. With the five-bit code, there are never more than three 0s in sequence, which maintains clocking on the ring. Each station provides its own clocking in FDDI, in contrast to token ring, in which the active monitor provides a master clock.

The MAC layer of the protocol defines a maximum token rotation time (TRT), which is established by a bidding process among all stations when the ring is initialized. When a station seizes a token, it can transmit frames up to the maximum value contained in its TRT. If the token fails to arrive after an interval determined by the protocol, a station initiates a claim token mode, which regenerates the token. If a station does not see its claim token frame return, it assumes that a ring failure has occurred.

If the ring fails, the stations enter a *beacon* mode that is used to isolate the failure. In the beacon mode, a station sends a continuous string of beacon frames until it receives a beacon frame from an upstream neighbor. When a station receives an upstream beacon frame, it quits sending its own beacon frames, and begins repeating frames from the neighbor. All stations repeat this process until the only station left beaconing is the one immediately downstream from the fault. That station connects the

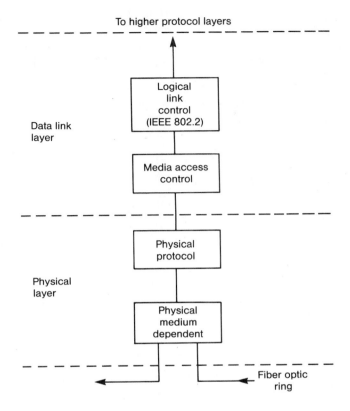

Figure 29.4   FDDI protocol layers.

primary ring to the secondary ring, a process known as a *wrap*. When the network wraps, the two rings are initialized as a single ring, and traffic resumes. The self-healing process in FDDI ensures a high degree of reliability and effectively insulates most stations from loss of service if the ring or a station fails.

FDDI Applications

Currently, FDDI attachment prices are high, which limits the applications to those companies that can justify spending $3000 to $5000 or more per node to gain the benefits of high bandwidth. As with other network technologies, prices will fall as demand

HEXADECIMAL	4-BIT BINARY	5-BIT BINARY
0	0000	11110
1	0001	01001
2	0010	10100
3	0011	10101
4	0100	01010
5	0101	01011
6	0110	01110
7	0111	01111
8	1000	10010
9	1001	10011
A	1010	10110
B	1011	10111
C	1100	11010
D	1101	11011
E	1110	11100
F	1111	11101

Figure 29.5   FDDI 4B/5B code.

develops. Many observers believe that FDDI will eventually replace slower LANs such as token ring. In the near term, the primary application for FDDI will be as a backbone network to link departmental LANs.

As with other networks, the base speed of the network is not translated into throughput of the same dimensions. Depending on the transfer protocol, the 100 mb/s speed may drop to 20% or less of the network speed. Even at top speed, the token-passing overhead consumes some 20% of the throughput, which limits the potential throughput to approximately 80 mb/s. An OSI-compliant protocol known as Express Transfer Protocol (XTP), which is currently under development, will improve throughput.

A major selling point of FDDI is its ability to transfer data between applications that are otherwise incompatible. For example, a DEC computer operating on an Ethernet connected to an FDDI backbone could transfer data to an IBM computer operating on an FDDI-connected token ring. This kind of transfer, however, requires that the protocols be fully FDDI-compliant. One method of making the FDDI connection is to encapsulate the data, including its own protocol, into an FDDI frame. This method would be effective for connecting, say, two Ethernets, using FDDI as a transport mechanism, but it does nothing to ensure multivendor connectivity.

Fiber Distributed Data Interface-II

The potential for delays in a packet network makes FDDI unacceptable for voice. The FDDI-II standard, which is not approved as of the writing of this book, divides the 100 mb/s bandwidth into separate voice and data segments. As many as 16 6.144 mb/s segments can be allocated for voice or non-packetized data. Designers chose this bandwidth because it can carry four North American or three European T-1 systems. The voice portion of the bandwidth is transmitted in serial format, while the data portion follows the normal FDDI protocol.

When this standard is developed, it will overcome a major drawback of FDDI—its inability to handle voice and compressed video. Many observers believe, however, that the 100 mb/s speed will prove to be too slow to handle these applications plus the other broadband applications that justify FDDI. IEEE 802.6 has a superior access protocol and may replace FDDI in private as well as public MANs.

The IEEE 802.6 Metropolitan Area Network

The arrival of powerful desktop computers and computer-aided drawing (CAD) applications led to demand for greater amounts of bandwidth and higher speeds over a wider range. FDDI fills these requirements for privately owned networks. FDDI breaks the range limitations of the 802.3, 802.4, and 802.5 protocols and increases the throughput by an order of magnitude or more, but it remains a single-organization network. An FDDI network could be extended throughout a metropolitan area, but data circulating through multiple premises could theoretically be intercepted—a possibility that stimulated the development of a public, shared, high speed network architecture and protocol.

In 1982, before completion of work on the 802 LAN standards, IEEE formed a subcommittee designated as 802.6 to work on a MAN standard. The LAN standards that were then under development had an objective bandwidth of 20 mb/s and were generally intended for a range of about two kilometers, which was too restrictive for many applications. Also, LANs were not designed as multicompany networks. The 802.6 committee adopted the following as goals for a metropolitan area network:

- A MAN requires fast and robust signaling schemes.

- The network should guarantee security and privacy, permitting the establishment of virtual private networks within the MAN.

- The network should have high availability, reliability, and maintainability.

- The MAN should perform efficiently despite its size.

Unlike the LAN committees, which were dedicated to specific access protocols, the 802.6 committee investigated several competing technologies before adopting, in November, 1987, a dual-bus proposal known as *Distributed Queued Dual Bus* (DQDB). The system was originally known as QPSX, for Queued Packet Synchronous Exchange (QPSX), but it was renamed to avoid confusion with the Australian company, QPSX Communications Limited, that developed the protocol.

The logical transmission medium for a high speed metropolitan network is fiber optics. The LECs have placed large amounts of fiber cable in most metropolitan areas but find it difficult to carve up the bandwidth and share it among multiple customers. Fiber optics by itself is an excellent point-to-point transmission medium, but it is difficult to administer in a multibuilding environment where bandwidth needs are continually shifting. Some form of network is needed to deliver voice, data, and video where and when it is required, while protecting the privacy of the users. The IEEE 802.6 MAN is the current answer.

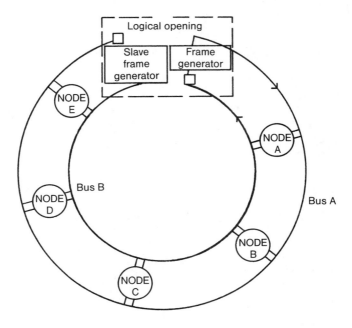

Figure 29.6   The architecture of the 802.6 metropolitan area network.

The 802.6 network makes use of both fiber optic and copper facilities that are already in place. It rides on common carrier facilities using the synchronous optical network (SONET) or broadband ISDN (B-ISDN) facilities, which are discussed in Chapters 13 and 26 respectively. Its initial transmission rate is 50 mb/s, but work is currently underway to develop a network at 155 mb/s, the lowest rate in the SONET hierarchy, with future transmission rates of 300 and 600 mb/s anticipated and strong indications that the rates will go even higher.

The MAN has two separate networks, a transport network and an access network. The transport network, which is located only on common carrier premises, carries the traffic of multiple users. The access network, which interconnects the user with the transport network, carries only a single user's traffic. This division is necessary to ensure privacy and security.

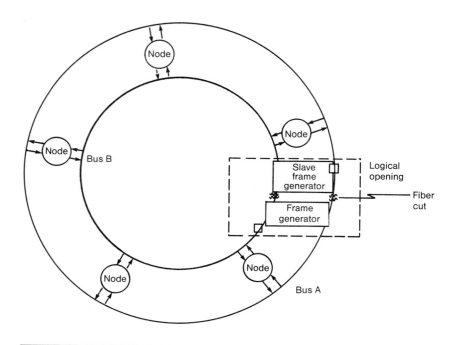

Figure 29.7   The 802.6 MAN shifts logical break to point of failure to close ring.

The 802.6 architecture, shown in Figure 29.6, is similar to FDDI. It uses two counter-rotating rings, which permit full duplex communications between any of the nodes. A logical break, at which clocking is introduced, is located between two of the nodes. The network is self-healing through one break in the fiber. As Figure 29.7 shows, if the fiber breaks between nodes, the logical break shifts to the point of failure and the ring closes to form the logical break at the point of the physical break.

Although the dual-ring architecture of DQDB topology appears to be a pair of rings, it is logically a looped dual bus, with each node appearing on each bus. Usually the transmission medium is fiber optics, but the standard allows use of coaxial cable; twisted pair does not have enough bandwidth to support transmission over a useful range. Twisted pair can be used, however, for the access network.

A frame generator at the master station emits 125 microsecond frames, which, not coincidentally, is the length of a T-1 frame. Each frame can contain a fixed number of fixed length slots. The number of slots depends on the bit rate of the bus, which in turn depends on the transmission medium. In a free-standing configuration, the network contains its own synchronization. When connected to a public network, however, the MAN must derive its synchronization from the public network.

Isochronous services such as digitized voice are time sensitive and therefore must be transported across the network with minimum delay. The network provides a prearbitrated access (PA) method, which reserves bandwidth on the network for a guaranteed bandwidth of 64 kb/s. The master station transmits empty PA frames every 125 microseconds. Each active station is assigned a fixed time slot that it uses for sending and receiving.

Non-isochronous applications such as bursty data are given queued arbitrated (QA) access only when they have data to send. DQDB uses an ingenious method of allocating QA access to the bus. Each node is equipped with a request counter and a packet countdown as Figure 29.8 shows. When a node has a packet ready for transmission, it transmits a request upstream. As the request passes the upstream nodes, each node increments its request counter by one, so each node knows at any time what its place in queue is by the contents of its request counter. As empty slots flow to the downstream nodes, each node decrements its request counter. Each node knows, therefore, how many packets were requested and how many were filled with passing slots that are intended for downstream stations. If a node's request counter is set at n, when the nth slot goes by, it knows that the next slot is intended for it. The node seizes the slot and sends its packet. This scheduling method provides a high degree of efficiency. Slots are never wasted while a station has traffic to send and no station can monopolize the network.

The 802.6 network nodes are constructed with side legs into the customers' premises. Traffic for the customer routes through the premises, while other traffic bypasses it. Security is not a problem because the only traffic entering a user's premises is its own traffic.

The logical structure of 802.6 is much like the other 802 standards. The physical layer corresponds to OSI and supports

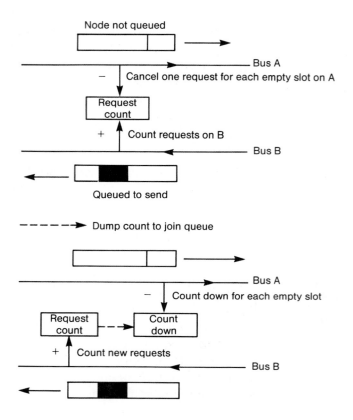

Figure 29.8   Queued arbitrated access to the 802.6 bus.

North American, European, and SONET standards. The 802.6 specification does not define a maximum network diameter or number of nodes. These are a function of the transmission system used by the network. The second layer of 802.6 is the DQDB layer, which corresponds to the OSI data link layer. The DQDB layer supports the following three types of services:

- Connection-oriented virtual circuit for bursty data.

- Connection-oriented virtual circuit for isochronous data, which has regular recurring signal characteristics.

- Connectionless or datagram service.

At this writing in late 1990, 802.6 is undergoing field trials in some Bell Operating Companies. Most LECs plan to introduce their service offerings in the early 1990s.

Applications

FDDI and 802.6 are intended for similar applications: high speed bandwidth on demand where the speed and distance limitations of local area networks are too restrictive. The technologies are too new to base their applications on the experience of others.

Standards

Unlike many other telecommunications technologies, metropolitan and campus network products are emerging from the standards instead of the other way around. The 802.6 standards are promulgated by IEEE as an expansion of the earlier 802 LAN standards. FDDI standards are driven by ANSI through its X3T9.5 Committee.

Evaluating Equipment

As this book was being written, the completed standards were just being introduced, so not many fully compliant products are on the market. The applications that exist use equipment that was developed in anticipation of the standards. The criteria discussed in this section is preliminary, and decisions will be based largely on the availability of products and services. Any reader contemplating a metropolitan or campus network should consult current publications.

Selection of FDDI Cable Types

Many organizations place fiber optic cable to support Ethernet or token ring with the expectation of converting to FDDI in the future. This strategy is sensible, but it is important to select the proper grade and type of fiber. LANs operate in the 850 nm. window of the fiber, while FDDI operates in the 1300 nm. window. Therefore, if the cable is to support a LAN now and FDDI in the future, it must have the proper characteristics in both windows.

The limiting factor in FDDI node spacing is the flux budget, which is the maximum amount of light that can be lost between two adjacent nodes while still maintaining communication. Both

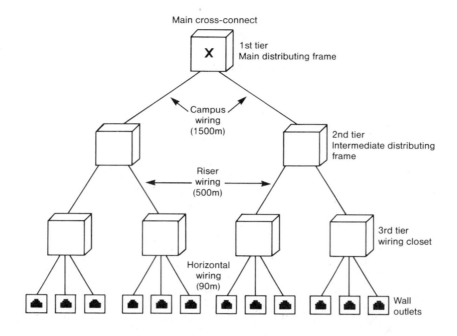

Figure 29.9   Three-tier wiring topology recommended by Electronics Industry Association.

62.5/125 and 50/125 micron cable can meet FDDI specifications. The 50/125 cable has a higher bandwidth but has approximately 2 dB lower flux budget. The 62.5/125 cable has a higher flux budget, but only the highest quality fiber can support the bandwidth of 500 MHz-km that the full two kilometer spacing requires. For all applications currently under development, multimode cable is sufficient. If fiber is being wired to the workstation, it may be advisable to install one or two pairs of single mode fibers for future applications that may require greater bandwidth.

FDDI Wiring Topology

The most effective topology for FDDI cable is the star-wired ring configuration. The EIA TR-41.8.1 working committee in its proposed building wiring standard recommends a three-tier wiring arrangement with maximum distances for fiber shown in Figure

29.9. The horizontal wiring is the most important to install in sufficient quantity and of the proper type because it is normally the least accessible for making future changes. Although the wiring arrangement shown in Figure 29.9 is point-to-point, it can easily be wired in a ring for FDDI or wired to a star hub for Ethernet.

FDDI Fiber Quantities

For non-FDDI applications separate transmit and receive fibers are required. FDDI's dual-ring architecture requires two fiber pairs for Class A stations and one pair for Class B stations. Most workstation applications will be adequately served by a single appearance on the ring. It may be difficult, however, to plan which nodes will have only single appearances, so in many applications the extra cost of installing two-pair fiber will be justified.

Selected FDDI and Metropolitan Area Network Equipment Manufacturers

Note: At the time of this writing FDDI and MAN standards were newly approved, and equipment alternatives had not reached the market in great supply. Therefore, the list of manufacturers producing the equipment will grow considerably in the future.

FDDI Equipment

AT&T

FiberCom, Inc.

Fibronics Fiber Optic
Communications

IBM

Raycom Systems

Private Networks

The forces discussed in this book are transforming private networks. The old networks will survive for a time because they revolve around mainframe computers that are expensive to replace and support applications that would be costly to redesign. In many applications, however, hierarchical networks are giving way to flat networks of peer devices. The principal driving forces are these:

- High powered personal computers are replacing dumb terminals.

- T-1 and fractional T-1 circuits are replacing analog circuits. The new circuits have several times the bandwidth of and considerably better error performance than their predecessors.

- Local area networks are replacing cluster controller-dumb terminal networks in many applications.

- Client-server applications are replacing the traditional mainframe data base.

- Information is being distributed throughout the network instead of being centrally located.

- Economical and high speed bridges, routers, and gateways make it feasible to create networks of LANs.

- Interexchange carriers, grappling for market share, offer intriguing discounts on their premier services, which, increasingly, are being marketed by outside companies.

The key word for any private network designer is flexibility. It is difficult to foresee what products and services will emerge in the highly competitive market that telecommunications has become, but the most effective network managers will avoid locking themselves into a single vendor or a particular architecture. The devices on today's and tomorrow's networks are intelligent and are continually getting smarter. Coupled with inexpensive circuits, networks are changing the social fabric of the world as it becomes feasible to move information instead of people.

Why Private Networks?

This chapter brings together the building blocks that previous chapters have discussed and attempts to integrate them in a discussion of the shapes private networks are assuming. Companies that have never considered a network beyond, perhaps, a few data circuits to tie remote terminals to the corporate mainframe are considering more extensive networks at this time. The obvious motivation is saving money, but cost-saving is often insignificant compared to other benefits that this section discusses.

Integrate the Company More Tightly

Human endeavor revolves around communication, and the more personalized the communication, the more effective the organization. Multilocation companies can be more closely knit with easy access to voice communication. Meetings can be more productive with video conferencing and presentation graphics equipment.

Tie the Company to Its Customers

The strategic use of telecommunications to integrate a company's business to that of its major customers has been well documented. By giving customers direct access to the company data base through the telecommunications network, companies have closely intertwined their businesses with their customers' businesses, making it easier for the customers to do business and more difficult for them to draw apart.

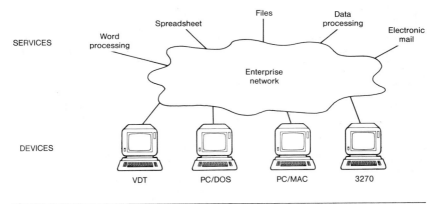

Figure 30.1   An enterprise network.

Tie the Company to Its Major Suppliers

Businesses can become more competitive by tying their ordering procedures with those of their major suppliers using such processes as electronic data interchange (EDI). Costs drop as inventories shift from purchaser to supplier and the time between manufacture of subcomponents and delivery of completed products is reduced.

Integrate Voice and Data Communications

The single-purpose networks of the past are giving way to multi-purpose networks. There are economies of scale from acquiring circuits in bulk, and it is almost invariably effective to merge voice and data requirements when networks are developed. The merger is particularly effective in the local loop. The major IECs are making T-1 based long distance service increasingly attractive. The same T-1 circuit that delivers switched voice service also can carry the local loops of data services.

Enterprise Networks

The term industry increasingly uses to describe the network discussed here is the *enterprise network*. An enterprise network, which Figure 30.1 shows conceptually, extends to the desktop where it can support a variety of devices regardless of the application or the operating system. The enterprise network recognizes that users' personal preferences dictate what kind of workstation they have. Instead of converting Apple users to MS-DOS or vice versa, it is easier to let the network do the translation. Instead of concerning users with routes and protocols, the network enables them to address servers, wherever they are located, as virtual drives on their workstations.

The enterprise network is also multivendor. The telecommunications market increasingly is composed of niche players who happen to produce a very good device, which might be a bridge, a router, or a network operating system, that fills a particular need better than any competing product from the major manufacturers. To remain with one vendor in today's market is to pay a premium in cost or a penalty in functionality, so increasingly, companies are drifting away from the single-vendor solution.

The globalization of business means the enterprise network is multilocation and even multinational. The strategic implications of the network also mean that it is likely to be multicompany. The multilocation/multicompany network is difficult to control. As companies do business electronically with their strategic partners, conflicts arise in protocols, governmental regulations, and standards. The enterprise network ties the parts together as if the design and architecture were unified.

Building Blocks of the Enterprise Network

This section discusses the elements of an enterprise network. These have been discussed in earlier chapters and are presented here with applications to show how they fit as an integrated whole.

Terminal Equipment

Figure 30.2 shows the evolution of terminal equipment interfaces to a host computer. Most of today's networks resemble the upper part of the figure: a host computer superintends a network of dumb terminals. The terminals connect through a cluster controller or multiplexer to the host, which contains the data base and manages the network. The dumb terminal is rapidly being replaced by the personal computer—at first emulating the terminal and then operating as a peer. Even with terminal emulation, gateways, which are less

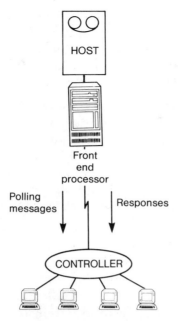

A. Dumb terminal interface

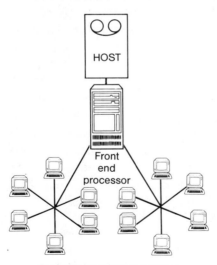

B. Intelligent terminal interface

Figure 30.2 **Evolution of terminal equipment interfaces to a host computer.**

expensive and more responsive, replace the cluster controller. Local area networks, usually using twisted pair wire, replace the coaxial and EIA-232 wiring to controllers and multiplexers.

Local Area Networks

The high growth area of private networks today is the LAN, and that growth is expected to continue. The basic building blocks: the network interface card, transmission medium, servers, and network operating system are becoming so common as to be practically commodities. Interest is high and expected to remain so for devices such as bridges, routers, and gateways that interconnect LANs over the facilities discussed in following sections.

Circuits

The circuit building block of the network of the past was the voice grade circuit. With conditioning it supports data, and with signaling it supports voice. The limited bandwidth of the voice grade circuit gave rise to DDS, a fully synchronized digital service operating at speeds up to 56 kb/s. Based on the bit-robbed signaling of a T-1 backbone, DDS is expensive and incapable of providing 64 kb/s clear channel circuits. As the demand for greater bandwidths increased, the major IECs provided T-1 facilities and, increasingly, are delivering T-3. The trend clearly is toward providing circuits in bulk. A T-1 can be leased for the price of six or seven voice grade circuits; a T-3 can be obtained for the price of the same number of T-1s.

Fractional T-1 now holds the limelight, not so much because companies don't need a full T-1 (which many don't), but because it is the migration path away from analog services that carriers have chosen. Anyone designing a network today should evaluate fractional T-1, which is superior to voice grade analog circuits except for two things: it isn't universally available, and it may not be suitable for bridging. At the time of this writing, fractional T-1 is largely a point-to-point service between major metropolitan areas, but that limitation will inevitably disappear.

Common Carrier Switched Facilities

IECs and LECs offer strong incentives to remain on the public switched networks. Dedicated circuits are effective for high volume voice and most data applications, but every enterprise network makes some use of the PSTN. One of the theories behind divestiture was that competition would drive down long distance costs, and that has proved to be true. Costs are nearing the bottom, however, because IECs' costs and the access charges they must pay to the LECs for the local network support prices on the downside.

In the past, switched long distance networks offered two alternatives: WATS for the heavy users and direct distance dialing for everyone else. Now, WATS is a dying service. T-1 services are replacing it for large users, and discounted long distance or "dial 1 WATS" is cost-effective for all but the smallest users, who will remain on direct distance dialing. T-1 access is particularly attractive for companies because the service charge is low (about the price of a WATS line of a few years ago), the usage charges are low, and the T-1 can be justified by a combination of services. T-1 lines can support outbound, inbound, data, and switched 56, which companies use for video conferencing, Group 4 facsimile, and other broadband services.

T-1 services also are effective for accessing the virtual network services of IECs. Instead of developing a network of fixed circuits, the IECs define the network in software and switch the call over the same trunks and switching systems they use for other services. If T-1 is used as the access facility to the IEC, the call carries a lower rate than the switched access alternative. Calls between points that both have dedicated access carry the lowest rates. Virtual network services are equivalent to fixed private network services in all respects except the IECs charge for usage and the fixed charges that are based on call volume rather than circuit costs.

Companies obtain local switched services from the LECs as direct inward dial and central office trunks. For data communications, packet services such as Tymnet and Telenet are available, and within the LATA many LECs also offer packet services.

Premises Switching Systems

The PBX is the most familiar kind of circuit switch in private networks. Larger networks use tandem switches, but most private networks use all or part of a PBX for the purpose. Common carrier

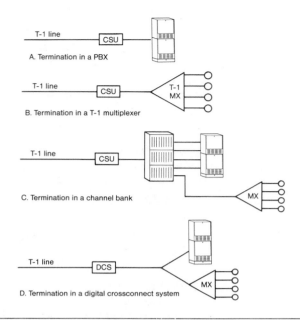

Figure 30.3   T-1 line termination options.

switching services also are available and gaining increased attention. The most familiar type is the Centrex service that most LECs offer. With few exceptions, Centrex systems can support the tie lines, T-1 long distance services, and special trunks that PBXs support. The data PBX, cousin of the voice/data PBX, is a circuit switching device used only for data.

Although they are not switching services in the strictest sense of the word, digital crossconnect services are offered by many LECs and IECs. These services do not switch one call at a time but reroute individual circuits or bandwidth on demand.

Increasingly, fast packet switching is used for both voice and data. A fast packet network not only can route and transport calls, it also can compress voice calls into narrower bandwidth.

Facility Termination Equipment

Private facilities must be terminated in equipment that provides testing access, conditions the signal to meet the line protocol, and divides the bandwidth among the users. Digital facilities terminate in a channel service unit (CSU) that converts the bipolar line signal

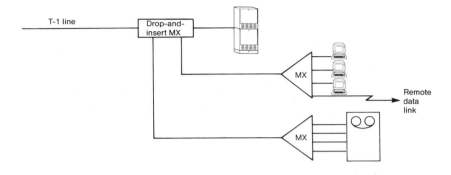

Figure 30.4 Using a drop-and-insert multiplexer to split a T-1 line.

to the T-1 format. Individual channels are derived by terminating the line in channel banks or T-1 multiplexers as Figure 30.3 shows. Circuits also are terminated on customer premises in digital crossconnect systems.

Time division and statistical multiplexers divide both analog and digital circuits, and increasingly the voice/data multiplexer is used to combine voice and data on the same digital facility. Where it is necessary to separate channels on a T-1 system, a drop-and-insert multiplexer can divide and combine the T-1 routes. Figure 30.4 illustrates the use of drop-and-insert multiplexers.

Although the use of analog circuits is declining, families of analog network channel terminating equipment (NCTE) are still used. These devices include repeaters, signaling systems, and other devices designed to amplify, convert, and condition the line. The shift from analog has not displaced the modem, a device that continues to be used in quantity, with special emphasis on high speed dial-up modems.

Private Network Development Issues

This overview of the building blocks of telecommunications networks shows that there is no shortage of options. In fact, network designers are faced with a surplus of options. This book and chapter do not attempt to explain the network design process. It discusses, instead, some of the principal design issues that managers must consider in implementing networks.

The Hybrid Network

Networks of today are not composed of any pure form of facilities or ownership. These "hybrid" networks have most or all of the following characteristics:

- *Multivendor*. In terms of circuits, equipment, and perhaps even management, the modern network involves many vendors.

- *Multiapplication*. Networks carry all of a company's applications—voice, data, video, text, graphics, and electronic mail—over the same transmission medium and possibly through the same switches.

- *Multiprotocol*. It is difficult to use a single protocol to support an enterprise network because of its multivendor characteristics. Protocol conversions are the rule for more elaborate networks.

- *Circuit or packet switched*. The design rules are changing. In the past, packet switching was avoided for voice, and circuit switching was avoided for most data. Today's hybrid network may have a circuit switched PBX feeding voice and data over a fast packet switched backbone, and many data applications are well suited to being switched through a PBX.

- *Private or public*. Even the largest private networks still find it necessary to use public facilities for some applications.

Security

In 1989 the breach of the Internet by a virus that destroyed data raised the security consciousness of every network manager. Everyone knows about the hackers who find it a challenge to invade private networks. An even more subtle threat to security are the network's users, who are authorized access to the network itself, but who attempt to obtain access to unauthorized files. Network security involves the following issues:

- *Physical Security*. Network and computer equipment and the circuits that connect them must be physically secure. Equipment rooms and wiring closets must be kept locked, and the keys under control. Fire prevention precautions should be taken. The facilities should be kept clean and free of debris.

- *Terminal Security*. Access to the network must be controlled. Dial-up circuits should use a system such as dial-back security to prevent unauthorized access. Passwords must be controlled and reissued. Terminals should be kept physically secure, and the keyboards locked if possible.

- *Disaster Recovery*. Every network should have a plan for restoring service in case common carrier services fail or major equipment is lost because of fire, earthquake, sabotage, or other disaster.

- *Data Security*. It is impossible to prevent unauthorized access to many types of telecommunications circuits, particularly those that are carried over radio. An organization's telecommunications plan must include methods of preventing unauthorized people from obtaining access to the information. Often, this requires encryption of data and scrambling of voice or video.

Network Intelligence

Networks composed of dedicated facilities tend to have static configurations because of the delays and high cost of facility rearrangements. Static networks, however, fail to meet the need for information flow in most modern organizations and contribute to low utilization of facilities. Network intelligence allows an organization to reconfigure the network based on instantaneous service demands. Products to accomplish this objective are based on digital circuit switches or on a digital crossconnect system that operates under some form of network management system. The critical issue is whether intelligence is on the user's premises or at the common carrier's facility. In either case, the intelligent network provides users with a greater degree of control.

Figure 30.5 shows an intelligent network. User services home on a service node that directs digital bandwidth where it is

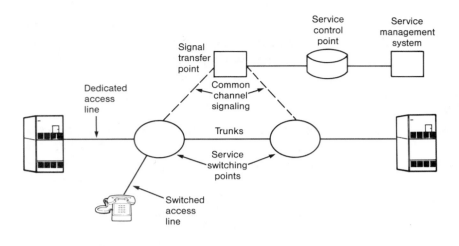

Figure 30.5   An intelligent network.

needed. Bit compression multiplex equipment compresses the bit stream to make the most effective use of digital facilities. The digital crossconnect system routes traffic to dedicated or switched services as needed. The network control system located on the user's premises dynamically monitors load and service and changes the network configuration in response to demand. For example, an airline reservation system extending across several time zones can be reconfigured to move calls to different answering centers as the load shifts during the day. Also, an intelligent network could give the airline the capability of offering priority treatment to their best customers when all positions in the nearest reservation center are occupied. For example, a call from a customer identified as a frequent flier could be shifted over the intelligent network to the opposite end of the country while less important customers wait in queue at the local automatic call distributor.

Network intelligence is most effective with all-digital circuits where bandwidth can be reallocated according to demand. Digital circuits that normally are used for individual voice channels can be rerouted during off-peak hours to a computer center for high speed data transmission or reallocated to a video conference center. The availability of low cost bulk digital facilities has a significant impact on the demand for network intelligence.

The growth of network intelligence greatly improves the utility of information resources and demands a higher level of knowledge to use the network effectively. Users will have greater flexibility and control and will undoubtedly have to employ computer-based tools to make the maximum use of the network.

Future Compatibility

Network products and services are changing so rapidly that it is difficult to be sure a current design will be compatible with the future shape of the network. New services, including Fiber Distributed Data Interface (FDDI), 802.6 metropolitan area networks, frame relay, cell relay, asynchronous transfer mode, SMDS, and other services, are on the horizon. The importance of ISDN and broadband ISDN is yet to be demonstrated, but both will undoubtedly play a role in future networks.

Services that demand high bandwidth are here now and will gain importance in the future. Some will have a strong impact, and others may fizzle. The key to designing a network is to remain flexible—not locked into any single technology that will limit the organization's ability to follow the shifting telecommunications environment in the future.

On-Premises Distribution

Debates on the best method for distributing information on the user's premises have raged for several years. Some services are suited to coaxial cable. Others can be served on twisted pair wire, but then the question of whether shielded or unshielded is best must be answered. Arguments can be made favoring all three media, but companies planning for the future must decide what to do about fiber. FDDI is available, but it is too expensive to use for ordinary office applications now. But what of the future? Will FDDI or another technology replace the present token ring and Ethernet networks? Many experts contend that FDDI is not fast enough for the network of the future, and there are even some present applications for which it is not fast enough. The relative importance of these factors is, of course, different for every company, so there are no principles to suggest except that the applications must be thoroughly understood before equipment is chosen.

How to Interconnect LANs

As mentioned earlier, the enterprise network of the future will appear to be networks of interconnected LANs, and unless a company deals with only one computer vendor, LANs are likely to be of different types. An important issue will be how these are interconnected. Will the network use bridges with their high throughput, simple architecture, and generally low cost? Will the lack of alternate routing cause the router to replace the bridge, or will the replacing device be a combination of the two, the brouter? Will multiple protocols, meaning the organization will use gateways with their high flexibility but low throughput, be the order of the day? The LAN interconnection field is changing so rapidly that companies should invest with the expectation that the equipment will be obsolete and replaced in three or four years.

Vendor Dependence or Independence

In the past, most of the components of the network were likely to be furnished by one vendor, who also probably furnished the mainframe computer at its head end. Network designers must determine whether a past vendor preference will be continued into the future. The penalty for not doing so is the risk of incompatibility and difficulties in testing and clearing trouble. The penalty for remaining dependent on one vendor, however, may be a loss of performance. No vendor has a monopoly on technology, and niche players are more apt to exhibit superior performance in one family of products because their developmental efforts are more concentrated.

Network Management Issues

Chapter 32 and 33 discuss principles of testing and managing networks. The hierarchical networks of the past had a significant advantage over the peer-to-peer networks of the present and future: they were easier to manage. Vendor-specific network management products make it possible to look into the network's components and diagnose and sometimes clear trouble. As the network becomes multivendor, these management capabilities diminish.

National, International, or Proprietary Standards?

The ideal route to follow in developing a network would be to use only products that meet an international standard. As the standard develops, production costs decline, and prices drop with them. Most companies, however, will find it effective to deviate from the ideal simply because standards take too long to develop. If the payback period is short, it is often desirable to use proprietary standards to gain an immediate advantage. The course to follow depends on the company's tolerance for uncertainty.

How to Plan Networks

Many managers today face a dilemma. Control of computing budgets is moving from the management information department to the end users. Users purchase computers today as they purchased office machines in the past: they are justified on an individual basis. The arrival of stand-alone computers almost inevitably leads to a demand for networking, and the network manager may find it almost impossible to plan because he or she lacks control over the applications. Organizations that have control over equipment standards are in the best position to plan the network. If the information in desktop devices is of any value, someone also must plan for such factors as security, regular data backup, and network capacity.

Applications

With the trend toward obtaining digital circuits in bulk—as either full or fractional T-1—the most cost-effective networks are those that integrate different applications at the transmission level. Devices such as PBXs, T-1 multiplexers, drop-and-insert multiplexers, and digital crossconnect systems are the means of integrating the applications onto the circuit backbone. Developing a network generally involves the following:

- *Identify the Applications.* Present and future applications including voice, data, video, facsimile, imaging, and all other foreseeable communications services should be identified. It is not enough to consider only present applications. Knowledge of future plans and expected growth is essential.

- *Identify Locations to Serve.* The geographic location of all points on the network must be identified. Although some locations are obviously too small to justify dedicated voice circuits, such locations often require data and may have enough volume to justify equipment such as voice-data multiplexers.

- *Determine Traffic Volume.* The amount of traffic, both terminating and originating, should be identified at each location. Determine the volume, type, and length of data transactions from such sources as multiplexers and front end processors. Determine the quantity of voice traffic from sources such as common carrier bills, traffic usage recorders, and call accounting systems. Identify both on-net and off-net traffic. It is usually useful to create a matrix of traffic volumes and costs between on-net locations.

- *Determine Network Type.* Each application will have an optimum network type to support it. For example, short range, high speed data applications are usually best served by a local area network. Geographically dispersed LANs with a common interest can often be served by remote bridges.

- *Develop Network Topology.* The topology of the network is based on the application, using techniques discussed in Chapter 31. Costs of alternative transmission methods are calculated, and where the volume and cost off traffic is enough to justify private circuits or a public network such as a virtual network, these are added to the design. Optimize the design by trying different combinations of circuits and by selecting alternative concentration points.

31

Network Design Principles

Establishing a telephone network is somewhat analogous to assembling a stereo or personal computer system. You begin with a variety of components, each of which has a particular purpose and certain characteristics. There are rules that must be followed, but within the guidelines there are many ways the components can be assembled to achieve the desired result. Telecommunications system designers are not concerned with design in the sense of creating the components. Instead, designers deal with such factors as:

- How many circuits—trunks, lines, voice mail ports, DTMF registers, etc.—are required?
- What are the interfaces between the circuits—tip and ring, EIA-232-C, E & M, etc.?
- What are the capacities of the component in Hz, bits per second, etc.?
- In what topology are the components assembled—star, ring, point-to-point, etc.?
- What type of circuit—digital or analog—will be used?

Telecommunication system design is beyond the scope of this book, but an understanding of several principles is essential to understanding the telecommunications network. This chapter presents the vocabulary and the basic principles of network design. This information, with the circuit design tables contained in Appendix E, supplies enough information to enable you to find how many circuits to provide for an objective level of service if the traffic load is known. *The Dow Jones-Irwin Handbook of Telecommunications Management* or any of the design books listed in the bibliography provide more detailed explanations.

Integrating switching systems and trunks into a network requires that the designer determine the number of trunks and the amount of shared network equipment needed to reach a reasonable balance between service and costs. The telecommunications industry calls this function *network design* or *traffic engineering*. Designers base trunk group size and shared equipment quantities on the probability of occurrence of some value of offered traffic load. When the load is less than the network capacity, the unused capacity is a waste of money. When demand exceeds the designed load, service is affected by ineffective attempts and delays, and lost revenues and unproductive employee time waste money. The designer's job is to balance cost and service.

Telecommunications traffic engineering is similar in many respects to highway traffic engineering. In highway engineering, the traffic capacity depends on the number of lanes. Each circuit in a group has a given capacity and is analogous to a lane on a highway. It is impossible in either a highway or a circuit group to achieve full utilization. The objective is to keep the lanes reasonably full without impeding traffic. The amount of load offered to the highway or circuit group varies with time of the day, day of the week, and season of the year. Within limits, these variations are predictable. The network is designed for anticipated peaks—called the *busy hour* in network design terms. When the offered traffic load exceeds the designed capacity, blockage results.

The design is a composite of the following information about the character of the network:

- Network owner's *grade of service* objectives.
- Anticipated *load* measured in number of call attempts and call holding time distributed by hourly, daily, and seasonal variations.
- *Behavior* of users in placing and holding calls.
- *Capacity* of the network elements—trunks, ports, switching network, common equipment, and processors.

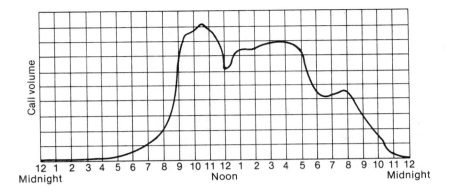

Figure 31.1 **Hourly variations in call volume for a typical central office.**

The Network Design Problem

The essential problem in designing a telecommunications network is to find how much equipment and trunking is required to reach an objective balance between service and cost. The process used to reach this balance is somewhat complex and requires special formulas, software tools, tables, and training. This chapter explains only the concepts and gives a few examples in the Applications section to show how to reach the balance.

Network design is the process of predicting future demand based on past results, evaluating the capacity of equipment and facilities, and providing the correct amount of capacity, in the proper configuration, in time to meet service objectives. The primary complication in network design is how to provide the right amount of equipment and facilities to meet a constantly fluctuating demand. In any part of the network, demand fluctuates from minute to minute as users originate and terminate calls. Hourly fluctuations also occur, as Figure 31.1 shows, because of changes in usage as the business day peaks and wanes during breaks and lunch hours. Also, demand varies by season of year, by class of service, and by type of call—local or long haul.

Queuing Theory

The most common design method involves modeling the network according to principles of queuing theory, which describes how customers or users behave in a queue. Three variables are considered in network design. The first variable is the *arrival* or *input process* that describes the way users array themselves as they arrive to request service. Examples are arrivals of users at a group of DTMF receivers to begin dialing or at a group of trunks to a distant office. The second variable is the *service process*, which describes the way servers handle the users when they leave the queue and enter the service-providing mechanism. The third variable is the *queue discipline*, which is the way users behave when they encounter blockage in the network. The network is designed by observing how users behave and selecting the appropriate design formula. Three disciplines or reactions to blockage are possible:

- *Blocked Calls Held (BCH)*. When users encounter blockage, they immediately redial and reenter the queue.

- *Blocked Calls Cleared (BCC)*. When users encounter blockage, they wait for some time before redialing.

- *Blocked Calls Delayed (BCD)*. When users encounter blockage, the service mechanism holds them in queue until capacity to serve them is available.

Traffic engineers apply different formulas or tables corresponding to their assumption about how users behave when blockage occurs. Service systems are grouped into two categories—loss systems and delay systems. In a loss system, when users encounter blockage they are turned away. An example is the "fast busy" tone that signals that all trunks are busy. In a delay system, the system holds the user in queue until a server is available. An example is the queue for an idle DTMF receiver. When DTMF receivers are all busy, users do not receive dial tone, but if they wait, dial tone will be provided.

Traffic Load

In a given, hour the load on any part of the network is expressed as the product of the number of call attempts and the average holding time of all attempts. For example, if a circuit experienced six call attempts that averaged 600 seconds (ten minutes) each, the group would have carried 3600 call-seconds of load. To express the load in more convenient terms, traffic engineers divide the number of call-seconds by 100 and express the result as hundreds of call seconds, abbreviated as CCS. A load of 36 CCS represents 100% occupancy of a single circuit for one hour.

Traffic loads are also expressed in Erlangs, units named for A. K. Erlang, a Danish mathematician. One Erlang is equal to 36 CCS; both represent full occupancy of a circuit for one hour. Designers can choose to use either unit. CCS is generally more convenient for small units of traffic. Most measuring devices such as the traffic usage registers in a PBX use CCS as the unit. Erlangs are usually more convenient when demand is expressed in hours or minutes because it is easier to convert to Erlangs than to CCS.

It is important to distinguish between the *carried* and *offered* loads of a network. The difference between the two is the ineffective attempts that the network did not carry because of blockage or failures. The offered load can be estimated from the carried load but it is impossible to determine accurately. When people encounter blockage, they tend to generate additional attempts. When the blockage is removed, the total number of attempts drops.

One hundred percent occupancy in a circuit group is un-achievable in the real world because of variations in timing and duration of access attempts. Calls do not align themselves neatly so that when one terminates, another is waiting to occupy the vacated capacity. As discussed in Chapter 8, calls can be queued on a trunk group to improve utilization, but even with queueing the full 36 CCS capacity of a circuit cannot be reached. The reason for this can be seen in the queuing formula:

$$\text{Average waiting time} = \frac{\text{average arrival rate}}{\text{service rate} \times (\text{service rate} - \text{arrival wait})}$$

When the service rate and arrival rate are equal, as they would be at 100% occupancy, the denominator of the equation is 0, which means the waiting time will be infinite. Figure 31.2 illustrates the relationship between occupancy and length of queue.

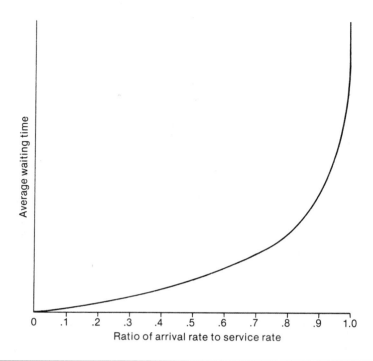

Figure 31.2   Waiting time as a function of circuit occupancy.

Network design becomes a task of determining how long the queue can be allowed to extend before the cost of delays outweighs the cost of adding capacity. It is evident, therefore, that network design requires a service objective, of which more will be said later.

The unpredictability of users further complicates the network design problem. Users vary widely in the number of calls they attempt per hour and the length of time they hold a circuit. Unless the network blocks them, users place calls at random. That is, the attempts and holding time of any user are independent of activities of other users. Users are far from uniform in their behavior. Some dial faster than others; some frequently dial a few digits and hang up (called *partial dial*); some redial immediately when a reorder or busy is encountered, while others wait for a time before redialing. If we observe this randomness in user behavior, it

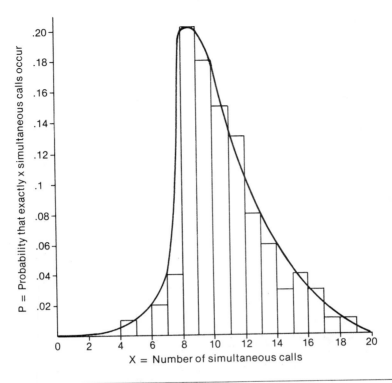

Figure 31.3   Poisson distribution of call arrivals.

begins to fall into a pattern that can be used to predict how load in a network element will be distributed.

   To illustrate how random behavior is used in network design, assume that we make many observations of the habits of customers attempting to access a group of DTMF receivers. With enough observations, it becomes possible to predict the probability that a given number of attempts will occur in the busy hour. Probability is stated as a decimal number between 0 and 1; the sum of the probabilities always equals 1.0. If we plot probabilities in a bar chart such as Figure 31.3, a pattern begins to develop. Countless observations have shown that arrivals tend to array themselves according to the curve shown by the solid line in Figure 31.3. This curve can be described by a formula known as

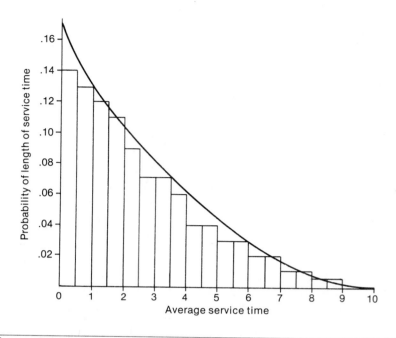

Figure 31.4   Exponential distribution of service times.

Poisson distribution, so named after the French mathematician S.D. Poisson. Although Poisson distribution is not a perfect match for the distribution of incoming service arrivals, its accuracy is sufficient for network design.

With a good estimate of patterns of call attempts, the second question is how long the average holding time of the group of DTMF registers will be. If we plot holding times, they tend to follow the exponential curve shown by the solid line in Figure 31.4.

These distributions of attempts and holding time are modeled by tables or software that designers select according to the disposition of blocked calls. Assuming the arrival rate is random, we choose the traffic formula according to the behavior of users in the queue. The Erlang B formula assumes blocked calls are cleared, that is, when users encounter blockage they do not immediately reenter the system. The Poisson formula assumes blocked calls are held. They are not actually held, but instead,

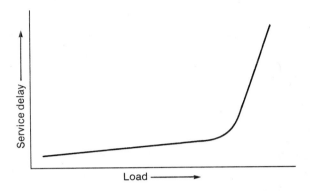

Figure 31.5   Load/service curve of typical common control equipment.

users immediately redial when they encounter blockage. For a given grade of service, the Poisson tables require slightly more trunks than Erlang B. Erlang C tables are used for the blocked calls delayed or queued assumption.

It is important to understand that traffic formulas are valid only if the attempts are random. Several things can affect randomness. A national or local emergency can drive the number of attempts far beyond the capacity of the network. This causes blockage and results in many retrials, which in turn generates more attempts. Most common control switching equipment exhibits a load-service response curve similar to that shown in Figure 31.5. With a gradually increasing load, service, as measured in amount of delay, follows a slope that is almost flat until a critical point is reached. At that point service degenerates rapidly, and the network, for all practical purposes, collapses. Networks are protected from overload by flow control, which is a series of procedures, described in a later section, to keep additional traffic off the network when excessive congestion will result.

It is also important to understand that in a common control network, overloading one critical element can cause the entire network to collapse. For example, if a central office with ample trunks and switching capacity has too few DTMF receivers, the trunk and switching capacity will be unused because users will not receive dial tone, and therefore will be unable to access the trunks. Because designers select the quantity of equipment to handle a given amount of usage, suppression in one portion of the network makes it appear that other parts of the network have excess capacity. When the cause of suppression is removed the true demand becomes apparent.

Common carriers, particularly those operating in a competitive environment, are well aware that blockage can result in loss of customers. Therefore, most common carriers design to avoid blockage in all but a few attempts. Blockage is often greater in private networks, however, because of the attempt to control communications costs by underproviding network capacity. Private networks usually can afford to provide a lower grade of service than public networks. If carried too far, however, the risk is great that the randomness of attempts will be lost, service will be poor, measurements will be invalid, and productivity will deteriorate.

Busy Hour Determination

Since networks must handle peak loads, a designer needs to know the heaviest load periods, called the busy hour. The busy hour is not a single hour, but rather is a composite network design point, leveled to represent the design peak. A common factor for engineering switching machines is the ten-high-day (10HD) busy period. This factor is determined by averaging the amount of traffic in the busiest hour of the ten days during the year when the highest traffic load is carried. PBX managers often use the average bouncing busy hour (ABBH) as the busy hour for sizing trunk groups. The ABBH is the average of the daily busy hour over the study period, which is usually one week.

The busy hour for the network as a whole is not necessarily the busy hour for all circuit groups or all equipment. Each group is likely to have its own busy hour because of the varying traffic flow between nodes, particularly when they are in different time zones. Unless the designer chooses these load peaks carefully as design criteria, congestion in some parts of the network will result.

Grade of Service

The service grade in a loss system such as a trunk group is expressed as the probability of blockage. Designers size trunk groups by using tables or computer programs that express blockage as a decimal number. For example, a P.01 grade of service means that a call has a 99% chance of finding a vacant circuit and a 1% chance of being blocked. Traffic tables used for sizing circuit groups are indexed by grade of service; therefore, selecting a grade of service objective is the starting point in designing a network.

The grade of service for a delay system such as access to service circuits is expressed in terms of the percent of calls that encounter a delay higher than the objective. For example, the dial tone delay objective is often expressed as "no more than 1.5% of the attempts will be delayed more than 3 seconds."

It must be understood that a network has several elements connected in tandem, each of which has a possibility of blockage. For example, after a call is dialed, it must contend for a path through the switching network, next for a trunk to the destination, then for a path through the terminating switching network. As each of these elements has its own probability of blockage, the probability of completing a call is the sum of the individual probabilities.

This additive nature of blockage probability can result in a network design that is wasteful of capacity if it is not carefully controlled. For example, if a circuit group is designed to a P.005 grade of service (0.5 % blockage probability), but incoming calls encounter a terminating switching network with a high degree of blockage, a considerable amount of trunk capacity will be wasted in carrying calls that cannot be completed because of blockage in the final link of the chain. This waste of circuit capacity is not detected by traffic load measurements because measures of attempts and holding time do not discriminate between successful and unsuccessful calls.

Traffic Measurements

The most difficult task in network design is obtaining accurate load data. With accurate data a skilled designer can design a network that meets service objectives. In public networks with a clientele that remains constant, the load can be predicted with reasonable accuracy. The number of call attempts and holding time can be predicted, and change occurs gradually enough that it can be accommodated with minor adjustments in capacity.

When major fluctuations in load occur, however, it is sometimes impossible to adjust capacity quickly enough, and users experience slow dial tone or blocked calls.

The best predictor of traffic load is a historical analysis of past usage, but in many networks historical information is unavailable for predicting the traffic load. When an organization first establishes a new private network the only source of information may be records of long distance calls billed by the telephone company. If WATS lines, foreign exchange lines and tie lines share the load and have not been detail-billed, insufficient data may exist to make a reliable prediction. The required capacity of circuits and equipment is predicted by observing past calling patterns. Historical information is a good predictor of the future if the conditions that generated the original demand remain unchanged. When changed conditions affect demand, however, the original design may be rendered invalid and require modification.

Traffic usage equipment measures usage either with an external device attached to the circuit for measuring attempts and holding time or in software registers assigned to groups of circuits and equipment items. Measurements are produced in raw number form and must be processed before the results can be applied to network design. For example, assume that a group of circuits is connected between two switching systems. TUR readings express the load in CCS. The designer consults traffic tables derived from the Poisson or Erlang formulas to determine the number of circuits needed to fill the demand for an objective grade of service. Table 31.1 is an example of a typical table and shows how it is used to determine the required number of circuits. Poisson and Erlang B tables are included for up to 100 circuits in Appendix E.

If the data in Table 31.1 is converted to call carrying capacity in CCS per circuit, the curve shown in Figure 31.6 is obtained. This curve shows an important factor in network design; large circuit groups are much more efficient in their per circuit traffic carrying ability than small groups, because large groups have less idle circuit time for a given grade of service.

Often, usage data sufficient to predict demand accurately is unavailable. For example, it may be known that an organization change or a circuit routing change will affect demand on the trunk

Table 31.1   Partial Poisson Traffic Table

	CARRIED TRAFFIC LOAD IN CCS		
TRUNKS	P.02	P.05	P.10
1	0.4	1.9	3.8
2	5.4	12.9	19.1
3	16	29.4	39.6
4	30	49	63
5	46	71	88
6	64	94	113
7	84	118	140
8	105	143	168
9	126	169	195
10	149	195	224
20	399	477	523
30	675	778	836
40	964	1088	1157
50	1261	1403	1482

Steps in using traffic tables:
1. Choose the appropriate queuing discipline.
2. Choose the objective grade of service.
3. Locate the load in CCS in the proper column.
4. Read the number of trunks required.

group between systems. Without valid measurements, the designer must estimate circuit numbers based on experience or rules of thumb until measurements can be made. Usage measurements show only the load that was carried. Besides usage it is important to measure ineffective attempts, the number of calls queued, and length of time in queue (if queuing is used) to derive a valid indication of the true demand.

A network can be visualized as a black box consisting of sources and dispositions (also called *sinks*) of calls as Figure 31.7 shows. Every attempt must be accounted for by its possible dispositions. The network administrator must determine whether the service provided by dispositions meets the organization's cost and service

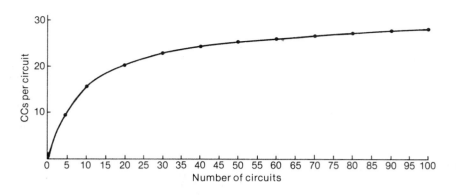

Figure 31.6   Circuit capacity as a function of size of circuit group.

objectives. The combination of all calls—including intramachine, those terminating on a tone trunk such as busy or reorder, off-net local calls, toll calls, and WATS calls—comprise the total load on the switching network. The various ports must be sized to fit the offered load, or blockage will result. The network design task becomes one of computing the numbers, circuits and pieces of equipment needed to fit the possible call dispositions.

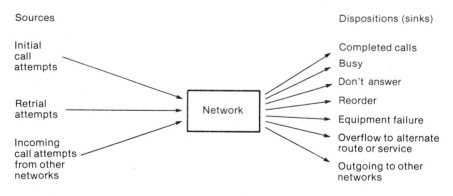

Figure 31.7   Sources and dispositions of network load.

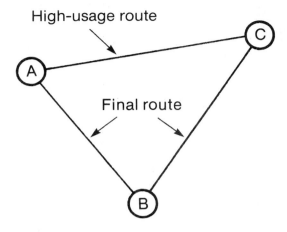

Figure 31.8   High usage and final routes in a three-node network.

Alternate Routing

One possible disposition of a call, as Figure 31.7 shows, is over-flow to an alternate route. Alternate routing is one of several techniques used to maintain circuit occupancy at a high level. The decision whether to use alternate routing is based on cost. For example, assume that a network consists of three nodes as in Figure 31.8. The circuits between A and C are designed for a high level of occupancy and are called *high usage* circuits. When the A-C trunk group is blocked, calls route through the tandem switch B over a *final route*. Different design criteria must be used on final and high usage trunk groups. On high usage groups an Erlang B table is used to size the group. For example, it may be economical to have as much as 10% of the traffic overflow to the final group, so the P.10 column of the Erlang B table would be used. On final groups the Poisson table is used at a higher grade of service.

Simulation

The techniques discussed so far for determining demand and capacity use mathematical modeling to calculate required capacity

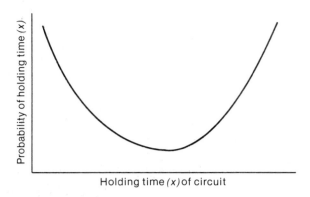

Figure 31.9   **Distribution of holding time probability in a data network.**

given an objective grade of service and estimated demand. Modeling is a valid way of designing a network if the demand is random and if it follows a known distribution of arrivals and holding time. Also, modeling is an inexpensive way of designing a network. Although computer design tools are useful in modeling, manual design using traffic tables is equally valid and can be done by a trained person with little apparatus beyond a book of tables and a hand calculator.

The modeling technique falls apart, however, when demand is not random and fails to follow predictable arrival and service rates. As shown previously, this occurs during high blockage conditions. It is impossible to compute what happens to service when a network is blocked. Therefore a design is valid only within the limits prescribed by the original assumptions. In addition, the modeling technique is often unable to describe the load when the network handles a significant amount of data traffic. Data terminals and computers behave entirely differently than people using voice communications.

The holding time of data terminals tends to follow the probability distribution shown in Figure 31.9. Many computer calls are established only long enough to send one page or less of text, which at 2400 b/s takes about 8 seconds—much less than the average telephone call. Other circuits used for bulk data transfer may have holding times much longer than average telephone calls—on the order of 30 minutes or more. Also, the data busy hour may be different from the telephone busy hour. For example, workers may dial their electronic mailboxes immediately upon returning from lunch, imposing on the system a high momentary load that is unlike that imposed by voice traffic.

Where this randomness and lack of uniform distribution occur, *simulation* can be employed to find how costs will be affected by service or capacity changes. A simulation program treats the network as a black box and varies the parameters to show the designer the costs and effects on service. Unlike modeling, simulation requires an elaborate program and a trained operator to produce valid designs. Data from traffic measurements is still required to operate the program, but simulation differs from modeling in that service results can be observed outside the limits of the modeling formulas.

The chief limitation on any network design is the validity of observations about users. Also, this behavior rarely remains constant. The smaller the network, the more difficult it is to predict behavior because small perturbations tend to have a large effect. For example, in a small private network a reorganization can change the calling patterns of the users, and blockage may occur where previously capacity was ample.

Network Topology

Choice of topology, which is the pattern of interconnection of circuits and nodes in the network, is another element of network design. Chapter 3 discusses the principal topologies. In both voice and data networks, all nodes can be afforded an equal access level, or they can be configured hierarchically. Private networks also can be ordered hierarchically with high usage trunks between low level nodes and final routing through a higher level node. The chief advantage of a hierarchical network is in the ability to conserve circuits by concentrating traffic in shared final circuit groups where insufficient traffic exists to justify high usage groups.

Data Network Design

The data network designer has many more alternatives than the voice network designer has. The building blocks of a voice network are generally limited to switches and circuits. Circuits are obtained individually or in bulk, and in the latter case multiplexers may be required. The grade of service in a voice network is usually expressed as percentage of blockage.

Data networks, on the other hand, use a combination of devices, including multiplexers, concentrators, front end processors, cluster controllers, modems, and switches, to develop a network. The grade of service in a data network usually is expressed as response time, which is the time between the issuance of a request to the host computer and the arrival of the first character of the response.

An important factor in data network design is the location of concentration points. Figure 31.10 shows two different ways of interconnecting multiple points on a circuit. The network design task is to minimize the cost of circuits, modems, and concentrators while keeping throughput at an acceptable level. In a large multipoint network, the number of possible configurations is substantial. Network designers use one of several empirical algorithms in reaching an optimum configuration. Two such algorithms are:

- *Add Algorithm.* All sites are initially assumed to be connected to the host. The designer chooses a concentrator location and calculates the cost of connecting each site to the concentrator. Additional concentrator locations are chosen and sites moved from the host or other concentrators until adding concentrators no longer improves cost.

- *Drop Algorithm.* The designer chooses several provisional concentrator locations and calculates the cost of connecting devices. Concentrators are then dropped and devices reassigned to other concentrators. If the total cost increases, the concentrator is restored; otherwise it is dropped.

Neither approach is necessarily superior. In complex networks with many nodes, different answers may be obtained from the different approaches. The solution is likely to be dictated by other variables, such as location of administrative headquarters, availability of technical support, and floor space.

Closely related to the location of concentration points is network topology, which refers to the configuration in connecting

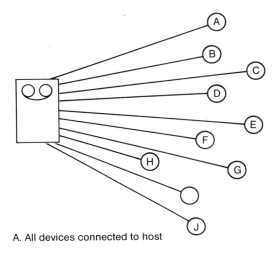

A. All devices connected to host

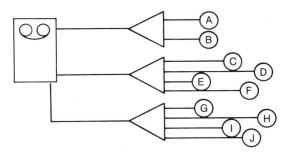

B. Devices connected to host through multiplexers

Figure 31.10   Two possible network topologies. The design task is to optimize cost and service.

circuits. The topologies shown in Figure 31.11 are usually a function of the network access method. Circuit switched networks are usually deployed in a star or hierarchical configuration. Packet switched networks normally employ a mesh topology, while polled networks employ a tree or bus topology. The ring topology is most commonly applied in local area networks that use a token passing access method.

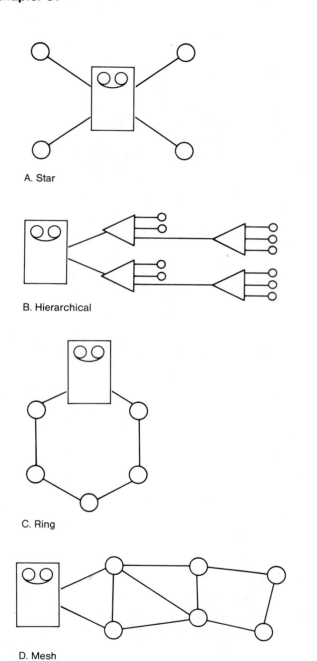

Figure 31.11   Network topologies.

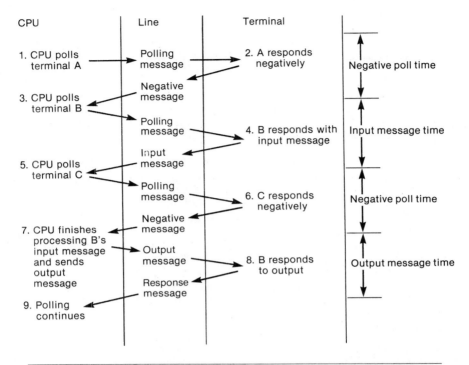

Figure 31.12   Multidrop polled network generalized response time model.

Many of the principles used in voice network design are applicable to data network design. Queuing theory is used to design data concentrator and statistical multiplexer networks. Other shared data equipment such as dial-up ports into a computer and pooled modems can be designed by measuring usage and comparing it to capacity determined from traffic tables.

Other types of data networks, however, have no counterparts in voice networks. Two examples are polled multidrop and packet switched data networks. Like voice networks, these can be sized by modeling or simulation—using different techniques.

A multidrop network is a typical application. Response time is expressed as the interval between the time a request is sent to the CPU and the time the first character of the response is received. A generalized response time model is shown in Figure 31.12. A terminal in a polled network either sends a block of data or returns a negative response to indicate that it has no data to send. The terminal response time of a network depends on these factors:

- CPU response time.
- Transmission speed.
- Error rate.
- Data block size.
- Number of overhead bits—NAK messages, CRC, headers, etc.
- Modem turnaround time (for a half duplex circuit).
- Propagation speed of the transmission medium.
- Protocol error recovery method.

If these factors are known, network throughput and terminal response time can be calculated.

Packet switched networks are designed with similar criteria. The network throughput is related to transmission speed, block length, error rate, the number of overhead bits, propagation speed, and the network's packet routing algorithm. Throughput can be increased by using an efficient algorithm. The primary algorithms are:

- *Flooding.* The node transmits packets on every route except the one they arrived on.
- *Static.* Incoming packets are transmitted according to a fixed routing table.
- *Centralized.* A network control center optimizes the route based on load and congestion reports from the nodes.
- *Isolated.* Nodes adjust their routing tables using their knowledge of network load and congestion.
- *Distributed.* Nodes adjust their routing tables by exchanging information about network load and congestion.

Local area networks are a specialized form of packet switching network that uses design criteria similar to those used for long haul packet networks. Contention networks present a unique design problem because not only are the other criteria of transmission speed, block length, error rate, and protocol important, but the frequency of collisions presents an additional factor that is difficult to model. Generalized design criteria are impossible to specify because of variations in the method of implementing contention networks. Such networks usually are sized by the experience of the designer. If overloads develop, the designer sectionalizes the network with the segments linked by a bridge that keeps traffic on its own segment unless it is addressed to a node on the other segment.

Token passing networks with their deterministic access method are easier to design. Given the characteristics of the input data and the number, length, and frequency of messages, throughput for any terminal becomes a function of network transmission speed, error rate, and the priority of the individual terminal. With all local networks, the manufacturer's instructions should be followed for design.

Like voice networks, data networks require flow control to prevent congestion. The network access nodes queue incoming messages and allow them on the network up to the capacity limits, holding the remainder in a buffer or stopping them at the source. The physical layer protocol provides a method of flow control by actuating the clear to send (CTS) lead of the interface. To stop a terminal from overloading the network, its control node turns off the CTS signal until congestion has cleared, thereby holding the message in the terminal. Similarly, a receiving device can stop a transmitting terminal from overrunning its buffer capacity by sending an X OFF character. When it can receive data again, it sends an X ON character.

Network Management

A network is a dynamic thing. The original premises on which it was designed never remain static, which means the network must be monitored continually and adjusted when change is indicated by the results. The process of monitoring and adjusting the network is called *network administration.*

Network Administration Tools

Network administration requires skills and tools to keep the network in the proper cost/service balance. The first requirement is a current and valid report of the demand on all network elements. These reports, as previously discussed, must include attempts, usage, and ineffective attempts on every circuit and equipment group in the network.

Next, the administrator must have a full understanding of the network itself. Current records of circuits and equipment, including circuit identification, end points, and capacity should be maintained. A network administrator must have a comprehensive knowledge of how the network functions, what the service objectives are, and what the capacity of each element is. The administrator also must have information on common carrier services and rates. When the service results indicate that capacity adjustments are needed, the administrator must add or drop circuits to retain the best cost/service balance. This requires knowledge of common carrier tariffs and the cost of other alternatives.

Network administration also requires knowledge of the status of circuits and apparatus. Although the administrator may not be directly responsible for maintenance, knowledge of trouble frequency and history is essential for diagnosing service results and timing adjustments of capacity. Status records should show, preferably on a real time basis, all cases of equipment and circuits out of service. The length of outage should be monitored carefully so excessive clearing times can be reported to maintenance personnel or the common carrier.

When the administrator observes blockage beyond planned levels, he or she should administer controls to relieve the blockage. The tools for relieving blockage include these:

- Additional capacity can be provided. This may require temporarily removing restrictions on overflow to other networks.

- Some code groups can be blocked. This may require the ability to block codes in an originating machine to keep congestion caused by ineffective attempts off the network.

- Circuit groups can be rerouted temporarily. It may be necessary to cancel alternate routing or to revise the rerouting tables in some machines temporarily to relieve congested machines or circuit groups.

■ Trunk directionalization can be applied. Two-way trunks can be temporarily converted to one-way trunks to allow a congested system to place outgoing calls while insulating it from excessive incoming traffic.

Managing flow controls such as these requires that the administrator have the necessary skills and understand the network well enough to know where and how to apply controls to relieve blockage. The feasibility of applying these controls depends on the complexity of the network. In complex networks, mechanized assistance may be required.

Automatic Network Controls

Administration of a network composed of stored program control switching machines that are designed for mechanized network management can be simplified by applying automatic controls. Mechanized network management requires a central computer with a map of the total network and two-way data links to the network nodes. The network control system monitors load and transmits orders to the nodes to relieve congestion. Such systems are complex, expensive, and warranted only for networks composed of multiple nodes and large numbers of trunks.

Applications

Network design is a complex topic that is beyond the scope of this book. This section presents typical design problems and shows how the tables in Appendix E are used to solve them. For additional examples and more information on how to apply these techniques, readers are referred to *The Dow Jones-Irwin Handbook of Telecommunications Management*.

Determining Trunk Quantities

Most PBXs contain traffic usage measuring equipment that states usage in CCS. Assume that management wants no more than 1% of the incoming or outgoing calls in a two-way trunk group to be blocked. Also, assume that the trunk group contains 15 circuits and the PBX's traffic usage equipment shows that the average bouncing busy hour traffic load was 324 CCS. Refer to the Erlang

B traffic tables in Appendix E. Look at the row containing 15 trunks, and follow across the table to the column to find the load figure nearest 324 CCS. At 1% blockage, 15 trunks can carry 292 CCS, so it is evident that we have too few trunks. At 2% blockage, 15 trunks can carry 347 CCS, so the actual blockage is just under 2%. The exact amount is not important. If we add one trunk, we will be able to carry 319 CCS at 1% blockage, which is just under the objective. To carry the full 324 CCS, 17 trunks are required, so we must add two trunks.

Often, the amount of traffic carried during the busy hour is unknown. Designers must, therefore, use rules of thumb to reach a starting point for calculating circuit quantities. One rule of thumb states that during the busy hour for an organization working eight hours per day, approximately 17% of the traffic is carried during the busy hour. If a long distance bill shows, for example, that 100 hours of traffic were carried during a month with 20 working days, 5 hours (or 5 Erlangs) of traffic were carried per day. If 17% was carried during the busy hour, the busy hour was 0.85 Erlangs of traffic, which Appendix E shows could be carried by four trunks at 1% blockage.

Another rule of thumb often used by designers who have no usage data is that the average business station uses 6 CCS of traffic during the busy hour. From knowledge of the organization, this is broken down into incoming, outgoing, and intrasystem traffic. For example, a telemarketing organization would have a high portion of incoming and outgoing traffic compared to a city or county government, which would have high intrasystem traffic.

Designers are also faced with deciding which tables to use. Where data is not precise, most designers use Erlang B tables. Common carriers, who have accurate measuring equipment and collect data regularly, use Erlang B for high usage trunks and Poisson tables for final trunk groups. Erlang C tables are used for queuing situations such as automatic call distributors.

Determining Numbers of Voice Mail Ports

Managers who are installing voice mail for the first time are faced with the question of how many ports and how much storage to provide. Most voice mail systems furnish information that can be used to measure service, but these are no help in initially sizing the system.

Studies have shown that the average voice mail user uses about 3 minutes of storage capacity per day. If a system had 100 users, it would need 300 minutes, or 5 hours, of capacity. If 17% of this occurs during the busy hour, 0.85 Erlangs of port capacity are needed, which requires four ports. It may be advisable to provide more capacity, but this process provides a starting point.

Determining Service Positions in an Automatic Call Distributor

An ACD manager is always faced with the necessity of deciding how many service positions to staff at any time. Most ACDs provide load and service information that the manager can use to balance load and service. Erlang C tables are used to evaluate service.

To illustrate the process, assume that ACD data indicates that the busy hour traffic load is 2.0 Erlangs and that the average holding time per call is 3.7 minutes. Also, assume that the ACD manager has an objective of having no more than 10% of the calls delayed.

The Erlang C table in Appendix E (Column N) gives a choice of from three to nine servers for 2.0 Erlangs (Column A). To stay within the objective of 10% or less of the calls delayed, Column P_d shows that five servers are required. To find the average delay for all calls, multiply the average holding time by Column D1. In this case the result is:

$$3.7 \text{ minutes x } .02 = 0.074 \text{ minutes} = 4.4 \text{ seconds.}$$

The average delay for all calls tells us little about how long the delayed calls are delayed. To find this factor, multiply the average holding time by Column D2. The result is:

$$3.7 \text{ minutes x } .333 = 1.23 \text{ minutes.}$$

The remaining columns show the probability that calls will be delayed longer than a specific time. For example, the factor .0333 is shown in the column headed .2. This means there is a 3.3% probability that calls will be delayed longer than 20% of the holding time, or 0.74 minutes.

Standards

Network design and administration are not covered by standards. Instead, networks are designed and administered to cost and service objectives that are achieved by applying network design principles. The bibliography lists publications that describe these principles more fully.

Chapter

32

Network Testing Principles

Some degree of testing capability is essential for most telecommunications networks. Even if the test is as simple as a check at the common carrier's demarcation point to determine whether trouble is in company or carrier facilities, the ability to make these tests can pay dividends in reduced maintenance costs. Companies with complex networks find that testing capability is essential, not only to control costs but to restore failed service quickly.

Telecommunications network testing has two objectives:

- To establish benchmarks that serve as references or to confirm that design objectives have been achieved.

- To locate faulty network elements by sectionalizing and isolating defective pieces of equipment.

The first category of tests is usually called acceptance or proof-of-performance. These are conducted to establish a data base that can later be the basis for fault locating tests. The second category of tests usually does not require the depth and sophistication of the first. It is often sufficient to measure a single variable such as circuit loss when searching for a defective element. When the cause of excessive loss is found, the tester may also locate the source of poor frequency response or excessive noise. Therefore, the tests used for routine circuit verification can be reduced to single frequency measurements, which in turn can be automated to survey a complex network rapidly and reliably.

Network reliability has increased dramatically over the years in spite of the ever-increasing complexity of the network. Nevertheless, every element of a telecommunications system is subject to failure, and when a circuit or service is in trouble, it is often difficult to find what portion of the network is at fault. Service irregularities and end-to-end tests can reveal the presence of a fault, but the defective element can be identified only by testing to sectionalize the trouble.

As we evolve into an integrated digital network, testing will be simplified in comparison with today's networks. A bit stream will originate on the user's premises and be carried over the network to the distant end without crossing the physically wired interfaces that circuits cross today. Circuit operation will either be near-perfect or catastrophically failed, although with properly designed diversity, total failures should be rare. With today's networks, testing is complicated by several factors:

- Network elements are obtained from multiple vendors

- Trouble must be sectionalized by testing to interfaces between vendors

- The responsibility for impairments such as high noise and data errors often is unclear, and vendors are not quick to claim responsibility

- Incompatibility at interfaces may arise under some conditions, and lacking interface standards, the user may be left to negotiate the solution between vendors.

Until low cost processors became available, network testing was almost entirely manual. Some electromechanical equipment was used (and sometimes still is) to test switching systems and circuits. Most of this equipment has been replaced by automatic equipment for bulk testing, but many individual tests are still made manually. Tests are designed specifically for a particular class of equipment; the testing principles are essentially the same whether the test is manual or automatic. This chapter describes the principles of testing the major components of a telecommunications network and, where appropriate, discusses the results that should be expected.

Transmission and switching systems require specialized test equipment to perform general tests and some tests that are unique to the manufacturer. For example, two types of tests are required on microwave radio—system performance and service. FCC-required system performance tests include frequency and bandwidth measurements and are similar for both analog and digital microwave. However, service criteria for the two types of microwave is different. Analog microwave service is closely related to its channel noise performance; the primary service indicator of digital microwave is its error rate.

Switching systems, nearly all of which contain microprocessors, require test systems that are similar to those used for maintaining computers. Because of the specialized nature of switching systems and their complexity, they are excluded from this discussion.

Test Access Methods

A common problem for all types of circuit tests is how to obtain test access to the circuit. Access is obtained by one of three methods:

- Manual access through jacks, test points, or distributing frames.
- Switched access.
- Permanently wired test equipment.

Manual access methods include jacks and terminal strips that allow direct connection of test equipment to the circuit conductors. The primary drawbacks to manual access methods are that they are labor intensive and often result in delays while a technician is being dispatched to a remote location. Switched access methods provide circuitry for connecting remote test equipment to a circuit from a distant location. Switched circuits are often accessible through the switching system. Dedicated circuits may be connected through a separate switching matrix that connects the transmission path to colocated test equipment. Test equipment also may be inserted into a circuit or designed into the terminating equipment. For example, some modems provide lights to show circuit status and a low speed channel for performing tests while the circuit is in operation.

A fundamental principle in designing a network is that it must include a plan for testing, sectionalizing, and clearing trouble. It is sometimes possible to obtain network services from a vendor who assumes full end-to-end testing and maintenance responsibility, but this may be more expensive for many organizations than the alternative of providing that service in-house. In any event, it is rare that an organization's total communications needs can be supplied by a single vendor who assumes full responsibility for performance, which means that the responsibility falls on telecommunications managers.

Analog Circuit Testing Principles

Certain tests are common to all elements of the network. The testing equipment may vary widely, but the principles are identical. The tests discussed in this section are applied to both voice frequency and data circuits and, where indicated, also may be applied to broadband transmission facilities. Analog data circuits require all the tests described in this section, but many impairments that cause trouble on data circuits are undetectable when the circuit is used for voice. The following discussion points out differences between data and voice tests.

Loss Measurements

Loss (and gain) measurements are made by injecting a signal source into the input of a circuit and reading the result at the output. Voice frequency measurements are made at a nominal frequency of 1000 Hz; 1004 Hz is actually used to prevent interference with digital transmission equipment. The frequency source, or *oscillator*, generates a pure audio tone. The signal is applied across the input of a circuit and measured at the output as shown in Figure 32.1. The difference between the two readings is the loss or gain of the circuit. This same principle is applied in measuring loss on analog radio and carrier systems. High frequency signal sources and level measuring sets are used to measure loss at baseband or at carrier or radio frequencies.

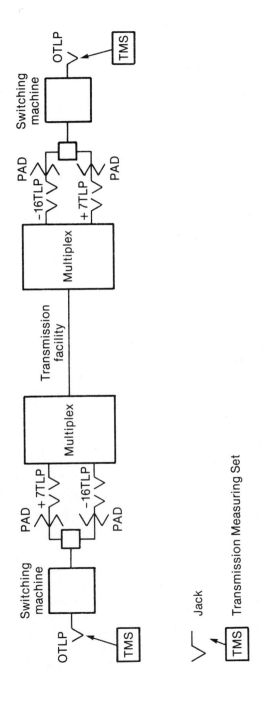

Figure 32.1   Transmission measurement on a circuit between TLPS.

In addition to single-frequency loss measurements, the gain-frequency, or attenuation distortion, characteristics of most apparatus is of interest. Attenuation distortion is a variation in loss at the audio frequencies within a circuit passband. It is measured by sending and receiving tones across the audio passband or by sweeping the circuit with a signal that varies continually in frequency. A *swept* channel can be displayed on a cathode ray tube to present a visual display of the circuit passband. Similar tests are made at carrier and radio frequencies to examine the linearity of a broadband facility. Spectrum occupancy and the presence of extraneous or high level frequencies are readily determined with a spectrum analyzer, a test instrument that displays the frequency domain of a signal.

Transmission level measurements typically are expressed as dB related to one milliwatt (dBm) as explained in Chapter 2. To ensure accurate results, test equipment must be calibrated by comparing the test set to a reference frequency and level standard.

Noise Measurements

As explained in Chapter 2, noise is expressed in dB compared to a reference noise level of -90 dBm (dBrn). Noise measurements are made with a measuring set that reads the noise power through a weighting filter and registers it on a digital or meter readout. Voice frequency circuits normally are measured through a C message filter, which approximates the human perception of the interfering effect of noise on a telephone conversation. Special service and program lines are measured through flat weighting filters, which weight all frequencies within the pass band equally.

When power is applied to a circuit, noise may increase because the greater loading reacts with nonlinearities in the circuit to increase the intermodulation noise. This effect is measured by injecting a single frequency into the circuit at the sending end and removing it with a filter at the receiving end so that only the intermodulation products remain. Circuits that are equipped with companders exhibit very low noise in the idle state because the receiving end expander has no signal and consequently reduces the volume level of its output. To obtain a realistic estimate of the noise that will be interfering with a live conversation it is necessary to place a test tone of appropriate level on the circuit to activate the compressor and expander combination and permit a useful assessment of the circuit's noise performance. The test tone is removed at the receiving end by a narrow band filter so that only the residual noise under approximately active conditions is measured. When the residual noise is measured through a C weighted filter by this technique it is designated as C-notched noise.

Impulse noise measurements are of particular interest in evaluating a circuit for data transmission. A common source of impulse noise is electromechanical relay operations that induce a sharp spike of noise into a circuit. Impulse noise has little effect on voice communication, but it can be devastating to data transmission. An impulse noise measuring set establishes a threshold level and counts the number of impulses that exceed the threshold. The set also includes a timer so impulses above reference level can be measured over a fixed time period.

Envelope Delay

Envelope delay expresses the difference in propagation speed of the various frequencies within the audio pass band. It is made with an envelope delay measuring set, which applies a pair of frequencies at the originating end of the circuit and registers the relative delay of each frequency at the receiver as the test signals move through the transmission band. Envelope delay affects high speed data but has no discernible effect on voice transmission.

Return Loss

Return loss measurements determine the amount of energy returned from a distant impedance irregularity such as the mismatch between a two-wire circuit and the network on the balancing port of a hybrid. Return loss measurements are made over a band of frequencies between 500 and 2500 Hz by transmitting a white noise signal source on the circuit as described in Chapter 2.

Phase Jitter

Phase jitter is any variation in the phase of a signal as illustrated in Figure 32.2. Jitter is measured with a special test set that detects

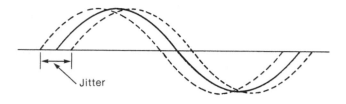

Figure 32.2   Phase jitter.

phase variations in a steady state tone injected at one end of a circuit and measured at the other.

Peak-to-Average Ratio

A peak-to-average ratio (P/AR) test gives an effective index of the quality of an analog circuit for data transmission. A P/AR transmitter sends a repetitive pulse consisting of a complex combination of signals. The P/AR receiver measures the envelope of the received signal and indexes the circuit quality on a scale of 0 to 100. The P/AR measurement attempts to provide a single composite indicator of circuit quality.

Harmonic Distortion

As described in Appendix A, a harmonic is a multiple of the fundamental frequency applied to a circuit. For reliable data communication, the second harmonic must be at least 25 dB lower than the fundamental frequency, and the third harmonic 28 dB lower than the fundamental. Harmonic distortion is measured with a special test set that reads directly the amount of second and third harmonic distortion.

Subscriber Loop Measurements

As Chapter 6 discusses, the subscriber loop is the part of a telecommunications circuit most susceptible to transmission impairment. Tests on the subscriber loop can be grouped into three categories: manual tests from a local test desk attached to a switching system, automatic tests through a switching system, and manual tests from the user's premises or intermediate points on the cable to the central office. Subscriber loop tests differ from

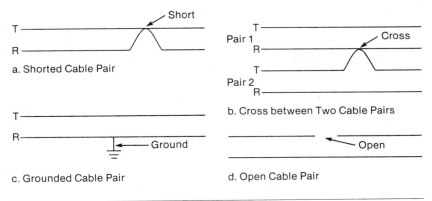

Figure 32.3   Common cable faults.

trunk tests in that full loss and noise measurements on a loop require manual or remotely controlled tests from the user's end of the circuit. Equipment to perform remote measurements can be justified only in locations with large concentrations of high cost circuits. Because such tests are labor intensive, they normally are made only to locate the cause of repeated trouble.

Local Test Desks

A local test desk (LTD) is a manually operated system that accesses a cable pair through the switching system or over a trunk to the main distributing frame. The latter connection requires manually placing a device called a test shoe at the main distributing frame to access the cable pair directly. Many local loops are inaccessible through switching systems because they are dedicated to special services. These circuits may be tested from an LTD through an MDF shoe or through switched access connectors and special service testing apparatus as described later. The principal faults that occur in local cable pairs are shorts, crosses, grounds, and opens, as Figure 32.3 shows. Crosses and grounds cause a high level of noise on the cable pair and often result in unwanted voltage (called foreign EMF) from the central office battery of the interfering pair.

Figure 32.4 shows a diagram of a properly functioning circuit and its access from an LTD. The LTD accesses the line through a circuit in the switching system that connects the LTD to the line

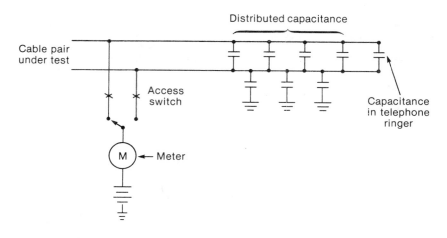

Figure 32.4 Local test desk cable testing circuit.

without ringing the telephone. The LTD evaluates the circuit by measuring capacitance between the two conductors of a cable pair, and from each conductor to ground. Because the pair consists of two parallel conductors separated by an insulator, the conductors form the two plates of a capacitor. When test voltage is applied, the meter on the LTD registers the amount of current flowing in the line as the capacitor charges. When the line reaches full charge, current ceases to flow and the meter returns to 0.

An experienced test board operator or automatic test apparatus can diagnose the condition of the line from the amount of *kick* to the meter. Shorted and open lines kick only a small amount. Properly functioning lines kick to a greater degree, with the amount of kick proportional to the length of the cable pair and the number of telephone sets installed on the line (the measurement charges the capacitor in the telephone ringer when the cable pair is charged, so more ringers increase the amount of capacitance).

Foreign EMF is detected by using the LTD voltmeter to measure the battery from each side of the line to ground. When the line is connected to the testing circuit, the central office battery is removed. Any voltage observed is coming from an interfering source such as a cross with a line that is connected to central office battery. When water enters a cable, it often provides a conductive path permitting foreign EMF to reach many lines simultaneously.

The LTD also can make loss measurements on the line. Loss measurements require someone at the distant end of the circuit. Noise measurements can be made at the central office end of a circuit, but because the noise signal is attenuated by the loss of the cable pair, noise measurements made at only the central office end of a circuit do not fully express the degree to which noise interferes with the user.

Automatic Testing

Automatic test equipment accesses local loops through the switching system to perform tests similar to LTD tests. The least complex type of automatic subscriber loop test system is the line insulation test (LIT), which has been used in central offices for many years. An LIT machine steps through each line in a central office, accessing the line through the switching system and applying to each line tests similar to those applied by the LTD. LIT machines look for shorted and grounded cable pairs and for foreign EMF. The results of the test are printed on a teletypewriter.

LIT machines are capable only of qualitative tests and offer few clues to the nature and location of the trouble. More sophisticated automatic test equipment also accesses the subscriber loop through the switching system. It can profile the impedance of the subscriber loop and determine more accurately what and where the trouble is. A mechanized line testing system functions by storing the electrical characteristics of normal lines and those with various faults in its data base. A remote test unit is accessed manually through a console or driven automatically by a computer to perform routine measurements.

Manual Loop Tests

Local test desks and mechanized line testing equipment are limited in their ability to locate certain types of cable faults. Open and wet cable pairs are among the most difficult faults to locate and often require measuring interactively with a technician in the field. The time domain reflectometer (TDR) locates trouble with a high degree of accuracy in all types of cable including coaxial cable and fiber optics. It uses the same principle in cable with which radar operates in free space. The TDR sends a pulse on the line. Any irregularity in the cable returns a reflected pulse that is displayed on a cathode ray tube calibrated in distance to the fault.

TDRs are excellent devices for locating all types of impedance irregularities, but their cost prevents their widespread use for less complex testing. Shorted and open cable pairs can be located by making precise resistance and capacitance measurements to a fault. Electronic instruments for these measurements are less expensive than TDRs and locate trouble with a satisfactory degree of accuracy.

Subscriber loop loss and noise measurements must be made from the user's premises to be accurate. Specialized test sets are available to measure the three variables that affect subscriber loop transmission—loss, noise, and loop current. Loss measurements are made by dialing a test signal supply in the central office. Noise measurements are made by dialing a termination, or *quiet line*, in the central office. Current measurements are made by measuring the off-hook current that would be drawn by a telephone set.

Network Interface Devices

Test equipment located in the central office is generally unable to distinguish between troubles located in outside cable plant and troubles in customer premises wiring and equipment. To aid in sectionalizing trouble, many types of network interface devices (NIDs) are available and sometimes installed at the interface between the customer's wiring and the telephone company's equipment. By applying voltage or an actuating tone from the LTD, the NID opens the line at the interface. Some types of NID also short the cable pair so tests can be made from the central office to the interface. With the NID actuated, if the trouble observed by the LTD remains, it is evidence that the fault is in the loop facilities. If the trouble disappears, the fault is in the customer premises wiring or equipment. NIDs are not universally applied because most ordinary telephone services do not experience trouble often enough to justify the cost of the NID. On data circuits, many data modems are equipped with loop-around capability that performs a similar function.

Trunk Transmission Measurements

The voice frequency measurements described earlier are of critical importance on all trunks. Transmission measurements are made either manually or automatically between TLPs, and adjustments are made by changing fixed loss pads or adjusting amplifier gains.

Manual Switched Circuit Test Systems

Circuit access for manual testing is obtained through jacks wired to the circuit, by access through the switching system, by removing jumper wires at a crossconnect point, or by switched access connectors. Both portable and fixed test equipment measures transmission variables and supervision. Supervision tests, which Chapter 11 discusses, are made on the signaling leads. These tests detect and register the status of supervisory leads under various conditions of circuit operation.

Manual tests are made either to a manual test board at the distant end or to responders. As described in Chapter 10, trunks may be equipped with a variety of test lines that are accessed by dialing special codes over the trunk. A typical test line is the 105, which permits two-way loss and noise measurements from an office equipped with a remote office test line (ROTL) and responder.

Automatic Switched Circuit Test Systems

In offices equipped with large numbers of circuits, the most economical way of testing is with automatic test equipment that conducts the tests under computer control. Figure 32.5 is a diagram of automatic circuit test equipment of the type discussed in Chapter 10. A computer-driven device actuates a ROTL, which communicates with a test line at the distant end. A full range of transmission and supervision tests can be made with such a system. The results are stored in memory and printed out. Trunks exceeding design limits are automatically taken out of service.

Tests on Special Service Trunks

Tests on special service lines cannot be made with the test equipment described in this section because they are not accessible through a switching system. Manual testing is particularly difficult in multipoint private lines because of the number of

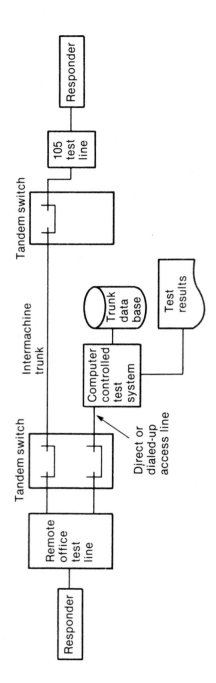

Figure 32.5   Automatic remote trunk testing system.

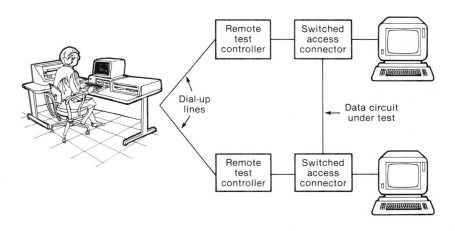

Figure 32.6   Switched access remote testing.

technicians needed to sectionalize trouble. In locations with large concentrations of special services, switched access systems, illustrated in Figure 32.6, can be justified. Circuits are wired through electromechanical crosspoints that monitor the circuit or open it to sectionalize trouble. Testing terminations and signal sources can be connected to the circuit through switched access connectors. The test console, which is typically located centrally for a company or region, is connected to a near end testing unit. Each remote location is equipped with a matching test unit, and the two units communicate over a dedicated or dialed access line.

Switched access connectors can provide the same types of access to circuits as jacks. Connectors are available to operate two, four, or six wires and allow the operator to monitor, split, test, and busy-out connections. Circuits also can be wired to enable patching hot standby spare equipment or circuits. Most systems also provide computer-supported operational functions such as logging trouble, recording circuit outage time, and maintaining trouble histories.

With a switched access testing system, a technician can obtain remote access to all points that are equipped. For example, if a multipoint circuit is singing, the technician can remotely terminate the legs of the circuit until the one causing the trouble is found. Circuit lineup tests can be made by performing two-way transmission measurements to test equipment that is accessed through the switched access connector.

Data Circuit Testing

Although non-conditioned data networks and voice networks share the same voice frequency facilities, data networks are more complex to test than voice networks. Voice networks are used by people who can give a qualitative analysis of what the trouble is. Data network troubles are apt to be reported as "slow response time," with no clue to whether the trouble is high error rate, CPU problems, noise, or momentary interruptions. Also, data circuits are subject to incompatibilities such as protocol and addressing faults that can be caused by troubles in DCE, DTE, or software.

Tests are applied to data circuits for one of three purposes: to resolve specific trouble reports, to monitor the circuit for proper operation, or to prevent trouble by detecting incipient faults with a preventive maintenance program. Many data network problems are found in the user's equipment—the software, the interface between the DTE and DCE, or a hardware element. Because each data network has a custom design, it is imperative that the manager analyze the trouble before referring it to a vendor. Such analysis will save time and money and will solve many problems without the help of an outside vendor.

Interface Tests

Many test sets are available to test the EIA-232-D or equivalent interface. The test set plugs between the DCE and the DTE and provides access points to the principal signaling and communication leads. The status and polarity of the leads are often displayed with colored lamps. Switches are provided to reconfigure the interface. A breakout box provides access for connecting test probes and injecting test signals.

Loopback Tests

A loopback test on a full duplex circuit is an effective way of locating faults and impairments in a data circuit. Figure 32.7

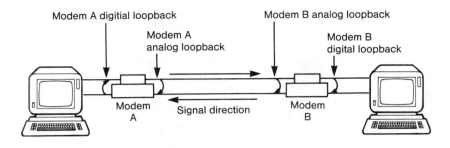

Figure 32.7   Modem loopback paths.

shows the different points at which a data circuit can be looped. Many modems contain integral loopback capability. If not, circuits can be looped with an adapter plug. Tests are performed either by sending a phrase that uses all letters of the alphabet, such as "fox" (the quick brown fox jumped over the lazy dog's back 1234567890), or by sending a standard test pattern and monitoring for errors with a bit error rate (BER) test set. Many modems also include built-in BER testing capability. By looping the circuit at progressively further points, the element causing the complaint can be identified.

Although loopback tests are useful in locating hard faults, some impairments such as data errors, phase jitter, and envelope delay are cumulative over the length of a circuit. Therefore the results of a loopback test must be tempered with the knowledge that the amount of impairment will be doubled because the length of the circuit is doubled. Such tests are more effectively made end-to-end.

Protocol Analyzers

Protocol analyzers are devices that are either inserted in or bridged on the digital portion of a data communications line to provide a character-by-character analysis of the data signal. Protocol analyzers such as the Hewlett-Packard 4952A, shown in Figure 32.8, typically include several digital test functions in the same test set. Many analyzers measure bit error rate, block error rate, and percent error-free (or errored) seconds. These variables are useful for detecting the character of noise in a data circuit. For

Figure 32.8   A Hewlett-Packard 4952A protocol analyzer.
Courtesy, Hewlett-Packard Corporation

example, if a circuit has a high bit error rate but a low block error rate, it indicates that errors are coming in bursts with error-free intermediate periods. A low bit error rate with a high block error rate indicates that errors are more equally spaced.

Protocol analyzers operate in a monitor or simulation mode. In the monitor mode the test set is a passive observer of the bit stream between two devices. In the simulation mode, the circuit is opened and the test set simulates circuit elements. Test sets can simulate terminals, modems, and CPUs. Among the features commonly included is a terminal exerciser to facilitate diagnosing terminal troubles by sending data messages into a terminal. Some systems contain a polling generator to simulate the CPU in polling a multidrop line. Most units include some form of storage so an error sequence can be captured for off-line diagnosis. Programmable units allow the operator to set triggers or test sequences for trapping error conditions. Many such devices can remember test sequences so they can be recalled without reprogramming.

PCM Test Sets

PCM test sets are used by both common carriers and end users to diagnose the condition of a PCM line. Test sets are available to monitor bipolar line violations, which are two consecutive pulses of the same polarity. Bipolar violations, however, are not available at the terminals of a high speed data line—a DS-1 bit stream, for example—that transits any multiplexing equipment. In this case, other indicators such as framing errors must be relied upon for performance measurement.

Applications

Anyone who has reviewed the advertisements for testing systems and equipment is aware that the market is flooded with options. Any organization that owns or is planning to develop a telecommunications network must attend to testing strategy at the outset. After the overall strategy is developed, individual test systems can be selected.

In general, the more sophisticated and expensive the test equipment, the higher the skill level or the more elaborate the software that is needed to obtain and interpret the results. Equipment should match the level of communications expertise within the organization. It is a waste of money to purchase sophisticated equipment that is beyond the capabilities of the personnel, and it is also a waste of money to buy simple equipment when more complex equipment can rapidly pay for itself in the hands of an experienced technician.

Standards

Standard-setting agencies issue standards on testing methods and procedures but generally do not produce standards on test equipment. Instead, manufacturers design test equipment to their specifications to conform to the standards of the circuits under test.

Evaluation Criteria

Accuracy

Accuracy and stability are of concern in all testing equipment and systems. This is of particular importance with analog test equipment, which must be held to precise level and frequency standards. Improperly calibrated test equipment and the failure to match the impedance of test equipment to the circuit are frequent causes of inaccuracy in measuring circuits and setting net loss. Every testing program must, therefore, include a procedure to ensure test equipment accuracy.

Portability

Test equipment is produced in three levels of portability—hand-held, portable, and fixed. Portable test equipment is packaged in cases for mobility but is often heavy enough that it is not easily moved. Fixed test equipment is mounted in relay racks and is used in test centers where circuits are accessed through jacks or switched access connectors. The type of equipment selected for an application is based on the need for portability and the number of functions included in a single package. Hand-held test equipment generally is as accurate as portable or fixed equipment, but several units may be needed to perform the functions that are contained in one package with larger equipment.

Analog vs. Digital Tests

On dedicated data circuits, tests can be made between either the analog or the digital side of modems. Digital tests are of little value in finding totally failed circuit conditions and of no value in voice frequency circuit tests. Analog tests are useful only on dedicated circuits or in verifying the condition of a circuit up to the point of interface with a common carrier. There is little reason for a user to conduct analog tests over a dial-up circuit. When trouble is experienced on dial circuits, equipment can be tested to the interface and then referred to the common carrier.

Analog test sets designed to measure most transmission variables are available. Measurements include attenuation distortion, intermodulation distortion, steady state and impulse noise, peak-to-average ratio, envelope delay, and phase jitter. Test sets that combine all these measurements in the same unit are more flexible and more expensive than single-purpose units.

Centralized vs. Distributed Testing

As networks become more complex, the usefulness of centralized testing becomes more apparent. From a central location where circuit status is continually monitored, reports of congestion and blockage can be most efficiently handled. The primary concern in determining whether to centralize is the availability of switched access connections to the circuits under test. If only jack access is provided, centralized testing is useful only on circuits terminating in the central location. In general, the larger and more complex the network, the greater the benefit from centralized testing. Also, the larger the network, the greater the benefit of automated testing.

Protocol Flexibility

The cost of protocol test equipment is proportional to its flexibility in testing various data protocols. In selecting this type of test set, present and planned protocols should be examined. The test equipment acquired should have the necessary capability without the cost of unneeded features. Programmable test sets have the greatest flexibility in implementing new protocols.

Security

A critical feature of any remote testing system is its provision for preventing unauthorized access. Because these systems enable monitoring and testing of operating circuits, it is very important that unauthorized access be prevented. The most secure form of access is the use of dedicated circuits between the test console and the remote units, but over long distances, dedicated access is uneconomical. Access to long haul facilities is usually provided over dial-up units. Where dial-up circuits are used, the telephone number of the remote units is difficult to keep secret, so means must be provided to prevent unauthorized access. A complex handshake between the master and the remote unit may deter anyone who lacks knowledge of the protocol. Passwords are also useful but far from foolproof. The most effective method is to use a dialer at the remote to dial the master back from the remote.

Selected Testing Systems and Equipment Manufacturers

Centralized Trunk Testing Systems

ADC Telecommunications
AT&T
Northwest Electronics

Wilcom
Telecommunications
Technologies, Inc.

Circuit Testing Equipment

ADC Telecommunications
Ameritec
Ando Corp.
AT&T
Atlantic Research Corporation
Biddle Instruments
ComData Systems
CXR/Telecom
Digilog
Dynatel 3M
Electrodata
Fluke Mfg. Co., Inc.
Frederick Engineering
Hekimian Laboratories, Inc.
Hewlett-Packard Co.

International Data Sciences
Navtel, Inc.
Northeast Electronics Div. of
Tau-Tron
Scientific-Atlanta, Inc.
Siemens Corporation
Sierra Transmission Products
Systron-Donner Corp.
Tekno Industries, Inc.
Tektronix, Inc.
Telenex Corporation
Marconi Instruments
Wilcom
Wandel & Goltermann, Inc.
Wiltron Company

T-1 Testing Equipment

DCM
Electrodata, Inc.
Frederick Engineering
International Data Sciences

Phoenix Microsystems, Inc.
T-Com Corporation
Tau-Tron, Inc.

Data Test Equipment and Protocol Analyzers

ADC Telecommunications

AR Division of Telenex

AT&T

Consultronics

Digitech Industries, Inc.

Dynatech Communications

Fluke Mfg. Co., Inc.

Frederick Engineering

General Datacomm, Inc.

Hekimian Laboratories, Inc.

Hewlett-Packard Co.

Northeast Electronics Div. of Tau-tron

Phoenix Microsystems, Inc.

Porta Systems Corp.

Sage Instruments

Scientific-Atlanta, Inc.

Siemens Corporation

Sierra Transmission Products

Systron-Donner Corp.

Tau-Tron, Inc.

Tekno Industries, Inc.

Tektronix, Inc.

Telecommunications Techniques Corp.

Teradyne Central, Inc.

Wandel & Goltermann, Inc.

Wiltron Company

Local Area Network Testing Equipment

Digilog

Digital Technology, Inc.

FTP Software, Inc.

Microtest

Network General

Spider Systems

Thomas-Conrad Corp.

33

Network Management

Ask the chief executive officer of any large corporation to rank company resources in the order of their importance, and certain responses are predictable. Nearly every company rates its employees at the top of the list. Management information systems and telecommunications systems too, will rank near the top in most companies. Because of their replaceable nature, real estate and motor vehicles usually rank well down the list, but ironically, many companies spend more to manage real estate and vehicles than they do to manage telecommunications. The reason for this apparent imbalance has nothing to do with the value of the resource; it is because tangible assets are so much easier to manage, and the principles are more clearly understood.

No one disputes the need to manage telecommunications, and there is no shortage of solutions. The market is replete with network control products, but the industry has few standards, and most of the available systems work on proprietary networks.

As networks become more complex and skilled labor to maintain them climbs in cost and shrinks in supply, it becomes logical to mechanize network management to the greatest degree feasible. The equipment that comprises large networks can support automation to an ever-increasing degree. Processors built into such devices as channel banks, multiplexers, and even modems can report status and accept orders to reconfigure themselves for testing or a different method of operation. As the equipment reports status and accepts orders in digital data form, it becomes feasible to control the network from a computer.

Human beings are needed to make the decisions that cannot easily be formulated into yes and no choices, but computers can react faster and weigh and discard alternatives at a speed that humans cannot match.

As the science of artificial intelligence develops, it will support the needs of network management. The uniqueness of every network makes it difficult to adopt standard rules and procedures, but the knowledge of managers who know how the network is to function and the relative importance of different phases of the operation can be captured in an artificial intelligence program and used to augment the available staff.

The shift from analog to digital circuits will require major changes in data network administration that artificial intelligence will be required to support. The rapid decline in digital circuit costs makes private networks more attractive, particularly to large organizations. Also, as the strategic importance of the network increases, it becomes critical that failed services be restored rapidly. Automated equipment and artificial intelligence become the vehicles for rapid diagnosis and restoral.

Managers have the problem of how to keep network and related systems from getting out of control. Many companies are experiencing rapid network growth. The budgets are often in the hands of end users who are familiar with the objectives but have no knowledge of how to administer or control the networks. Simultaneously, users' expectations are growing along with their familiarity with personal computers. They expect the network to be sophisticated in its interfaces, yet easy to understand and manage. These trends are causing the network manager's job to become more complex.

The primary hope of network managers is to automate the management task. The automation engine must gather information from multiple vendors and diverse sources, process the information, and enter it in a data base so it can be massaged and presented to operators in an understandable, preferably graphic, manner.

A primary obstacle to mechanized network management is that many applications are becoming peer-to-peer, but the management systems are still hierarchical. A second problem is the lack of standards. Many proprietary systems, including IBM's

Netview, AT&T's Unified Network Management Architecture (UNMA), Digital Equipment's Enterprise Management Architecture, Hewlett-Packard's Open View, and the OSI Network Management Protocol, have been proposed. None has reached the status of even a de facto standard at this point, and network managers are left with a bewildering array of products that will do a good job if the network has a single-vendor architecture but will fall short of the ideal if multiple vendors are involved.

Local area networks present a special management challenge because they are so closely integrated with the end users' operations. The management of a LAN is not a great deal different from the management of a data center. This means the following functions, which are typical of data centers, must be provided:

- Capacity planning.
- Change management.
- Disaster planning and recovery.
- Fault management.
- Power conditioning.
- Security management.
- Service management.
- Storage medium backup and recovery.

This chapter explains briefly the elements of a telecommunications management program. The principles apply whether the system is owned or leased. Telecommunications management applies to both large and small systems, although in small networks some functions are more likely to be contracted out than performed by in-house staff. For a more detailed discussion of telecommunications system management, refer to *The Dow Jones-Irwin Handbook of Telecommunications Management*.

Network Management and Control

Technical control is a term applied to centralized network management and control systems that monitor status and manage capacity in large networks. These systems include provisions for accessing data circuits by jacks or computer controlled switched access similar to that described in Chapter 32. In addition to providing testing capability, technical control centers include alarm reporting, trouble history, and, usually, a mechanized inventory of circuit equipment. Network control center operations can be divided into the following classifications:

- *Configuration Management.* Retains records and, where possible, configures network equipment remotely. Retains a complete record of users, assignments, equipment, and other records needed to administer the telecommunications system.
- *Cost Management.* Tracks vendor bills and distributes costs to organizational units.
- *Fault management.* Receives reports from users, diagnoses trouble, corrects trouble, and restores service to the users.
- *Performance Management.* Monitors service levels and measures response time, availability, and other measures of user satisfaction.
- *Security Management.* Ensures that network and files are accessible only to authorized personnel. Assigns passwords and user numbers and detects unauthorized attempts to penetrate the network.

System Records

A complete record of telecommunications resources is essential in any organization with a system that has more than single-line telephones. Records should consist of at least these elements:

- Equipment identification.
- Equipment documentation.
- Equipment location.
- System layout.
- Circuit identification.

These records are kept along with the property records that most companies keep for depreciation and accounting purposes. If the system is leased, the lessor probably will retain some of the above records, but they should be available to the lessee because they are essential for studies of future growth and rearrangement.

Equipment Identification

An inventory of equipment by type, model number, manufacture date or equipment list number, and wiring options is essential for managing a telecommunications system. For stored program controlled equipment the program identification, serial number, and issue number also should be retained. Most equipment manufacturers have a systematic process for upgrading their equipment as they improve hardware and software. When manufacturers announce these improvements, the user must decide whether to upgrade. Equipment records are necessary for maintaining an upgrade program and for answering compatibility questions.

Equipment Documentation

Manufacturers typically document telecommunications equipment with installation and maintenance manuals, schematic diagrams, wiring or interconnection diagrams, and circuit descriptions. All such documents should be obtained with the equipment and filed, even if the vendor is maintaining the equipment under contract, because such documentation is the key to changing maintenance contractors if the need arises. Software documentation also should be obtained with any stored program-controlled equipment. Review the documentation to ensure that it covers restart and error recovery procedures.

Location Records

The location of fixed equipment should be documented, possibly on the equipment identification records. Location records are not needed for simple systems such as small PBX and key telephone systems, but they are vital for more complex networks that include transmission equipment. Location records are particularly essential for concealed LAN equipment such as repeaters and junction boxes.

System Layout

Telecommunications circuits consist of interconnected assemblies of equipment. Records of assignments and interconnection are essential for trouble shooting. Such records normally include both the drawings that the vendor assembles when equipment is installed and the records of connections that are made when it is assigned. Interconnection drawings should show all options wired at the time of installation, designation of the wiring, and identification of the crossconnection and testing points. Records of assignments of services supplied by outside vendors should be kept. Station records should identify the user and the features of each station. Most modern PBX systems also require software translations. The manager should keep records or backup data files of these.

Circuit Identification Records

Every circuit in the network should be documented with such details as the circuit identification number, vendor, end points, route, date installed, type of medium (analog, fractional T-1, DDS, etc.), and cost. Record trouble reporting numbers where maintenance personnel can find them.

System Usage Management

Although a telecommunications system is a high cost resource, personnel costs outweigh equipment costs in most organizations. The objective of an effective telecommunications system is to ensure that the productivity of the users is not hampered by non-availability of the service, poor response time, or cumbersome operating procedures. Also, it is essential to control telecommunications costs. Costs should be controlled through policies and supervision, not through under-design of the network. The essential part of a telecommunications management system is usage monitoring and translating the result into capacity changes. A second consideration in many organizations is allocating telecommunications costs to the unit incurring the expense.

These two elements are both measurable in switched networks equipped with a PBX or key system. Normally, cost allocation is based on line usage, while system utilization is measured by load indicators on the system components.

Line Usage Measurements

Line usage is determined by common carrier bills, user dialed identification digits, or reports from the call accounting system. In Centrex systems and PBXs with automatically identified outward dialing (AIOD), the LEC renders the toll bill directly to the end user's telephone number. Systems sharing a common group of trunks without AIOD need another form of cost allocation.

The simplest form, but the one that is least convenient from a user's standpoint, is for the user to dial accounting digits with each call. Typically, the user dials the telephone number followed by an accounting code, and software in the switching machine or in an external computer tabulates costs by account code. The account code may be programmed into a smart telephone set that automatically pulses the code with the dialed digits. This technique is not feasible for allocating the cost of telecommunication services from common facilities such as conference rooms.

A PBX or key telephone system may be equipped with a call accounting system or simply a station message detail recorder port (SMDR) to register calls in systems that lack call accounting software. A call accounting system is a valuable tool for preventing abusive personal use of telephone services. As discussed in Chapter 20, the call accounting system logs complete details of each outgoing call and produces a summary at the end of the accounting period. The call accounting system screens authorized calls automatically through a data base and flags unauthorized and unidentified calls for administrative action. Dedicated voice and data circuits are billed directly to the department incurring the expense.

Traffic Usage

The second type of usage monitoring is system-focused rather than user-focused. Traffic usage monitoring supplies the information needed to determine when it is time to adjust circuit capacities. In PBXs and central offices with processor-controlled switching, the system usually includes software usage registers. Older electromechanical PBXs, many hybrids, and KTSs lack provision for usage measuring, so external recorders are required. In central office-based systems such as Centrex, the telephone company monitors usage and recommends capacity changes. Many data networks include usage monitoring software in the front end processor, multiplexer, concentrator, or host computer.

The traffic usage system monitors three separate elements of a telecommunications system—line usage, trunk usage, and common equipment usage. As Chapter 31 discusses, usage measurements normally include peg count (the number of times a circuit is accessed), the total minutes of use for all circuits of the same type, and the amount of overflow. Traffic usage readings must be distilled, interpreted, and translated into capacity changes. Any network management system requires the traffic usage monitoring function.

In addition to usage measurements, network service measurements also should be made. On line circuits, the average amount of dial tone delay and, on trunk and common equipment, the amount of blockage should be monitored as service indicators. Common equipment such as DTMF registers should be monitored because a shortage of these will delay calls. The objective of usage measurements is to detect bottlenecks so they can be corrected before service degenerates and to optimize line and equipment utilization.

Trouble Handling Procedures

Every telecommunications system, including those too small to justify a network management system, should have a procedure for handling trouble reports. In smaller offices the receptionist or attendant is usually the focal point for trouble reports. In systems with full time network management, trouble report handling and analysis is handled by the help desk.

A trouble log is essential in either case. At a minimum, the log should include the following information:

- Name of the person reporting trouble.
- Date and time of the trouble report.
- Nature of the trouble.
- Date, time, and name of person receiving the trouble referral.
- Date, time, and name of person clearing trouble.
- Description of cause and work done to clear trouble.

Trouble reports should be summarized periodically, with frequency depending on the size of the system. Without regular analysis of trouble reports, undesirable trends may escape management's notice. The trouble report summary should reveal patterns of excessive trouble reports, excessive clearing time, and recurring failures of the same type. These patterns can be used to initiate corrective action with common carriers, equipment suppliers, and service organizations.

Unless cost is no object, telecommunications system owners should be prepared to do a limited amount of maintenance in-house. Simple tests can sectionalize trouble so the right service technician is called. Large organizations may have network testing centers. Small organizations can train one or two people to make simple tests.

The network management center or, in smaller networks, the PBX attendant, is also the focal point for receiving system alarms. In an effective network, major trunk groups and critical equipment are equipped with alarm points and bring the alarm indications into a center for trouble diagnosis.

Telecommunications Costs

Every organization should maintain a detailed record of telecommunications costs segregated by major service categories such as:

- Local telephone service.
- Long distance telephone service.
- Special services, including data, private lines, and foreign exchange.
- Maintenance and repair.
- Equipment lease costs.
- Administrative costs.

These costs are used to allocate overhead to the operating entities and form a basis for comparing alternative sources of telecommunications services. Long distance records are essential for evaluating alternative carriers and for determining when it is economical to replace toll telephone service with some form of special service such as foreign exchange and leased tie trunks.

Organizations with large networks should continually be monitoring the use of common carrier message toll services to determine the most economical point at which to add trunks. Busy line
or overflow studies for 800 numbers should be made to project a
potential loss of revenue because of inability of customers to reach
an incoming line.

Local service costs should be monitored to discover whether
the most economical number of local service lines has been
provided. LECs can monitor the number of busy signals to a
telephone number to project a potential loss of revenue because
of busies that customers encounter. Where the LEC measures
local service, records of message charges can aid in determining
when alternative types of service are economical. For example,
the use of dial-up data on local lines may be more expensive than
installing a private line to a public data network.

Trouble and cost records are useful for determining whether to
maintain a system on an on-call basis, under a maintenance contract,
or by internal staff. The service provider usually bases the cost of a
maintenance contract on a worst-case assumption, and a contract is
often more expensive than paying for repairs as needed. Maintenance contracts often include parts, preventive maintenance services, and equipment upgrades, however, and from that standpoint
they are a type of insurance that may be worthwhile. Also, most
vendors give preferential treatment to maintenance contract
customers when there is a conflict of priorities. A combination of
trouble records and costs will aid in determining the best option.

Administrative costs, including the costs of internal maintenance staff, accounting for and billing the system, processing
requests for additions and changes, and handling trouble reports,
also should be monitored.

Service Monitoring

An effective network management system includes a procedure for
measuring service levels. The key question is whether the system is
supporting or hampering the productivity of its users. In a network
with privately owned or leased facilities, the network management
center should monitor call completions. Calls not completed because of blockage or equipment failures indicate lost time and are

the responsibility of the network management center to correct. Busy signals are equally important because of the expense of setting up a circuit and consuming circuit time, only to find it blocked by a busy signal at the far end. Call completions can often be improved by adding lines or forwarding busy calls to another number at the distant end. In data networks the error rate, response time, and throughput should be measured.

Preventing and Recovering from Disasters

Within the memory of most telecommunications managers are disasters that have drastically affected service. These have ranged from common carrier failures with national implications such as the 1989 Hinsdale, Illinois, fire, which destroyed an important tandem switch, to single circuit failures that affected only a single company and its customers. Every network manager must have a plan for preventing and recovering from disasters. Many of the principles involved in creating such a plan are the same principles computer center managers have been using for years: avoid centers made of flammable materials, provide automatic fire extinguishing apparatus, back up storage media frequently, and store the backup copies away from the center.

Telecommunications disaster plans go further, however, because they look outside the company environment to the common carriers and evaluate their facilities for service continuity. Backup plans may involve serving the company from more than one wire center, providing alternative cable entrance facilities, and providing emergency power and emergency microwave radio facilities for rapid circuit restoration.

Disaster planning is a detailed and technical field, and space limitations prevent covering it in any depth here. The following section discusses some principles that should be considered in any network management center.

Network Reconfiguration

A major goal of the network management center is to bypass failures when they occur and to reconfigure the network in

Figure 33.1   A network status map.
Courtesy, General Datacomm, Inc.

response to changes in load. Ideally, the network will be reconfigured dynamically as load patterns change and as failures occur. In networks composed of conventional private line services, network reconfiguration can take weeks or months because of the long lead times involved in ordering new circuits or equipment. As discussed in Chapter 4, the advent of digital crossconnect systems facilitates rearrangement under control of the user and aids in achieving the goal of rapid reconfiguration.

The matrix switch is one device that can be used for rapid network reconfiguration. Matrix switches, which can switch any of their ports to any other port, are not used for disaster recovery alone. In normal operation, it may be desirable to reroute ports on a computer or PBX. The matrix switch terminates circuits and ports on its input ports and makes it easy to reconfigure them either locally or remotely. The switch also provides the capability of triggering an alarm when an event such as a lost carrier on a data circuit occurs.

A network management system also provides status information on all parts of the network. Figure 33.1 shows a network status map, which is displayed on a VDT and updated in real time. Alarms and circuit and equipment failures are shown in red, and less critical alerts are shown in other colors. If this status information is available in real time, the network management center can react quickly to changes.

Preventing Failures

The most important goal of network management is to prevent failures. The network management center should control preventive maintenance on all network elements, including transmission testing on circuits and equipment adjustments, if any are required.

The design of the system is the first line of defense against failures. Redundant equipment should be provided where failures cannot be tolerated. Diverse routes can be used to keep the system functioning with degraded service when one route fails. Backup equipment or facilities should be provided to restore a failed service rapidly. Dial-up facilities provide an excellent means of backing up dedicated voice and data services and should be considered for most networks.

Stored program-controlled equipment relies heavily on its software to prevent failures. All SPC software should devote a substantial portion of its resources to diagnosing the system and searching for potential weak spots.

Applications

Network management systems are often not acquired as a single product from a single vendor. Instead, they are assembled from equipment and software packages provided by a variety of sources and contain custom software to accommodate the uniqueness of the network.

Standards

Standard-setting agencies recommend few standards for network management, although they have done considerable work on an OSI network management standard. Networks in the United States are managed according to the policies of each network's owner and may include systems made by a variety of manufacturers. IBM's Netview is an important data network management tool, because there are so many SNA networks in service. Many other vendors provide Netview-compatible equipment, but the product has not yet become a de facto standard. One standard that is gaining in popularity is Simple Network Management Protocol (SNMP).

Simple Network Management Protocol (SNMP)

Few managers dispute the need to monitor and control their networks, but in the past they were hampered by a lack of a standard network management protocol. Ultimately, an OSI-based management protocol will be developed, but as discussed in Chapter 3, OSI is developing slowly, and meanwhile TCP/IP is the protocol of choice for interconnecting devices of multiple vendors. It is appropriate, therefore, that a TCP/IP-based protocol, Simple Network Management Protocol (SNMP), is gaining acceptance by many manufacturers.

SNMP is an application layer protocol consisting of three parts: the SNMP protocol itself, the Structure of Management Information (SMI) specification, and the Management Information Data Base (MIB).

SNMP is designed for large internets. Vendors are free to establish the user interface. Most products are based on a graphical interface with icons, pull-down menus, and network maps. These run in the Network Management Station (NMS), which is a graphical workstation.

The NMS contains the software that oversees the network. The devices on the network contain agent software that is deliberately kept simple to conserve processing power for the tasks for which the device is intended. The NMS polls the agents, which respond with alarms, statistical information, and indications of thresholds exceeded. The NMS also can send commands to agents through its SET command structure. The agent could be remotely reconfigured, rebooted, or even shut down if the vendor's implementation of SNMP permits it.

The SNMP protocol is the language that agents and management stations use to communicate. SNMP can perform the following functions:

- Reconfigure devices.
- Collect network statistics.
- Isolate faults before they become hard failures.
- Monitor performance of devices on the network.
- Maintain event logs.

When TCP/IP is eventually displaced by OSI, SNMP will disappear. Until then, the many TCP/IP networks in use indicate a future for SNMP.

Evaluation Criteria

As networks grow increasingly complex, network management systems likewise grow in complexity. Also, as networks are continually changing, network management systems must have the flexibility to accommodate the growth and rearrangement of the network without becoming so complicated that only experts can administer them. Network management can be simplified by using processors, and as with any mechanized system the user interface is essential to keeping it understandable. At the present state of development, network management is not a single entity but a collection of techniques, most of which are computer-supported. The primary issues in keeping a network management system manageable are:

- All aspects of management are covered in some way by a system—either manual or mechanical.
- The systems are interactive to drive each other to the maximum extent possible.
- The network layout records are accessible and easily understood.
- The system can infer the cause of trouble from a diagnosis of a variety of inputs. For example, a hardware alarm could be diagnosed as the cause of a group of circuit failures.
- The system should aid the operators in determining appropriate action for alleviating symptoms.
- The system should automatically reroute failed circuits and patch in standby equipment to guard against total failure.

- The system should provide output data summarized and sorted for analysis or should provide a port to an external system to accomplish the same objective.
- The system should provide a trouble history log.

Method Of Data Collection

A critical issue in any network management systems is how it collects data from circuits and equipment and sends it to a management center. The cost of equipment and facilities to connect data to the center can represent a significant portion of the network cost and must be justified by saving expense. Access switches, responders, and remote test equipment are most easily justified with large concentrations of circuits. In less dense locations, it may be most economical to collect information manually and to access circuits through jacks. The network manager must examine each element of the network management system based on value gained from the system compared to the costs of implementing it.

Centralized vs. Decentralized Network Management

It is not possible to generalize about centralization or decentralization of a network management system because the benefits of centralization depend on the character of the network, the types of services being carried, the penalty for outage, the ability of trained people to administer the system locally, and the nature of the organization that owns the network. If centralization can be justified, it is usually the most effective method of managing a network because diagnosing network trouble requires information that often can be analyzed more meaningfully from a central site. The people on the spot, however, are usually the best equipped to take corrective action when troubles occur. Some of the most complex networks in the world, the telephone networks, are administered locally with central sites monitoring traffic flow and dealing with congestion. The issue of centralization is one that must be dealt with as part of the fundamental network design and reexamined as new services and equipment make it feasible to change the basic plan.

A parallel issue to that of centralization is whether testing will be done manually or automatically. As networks gain intelligence, automatic testing becomes more the rule than the exception. The network must be large enough, however, to justify the cost of automatic testing before it can be considered. Equipment to do automatic tests is advancing rapidly, and network management strategies should be reexamined periodically in the light of new developments.

Multiple Vendor Issues

With the demise of the end-to-end service responsibility of the LECs, network users increasingly must obtain their equipment from multiple vendors. Although this offers opportunities for cost saving, it thrusts a much greater responsibility on the network manager to monitor service and develop techniques for dealing with multiple vendors.

One problem is the lead time for obtaining additional capacity. Projects involving multiple vendors must be coordinated, or one vendor may install capacity that cannot be used because another vendor has not completed its work. Procurement policies must be closely administered to ensure that equipment is procured to the user's specifications. Compatibility problems become the user's responsibility—a responsibility that can be exercised best by preparing precise procurement requirements and specifications when acquiring equipment and services.

An allied issue is the degree of internal network management expertise that an organization develops. Although it is possible to turn the problem of network administration over to an outside contractor, to do so is to incur both a risk and an expense. The risk and the expense may be preferable to developing internal resources, but this is a decision that should be made only after an analysis of the alternative of developing internal staff.

Organizational Considerations

Many companies have not yet aligned their internal organizations with the realities of the new telecommunications networks. In most companies data processing people administer the data network, and a separate staff administers the voice network. The information resource that both support may be managed by yet a third group. In the future the integration of voice and data networks is inevitable for most large organizations. Though the two may be separated at the source, bulk circuit procurement is more economical and flexible than obtaining individual circuits. When failures occur, a single organizational unit will be the most effective in dealing with the problems of restoring services and rerouting high priority circuits over alternative facilities. In most organizations, the most effective structure will separate the information-generating entities from the information-transporting entities. As this is contrary to the way most companies are organized, this issue should be dealt with as the character of the network becomes more integrated.

Another issue that must be dealt with is flexibility of network planning. Changing tariffs and rates of long haul carriers, access charges, and measured local service of local telephone companies make it essential that managers continually reexamine network plans. Plans should be flexible enough to enable the organization to react quickly as changes in tariffs and grades of service occur.

Vendors

Manufacturers of Matrix Switches

Bytex Corp.

Codex Corp.

Data Switch Corporation

Datacomm Management Sciences

Datatran Corp.

Dynatech Corp.

Redcom Laboratories

Telenex Corp.

Companies that Support SNMA

Cisco Systems, Inc.

Proteon

IBM

Digital Equipment Corp.

Sun Microsystems, Inc.

Hewlett-Packard

Advanced Computer Communications

Hughes

LAN Systems

Wellfleet

Synoptics

Selected Network Management Systems Manufacturers

Alcatel Network Systems

AR Division, Telenex Corp.

AT&T Paradyne

BBN, Inc.

Codex Corporation

Data Switch Corporation

Dynatech Corp.

Frederick Engineering, Inc.

General Datacomm, Inc.

Hekimian Laboratories, Inc.

Hewlett-Packard

Infotron Systems Corporation

Network Communications Corp.

Network Equipment Technologies

Newbridge Networks, Inc.

Northern Telecom

Phoenix Microsystems

Racal Milgo

RAD Network Devices

Rockwell International

Stratacom

Tekelec

Tellabs

Timeplex, Inc.

Ungermann-Bass, Inc.

Universal Data Systems

Wandel & Goltermann, Inc.

Future Developments in Telecommunications

The exact shape of the future network is not yet well defined. It is clear that unlike the predivestiture network, which was essentially a single entity, future networks in the United States will be combinations owned by a variety of competing carriers. Not only will the carriers compete; many of the technologies also will compete to carry a variety of information, most of which will be in digital form. Analog information will remain on local loops, but even that will eventually disappear as residential users embrace ISDN. How quickly this will happen is impossible to predict, but there are no compelling services on the horizon to inspire a widespread adoption of ISDN in the next few years.

Whatever shape the network takes, it is likely that ISDN will play only an incidental role in non-voice services. Although one of ISDN's selling points has been its suitability for data and video, competing technologies offer greater promise. Many services will be satisfactorily supported by the 2B+D basic ISDN service, but many bandwidth-hungry applications will require other facilities.

The question is who will be the dominant carrier of broadband services. The LECs appear to have accepted ISDN's limitations in their adoption of the IEEE 802.6 metropolitan area network. The LECs seem ideally suited to transport broadband with their network of conduit in major metropolitan areas, which provides the infrastructure for the fiber optic cable that will undoubtedly be the preferred medium. They are being pushed, however, by independent metropolitan fiber optic carriers, who may capture a significant market share in large cities.

ISDN also will increase, if only because of the commitment the LECs' have made to it as the vehicle for modernizing their networks. Less clear is whether users will embrace ISDN as an essential solution to their communication problems. The LECs' broadband technologies, including Switched Multimegabit Data Service (SMDS) and broadband ISDN, will doubtless achieve a share of the broadband market.

It is easy to see the forces that are driving telecommunications; it is less obvious what the results will be. This chapter is not an attempt to forecast what developments will occur. Instead, it discusses the trends that the technological and political climate already have set in motion.

Computer Technologies

Probably no force has had a greater effect on telecommunications than the development of microelectronics. Chip densities are increasing at the rate of 40 to 50% per year, with the limits not yet in sight. A decade ago the 64 kilobit RAM chip was on the forefront of technology; in 1990 Hitachi Corporation announced development of a 64 *mega*bit chip. As microprocessors grow more powerful and memory becomes less expensive, the telecommunications networks increasingly become extensions of computer systems. Personal computers have driven a revolution in software that was unthinkable with earlier mainframes. The graphic user interface is becoming the standard even as the stand-alone personal computer is losing ground to networked devices.

Computer technology not only drives demand for telecommunications service, it is also an important means of providing it. Microprocessors and memory are embedded in systems ranging from simple test equipment to digital switches. We have not yet glimpsed the limits of the microelectronics revolution, nor can we imagine the products that will result.

One of the next major computing trends will likely be cooperative processing, or *groupware*. Today's network software is designed with file and record locking to prevent simultaneous use and potential damage of records. Cooperative software enables a group to work collectively on a project in real time. The products that will make groupware possible are just entering the market, but they promise to make telecommunications even more important in linking computers over a wide range.

The Compact Disk/Read Only Memory (CD/ROM) is another development that will reshape telecommunications. CD/ROM offers low storage cost per byte, speed of access, and reproducibility that are unequalled by other storage technologies. As these devices come into general use, they will result in ever-increasing amounts of data being transferred across the network.

Telecommunications Technologies

For the future, there is no question that voice will continue as the primary means of personal communication. The use of video will increase, but its applications will remain specialized and formal until ISDN brings digital circuits to many desktops. Electronic mail also will gain importance as information service providers offer enhancements such as text-to-voice translation and notification of electronic mail messages through voice mail and vice versa. Electronic mail is, and will remain, an effective mode of non-real-time communication. It is an effective method within a closed private network, but its growth is hampered by the need for a terminal with which to access it, lack of uniformity in addressing, and lack of a universal directory assistance feature. As the X.400 and X.500 standards become more widely supported, e-mail will increase in importance.

It is safe to predict that several existing trends will continue to affect telecommunications. For example, fiber optics will continue to replace other technologies in the interoffice plant. Before the end of the century, practically all interoffice transmission will be carried over fiber optics.

Electromechanical switching will all but disappear in the next few years. Sometime in the next few years, the country will reach the crossover point between analog and digital switching, and more than half the lines in the United States will be served by digital central offices. By the end of the decade, analog offices will effectively have disappeared.

Even more difficult to predict is the future of embryonic telecommunications technologies. Several of these are recently announced as this book is written.

For example, wireless LANs offer considerable promise if the products can be made to function as economically as wired LANs. The cost of cabling and the difficulty of rearranging LANs remains an impediment for many organizations. If a LAN can be made to "plug and play" as easily as a personal computer, the difficulties of installing one will be greatly reduced.

Work has just begun on a Personal Communications Network (PCN), which is a type of cellular radio system with a maximum cell radius of about eight miles. It is intended for hand-carried, rather than vehicular traffic. The FCC has been petitioned to provide new frequencies in the 1.7 to 2.3 GHz range for this service. If the petitioners are successful, demand for this service could be substantial.

Fiber Distributed Data Interface (FDDI), which is just emerging as this book goes to press, will become an important local network technology. High prices will hold growth down for the first few years, but as demand increases and development costs are recovered, prices should drop, and FDDI will replace Ethernet and token ring in many applications. The present LAN types will not disappear altogether, however, because many organizations do not need the bandwidth of FDDI.

Broadband Technology

The broadband technologies show considerable promise for the future. Driven by applications such as LAN interconnection and broadband services such as video, and by new technologies such as metropolitan area networks, frame relay, and fast packet switching, the use of broadband should gradually increase through the 1990s. The following factors are driving the development of broadband transmission systems:

- A nationwide surplus of fiber optic capacity. By the end of 1990, there were 1.3 million miles of fiber in place, much of it not in use. Its capacity can be multiplied several times over by higher speeds and wave division multiplexing.

- High speed LANs. High speeds are being carried to the desktop for functions such as CAD/CAM, desktop publishing, and imaging. These LANs need to be linked.

- Supercomputers that are capable of large scale simulations of such phenomena as weather.

- Powerful desktop devices such as graphic workstations.

- Emerging applications, such as imaging and video, that use large amounts of bandwidth. The paperless office may finally emerge from widespread use of images for document storage and retrieval

- Medical and scientific applications such as CAT scan, magnetic resonance image scanning, and digital X-rays

- Standards such as FDDI, 802.6, ISDN, SONET, OSI, frame relay (Q.921), and cell relay (Q.931) are all driving the use of high bandwidths.

The technologies required to implement this ideal are nearing completion. Much of the physical structure is in place, although it is subdivided by asynchronous DS-0, DS-1, and DS-3 equipment. The DS digital hierarchy will be replaced by Synchronous Optical Network (SONET), which LECs are accepting as the standard for multiplexing their fiber optic capacity. The bit-robbed signaling of T-1 will disappear to be replaced by clear channel extended superframe.

Higher level protocols will use SONET (or bare fiber) as the physical medium. Many standards such as frame relay, asynchronous transfer mode, cell relay, and broadband ISDN are under development. Others such as 802.6 and FDDI are complete in their first versions, but are certain to undergo further modification. Whether these will survive is open to question, but each fits a niche that the others do not fill. It is likely that additional protocols will emerge to envelop other standards.

Which of the broadband technologies the private metropolitan fiber carriers will adopt is also unclear. So far they, like the LECs, have used their fiber resources as a point-to-point medium, but their customers will find that too limiting. In the future, customers will gravitate toward the carrier that can provide bandwidth on demand and deliver the data it carries to any address—first in a metropolitan area, then in the country, and finally anywhere in the world.

Even with some exciting developments on the horizon, changes in the shape of telecommunications are likely to be evolutionary rather than revolutionary. The investments IECs, LECs, and private users have in present facilities is enormous and will not be replaced until the carriers see a clear advantage in the new technology. The demand for more bandwidth at the desktop will develop, but currently it is needed by only a small minority of users, who will blaze the trail for their successors.

The remaining users are just becoming accustomed to the bandwidth of a local area network, and it is such an improvement over the 1200 b/s modems of yesterday, that it will take a while for the demand for gigabit networks to develop. High speed networks will ultimately be required by everyone, however, if imaging replaces the file cabinet and finally delivers the paperless office that has been promised for the past decade.

Group 4 facsimile will arrive over the next few years, and when demand rises and prices drop, it will be as necessary as the Group 3 facsimile machine and laser printer of today. Facsimile machine, printer, and copy machine could even be integrated into a single product that is accessible from the desktop over the office network. Group 4 facsimile will probably be a limited commodity until ISDN brings 64 kb/s circuits to the office. Without ISDN, a dedicated line to the LEC is required, and this is feasible only for large companies, many of which already use T-1 circuits for their local loops.

Switching Technology

The future of switching technology is also unclear. At the beginning of the 1990s, fast packet products are just entering the market, and with their ability to compress voice, they undoubtedly will capture some of the market that is now handled by circuit switching. The LECs are basing their future voice switching plans on ISDN, which continues to use circuit switching technology.

There is no indication that circuit switching will disappear in the near term, although fast packet could eventually displace circuit switching. Slower packet protocols such as X.25 seem destined to disappear because they have overhead and delay that were necessary for the high error analog facilities of the past but are not needed for today's fiber optic circuits.

PBXs will continue to use circuit switching in the future. A few packet switching products have entered the market, but they have not made an impact so far. The PBX market is not in a high growth mode, so it appears that most manufacturers will continue to develop their present PCM switching technologies, with upgrades periodically announced to remain competitive in a market that is advancing slowly.

The technology with the most intriguing future is photonic switching, which is 1000 times faster than present switching products. Bell Laboratories has announced products that appear to offer considerable promise for both switching systems and computers. As fiber optics extends to the desktop, a photonic switch, which fits neatly at the hub of a star-wired fiber configuration, may be just what the office requires for linking high bandwidth facilities.

Regulation

Regulation is an unpredictable force in the future of telecommunications. The slow pace of regulatory authorities, principally the FCC, has impeded the advancement of more than one new technology. The courts still play more than an incidental role in regulation as well, keeping a strong hand on the Regional Bell Holding Companies and preventing their entry into manufacturing and some new services. Regulatory authorities are subject to pressures from many companies who fought for open competition in the telecommunications arena and now, ironically, combat attempts by AT&T and the RBHCs to free themselves from regulatory restraints.

The future of telecommunications also is affected by the pace of standard-setting agencies. The standard-setting process is affected by the open participation of many private and public organizations, some of which have a vested interest in promoting or impeding the development of a particular standard. This open exchange is beneficial in preventing telecommunications technology from being driven by a few dominant market forces, but it sometimes results in less-than-optimum standards and invariably delays the entry of new products. Meanwhile, companies with a particular technology to promote enter the market with proprietary products, further diluting the effectiveness of standards. Though international standards are playing a much bigger role in the United States now than in the past, there is little in the future to diminish the influence of proprietary products in the emerging technologies.

The Information Revolution

The transformation of the American economy from a manufacturing to an information-based economy is well documented, but its implications are barely understood. Information is a valuable resource to companies in several ways. At one level, information is generated and sold outright. Publishing companies, legal firms, and accounting firms are examples of organizations whose mission is the production, distillation, and distribution of information.

From another point of view, information can be viewed as part of the content of manufactured goods. Products assume a value far in excess of their size or of the resources required for their manufacture. High technology products such as microprocessors and random access memory are constructed from resources that are only partially physical—the bulk of the resources are information-based.

From a third point of view, many organizations that are not considered to be in the direct stream of the information economy, possess an information resource that is valuable to their customers. For example, an airline is in the business of moving freight and passengers; yet without its information base of schedules, aircraft capacity, and seat vacancies, it would be unable to function. Almost every organization has an information base of some sort that distinguishes it from its competitors and enables it to function efficiently.

The role of telecommunications in this information society is clear because telecommunications is the movement of information. The companies that learn how to use and move information and to make it accessible to their customers will be the strongest competitors in the future. This means that organizations must learn to manage their telecommunications resources as an extension of their information resources.

Effects of Competition

The theory of the pre-divestiture Bell System was that a regulated monopoly was a more efficient way to deliver services because it avoided wasteful duplication of facilities. The theory of the Modified Final Judgement that split the Bell System was that the Bell Operating Companies would retain a monopoly on local exchange service and would remain regulated. AT&T's long distance service would remain regulated while it was a dominant carrier. The more competitive aspects of AT&T's business, such as PBX and computer products, would be unregulated.

Competition has permanently altered the character of the American telecommunications system. Although AT&T retains a commanding lead in interexchange services, the market in customer premises equipment is more evenly divided among the top competitors. The remaining bastion of the telecommunications monopoly is the local exchange, and cracks are beginning to appear there.

The Bell Operating Companies have argued before courts and regulatory commissions, with limited success, that they should be released from regulation because their services are increasingly subject to competition. At first it seemed that cable television might be the chink in the LECs' armor, but the use of CATV for voice transmission is nil, and its impact on data transmission is insignificant.

One important form of competition is just beginning to emerge in the major metropolitan areas with the development of local access carriers, or LACs, also known as metropolitan fiber carriers. The two largest LACs, Teleport Communications of New York and Metropolitan Fiber Systems of Chicago, have built fiber optic networks in the 15 top metropolitan areas in direct competition with the LECs. Other LACs are installing fiber in the smaller metropolitan areas.

History seems to be repeating itself with the advent of the LACs. Predictably, they are interested in serving only high volume metropolitan areas, at least in the near term. This leads to the same charges of "cream skimming" that the Bell companies leveled in the early 1970s against the fledgling IECs, who then were interested in serving only high volume long distance routes. Also, the LACs, seeking to overcome the limitations of non-switched point-to-point traffic, have requested permission to interconnect with the LECs' local networks. In at least one instance, under a ruling by the New York Public Service Commission, they have been successful.

The LECs themselves see a lucrative market in the information service provider (ISP) business. In exchange for some freedom to provide information services, the LECs have proposed open network architecture (ONA) for assuring competing ISPs that they will have equal access to the LECs' networks. ONA has been in the conceptual stages for several years with little progress or agreement about its ultimate shape. It is not clear what, if any, effect ONA will have on competition in the local network.

The inroads of the LACs are likely to have little effect on most users. More critical is the question of who will provide a broadband information channel to end users over the local loop. The LECs are rapidly deploying fiber in loops to major users, but most fiber-to-the-home applications have so far been only trials. These applications will develop slowly because the immediate demand is not sufficient to repay the cost of replacing the enormous amount of copper cable that is already in place.

Cellular radio offers another form of competition to the LECs. Currently, cellular is too expensive and the frequencies are too limited to make a substantial impact on the LECs' markets. If digital cellular develops as expected and if the FCC opens more frequencies, the demand will probably expand.

The pace of technology is accelerating on a geometric curve, and there are no signs of it slowing. The regulatory restraints that slowed development in the past are beginning to loosen, even in some countries that have a governmental strangle hold on telecommunications. Whatever the future of telecommunications holds, it is bound to be unpredictable and exciting.

A

Principles of Electricity
Applied to Telecommunications

Although it is possible to gain an appreciation of telecommunications with little or no technical background, the technology is based on the applied science of electronics. Without some understanding of the principles, the reader is apt to be confused by some concepts. A complete understanding of communications technology cannot be developed without understanding the mathematics involved, some of it complex. However, a working knowledge of the concepts presented in this book can be gained with no more than elementary mathematics and some fundamental principles of electrical theory. For those readers who lack understanding of electricity, this appendix is an overview of the basic principles of electricity as used in telephony. This appendix also explains most of the terminology used in basic electricity.

An understanding of the terminology begins with the units of measure. These are multiplied or divided by factors ranging from one to one billion. For those who are unfamiliar with electrical units, Table A.1 lists the ones most frequently encountered.

Electricity and Magnetism

The characteristics of permanent magnets are familiar to all who have experimented with magnetized iron bars. In the natural state of materials such as iron, electrons array themselves in disorderly patterns and have no attracting force. When the mate-

Table A.1 Common Units of Electrical Measurements

	PREFIX	ABBREVIATION	FREQUENCY	POWER	CURRENT	RESISTANCE	VOLTAGE	OTHER	DATA
1,000,000,000	Giga	g	Gigahertz (GHz)						Gigabit (gb)
1,000,000	Mega	Meg or M	Megahertz (MHz)	Megawatt (Mw)		Megohm	Megavolt		Megabit (mb)
1000	Kilo	K	Kilohertz (KHz)	Kilowatt (Kw)		Kilohm	Kilovolt		Kilobit (kb)
1			Hertz (Hz)	Watt (w)	Ampere (amp or A)	Ohm (Ω)	Volt (V)		Bit
1/10	Deci	d							
1/1000	Milli	m		Milliwatt (mw)	Milliamp (ma)	Milliohm (mΩ)	Millivolt (mv)	Decibel (dB)	
1/1,000000	Micro	μ		Microwatt (μw)	Microamp (μa)		Microvolt (μv)	Microfarad ((μf) Microhenry (μh)	
1/1,000,000,000 Pico		p					Picovolt (pv)	Picofarad (pf)	

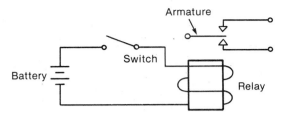

Figure A.1   Schematic diagram of a relay.

rial is magnetized, the electrons align themselves neatly, creating the power to attract and repel other elements. The opposite ends of magnetized material are called its *poles*. Anyone who has experimented with magnets knows that like poles repel and opposite poles attract, and that either pole attracts some metals, but not others. Metals such as iron and its alloys exhibit strong magnetic properties but others such as copper and aluminum cannot be magnetized.

Relays and Solenoids

Permanently magnetized materials have application in telecommunications; for example, loudspeakers and the receiver in an ordinary telephone set contain permanent magnets. A more important application of magnetism in telecommunications is the *electromagnet*, a device that becomes magnetized when external current is applied, and nonmagnetized when it is removed. The millions of relays and electromechanical switches in telephone central offices use this principle. Although solid state electronic circuits are replacing relays, vast numbers of relays remain in service, and are important to understanding telecommunications.

A relay is shown schematically in Figure A.1. When the coil surrounding the relay's core is energized by closing a switch to the battery, the core attracts the armature and the movement closes or opens contacts. Relays control large electric currents with a small current flowing through the winding. For example, the starter solenoid in an automobile allows the ignition switch, which is a low current device, to control the large amount of current needed to connect the starter to the battery. Relays often

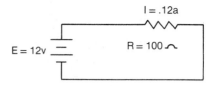

Figure A.2   **Current flow in a resistive circuit.**

---

are made with multiple sets of contacts so that a single source can control current to multiple paths. A relay is a binary device; that is, its coil and contacts are either open or closed, corresponding to the zeros and ones of logic circuitry. These principles are used in chaining relays to form logic circuits in electromechanical central offices.

Electric Current and Voltage

When an electric source is applied to a circuit by closing a switch, *current* begins to flow. A circuit is composed of three variables: *current*, *voltage*, and *resistance*.

- *Current* is the quantity of electricity flowing in a circuit. The unit of current is the *ampere* or "amp." Its symbol in circuits and formulas is "I."

- *Voltage* (sometimes called *electromagnetic force* or EMF) is the pressure forcing current to flow. The unit of voltage is the *volt*. Its symbol is "E."

- *Resistance* is the opposition to flow of current. The unit of resistance is the *ohm*. Its symbol is "R."

These three variables are interrelated by Ohm's law, which states that the amount of current flowing in an electric circuit is directly proportional to the voltage and inversely proportional to the resistance. Stated as a formula, Ohm's law is:

$$I = \frac{E}{R}$$

This simple formula is the basis for understanding the behavior of electricity. To illustrate with a simple example, assume the circuit in Figure A.2. A 12-volt battery such as that used in automobiles is feeding current to a 100-ohm resistance such as a light bulb. In this circuit, 12 volts/100 ohms, or 120 milliamps, of current flows.

Power

Because current and voltage are inversely related and may vary with changing circuit conditions, neither is an adequate measure of the power consumed. The power in a circuit is the product of the current and voltage, and is measured in *watts*. For example, the circuit in Figure A.2 consumes 12 volts x .12 amps = 1.44 watts of power. The measurement of power is usually combined with the length of time the current flows and is expressed in *kilowatt hours* (abbreviated KWH). One KWH is equal to 1,000 watts of power being supplied for one hour.

The Decibel

The power in telecommunications circuits is so low that it is usually measured in milliwatts. The milliwatt is an effective way of expressing how much power is supplied to a circuit, but it is not a convenient way to express differences in power between circuits or between two points on the same circuit. Voice frequency circuits are designed around the human ear, which has a logarithmic response to changes in power. Therefore, in telephony the *decibel* (dB), which is a logarithmic rather than a linear measurement, is used as a measure of relative power between circuits or transmission level points. A change in level of 1 dB is barely perceptible under ideal conditions. The number of dB corresponding to a power ratio is expressed as:

$$dB = 10 \log \frac{P2}{P1}$$

The dB also can express voltage and current ratios if the impedance, which will be discussed in a later section, is the same for both values of voltage or current. The dB ratio between voltage and current is:

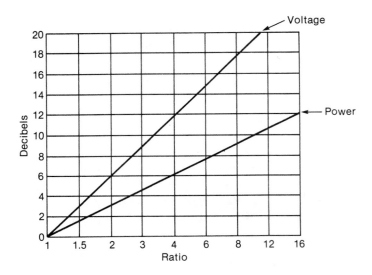

Figure A.3   **Chart of power and voltage ratios versus decibels.**

$$dB = 20 \log \frac{E2}{E1}$$

$$dB = 20 \log \frac{I2}{I1}$$

Figure A.3 is a chart showing the ratios between power, voltage, and current plotted as a function of decibels. Note that the horizontal scale is logarithmic. Also note that increases or reductions of 3 dB result in doubling or halving the power in a circuit. This ratio is handy to remember when evaluating power differences. The corresponding figure for doubling or halving voltage and current is 6 dB.

Series and Parallel Resistance

Figure A.4 shows resistors connected in series and parallel. In a series circuit the total resistance is the sum of the individual resistors. In a parallel circuit current divides between the resistors. If the resistors

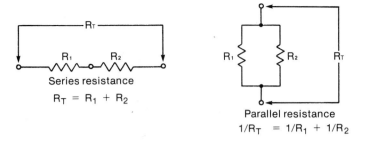

Figure A.4   Series and parallel resistance.

are of equal value the current divides equally; if they are unequal a greater current flows through the smaller resistance.

The formula for calculating the total resistance of series resistors is:

$$RT = R1 + R2 + R3 \dots$$

The formula for calculating the total resistance of parallel resistors is

$$RT = \frac{1}{R1} + \frac{1}{R2} + \frac{1}{R3} \dots$$

Direct and Alternating Current

So far we have been discussing only the flow of direct current (DC) in a circuit. In a DC circuit the source or battery supplies voltage with fixed *polarity*. The polarity in a battery corresponds to the poles in an electromagnet, and is designated as positive (+) or negative (–). All telecommunications apparatus is powered by a DC source. However, the signals carried by the telecommunications apparatus and the power source that charges the batteries or powers the converters come from commercial alternating current (AC).

The polarity from an AC source is constantly reversing. If voltage is measured against time, the result is a *sine wave* as in

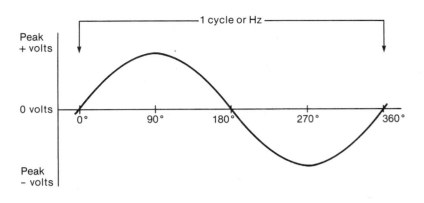

Figure A.5   Alternating current sine wave.

Figure A.5. The sine wave is so named because it describes the shape of the wave that results from plotting the sine of the angles from 0 to 360 degrees.

In AC circuit analysis, we are not only concerned with the magnitude or voltage of the source but also with *frequency* of its reversals. A complete cycle carries the voltage from its zero starting point, to peak positive, back through zero to peak negative, and back to zero again. The unit of measurement of frequency is the *hertz* (Hz). One Hz is equivalent to one cycle. The distance between corresponding points on a cycle is called its *wavelength*, which is inversely proportional to frequency. Table A.2 shows the frequency and corresponding wavelengths of the radio frequency spectrum.

Another property of AC is *phase*, which describes the relationship between the zero-crossing points of signals. Figure A.6 shows two voltages that are 90 degrees out of phase with each other. Phase is measured in degrees as illustrated in the figure. A full cycle describes a 360 degree arc. The two signals shown are out of phase, with Curve B lagging Curve A by 90 degrees.

AC follows Ohm's law in a circuit composed only of resistance. Because the voltage in an AC circuit varies continually, the current flow in such a circuit is proportional to the *root mean square* (RMS) voltage, which is .707 of the peak voltage. RMS voltage is

Table A.2 Frequencies and Wavelengths of Radio Frequencies

FREQUENCY	WAVELENGTH (METERS)	CLASS (FREQUENCY)	ABBREVI-ATION
30 KHz	10,000	Very low	VLF
300 KHz	1000	Low	LF
3000 KHz	100	Medium	MF
30 MHz	10	High	HF
300 MHz	1	Very high	VHF
3000 MHz	0.1	Ultra high	UHF
30,000 MHz	0.01	Superhigh	SHF

normally used in describing AC; for example, the 120 volts of electric house current actually has a peak value of 170 volts.

A sine wave has a single fundamental frequency. Voice signals, on the other hand, are a complex composite of several fundamental tones rapidly varying in both frequency and amplitude. Because of the limited passband of a voice frequency telecommunications channel, higher and lower frequencies are cut off, but enough frequencies remain to ensure intelligibility. A digital signal, however, is not a sine wave. Instead, it takes the shape of a square wave as in Figure A.7.

If a square wave is examined, it is found to consist of a fundamental frequency and numerous *harmonics*, which are

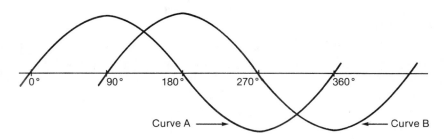

Figure A.6 Phase relationship between two sine waves.

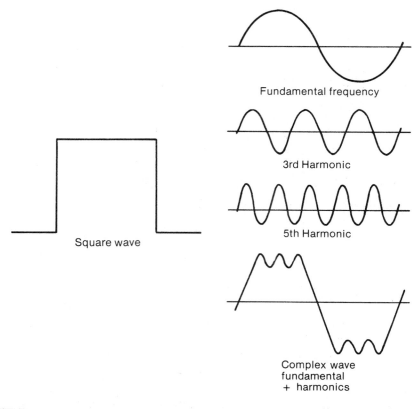

Fundamental frequency

3rd Harmonic

5th Harmonic

Square wave

Complex wave
fundamental
+ harmonics

Figure A.7   Derivation of a square wave from its harmonics.

multiples of the fundamental frequency. Figure A.7 shows the
derivation of a square wave from the fundamental frequency and
its harmonics. The harmonics consist of high frequency components, many of which are filtered out by a telephone channel. As
Figure A.8 shows, the attenuation in a cable pair is generally
limited, but as loading is applied, as described in Chapter 2, the
cutoff frequency becomes sharper. The filters in amplifiers and
multiplex equipment are sharper yet, approximating the curve
shown in Figure A.9.

When a square wave signal passes through a voice channel,
the high frequency components are filtered out. The signal is

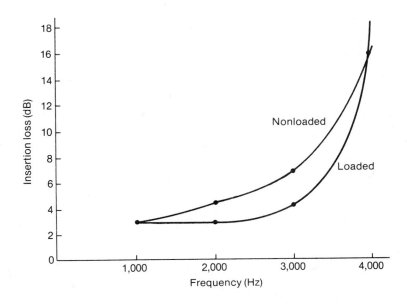

Figure A.8   Frequency response of loaded and nonloaded cable.

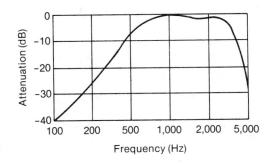

Figure A.9   Frequency response of a typical telephone channel.

reduced to its fundamental frequency and assumes the shape of a sine wave. The degree of filtering in a voice channel is in direct proportion to the frequency of the square wave (or speed of a data signal), and the distance the signal travels. It is this filtering effect that makes it necessary to use modems to pass data signals over voice frequency channels.

Inductance and Capacitance

All circuits also contain two more variables: capacitance, which is the property of storage of an electric charge, and inductance, which is the property of an electric force field built up around a conductor. Although inductance and capacitance are present in all circuits, their effects are slight in many circuits and can be ignored. In other circuits, however, they are deliberately introduced to produce an intended effect.

Capacitance

The capacitance effect occurs when two plates of conducting material are separated by an insulator called a *dielectric*. Common dielectrics are air, mica, ceramics, and plastics. Capacitance has the property of blocking the flow of DC but permitting some AC to flow. Capacitors are constructed with fixed values or with movable plates so the amount of capacitance is variable.

The unit of capacitance is the *farad*, although the farad is so large that capacitors are measured in microfarads or picofarads. The amount of capacitance is proportional to the amount of area of the conducting plates and the insulating properties or *dielectric constant* of the insulator.

Alternating current does not flow through a capacitor without some opposition, called the *reactance* of a capacitor. The reactance for a capacitor of a given size is inversely proportional to the AC frequency of the current flowing in the circuit. Capacitors are used in any electronic circuit where it is desirable to block the flow of DC while permitting the flow of AC, or to permit higher frequencies to pass while attenuating lower frequencies.

Of great pertinence to telecommunications is the fact that capacitance occurs naturally whenever two conductors parallel one another. The capacitance effect occurs in a cable pair where the two wires form the plates of a capacitor and the insulation forms the dielectric. In a voice-frequency circuit, some current flows between the two wires, attenuating the higher frequencies more than the low. The capacitance effect causes the shoulders of a square wave to become rounded as the high-frequency components are attenuated.

When capacitors are connected in parallel, the effect is directly additive. For example, if two 1.0 mf capacitors are connected in parallel, the resulting capacitance is 2.0 mf. When they are connected in series, the total capacitance is reduced. The formula for calculating the total capacitance of capacitors connected in series is

$$CT = \frac{1}{C1 + C2 + C3...}$$

The formula for calculating the total capacitance of parallel capacitors is

$$C_T = C_1 + C_2 + C_3$$

$$CT = \frac{1}{C1} + \frac{1}{C2} + \frac{1}{C3}\ ...$$

Inductance

An *inductor* is formed by winding a conductor into a coil. The amount of inductance is a function of the number of turns, the length and diameter of the coil, and the material used in the core of the coil. Many coils are wound with air cores, but the inductance of an air core coil can be increased by using magnetic material such as iron as its core. Inductors made with a moveable core inside the winding have a variable amount of inductance.

When current flows through a wire, lines of force are built up around the wire. The field created by DC current is steady and unvarying, but when AC flows through a wire, the lines of force are constantly building up and collapsing. These lines of force impede the flow of AC in a coil. The effect of inductance on current flow is the opposite of the effects of capacitance: the flow of AC is impeded by an inductor, while DC passes through with little effect. The unit of inductance is the *henry*, or in smaller coils, the millihenry or microhenry. The higher the frequency of an AC signal, the higher the *inductive reactance* of the coil.

The paralleling wires of a cable pair present some inductive reactance, but the effect is outweighed by the much greater effects

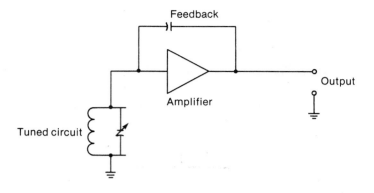

Figure A.10   Oscillator circuit.

of capacitive reactance. To counter capacitive reactance, inductance is often deliberately introduced into telephone circuits. For example, inductors known as *load coils* are connected in series with the two wires of long subscriber loops to counteract the effects of capacitive reactance, and reduce the loss of the loop as shown in Figure A.8. Inductors behave in the same way as resistors when connected in series and parallel; that is, paralleling inductors reduces inductance, and adding them in series increases the inductance.

Impedance

The algebraic sum of inductive and capacitive reactance effects is known as the *impedance* of a circuit. Impedance in a circuit describes the opposition to the flow of current, and varies with the frequency of an AC signal. Mathematically, the impedance of a circuit is the ratio of voltage to current. In a purely resistive circuit, impedance is independent of frequency, but in a reactive circuit, impedance varies with frequency.

When capacitive reactance and inductive reactance are equal to each other, the circuit is said to be in *resonance*. A circuit offers maximum opposition to current flow at its resonant frequency,. The principles of resonance are used in electronics to tune circuits to a desired frequency. When a small amount of energy is added to a resonant circuit and some output is fed back into the input, the circuit *oscillates* at its resonant fre-

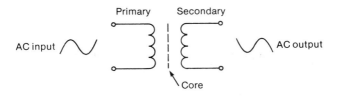

Figure A.11   Transformer.

quency. Figure A.10 illustrates the concept of oscillation in a parallel resonant circuit. Oscillators are widely used in telecommunications to generate audio tones and radio frequencies.

Transformers

When a coil is moved into the electrical field caused by the rising and collapsing lines of force surrounding another coil fed by an AC source, a portion of the energy couples from the first coil into the second. This effect, shown in Figure A.11, is known as *mutual inductance* or the *transformer* effect. The transformer windings connected to the source are known as the primary, and those connected to the load, the secondary. The amount of voltage induced into the secondary is a function of how closely coupled the two windings are, the frequency of the AC source, and the ratio of turns between the primary and secondary windings. If the secondary consists of more turns than the primary, the voltage is stepped up; with fewer turns in the secondary the voltage is stepped down.

Many transformers have multiple windings in the secondary to create several voltages from a single source, but of course, the total power in the secondary windings cannot exceed the power of the primary. For example, if a transformer that draws one amp of current at 120 volts in the primary has a 1:2 turns ratio, the voltage in the secondary is 240 volts. However, no more than 0.5 amps of current can be supplied by the secondary winding. Actually, the power supplied in the secondary is somewhat less because the transformer is not 100 percent efficient.

Transformers are widely used in telecommunications, where they are often called *repeat coils*. Not only do transformers convert

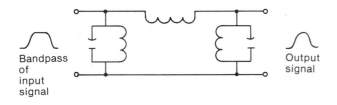

Figure A.12   Bandpass filter.

AC power to the voltages used to charge batteries and to power apparatus, they also are used as impedance matching devices.

When two circuits are interconnected, the maximum transfer of power occurs when their impedances are exactly matched. Telephone circuits are designed with characteristic impedances of 600 ohms or 900 ohms. These impedances were chosen because of the characteristic impedances of wire transmission lines. The characteristic impedance of equipment used in amplifiers and multiplex is much higher than the 600 or 900 ohms of telephone circuits. Therefore, wherever equipment connects to external telephone circuits the impedances are matched by repeat coils or other matching circuits that are beyond the scope of this discussion.

All users of telecommunications services must be alert to the hazards of mismatched impedances. Wherever a mismatch occurs, part of the signal reflects toward the source, and a reduced transfer of energy results. Impedance mismatches are the source of echo, unwanted oscillations, and excessive loss. It is important in telecommunications not to connect circuits without the use of impedance matching devices.

Filters

A *filter* is any device that rejects a frequency or band of frequencies while allowing other frequencies to pass. Capacitors and inductors, as we have seen, make effective filters with opposite effects. A capacitor presents high impedance to low-frequency signals, blocks DC entirely, and allows high-frequency signals to pass with little or no attenuation. Inductors, on the other hand, offer little resistance to the flow of DC, but high resistance to AC. As a

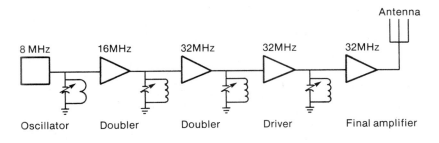

Figure A.13 Block diagram of a radio transmitter.

practical matter, an instantaneous impedance is offered to AC by a capacitor until an initial charge is established. Similarly, an initial impedance is offered to the flow of DC by an inductor until the lines of force are built up. These effects are used in pulse generating circuits, but in filters where the flow of current is fairly steady, this effect can be ignored.

Capacitors and inductors are used in filter networks such as that shown in Figure A.12. As shown in the figure, if a broad band of frequencies is applied to the input of the circuit, the upper and lower frequencies are attenuated while the mid-band is passed. Although such a passband is adequate where it is unnecessary to reject the high and low frequencies entirely, in many telecommunications applications this "leak through" of signal power is unacceptable. For example, if two channels share the same medium and both have response curves similar to those shown in the output of Figure A.12, the overlapping passbands would result in audible crosstalk, which is clearly undesirable. For most telecommunications circuits, filters with steep-skirted response curves and a passband with little amplitude distortion are required. This is accomplished by inserting piezoelectric crystals in the filter, resulting in a passband similar to that in Figure A.9.

Radio

The principles of radio transmission are fundamental to understanding telecommunications. Not only is radio widely used for carrying voice channels and for mobile telephones, the same

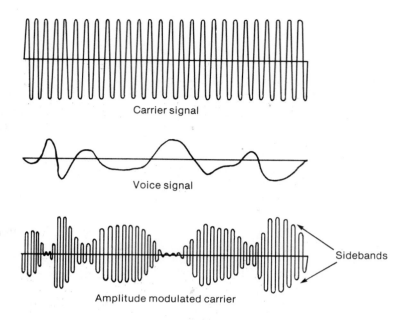

Carrier signal

Voice signal

Amplitude modulated carrier

Sidebands

Figure A.14   Amplitude modulation.

principles are also used in analog multiplex. An analog carrier system resembles a multi-channel radio except the signal is low-powered and is not radiated into free space.

Transmitters

Tuned or resonant circuits are at the heart of every radio. A tuned circuit is a type of filter in which the capacitance and inductance are tuned to a resonant frequency and pass only a very narrow band of frequencies. As we discussed earlier, when amplification is added to a tuned circuit and a portion of the output is fed back into the input of the amplifier, the amplifier oscillates. Oscillators are used to generate radio frequencies (rf). Piezoelectric crystals are often employed in oscillator circuits to ensure frequency stability and accuracy. The output of the oscillator is a sine wave of a fundamental frequency and is often rich in harmonic frequencies as well.

Harmonic frequencies are used in circuits called *frequency multipliers*. In the block diagram of Figure A.13, an oscillator and a chain of frequency multipliers raise the fundamental frequency to the desired rf output frequency. Low-frequency oscillators are used in radio because it is easier to control the stability at low frequencies than at high.

Frequency multiplier stages employ tuned circuits to select the desired harmonic. For example, in Figure A.13 the first-stage frequency doubler is tuned to the second harmonic of the 8 MHz oscillator to select an output frequency of 16 MHz.

The output of the multipliers is connected to a *driver* that amplifies the signal to the higher level required by the final rf amplifier. The final amplifier boosts the signal to the desired output level. The output may range from a watt or less in some microwave transmitters to a megawatt or more in high-power broadcast transmitters.

Modulation

The transmitter described in the last section produces only a single high-powered radio frequency wave known as a *carrier*. The carrier contains no intelligence. Radio telegraph transmitters carry information by interrupting the carrier with a coded signal of dots and dashes. This type of modulation is known as *continuous wave* (cw).

Amplitude Modulation

Voice communication is far more essential to telecommunications than cw, which is disappearing as a means of communication. A voice signal is impressed on an rf carrier by a process called *modulation*. The simplest form is called *amplitude mondulation* (AM). An AM modulator consists of several stages of audio amplification that are coupled to an rf amplifier through a transformer. The resultant signal is shown in Figure A.14.

Single Sideband

When amplitude modulation occurs, four frequencies result: the original voice frequency, the carrier frequency, the sum of the two frequencies, and the difference between the two frequencies. The sum and difference frequencies are called *sidebands*. In an AM signal all the information is contained in either of the two sidebands. The carrier contributes nothing to communication, and the two sidebands are redundant. Moreover, 75 percent of the

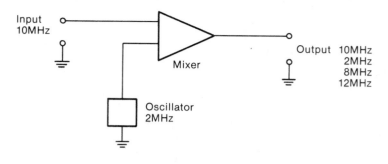

Figure A.15   Mixer.

signal power is contained in the carrier and the redundant side-band. A large improvement in efficiency is obtained by using *single sideband* (ssb) telephony.

In an ssb transmitter the carrier is suppressed in a circuit called a *balanced modulator*. The output of this modulator consists of the upper and lower sidebands, only one of which is needed. The unwanted sideband is eliminated with a filter. The carrier suppression and filtering are done in low-level stages of the transmitter where little power handling capacity is needed. After filtering, the ssb signal is boosted to the desired output power by the rf amplifier.

Frequency Modulation

Telecommunications apparatus also makes wide use of *frequency modulation* (FM) in radio, and, to a limited degree, in multiplex systems. In an FM transmitter an rf signal is generated by an oscillator. With no modulating voice signal, the carrier rests at its center frequency. The modulating signal shifts the carrier above and below its center frequency in proportion to the frequency and amplitude of the modulating signal. The result is a broadband signal of varying frequencies.

FM passes a wide band signal with a great deal of linearity. Noise, which tends to affect the amplitude of a signal, can be eliminated in the receiver by filtering the received signal through limiting amplifiers that chop off the noise peaks. The result is a low noise output with wide bandwidth. FM is widely used in

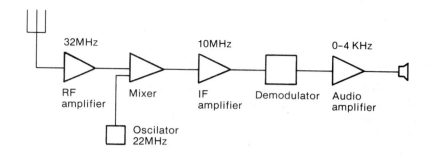

Figure A.16   Block diagram of a superheterodyne radio receiver.

mobile and microwave radio, but it is rarely used in analog multiplex systems.

Heterodyning

The transmitter in Figure A.13 uses frequency multipliers to generate the desired transmitting frequency. Both transmitters and receivers also use an effect called *heterodyning* to raise or lower the fundamental frequency. Figure A.15 is a block diagram that illustrates the principle. As discussed in the modulation section, when two frequencies are applied to a mixer, the output consists of the two original frequencies, the sum of the two frequencies, and the difference between the frequencies. Tuned circuits select the desired frequency.

Heterodyning is used in many microwave repeaters to change the frequency of the received signal to a different transmit frequency. Most receivers also use heterodyning to change an incoming signal to a fixed intermediate frequency as we discuss in the next section.

Receivers

A block diagram of a typical radio receiver using *superheterodyne* technology is shown in Figure A.16. The signal from the antenna is boosted by an rf amplifier and coupled to a mixer. A signal from an oscillator is coupled into the other mixer port. The selected output is a fixed *intermediate frequency* (if) that is coupled to succeeding if amplifier stages. The superheterodyne technique improves selectivity. Intermediate frequency amplifier stages have steep-skirted filters to reject unwanted frequencies.

The superheterodyne technique is used in virtually all receivers, ranging from simple broadcast receivers to microwave radios. The intermediate frequency is chosen to be high enough to pass the entire range of desired frequencies. Broadcast band radios, which are tuned to only one voice channel, typically use a 455 kHz if, FM radios use 10.7 mHz, and most microwave systems use 70 MHz as the if. An intermediate frequency this high is required to handle the bandwidth of a microwave system. Bandwidths of 10 or 20 MHz are common.

The demodulator stage in a receiver selects the audio output from the if stages. In a broadcast receiver only a simple device such as a diode is needed to detect the audio envelope from the AM signal. In single sideband receivers a frequency identical to the original suppressed carrier frequency must be injected into the detector by an oscillator. In FM receivers the detector is a linear circuit known as a *discriminator* that translates the frequency excursions into a signal identical to the original modulating frequencies.

This overview of electrical theory has only brushed the surface of the technology. Readers who require more information are advised to consult one of the many manuals on electric theory that are available in most bookstores.

Selected Standards and Publications Pertaining to Telecommunications

American National Standards Institute (ANSI)

ANSI/IEEE

ANSI/IEEE 145	Definition of Terms For Antennas
ANSI/IEEE 149	Test Procedure For Antennas
ANSI/IEEE 269	Method of Measuring Transmission Performance of Telephone Sets
ANSI/IEEE 312	Definitions of Terms for Communication Switching
ANSI/IEEE 377	Measurement of Spurious Emission from Land Mobile Communication Transmitters
ANSI/IEEE 455	Test Procedure for Measuring Longitudinal Balance of Telephone Equipment Operating in the Voice Band
ANSI/IEEE 487	Guide for the Protection of Wire-Line Communication Facilities Serving Electric Power Stations
ANSI/IEEE 661	Method for Determining Objective Loudness Ratings of Telephone Connections

ANSI/IEEE 753	Standard Functional Methods and Equipment for Measuring Performance of Dial-Pulse (DP) Address Signaling Systems
ANSI/IEEE 802.2	Local Area Networks: Logical Link Control
ANSI/IEEE 802.3	Local Area Networks: Carrier Sense Multiple Access with Collision Detection (CSMA/CD) Access Method and Physical Layer Specifications
ANSI/IEEE 802.4	Local Area Networks: Token-Passing Bus Access Method
ANSI/IEEE 820	Telephone Loop Performance Characteristics
ANSI T1.101-1986	Telecommunications-Synchronization Interface Standards for Digital Networks
ANSI T1.102-1987	Telecommunications—Digital Hierarchy—Electrical Interfaces
ANSI T1.103-1987	Telecommunications—Digital Hierarchy—Synchronous DS3 Format Specifications
ANSI T1.110-1987	Telecommunications—Signaling System Number 7 (SS7)—General Information
ANSI T1.112-1987	Telecommunications—Signaling System No. 7—Functional Description of the Signalling Connection Control Part (SCCP)
ANSI T1.201-1987	Telecommunications—Information Interchange—Structure for the Identification of Location Entities for the North American Telecommunications System
ANSI T1.301-1987	Telecommunications—Digital Processing of Voice-Band Signals—Algorithm and Line Format for 32 kb/s Adaptive Differential Pulse-Code Modulation (ADPCM)
ANSI T1.202-1988	Telecommunications—Internetwork Operations—Guidelines for Network Management of the Public Switched Networks Under Disaster Conditions
ANSI T1S1/88-224R2	Frame Relay Bearer Service—Architectural Framework and Service Description.
ANSI X3.1-1987	Information Systems—Data Transmission—Synchronous Signaling Rates

ANSI X3.4-1986	Coded Character Set—7-Bit American National Standard Code for Information Interchange
ANSI X3.15	Sequencing of the American National Standard Code for Information Interchange iN Serial-by-Bit Data Transmission
ANSI X3.16-1976(R1983)	Character Structure and Character Parity Sense for Serial-by-Bit Data Communication in the American National Standard Code for Information Interchange
ANSI X3.25-1976(R1983)	Character Structure and Character Parity Sense for Parallel-by-Bit Data Communication in the American National Standard Code for Information Interchange
ANSI X3.28-1976(R1986)	Communications Control Characters of American National Standard Code for Information Interchange in Specified Data Communications Links, Procedures for the Use of the
ANSI X3.36	Synchronous High Speed Data Signaling Rates Between Data Terminal Equipment and Data Communications Equipment
ANSI X3.41	Code Extension Techniques for Use With the 7-Bit Coded Character Set of American National Standard Code for Information Interchange (ASCII)
ANSI X3.44-1974	Determination of Performance of Data Communication Systems
ANSI X3.64	Additional Controls for Use With the American National Standard Code for Information Interchange
ANSI X3.66-1979	Advanced Data Communication Control Procedure (ADCCP)
ANSI X3.79-1981	Data Communications Systems that Use Bit-Oriented Communications Control Procedures, Determination of Performance of
ANSI X3.92-1981(R1987)	Data Encryption Algorithm
ANSI X3.98	Text Information Interchange in Page Image Format, (PIF)
ANSI X3.100-1983	Interface between Data Terminal Equipment and Data Circuit-Terminating Equip-

	ment for Packet Mode Operation with Packet Switched Data Communications Networks
ANSI X3.102-1983	Data Communication User-Oriented Performance Parameters
ANSI X3.105-1983	Data Link Encryption
ANSI X3.106-1983	Data Encryption Algorithm, Modes of Operation for the
ANSI X3.117	Printable/image Areas For Text and Facsimile Communication Equipment
ANSI X3.139-1987	Information Systems—Fiber Distributed Data Interface (FDDI)—Token Ring Media Access Control (MAC)
ANSI X3.141-1987	Information Systems—Data Communication Systems and Services—Measurement Methods for User-Oriented Performance Evaluation
ANSI X3T9.5	Local Distributed Data Interface (LDDI), 70 mb/s Coaxial Cable Network and Fiber Distributed Data Interface (FDDI), Token Passing Ring Architecture For Local Networks Using Optical Fiber Cable.
ANSI X12B86-005	Common U.S. Data Dictionary, DRAFT STANDARD (also referred to as the EDI Dictionary)
ANSI X12.1-1986	Purchase Order Transaction Set (850)
ANSI X12.3-1986	Data Element Dictionary
ANSI X12.4	Payment Order/Remittance Advice Transaction Set, DRAFT STANDARD
ANSI X12.5-1987	Electronic Business Data Interchange—Interchange Control Structure
ANSI X12.6-1986	Electronic Business Data Interchange—Application Control Structure
ANSI X12.7-1986	Request for Quotation Transaction Set (840)
ANSI X12.8-1986	Response to Request for Quotation Transaction Set (843)
ANSI X12.9-1986	Purchase Order Acknowledgment Transaction Set (855)
ANSI X12.10-1987	Electronic Business Data Interchange—Ship Notice/Manifest Transaction Set (856)

ANSI X12.12-1986	Receiving Advice Transaction Set (861)
ANSI X12.13-1986	Price/Sales Catalog Transaction Set (832)
ANSI X12.14-1986	Planning Schedule with Release Capability Transaction Set (830)
ANSI X12.15-1986	Purchase Order Change Request Transaction Set (860)
ANSI X12.16-1986	Purchase Order Change Request Acknowledgment Transaction Set (865)
ANSI X12.20-1986	Electronic Business Data Interchange—Functional Acknowledgement (997)
ANSI X12.22-1986	Electronic Business Data Interchange—Data Segment Directory (includes revision service)
ANSI/EIA TSB-19-1985	Optical Fiber Digital Transmission Systems—Considerations for Users and Suppliers
ANSI/EIA 195-C-1985	Terrestrial Microwave Relay System Antennas and Passive Reflectors, Electrical and Mechanical Characteristics for
ANSI/EIA 199-A-1972 (R1983)	Solid and Semi-Solid Dielectric Transmission Lines, Requirements for
ANSI/EIA 200-A-1965	Circular Waveguides
ANSI/EIA 222-D-1986	Steel Antenna Towers and Antenna Supporting Structures, Structural Standards for
ANSI/EIA 225-1959	Rigid Coaxial Transmission Lines-50 Ohms, Requirements for
ANSI/EIA 250-B-1976	Electrical Performance Standards for Television Relay Facilities
ANSI/EIA 329-A-1978	Land Mobile Communication Antennas, Part 1—Base or Fixed Station Antennas, Minimum Standards for
ANSI/EIA 334A-1985	Signal Quality at Interface Between Data Terminal Equipment and Synchronous Data Circuit-Terminating Equipment for Serial Data Transmission
ANSI/EIA 375-A-1974	Electrical Performance Standards for Direct View Monochrome Closed Circuit Television Monitors 525/60 Interlaced 2:1
ANSI/IEEE 81-1983	Earth Resistivity, Ground Impedance, and Earth Surface Potentials of a Ground System, Guide for Measuring

ANSI/IEEE 142-1982	Grounding of Industrial and Commercial Power Systems, Practice for
ANSI/IEEE 145-1983	Antennas, Definitions of Terms for
ANSI/IEEE 146-1980	Waveguide Terms, Definitions of Fundamental
ANSI/IEEE 146-1979(R1987)	Antennas, Test Procedure for
ANSI/IEEE 167-1966	Facsimile, Test Procedure for
ANSI/IEEE 168-1956	Facsimile, Definitions of Terms on
ANSI/IEEE 184-1969	Frequency Modulated Mobile Communications Receivers, Test Procedure for
ANSI/IEEE 201-1979	Television—Definitions of Terms
ANSI/IEEE 211-1977	Radio Wave Propagation, Definition of Terms for
ANSI/IEEE 269-1983	Transmission Performance of Telephone Sets, Method of Measuring
ANSI/IEEE 312-1977	Communication Switching, Definitions of Terms for

Bell Communications Research

TR-190-23140-84-01	No. 2 SCCS Interface Specifications for Asynchronous Interactive Data Channels
TR-533-23112-84-01	Description of Interface Between a 1/1A ESS Switching System and a Customer Premises Detail Recording System
TR-795-25540-84-02	Common Language Identification of Manufacturers of Telecommunications Products
TR-820-23125-84-01	Voice Band Signaling for Delivery of Network Data on Local Exchange Lines
TR-880-22135-84-01	Circuit Switched Digital Capability Network Access Interface Specification
TR-EOP-000001	Lightning, Radio Frequency, and 60 Hz Disturbances at the Bell Operating Company Network Interface
TR-NPL-000002	Estimated Transmission Performance of Switched Access Service Feature Group-D
TR-TSY-000004	System Engineering Requirements for the 1ESS Switch Automatic Message Accounting Transmitter (AMAT)
TR-TSY-000005	Pressure Tight Splice Closures for Fiber Optic Cable

TR-TSY-000007	Functional Criteria Voice Frequency Network Channel Terminating Equipment Metallic Facilities
TR-TSY-000008	Digital Interface Between the SLC 96 Digital Loop Carrier System and a Local Digital Switch
TR-TSY-000009	Asynchronous Digital Multiplexer Requirements and Objectives
TR-TSY-000010	Synchronous DS3 Add-Drop Multiplex (ADM 3/X) Requirements and Objectives
TR-NPL-000011	Asynchronous Terminal and Host Interface Reference
TR-TSY-000012	Bell Communications Research MML Requirements
TR-TSY-000016	BELLCORE-STD-100 and BELLCORE-STD-200 Inspection Resource Allocation Plans
TR-TSY-000019	Traffic Data Administration System (TDAS) Binary Editor Interface Specifications
TR-TSY-000020	Generic Requirements for Optical Fiber and Optical Fiber Cable
TR-TSY-000021	Synchronous DS3 Format Interface Specification
TR-TSY-000023	4 GHz Digital Radio Requirements and Objectives
TR-TSY-000024	Service Switching Points (SSPs) Generic Requirements
TR-TSY-000026	Below Ground Electronic Equipment Enclosures
TR-TSY-000027	Environmental Control Systems for Electronic Equipment Enclosures
TR-TSY-000031	CLASS Feature: Calling Number Delivery
TR-TSY-000032	CLASS Feature: Bulk Calling Line Identification
TR-NPL-000037	1983 Exchange Access Study: Analog Voice and Voice Band Performance Characterization Data Transmission of the Exchange Access Plant
TR-TSY-000039	Quality Program Analysis
TR-TSY-000041	Splicing Machines for Single-Mode Fiber Optic Cable

TR-TSY-000042	Mechanical Splicing Devices for Optical Fibers
TR-TSY-000043	Above Ground Electronic Equipment Enclosures (AG/EEE)
TR-TSY-000048	Cable Sheath Repair
TR-TSY-000049	Outdoor Telephone Network Interfaces—One- and Two-Line
TR-TSY-000050	Functional Criteria—Public Telephone Mounting Accessories
TR-TSY-000051	Public Telephone Mountings
TR-TSY-000052	Below Ground Repeater Enclosures
TR-TSY-000056	Repeater Housings for T1, T1C, T1D, and T1G
TR-TSY-000057	Functional Criteria for Digital Loop Carrier Systems
TR-TSY-000058	Cable Pressurization Pipe Panels and Distribution Panels
TR-EOP-000063	Network Equipment—Building System (NEBS) Generic Requirements
TR-TSY-000064	LATA Switching Systems Generic Requirements
TR-NPL-000065	Interexchange Packet Interface
TR-EOP-000066	Space Planning Documentation Requirements
TR-NPL-000067	EADAS/NM System: Requirements for the 1NM8 Generic
TR-TSY-000069	Comptrollers' Automatic Message Accounting Format Description (CAFD)
TR-TSY-000070	Customer Station Gas Tube Protector Units
TR-TSY-000071	One-Pair and Two-Pair Customer Station Protectors with Carbon Blocks or Two-Element Gas Tubes
TR-TSY-000072	Central Office and 5ESS Gas Tube Protector Units
TR-TSY-000073	Customer Station Three-Element Gas Tube Protectors
TR-TSY-000078	Generic Physical Design Requirements for Telecommunications Products and Equipment

TR-TSY-000079	Pressure Contactors for Repeater Cases
TR-TSY-000080	Station Management System (SMS) Requirements for a Data Collection Device (DCD)
TR-TSY-000082	Signaling Transfer Point Generic Requirements
TR-TSY-000100	PIC Filled ASP Cable
TR-TSY-000101	Aircore PIC ALPETH Cable
TR-TSY-000102	PIC Self-Support Cable
TR-TSY-000103	Pulp Bonded STALPETH Cable
TR-TSY-000104	Pulp Bonded PASP Cable
TR-TSY-000105	Pulp Bonded Steam Resistant Cable
TR-TSY-000106	Underground Foam-Skin PIC Bonded STALPETH Cable
TR-TSY-000107	PIC Bonded PASP Cable
TR-TSY-000108	PIC Reinforced Self-Support Cable
TR-TSY-000109	PIC Filled Screened ASP Cable
TR-TSY-000110	PIC Bonded Steam Resistant Cable
TR-TSY-000111	PIC Riser Cable
TR-TSY-000112	PIC Bonded Screened PASP Cable
TR-TSY-000113	PIC PAP Cable
TR-TSY-000114	PIC Screened PAP Cable
TR-TSY-000115	Inter-City PIC Filled Screened ASP Cable
TR-TSY-000116	Inter-City PIC Bonded Screened STAPETH Cable
TR-TSY-000117	Inter-City PIC Bonded Screened PASP Cable
TR-TSY-000118	Cable Outer Protection
TR-TSY-000119	PIC Filled Bonded ASP Cable
TR-TSY-000143	Call Assembly Requirements for the 2ESS Switch Automatic Message Accounting Transmitter (AMAT)
TR-NPL-000145	Compatibility Information for Interconnection of a Cellular Mobile Carrier and a Local Exchange Carrier Network
TR-EOP-000146	Engine-Alternator Standby AC Systems
TR-TSY-000148	Loudspeaker Paging Equipment: Interface Between a 1/1A and 2/2B ESS Centrex Offices and Customer Premises Equipment

TR-TSY-000149	Recorded Telephone Dictation Equipment: Interface Between 1/1A and 2/2B ESS Centrex Offices and Customer Premises Equipment
TR-TSY-000150	Radio Paging Equipment: Interface Between 1/1A and 2/2B ESS Centrex Offices and Customer Premises Equipment
TR-EOP-000151	Generic Requirements for 24-, 48-, 130-, and 140-Volt Central Office Power Plant Rectifiers
TR-ISD-000152	Guidelines for Mechanized Invoicing
TR-EOP-000154	Generic Requirements for 24-, 48-, 130-, and 140-Volt Central Office Power Plant Control and Distribution Equipment
TR-TSY-000156	Drop Wire Splice for Single Pair Aerial Drop Wire
TR-NPL-000157	Secondary Channel in the Digital Data System: Channel Interface Requirements
TR-EOP-000158	Distributing Frame
TR-EOP-000159	Distributing Frame Interfaces
TR-EOP-000160	Conventional Distributing Frame System
TR-EOP-000161	Modular Distributing Frame System
TR-EOP-000162	Conventional Distributing Frame Framework
TR-EOP-000163	Modular Distributing Frame Framework
TR-TSY-000170	Digital Crossconnect System Requirements and Objectives
TR-TSY-000171	96 Channel Digital Paired-Cable Transmission System Requirements and Objectives
TR-TSY-000172	General Compatibility Information—Loop Fiber System
TR-TSY-000174	Automated Digital Terminal System (ADTS) Requirements and Objectives
TR-NPL-000175	Compatibility Information for Feature Group B Switched Access Service
TR-TSY-000177	Digital Channel Bank Low Speed Signaling Channel Units Generic Requirements
TR-TSY-000180	Hardware Attachments for Steel and Concrete Telephone Poles

TR-TSY-000181	Dual-Tone Multifrequency Receiver Generic Requirements for End-to-End Signaling Over Tandem-Switched Voice Links
TR-TSY-000183	Cable Pressurization—Flow Transducers
TR-TSY-000184	Fiberglass Extension Ladders
TR-TSY-000187	Optical Cable Placing Winches
TR-TSY-000188	Plugged Cable Stubs
TR-TSY-000191	Alarm Indication Signals Requirements and Objectives
TR-TSY-000194	Extended Superframe Format Interface Specification
TR-TSY-000196	Optical Time Domain Reflectometers
TR-TSY-000197	Tone Generator Test Sets
TR-TSY-000198	Optical Loss Test Equipment
TR-TSY-000206	Cable Pressurization Air Feeder Pipe
TR-EOP-000208	Stored Program Control Proposed Software Documentation Requirements for C.O. Switching Systems
TR-EOP-000209	Guidelines for Product Change Notices
TR-TSY-000210	Low Bit Rate Voice (LBRV) Terminals
TR-TSY-000216	CLASS Feature: Customer Originated Trace
TR-TSY-000217	CLASS Feature: Selective Call Forwarding
TR-TSY-000218	CLASS Feature: Selective Call Rejection
TR-TSY-000219	CLASS Feature: Distinctive Ringing/Call Waiting
TR-EOP-000221	Interface and Functional Requirements for Microprocessor Control of 24-, 48-, 130-, and 140-Volt Central Office Power Plants
TR-TSY-000222	InterLATA Dial Pulsing Requirements
TR-EOP-000230	Guidelines for Engineering Complaints and Operational Trouble Reports
TR-TSY-000231	Generic Automated Loop Test Systems
TR-EOP-000232	Generic Requirements for Lead-Acid Storage Batteries
TR-TSY-000235	Machine Interface Codes for Voice Grade Switched Exchange Access Service
TR-TSY-000238	Digital Channel Bank Dual Tone Multifrequency Code Select Signaling Channel Unit

TR-TSY-000239	Indoor Telephone Network Interfaces
TR-EOP-000246	Network Interface for Nonregistered Voice Band Analog Private Line Services
TR-NPL-000246	Bell Communications Research Specification of Signaling System Number 7
TR-TSY-000251	Service Wire Splice for Buried Service Wire
TR-TSY-000252	Emergency Restoration Facilities for Electronic Equipment Enclosures
TR-NPL-000258	Compatibility Information for Feature Group D Switched Access Service
TR-TSY-000264	Optical Fiber Cleaving Tools
TR-TSY-000265	Cable Entrance Splice Closures for Fiber Optic Cable
TR-TSY-000266	Optical Patch Panels
TR-TSY-000267	Drop Wire Clamp for Single-Pair Aerial Service Wire
TR-TSY-000268	ISDN Basic Access Call Control Switching and Signaling Requirements
TR-TSY-000271	Operator Service Systems Generic Requirements
TR-NPL-000275	Notes on the BOC IntraLATA Networks— 1986
TR-TSY-000276	Description of the Interface Between 1/1A or 2/2B ESS Switching Equipment and a Non-Data-Linked Centrex/ESSX Attendant Position System
TR-EOP-000277	Datapath Network Access Interface Specification
TR-TSY-000282	Software Reliability and Quality Acceptance Criteria (SRQAC)
TR-TSY-000283	Interface Description—Interface Between Customer Premises Equipment; Simplified Message Desk and Switching System: 1AESS
TR-TSY-000284	Reliability and Quality Switching Systems Generic Requirements (RQSSGR)
TR-TSY-000294	Cable Pressurization Pressure Transducer Housing
TR-EOP-000295	Isolated Ground Planes: Definition and Application to Telephone Central Offices

TR-TSY-000297	LMOS/MLT-1 Compatible Interface Requirements for a Loop Test System
TR-TSY-000299	Indoor Building Entrance Terminals and Associated Plug-In Protector Units
TR-TSY-000300	Plug-In Carbon Block Protector Units for Use in Central Office Connectors and Building Entrance Terminals
TR-TSY-000301	Public Packet Switched Network Generic Requirements (PPSNGR)
TR-TSY-000303	Integrated Digital Loop Carrier System Generic Requirements, Objectives, and Interface
TR-TSY-000306	Automatic Call Distributor/Management Information System: Interface Between 1/1A ESS Switch Central Office and Customer Premises Equipment
TR-TSY-000312	Functional Criteria for the DS1 Interface Connector
TR-NPL-000314	Generic Requirements for Telephone Headsets at Operator Consoles
TR-EOP-000316	Vendor/BOC Information Requirements for Servicing Defective Units Through the NPIAC
TR-TSY-000317	Switching System Requirements for Call Control Using the Integrated Services Digital Network User Part (ISDNUP)
TR-TSY-000319	Customer Traffic Report Feature: Interface Between a 1/1A ESS Centrex Office and Customer Premises Equipment
TR-NPL-000320	Fundamental Generic Requirements for Metallic Digital Signal Crossconnect Systems—DSX-1, -1C, -2, -3
TR-NPL-000322	Generic Requirements for Partially Automated Digital Signal Crossconnect Frames Using Concentrated Test Access
TR-ISD-000325	Equipment Information Required from Suppliers for Operations Systems
TR-TSY-000326	Fiber Optic Connectors for Single-Mode Optical Fibers
TR-TSY-000332	Reliability Prediction Procedure for Electronic Equipment

TR-NPL-000334	Voice Grade Switched Access Service—Transmission Parameter Limits and Interface Combinations
TR-NPL-000335	Voice Grade Special Access Service
TR-NPL-000336	Metallic and Telegraph Grade Special Access Service Transmission Parameter
TR-NPL-000337	Program Audio Special Access and Local Channel Services
TR-NPL-000338	Television Special Access and Local Channel Services—Transmission Parameter Limits and Interface Combinations
TR-NPL-000339	Wideband Analog Special Access Service Transmission Parameter Limits and Interface Combinations
TR-NPL-000340	Wideband Data Special Access Service Transmission Parameter Limits and Interface Combinations
TR-TSY-000343	Description for a Generic Interface Between SARTS and Digital Crossconnect or Digital Test Access Systems
TR-TSY-000344	Generic Requirements for the Craftsperson's Handset
TR-TSY-000348	Centrex Data Link Interface Between 1/1AESS switch and Customer Premises Equipment
TR-TSY-000349	Interface Between Miscellaneous Control Functions of Customer Premises Equipment and 1/1A ESS Centrex Switching Systems
TR-TSY-000350	E911 Public Safety Answering Point: Interface Between a 1/1AESS Switch and Customer Premises Equipment
TR-EOP-000352	Cellular Mobile Carrier Interconnection Transmission Plans
TR-TSY-000356	Optical Cable Ductliner
TR-TSY-000357	Component Reliability Assurance Requirements for Telecommunications Equipment
TR-TSY-000359	Bellcore AMA Format Design Guidelines
TR-TSY-000360	Nail-Up of Non-Switched Circuits on a Local Switch
TR-TSY-000362	Centrex Update Interface to COSMOS

TR-TSY-000366	Customer Control and Management (CCM) Controller Requirements and Objectives
TR-NPL-000377	Compatibility Information for Feature Group A Switched Access Service
TR-TAP-000383	Generic Requirements for Common Language Bar Code Labels
TR-TSY-000385	Automatic Message Accounting Teleprocessing System (AMATPS) Generic Requirements
TR-TSY-000387	Interim Defined Central Office Interface (IDCI) to the Switching Control Center System (SCCS)
TR-TSY-000391	CLASS Feature: Calling Number Delivery Blocking
TR-TSY-000393	ISDN Basic Access Digital Subscriber Lines
TR-TSY-000394	Switching System Requirement for Interexchange Carrier Interconnection Using the ISDNUP
TR-TSY-000402	Additional Service Switching Point and Related End Office Capabilities (Including Private Virtual Network Services)
TR-TSY-000406	DC Bulk Power System for Confined Locations
TR-TSY-000409	Generic Requirements for Intrabuilding Optical Fiber Cable
TR-TSY-000411	Manufacturing Program Analysis for Quality and Reliability
TR-RGS-000414	Mechanized Remittance/Payment Advice Interface
TR-TSY-000416	Call Waiting Deluxe Feature Requirements
TR-TSY-000418	Generic Reliability Assurance Requirements for Fiber Optic Transport Systems
TR-TSY-000421	Generic Requirements for Metallic Telecommunication Cables
TR-TSY-000430	7.5 KHz Digital Program Terminal or Channel Unit Requirements and Objectives
TR-TSY-000431	15 KHz Digital Audio Terminal for Program or Television Requirements and Objectives
TR-TAP-000437	Program Document Microfiche Requirements

TR-TSY-000438	The Quality Measurement Plan (QMP)
TR-TSY-000471	Operations Technology Generic Requirements (OTGR): Introduction, Section 1.
TR-TSY-000472	Operations Technology Generic Requirements (OTGR): Memory Administration, Section 2
TR-TSY-000473	Operations Technology Generic Requirements (OTGR): Network Maintenance: Common, Section 3
TR-TSY-000474	Operations Technology Generic Requirements (OTGR): Network Maintenance: Network Element, Section 4
TR-TSY-000475	Operations Technology Generic Requirements (OTGR): Network Maintenance: Transport Surveillance, Section 5
TR-TSY-000476	Operations Technology Generic Requirements (OTGR): Network Maintenance: Access and Testing, Section 6
TR-TSY-000478	Operations Technology Generic Requirements (OTGR): Measurements and Data Generation, Section 8
TR-TSY-000479	Operations Technology Generic Requirements (OTGR): Message Accounting, Section 9
TR-TSY 000480	Operations Technology Generic Requirements (OTGR): User System Interface, Section 10
TR-TSY-000824	Operations Technology Generic Requirements (OTGR): User System Interface-User System Access, Section 10.1
TR-TSY-000825	Operations Technology Generic Requirements (OTGR): User System Interface-User System Language, Section 10.A
TR-TSY-000481	Operations Technology Generic Requirements (OTGR): Generic Operations Interface, Section 11
TR-TSY-000482	Operations Technology Generic Requirements (OTGR): Operations Applications Messages—Directory, Section 12
TR-TSY-000831	Operations Technology Generic Requirements (OTGR): Operations Application

	Messages—Language for Operations Application Messages, Section 12.1
TR-TSY-000832	Operations Technology Generic Requirements (OTGR): Operations Application Messages—Memory Administration Messages, Section 12.2
TR-TSY-000833	Operations Technology Generic Requirements (OTGR): Operations Application Messages—Network Maintenance: Network Element and Transport Surveillance Messages, Section 12.3
TR-TSY-000834	Operations Technology Generic Requirements (OTGR): Operations Application Messages—Network Maintenance: Access and Testing Messages, Section 12.4
TR-TSY-000483	Operations Technology Generic Requirements (OTGR): Embedded Operations Interfaces, Section 13
TR-TSY-000484	Operations Technology Generic Requirements (OTGR): Documentation, Training and Supplier Support Directory, Section 14
TR-TSY-000839	Operations Technology Generic Requirements (OTGR): Documentation, Training and Supplier Support—Vendor Generic Training Requirements, Section 14.2
TR-TSY-000440	Transport Systems Generic Requirements (TSGR)
TR-TSY-000452	Generic Requirements for Public Telephone Handsets
TR-TSY-000461	X.75 Interfaces to BOC/IDC Network
TR-TSY-000462	Public Packet Switched Network (PPSN) X.25 Interface Description
TR-TSY-000465	Interface Between Loop Carrier Systems and Loop Testing Systems
TR-TAP-000485	Common Language CLEI Code Assignment and Equipment Marking Requirements
TR-TSY-000499	Transport Systems Generic Requirements (TSGR): Common Requirements, a Module of TSGR, TR-TSY-000440

TR-TSY-000500	LSSGR: Index and Feature Definitions, Network Plan, System Architecture, and Feature Definitions, Section 1-4
TR-TSY-000505	LSSGR: Call Processing, Section 5
TR-TSY-000506	LSSGR: Signaling, Section 6
TR-TSY-000507	LSSGR: Transmission, Section 7
TR-TSY-000508	LSSGR: Automatic Message Accounting, Section 8-8.1
TR-TSY-000541	LSSGR: Measurements and Administration, Section 8.2-8.6
TR-TSY-000776	Network Interface Description for ISDN Customer Access

Consultative Committee on International Telephone and Telegraph (CCITT)

E.180	Characteristics of the dial tone, ringing tone, busy tone, congestion tone, special information and warning tone
E.210, F.120, Q.11 *ter*	Ship station identification for VHF/UHF and maritime mobile-satellite services
E.211, Q.11 *quater*	Numbering and dialing procedures for VHF/UHF and maritime mobile-satellite telephone services
F.160	General operational provisions for the international public facsimile services
F.170	Operational provisions for the international public facsimile service between public bureaux (bureaufax)
F.180	Operational provisions for the international public facsimile service between subscribers' stations
F.200	Teletex service
G.101	The transmission plan
G.102	Transmission performance objectives and recommendations
G.113	Transmission impairments
G.114	Mean one-way propagation time

G.117	Transmission aspects of unbalance about earth
G.120	Transmission characteristics of national networks
G.122	Influence of national networks on stability and echo losses in national systems
G.123	Circuit noise in national networks
G.125	Characteristics of national circuits on carrier systems
G.131	Stability and echo
G.132	Attenuation distortion
G.133	Group-delay distortion
G.134	Linear crosstalk
G.141	Transmission characteristics of exchanges
G.143	Circuit noise and the use of compandors
G.152	Characteristics appropriate to long distance circuits of a length not exceeding 2500 km
G.153	Characteristics appropriate to international circuits more than 2500 km in length
G.161	Echo suppressors suitable for circuits having either short or long propagation times
G.162	Characteristics of compandors for telephony
G.163	Call concentrating systems
G.164	Echo suppressors
G.165	Echo cancelers
G.171	Transmission characteristics of leased circuits forming part of a private telephone network
G.221	Overall recommendations relating to carrier-transmission system
G.222	Noise objectives for design of carrier-transmission systems of 2500 km
G.224	Maximum permissible value for the absolute power level (power referred to one milliwatt) of a signaling pulse
G.225	Recommendations relating to the accuracy of carrier frequencies
G.231	Arrangement of carrier equipment

G.232	12-channel terminal equipment
G.241	Pilots on groups, supergroups, etc.
G.242	Through-connection of groups, super-groups, etc.
G.243	Protection of pilots and additional measuring frequencies at points where there is a through-connection
G.299	Unwanted modulation and phase jitter
G.332	12 MHz systems on standardized 2.6/9.5 mm coaxial cable pairs
G.333	60 MHz systems on standardized 2.6/9.5 mm coaxial cable pairs
G.334	18 MHz systems on standardized 2.6/9.5-mm coaxial cable pairs
G.411	Use of radio-relay systems for international telephone circuits
G.412	Terminal equipment of radio-relay systems forming part of a general telecommunications network.
G.423	Interconnection at the baseband frequencies of frequency-division multiplex radio-relay systems.
G.434	Hypothetical reference circuit for communications satellite systems.
G.441	Permissible circuit noise on frequency-division multiplex radio-relay systems.
G.445	Noise objectives for communications satellite system design.
G.473	Interconnection of a maritime mobile satellite system with the international automatic switched telephone service; transmission aspects.
G.611	Characteristics of symmetric cable pairs for analog transmission
G.612	Characteristics of symmetric cable pairs designed for the transmission of systems with bit rates of the order of 6 to 34 mb/s
G.651	Characteristics of 50/125 micrometer graded index optical fibre cables

G.702	Vocabulary of pulse code modulation (PCM) and digital transmission terms
G.703	General aspects of interfaces
G.704	Maintenance of digital networks
G.705	Integrated services digital network (ISDN)
G.711	Pulse code modulation (PCM) of voice frequencies
G.712	Performance characteristics of PCM channels at audio frequencies
G.731	Primary PCM multiplex equipment for voice frequencies
G.733	Characteristics of primary PCM multiplex equipment operating at 1544 kb/s
G.735	Characteristics required to terminate 1544-kb/s digital paths on a digital exchange
G.736	Characteristics of synchronous digital multiplex equipment operating at 1544 kb/s
G.791	General considerations on transmultiplexing equipment
G.792	Characteristics common to all transmultiplexing equipment
G.793	Characteristics of 60-channel transmultiplexing equipment
G.7ZZ	Proposed 32 kb/s low bit rate voice algorithm
G.901	General considerations on digital line — sections and digital line systems
G.911	Digital line sections and digital line systems on cable at 1544 kb/s
G.917	Digital line sections and digital line systems on cable at 736 kb/s
H.41	Phototelegraph transmissions on telephone-type circuits
H.42	Range of phototelegraph transmissions on a telephone-type circuit
H.43	Document facsimile transmissions on leased telephone-type circuits
I.112	Vocabulary of terms for ISDNs
I.120	Integrated Service Digital Networks (ISDNs)

I.122	Framework for additional packet mode bearer services
I.130	Attributes for the characterization of telecommunications services supported by an ISDN and network capabilities of an ISDN
I.210	Principles of telecommunications services supported by an ISDN
I.211	Bearer services supported by an ISDN
I.212	Teleservices supported by an ISDN
I.310	ISDN-Network functional principles
I.320	ISDN protocol reference model
I.330	ISDN numbering and addressing principles
I.331 (E.164)	Numbering plan for the ISDN era
I.340	ISDN connection types
I.410	General aspects and principles relation to recommendations on ISDN user-network interfaces
I.411	ISDN user-network interfaces—Reference configurations
I.412	ISDN user-network interfaces—Interface structures and access capabilities
I.420	Basic user-network interface
I.421	Primary user-network interface
I.430	Basic user-network interface—Layer 1 specification
I.431	Primary user-network interface—Layer 1 specification
I.440 (Q.920)	ISDN user-network interface—General aspects
I.441 (Q.921)	ISDN user-network interface data link layer specification
I.450 (Q.930)	ISDN user-network interface Layer 3—General aspects
I.451 (Q.931)	ISDN user-network interface Layer 3 specification
I.461 (X.30)	Support of X.21 and X.21 *bis* based Data Terminal Equipment (DTE) by an Integrated Services Digital Network (ISDN)

I.462 (X.31)	Support of packet mode terminal equipment by an ISDN
I.463	Support of Data Terminal Equipment (DTE) with V-series type interfaces by an Integrated Services Digital Network (ISDN)
I.464	Multiplexing, rate adaptation and support of existing interfaces for restricted 64 kb/s transfer capability
J.61	Transmission performance of television circuits designed for use in international connections
J.62	Single value of signal-to-noise ratio for all television systems
J.63	Insertion of test signals in the field-blanking interval of monochrome and color television signals
J.64	Definitions of parameters for automatic measurement of television insertion test signals
J.65	Standard test signal for conventional loading of a television channel
J.66	Transmission of one sound program associated with analog television signal by means of time division multiplex in the line synchronizing pulse
J.73	Use of a 12 MHz system for the simultaneous transmission of telephony and television
J.74	Methods for measuring the transmission characteristics of translating equipment
J.75	Interconnection of systems for television transmission on coaxial pairs and on radio-relay links
J.77	Characteristics of the television signals transmitted over 18 MHz and 60 MHz systems
K.11	Protection against overvoltages
K.12	Specification clauses for the requirements to be met by gas discharge protectors for the protection of telecommunication installations

O.22	Specification for the CCITT automatic transmission measuring and signaling testing equipment ATME No.2
P.10	Vocabulary of terms on telephone transmission quality and telephone sets
P.11	Effect of transmission impairments
P.16	Subjective effects of direct crosstalk: thresholds of audibility and intelligibility
P.62	Measurements on subscribers' telephone equipment
P.63	Methods for the evaluation of transmission quality on the basis of objective measurements
P.64	Determination of sensitivity/frequency characteristics of local telephone systems to permit calculation of their loudness ratings
P.71	Measurement of speech volume
P.74	Methods for subjective determination of transmission quality
P.77	Method for evaluation of service from the standpoint of speech transmission quality
Q.9	Vocabulary of switching and signaling terms
Q.14	Means to control the number of satellite links on an international telephone connection.
Q.29	Causes of noise and ways of reducing noise in telephone exchanges
Q.35	Characteristics of the dial tone, ringing tone, busy tone, congestion tone, special information tone, and warning tone
Q.40	The transmission plan
Q.43	Transmission losses, relative levels
Q.44	Attenuation distortion
Q.46 and Q.47	Characteristics of primary PCM multiplex equipment
Q.60	General requirements for the interworking of the terrestrial telephone network and the Maritime Mobile-Satellite Service.
Q.254 and Q.258	Telephone signals

Q.256	Management signals
Q.260	Management signals
Q.311	2600 Hz line signaling
Q.314	PCM line signaling
Q.320	Signal code for register signaling
Q.330	Automatic transmission and signaling testing
Q.331	Test equipment for checking equipment and signals operating at 2048 kb/s and 1544 kb/s
Q.506	Network management functions
Q.704	Signaling network functions and messages
Q.705	Signaling network structure
Q.723	Formats and codes
Q.921	Layer 2 protocol used in the ISDN D channel
Q.931	Layer 3 protocol used in the ISDN D channel
Q.932	Generic procedures for the control of ISDN supplementary services
T.0	Classification of facsimile apparatus for document transmission over the public networks.
T.1	Standardization of phototelegraph apparatus
T.2	Standardization of Group 1 facsimile apparatus for document transmission
T.3	Standardization of Group 2 facsimile apparatus for document transmission
T.4	Standardization of Group 3 facsimile apparatus for document transmission
T.10	Document facsimile transmissions on leased telephone-type circuits
T.10 *bis*	Document facsimile transmissions in the general switched telephone network
T.11	Phototelegraph transmissions on telephone-type circuits
T.12	Range of phototelegraph transmissions on a telephone-type circuit
T.13	Phototelegraph transmission over combined radio and metallic circuits
T.20	Standardized test chart for facsimile transmissions

T.21	Standardized test chart for document facsimile transmissions
T.30	Procedures for document facsimile transmission in the general switched telephone network
U.60	General requirements to be met in interfacing the international telex network with maritime satellite systems.
U.61	Detailed requirements to be met in interfacing the international telex network with maritime satellite systems.
V.2	Power levels for data transmission over telephone lines
V.5	Standardization of data signaling rates for synchronous data transmission in the general switched telephone network
V.6	Standardization of data signaling rates for synchronous data transmission on leased telephone-type circuits
V.7	Definitions of terms concerning data communication over the telephone network
V.15	Use of acoustic coupling for data transmission
V.20	Parallel data transmission modems standardized for universal use in the general switched telephone network
V.22	1200 bits per second duplex modems standardized for use on the general switched telephone network
V.22 *bis*	2400 bits per second duplex modems standardized for use on the general switched telephone network
V.24	Functions and electrical characteristics of circuits at the interface between data terminal equipment and data circuit-terminating equipment.
V.29	9600 bits per second modem standardized for use on point-to-point leased telephone-type circuits

V.32	9600 bits per second modem standardized for duplex use in the general switched telephone network
V.50	Standard limits for transmission quality of data transmissions
V.53	Limits for the maintenance of telephone-type circuits used for data transmission
V.54	Loop test devices for modems
V.110	Data transfer protocol for the B channel
V.120	Data transfer protocol for the D channel
X.2	International user services and facilities in public data networks.
X.3	Packet assembly/disassembly facility (PAD) in a public data network.
X.15	Definitions of terms concerning public data networks
X.20	Interface between data terminal equipment (DTE) and data circuit-terminating equipment (DCE) for start-stop transmission services on public data networks.
X.20 *bis*	Use on public data networks of data terminal equipment (DTE) which is designed for interfacing to asynchronous duplex V-Series modems
X.21	Interface between data terminal equipment (DTE) and data circuit-terminating equipment (DCE) for synchronous operation on public data networks.
X.21 *bis*	Use on public data networks of data terminal equipment (DTE) which is designed for interfacing to synchronous V-Series modems
X.24	List of definitions for interchange circuits between data terminal equipment (DTE) and data circuit-terminating equipment (DCE) on public data networks
X.25	Interface between data terminal equipment and data circuit-terminating equipment for terminals operating in the packet mode on public data networks.

X.28	DTE/DCE interface for start-stop mode data terminal equipment accessing the packet assembly/disassembly facility (PAD) in a public data network situated in the same country.
X.29	Procedures for the exchange of control information and user data between a packet assembly/disassembly facility (PAD) and a packet mode DTE or another PAD.
X.60	Common channel signaling for circuit switched data applications.
X.75	Terminal and transit call control procedures and data transfer system on international circuits between packet switched data networks.
X.121	International numbering plan for public data networks.
X.150	DTE and DCE test loops for public data networks.

FCC Rules and Regulations

Part 21	Rules and Regulations Domestic Public Fixed Radio Service (Common Carrier)
Sub Part B	Public Safety Radio Services
Sub Part C	Special Emergency Radio Services
Sub Part D	Industrial Radio Services
Sub Part E	Land Transportation Radio Services
Sub Part K	Offshore Radio Telephone Service
Part 22	Public Mobile Services
Sub Part G	Public Land Mobile Service
Sub Part K	Domestic Public Cellular Radio Telephone Service
Part 25	Satellite Communications
Part 68	Connection of Terminal Equipment to the Telephone Network
Subpart C	Registration Procedures
Subpart F	Connectors
Part 76	Cable Television Service
Part 90	Private Land Mobile Radio Services

Part 94	Rules and Regulations Private Operational Fixed Radio Service
Subpart F	Digital Termination Systems
Subpart I	Point-to-Point Microwave Radio Service
Part 100	Direct Broadcast Satellite Service

Electronic Industries Association Standards Pertaining to Telecommunications

Interim Standards

EIA/IS-3-D	Cellular Systems Mobile Station—Land Station Compatibility Specification
EIA/IS-4	Transmission Loss Plan of a mu-Law Compatibility PBX
EIA/IS-15	Standard Baseband (Audio/Video) Interface Between NTSC Television Receiving Devices and Peripheral Devices
EIA/IS-19-B	Recommended Minimum Standards for 800 MHz Cellular Subscriber Units
EIA/IS-20-A	Recommended Minimum Standards for 800 MHz Cellular Land Stations
EIA/IS-21	Interim Sectional Specification for Fiber Optic Transmitters with Digital Input
EIA/IS-22	Blank Detail Specifications for Fiber Optic Transmitters with Digital Input
EIA/IS-26	Interim Sectional Specification for Fiber Optic Receivers with Digital Output
EIA/IS-27	Interim Blank Detail Specification for Fiber Optic Receivers with Digital Output
EIA/IS-41.1	Cellular Radiotelecommunications Intersystem Operations: Functional Overview
EIA/IS-41.2	Cellular Radiotelecommunications Intersystem Operations: Intersystem Handoff
EIA/IS-41.3	Cellular Radiotelecommunications Intersystem Operations: Automatic Roaming

EIA/IS-41.4	Cellular Radiotelecommunications Inter-system Operations: Operations, Administration and Maintenance
EIA/IS-41.5	Cellular Radiotelecommunications Inter-system Operations: Data Communication
NQ-EIA/IS-43	Omnibus Specification—Local Area Network Twisted Pair Data Communications Cable
NQ-EIA/IS—43AA	Cable for LAN Twisted Pair Data Communications—Detail Specification for Type 1, Outdoor Cable
NQ-EIA/IS—43AB	Cable for LAN Twisted Pair Data Communications—Detail Specification for Type 1, Non-Plenum Cable
NQ-EIA/IS—43AC	Cable for LAN Twisted Pair Data Communications—Detail Specification for Type 1, Riser Cable
NQ-EIA/IS—43AD	Cable for LAN Twisted Pair Data Communications—Detail Specification for Type 1, Plenum Cable
NQ-EIA/IS—43AE	Cable for LAN Twisted Pair Data Communications—Detail Specification for Type 2, Non-Plenum Cable
NQ-EIA/IS—43AF	Cable for LAN Twisted Pair Data Communications—Detail Specification for Type 2, Plenum Cable
NQ-EIA/IS—43AG	Cable for LAN Twisted Pair Data Communications—Detail Specification for Type 6, Office Cable
NQ-EIA/IS—43AH	Cable for LAN Twisted Pair Data Communications—Detail Specification for Type 8, Undercarpet Cable
NQ-EIA/IS—43AJ	Cable for LAN Twisted Pair Data Communications—Detail Specification for Type 9, Plenum Cable

EIA Standards

| EIA-152-C | Minimum Standards for Land Mobile Communication, FM or PM Transmitters, 25-866 MHz (ANSI/EIA-152-C-88) |

EIA-170	Electrical Performance Standards—Monochrome Television Studio Facilities
EIA-189-A	Encoded Color Bar Signal
EIA-195-C	Electrical and Mechanical Characteristics for Terrestrial Microwave Relay System Antennas and Passive Reflectors (ANSI/EIA-195-C-85)
EIA-199-A	Solid and Semi-Solid Dielectric Transmission Lines (ANSI/EIA-199-A-72)
EIA-200-A	Circular Waveguides (ANSI/EIA-200-A-69)
EIA-204-C	Minimum Standard for Land Mobile Communication FM or PM Receivers 25-947 MHz
EIA-210	Terminating and Signaling Equipment for Microwave Communication Systems, Part 1: Telephone Equipment
EIA-220-B	Minimum Standards for Land Mobile Communication Continuous Tone-Controlled Squelch Systems (CTCSS) (ANSI/EIA-220-B-88)
EIA-222-D	Structural Standards for Steel Antenna Towers and Antenna Supporting Structures (ANSI/EIA-222-D-86)
EIA-225	Requirements for Rigid Coaxial Transmission Lines, 50 Ohms
EIA-232-D	Interface Between Data Terminal Equipment and Data Communication Equipment Employing Serial Binary Data Interchange (ANSI/EIA-232-D-86)
EIA-250-B	Electrical Performance Standards for Television Relay Facilities (ANSI/EIA-250-B-76)
EIA-252-A	Standard Microwave Transmission Systems
EIA-261-B	Rectangular Waveguides (WR3 to WR 2300)
EIA-266-A	Registered Screen Dimensions for Monochrome Picture Tubes
EIA-271-A	Waveguide Flanges—Pressurizable Contact Types for Waveguide Sizes WR90 to WR2300
EIA-285	Waveguide Flanges—Dual Contact Pressurizable and Miniature Type for Waveguide Sizes WR90 to WR975
EIA-310-C	Racks, Panels, and Associated Equipment (ANSI/EIA-310-C-77)

EIA-312-A	Engineering Specifications Outline for Monochrome CCTV Camera Equipment (ANSI/EIA-312-A-76)
EIA-316-B	Minimum Standards for Portable/Personal Radio Transmitters, Receivers and Transmitter/Receiver Combination Land Mobile Communications FM or PM Equipment 25-1000 MHz
EIA-324-A	Registered Screen Dimensions for Color Picture Tubes (ANSI/EIA-324-A-82)
EIA-329-A	Minimum Standards for Land Mobile Communication Antennas Part I: Base or Fixed Station Antennas (ANSI/EIA-329-A-78)
EIA-329-1	Minimum Standards for Land Mobile Communication Antennas Part II: Vehicular Antennas
EIA-330	Electrical Performance Standards for Closed Circuit Television Camera 525/60 Interlaced 2:1 (ANSI/EIA-330-68)
EIA-334-A	Signal Quality at Interface Between Data Terminal Equipment and Synchronous Data Circuit-Terminating Equipment for Serial Data Transmission
EIA-334-A-1	Addendum No. 1 to EIA-334-A and EIA-404 Application of Signal Quality Requirements to EIA-449
EIA-343-A	Electrical Performance Standards for High Resolution Monochrome Closed Circuit Television Camera
EIA-363	Standard for Specifying Signal Quality for Transmitting and Receiving Data Processing Terminal Equipment Using Serial Data Transmission at the Interface with Non-Synchronous Data Communication Equipment
EIA-366-A	Interface Between Data Terminal Equipment and Automatic Calling Equipment for Data Communication
EIA-368	Frequency Division Multiplex Equipment Standard for Nominal 4 KHz Channel

	Bandwidths (Non-Compandored) and Wideband Channels (Greater than 4 KHz)
EIA-374A	Land Mobile Signaling Standard
EIA-375-A	Electrical Performance Standards for Direct View Monochrome Closed Circuit Television Camera 525/60 Interlaced 2:1 (ANSI/EIA-375-A-76)
EIA-378	Measurement of Spurious Radiation From FM and TV Broadcast Receivers in the Frequency Range of 100 to 1000 MHz—Using the EIA Laurel Broadband Antenna
EIA-384	Time Division Multiplex Equipment for Nominal 4 KHz Channel Bandwidths
EIA-404-A	Standard for Start-Stop Signal Quality Between Data Terminal Equipment and Non-Synchronous Data Communication Equipment
EIA-411	Electrical and Mechanical Characteristics of Earth Station Antennas for Satellite Communications (ANSI/EIA-411-A-86).
EIA-412-A	Electrical Performance Standards for Direct View High Resolution Monochrome Closed Circuit Television Monitors (ANSI/EIA-412-A-76)
EIA-420	Electrical Performance Standards for Monochrome Closed Circuit Television Cameras 525/60 Random Interlace (ANSI/EIA-420-76)
EIA-422-A	Electrical Characteristics of Balanced Voltage Digital Interface Circuits
EIA-423-A	Electrical Characteristics of Unbalanced Voltage Digital Interface Circuits
EIA-439	Engineering Specifications for Color CCTV Camera Equipment
EIA-440-A	Fiber Optic Terminology (ANSI/EIA-440-A-89)
EIA-449	General Purpose 37-Position and 9-Position Interface for Data Terminal Equipment and Data Circuit-Terminating Equipment Employing Serial Binary Data Interchange.

EIA-449-1	Addendum to EIA-449 General Purpose 37-Position and 9-Position Interface for Data Terminal Equipment and Data Circuit-Terminating Equipment Employing Serial Binary Data Interchange.
EIA-450	Standard Form For Reporting Measurements of Land Mobile, Base Station and Portable/Personal Radio Receivers in Compliance with FCC Part 15 Rules
EIA-455	Standard Test Procedures for Fiber Optic Fibers, Cables, Transducers, Connections and Terminating Devices (with 27 addenda covering specific tests)
EIA-458-A	Standard Optical Waveguide Fiber Material Classes and Preferred Sizes (ANSI/EIA-458-A-84)
EIA-464	Private Branch Exchange (PBX) Switching Equipment for Voice Band Applications.
EIA-464-1	Addendum No. 1 to EIA-464.
EIA-465	Group 3 Facsimile Apparatus for Document Transmission
EIA-466	Procedures for Document Facsimile Transmission
EIA-470-A	Telephone Instruments with Loop Signaling for Voice Band Application.
EIA-4720000	Generic Specification for Fiber Optic Cables (ANSI/EIA-4720000)
EIA-472A000	Sectional Specification for Fiber Optic Communication Cables for Outside Aerial Use (ANSI/EIA-472A000-85)
EIA-472B000	Sectional Specification for Fiber Optic Communication Cables for Underground and Buried Use (ANSI/EIA-472B000-85)
EIA-472C000	Sectional Specification for Fiber Optic Communication Cables for Indoor Use (ANSI/EIA-472C000-85)
EIA-472D000	Sectional Specification for Fiber Optic Communication Cables for Outside Telephone Plant Use (ANSI/EIA-472D000-85)

EIA-472AXX0	Blank Detail Specification for Fiber Optic Communication Cables for Outside Aerial Use (ANSI/EIA-472AXX0-86)
EIA-472BXX0	Blank Detail Specification for Fiber Optic Communication Cables for Underground and Buried Use (ANSI/EIA-472BXX0-86)
EIA-472CXX0	Blank Detail Specification for Fiber Optic Communication Cables for Indoor Use (ANSI/EIA-472CXX0-86)
EIA-472DXX0	Blank Detail Specification for Fiber Optic Communication Cables for Outside Telephone Plant Use (ANSI/EIA-472DXX0-86)
EIA-4750000-A	Generic Specification for Fiber Optic Connectors (ANSI/EIA-475-A-86)
EIA-478	Multiline Key Telephone Systems (KTS) for Voice Band Application.
EIA-484	Electrical and Mechanical Interface Characteristics and Line Control Protocol Using Communication Control Characters for Serial Data Link Between a Direct Numerical Control System and Numerical Control Equipment Employing Asynchronous Full Duplex Transmission
EIA-491	Interface Between a Numerical Control Unit and Peripheral Equipment Employing Asynchronous Binary Data Interchange Over Circuits Having EIA-423-A Electrical Characteristics
EIA-4920000-A	Generic Specification for Optical Waveguide Fibers (ANSI/EIA-4910000-A-87)
EIA-492A000	Generic Specification for Class 1a Multimode, Graded-Index Optical Waveguide Fibers (ANSI/EIA-491A000-87)
EIA-492AA00	Blank Detail Specifications for Class 1a Multimode, Graded-Index Optical Waveguide Fibers (ANSI/EIA-491AA00-87)
EIA-492B000	Sectional Specification for Class IV Single-Mode, Optical Waveguide Fibers (ANSI/EIA-491B000-88)

EIA-492BA00	Blank Detail Specification for Class IVa Dispersion Unshifted Single-Mode, Optical Waveguide Fibers (ANSI/EIA-491BA00-88)
EIA-496	Interface Between Data Circuit-Terminating Equipment (DCE) and the Public Switched Telephone Network (PSTN) (ANSI/EIA-496-84)
EIA-497	Facsimile Glossary
EIA-499	Call Sequencer Interface to 1A/1A2 Generic Key Telephone System (ANSI/EIA-499-86)
EIA-504	Magnetic Field Intensity Criteria for Telephone Compatibility with Hearing Aids
EIA-508	Electrical Performance Standards for Television Broadcast Transmitters (ANSI/EIA—508-87)
EIA-514	Telephone Exclusion-Key Interface (ANSI/EIA-514-85)
EEIA-516	Joint EIA/CVCC Recommended Practice for Teletext: North American Basic Teletext Specification (NABTS) (ANSI/EIA-516-88)
EIA-530	High Speed 25-Position Interface for Data Terminal Equipment and Data Circuit-Terminating Equipment (ANSI/EIA-530-87)
EIA-533	Optical Fiber Interface that may be Employed for Synchronous or Asynchronous Point-to-Point Interconnection of Digital Equipment (ANSI/EIA-533-87)
EIA-536	General Aspects of Group 4 Facsimile Equipment (ANSI/EIA-536-88)
EIA-537	Control Procedures for Telematic Terminals (ANSI/EIA-537-88)
EIA-538	Facsimile Coding Schemes and Coding Control Functions for Group 4 Facsimile Equipment (ANSI/EIA-538-88)
EIA-5090000	Generic Specifications for Fiber Optic Terminal Devices (ANSI/EIA-509-84)
EIA-5150000	Generic Specification for Optical Fiber and Cable Splices (ANSI/EIA-5150000-87)

EIA-515B000	Sectional Specification for Splice Closures for Pressurized Aerial, Buried and Underground Fiber Optic Cable Splices (ANSI/EIA-515B000-87)
EIA-5230000	Generic Specification for Field Portable Optic Fiber Cleaving Equipment (ANSI/EIA-5230000-87)
EIA-5390000	Generic Specification for Field Portable Polishing Device for Preparation of Optical Fibers (ANSI/EIA-5390000-88)
NQ-EIA-5460000	Generic Specification for a Field Optical Inspection Device (ANSI/EIA-5460000 -88)

Selected Manufacturers and Vendors of Telecommunications Products and Services

This appendix lists manufacturers and vendors whose products are included in the lists at the ends of the chapters. This list is not a complete buyer's guide. This list and the lists at the ends of the chapters offer a representative sample of the vendors on the market. Because addresses and telephone numbers change frequently, it is advisable to check these against sources that are kept updated. Readers are advised to consult one of the following sources for current and more complete manufacturer information:

Data Communications Buyer's Guide Issue Data Communications Magazine, McGraw-Hill Building, 1221 Avenue of the Americas, New York, NY 10020 (212) 512-2000

Datapro Reports on Telecommunications and Data Communications Data Pro Research Corporation, 1805 Underwood Blvd., Delran NJ 08075 (609) 764-0100

Telecommunications Reference Data and Buyers Guide Telecommunications, 610 Washington St., Dedham, MA 02026 (617) 326-8220

Telephone Engineer and Management Directory Telephone Engineer and Management Magazine, 124 S. First St., Geneva, IL 60134 (312) 232-1400

Teleconnect Magazine 12 W. 21st St., New York, NY 10010 (212) 691-8215

Telephony Directory and Buyers Guide   Telephony Publishing Co.,
55 E. Jackson Blvd., Chicago, IL 60604

Manufacturers and Vendors of Telecommunications Products and Services

ABS Systems   2500 Shames Dr., Westbury, NY 11590 (516) 333-7900

Account-A-Call Corporation   4450 Lakeside Dr., #300, Burbank, CA 91505 (818) 846-3340

Acoustics Development Corporation.   3800 S. 48th Ter., St. Joseph, MO 64508 (816) 233-8061

Active Voice   101 Stewart St., Seattle, WA 98101 (206) 441-4700

ADC Kentrox Industries, Inc.   P.O. Box 10704, Portland, OR 97201 (503) 643-1681

ADC Telecommunications   5501 Green Valley Dr., Bloomington, MN 55437 (612) 835-6800

Adco   3899 S. 48th Ter., St. Joseph, MO 64503   (816) 233-8061

Adirondack Wire & Cable   New Britain Ave., Farmington, CT 06032 (203) 677-2657

Adtech   6725 Mesa Ridge Rd., Suite 104, San Diego, CA 92121 (619) 455-5353

Advanced Compression Technology, Inc.   31368 Via Colinas, Suite 104, Westlake Village, CA 91362 (818) 889-3618

Advanced Computer Communications   720 Santa Barbara St., Santa Barbara, CA 93101   (800) 444-7854

Advanced Voice Technologies   1895 Airlane Dr., Nashville, TN 37210 (615) 885-4170

Advantest America, Inc.   300 Knightsbridge Pkwy., Lincolnshire, IL 60069 (708) 634-2552

AEC   11501 Dublin Blvd., Dublin, CA 94568   (415) 828-2880

AEG   Olympia, Rt. 22, Orr Dr., Somerville, NJ 08876   (908) 231-8300

Alcatel Cable Systems   7635 Plantation Rd., Roanoke, VA 24019 (703) 265-0510

Alcatel Network Systems Corporation.   2912 Wake Forest Rd., Raleigh, NC 27609 (919) 872-3359

Alcatel, Inc.   10800 Parkridge Blvd., Reston, VA 22091   (703) 476-7300

Alcatel/Cortelco   P.O. Box 831, Corinth, MS 38834   (601) 287-3771

Alcoa Fujikura   P.O. Box 5631, Spartanburg, SC 29304 (803) 439-1739

Allen Bradley Communication Division   747 Alpha Dr., Highland Heights, OH 44143 (216) 449-6700

Alpha Wire   711 Lidgerwood Ave., Elizabeth, NJ 07207 (908) 925-8000

Alston   1600 S. Mountain Ave., Duarte, CA 91010 (818) 357-2121

Amdahl Communications   1250 E. Arques Ave., Sunnyvale, CA 94088-3470 (408) 492-1077

America's Business Software   3317 Julliard Dr., Suite 123, Sacramento, CA 95826 (916) 483-7266

American Data Technology, Inc.   44 W. Bellevue Dr., Suite 6, Pasadena, CA 91105 (818) 578-1264

American Digital   P.O. Box 523, Holmdel, NJ 07733 (908) 946-9288

American Laser Systems, Inc.   106 James Fowler Rd., Goleta, CA 93117 (805) 967-0423

American Lightwave Systems, Inc.   358 Hall Ave., Wallingford, CT 06492 (203) 265-8880

American Power Conversion   350 Columbia St., Peace Dale, RI 02880 (401) 789-3710

American Specialties, Inc.   441 Saw Mill River Rd., Yonkers, NY 10701   (914) 476-9000

American Telesystems   7 Piedmont Center, Suite 200, Atlanta, GA 30305 (404) 266-2500

Ameritec Corporation.   760 Arrow Grand Circle, Covina, CA 91722 (818) 915-5441

Amfas, Inc.   4062 Fabian Way, Palo Alto, CA 94303   (415) 321-5520

AMP, Inc.   P.O. Box 1776, Valley Forge, PA 19482 (215) 647-1000

Amphenol Corporation   1925A Ohio St., Lisle, IL 60532 (312) 960-1010

Anderson-Jacobson   521 Charcot Ave., San Jose, CA 95131 (408) 435-8520

Ando Corporation   480 Oakmead Pkwy., Sunnyvale, CA 94086 (408) 738-2636

Andrew Corporation   10500 W 153rd St., Orlane Park, IL 60462 (708) 349-3300

Anritsu America, Inc.   15 Thornton Rd., Oakland, NJ (201) 337-1111

APA Optics   2950 N.E. 84th Lane, Minneapolis, MN 55434 (612) 784-4995

Apple Computer, Inc.   Cupertino, CA (408) 996-1010

Applied Innovation   651 Lakeview Plaza Blvd., Suite C, Columbus, OH 43085 (800) 247-9482

Applied Knowledge Groups   1608 17th Ave., S., Nashville, TN 37212 (615) 269-9071

Applied Voice Technology   2445 140th Ave., N.E., Bellevue, WA 98007 (206) 641-1760

Applitek Corporation   107 Audubon Rd., Wakefield, MA 01880 (617) 246-4500

AR Division of Telenex Corporation.   7401 Boston Blvd., Springfield, VA 22153 (703) 644-9190

Artel Communications Corporation.   22 Kane Industrial Dr., Hudson, MA 01749 (508) 562-2100

Aspect Telecomunications   1730 Fox Dr., San Jose,CA 95131 (800) 541-7799

AT&E Laboratories   10450 S.W. Nimbus Ave., Beaverton, OR 97005 (503) 620-7787

AT&T Business Products Group   55 Corporate Dr., Bridgewater, NJ 08807 (908) 658-6000

AT&T Consumer Products   5 Wood Hollow Rd., Parsippany, NJ 07054   (201) 581-3250

AT&T Data Systems Group   1 Speedwell Ave., Morristown, NJ 07960 (800) 247-1712

AT&T Information Systems   100 Southgate Pkwy., Morristown, N.J. 07962 (201) 898-8000

AT&T Network Systems   475 South St., Morristown, NJ 07962 (201) 631-7019

AT&T Paradyne Corporation.   8545 126th Ave., N. , Largo, FL 34649-2826 (813) 530-2000

Atelco US, Inc.   6611 Bay Circle, Norcross, GA 30071 (800) 262-8835

ATIS   1225 Northmeadow Pkwy., Suite 114, Roswell, GA 30076 (404) 664-4744

Audiocom   8100 Oak Lane, No. 401, Miami Lakes, FL 33016 (305) 825-4653

Automation Electronics Corporation.   11501 Dublin Blvd., Dublin, CA 94568 (415) 828-2880

Avanti Communications   Aquidneck Industrial Park, Newport, RI
02840   (401) 849-4660

Axon Computers   9025 Wilshire Blvd., Suite 321, Beverly Hills, CA
90211   (800) 422-2966

Avantek, Inc.   3175 Bowers Ave., Santa Clara, CA 95054
(408) 727-0700

Aydin Microwave Division   30 Great Oakes Blvd., San Jose, CA
95119   (408) 432-6300

Aydin Monitor System   502 Office Center Dr., Ft. Washington, PA
19034   (215) 646-8100

BBL Industries   2935 Northeast Pkwy., Atlanta, GA 30360   (404) 662-
1840

BBN Communications Corporation   150 Cambridge Park Dr.,
Cambridge, MA 02238   (617) 873-2678

Belden Corporation.   2200 US Highway 27 S., Richmond, IN
47374   (317) 983-5200

Bellcore   290 W. Mt. Pleasant Ave., Livingston, NJ 07039   (800) 521-
3673

Bell-Northern Research   3500 Carling, Station C, Ottawa, ON K1Y
4H7 Canada (613) 763-2211

Benner-Nawman, Inc.   3070 Bay Vista Ct., Benicia, CA 94510
(707) 746-0500

Biddle Instruments   510 Township Line Rd., Blue Bell, PA 19422
(215) 646-9200

Bitek International, Inc.   6010 Parmount Blvd., Long Beach, CA
90805   (213) 634-8950

Bogen   50 Spring St., P.O. Box 575, Ramsey, NJ 07446   (201) 934-
8500

Boston Technology   1 Kendall Square, Cambridge, MA 02139   (617)
225-0500

Bowmar Telecommunications Division   531 Main St., Acton, MA
01826   (508) 263-8365

Bridge Communications   2081 Stierlin Rd., Mountain View, CA
94043   (415) 969-4400

Broadband Communications Products   1918 Waverly Pl.,
Melbourne, FL 32901   (407) 984-3671

Broadband Technologies   P.O. Box 13737, Research Triangle Park,
NC 27709 (919) 544-0015

Brooktrout Technology, Inc.   110 Cedar St., Wellesley Hills, MA
02181   (617) 235-3026

Brother International Corporation.   200 Cottontail Lane, Somerset, NJ (908) 981-0300

BT Tymnet   2560 N. First St., San Jose, CA 95161-9019 (800) 872-7654

BT&D Technologies   2 Righter Pkwy., Suite 200, Wilmington, DE 19803 (302) 479-0300

C-COR Electronics   60 Decibel Rd., State College, PA 16801 (814) 238-2461

Cabletron   P.O. Box 6257, East Rochester, NH 03867 (603) 332-9400

California Microwave   990 Almanor Ave., Sunnyvale, CA 94086 (408) 732-4000

Canoga Perkins Corporation.   21012 Lassen St., Chatsworth, CA 91311 (818) 718-6300

Canon USA   One Cannon Plaza, Lake Success, NY 11042 (516) 488-6700

Case Communications   7200 Riverwood Dr., Columbia, MD 21046 (301) 290-7710

Case/Datatel, Inc.   Cherry Hill Industrial Center, 55 Carnegie Pl. Cherry Hill, NJ 08003 (609) 424-4451

CCMI/McGraw-Hill   50 S. Franklin Tpk., Ramsey, NJ 07446 (201) 825-3311

CDA Industries South, Inc.   One CNN Center, Suite 370, Atlanta, GA 30303-2705 (404) 659-7608

Centigram   4415 Fortran Ct., San Jose, CA 95134 (408) 942-3500

Cermetek Microelectronics, Inc.   1308 Borregas Ave., Sunnyvale, CA 94088-3565 (408) 752-5000

Chipcom   195 Bear Hill Rd., Waltham, MA 02154 (617) 890-6844

Cinch   1501 Morse Ave., S., Grove Village, IL 60007 (312) 981-6010

Cisco Systems, Inc.   1350 Willow Rd., Menlo Park, CA 94025 (415) 326-1941

CMX Communications   1111 Industry Ave., Roanoke, VA 24013 (800) 345-2670

Coastcom   2312 Stanwell Dr., Concord, CA 94520 (415) 825-7500

Cobotyx Corporation.   20 Miry Brook Rd., Danbury, CT 06810-9825 (203) 748-0095

Code-A-Phone Corporation   16261 S.E. 130th Ave., Clackamas, OR 97015 (503) 655-8940

Codex Corporation.   7 Blue Hill River Rd., Canton, MA 02021-1097 (617) 364-2000

Coherent Communications Systems Corporation.   60 Commerce Dr., Hauppauge, NY 11788   (516) 231-1550

Coin-Op-Telecommunications   50-06 49th St., Woodside, NY 11377   (718) 937-6817

Colorado Video   Box 928, Boulder, CO 80306   (303) 530-9580

Com Dev   2150 Whitefield Industrial Way, Sarasota, FL 34243   (813) 753-6411

Comdial Corporation   1180 Seminole Trail, Charlottesville, VA 22906 (804) 978-2200

Commtex   1655 Crofton Blvd., Crofton, MD 21114   (301) 721-3666

Complete PC   521 Cottonwood Dr., Milpitas, CA 95035   (408) 434-0145

Compression Labs, Inc.   2860 Junction Ave., San Jose, CA 95134 (408) 435-3000

Compucom   333 N. Alabama St., Indianapolis, IN 46204 (317) 262-4666

CompuServe, Inc.   5000 Arlington Centre Blvd., Columbus, OH 43220   (614) 457-8600

Computer Pathways   19102 North Creek Pkwy., Bothell, WA 98011 (206) 487-1000

Comsat World Systems   950 L'Enfant Plaza S.W., Washington, D.C. 20024   (202) 863-6295

Comtech Systems, Inc.   3100 Communications Rd., St. Cloud, FL 32769   (407) 892-6111

Concord   9025 Wilshire Blvd., Suite 321, Beverly Hills, CA 90211 (213) 273-2993

Concord Data Systems, Inc.   45 Bartlett St., Marlborough, MA 01752   (617) 460-0808

Consultronics   160 Drumlin Circle, Concord, ON Canada L4K 3E5 (416) 738-3741

Contel ASC   1801 Research Blvd., Rockville, MD 20850   (301) 251-8481

Conveyant Systems   2332 McGaw Ave., Irvine, CA 92714   (714) 756-7100

Corning Glass Works, Telecommunications Products Division   Corning, NY 14831   (607) 974-7181

Corvus Systems, Inc.   2100 Corvus Dr., San Jose, CA 95124   (408) 281-4100

Crest Industries, Inc. 201 Frontage Rd. N., Suite B, Pacific, WA 98047 (206) 927-6922

Cross Comm Corporation. 133 E. Main St., Marlborough, MA 01752 (508) 481-4216

Crosspoint Systems, Inc. 1200 Charleston Rd., Mountain View, CA 94043 (415) 966-1911

Cryptall Communications Corporation. 1110 Wellington Ave., Cranston, RI 02910 (401) 941-7600

Crystal Technology, Inc. 1060 East Meadow Circle, Palo Alto, CA 94303 (415) 856-7911

CXC 2332 McGaw Ave., Irvine, CA 92714 (714) 756-7100

Cylink 110 S. Wolfe Rd., Sunnyvale, CA 94086 (408) 735-5800

Cylix 2637 Townsgate Rd., Suite 200, Westlake Village, CA 91361 (805) 379-3155

Dacon Electronic, Inc. 8 Industrial Ave., Upper Saddle River, NJ 07458 (201) 825-4640

Darome Teleconferencing Systems 8750 W. Bryn Mawr Ave., Suite 850, Chicago, IL 60631 (800) 327-6631

Data General Corporation 3400 Computer Dr., Westborough, MA 01580 (508) 898-4306

Data Race, Inc. 12758 Cimarron Path, Suite 108, San Antonio, TX 78249 (512) 692-3909

Data Switch Corporation One Enterprise Dr., Shelton, CT 06484 (203) 926-1801

Datagraf, Inc. 6101 W. Courtyard Dr., Bldg. 1. Austin, TX 78730 (512) 346-6866

Datapoint Corporation 9725 Datapoint Dr., San Antonio, TX 78284 (512) 699-7000

DataProducts New England, Inc. P.O. Box 30, Wallingford, CT 06492 (203) 265-7151

Datatel Inc. Bldg 55, Carnegie Plaza, Cherry Hill, NJ 08003 (609) 424-4451

Datec Inc. 200 Eastowne Dr., Suite 116, Chapel Hill, NC 27709 (919) 929-2135

David Systems 701 E. Evelyn Ave., Sunnyvale, CA 94086 (408) 720-6867

DCM 13666 E. 14th St., San Leandro, CA 94578 (415) 352-5330

Deka 416 Aldo Ave., Santa Clara, CA 95054 (408) 988-8629

Develcon Electronics, Inc.   6701 Sierra Ct., Dublin, CA 94568 (415) 829-6200

DiCon Fiberoptics   950-C Gilman St.. Berkeley, CA 94710 (415) 528-0427

Dictaphone Corporation   3191 Broadbridge Ave., Stratford, CT 06497-2559 (203) 381-7000

Digilog   1370 Welsh Rd., Montgomeryville, PA 18936 (215) 628-4530

Digital Communications Associates, Inc.   1000 Alderman Dr., Alpharetta, GA 30201 (404) 442-4000

Digital Equipment Corporation,   146 Maine St., Maynard, MA 01754 (508) 493-5111

Digital Link Corporation.   133 Caspian Ct., Sunnyvale, CA 94089 (408) 745-6200

Digital Microwave Co.   170 Rose Orchard Way, San Jose, CA 95134 (408) 943-0777

Digital Products   108 Water St., Watertown, MA 02172   (800) 243-2333

Digital Services   3261 S. Highland Ave., Suite 605 Las Vegas, NV 89109   (702) 735-9211

Digital Speech   1840 N Greenville, Suite 156, Dallas, TX 75081 (214) 235-2999

Digital Technology, Inc.   2300 Edwin C. Moses Blvd., Dayton, OH 45408 (800) 852-1252

Digitcom   405 S. Beverly Dr., Beverly Hills, CA 90212 (213) 277-1220

Digitech Industries, Inc.   66 Grove St., Ridgefield, CT 06877 (203) 438-3731

Dowty Information Systems   26 Springdale Rd., Bldg. 27, Cherry Hill, NJ 08003-9913 (800) 553-6989

DSC Communications Corp.   1000 Coit Rd., Plano, TX 75075 (214) 519-3000

Dukane   2900 Dukane Dr., St. Charles, IL 60174 (312) 584-2300

Durant Technologies   5627 W. Howard Ave., Niles, IL 60648 (312) 647-6707

Dynatech Communications   991 Annapolis Way, Woodbridge, VA 22191 (703) 550-0011

Dynatech Communication Systems   8500 Cinderbed Rd., Newington, VA 22122 (703) 550-0066

E Comms, Inc.   5720 144th St. N.W., Gig Harbor, WA 98335 (800) 247-1431

E.F. Johnson Company   299 Johnson Ave., Waseca, MN 56093 (507) 835-6222

Eagle Telephonics, Inc.   375 Oser Ave., Hauppauge, NY 11788 (516) 273-6700

Eastman Kodak Co.   343 State St., Rochester, NY 14650 (800) 445-6325

EFI Electronics   2415 S. 2300 W., Salt Lake City, UT 84119 (800) 221-1170

Elcotel, Inc.   6428 Parkland Dr., Sarasota, FL 34243 (813) 758-0389

Electrodata, Inc.   23020 Miles Rd., Bedford Heights, OH 44128 (216) 663-3333

Electronic Tele-Communications Inc.   1915 Macarthur Rd., Waukesha, WI 53188 (414) 542-5600

Eltrex   2 Columbia Dr., Amherst, NH 03031 (603) 886-3500

Enclosures, Inc.   7234 W. North Ave., Elmwood Park, IL 60635 (312) 456-7005

Energy Control Systems   500 E Loop 820 South 205, Fort Worth, TX 76119 (817) 483-8497

Ensign-Bickford Optics Co.   150 Fisher Dr., Avon, CT 06001 (203) 678-0371

Equatorial Communications Co.   300 Ferguson Dr., Mountain View, CA 04043 M (415) 969-9500

Equinox Systems, Inc.   14260 S.W. 119th Ave., Miami, FL 33186 (305) 255-3500

Ericsson Business Communications   715 N. Glenville, Richardson, TX 75044 (214) 997-0487

Ernest Telecom, Inc.   6475 Jimmy Carter Blvd., Norcross, GA (404) 448-7788

Excelan   2180 Fortune Dr., San Jose, CA 95131 (408) 434-2300

Executone Information Systems   6 Throndal Circle, Darien CT 06820 (203) 655-8500

Exide Corporation   645 Penn St., Reading, PA 19601 (215) 378-0500

Expert Systems   1010 Huntcliff, Suite 2235, Atlanta, GA 30350 (404) 642-7575

Fabrication Technologies of America, Inc.   2197 Canton Rd., Marietta, GA 30066 (404) 425-1837

Fairchild Data Corporation.   350 N. Hayden Rd., Scottsdale, AZ 85257-4692   (602) 949-1155

Farinon Division, Harris Corporation   1691 Bayport Ave., San Carlos, CA 94070 (415) 594-3000

Fibercom, Inc.   3353 Orange Ave. N.E., Roanaoke, VA 24012   (703) 342-6700

FiberLAN, Inc.   P.O. Box 12726, Research Triangle Park, NC 27709 (919) 549-4195

Fibermux Corporation.   9428 Eton Ave., Chatsworth, CA 91311 (818) 709-6000

Fibronics   Independence Park, Hyannis, MA 02601 (508) 778-0700

Fiskars   Newtown Rd., Box 1490, Littleton, MA 01460-4490 (508) 486-9551

Fluke Mfg. Co., Inc.   P.O. Box C9090, Everett, WA 98206 (206) 347-6100

Fortech, Inc.   W226 N825 Eastmound Dr., Waukesha, WI 53186 (414) 544-4300

Frederick Engineering Corporation.   10200 Old Columbia Rd., Columbia, MD 21046   (301) 290-9000

FTP Software, Inc.   26 Princess St., Wakefield, MA 01880-3004 (617) 246-0900

Fujitsu America, Inc.   3055 Orchard Dr., San Jose, CA 95134 (408)-432-1300

Fujitsu Business Communications   3190 Miraloma Ave., Anaheim, CA 92806 (714) 630-7721

Fujitsu Imaging Systems of America, Inc.   Corporate Dr., Commerce Park, Danbury, CT 06810 (203) 796-5400

Gabriel Electronics, Inc.   P.O. Box 70, Scarborough, ME 04704 (207) 883-5161

GAI-Tronics   5600 Oakbrook Pkwy., Suite 100, Norcross, GA 30093 (404) 446-6000

Galaxy Communications   141 W. 36th St., New York, NY 10018 (212) 967-7111

GammaLink, Inc.   2452 Embarcadero Way, Palo Alto, Ca 94303 (415) 856-7421

Gandalf Technologies, Inc.   1020 S. Noel Ave., Wheeling, IL 60090 (312) 541-6060

Gates Energy Products   P.O. Box 861, Gainesville, FL 32602 (904) 462-3911

Gateway Communications, Inc.   2941 Alton Ave., Irvine, CA 92714 (714) 553-1555

General Cable Co.   Communications Systems Div., 1748 Independence Blvd., Bldg. A, Sarasota, FL 33580 (813) 355-2757

General Cable Company   1 Woodbridge Center, Woodbridge, NJ 07095 (908) 636-5500

General Datacom, Inc.   1475 Straits Tpk., Middlebury, CT 06762-1299 (203) 574-1118

General Electric Mobile Communications Division   P.O. Box 4197, Lynchburg, VA 24502 (804) 528-7000

General Instrument   2200 Bayberry Rd., Hatboro, PA 19040 (215) 674-4800

General Semiconductor   2001 W. 10th Pl., Tempe, AZ 85281 (602) 986-3101

Genesis Electronics   3078 Prospect Park Dr., Rancho Cordoba, CA 95670 (916) 638-7575

Glenayre Electronics   12 Pacific Hwy. Blaine, WA 98230 (206) 676-1980

Gordon Kapes   5520 W. Touhy Ave., Skokie, IL 60077 (312) 676-1750

Gould Inc. Fiber Optics Operation   6730 Baymeadow Dr., Suite D, Glen Burnie, MD 21061 (301) 787-8300

GPT Video Systems   737 Canal St., Building 35A, Stamford, CT 06902 (203) 348-6600

Granger-Teleratta   2940 N. First St., San Jose, CA 95134 (408) 954-5097

Grass Valley Group, Inc.   P.O. Box 1114, Grass Valley, CA 95945 (916) 478-3000

GTE Communication Systems   2500 W. Utopia Rd., Phoenix, AZ 85027 (602) 582-7000

GTE Fiber Optic Products   2401 Reach Rd., Williamsport, PA 17701 (717) 326-6591

GTE Spacenet   1700 Old Meadow Rd., McLean, VA 22102 (703) 848-1000

Hard Engineering Inc. Test Equipment Division   3005 L&N Dr., Huntsville, AL 35801 (205) 533-2663

Harris Corporation, RF Communications Group   1680 University Ave., Rochester, NY 14610 (716) 244-5830

Harris Telephone Systems   300 Bel Martin Keys Blvd., Novato, CA 94949 (415) 382-5000

Harris/3M   2300 Parklake Dr. N.E., Atlanta, GA 30345-2979   (404) 496-9500

Harris/Dracon.   1809 Calle Plano, Camarillo, CA 93010   (805) 987-9511

Harris/Lanier   1700 Chantilly Dr. N.E., Atlanta, GA 30324   (404) 329-8000

Hayes Microcomputer Products, Inc.   P.O. Box 105203, Atlanta, GA 30348   (404) 449-8791

Hekimian Laboratories, Inc.   9298 Gaither Rd., Gaithersburg, MD 20877   (301) 590-3600

Hewlett-Packard Co.   1501 Page Mill Rd., Palo Alto, CA 94304 (415) 493-1501

Hewlett-Packard Roseville Networks Division   8000 Foothills Blvd., Roseville, CA 95678   (408) 407-2180

Hitachi America, Telecommunications Research and Sales Division   2990 Gateway Dr., Suite 1000, Norcross, GA 30071   (404) 446-8820

Hubbell, Pulsecom Division   2900 Towerview Rd., Herndon, VA 22071 (703) 471-2900

Hughes Network Systems   11717 Exploration Lane, Germantown, MD 20874 (301) 428-5500

Hybrid Fax, Inc.   1733 Woodside Rd., Redwood City, CA 94061 (415) 369-0600

IBM Corporation   Old Orchard Rd., Armonk, NY 10504   (914) 765-1900

Idacom Electronics, Inc.   17972 Skypark Circle E, Irvine, CA 92714 (714) 261-7663

Industrial Technology, Inc.   P.O. Box 190, Mineral Wells, TX 76067 (817) 325-9461

Infortext Systems   1067 E. State Pkwy. Schaumburg, IL 60173 (312) 490-1155

Infotron Systems Corporation   Cherry Hill Industrial Center, #9, Cherry Hill, NJ 08003-1688   (609) 424-9400

Innings Telecom   251 Bartley Dr., Toronto, ON Canada (416) 757-3251

Innovative Technology   1000 Holcomb Woods Pkwy., Suite 422, Roswell, GA 30076   (404) 998-9970

Intecom, Inc.   601 Intecom Dr., Allen TX 75002   (214) 727-9141

Integrated Network Corporation.   757 Route 202, Bridgewater, NJ 08807   (908) 218-1600

Intel Personal Computer Enhanced Operations   5200 N.E. Elam Young Pkwy., CO3-7, Hillsboro, OR 97214-6497 (503) 629-7354

Intellicall, Inc.   2155 Chenault, Suite 410, Carrollton, TX 75006-5023   (214) 416-0022

Inter-Tel   6505 W. Chandler Blvd., Chandler, AZ 85226 (602) 961-9000

Interalia   6277 Bury Dr., Eden Prarie, MN 55346 (612) 934-7766

Interlan, Inc.   155 Swanson Rd., Boxborough, MA 01719 (508) 263-9929

Intraplex, Inc.   P.O. Box 2427, Littleton, MA 01460 (508) 486-3722

IRC   Greenway Rd., Boone, NC 28607 (704) 264-8861

ITT Communications Services, Inc.   100 Plaza Dr., Secaucus, NJ 07096 (201) 330-5000

Iwatsu America   430 Commerce Blvd., Carlstadt, NJ 07072   (201) 935-8580

Jerrold Communications   2200 Bayberry Rd. Hatboro, PA 19040 (215) 674-4800

JM Industries, Inc.   6300 Midvale, Houston, TX 77087   (713) 643-2992

Johnson, E.F. Co.   11095 Viking Dr., Suite 220, Eden Prairie, MN 55459 (612) 942-1000

Joslyn Electronic Systems   Box 817, Goleta, CA 93116 (805) 968-3551

Kanda Telecom   1807 Braker Lane, Austin, TX 78758 (512) 834-8711

Kaptron, Inc.   2525 E. Bayshore Rd., Palo Alto, CA 94303 (415) 493-8008

Keptel   56 Park Rd., Tinton Falls, NJ 07724 (908) 389-8800

Konica Business Machines USA, Inc.   500 Day Hill Rd., Windsor, CT 06095 (203) 683-2222

Lanex Corporation.   10727 Tucker St., Beltsville, MD 20705 (301) 595-4700

Lanier Voice Products   1700 Chantilly Dr. N.E., Atlanta, GA 30324 (404) 329-8000

Larus Corporation.   848-3 E. Gish Rd., San Jose, CA 95112 (408) 275-9505

Laser Precision Corporation.   1231 Hart St., Utica NY 13502 (315) 797-4449

LDC Inc. Fiber Optics Communications   4971 Antioch Loop, Union City, CA 94587 (415) 471-4811

Lear Siegler, Inc. Telecommunications Division   714 N. Brookhurst St., Anaheim, CA 92803 (714) 774-1010

Leviton Telecom   2222 222nd St. S.E., Bothell, WA 98021 (206) 486-2222

Licom   200 Fairbrook Dr., Herndon, VA 22070 (703) 689-0500

Light Communications Corporation   25 Van Zant St., New Canaan, CT 06855 (203) 866-6858

Light Control Systems, Inc.   2 Bridgeview Circle, Tyngsboro, MA 01879 (508) 649-9870

Link Technologies, Inc.   47339 Warm Springs Blvd., Fremont, CA 94539 (415) 651-8000

Lorain Products   1122 F St., Lorain OH 44052   (216) 288-1122

Loral Terracom Corporation.   9020 Balboa Ave., San Diego, CA 92123 (619) 278-4100

LorTec Power Systems, Inc.   145 Keep Ct., Elyria, OH 44035 (216) 327-5050

Lytel, Inc.   61 Chubb Way, Somerville, NJ 08876 (908) 685-1282

M/A-COM Land Mobile Communications, Inc.   21 Continental Blvd., Merrimack, NH 03054 (603) 424-3400

M/A-COM MAC, Inc.   5 Omni Way, Chelmsford, MA 01824 (617) 272-3100

MacKenzie Laboratories   5507 Peck Rd., Arcadia, CA 91006 (818) 579-0440

MacroTel International   3540 N.W. 56th St., Ft. Lauderdale, FL 33309 (305) 484-4000

Marconi Instruments, Inc.   3 Pearl Ct., Allendale, NJ 07401 (201) 934-9050

Marubeni America   200 Park Ave., New York, NY 10166   (212) 599-7146

McDonnell-Douglas   5299 DTC Blvd., Suite 1400, Englewood, CO 80111 (303) 220-6000

MCI Communications Corporation   1133 19th St. N.W., Washington, DC 20036 (202) 872-1600

MCI International   2 International Dr., Rye Brook, NY 10573 (914) 934-6324

Meridian Networx   14044 Ventura Blvd. Suite 303, Sherman Oaks, CA 91423 (818) 501-7410

Metro Tel   490 Gianni St., Santa Clara, CA 95054 (408) 988-5200

MetroTel Corporation.   485-13 S. Broadway, Hicksville, NY 11801 (516) 937-3420

Miami Voice   5215 N.W. 74th Ave., Miami, FL 33166 (305) 593-6077

Micom Systems, Inc.   4100 Los Angeles Ave., Simi Valley, CA 93063 (805) 583-8600

Microcom   500 River Ridge Dr., Norwood, MA 02062 (617) 551-1000

Microlog   20270 Goldenrod Lane, Germantown, MD 20874 (301) 428-3227

Microscience   8601 Dunwoody Pl., Atlanta, GA 30350   (404) 998-6551

Microtek Lab, Inc.   680 Knox St., Torrance, CA 90502 (213) 321-2121

Microtel Ltd.   2100-401 W. Georgia St., Vancouver, BC V6B 5C8 Canada   (604) 683-3575

Microtest   3519 E. Shea Blvd., Phoenix, AZ 85028 (800) 526-9675

Microwave Networks Corporation.   10795 Rockley Rd., Houston, TX (713) 495-7123

Miltimil   670 International Pkwy., Suite 190, Richardson, TX 75081 (214) 644-7724

Mita   777 Terrace Ave., Hasbrouck Heights, NJ 07604 (201) 288-6900

Mitel Datacom, Inc.   13873 Park Center Rd., Herndon, VA 22071 (703) 471-1000

Mitel, Inc.   5400 Broken Sound Blvd. N.W., Boca Raton, FL 33487 (407) 994-8500

Mitsubishi   5757 Plaza Dr., Cyprus, CA 90630-0007 (714) 220-2500

MOD-TAP System   285 Ayer Rd., Harvard, MA 01451 (508) 772-5630

Modular Systems, Inc.   169 W. Park St., Fruitport, MI 49415 (616) 865-3167

Montrose Products Co.   Auburn Industrial Park, Auburn, MA 01501 (508) 793-9862

Moscom   300 Main St., East Rochester, NY 14445 (716) 385-6440

Motorola Communications & Electronics, Inc.   1301 E. Algonquin Rd., Schaumburg, IL 60196 (312) 576-6602

MPSI   8848 Red Oak Blvd., Charlotte, NC 28217 (704) 527-8888

Multitech Systems   82 Second Ave. S.E., New Brighton, MN 55112 (612-631-3550

Murata Business Systems, Inc.   4801 Spring Valley Rd., 108B, Dallas, TX 75244 (214) 392-1622

Navtel, Inc.   55 Renfrew Dr., Markham, ON L3R 8H3 Canada (416) 479-8090

NEC America Inc. Switching Systems Division   1525 Walnut Hill Lane, Irving, TX 75038 (214) 580-9100

NEC America Inc., Radio & Transmission Systems Group   14040 Park Center Rd., Herndon, VA 22071 (703) 834-4000

NEC America, Inc. PBX Division   8 Old Sod Farm Rd., Melville, NY 11747 (516) 753-7000

NEC Information Systems   1414 Massachussetts Ave., Boxborough, MA 01719 (508) 264-8000

Netcom Technologies, Inc.   200 Girard St., Suite 201, Gaithersburg, MD 20877 (301) 670-0486

Network Equipment Technologies, Inc.   800 Saginaw Dr., Redwood City, CA 94063 (415) 366-4400

Network General   1945A Charleston Rd., Mountain View, CA 94043 (800) 952-6300

NetWorth, Inc.   8101 Ridgepoint Dr., Suite 107, Irving, TX 75063 (214) 869-1331

Nevada Western   615 N Tasman Dr., Sunnyvale, CA 94089 (408) 734-2700

Newbridge Networks   13873 Park Center Rd., Herndon, VA 22071 (703) 834-3600

Newton Instrument Co., Inc.   111 East A St., Butner, NC 27509 (919) 575-6426

Northeast Electronics Division of Tau-Tron   57 Regional Dr., Concord, NH 03302 (603) 228-3700

Northern Telecom, Inc.   200 Athens Way, Nashville, TN 37228-1803 (615) 734-4000

Northern Telcom Inc., Integrated Carrier Systems Divisiom   1201 E. Arapaho Rd., Richardson, TX 75081 (214) 234-7500

Northern Telecom Cook Division   6201 Oakton St., Morton Grove, IL 60053 (708) 967-6600

Novell, Inc.   122 E 1700 S, Orem, UT 84606 (801) 379-5900

OAZ Communications, Inc.   1362 Bordeaux Dr., Sunnyvale, CA 94089 (408) 745-1750

Octel Communications   890 Tasman Dr., Milpitas, CA 95035
(408) 942-6500

OFTI   5 Fortune Dr., Billerica, MA 01821-9919 (508) 663-6629

Oki Telecom Div.   2208 Rt. 208, Fair Lawn, NJ 07410 (908) 654-1414

Olivetti USA   765 US Highway 202, Somerville, NJ 08876-1289
(908) 526-8200

Ominfax/Telautograph   8700 Bellenca Ave., Los Angeles, CA 90045
(213) 641-3690

Omniphone   P.O. Box 8739, Mobile, AL 36689   (205) 666-6333

Omnivoice   280 N. Park Ave., Suite 108, Warren, OH 44482   (216)
393-3246

Optical Data Systems   1226 Exchange Dr., Richardson, TX 75081-9990 (214) 234-6400

Optilink   1310 Redwood Way, Petaluma, CA 94975 (707) 795-9444

Opto-Electronics, Inc.   775 Main St., Buffalo, NY 14202   (716) 856-1322

OST   14225-F Sullyfield Circle, Chantilly, VA 22021 (703) 817-0400

Pacific Image Communications, Inc.   1111 S. Arroyo Pkwy., #420,
Pasadena, CA 91105 (818) 441-0104

Pacific Netcom, Inc.   8835 S.W. Canyon Lane, #307, Portland, OR
97225 (503) 297-6945

Panafax Corporation   10 Melville Park Rd., Melville, NY 11747
(516) 420-0250

Panasonic Co. Telephone Products Division   1 Panasonic Way
Secaucus, NJ 07095 (201) 348-7000

Panduit   17301 Ridgeland Ave., Tinley Park, IL 60477   (312) 532-1800

Para Systems, Inc.   1455 LeMay Dr., Carollton, TX 75007   (214)
238-7272

PCO Inc.   20200 Sunburst St., Chatsworth, CA 91311   (818) 700-1233

Pennil Corp.   1300 Quince Orchard Blvd., Gaithersburg, MD
20878   (301) 417-0552

Performance Technology, Inc.   7800 IH-10 W., San Antonio, TX
78230 (512) 349-2000

Perimeter Technology   102 Perimeter Rd., Nashua, NH 03063
(603) 882-2900

Phillips & Brooks, Inc.   1485 Redi Rd., Cumming, GA 30130   (404) 887-9901

Phoenix Microsystems, Inc.   991 Discovery Dr., Huntsville, AL 35806   (205) 826-6798

Photon Kinetics   9350 S.W. Gemini Dr., Beaverton, OR 97005   (503) 644-1960

Pitney Bowes Facsimile Systems   Walker Wheeler Dr., Stamford, CT 06926   (203) 356-5000

Plantronics   P.O. Box 635, Santa Cruz, CA 95060   (408) 426-5858

Porta Systems Corporation.   575 Underhill Blvd., Syosset, NY 11791   (516) 364-9300

Power Battery   543-53 E. 42nd St., Paterson, NJ 07513   (201) 523-8630

Power Conversion Products, Inc.   42 East St., Crystal Lake, IL 60014   (815) 459-9100

Power Technology, Inc.   Box 9769, Little Rock, AR 72219   (501) 568-1995

Precision Components   1110 W. National Ave., Addison, IL 60101   (312) 543-6400

Preformed Line Products Company   P.O. Box 91129, Cleveland, OH 44101   (216) 461-5200

Prentice Corporation.   1972 Concourse, San Jose, CA 95131   (408) 432-1515

Proctor & Associates Co., Inc.   15050 N.E. 36th, Redmond, WA 98052   (206) 881-7000

Proteon   Two Technology Dr., Westborough, MA 01581   (508) 898-2100

Pulsecom Division, Harvey Hubbell, Inc.   2900 Towerview Rd., Herndon, VA 22071   (703) 471-2900

Quadram Corporation.   One Mecca Way, Norcross, GA 30093   (404) 923-6666

Quality Industries   130 Jones Blvd., LaVergne, TN 37086-0250   (615) 793-3000

Quasitronics   211 Vandale Dr., Houston, PA 15342   (412) 745-2663

Racal-Vadic   1525 McCarthy Blvd., Milpitas, CA 95035   (408) 432-8008

Racom   5504 State Rd., Cleveland, OH 44134   (216) 351-1755

Racon   12628 Interurban Ave., Seattle, WA 98168   (800) 426-5245

RAD Data Communications, Inc.   151 W. Passaic St., Rochelle Park, NJ 07662   (201) 587-8822

Rainbow Communications   1219 Abrams, Suite 117, Richardson, TX 75081   (214) 690-6264

Raycom Systems, Inc.   6395 Gunpark Dr., Boulder, CO 80301 (303) 530-1620

RCA American Communications   4 Research Way, Princeton, NJ 08540   (609) 734-4000

Redcom Laboratories   1 Redcom Center, Victor, NY 14564   (716) 924-7550

Reliable Electric   11333 Addison St., Franklin Park, IL 60131   (312) 451-5549

Reliance Comm/Tec Lorain Products   1122 F. St., Lorain, OH 44052-2293   (216) 226-1122

Reliance Comm/Tec R-Tec Systems   2100 Reliance Pkwy., Bedford, TX 76021   (817) 267-3141

Reliance Comm/Tec Reliable Electric/Utility Products   11333 Addison St., Franklin Park, IL 60131   (312) 455-8010

Retix   2644 30th St., Santa Monica, CA 90405-3009   (213) 399-2200

Ricoh Corporation.   5 Didrick Pl., West Caldwell, NJ 07006   (201) 882-2000

Rockwell International Corporation.   P.O. Box 568842, Dallas, TX 75356-8842   (214) 996-5000

Rockwell International Corporation. Switching Systems Division   1431 Opus Pl., Downers Grove, IL 60515   (312) 960-8000

Rolm Corporation   4900 Old Ironsides Dr., Santa Clara, CA 95050 (408) 986-1000

Sage Instruments   240 Airport Blvd., Freedom, CA 95019-9986 (408) 761-1000

San/Bar Corporation   201 Technology Dr., Irvine, CA 92718   (714) 727-1911

Sanyo Business Systems Corporation.   51 Joseph St., Moonachie, NJ 07074   (201) 440-9300

Satellite Business Systems   8283 Greensboro Dr., McLean, VA 22102   (703) 442-5000

Satellite Transmission Systems, Inc.   125 Kennedy Dr., Hauppauge, NY 11788   (516) 231-1919

Scientific Atlanta, Inc.   4One Technology Parkway, Atlanta, GA 30348 (404) 441-4000

SDI   375 Franklin Rd., Suite 460, Marietta, GA 30214   (404) 423-9485

Seiscor Inc.   P.O. Box 470580, Tulsa, OK 74147-0580   (918) 252-1578

Sharp Electronics   Sharp Plaza, Mahwah NJ 07430   (201) 529-9500

Shure Teleconferencing Systems   222 Hartrey Ave., Evanston, IL 60204   (312) 866-2400

Siecor Corporation   489 Siecor Pk., Hickory, NC 28603   (704) 327-5000

Siecor Corporation Electro Optic Products   P.O. Box 13625, Research Triangle Park, NC 27709   (800) 888-5261

Siemens Information Systems   5500 Broken Sound Blvd., Boca Raton, FL 33487   (407) 994-8800

Siemens Transmission Systems   8620 N. 22nd Ave., Phoenix, AZ 85021   (602) 395-5000

Sierra Transmission Products   970 McLaughlin Ave., San Jose, CA 95122-2696   (408) 292-4025

SNC Manufacturing Co., Inc.   101 Waukau Ave., Oshkosh, WI 54901   (414) 231-7370

Soft-Com, Inc.   140 W. 22nd St., New York, NY 10011   (212) 242-9595

Sola Electric   1717 Busse Rd., Oak Grove Village, IL 60007   (312) 439-2800

Solitare   2100 Roswell, Suite 200C, Marietta, GA 30062   (404) 971-4811

Sony Corporation Videoconferencing and Satellite Systems Division   Sony Dr., Park Ridge, NJ 07656   (201) 930-7829

Southwestern Bell   7486 Shadeland Station Way, Indianapolis, IN 46256   (317) 841-8006

SpectraFAX Corporation.   209 S. Airport Rd., Naples, FL 33942   (813) 643-5070

Spider Systems, Inc.   12 New England Executive Park, Burlington, MA 01803   (617) 270-3510

SRX   17919 Waterview Pkwy., Dallas, TX 75252   (214) 907-6700

Startel   17661 Cowan Ave., Irvine, CA 92714   (714) 863-8700

STC Telecom   450 Fairway Dr., Suite 107, Deerfield Beach, FL 33441   (305) 426-4100

StrataCom, Inc.   3175 Winchester Blvd., Campbell, CA 95008   (408) 370-2333

Stromberg Carlson Corporation.   400 Rinehart Rd., Lake Mary, FL 32746   (407) 333-5000

Sumitomo Electric Fiber Optics Corporation. 78 Alexander Dr., Research Triangle Park, NC 27709 (919) 541-8100

Summa Four One Sundial Ave., Manchester, NH 03103 (603) 624-4424

Sun MicroSystems, Inc. 2550 Garcia Ave., Mountain View, CA 94043 (415) 960-1300

Superior Electric 383 Middle St., Bristol, CT 06010 (203) 582-9561

Superior Optics 1349 Old 41 Hwy., Marietta, GA 30060

Suttle Apparatus 223 S. Main. Hector, MN 55342 (612) 848-6711

Sykes Datatronics, Inc. 375 Orchard St., Rochester, NY 14606 (716) 647-8000

SynOptics Communications, Inc. 501 E. Middlefield Rd., Mountain View, CA 94043-4015 (800) 872-8023

Systron-Donner Corporation. 2700 Systron Dr., Concord, CA 94518 (415) 671-6400

Sytek, Inc. 1225 Charleston Rd., Mountain View, CA 94043 (415) 966-7333

3Com 3165 Kifer Rd., Santa Clara, CA 95052 (408) 562-6400

3M Company, Business Communication Products Division 3M Center, St. Paul, MN 55101 (612) 733-1110

3M Fiber Optic Products, Inc. 10 Industrial Way E., Eatontown, NJ 07724 (908) 544-0938

T-Com Corporation 805 E. Middlefield Rd., Mountain View, CA 94043 (415) 964-3415

Tadiran Electronic Industries 5733 Myerlane Circle, Clearwater, FL 34620 (813) 535-3506

Talking Technology 4383 Piedmont Ave., Suite B, Oakland, CA 94611 (415) 652-9600

Tatung Telecom 599A Fairchild Dr., Mountain View, CA 94043 (415) 961-6193

Tau-Tron, Inc. 10 Liberty Way, Westford, MA 01886 (603) 228-3700

TDS 17993 Cowan, Irvine, CA 92714 (800) 634-8513

Teac America, Inc. 7733 Telegraph Rd., Montebello, CA 90640 (213) 726-0303

Tecom Northwest 17624 15th Ave. S.E., Suite 109A, Bothell, WA 98012 (206) 485-1624

Tekelec 26580 W. Agoura Rd., Calabasas, CA 91302 (818) 880-5656

Teknekron Infoswitch 4401 Cambridge Rd., Fort Worth, TX 76155 (800) 992-6119

Tekno Industries, Inc.   795 Eagle Dr., Bensenville, IL 60106   (312) 766-6960

Tektronix, Inc.   P.O. Box 500, Beaverton, OR 97077   (503) 627-7111

Tel Electronics   705 E. Main St., American Fork, UT 84003   (801) 756-9606

Telautograph/Omnifax   8700 Bellanca Ave., Los Angeles, CA 90045 (213) 641-3690

Telco Research   1207 17th Ave. S., Nashville, TN 37212   (615) 329-0031

Telco Systems Fiber Optics Corporation.   63 Nahatan St., Norwood, MA 02062   (800) 447-2537

Telco Systems Network Access Corporation.   48430 Milmont Dr., Fremont, CA 94537   (800) 227-0937

Telcom Technologies   981 Corporate Center Dr., Pomona, CA 91768 (714) 620-7711

Tele-Source Corporation.   2600 Laskey Rd., Toledo, OH 43613 (419) 472-8353

Telebit Corporation.   1315 Chesapeake Terrace, Sunnyvale, CA 94089   (408) 734-4333

Telebyte Technology, Inc.   270 E. Pulaski Rd., Greenlawn, NY 11740   (516) 423-3232

Telecom Solutions   85 W. Tasman Dr., San Jose, CA 95134-1703 (408) 433-0910

Telecom USA   500 2nd Ave. S.E., Cedar Rapids, IA 52401   (319) 366-6600

Telecommunications Software   93 Centre Pointe Dr., St. Charles, MO 63303   (314) 441-6100

Telecommunications Techniques Corporation.   20410 Observation Dr., Germantown, MD 20874   (301) 353-1550

Telecommunications Technologies   761 Corporate Center Dr., Pomona, CA 91768   (714) 620-7711

Telecorp Products   20830 Rutland Dr., Suite 106, Southfield, MI 48075   (313) 569-7100

Teledex   25 E. Trimble Rd., Suite 200, San Jose, CA 95131   (408) 432-3100

Teledial Devices   125 Schmidtt Blvd., Farmingdale, NY 11735 (516) 293-8400

Telemon   5648 W. 73rd St., Indianapolis, IN 46278   (317) 298-6440

Telenet Communications Corporation   12490 Sunrise Valley Dr., Reston, VA 22096 (703) 689-6000

Telenetics 5109 E. La Palma Ave., Anaheim, CA 92808 (800) 826-6336

Telenex Corporation 13000 Midatlantic Dr., Mt. Laurel, NJ 08054 (609) 234-7900

Teleos Communications, Inc. 2 Meridian Rd., Eatontown, NJ 07724 (908) 389-5700

TeleProcessing Products, Inc. 4565 E. Industrial St., Bldg. 7K, Simi Valley, CA 93063 (805) 522-8147

Telerad 135 Crossways Park Dr., Woodbury, NY 11790 (516) 921-8300

Telescan 10679 Midwest Ind. Blvd., St. Louis, MO 63132 (314) 426-7662

Telesciences Transmission Systems 48761 Kato Rd., Fremont, CA 94538 (415) 651-0300

Telesciences, Inc. 351 New Albany Rd., Moorestown, NJ 08057-1177 (609) 866-1000

TeleVideo Systems, Inc. 550 E. Brokaw Rd., San Jose, CA 95161-9048 (408) 954-8333

TelFab, Inc. P.O. Box 388, Willoughby, OH 44094 (216) 442-0059

Telindus, Inc. 330 E. 58th St., New York, NY 10157 (212) 682-2595

Tellabs Inc. 4951 Indiana Ave., Lisle, IL 60532 (312) 969-8800

Telrad 135 Crossways Park Dr., Woodbury, NY 11797 (516) 921-8300

Teltone Corporation 10801 120th N.E., Kirkland, WA 98033 (206) 827-9626

Teradyne, Inc. Telecommunications Division 1405 Lake Cook Rd., Deerfield, IL 60015 (312) 940-9059

Thomas-Conrad Corporation 1908-R Kramer Lane, Austin, TX 78758 (800) 332-8683

Thomas & Betts 1001 Frontier Rd., Bridgewater, NJ 08807 (908) 685-1600

TIE/communications, Inc. 4 Progress Ave., Seymour, CT 06483 (203) 888-8000

TII Industries 1385 Akron St., Copiague, NY 11726 (516) 789-5000

Timeplex Inc. 400 Chestnut Ridge Rd., Woodcliff Lake, NJ 07675 (201) 930-4600

Times Fiber Communications, Inc. P.O. Box 384, Wallingford, CT 06492 (203) 265-8500

Tone Commander Systems, Inc.   4320 150th N.E., Redmond, WA 98052 (206) 883-3600

Toshiba America   9740 Irvine Blvd., Irvine, CA 92718 (714) 583-3700

Transaction Recording Systems   13865 N.W. Cornell Rd., Portland, OR 97229 (503) 646-5321

Tri-Data Systems, Inc.   1450 Kifer Rd., Sunnyvale, CA 94086-9707 (408) 746-2900

Triplett Corporation   One Triplett Dr., Buffton, OH 45817 (419) 358-5015

TRW Information Networks   23800 Hawthorne Blvd., Torrance, CA 90505 (213) 373-9161

Ungermann Bass Inc.   3900 Freedom Circle, Santa Clara, CA 95054-8030 (408) 496-0111

Uniden   15161 Triton Lane, Huntington Beach, CA 92649 (714) 898-0576

Unisys   P.O. Box 500, Blue Bell, PA 19424 (215) 542-4011

Universal Data Systems Inc.   5000 Bradford Dr., Huntsville, AL 35805 (205) 721-8000

US Fiber Optics, Inc.   96 Inverness Dr. E., Suite J, Englewood, CO 80112 (303) 790-2821

US Takachiho Corporation.   10722 Los Vaqueros Circle, Los Alamitos, CA 90720 (714) 761-3844

US Telecommunications   3118 62nd Ave. N., St. Petersburg, FL 33702 (813) 527-1107

US Teletron, Inc.   19255 San Jose Ave., City of Industry, CA 91748 (818) 810-8610

US Robotics   8100 McCormick Blvd., Skokie, IL 60076 (312) 982-5001

Verilink Corporation   145 Baytech Dr., San Jose, CA 95134 (408) 945-1199

Videoconferencing Systems, Inc.   5801 Goshen Springs Rd., Norcross, GA 30071 (404) 242-7566

VideoTelecom Corporation   1908 Kramer Lane, Austin, TX 78758 (512) 834-9734

Viking Electronics   1531 Industrial St., Hudson, WI 54016 (715) 386-8861

Vitalink Communications   6607 Kaiser Dr., Fremont, CA 94555 (415) 794-1100

VMX   110 Rose Orchard Way, San Jose, CA 94134 (408) 943-0878

Vodavi Communications Systems   8300 E. Rainbow Dr., Scottsdale, AZ 85260 (602) 948-5470

Voicemail International   2953 Bunker Hill Lane, Suite 110, Santa Clara, CA 95054 (408) 980-4000

Wandel & Goltermann, Inc.   1030 Swabia Ct., Research Triangle Park, NC 27709 (919) 941-5730

Wang Laboratories, Inc.   One Industrial Ave., Lowell, MA 01857 (617) 459-5000

Wellfleet Communications, Inc.   12 DeAngelo, Bedford, MA 01730-2204 (617) 275-2400

Wescom, Telephone Products Division   Rockwell Telecommunications, Inc. 8245 S. Lemont Rd., Downers Grove, IL 60515 (312) 985-9000

Western Digital   2445 McCabe Way, Irvine, CA 92714   (800) 638-5323

Western Telematic   5 Sterling St., Irvine, CA 92718   (714) 586-9950

Western Union Telegraph Co.   1 Lake St., Upper Saddle River, NJ 07458 (201) 825-5000

Westinghouse Communications   5 Westinghouse Building/Gateway, Pittsburgh, PA 15222 (412) 244-2000

Wilcom   P.O. Box 508, Laconia, NH 03247 (800) 528-3804

Williams Telecommunications Group   One Williams Center, Tulsa, OK 74121 (800) 642-2299

Wiltron Company,   490 Jarvis Dr., Morgan Hill, CA 95037-2809 (408) 778-2000

WIN Communications   200 Oser Ave., Hauppauge, NY 11788 (516) 435-1100

Wyse Technology   3571 N. First St., San Jose, CA 95134 (408) 433-1000

Xerox Corporation Information Products Division   1201 Ridgeview Dr., Lewisville, TX 75067 (214) 412-7200

Xerox Imaging Systems DataCopy Products   1215 Terra Bella Ave., Mountain View, CA 94043 (415) 965-7900

Xiox   577 Airport Blvd., Suite 700, Burlingame, CA 94010   (415) 375-8188

Xtend   171 Madison Ave., New York, NY 10016   (212) 725-2010

Zenith Electronics Corporation.   1000 Milwaukee Ave., Glenview, IL 60025 (312) 391-8000

D

Sources of Technical Information

Standards Information

American National Standards Institute

ANSI standards and ANSI's Catalog of American National Standards can be ordered from:

> American National Standards Institute
> 1430 Broadway
> New York, NY 10018
> (212) 642-4900

Electronic Industries Association

EIA standards and their publication Catalog of EIA and JEDC Standards and Engineering Publications are available from:

> Electronic Industries Association
> 1722 Eye St., N.W.
> Washington, D. C. 20006
> (202) 457-4966

Institute of Electrical and Electronic Engineers

IEEE standards are available from:

> IEEE Computer Society
> Suite 608
> 111 19th St, N. W.

Washington, D. C. 20036
(202) 785-0017

International Organization for Standardization

ISO standards are available from:

Central Secretariat
Case postale 56
CH-1211 Geneva 20, Switzerland
(022) 34 12 40

or

American National Standards Institute
1430 Broadway
New York, NY 10018
(212) 457-4966

International Radio Consultative Committee

CCIR standards are available from:

General Secretariat
International Telecommunications Union
Place de Nations
1211 Geneva 20, Switzerland

or

United Nations Bookstore
Room 32B
U. N. General Assembly Building
New York, NY 10017

International Telephone and Telegraph Consultative Committee

CCITT standards are available from:

General Secretariat
International Telecommunications Union
Place de Nations
1211 Geneva 20, Switzerland
or

United Nations Bookstore
Room 32B
U. N. General Assembly Building
New York, NY 10017

Technical Information

Bell Communications Research

Bell Communications Research publications and its Catalog of Technical Information listing publications of Bellcore and the seven operating telephone regions are available from:

Bell Communications Research, Inc.
Information Exchange Management
445 South St., P.O. Box 1910
Morristown, NJ 07960-1910
(201) 699-5800

Trade Publications

BCR Handbook of Telecommunications Management BCR Enterprises, Inc., 950 York Rd., Hinsdale, IL 60521 (312) 986-1432

Bellcore Digest of Technical Information Bellcore, 445 South St., P.O. Box 1910, Morristown, NJ 07960-1910

BOC Week Suite 444, 1101 King St., Alexandria, VA 22314 (703) 683-4100

Cellular Business P.O. Box 12901, Overland Park, KS 66212-0930 (913) 888-4664

Common Carrier Week 1836 Jefferson Pl. N.W., Washington, DC 20036 (202) 872-9200

Communications Daily 1836 Jefferson Pl. N.W., Washington, DC 20036 (202) 872-9200

Communications News Harcourt Brace Jovanovich, 124 S.W. First St., Geneva, IL 60134 (312) 232-1401

Communications Week CMP Publications, Inc., 600 Community Dr., Manhasset, NY 11030 (516) 365-4600

Data Communications McGraw-Hill, Inc. 1221 Avenue of the Americas, New York, NY 10020 (212) 512-2000

FCC Week Suite 444, 1101 King St., Alexandria, VA 22314 (703) 683-4100

IEEE Network IEEE Publishing Services 345 E. 47th St., New York, NY 10017-2394 (212) 705-7018

IEEE Communications IEEE Publishing Services, 345 E. 47th St., New York, NY 10017-2394 (212) 705-7018

International Communications Week Suite 444, 1101 King St., Alexandria, VA 22314 (703) 683-4100

ISDN Strategies 950 York Rd., Hinsdale, IL 60521 (312) 986-1432

LAN: The Local Area Network Magazine 12 West 21 St., New York, NY 10010 (212) 206-6660

Lightwave 235 Bear Hill Rd., Waltham, MA 02154 (617) 890-2700

Mobile Communications Business P.O. Box 2000-141, Mission Viejo, CA 92690 (714) 859-5502

Network World Box 9171 375, Cocituate Rd., Framingham, MA 01701-9171 (617) 879-0700

Pay Phone News P.O. Box 1218, McLean, VA 22101 (703) 734-7050

Report on AT&T Suite 444, 1101 King St., Alexandria, VA 22314 (703) 683-4100

Satellite Communications Cardiff Publishing Co., 6300 S. Syracuse Way, Suite 650, Englewood, CO 80111

Satellite Week 1836 Jefferson Pl. N.W., Washington, DC 20036 (202) 872-9200

State Telephone Regulation Report Suite 444, 1101 King St., Alexandria, VA 22314 (703) 683-4100

Telecom Manager Suite 444, 1101 King St., Alexandria, VA 22314 (703) 683-4100

Telecommunications Horizon House-Microwave, Inc., 685 Canton St., Norwood MA 02062

Telecommunications Products + Technology Pennwell Publishing Co., P.O. Box 1425, 119 Russell St., Littleton, MA 01460-4425 (617) 486-9501

Telecommunications Reports 1036 National Press Bldg., Washington, DC 20045 (202) 347-2654

Teleconnect 12 W. 21 St. New York, NY 10010 (212) 691-8215

Telephone Angles Suite 700N, 4550 Montgomery Ave., Bethesda, MD 20814 (301) 656-6666

Telephone Engineer and Management   Harcourt Brace Jovanovich Publications, Inc., 124 S. First St., Geneva, IL 60134

Telephone News   7811 Montrose Rd., Potomac, MD 20854 (301) 424-3700

Telephony   Telephony Publishing Corporation, 55 E. Jackson Blvd., Chicago, IL 60604 (312) 922-2435

Transnational Data & Communications Report   P.O. Box 2039, Springfield, VA 22152 (202) 488-3434

Voice Processing   P.O. Box 42382, Houston, TX 77242

E

Network Design Tables

Table E 1 Erlang B Table

TRUNKS	P.01		P.03		P.05		P.10	
	ERL	CCS	ERL	CCS	ERL	CCS	ERL	CCS
1	0.01	0.4	0.03	1.1	0.05	1.8	0.11	4.0
2	0.15	5.4	0.28	10.1	0.38	13.7	0.60	21.6
3	0.46	16.6	0.72	26.9	0.90	32.4	1.27	45.7
4	0.87	31.3	1.26	45.4	1.52	54.7	2.05	73.8
5	1.36	49.0	1.88	67.7	2.22	79.9	2.88	104.0
6	1.91	68.8	2.54	91.4	2.96	107.0	3.76	135.0
7	2.50	90.0	3.25	117.0	3.74	135.0	4.67	168.0
8	3.13	113.0	3.99	144.0	4.54	163.0	5.60	202.0
9	3.78	136.0	4.75	171.0	5.37	193.0	6.55	236.0
10	4.46	161.0	5.53	199.0	6.22	224.0	7.51	270.0
11	5.16	186.0	6.33	228.0	7.08	255.0	8.49	306.0
12	5.88	212.0	7.14	257.0	7.95	286.0	9.47	341.0
13	6.61	238.0	7.97	287.0	8.83	318.0	10.47	377.0
14	7.35	265.0	8.80	317.0	9.73	350.0	11.47	413.0
15	8.11	292.0	9.65	347.0	10.63	383.0	12.48	339.0
16	8.87	319.0	10.51	378.0	11.54	415.0	13.50	486.0
17	9.65	347.0	11.37	409.0	12.46	449.0	14.52	523.0
18	10.44	376.0	12.24	441.0	13.38	482.0	15.55	560.0
19	11.23	404.0	13.11	472.0	14.31	515.0	16.58	597.0

Table E 1   Erlang B Table

TRUNKS	P.01 ERL	P.01 CCS	P.03 ERL	P.03 CCS	P.05 ERL	P.05 CCS	P.10 ERL	P.10 CCS
20	12.03	433.0	14.00	504.0	15.25	549.0	17.61	634.0
21	12.84	462.0	14.89	536.0	16.19	583.0	18.65	671.0
22	13.65	491.0	15.78	568.0	17.13	617.0	19.69	709.0
23	14.47	521.0	16.68	600.0	18.08	651.0	20.74	748.0
24	15.29	550.0	17.58	633.0	19.03	685.0	21.78	784.0
25	16.12	580.0	18.48	665.0	19.99	720.0	22.83	822.0
26	16.96	611.0	19.39	698.0	20.94	754.0	23.88	860.0
27	17.80	641.0	20.30	731.0	21.90	788.0	24.94	898.0
28	18.64	671.0	21.22	764.0	22.87	823.0	26.00	936.0
29	19.49	702.0	22.14	797.0	23.83	858.0	27.05	974.0
30	20.34	732.0	23.06	830.0	24.80	893.0	28.11	1012.0
31	21.19	763.0	23.99	864.0	25.77	928.0	29.17	1050.0
32	22.05	794.0	24.91	897.0	26.75	963.0	30.23	1088.0
33	22.91	825.0	25.84	930.0	27.72	998.0	31.30	1127.0
34	23.77	856.0	26.77	964.0	28.70	1033.0	32.36	1165.0
35	24.64	887.0	27.71	998.0	29.68	1068.0	33.43	1203.0
36	25.51	918.0	28.64	1031.0	30.66	1104.0	34.50	1232.0
37	26.38	950.0	29.58	1065.0	31.64	1139.0	35.57	1281.0
38	27.25	981.0	30.51	1098.0	32.63	1175.0	36.64	1319.0
39	28.13	1013.0	31.45	1132.0	33.61	1210.0	37.71	1358.0
40	29.01	1044.0	32.39	1166.0	34.60	1246.0	38.79	1396.0
41	29.89	1076.0	33.34	1200.0	35.59	1281.0	39.86	1435.0
42	30.77	1108.0	34.29	1234.0	36.58	1317.0	40.94	1474.0
43	31.66	1140.0	35.24	1269.0	37.57	1353.0	42.01	1512.0
44	32.54	1171.0	36.19	1303.0	38.56	1388.0	43.09	1551.0
45	33.43	1203.0	37.15	1336.0	39.55	1424.0	44.16	1590.0
46	34.32	1236.0	38.10	1372.0	40.54	1459.0	45.24	1629.0
47	35.21	1268.0	39.06	1406.0	41.54	1495.0	46.32	1668.0
48	36.11	1300.0	40.02	1440.0	42.54	1531.0	47.40	1706.0
49	37.00	1332.0	40.98	1475.0	43.54	1567.0	48.48	1745.0
50	37.90	1364.0	41.93	1509.0	44.53	1603.0	49.56	1784.0
51	38.80	1397.0	42.90	1544.0	45.50	1638.0	50.60	1822.0
52	39.70	1429.0	43.90	1580.0	46.50	1674.0	51.70	1861.0
53	40.60	1462.0	44.80	1613.0	47.50	1710.0	52.80	1901.0
54	41.50	1494.0	45.80	1649.0	48.50	1746.0	53.90	1940.0
55	42.40	1526.0	46.70	1681.0	49.50	1782.0	55.00	1980.0
56	43.30	1559.0	47.70	1717.0	50.50	1818.0	56.10	2020.0

Table E 1   Erlang B Table

TRUNKS	P.01 ERL	P.01 CCS	P.03 ERL	P.03 CCS	P.05 ERL	P.05 CCS	P.10 ERL	P.10 CCS
57	44.20	1591.0	48.70	1753.0	51.50	1854.0	57.10	2056.0
58	45.10	1624.0	49.60	1786.0	52.60	1894.0	58.20	2095.0
59	46.00	1656.0	50.60	1822.0	53.60	1930.0	59.30	2135.0
60	46.90	1688.0	51.60	1858.0	54.60	1966.0	60.40	2174.0
61	47.90	1724.0	52.50	1890.0	55.60	2002.0	61.50	2214.0
62	48.80	1757.0	53.50	1926.0	56.60	2038.0	62.60	2254.0
63	49.70	1789.0	54.50	1962.0	57.60	2074.0	63.70	2293.0
64	50.60	1822.0	55.40	1994.0	58.60	2110.0	64.80	2333.0
65	51.50	1854.0	56.40	2030.0	59.60	2146.0	65.80	2369.0
66	52.40	1886.0	57.40	2066.0	60.60	2182.0	66.90	2408.0
67	53.40	1992.0	58.40	2102.0	61.60	2218.0	68.00	2448.0
68	54.30	1955.0	59.30	2135.0	62.60	2254.0	69.10	2448.0
69	55.20	1987.0	60.30	2171.0	63.70	2293.0	70.20	2527.0
70	56.10	2020.0	61.30	2207.0	64.70	2329.0	71.30	2567.0
71	57.00	2052.0	62.30	2243.0	65.70	2365.0	72.40	2606.0
72	58.00	2088.0	63.20	2275.0	66.70	2401.0	73.50	2646.0
73	58.90	2120.0	64.20	2311.0	67.70	2437.0	74.60	2686.0
74	59.80	2153.0	65.20	2347.0	68.70	2473.0	75.60	2722.0
75	60.70	2185.0	66.20	2383.0	69.70	2509.0	76.70	2761.0
76	61.70	2221.0	67.20	2419.0	70.80	2549.0	77.80	2801.0
77	62.60	2254.0	68.10	2452.0	71.80	2585.0	78.90	2840.0
78	63.50	2286.0	69.10	2488.0	72.80	2621.0	80.00	2880.0
79	64.40	2318.0	70.10	2524.0	73.80	2657.0	81.10	2920.0
80	65.40	2354.0	71.10	2560.0	74.80	2693.0	82.20	2959.0
81	66.30	2387.0	72.10	2596.0	75.80	2729.0	83.30	2999.0
82	67.20	2419.0	73.00	2628.0	76.90	2768.0	84.40	3038.0
83	68.20	2455.0	74.00	2664.0	77.90	2804.0	85.50	3078.0
84	69.10	2488.0	75.00	2700.0	78.90	2840.0	86.60	3118.0
85	70.00	2520.0	76.00	2736.0	79.90	2876.0	87.70	3157.0
86	70.90	2552.0	77.00	2772.0	80.90	2912.0	88.80	3197.0
87	71.90	2588.0	78.00	2808.0	82.00	2952.0	89.90	3236.0
88	72.80	2621.0	78.90	2840.0	83.00	2988.0	91.00	3276.0
89	73.70	2653.0	79.90	2876.0	84.00	3024.0	92.10	3316.0
90	74.70	2689.0	80.90	2912.0	85.00	3060.0	93.10	3352.0
91	75.60	2722.0	81.90	2948.0	86.00	3096.0	94.20	3391.0
92	76.60	2758.0	82.90	2984.0	87.10	3136.0	95.30	3431.0
93	77.50	2790.0	83.90	3020.0	88.10	3172.0	96.40	3470.0

Table E 1   Erlang B Table

TRUNKS	P.01		P.03		P.05		P.10	
	ERL	CCS	ERL	CCS	ERL	CCS	ERL	CCS
94	78.40	2822.0	84.90	3056.0	89.10	3208.0	97.50	3510.0
95	79.40	2858.0	85.90	3092.0	90.10	3244.0	98.60	3550.0
96	80.30	2891.0	86.80	3125.0	91.10	3280.0	99.70	3589.0
97	81.20	2923.0	87.80	3161.0	92.20	3319.0	100.80	3629.0
98	82.20	2959.0	88.80	3197.0	93.20	3355.0	101.90	3668.0
99	83.10	2992.0	89.80	3233.0	94.20	3391.0	103.00	3708.0
100	84.10	3028.0	90.80	3269.0	95.20	3427.0	107.00	3748.0

Table E 2   Poisson Table

TRUNKS	P.01		P.03		P.05		P.10	
	ERL	CCS	ERL	CCS	ERL	CCS	ERL	CCS
1	0.01	0.4	0.03	1.1	0.05	1.9	0.11	3.8
2	0.15	5.4	0.27	9.7	0.36	12.9	0.53	19.1
3	0.44	15.7	0.67	24.0	0.82	29.4	1.10	39.6
4	0.82	29.6	1.16	41.6	1.37	49.1	1.75	63.0
5	1.28	46.1	1.71	61.6	1.97	70.9	2.44	88.0
6	1.79	64.4	2.30	82.8	2.61	94.1	3.14	113.0
7	2.33	83.9	2.92	105.0	3.28	118.0	3.89	140.0
8	2.91	105.0	3.58	129.0	3.97	143.0	4.67	168.0
9	3.50	126.0	4.25	153.0	4.69	169.0	5.42	195.0
10	4.14	149.0	4.94	178.0	5.42	195.0	6.22	224.0
11	4.78	172.0	5.67	204.0	6.17	222.0	7.03	253.0
12	5.42	195.0	6.39	230.0	6.92	249.0	7.83	282.0
13	6.11	220.0	7.11	256.0	7.69	277.0	8.64	311.0
14	6.78	244.0	7.83	283.0	8.47	305.0	9.47	341.0
15	7.47	269.0	8.61	310.0	9.25	333.0	10.28	370.0
16	8.18	294.0	9.36	337.0	10.06	362.0	11.14	401.0
17	8.89	320.0	10.14	365.0	10.83	390.0	11.97	431.0
18	9.61	346.0	10.89	392.0	11.64	419.0	12.83	462.0
19	10.36	373.0	11.67	420.0	12.44	448.0	13.67	492.0
20	11.08	399.0	12.47	449.0	13.25	477.0	14.53	523.0
21	11.83	426.0	13.28	478.0	14.08	507.0	15.39	554.0
22	12.58	453.0	14.08	507.0	14.89	536.0	16.25	585.0
23	13.33	480.0	14.89	536.0	15.72	566.0	17.11	616.0
24	14.08	507.0	15.67	564.0	16.56	596.0	17.97	647.0
25	14.86	535.0	16.47	593.0	17.39	626.0	18.83	678.0
26	15.61	562.0	17.31	623.0	18.22	656.0	19.72	710.0
27	16.39	590.0	18.11	652.0	19.06	686.0	20.58	741.0
28	17.17	618.0	18.94	682.0	19.92	717.0	21.47	773.0
29	17.97	647.0	19.75	711.0	20.75	747.0	22.36	805.0
30	18.75	675.0	20.59	741.0	21.61	778.0	23.22	836.0
31	19.53	703.0	21.42	771.0	22.47	809.0	24.11	868.0
32	20.33	732.0	22.25	801.0	23.33	840.0	25.00	900.0
33	21.11	760.0	23.08	831.0	24.19	871.0	25.89	932.0
34	21.92	789.0	23.92	861.0	25.06	902.0	26.78	964.0
35	22.72	818.0	24.75	891.0	25.92	933.0	27.67	996.0
36	23.53	847.0	25.61	922.0	26.78	964.0	28.56	1028.0
37	24.33	876.0	26.44	952.0	27.64	995.0	29.44	1060.0
38	25.14	905.0	27.28	982.0	28.50	1026.0	30.33	1092.0
39	25.97	935.0	28.14	1013.0	29.36	1057.0	31.25	1125.0

Table E 2   Poisson Table

TRUNKS	P.01 ERL	CCS	P.03 ERL	CCS	P.05 ERL	CCS	P.10 ERL	CCS
40	26.78	964.0	28.97	1043.0	30.22	1088.0	32.14	1157.0
41	27.58	993.0	29.83	1074.0	31.11	1120.0	33.06	1190.0
42	28.42	1023.0	30.67	1104.0	31.97	1151.0	33.94	1222.0
43	29.22	1052.0	31.53	1135.0	32.86	1182.0	34.86	1255.0
44	30.06	1082.0	32.39	1166.0	33.72	1214.0	35.75	1287.0
45	30.89	1112.0	33.25	1197.0	34.61	1246.0	36.67	1320.0
46	31.72	1142.0	34.11	1228.0	35.47	1277.0	37.56	1352.0
47	32.53	1171.0	34.97	1259.0	36.36	1309.0	38.47	1385.0
48	33.36	1201.0	35.86	1291.0	37.22	1340.0	39.36	1417.0
49	34.19	1231.0	36.72	1322.0	38.11	1372.0	40.28	1450.0
50	35.03	1261.0	37.58	1353.0	38.97	1403.0	41.17	1482.0
51	35.86	1291.0	38.44	1384.0	39.86	1435.0	42.08	1515.0
52	36.72	1322.0	39.33	1416.0	40.75	1467.0	43.00	1548.0
53	37.56	1352.0	40.19	1447.0	41.64	1499.0	43.92	1581.0
54	38.40	1382.0	41.06	1478.0	42.53	1531.0	44.83	1614.0
55	39.22	1412.0	41.92	1509.0	43.42	1563.0	45.72	1646.0
56	40.08	1443.0	42.81	1541.0	44.31	1595.0	46.64	1679.0
57	40.92	1473.0	43.69	1572.0	45.19	1627.0	47.56	1712.0
58	41.78	1504.0	44.56	1604.0	46.08	1659.0	48.47	1745.0
59	42.61	1534.0	45.41	1635.0	46.97	1691.0	49.39	1778.0
60	43.47	1565.0	46.31	1667.0	47.86	1723.0	50.31	1811.0
61	44.31	1595.0	47.17	1698.0	48.75	1755.0	51.22	1844.0
62	45.17	1626.0	48.06	1730.0	49.64	1787.0	52.14	1877.0
63	46.03	1657.0	48.94	1762.0	50.53	1819.0	53.06	1910.0
64	46.86	1687.0	49.83	1794.0	51.42	1851.0	53.97	1943.0
65	47.72	1718.0	50.69	1825.0	52.33	1884.0	54.89	1976.0
66	48.58	1749.0	51.58	1857.0	53.22	1916.0	55.81	2009.0
67	49.44	1980.0	52.47	1889.0	54.11	1948.0	56.72	2042.0
68	50.31	1811.0	53.36	1921.0	55.02	1981.0	57.67	2076.0
69	51.17	1842.0	54.25	1953.0	55.92	2013.0	58.58	2109.0
70	52.03	1873.0	55.14	1985.0	56.83	2046.0	59.50	2142.0
71	52.89	1904.0	56.03	2017.0	57.72	2078.0	60.42	2175.0
72	53.75	1935.0	56.89	2048.0	58.64	2111.0	61.36	2209.0
73	54.61	1966.0	57.78	2080.0	59.53	2143.0	62.28	2242.0
74	55.47	1997.0	58.67	2112.0	60.44	2176.0	63.22	2276.0
75	56.33	2028.0	59.58	2145.0	61.33	2208.0	64.14	2309.0
76	57.19	2058.0	60.44	2176.0	62.25	2241.0	65.06	2342.0
77	58.08	2091.0	61.36	2209.0	63.17	2274.0	66.00	2376.0
78	58.94	2122.0	62.25	2241.0	64.06	2306.0	66.94	2410.0

Table E 2   Poisson Table

TRUNKS	P.01 ERL	P.01 CCS	P.03 ERL	P.03 CCS	P.05 ERL	P.05 CCS	P.10 ERL	P.10 CCS
79	59.81	2153.0	63.14	2273.0	64.97	2339.0	67.86	2443.0
80	60.67	2184.0	64.03	2305.0	65.89	2372.0	68.81	2477.0
81	61.54	2215.0	64.92	2337.0	66.81	2405.0	69.72	2510.0
82	62.42	2247.0	65.83	2370.0	67.69	2437.0	70.64	2543.0
83	63.28	2278.0	66.72	2402.0	68.61	2470.0	71.58	2577.0
84	64.17	2310.0	67.64	2435.0	69.53	2503.0	72.50	2610.0
85	65.03	2341.0	68.53	2467.0	70.44	2536.0	73.44	2644.0
86	65.92	2373.0	69.42	2499.0	71.36	2569.0	74.39	2678.0
87	66.78	2404.0	70.33	2532.0	72.25	2601.0	75.31	2711.0
88	67.67	2436.0	71.22	2564.0	73.17	2634.0	76.25	2745.0
89	68.53	2467.0	72.11	2596.0	74.08	2667.0	77.17	2778.0
90	69.42	2499.0	73.03	2629.0	75.00	2700.0	78.11	2812.0
91	70.28	2530.0	73.92	2661.0	75.92	2733.0	79.06	2846.0
92	71.17	2562.0	74.83	2694.0	76.83	2766.0	80.00	2880.0
93	72.06	2594.0	75.72	2726.0	77.72	2798.0	80.92	2913.0
94	72.92	2625.0	76.64	2759.0	78.64	2831.0	81.86	2947.0
95	73.81	2657.0	77.53	2791.0	79.56	2864.0	82.81	2981.0
96	74.69	2689.0	78.44	2824.0	80.47	2897.0	83.72	3014.0
97	75.58	2721.0	79.36	2857.0	81.39	2930.0	84.67	3048.0
98	76.44	2752.0	80.25	2889.0	82.31	2963.0	85.61	3082.0
99	77.33	2784.0	81.14	2921.0	83.22	2996.0	86.56	3116.0
100	78.22	2816.0	82.06	2954.0	84.17	3029.0	87.47	3149.0

Table E 3 Erlang C Table

A	N	Pd	D1	D2	PROBABILITY OF DELAY (ALL CALLS) OF TIME t						
					.2	.4	.6	.8	1	2	3
.05	1	.0500	.053	1.05	.041	.034	.028	.023	.019	.007	.003
	2	.0012	.001	.513	.001	.001					
.10	1	.1000	.111	1.11	.084	.070	.058	.049	.041	.017	.007
	2	.0048	.003	.526	.003	.002	.002	.001	.001		
	3	.0002		.345							
.15	1	.1500	.176	1.18	.127	.107	.090	.076	.064	.027	.012
	2	.0105	.006	.541	.007	.005	.003	.002	.002		
	3	.0005		.351							
.20	1	.2000	.250	1.25	.170	.145	.124	.105	.090	.040	.018
	2	.0182	.010	.556	.013	.009	.006	.004	.003		
	3	.0012		.357	.001						
	4	.0001		.263							
.25	1	.2500	.333	1.33	.215	.185	.159	.137	.118	.056	.026
	2	.0278	.016	.571	.020	.014	.010	.007	.005	.001	
	3	.0022	.001	.364	.001	.001					
	4	.0001		.267							
.30	1	.3000	.429	1.43	.261	.227	.197	.171	.149	.074	.037
	2	.0391	.023	.588	.028	.020	.014	.010	.007	.001	
	3	.0037	.001	.370	.002	.001	.001				
	4	.0003		.270							
.35	1	.3500	.538	1.54	.307	.270	.237	.208	.183	.095	.050
	2	.0521	.032	.606	.037	.027	.019	.014	.010	.002	
	3	.0057	.002	.377	.003	.002	.001	.001			
	4	.0005		.274							
.40	1	.4000	.667	1.67	.355	.315	.279	.248	.220	.120	.066
	2	.0667	.042	.625	.048	.035	.026	.019	.013	.003	.001
	3	.0082	.003	.385	.005	.002	.001	.001			
	4	.0008		.278							
	5	.0001		.217							
.45	1	.4500	.818	1.82	.403	.361	.324	.290	.260	.150	.086
	2	.0827	.053	.645	.061	.044	.033	.024	.018	.004	.001
	3	.0114	.004	.392	.007	.004	.002	.001	.001		
	4	.0012		.282	.0001						
	5	.0001		.220							

A = Offered load in Erlangs
N = Number of trunks (servers) required
P_d = Probability that a call will be delayed

D1 = Average delay of all calls
D2 = Average delay of delayed calls

Table E 3   Erlang C Table

A	N	Pd	D1	D2	PROBABILITY OF DELAY (ALL CALLS) OF TIME t						
					.2	.4	.6	.8	1	2	3
.50	1	.5000	1.00	2.00	.452	.409	.370	.335	.303	.184	.112
	2	.1000	.067	.667	.074	.055	.041	.030	.022	.005	.001
	3	.0152	.006	.400	.009	.006	.003	.002	.001		
	4	.0018	.001	.286	.001						
	5	.0002		.222							
.55	1	.5500	1.22	2.22	.503	.459	.420	.384	.351	.224	.143
	2	.1186	.082	.690	.089	.066	.050	.037	.028	.007	.002
	3	.0196	.008	.408	.012	.007	.004	.003	.002		
	4	.0026	.001	.290	.001	.001					
	5	.0003		.225							
.60	1	.6000	1.50	2.50	.554	.511	.472	.436	.402	.270	.181
	2	.1385	.099	.714	.105	.079	.060	.045	.034	.008	.002
	3	.0247	.010	.417	.015	.009	.006	.004	.002		
	4	.0035	.001	.294	.002	.001					
	5	.0004		.227							
.65	1	.6500	1.86	2.86	.606	.565	.527	.491	.458	.323	.227
	2	.1594	.118	.741	.122	.093	.071	.054	.041	.011	.003
	3	.0304	.013	.426	.019	.032	.007	.005	.003		
	4	.0046	.001	.299	.002	.001	.001				
	5	.0006		.230							
	6	.0001		.187							
.70	1	.7000	2.33	3.33	.659	.621	.585	.551	.519	.384	.285
	2	.1815	.140	.769	.140	.108	.083	.064	.049	.013	.004
	3	.0369	.016	.435	.023	.015	.009	.006	.004		
	4	.0060	.002	.303	.003	.002	.001				
	5	.0008		.233							
	6	.0001		.189							
.75	1	.7500	3.00	4.00	.713	.679	.646	.614	.584	.455	.354
	2	.2045	.164	.800	.159	.124	.097	.075	.059	.017	.005
	3	.0441	.020	.444	.028	.018	.011	.007	.005		
	4	.0077	.002	.308	.004	.002	.001	.001			
	5	.0011		.235							
	6	.0001		.190							

A = Offered load in Erlangs
N = Number of trunks (servers) required
P_d = Probability that a call will be delayed

D1 = Average delay of all calls
D2 = Average delay of delayed calls

Table E 3   Erlang C Table

A	N	Pd	D1	D2	.2	.4	.6	.8	1	2	3
					\multicolumn{7}{PROBABILITY OF DELAY (ALL CALLS) OF TIME t}
.80	1	.8000	4.00	5.00	.769	.738	.710	.682	.655	.536	.439
	2	.2286	.190	.833	.180	.141	.111	.088	.069	.021	.006
	3	.0520	.024	.455	.034	.022	.014	.009	.006	.001	
	4	.0096	.003	.312	.005	.003	.001	.001			
	5	.0015		.238	.001						
	6	.0002		.192							
.85	1	.3500	5.67	6.67	.825	.800	.777	.754	.732	.630	.542
	2	.2535	.220	.870	.201	.160	.127	.101	.080	.025	.008
	3	.0607	.028	.465	.039	.026	.017	.011	.007	.001	
	4	.0118	.004	.317	.006	.003	.002	.001	.001		
	5	.0019		.241	.001						
	6	.0003		.194							
.90	1	.9000	9.00	10.0	.882	.865	.848	.831	.814	.737	.667
	2	.2793	.254	.909	.224	.180	.144	.116	.093	.031	.010
	3	.0700	.033	.476	.046	.030	.020	.013	.009	.001	
	4	.0143	.005	.323	.008	.004	.002	.001	.001		
	5	.0024	.001	.244	.001						
	6	.0004		.196							
.95	1	.9500	19.0	20.0	.941	.931	.922	.913	.904	.860	.818
	2	.3059	.291	.952	.248	.201	.163	.132	.107	.037	.013
	3	.0801	.039	.488	.053	.035	.023	.016	.010	.001	
	4	.0172	.006	.328	.009	.005	.003	.001	.001		
	5	.0031	.001	.247	.001						
	6	.0005		.198							
	7	.0001		.165							
1.0	2	.3333	.333	1.00	.273	.223	.183	.150	.123	.045	.017
	3	.0909	.045	.500	.061	.041	.027	.018	.012	.002	
	4	.0204	.007	.333	.011	.006	.003	.002	.001		
	5	.0038	.001	.250	.002	.001					
	6	.0006		.200							
	7	.0001		.167							

A = Offered load in Erlangs
N = Number of trunks (servers) required
P_d = Probability that a call will be delayed

D1 = Average delay of all calls
D2 = Average delay of delayed calls

Table E 3   Erlang C Table

A	N	Pd	D1	D2	PROBABILITY OF DELAY (ALL CALLS) OF TIME t						
---	---	----	----	----	.2	.4	.6	.8	1	2	3
1.1	2	.3903	.434	1.11	.326	.272	.227	.190	.159	.065	.026
	3	.1146	.060	.526	.078	.054	.037	.025	.017	.003	
	4	.0279	.010	.345	.016	.009	.005	.003	.002		
	5	.0057	.001	.256	.003	.001	.001				
	6	.0010		.204							
	7	.0002		.169							
1.2	2	.4500	.562	1.25	.383	.327	.278	.237	.202	.091	.041
	3	.1412	.078	.556	.098	.069	.048	.033	.023	.004	.001
	4	.0370	.013	.357	.021	.012	.007	.004	.002		
	5	.0082	.002	.263	.004	.002	.001				
	6	.0016		.208	.001						
	7	.0003		.172							
1.3	2	.5121	.732	1.43	.445	.387	.336	.293	.254	.126	.063
	3	.1704	.100	.588	.121	.085	.061	.044	.031	.006	.001
	4	.0478	.018	.370	.028	.016	.009	.006	.003		
	5	.0114	.003	.270	.005	.003	.001	.001			
	6	.0023		.213	.001						
	7	.0004		.175							
	8	.0001		.149							
1.4	2	.5765	.961	1.67	.511	.453	.402	.357	.316	.174	.095
	3	.2024	.126	.625	.147	.107	.077	.056	.041	.008	.002
	4	.0603	.023	.385	.036	.021	.013	.008	.004		
	5	.0153	.004	.278	.007	.004	.002	.001			
	6	.0034	.001	.217	.001	.001	.001				
	7	.0006		.179							
	8	.0001									
1.5	2	.6429	1.29	2.00	.582	.526	.476	.431	.390	.236	.143
	3	.2368	.158	.667	.175	.130	.096	.071	.053	.012	.003
	4	.0746	.030	.400	.045	.027	.017	.010	.006	.001	
	5	.0201	.006	.286	.010	.005	.002	.001	.001		
	6	.0047	.001	.222	.002	.001					
	7	.0010		.182							
	8	.0002		.154							

A = Offered load in Erlangs
N = Number of trunks (servers) required
P_d = Probability that a call will be delayed

D1 = Average delay of all calls
D2 = Average delay of delayed calls

Table E 3   Erlang C Table

A	N	Pd	D1	D2	PROBABILITY OF DELAY (ALL CALLS) OF TIME t						
					.2	.4	.6	.8	1	2	3
1.6	2	.7111	1.78	2.50	.656	.606	.559	.516	.477	.320	.214
	3	.2738	.196	.714	.207	.156	.118	.089	.068	.017	.004
	4	.0907	.038	.417	.056	.035	.021	.013	.008	.001	
	5	.0259	.008	.294	.013	.007	.003	.002	.001		
	6	.0064	.001	.227	.003	.001					
	7	.0014		.185							
	8	.0003		.156							
1.7	2	.7811	2.60	3.33	.736	.693	.652	.614	.579	.429	.318
	3	.3131	.241	.769	.241	.186	.144	.111	.085	.023	.006
	4	.1087	.047	.435	.069	.043	.027	.017	.011	.001	
	5	.0326	.010	.303	.017	.009	.005	.002	.001		
	6	.0085	.002	.233	.004	.002	.001				
	7	.0020		.189	.001						
	8	.0004		.159							
	9	.0001		.137							
1.8	2	.8526	4.26	5.00	.819	.787	.756	.727	.698	.572	.468
	3	.3547	.296	.833	.279	.220	.173	.136	.107	.032	.010
	4	.1285	.058	.455	.083	.053	.034	.022	.014	.002	
	5	.0405	.013	.312	.021	.011	.006	.003	.002		
	6	.0111	.003	.238	.005	.002	.001				
	7	.0027	.001	.192	.001						
	8	.0006		.161							
	9	.0001		.139							
1.9	2	.9256	9.26	10.0	.907	.889	.872	.854	.838	.758	.686
	3	.3985	.362	.909	.320	.257	.206	.165	.133	.044	.015
	4	.1503	.072	.476	.099	.065	.043	.028	.018	.002	
	5	.0495	.016	.323	.027	.014	.008	.004	.002		
	6	.0143	.003	.244	.006	.003	.001	.001			
	7	.0036	.001	.196	.001						
2.0	3	.4444	.444	1.00	.364	.298	.244	.200	.164	.060	.022
	4	.1739	.087	.500	.117	.078	.052	.035	.024	.003	
	5	.0597	.020	.333	.033	.018	.010	.005	.003		
	6	.0180	.005	.250	.008	.004	.002	.001			
	7	0048	.001	.200	.002	.001					
	8	.0011		.167							
	9	.0002		.143							

A = Offered load in Erlangs
N = Number of trunks (servers) required
P_d = Probability that a call will be delayed

D1 = Average delay of all calls
D2 = Average delay of delayed calls

Table E 3   Erlang C Table

A	N	Pd	D1	D2	.2	.4	.6	.8	1	2	3
				PROBABILITY OF DELAY (ALL CALLS) OF TIME t							
2.1	3	.4923	.547	1.11	.411	.343	.287	.240	.200	.081	.033
	4	.1994	.105	.526	.136	.093	.064	.044	.030	.004	.001
	5	.0712	.025	.345	.040	.022	.012	.007	.004		
	6	.0224	.006	.256	.010	.005	.002	.001			
	7	.0062	.001	.204	.002	.001					
	8	.0016		.169							
	9	.0003		.145							
	10	.0001		.127							
2.2	3	.5422	.678	1.25	.462	.394	.335	.286	.244	.109	.049
	4	.2268	.126	.556	.158	.110	.077	.054	.037	.006	.001
	5	.0839	.030	.357	.048	.027	.016	.009	.005		
	6	.0275	.007	.263	.013	.006	.003	.001	.001		
	7	.0080	.002	.208	.003	.001					
	8	.0021		.172	.001						
	9	.0005		.147							
	10	.0001		.128							
2.3	3	.5938	.848	1.43	.516	.449	.390	.339	.295	.146	.073
	4	.2560	.151	.588	.182	.130	.092	.066	.047	.009	.002
	5	.0980	.036	.370	.057	.033	.019	.011	.007		
	6	.0333	.009	.270	.016	.008	.004	.002	.001		
	7	.0101	.002	.213	.004	.002	.001				
	8	.0027		.175	.001						
	9	.0007		.149							
	10	.0001		.130							
2.4	3	.6472	1.08	1.67	.574	.509	.452	.400	.355	.195	.107
	4	.2870	.179	.625	.208	.151	.110	.080	.058	.012	.002
	5	.1135	.044	.385	.040	.024	.014	.008	.001		
	6	.0400	.011	.278	.019	.009	.005	.002	.001		
	7	.0126	.003	.217	.005	.002	.001				
	8	.0035	.001	.179	.001						
	9	.0009		.152							
	10	.0002		.132							

A = Offered load in Erlangs
N = Number of trunks (servers) required
Pd = Probability that a call will be delayed

D1 = Average delay of all calls
D2 = Average delay of delayed calls

Table E 3   Erlang C Table

A	N	Pd	D1	D2	PROBABILITY OF DELAY (ALL CALLS) OF TIME t						
					.2	.4	.6	.8	1	2	3
2.5	3	.7022	1.40	2.00	.635	.575	.520	.471	.426	.258	.157
	4	.3199	.213	.667	.237	.176	.130	.096	.071	.016	.004
	5	.1304	.052	.400	.079	.048	.029	.018	.011	.001	
	6	.0474	.014	.286	.024	.012	.006	.003	.001		
	7	.0154	.003	.222	.006	.003	.001				
	8	.0043	.001	.182	.002	.001					
	9	.0012		.154							
	10	.0003		.133							
	11	.0001		.118							
2.6	3	.7589	1.90	2.50	.701	.647	.597	.551	.509	.341	.229
	4	.3544	.253	.714	.268	.202	.153	.116	.087	.022	.005
	5	.1487	.062	.417	.092	.057	.035	.022	.013	.001	
	6	.0558	.016	.294	.028	.014	.007	.004	.002		
	7	.0188	.004	.227	.008	.003	.001	.001			
	8	.0057	.001	.185	.002	.001					
	9	.0016		.156							
	10	.0004		.135							
	11	.0001		.119							
2.7	3	.8171	2.72	3.33	.769	.725	.682	.643	.605	.448	.332
	4	.3907	.301	.769	.301	.232	.179	.138	.106	.029	.008
	5	.1684	.073	.435	.106	.067	.042	.017	.002		
	6	.0652	.020	.303	.034	.017	.009	.005	.002		
	7	.0227	.005	.233	.010	.004	.002	.001			
	8	.0071	.001	.189	.002	.001					
	9	.0020		.159	.001						
	10	.0005		.137							
	11	.0001		.120							
2.8	3	.8767	4.38	5.00	.842	.309	.778	.747	.718	.588	.481
	4	.4287	.357	.833	.337	.263	.209	.164	.129	.039	.012
	5	.1895	.086	.455	.122	.079	.051	.033	.021	.002	
	6	.0755	.024	.312	.040	.021	.011	.006	.003		
	7	.0271	.006	.238	.012	.005	.002	.001			
	8	.0088	.002	.192	.003	.001					
	9	.0026		.161	.001						

A = Offered load in Erlangs
N = Number of trunks (servers) required
P_d = Probability that a call will be delayed

D1 = Average delay of all calls
D2 = Average delay of delayed calls

Table E 3   Erlang C Table

A	N	Pd	D1	D2	PROBABILITY OF DELAY (ALL CALLS) OF TIME t						
					.2	.4	.6	.8	1	2	3
2.9	3	.9377	9.38	10.0	.919	.901	.883	.866	.848	.768	.695
	4	.4682	.426	.909	.376	.302	.242	.194	.156	.052	.017
	5	.2121	.101	.476	.139	.092	.060	.040	.026	.003	
	6	.0868	.028	.323	.047	.025	.014	.007	.004		
	7	.0320	.008	.244	.014	.006	.003	.001	.001		
	8	.0107	.002	.196	.004	.001	.001				
	9	.0032	.001	.164	.001						
3.0	4	.5094	.509	1.00	.461	.417	.377	.341	.309	.241	.187
	5	.2362	.118	.500	.193	.158	.130	.106	.087	.053	.032
	6	.0991	.033	.333	.073	.054	.040	.030	.022	.010	.005
	7	.0376	.009	.250	.025	.017	.011	.008	.005	.002	.001
	8	.0129	.003	.200	.008	.005	.003	.002	.001		
	9	.0040	.001	.167	.001	.001					
3.1	4	.5522	.614	1.11	.505	.461	.422	.385	.352	.281	.225
	5	.2616	.138	.526	.216	.179	.148	.122	.101	.063	.039
	6	.1126	.039	.345	.084	.063	.047	.035	.026	.013	.006
	7	.0439	.011	.256	.030	.020	.014	.009	.006	.002	.001
	8	.0155	.003	.204	.009	.006	.004	.002	.001		
	9	.0050	.001	.169	.003	.002	.001				
3.2	4	.5964	.746	1.25	.551	.508	.469	.433	.400	.327	.268
	5	.2886	.160	.556	.241	.201	.168	.140	.117	.075	.048
	6	.1271	.045	.357	.096	.073	.055	.041	.031	.016	.008
	7	.0509	.013	.263	.035	.024	.016	.011	.008	.003	.001
	8	.0185	.004	.208	.011	.007	.004	.003	.002	.001	
	9	.0061	.011	.172	.003	.002	.001	.001			
3.3	4	.6422	.917	1.43	.599	.558	.521	.485	.453	.380	.319
	5	.3169	.186	.588	.267	.226	.190	.161	.135	.089	.058
	6	.1427	.053	.370	.109	.083	.063	.048	.037	.019	.010
	7	.0585	.016	.270	.040	.028	.019	.013	.009	.004	.001
	8	.0219	.005	.213	.014	.009	.005	.003	.002	.001	
	9	.0074	.001	.175	.004	.002	.001	.001			
	10	.0023		.149	.001	.001					

A = Offered load in Erlangs
N = Number of trunks (servers) required
P_d = Probability that a call will be delayed

D1 = Average delay of all calls
D2 = Average delay of delayed calls

Table E 3   Erlang C Table

A	N	Pd	D1	D2	PROBABILITY OF DELAY (ALL CALLS) OF TIME t						
					.2	.4	.6	.8	1	2	3
3.4	4	.6893	1.15	1.67	.649	.611	.576	.542	.511	.440	.378
	5	.3467	.217	.625	.295	.262	.215	.183	.156	.104	.070
	6	.1595	.061	.385	.123	.095	.073	.056	.043	.023	.012
	7	.0670	.019	.278	.047	.033	.023	.016	.011	.005	.002
	8	.0256	.006	.217	.016	.010	.006	.004	.003	.001	
	9	.0090	.002	.179	.005	.003	.002	.001	.001		
	10	.0029		.152	.001	.001					
3.5	4	.7379	1.48	2.00	.702	.668	.635	.604	.575	.507	.448
	5	.3778	.252	.667	.325	.280	.241	.207	.178	.123	.084
	6	.1775	.071	.400	.138	.108	.084	.065	.051	.027	.015
	7	.0762	.022	.286	.054	.038	.027	.019	.013	.006	.002
	8	.0299	.007	.222	.022	.014	.009	.006	.004	.001	
	9	.0107	.002	.182	.007	.004	.003	.001	.001		
	10	.0035	.001	.154	.002	.001	.001				
	11	.0011		.133	.001						
3.6	4	.7878	1.97	2.50	.757	.727	.699	.671	.645	.584	.528
	5	.4104	.293	.714	.357	.310	.270	.234	.204	.144	.101
	6	.1966	.082	.417	.153	.122	.096	.075	.059	.032	.018
	7	.0862	.025	.294	.061	.044	.031	.022	.016	.007	.003
	8	.0346	.008	.227	.022	.014	.009	.006	.004	.001	
	9	.0127	.002	.185	.007	.004	.003	.002	.001		
	10	.0043	.001	.156	.002	.001	.001				
3.7	4	.8390	2.80	3.33	.814	.790	.767	.744	.722	.670	.622
	5	.4443	.342	.769	.390	.343	.301	.264	.232		
	8	.0521	.013	.244	.035	.023	.015	.010	.007	.002	.001
	9	.0205	.004	.196	.012	.007	.004	.003	.002		
	10	.0074	.001	.164	.004	.002	.001	.001			
	11	.0025		.141	.001	.001					

A = Offered load in Erlangs   D1 = Average delay of all calls
N = Number of trunks (servers) required   D2 = Average delay of delayed calls
P_d = Probability that a call will be delayed

Table E 3   Erlang C Table

A	N	Pd	D1	D2	PROBABILITY OF DELAY (ALL CALLS) OF TIME t						
					.2	.4	.6	.8	1	2	3
3.8	4	.8914	4.46	5.00	.874	.856	.840	.823	.807	.767	.730
	5	.4796	.400	.833	.425	.377	.355	.297	.263	.195	.144
	6	.2383	.108	.455	.191	.153	.123	.099	.079	.046	.026
	7	.1089	.034	.312	.079	.057	.042	.030	.022	.010	.004
	8	.0457	.011	.238	.030	.020	.013	.009	.006	.002	.001
	9	.0176	.003	.192	.010	.006	.004	.002	.001		
	10	.0062	.001	.161	.003	.002	.001	.001			
	11	.0029		.139	.001						
3.9	4	.9451	9.45	10.0	.936	.926	.917	.908	.899	.877	.855
	5	.5162	.469	.909	.462	.414	.371	.332	.298	.226	.172
	6	.2609	.124	.476	.212	.271	.139	.113	.091	.058	.032
	7	.1215	.039	.323	.089	.065	.048	.035	.026	.012	.005
	8	.0521	.013	.244	.035	.023	.015	.010	.007	.002	.001
	9	.0205	.004	.196	.012	.007	.004	.003	.002		
	10	.0074	.001	.164	.004	.002	.001	.001			
	11	.0025		.141	.001	.001					
4.0	5	.5541	.334	1.00	.501	.454	.410	.371	.336	.262	.204
	6	.2848	.142	.500	.233	.191	.156	.128	.105	.064	.039
	7	.1351	.045	.333	.100	.074	.053	.041	.030	.014	.007
	8	.0590	.015	.250	.040	.027	.018	.012	.008	.003	.001
	9	.0238	.205	.200	.014	.009	.005	.003	.002	.002	
	10	.0088	.001	.167	.005	.003	.001	.001			
	11	.0030		.143	.002	.001					
4.1	5	.5933	.659	1.11	.542	.496	.453	.414	.378	.302	.241
	6	.3098	.263	.526	.256	.212	.176	.145	.120	.075	.046
	7	.1496	.052	.343	.112	.084	.063	.047	.035	.017	.008
	8	.0667	.017	.256	.045	.031	.021	.014	.009	.004	.001
	9	.0274	.006	.204	.017	.010	.006	.004	.002	.001	
	10	.0104	.002	.169	.006	.003	.002	.001	.001		
	11	.0036	.001	.145	.002	.001					
	12	.0012		.127	.001						

A = Offered load in Erlangs
N = Number of trunks (servers) required
Pd = Probability that a call will be delayed

D1 = Average delay of all calls
D2 = Average delay of delayed calls

Table E 3   Erlang C Table

					PROBABILITY OF DELAY (ALL CALLS) OF TIME t						
A	N	Pd	D1	D2	.2	.4	.6	.8	1	2	3
4.2	5	.6338	.792	1.25	.585	.540	.499	.460	.425	.348	.285
	6	.3360	.187	.556	.281	.234	.196	.164	.137	.087	.056
	7	.1651	.059	.357	.125	.094	.071	.054	.041	.020	.010
	8	.0749	.020	.263	.051	.035	.024	.016	.011	.004	.002
	9	.0314	.007	.208	.019	.012	.007	.005	.003	.001	
	10	.0122	.002	.172	.007	.004	.002	.001	.001		
	11	.0044	.001	.147	.002	.001	.001				
	12	.0015		.128	.001						
4.3	5	.6755	.965	1.43	.630	.587	.548	.511	.476	.400	.335
	6	.3634	.214	.588	.307	.259	.218	.184	.155	.102	.066
	7	.1815	.067	.370	.139	.106	.081	.062	.047	.024	.012
	8	.0839	.023	.270	.058	.040	.028	.019	.013	.005	.002
	9	.0358	.008	.213	.022	.014	.009	.005	.003	.001	
	10	.0142	.002	.175	.008	.005	.003	.001	.001		
	11	.0052	.001	.149	.003	.001	.001				
	12	.0018		.130	.001						
4.4	5	.7184	1.20	1.67	.667	.637	.600	.565	.532	.458	.394
	6	.3919	.245	.625	.334	.285	.243	.207	.176	.118	.079
	7	.1988	.076	.385	.153	.118	.091	.070	.054	.028	.015
	8	.0935	.026	.278	.065	.046	.032	.022	.015	.006	.003
	9	.0407	.009	.217	.026	.016	.010	.006	.004	.001	
	10	.0164	.003	.179	.009	.005	.003	.002	.001		
	11	.0061	.001	.152	.003	.002	.001				
	12	.0021		.132	.001						
4.5	5	.7625	1.52	2.00	.725	.690	.656	.625	.594	.524	.462
	6	.4217	.281	.667	.363	..312	.269	.231	.199	.137	.094
	7	.2172	.087	.400	.169	.132	.103	.080	.062	.033	.018
	8	.1039	.030	.286	.073	.052	.036	.026	.018	.008	.003
	9	.0460	.010	.222	.029	.019	.012	.008	.005	.002	.001
	10	.0189	.003	.182	.011	.006	.004	.002	.001		
	11	.0072	.001	.154	.004	.002	.001	.001			
	12	.0026		.133	.001	.001					

A = Offered load in Erlangs
N = Number of trunks (servers) required
P_d = Probability that a call will be delayed

D1 = Average delay of all calls
D2 = Average delay of delayed calls

F

Domestic and International Dialing Codes

North American Area Codes by State or Province

State	Area Code	State	Area Code
Alabama	205	Ontario	416
Alaska	907	Ontario	519
Arizona	602	Ontario	613
Arkansas	501	Ontario	705
Bermuda, Puerto Rico,		Ontario	807
Virgin Islands & other		Quebec	418
Caribbean Islands	809	Quebec	514
California	209	Quebec	819
California	213	Saskatchewan	306
California	310	Colorado	303
California	408	Colorado	719
California	415	Connecticut	203
California	510	Delaware	302
California	619	DIAL IT Services	900
California	707	District of Columbia	202
California	714	Florida	305
California	805	Florida	407
California	818	Florida	813
California	916	Florida	904
Canada:		Georgia	404
Alberta	403	Georgia	912
British Columbia	604	Govt. Spec. Svc.	710
Manitoba	204	Hawaii	808
New Brunswick	506	IC Services	700
Newfoundland	709	Idaho	208
Nova Scotia &		Illinois	217
Prince Edward Island	902	Illinois	309

Illinois	312	New York	315
Illinois	618	New York	516
Illinois	708	New York	518
Illinois	815	New York	607
Indiana	219	New York	716
Indiana	317	New York	718
Indiana	812	New York	914
800 Service	800	North Carolina	704
Iowa	319	North Carolina	919
Iowa	515	North Dakota	701
Iowa	712	Ohio	216
Kansas	316	Ohio	419
Kansas	913	Ohio	513
Kentucky	502	Ohio	614
Kentucky	606	Oklahoma	405
Louisiana	318	Oklahoma	918
Louisiana	504	Oregon	503
Maine	207	Pennsylvania	215
Maryland	301	Pennsylvania	412
Massachusetts	413	Pennsylvania	717
Massachusetts	508	Pennsylvania	814
Massachusetts	617	Rhode Island	401
Mexico City	905	South Carolina	803
Northwest Mexico	706	South Dakota	605
Michigan	313	Tennessee	615
Michigan	517	Tennessee	901
Michigan	616	Texas	214
Michigan	906	Texas	409
Minnesota	218	Texas	512
Minnesota	507	Texas	713
Minnesota	612	Texas	806
Mississippi	601	Texas	817
Missouri	314	Texas	915
Missouri	417	TWX	610
Missouri	816	Utah	801
Montana	406	Vermont	802
Nebraska	308	Virginia	703
Nebraska	402	Virginia	804
Nevada	702	Washington	206
New Hampshire	603	Washington	509
New Jersey	201	West Virginia	304
New Jersey	609	Wisconsin	414
New Jersey	908	Wisconsin	608
New Mexico	505	Wisconsin	715
New York	212	Wyoming	307

North American Area Codes by Area Code

Area Code	State or Province	Area Code	State or Province
201	New Jersey	412	Pennsylvania
202	District of Columbia	413	Massachusetts
203	Connecticut	414	Wisconsin
204	Manitoba	415	California
205	Alabama	416	Ontario
206	Washington	417	Missouri
207	Maine	418	Quebec
208	Idaho	419	Ohio
209	California	501	Arkansas
212	New York	502	Kentucky
213	California	503	Oregon
214	Texas	504	Louisiana
215	Pennsylvania	505	New Mexico
216	Ohio	506	New Brunswick
217	Illinois	507	Minnesota
218	Minnesota	508	Massachusetts
219	Indiana	509	Washington
301	Maryland	510	California
302	Delaware	512	Texas
303	Colorado	513	Ohio
304	West Virginia	514	Quebec
305	Florida	515	Iowa
306	Saskatchewan	516	New York
307	Wyoming	517	Michigan
308	Nebraska	518	New York
309	Illinois	519	Ontario
310	California	601	Mississippi
312	Illinois	602	Arizona
313	Michigan	603	New Hampshire
314	Missouri	604	British Columbia
315	New York	605	South Dakota
316	Kansas	606	Kentucky
317	Indiana	607	New York
318	Louisiana	608	Wisconsin
319	Iowa	609	New Jersey
401	Rhode Island	610	TWX
402	Nebraska	612	Minnesota
403	Alberta	613	Ontario
404	Georgia	614	Ohio
405	Oklahoma	615	Tennessee
406	Montana	616	Michigan
407	Florida	617	Massachusetts
408	California	618	Illinois
409	Texas	619	California

700	IC Services	809	Bermuda, Puerto Rico,
701	North Dakota		Virgin Islands & other
702	Nevada		Caribbean Islands
703	Virginia	812	Indiana
704	North Carolina	813	Florida
705	Ontario	814	Pennsylvania
706	Northwest Mexico	815	Illinois
707	California	816	Missouri
708	Illinois	817	Texas
709	Newfoundland	818	California
710	Govt. Special Services	819	Quebec
712	Iowa	900	DIAL IT Services
713	Texas	901	Tennessee
714	California	902	Nova Scotia & Prince
715	Wisconsin		Edward Island
716	New York	904	Florida
717	Pennsylvania	905	Mexico City
718	New York	906	Michigan
719	Colorado	907	Alaska
800	800 Service	908	New Jersey
801	Utah	912	Georgia
802	Vermont	913	Kansas
803	South Carolina	914	New York
804	Virginia	915	Texas
805	California	916	California
806	Texas	918	Oklahoma
807	Ontario	919	North Carolina
808	Hawaii		

International Dialing Plan Listed by Country Code

Country	Country Code	Country	Country Code
201	Egypt	251	Ethiopia
202	Egypt, Cairo	253	Afars and Issas (Djibouti)
203	Egypt, Alexandria	254	Kenya
204	Egypt	255	Tanzania
205	Egypt	257	Burundi
206	Egypt	258	Mozambique
207	Egypt	259	Zanzibar
208	Egypt	260	Zambia
209	Egypt	261	Madagascar
210	Spanish Sahara	262	Namibia
212	Morocco	263	Zimbabwe
213	Algeria	264	Reunion
216	Tunisia	265	Malawi
217	Tunisia	266	Lesotho
218	Libya	267	Botswana
219	Libya	268	Swaziland
220	Gambia	269	Comorro Islands
221	Senegal	270	South Africa
222	Mauritania	271	South Africa, Pretoria
223	Mali	272	South Africa, Capetown
224	Guinea	273	South Africa
225	Ivory Coast	274	South Africa
226	Burkina Faso	275	South Africa
227	Niger	276	South Africa
228	Togo	277	South Africa
229	Benin	278	South Africa
230	Mauritius	279	South Africa
231	Liberia	297	Aruba
232	Sierra Leone	300	Greece
233	Ghana	301	Greece, Athens
234	Nigeria	302	Greece, Rhodes
235	Chad	303	Greece
236	Central African Republic	304	Greece
237	Cameroon	305	Greece
239	Sao Tome & Principe	306	Greece
240	Equatorial Guinea	307	Greece
241	Gabon	308	Greece
242	Congo	309	Greece
243	Zaire	310	Netherlands
244	Angola	311	Netherlands, Rotterdam
245	Guinea-Bissau	312	Netherlands, Amsterdam
247	Niger	313	Netherlands
248	Seychelles	314	Netherlands
249	Sudan	315	Netherlands
250	Rwanda	316	Netherlands

317	Netherlands, The Hague	365	Hungary
318	Netherlands	366	Hungary
319	Netherlands	367	Hungary
320	Belgium	368	Hungary
321	Belgium	369	Hungary
322	Belgium, Brussels	370	East Germany
323	Belgium, Antwerp	371	East Germany
324	Belgium	372	East Germany, Berlin
325	Belgium	373	East Germany
326	Belgium	374	East Germany, Leipzig
327	Belgium	375	East Germany, Dresden
328	Belgium	376	East Germany
329	Belgium	377	East Germany
330	Andorra	378	East Germany
331	France, Paris	379	East Germany
332	France	380	Yugoslavia
333	France	381	Yugoslavia, Belgrade
334	France	382	Yugoslavia
335	France, Bordeaux	383	Yugoslavia
336	France	384	Yugoslavia
337	France	385	Yugoslavia
338	France	386	Yugoslavia
339	France - Monaco	387	Yugoslavia
340	Spain	388	Yugoslavia, Titograd
341	Spain, Madrid	389	Yugoslavia
342	Spain - Canary Islands	390	Italy
343	Spain, Barcelona	391	Italy
344	Spain	392	Italy, Milan
345	Spain, Seville	393	Italy
346	Spain	394	Italy, Venice
347	Spain	395	Italy, Florence, San Marino
348	Spain	396	Italy, Rome, Vatican City
349	Spain	397	Italy
350	Gibraltar	398	Italy, Naples
351	Portugal	399	Italy
352	Luxembourg	400	Romania, Bucharest
353	Ireland	401	Romania
354	Iceland	402	Romania
355	Albania	403	Romania
356	Malta	404	Romania
357	Cyprus	405	Romania
358	Finland	406	Romania
359	Bulgaria	407	Romania
360	Hungary	408	Romania
361	Hungary, Budapest	409	Romania
362	Hungary	410	Switzerland
363	Hungary	411	Switzerland, Zurich
364	Hungary	412	Switzerland, Geneva

413	Switzerland, Berne		460	Sweden
414	Switzerland, Lucerne		461	Sweden
415	Switzerland		462	Sweden
416	Switzerland		463	Sweden, Goteborg
417	Liechtenstein		464	Sweden
418	Switzerland		465	Sweden
419	Switzerland		466	Sweden
420	Czechoslovakia		467	Sweden
421	Czechoslovakia		468	Sweden, Stockholm
422	Czechoslovakia		469	Sweden
423	Czechoslovakia		470	Norway
424	Czechoslovakia		471	Norway
425	Czechoslovakia		472	Norway, Oslo
426	Czechoslovakia		473	Norway
427	Czechoslovakia		474	Norway
428	Czechoslovakia		475	Norway, Bergen
429	Czechoslovakia		476	Norway
430	Austria		477	Norway
431	Austria		478	Norway
432	Austria, Vienna		479	Norway
433	Austria		480	Poland
434	Austria		481	Poland
435	Austria, Innsbruck		482	Poland, Warsaw
436	Austria		483	Poland
437	Austria		484	Poland
438	Austria		485	Poland
439	Austria		486	Poland
440	United Kingdom		487	Poland
441	United Kingdom, London		488	Poland
442	United Kingdom, N. Ireland, Wales		489	Poland
			490	West Germany
			491	West Germany
443	United Kingdom, Edinburgh		492	West Germany, Bonn
444	United Kingdom, Glasgow		493	West Germany, Berlin
445	United Kingdom, Liverpool		494	West Germany, Hamburg
446	United Kingdom		495	West Germany
447	United Kingdom		496	West Germany, Frankfurt
448	United Kingdom		497	West Germany
449	United Kingdom		498	West Germany, Munich
450	Denmark		499	West Germany
451	Denmark, Copenhagen		501	Belize
452	Denmark, Copenhagen		502	Guatemala
453	Denmark		503	El Salvador
454	Denmark		504	Honduras
455	Denmark, Esbjerg		505	Nicaragua
456	Denmark		506	Costa Rica
457	Denmark		507	Panama
458	Denmark, Aalborg		509	Haiti
459	Denmark			

510	Peru	558	Brazil
511	Peru, Lima	559	Brazil
512	Peru	560	Chile
513	Peru	561	Chile
514	Peru	562	Chile, Santiago
515	Peru, Arequipa	563	Chile, Valparaiso
516	Peru	564	Chile, Concepcion
517	Peru	565	Chile
518	Peru	566	Chile
519	Peru	567	Chile
520	Mexico, Mexico City	568	Chile
521	Mexico, Chihuahua	569	Chile
522	Mexico, Puebla	570	Colombia
523	Mexico, Guadalajara	571	Colombia
524	Mexico, Leon	572	Colombia
525	Mexico, Mexico City	573	Colombia
526	Mexico, Tijuana	574	Colombia
527	Mexico, Acapulco	575	Colombia
528	Mexico, Monterrey	576	Colombia
529	Cancun, Mexico	577	Colombia
530	Cuba	578	Colombia
531	Cuba	579	Colombia
532	Cuba	580	Venezuela
533	Cuba	582	Venezuela, Caracas
534	Cuba	583	Venezuela
535	Cuba	584	Venezuela
536	Cuba	586	Venezuela, Maracaibo
537	Cuba	587	Venezuela
538	Cuba	588	Venezuela
539	Cuba	589	Venezuela
540	Argentina	590	Guadaloupe
541	Argentina, Buenos Aires	591	Bolivia
542	Argentina	592	Guyana
543	Argentina	593	Ecuador
544	Argentina	594	French Guinea
545	Argentina, Cordoba	595	Paraguay
546	Argentina, San Juan	596	French Antille
547	Argentina	597	Surinam
548	Argentina	598	Uruguay
549	Argentina	599	Netherland Antille
550	Brazil	600	Malaysia
551	Brazil, Sao Paulo	601	Malaysia
552	Brazil, Rio de Janeiro	602	Malaysia
553	Brazil	603	Malaysia
554	Brazil	604	Malaysia, Alor Star
555	Brazil	605	Malaysia
556	Brazil, Brasillia	606	Malaysia, Port Dickson
557	Brazil	607	Malaysia

608	Malaysia	657	Singapore
609	Malaysia	658	Singapore
610	Australia	659	Singapore
611	Australia	660	Thailand
612	Australia, Sydney	661	Thailand
613	Australia, Melbourne	662	Thailand, Bangkok
614	Australia	663	Thailand
615	Australia, Brisbane	664	Thailand
616	Australia	665	Thailand
618	Australia	666	Thailand
619	Australia, Perth	667	Thailand
620	Indonesia	668	Thailand
621	Indonesia	669	Thailand
622	Indonesia	671	Guam
623	Indonesia	672	Portuguese Timor
624	Indonesia	673	Brunei
625	Indonesia	674	Nauru
626	Indonesia	674	Papua New Guinea
627	Indonesia	676	Tonga
628	Indonesia	677	Solomon Islands
629	Indonesia	678	New Hebrides
630	Philippines	679	Fiji
631	Philippines	681	Wallis Futuna
632	Philippines, Manila	682	Cook Islands
633	Philippines	683	Nieuw Island
634	Philippines	684	American Samoa
635	Philippines	685	Western Samoa
636	Philippines	686	Kiribati
637	Philippines	687	New Caledonia
638	Philippines	688	Tuvalu
639	Philippines	689	French Polynesia
640	New Zealand	700-799	USSR
641	New Zealand	810	Japan
642	New Zealand	811	Japan
643	New Zealand, Christchurch	812	Japan
644	New Zealand, Wellington	813	Japan, Tokyo
645	New Zealand	814	Japan, Yokohama
646	New Zealand	815	Japan
647	New Zealand	816	Japan, Osaka
648	New Zealand	817	Japan, Kyoto
649	New Zealand, Aukland	818	Japan, Hiroshima
650	Singapore	819	Japan
651	Singapore	820	Korea
652	Singapore	821	Korea
653	Singapore	822	Korea, Seoul
654	Singapore	823	Korea
655	Singapore	824	Korea
656	Singapore	825	Korea, Pusan

826	Korea	917	India
827	Korea	918	India
828	Korea	919	India
829	Korea	920	Pakistan
840	Viet Nam	921	Pakistan
841	Viet Nam	922	Pakistan, Karachi
842	Viet Nam	923	Pakistan
843	Viet Nam	924	Pakistan
844	Viet Nam	925	Pakistan
845	Viet Nam	926	Pakistan
846	Viet Nam	927	Pakistan
847	Viet Nam	928	Pakistan
848	Viet Nam	929	Pakistan
849	Viet Nam	930	Afghanistan
852	Hong Kong	931	Afghanistan
853	Macao	932	Afghanistan
855	Kampuchea	933	Afghanistan
856	Laos	934	Afghanistan
860	China	935	Afghanistan
861	China, Beijing	936	Afghanistan
862	Taiwan	937	Afghanistan
863	China	938	Afghanistan
864	China	939	Afghanistan
865	China	941	Sri Lanka, Colombo
866	China	942	Sri Lanka
867	Taiwan	943	Sri Lanka
868	China	944	Sri Lanka, Matara
869	China	945	Sri Lanka
870	Maritime Mobile	946	Sri Lanka
880	Bangladesh	947	Sri Lanka
886	Taiwan	948	Sri Lanka
900	Turkey	949	Sri Lanka
901	Turkey, Istanbul	950	Burma
902	Turkey	951	Burma
903	Turkey	952	Burma
904	Turkey, Ankara	953	Burma
905	Turkey, Izmir	954	Burma
906	Turkey	955	Burma
907	Turkey	956	Burma
908	Turkey	957	Burma
909	Turkey	958	Burma
910	India	960	Maldives
911	India	961	Lebanon
912	India	962	Jordan
913	India, Calcutta	963	Syria
914	India	964	Iraq
915	India	965	Kuwait
916	India	966	Saudi Arabia

967	Yeman Arab Republic	979	Abu Dhabi
968	Oman	980	Iran
969	Yeman Peoples	981	Iran
	Democratic Republic	982	Iran
971	United Arab Emirates	983	Iran
972	Israel	984	Iran
973	Bahrain	985	Iran
974	Qatar	986	Iran
976	Mongolia, Bhutan	987	Iran
977	Nepal	988	Iran
978	Dubai	989	Iran

International Numbering Plan Listed by Country

Country	Country Code	Country	Country Code
Abu Dhabi	979	Belgium	326
Afars and Issas (Djibouti)	253	Belgium	327
Afghanistan	930-939	Belgium	328
Albania	355	Belgium	329
Algeria	213	Belgium, Antwerp	323
American Samoa	684	Belgium, Brussels	322
Andorra	330	Belize	501
Angola	244	Benin	229
Argentina	540	Bolivia	591
Argentina	542	Botswana	267
Argentina	543	Brazil	550
Argentina	544	Brazil	553
Argentina	547	Brazil	554
Argentina	548	Brazil	555
Argentina	549	Brazil	557
Argentina, Buenos Aires	541	Brazil	558
Argentina, Cordoba	545	Brazil	559
Argentina, San Juan	546	Brazil, Brasilia	556
Aruba	297	Brazil, Rio de Janeiro	552
Australia	610	Brazil, Sao Paulo	551
Australia	611	Brunei	673
Australia	614	Bulgaria	359
Australia	616	Burkina Faso	226
Australia	618	Burma	950-988
Australia, Brisbane	615	Burundi	257
Australia, Melbourne	613	Cameroon	237
Australia, Perth	619	Cancun, Mexico	529
Australia, Sydney	612	Central African Republic	236
Austria	430	Chad	235
Austria	431	Chile	560
Austria	433	Chile	561
Austria	434	Chile	565
Austria	436	Chile	566
Austria	437	Chile	567
Austria	438	Chile	568
Austria	439	Chile	569
Austria, Innsbruck	435	Chile, Concepcion	564
Austria, Vienna	432	Chile, Santiago	562
Bahrain	973	Chile, Valparaiso	563
Bangladesh	880	China	860
Belgium	320	China	863
Belgium	321	China	864
Belgium	324	China	865
Belgium	325	China	866

China	868	Egypt	209
China	869	Egypt, Alexandria	203
China, Beijing	861	Egypt, Cairo	202
Colombia	570-879	El Salvador	503
Comorro Islands	269	Equatorial Guinea	240
Congo	242	Ethiopia	251
Cook Islands	682	Fiji	679
Costa Rica	506	Finland	358
Cuba	530-839	France	332
Cyprus	357	France	333
Czechoslovakia	420	France	334
Czechoslovakia	421	France	336
Czechoslovakia	422	France	337
Czechoslovakia	423	France	338
Czechoslovakia	424	France - Monaco	339
Czechoslovakia	425	France, Bordeaux	335
Czechoslovakia	426	France, Paris	331
Czechoslovakia	427	French Antilles	596
Czechoslovakia	428	French Guinea	594
Czechoslovakia	429	French Polynesia	689
Denmark	450	Gabon	241
Denmark	453	Gambia	220
Denmark	454	Ghana	233
Denmark	456	Gibraltar	350
Denmark	457	Greece	300
Denmark	459	Greece	303
Denmark, Aalborg	458	Greece	304
Denmark, Copenhagen	451	Greece	305
Denmark, Copenhagen	452	Greece	306
Denmark, Esbjerg	455	Greece	307
Dubai	978	Greece	308
East Germany	370	Greece	309
East Germany	371	Greece, Athens	301
East Germany	373	Greece, Rhodes	302
East Germany	376	Guadaloupe	590
East Germany	377	Guam	671
East Germany	378	Guatemala	502
East Germany	379	Guinea	224
East Germany, Berlin	372	Guinea-Bissau	245
East Germany, Dresden	375	Guyana	592
East Germany, Leipzig	374	Haiti	509
Ecuador	593	Honduras	504
Egypt	201	Hong Kong	852
Egypt	204	Hungary	360
Egypt	205	Hungary	362
Egypt	206	Hungary	363
Egypt	207	Hungary	364
Egypt	208	Hungary	365

Hungary	366	Korea	821
Hungary	367	Korea	823
Hungary	368	Korea	824
Hungary	369	Korea	826
Hungary, Budapest	361	Korea	827
Iceland	354	Korea	828
India	910	Korea	829
India	911	Korea, Pusan	825
India	912	Korea, Seoul	822
India	914	Kuwait	965
India	915	Laos	856
India	916	Lebanon	961
India	917	Lesotho	266
India	918	Liberia	231
India	919	Libya	218
India, Calcutta	913	Libya	219
Indonesia	620-629	Liechtenstein	417
Iran	980-989	Luxembourg	352
Iraq	964	Macao	853
Ireland	353	Madagascar	261
Israel	972	Malawi	265
Italy	390	Malaysia	600
Italy	391	Malaysia	601
Italy	393	Malaysia	602
Italy	397	Malaysia	603
Italy	399	Malaysia	605
Italy, Florence,		Malaysia	607
San Marino	395	Malaysia	608
Italy, Milan	392	Malaysia	609
Italy, Naples	398	Malaysia, Alor Star	604
Italy, Rome, Vatican City	396	Malaysia, Port Dickson	606
Italy, Venice	394	Maldives	960
Ivory Coast	225	Mali	223
Japan	810	Malta	356
Japan	811	Maritime Mobile	870
Japan	812	Mauritania	222
Japan	815	Mauritius	230
Japan	819	Mexico, Acapulco	527
Japan, Hiroshima	818	Mexico, Chihuahua	521
Japan, Kyoto	817	Mexico, Guadalajara	523
Japan, Osaka	816	Mexico, Leon	524
Japan, Tokyo	813	Mexico, Mexico City	520
Japan, Yokohama	814	Mexico, Mexico City	525
Jordan	962	Mexico, Monterrey	528
Kampuchea	855	Mexico, Puebla	522
Kenya	254	Mexico, Tijuana	526
Kiribati	686	Mongolia, Bhutan	976
Korea	820	Morocco	212

Mozambique	258	Pakistan	926
Namibia	262	Pakistan	927
Nauru	674	Pakistan	928
Nepal	977	Pakistan	929
Netherland Antille	599	Pakistan, Karachi	922
Netherlands	310	Panama	507
Netherlands	313	Papua New Guinea	674
Netherlands	314	Paraguay	595
Netherlands	315	Peru	510
Netherlands	316	Peru	512
Netherlands	318	Peru	513
Netherlands	319	Peru	514
Netherlands, Amsterdam	312	Peru	516
Netherlands, Rotterdam	311	Peru	517
Netherlands, The Hague	317	Peru	518
New Caledonia	687	Peru	519
New Hebrides	678	Peru, Arequipa	515
New Zealand	640	Peru, Lima	511
New Zealand	641	Philippines	630
New Zealand	642	Philippines	631
New Zealand	645	Philippines	633
New Zealand	646	Philippines	634
New Zealand	647	Philippines	635
New Zealand	648	Philippines	636
New Zealand, Aukland	649	Philippines	637
New Zealand, Christchurch	643	Philippines	638
New Zealand, Wellington	644	Philippines	639
Nicaragua	505	Philippines, Manila	632
Nieuw Island	683	Poland	480
Niger	227	Poland	481
Niger	247	Poland	483
Nigeria	234	Poland	484
Norway	470	Poland	485
Norway	471	Poland	486
Norway	473	Poland	487
Norway	474	Poland	488
Norway	476	Poland	489
Norway	477	Poland, Warsaw	482
Norway	478	Portugal	351
Norway	479	Portuguese Timor	672
Norway, Bergen	475	Qatar	974
Norway, Oslo	472	Reunion	264
Oman	968	Romania	401
Pakistan	920	Romania	402
Pakistan	921	Romania	403
Pakistan	923	Romania	404
Pakistan	924	Romania	405
Pakistan	925	Romania	406

Romania	407	Sweden	464
Romania	408	Sweden	465
Romania	409	Sweden	466
Romania, Bucharest	400	Sweden	467
Rwanda	250	Sweden	469
Sao Tome & Principe	239	Sweden, Goteborg	463
Saudi Arabia	966	Sweden, Stockholm	468
Senegal	221	Switzerland	410
Seychelles	248	Switzerland	415
Sierra Leone	232	Switzerland	416
Singapore	650-689	Switzerland	418
Solomon Islands	677	Switzerland	419
South Africa	270	Switzerland, Berne	413
South Africa	273	Switzerland, Geneva	412
South Africa	274	Switzerland, Lucerne	414
South Africa	275	Switzerland, Zurich	411
South Africa	276	Syria	963
South Africa	277	Taiwan	862
South Africa	278	Taiwan	867
South Africa	279	Taiwan	886
South Africa, Cape Town	272	Tanzania	255
South Africa, Pretoria	271	Thailand	660
Spain	340	Thailand	661
Spain	344	Thailand	663
Spain	346	Thailand	664
Spain	347	Thailand	665
Spain	348	Thailand	666
Spain	349	Thailand	667
Spain - Canary Islands	342	Thailand	668
Spain, Barcelona	343	Thailand	669
Spain, Madrid	341	Thailand, Bangkok	662
Spain, Seville	345	Togo	228
Spanish Sahara	210	Tonga	676
Sri Lanka	942	Tunisia	216
Sri Lanka	943	Tunisia	217
Sri Lanka	945	Turkey	900
Sri Lanka	946	Turkey	902
Sri Lanka	947	Turkey	903
Sri Lanka	948	Turkey	906
Sri Lanka	949	Turkey	907
Sri Lanka, Colombo	941	Turkey	908
Sri Lanka, Matara	944	Turkey	909
Sudan	249	Turkey, Ankara	904
Surinam	597	Turkey, Istanbul	901
Swaziland	268	Turkey, Izmir	905
Sweden	460	Tuvalu	688
Sweden	461	United Arab Emirates	971
Sweden	462	United Kingdom	440

United Kingdom	446	West Germany	499
United Kingdom	447	West Germany	497
United Kingdom	448	West Germany, Berlin	493
United Kingdom	449	West Germany, Bonn	492
United Kingdom, Edinburgh	443	West Germany, Frankfurt	496
United Kingdom, Glasgow	444	West Germany, Hamburg	494
United Kingdom, Liverpool	445	West Germany, Munich	498
United Kingdom, London	441	Western Samoa	685
United Kingdom,		Yeman Arab Republic	967
N. Ireland, Wales	442	Yeman Peoples	
Uruguay	598	Democratic Republic	969
USSR	700-799	Yugoslavia	380
Venezuela	580	Yugoslavia	382
Venezuela	583	Yugoslavia	383
Venezuela	584	Yugoslavia	384
Venezuela	587	Yugoslavia	385
Venezuela	588	Yugoslavia	386
Venezuela	589	Yugoslavia	387
Venezuela, Caracas	582	Yugoslavia	389
Venezuela, Maracaibo	586	Yugoslavia, Belgrade	381
Viet Nam	840-849	Yugoslavia, Titograd	388
Wallis Futuna	681	Zaire	243
West Germany	490	Zambia	260
West Germany	491	Zanzibar	259
West Germany	495	Zimbabwe	263

Telecommunications
Acronym Dictionary

The telecommunications industry is as expansive in its use of acronyms as the computer industry. The following is a list of acronyms used in this book, without definitions. Definitions for all acronyms are indexed by their full name in the glossary.

AC	Alternating Current
ACD	Automatic Call Distributor
ACTS	Automatic Coin Telephone System
ADPCM	Adaptive Differential Pulse Code Modulation
AF	Audio Frequency
AIS	Automatic Intercept System
ALI	Automatic Location Information
AMA	Automatic Message Accounting
AMI	Alternate Mark Inversion
ANI	Automatic Number Identification
AOS	Alternate Operator Service
APD	Avalanche Photo Diode
ARQ	Automatic Repeat Request
ASCII	American Standard Code for Information Interexchange
ATM	Asynchronous Transfer Mode
AWG	American Wire Gauge
B8ZS	Bipolar with 8-Zero Substitution

BCD	Blocked Calls Delayed
BCH	Blocked Calls Held
BCR	Blocked Calls Released
BER	Bit Error Rate
BHCA	Busy Hour Call Attempts
BIOS	Basic Input/Output System
BLER	Block Error Rate
BOC	Bell Operating Company
BRI	Basic Rate Interface
BSA	Basic Service Arrangement
BSC	Binary Synchronous Communications
BSE	Basic Service Element
CAC	Carrier Access Code
CAD	Computer Aided Dispatch; Computer Aided Design
CAS	Centralized Attendant Service
CATV	Community Antenna Television
CBX	Computer Branch Exchange
CCIS	Common Channel Interoffice Signaling
CCITT	Consultative Committee on International Telephone and Telegraph
CCS	Centum Call Seconds
CCS	Common Channel Signaling
CCTV	Closed Circuit Television
CDO	Community Dial Office
CDR	Call Detail Recorder
CELP	Code Excited Linear Prediction
CEPT	Conference European on Post and Telecommunications
CGSA	Cellular Geographic Serving Area
CLASS	Custom Local Area Signaling Services
CNS	Complementary Network Services
CO	Central Office
CODEC	Coder/Decoder
CPE	Customer Premises Equipment
CPU	Central Processing Unit
CRC	Cyclical Redundancy Checking
CRSO	Cellular Radio Switching Office

CSM/CD	Carrier Sense Multiple Access with Collision Detection
CSU	Channel Service Unit
DAMA	Demand Assigned Multiple Access
dB	Decibel
DBS	Direct Broadcast Satellite
DC	Direct Current
DCE	Data Circuit-Terminating Equipment
DCS	Digital Crossconnect System
DDD	Direct Distance Dialing
DID	Direct Inward Dialing
DMI	Digital Multiplexed Interface
DNIC	Data Network Identification Code
DNIS	Dialed Number Identification Service
DOC	Dynamic Overload Control
DOV	Data Over Voice
DQDB	Distributed Queue Dual Bus
DSI	Digital Speech Interpolation
DSX	Digital Service Crossconnect
DTE	Data Terminal Equipment
DTMF	Dual Tone Multifrequency
EAS	Extended Area Service
EBCDIC	Expanded Binary Coded Decimal Interexchange Code
EDI	Electronic Data Interchange
EFS	Error Free Seconds
EIRP	Effective Isotropic Radiated Power
EMI	Electromagnetic Interference
ERL	Echo Return Loss
ESF	Extended Super Frame
ESP	Enhanced Service Provider
ESS	Electronic Switching System
ETN	Electronic Tandem Network
FDDI	Fiber Distributed Data Interface
FDMA	Frequency Division Multiple Access
FEC	Forward Error Correction
FX	Foreign Exchange
gb/s	Gigabits Per Second
GHz	Gigahertz

GOS	Grade of Service
HDTV	High Definition Television
Hz	Hertz
IC	Independent Company
IDF	Intermediate Distributing Frame
IEC	Interexchange Carrier
IMTS	Improved Mobile Telephone Service
INMARSAT	International Maritime Satellite Service
INWATS	Inward Wide Area Telephone Service
ISDN	Integrated Services Digital Network
IVR	Interactive Voice Response
kb/s	Kilobits Per Second
KHz	Kilohertz
KTS	Key Telephone System
LAN	Local Area Network
LAPD	Link Access Procedure D
LATA	Local Access Transport Area
LCR	Least Cost Routing
LEC	Local Exchange Carrier
LED	Light Emitting Diode
LIT	Line Insulation Test
LLC	Logical Link Control
LMX	L Multiplex
LTD	Local Test Desk
MAP/TOP	Manufacturing Automation Protocol/Technical and Office Protocol
mb/s	Megabits Per Second
MCVD	Modified Chemical Vapor Deposit
MDF	Main Distributing Frame
MHz	Megahertz
MLN	Main Listed Number
MTBF	Mean Time Between Failures
MTS	Message Telephone Service
MTTR	Mean Time to Repair
NAU	Network Access Unit
NCTE	Network Channel Terminating Equipment
NID	Network Interface Device

NMCC	Network Management Control Center
NPA	Numbering Plan Area
NT1	Network Termination 1
NT12	Network Termination 12
NT2	Network Termination 2
NTN	Network Terminal Number
ONA	Open Network Architecture
OPX	Off-Premises Extension
OSI	Open Systems Interconnect
OSS	Operations Support System
P/AR	Peak-to-Average Ratio
PABX	Private Automatic Branch Exchange
PAD	Packet Assembler/Disassembler
PAM	Pulse Amplitude Modulation
PASP	Public Service Answering Point
PBX	Private Branch Exchange
PCM	Pulse Code Modulation
PIC	Primary Interexchange Carrier
PIN	Personal Identification Number
Pixel	Picture Element
POP	Point of Presence
PRI	Primary Rate Interface
PSK	Phase Shift Keying
PSTN	Public Switched Telephone Network
QAM	Quadrature Amplitude Modulation
RCF	Remote Call Forwarding
RMATS	Remote Maintenance and Testing System
rms	Root Mean Square
rn	Reference Noise
ROTL	Remote Office Test Line
RSL	Received Signal Level
SCC	Satellite Communications Control
SDN	Software Defined Network
SF	Single Frequency
SMDR	Station Message Detail Recording
SMDS	Switched Multimegabit Data Service
SMSA	Standard Metropolitan Statistical Area

SNA	Systems Network Architecture
SONET	Synchronous Optical Network
SPC	Stored Program Control
SRL	Singing Return Loss
SSB	Single Sideband
SSTDMA	Spacecraft Switched Time Division Multiple Access
TCM	Trellis-Coded Modulation
TDM	Time Division Multiplexing
TDMA	Time Division Multiple Access
TDR	Time Domain Reflectometer
TE1	Terminal Equipment Type 1
TE2	Terminal Equipment Type 2
TLP	Transmission Level Point
TUR	Traffic Usage Recorder
UCD	Uniform Call Distribution
UPS	Uninterruptable Power Supply
VF	Voice Frequency
VNL	Via Net Loss
VPN	Virtual Private Network
VRU	Voice Response Unit
VU	Volume Unit
WATS	Wide Area Telephone Service
WDM	Wavelength Division Multiplexing
XPD	Cross Polarization Discrimination

Glossary

A Bit. In T-1 carrier, the signaling bit that is formed from the eighth bit of the sixth channel.

A Law. The coding law used in the European 30-channel PCM system.

Absorption. The attenuation of a lightwave signal by impurities or fiber core imperfections, or of a microwave signal by oxygen or water vapor in the atmosphere.

Access. The capability of devices on a network to be interconnected with one another.

Access Tandem. An LEC switching system that provides access for the IECs to the local network. The access tandem provides the IEC with access to more than one end office within a LATA.

Access Time. The time required for a hard disk to retrieve information requested by a file server. Access time consists of seek time plus rotate time.

Acoustic Coupler. A method of connecting a modem to a voice circuit with a handset adapter that picks up modem tones through the mouthpiece and sends them to the modem through the earpiece of a handset.

Adaptive Bridge.   See Learning Bridge.

Adaptive Differential Pulse Code Modulation (ADPCM). A method approved by CCITT for coding voice channels at 32 kb/s to increase the capacity of T-1 to either 44 or 48 channels.

Adaptive Equalizer. (1) Circuitry in a modem that allows the modem to compensate automatically for circuit conditions that impair high speed data transmission. (2) A circuit installed in a microwave receiver to compensate for distortion caused by multipath fading.

Adaptive Integration. A voice mail feature that enables the mail system to give personalized service to callers depending on the called party's personal preference. Includes such features as transfer to a personal assistant and variable treatment according to the time of day.

Addressing. The process of sending digits over a telecommunications circuit to direct the switching equipment to the station address of the called number.

Aerial Cable. Any cable that is partially or completely run aerially between buildings or poles.

Alerting. The use of signals on a telecommunications circuit to alert the called party or equipment to an incoming call.

Algorithm. A set of processes in a computer program used to solve a problem with a given set of steps.

Alternate Mark Inversion (AMI). See Bipolar Coding.

Alternate Operator Service (AOS). An operator service provider, not connected with a major IEC, that handles operator functions such as coin, third number, collect, and credit card billing.

Alternate Routing. The ability of a switching system to establish a path to another system over more than one circuit group.

Alternating Current (AC). Current flow that changes over time from a peak positive value to a peak negative value.

American Standard Code for Information Interexchange (ASCII). A seven-bit (plus one parity bit) coding system used for encoding characters for transmission over a data network.

American Wire Gauge (AWG). The American standard method of designating wire size. The higher the number, the finer the wire.

Ampere. A unit of measure of current flow.

Amplitude Distortion. Any variance in the level of frequencies within the pass band of a communication channel.

Analog. A transmission mode in which information is transmitted by converting it to a continuously variable electrical signal.

Angle of Acceptance. The angle of light rays striking an optical fiber aperture, within which light is guided through the fiber. Light outside the angle of acceptance escapes through the cladding.

Answer Supervision. A signal that is sent from a switching system through the trunking network to the originating end of a call to signal that a call has been answered.

Antenna Gain. The increase in radiated power from an antenna compared to an isotropic antenna.

Application Program. A computer program that performs a specific function such as word processing or spreadsheet.

Applications Processor. An ancillary processor to a PBX that performs a specific function such as message handling.

Area Code. See Numbering Plan Area.

Armored Cable. Multipair cable intended for direct burial that is armored with a metallic covering that serves to prevent damage from rodents and digging apparatus.

Aspect Ratio. The ratio between the width and the height of a video screen.

Asynchronous. A means of transmitting data over a network wherein each character contains a start and a stop bit to keep the transmitting and receiving terminals sychronized.

Asynchronous Transfer Mode (ATM). A connection-type transmission system carrying information in the form of headers followed by information blocks. Recurrence of blocks depends on instantaneous bandwidth requirements.

Atmospheric Loss. The attenuation of a radio signal because of absorption by oxygen molecules and water vapor in the atmosphere.

Audible Ring. A tone returned from the called party's switching machine to inform the calling party that the called line is being rung.

Audio Frequency (AF). A range of frequencies, nominally 20 Hz to 20 KHz, that the human ear can hear.

Audiotex. A method of delivering information from a voice processing system in response to DTMF tones that the caller dials.

Autodial. Automatic dialing of a number that is programmed into a telephone or PBX.

Automated Attendant. A feature of voice mail and stand-alone systems that answers calls, prompts callers to enter DTMF digits in response to menu options, and routes the call to an extension or call distributor.

Automatic Call Distributor (ACD). A system that directs incoming calls to a group of agents. Calls are directed to the first available agent or queued until an agent is available.

Automatic Coin Telephone System (ACTS). A coin telephone service that rates calls, collects coins, and completes other types of calls without intervention by an operator.

Automatic Intercept System (AIS). An LEC service system that intercepts calls to disconnected numbers and routes them to a call transfer announcement.

Automatic Location Information (ALI). Emergency equipment that enables the 911 center to determine the location of a caller using a table lookup function.

Automatic Message Accounting (AMA). Equipment that registers the details of chargeable calls and enters them on a storage medium for processing by an off-line center.

Automatic Number Identification (ANI). Circuitry in a switching system that automatically identifies the calling party's telephone number on a billable call.

Automatic Repeat Request (ARQ). A data communications protocol that automatically initiates a request to repeat the last transmission if an error is received.

Availability. (1) The ratio of circuit uptime to total elapsed time. (2) In a switching system, the ability of every input port to reach every output port.

Avalanche Photo Diode (APD). A light detector that generates an output current many times greater than the light energy striking its face.

B Bit. In T-1 carrier, the signaling bit that is formed from the eighth bit of the twelfth channel.

B Channel. See Bearer Channel.

Backboard. A board made of wood or plastic on which terminating blocks are mounted in a wiring system.

Backoff Algorithm. The formula, built into a contention network, used after collision by the media access controller to determine when to reattempt to acquire the network.

Backplane. A network of wiring with sockets into which printed circuit cards can be placed.

Back-to-Back Channel Bank. The interconnection of voice frequency and signaling leads between channel banks to allow dropping and inserting channels.

Balance. The degree of electrical match between the two sides of a cable pair or between a two-wire circuit and the matching network in a four-wire terminating set.

Balanced Modulator. An amplitude modulating circuit that suppresses the carrier signal, resulting in an output consisting of only upper and lower sidebands.

Balancing Network. A network used in a four-wire terminating set to match the impedance of the two-wire circuit.

Balun. A device that converts the unbalanced wiring of a coaxial terminal system to a balanced twisted pair system.

Band. A range of frequencies.

Bandpass. The range of frequencies that a channel will pass without excessive attenuation.

Bandwidth. The range of frequencies a communications channel is capable of carrying without excessive attenuation.

Bandwidth Manager. See Voice/Data Multiplexer.

Banyan Switch. A high speed switching system that takes its name from the many branches of a banyan tree. A banyan switch is bidirectional and chooses its path from the address contained in the header of an incoming packet. If an address bit is a 1, the upper path of the switch is taken. Otherwise the switch takes the lower, or 0, path.

Baseband. A form of modulation in which data signals are pulsed directly on the transmission medium without frequency division.

Basic Input/Output System (BIOS). A collection of software routines that a computer uses to communicate with its peripherals.

Basic Rate Interface (BRI). The basic ISDN interface that consists of two bearer (B) channels and one data (D) channel.

Basic Service Arrangement (BSA). An ONA term referring to the fundamental switching and transport service obtained by an information service provider to serve its customers over the PSTN.

Basic Service Element (BSE). Functions of the telephone network broken down into essentials that are defined in the FCC's Open Network Architecture plan.

Battery. A direct current voltage supply that powers telephones and telecommunications apparatus.

Baud. The number of signal events on a circuit per unit of time.

Beacon. In a token ring network, beacons are signals sent by stations to isolate and bypass failures.

Bell Operating Company (BOC). One of the 22 local exchange companies (LECs) that were previously part of the Bell System.

Bearer Channel. A 64 kb/s information-carrying channel that furnishes integrated services digital network (ISDN) services to end users.

Binary. A numbering system consisting of two digits   0 and 1.

Binary Synchronous Communications (BSC or Bisync). An IBM byte-controlled half duplex protocol using a defined set of control characters and sequences for data transmission.

Bipolar Coding. The T carrier line coding system that inverts the polarity of alternate 1s bits. Also called alternate mark inversion (AMI).

Bipolar Violation. The presence of two consecutive 1s bits of the same polarity on a T carrier line.

Bipolar with 8-Zero Substitution (B8ZS). A line coding scheme used with T-1 clear channel to send a string of eight zeros with a deliberate bipolar violation. The 1s bits in the bipolar violation maintain line synchronization.

Bit. The smallest unit of binary information; a contraction formed from the words BInary digIT.

Bit Error Rate (BER). The number of error bits in a signal expressed as a fraction of the number of transmitted bits.

Bit Rate. The number of bits per second a communications system carries.

Bit Robbing. The use of the least significant bit per channel in every sixth frame of a T-1 carrier system for signaling.

Bit Stream. A continuous string of bits transmitted serially in time.

Bit Stuffing. Adding bits to a digital frame for synchronizing and control. Used in T carrier to prevent loss of synchronization from 15 or more consecutive 0 bits.

Block Error Rate (BLER). In a given unit of time, BLER measures the number of blocks that must be retransmitted because of error

Blocked Call. A call that cannot be connected immediately because no path is available at the time the call arrives.

Blocked Calls Delayed (BCD). A variable used in queuing theory to describe the behavior of the input process when the user is held in queue upon encountering blockage.

Blocked Calls Held (BCH). A variable used in queuing theory to describe the behavior of the input process when the user immediately redials upon encountering blockage.

Blocked Calls Released (BCR). A variable used in queuing theory to describe the behavior of the input process when the user waits for a time before redialing when encountering blockage.

Blocking. A switching system condition in which no circuits are available to complete a call, and a busy signal is returned to the caller.

Bonding. The permanent connecting of metallic conductors to equalize potential between the conductors and carry any current that is likely to be imposed.

Boot. A program that starts another program.

Branch Feeder. A cable between distribution cable and the main feeder cable that connects users to the central office.

Branching Filter. A device inserted in a waveguide to separate or combine different microwave frequency bands.

Break. An interruption in transmission on a circuit.

Breakdown Voltage. The voltage at which electricity will flow across an insulating substance between two conductors.

Bridge. Circuitry used to interconnect networks with a common set of higher level protocols.

Bridged Tap. Any section of a cable pair that is not on the direct electrical path between the central office and the user's premises.

Bridger Amplifier. An amplifier installed on a CATV trunk cable to feed branching cables.

Broadband. A form of modulation in which multiple channels are formed by dividing the transmission medium into discrete frequency segments.

Broadcast Address. A network address that includes all stations on the network that are intended to receive a transmission.

Brouter. A local area network bridge that is capable of routing.

Buried Cable. A cable that is buried in the ground without being enclosed in conduit.

Bus. A group of conductors that connects two or more circuit elements, usually at a high speed for a short distance.

Busy Hour. The composite of various peak load periods selected for the purpose of designing network capacity.

Busy Hour Call Attempts (BHCA). The number of call originations that occur during the hour or hours in which a telecommunications system carries the maximum number of calls.

Busy Season. An annually recurring interval in which call volumes reach a peak for a specified period of time such as 10 days.

Bypass. Routing circuits around the facilities of a local exchange carrier by some form of technology such as lightwave or microwave.

Byte. A set of eight bits of information equivalent to a character. Also sometimes called an octet.°

C Message Weighting. A factor used in noise measurements to describe the lesser annoying effect on the human ear of high and low frequency noise compared to mid-range noise.

C Notched Noise. A measurement of C message-weighted noise in a circuit with a tone applied at the far end and filtered out at the near end.

Cable Racking. Framework fastened to bays to support inter-bay cabling.

Caching. The use of memory in a file server to read more information than is requested, storing it so the next information request can be served from memory instead of from the disk.

Call-Back Queueing. A trunk queueing system in which the switching system signals the users that all trunks are busy and calls them back when a trunk is available.

Call Detail Recorder (CDR). An auxiliary device attached to a PBX to capture and record call details such as called number, time of day, duration, etc.

Call Progress Tones. Tones returned from switching systems to inform the calling party of the progress of the call. Examples are audible ring, reorder, and busy.

Call Sequencer. An electronic device similar to an automatic call distributor that can answer calls, play an announcement, hold callers in queue, and provide limited statistical information.

Call Store. The temporary memory used in an SPC switching system to hold records of calls in progress and pending changes to permanent memory.

Call Warning Tone. A tone placed on a circuit to indicate that the call is about to route to a high cost facility.

Called Party Control. The provision in a 911 system for the called party to supervise a call and to hold it up for tracing.

Capacitance. The property of an electronic circuit element that stores an electrical charge.

Capacity. The number of call attempts and busy hour load that a switching system is capable of supporting.

Carbon Block Protector. A form of electrical protector that uses a pair of carbon blocks separated from ground by a narrow gap. When the voltage from the block to ground exceeds a specified value, the blocks arc across to ground the circuit.

Carried Load. The amount of traffic that a switching system or trunk group carries during a set period of time; usually one hour.

Carrier. (1) A company that carries telecommunications services for a fee. (2) A signal that can be modulated to carry intelligence from another signal. (3) A type of multiplexing equipment used to derive several channels from one communications link by combining signals on the basis of time or frequency division.

Carrier Access Code (CAC). A five-digit code consisting of the digits 10 plus a three-digit carrier identification code. For example, the CAC for MCI is 10222.

Carrier Sense Multiple Access with Collision Detection CSMA/CD). A system used in contention networks where the network interface unit listens for the presence of a carrier before attempting to send and detects the presence of a collision by monitoring for a distorted pulse.

Carrier to Noise Ratio. The ratio of the received carrier to the noise level in a satellite link.

Consultative Committee on International Telephone and Telegraph (CCITT). An element of the International Telecommunications Union, which establishes international telecommunications standards.

Cell. A hexagonal subdivision of a mobile telephone service area containing a cell-site controller and radio frequency transceivers. Also, a group of bytes conditioned for transmission across a network.

Cell Relay. A proposed method of transmitting information at high speed across a physical network.

Cell-Site Controller. The cellular radio unit that manages radio channels within a cell.

Cellular Geographic Serving Area (CGSA). A metropolitan area in which the FCC grants cellular radio licenses.

Cellular Radio Switching Office (CRSO). The electronic switching system that switches calls between mobile and wireline telephones, controls handoff between cells, and monitors usage. This equipment is known by various trade names.

Centralized Attendant Service (CAS). A PBX feature that enables an attendant at a centralized location to answer calls arriving at one or more distant PBXs.

Central Office (CO). A switching center that terminates and interconnects lines and trunks from users.

Central Office LAN. A service offered by many LECs that provides a data switching function inside the central office. Data is carried to the central office by data-over-voice carrier.

Central Processing Unit (CPU). The control logic element used to execute instructions in a computer.

Centrex. A class of central office service that provides the equivalent of PBX service from a telephone company switching system.

Centum Call Seconds (CCS). See Hundred Call Seconds.

Channel. A communications path that is capable of carrying a signal.

Channel Bank. Apparatus that converts multiple voice frequency signals to frequency or time division multiplexed signals for transmitting over a transmission medium.

Channel Service Unit (CSU). Apparatus that interfaces DTE to a line connecting to a dataport channel unit to enable digital communications without a modem. Used with DSU when DTE lacks complete digital line interface capability.

Chrominance. The portion of a television signal that carries color encoding information to the receiver.

Circuit. A transmission path between two points in a telecommunications system.

Circuit Pack. A plug-in electronic device that contains the circuitry to perform a specific function. A circuit pack is not capable of stand-alone operation but functions only as an element of the parent device.

Circuit Switching. A method of network access in which terminals are connected by switching together the circuits to which they are attached. In a circuit switched network, the terminals have full real-time access to each other up to the bandwidth of the circuit.

Cladding. The outer coating of glass surrounding the core in a lightguide.

Class 5 Office. The former designation for an end office in the AT&T/BOC switching hierarchy that directly serves end users. See End Office.

Class of Service. A classification assigned to a station in a PBX that defines the features and restrictions applied to that station.

Clear Channel. The elimination of bit-robbed signaling in a digital channel to enable use of all 64 kb/s for digital transmission.

Client. A workstation in a local area network that is set up to use the resources of a server.

Clock. A device that generates a signal for controlling network synchronization.

Closed Circuit Television (CCTV). A privately operated television system not connected to a public distribution network.

Cluster Controller. A device that controls access of a group of terminals to a higher level computer.

Coaxial Cable. A single-wire conductor, surrounded by an insulating medium and a metallic shield, that is used for carrying a telecommunications signal.

Code Blocking. The capability of a switching system to block calls to a specified area code, central office code, or telephone number.

Code Conversion. The process of registering incoming digits from a line or trunk and converting them to a different code required for call routing.

Code Excited Linear Prediction (CELP). A speech encoding algorithm that enables speech to be digitized at 8.0 kb/s with quality approximately equal to that of analog FM systems.

Coder/Decoder (codec). The analog-to-digital conversion circuitry in the line equipment of a digital CO. Also, a device in television transmission that compresses a video signal into a narrow digital channel.

Coherence Bandwidth. The bandwidth of a range of frequencies that are subjected to the same degree of frequency-selective fading.

Coin-Free Dialing. The ability of a caller from a coin telephone to reach an emergency or assistance operator without using a coin to place the call.

Collimate. The condition of parallel light rays in a fiber optic facility.

Collision. A condition that occurs when two or more terminals on a contention network attempt to gsin access to the network simultaneously.

Collision Window. The time it takes for a data pulse to travel the length of the network. During this interval, the network is vulnerable to collision.

Common Carrier. A company that carries communications services for the general public within an assigned territory.

Common Channel Interoffice Signaling (CCIS). The AT&T common channel signaling system used in North America.

Common Channel Signaling (CCS). A separate data network used to route signals between switching systems.

Common Control Switching. A switching system that uses shared equipment to establish, monitor, and disconnect paths through the network. The equipment is called into the connection to perform a function and then released to serve other users.

Communicating Word Processor. A word processor that includes protocols for enabling memory-to-memory transfer over a telecommunication circuit.

Communications Controller. See Front End Processor.

Community Antenna Television (CATV). A network for distributing television signals over coaxial cable throughout a community. Also called cable television.°

Community Dial Office (CDO). A small CO designed for unattended operation in a community, usually limited to about 10,000 lines.

Compandor. A device that compresses high level voice signals in the transmitting direction and expands them in the receiving direction with respect to lower level signals. Its purpose is to improve noise performance in a circuit.

Complement. A group of 50 cable pairs (25 pairs in small cable sizes) that are bound together and identified as a unit.

Complementary Network Services (CNS). An ONA term referring to a service residing on the user's side of the telephone line. The user purchases CNSs to connect to an information service provider.

Composite (CX) Signaling. A direct current signaling system that separates the signal from the voice band by filters.

Computer Aided Dispatch (CAD). A feature used by many public agencies that employs a computer to track the location and availability of emergency personnel.

Computer Branch Exchange (CBX). A computer-controlled PBX.

Concentration. The process of connecting a group of inputs to a smaller number of outputs in a network. If there are more inputs than outputs, the network has concentration.

Concentration Ratio. As applied to CO line equipment, it is the ratio between the number of lines in an equipment group and the number of links or trunks that can be accessed from the lines.

Concentrator. A device that can multiplex several sessions onto a single line.

Conditioning. The process of applying special treatment to a private line circuit to improve its ability to carry data.

Conference European on Post and Telecommunications CEPT). The European telecommunications standards-setting body.

Connectivity. The ability to connect a device to a network.

Contention. A form of multiple access to a network in which the network capacity is allocated on a first come first served° basis.

Control Equipment. Equipment used to transmit orders from an alarm center to a remote site to perform operations by remote control.

Converter. A device for changing central office voltage to another DC voltage for powering equipment.

Core. The inner glass element that guides the light rays in an optical fiber.

Critical Rain Rate. The amount of rainfall where the drops are of sufficient size and intensity to cause fading in a microwave signal.

Cross. A circuit impairment where two separate circuits are unintentionally interconnected.

Crossbar. A type of switching system that uses a centrally controlled matrix switching network consisting of electromechanical switches connecting horizontal and vertical paths to establish a path through the network.

Crossconnect. The interconnection of voice or signal paths between separate equipment units.

Cross-Polarization Discrimination (XPD). The amount of decoupling between radio waves that exists when they are cross polarized.

Cross Polarization. The relationship between two radio waves when one is polarized vertically and the other horizontally.

Crosstalk. The unwanted coupling of a signal from one transmission path into another.

Current. The flow of electrons through an electrical circuit.

Customer Premises Equipment (CPE). Any equipment such as telephones, PBXs, network channel terminating equipment, key telephone equipment, modems, etc. that is provided by the user and is normally located on the user's premises.

Custom Local Area Signaling Services (CLASS). A suite of services that LECs deliver to end users. Examples are calling party number identification, call transfer, and traffic information.

Cutover. The time at which a transition from one communications system to another takes place.

Cyclical Redundancy Checking (CRC). A data error-detecting system wherein an information block is subjected to a mathematical process designed to ensure that errors cannot occur undetected.

D Channel. The ISDN data 16 kb/s channel that is used for out-of-band signaling functions such as call setup.

Daisy Chain. A local area network configuration in which nodes are directly connected in series.

Data. Digitized information in a form suitable for storage or communication over electronic means.

Data Circuit-Terminating Equipment (DCE). Equipment designed to establish a connection to a network, condition the input and output of DTE for transmission over the network, and terminate the connection when completed.

Data Compression. A data transmission system that replaces a bit stream with another bit stream having fewer bits.

Datagram. A single unacknowledged packet of information that is sent over a network as an individual unit without regard to previous or subsequent packets.

Data Line Monitor. A data line impairment-measuring device that bridges the data line and observes the condition of data, addressing, and protocols.

Data Link. A circuit capable of carrying digitized information.

Data Network Identification Code (DNIC). A 14-digit number used for worldwide numbering of data networks.

Data Over Voice (DOV). A device that multiplexes a full duplex data channel over a voice channel using analog modulation.

Dataport. A PCM channel unit that provides direct access to a digital bit stream for data transmission.

Data Service Unit (DSU). Apparatus that interfaces DTE to a line connecting to a dataport channel unit to enable digital communications without a modem. Used with CSU when DTE lacks complete digital line interface capability or alone when DTE includes digital line interface capability.

Data Terminal Equipment (DTE). Any form of computer, peripheral, or terminal that can be used for originating or receiving data over a communication channel.

DBm. A measure of power level relative to the power of 1 milliwatt.

DBrn. A measure of noise power relative to a reference noise of -90 dBm.

DBrnc. A measure of noise power through a C message weighting filter.

DBrnc0. A measure of C message noise referred to a zero test level point.

Decibel (dB). A measure of relative power level between two points in a circuit.

Dedicated Access. The interconnection of a station to an IEC through a dedicated line.

Delay. (1) The time a call spends in queue. (2) The time required for a signal to transit the communications facility.

Delta Modulation. A system of converting analog to digital signals by transmitting a single bit indicating the direction of change in amplitude from the previous sample.

Demand Assigned Multiple Access (DAMA). A method of sharing the capacity of a communications satellite by assigning capacity on demand to an idle channel or time slot from a pool.

Demarcation Point. The point at which customer-owned wiring and equipment interfaces with the telephone company.

Demodulation. The process of extracting intelligence from a carrier signal.

Diagnostics. A software program that determines the cause of faults in a telecommunications system.

Dialed Number Identification Service (DNIS). A service offered by 800 carriers that carries the number dialed by the calling party to the user's premises where it is routed within the PBX to the appropriate answering point.

Dial-Up. A data communications session that is initiated by dialing a switched telephone circuit.

Digital. A mode of transmission in which information is coded in binary form for transmission on a network.

Digital Crossconnect System (DCS). A specialized digital switch that enables crossconnection of channels at the digital line rate.

Digital Multiplexed Interface (DMI). A T-1 interface between a PBX and a computer.

Digital Service Crossconnect (DSX). A physically wired crossconnect frame to enable connecting digital transmission equipment at a standard bit rate.

Digital Speech Interpolation (DSI). A method of increasing the carrying capacity of a circuit group by dynamically assigning voice channels only when the users are speaking.

Digital Switching. A process for connecting ports on a switching system by routing digital signals without converting them to analog.

Digroup. Two groups of 12 digital channels integrated to form a single 24-channel system.

Diplexer. A device that couples a radio transmitter and receiver to the same antenna.

Dipole. An antenna that has two radiating elements fed from a central point.

Direct Broadcast Satellite (DBS). A television broadcast service that provides television programming services throughout a country from a single source through a satellite.

Direct Control Switching. A system in which the switching path is established directly through the network by dial pulses without central control.

Direct Current (DC). Current that flows through a circuit in only one direction.

Direct Distance Dialing (DDD). A long distance calling system that enables a user to place a call without operator assistance.

Direct Inward Dialing (DID). A method of enabling callers from outside a PBX to reach an extension by dialing the access code plus the extension number.

Directional Coupler. A device inserted in a waveguide to couple a transmitter and receiver to the same antenna. Also a passive device installed on a CATV cable to isolate the feeder cable from another branch.

Direct-to-Line Multiplex. A system that modulates individual channel frequencies directly to their final carrier line frequencies.

Direct Trunks. Trunks dedicated exclusively to traffic between the terminating offices.

Dispersion. The rounding and overlapping of a light pulse that occurs to different wavelengths because of reflected rays or the different refractive index of the core material.

Dispersive Fade Margin. A property of a digital microwave signal that expresses the amount of fade margin under conditions of distortion caused by multipath fading.

Distortion. An unwanted change in a waveform.

Distributed Control. A switching system architecture in which more than one processor controls certain functions.

Distributed Processing. The distribution of call processing functions among numerous small processors rather than concentrating all functions in a single central processor.

Distributed Queue Dual Bus (DQDB). The protocol used in the 802.6 metropolitan area network.

Distributed Switching. The capability to install CO line circuits close to the served subscribers and connect them over a smaller group of links or trunks to a CO that directly controls the operation of the remote unit.

Distributing Frame. A framework holding terminal blocks that interconnect cable and equipment and provide test access.

Distribution Cable. Cable that connects the user's serving terminal to an interface with a branch feeder cable.

Diversity. A method of protecting a radio signal from failure of equipment or the radio path by providing standby equipment.

Downlink. The radio path from a satellite to an earth station.

Download. To send information from a host computer to a remote terminal.

Downstream Channel. The frequency band in a CATV system that distributes signals from the headend to the users.

Drop Wire. Wire leading from the user's serving terminal to the station protector.

Dual Tone Multifrequency (DTMF). A signaling system that uses pairs of audio frequencies to represent a digit. Usually synonymous with the AT&T trademark Touchtone.

Dumb Terminal. A terminal that has no processing capability. It is functional only when connected to a host.

Duplex (DX) Signaling. A direct current signaling system that transmits signals directly over the cable pair.

Dynamic Overload Control (DOC). The ability of the translation and routing elements in a CO to adapt to changes in traffic load by rerouting traffic and blocking call attempts.

E & M Signaling. A method of signaling between offices by voltage states on the transmit and receive leads of signaling equipment at the point of interface.

Earth Station. The assembly of radio equipment, antenna, and satellite communication control circuitry that provides access from terrestrial circuits to a satellite.

Echo. The reflection of a portion of a signal back to its source.

Echo Cancelation. A protocol used to obtain full duplex data communication over a two-wire line.

Echo Canceler. An electronic device that processes the echo signal and cancels it out to prevent annoyance to the talker.

Echo Checking. A method of error checking in which the receiving end echoes received characters to the transmitting end.

Echo Return Loss (ERL). The weighted return loss of a circuit across a band of frequencies from 500 to 2500 Hz.

Echo Suppressor. A device that opens the receive path of a circuit when talking power is present in the transmit path.

Effective Isotropic Radiated Power (EIRP). Power radiated by a transmitter compared to the power of an isotropic antenna, which is one that radiates equally in all directions.

Electromagnetic Interference (EMI). An interfering signal that is radiated from a source and picked up by a telecommunications circuit.

Electronic Data Interchange (EDI). A standard method of enabling organizations to exchange information over a data circuit.

Electronic Mail. A service that allows text-form messages to be stored in a central file and retrieved over a data terminal by dialing access and identification codes.

Electronic Switching System (ESS). A stored program controlled switching system used in offices.

Electronic Tandem Network (ETN). A private telecommunications network that consists of switching nodes and interconnecting trunks.

Emergency Ringback. A feature that enables a 911 center to connect a caller to the appropriate Public Service Answering Point (PASP) and to enable the PASP to re-ring the circuit if the caller disconnects. This enables the PASP to connect to the caller to get additional emergency information.

End Office. The central office in the LEC's network that directly serves subscriber lines.

End-to-end Signaling. A method of connecting signaling equipment so it transmits signals between the two ends of a circuit with no intermediate appearances of the signaling leads.

Enhanced 911. A 911 service in which information relative to the specific caller, such as identity and location, is forwarded to the 911 agency by the serving central office.

Enhanced Service Provider (ESP). Companies that use the PSTN to provide services to the public.

Enterprise Network. A private network of both switched and dedicated facilities that enables users to connect to services wherever they are located without concern about how to establish the session.

Entrance Link. A coaxial or fiber optic facility used to connect the last terminal in a microwave signal to multiplex or video terminating equipment.

Envelope Delay. The difference in propagation speed of different frequencies within the pass band of a telecommunications channel.

Equal Access. A central office feature that allows all interexchange carriers to have access to the trunk side of the switching network in an end office.

Erlang. A unit of network load. One Erlang equals 36 CCS and represents 100% occupancy of a circuit or piece of equipment. Also used to define the input process under the BCC (Erlang B) and BCD (Erlang C) blockage conditions.

Error. Any discrepancy between a received data signal from the signal as it was transmitted.

Error Free Seconds (EFS). The number of seconds per unit of time that a circuit vendor guarantees the circuit will be free of errors.

Ethernet. A proprietary contention bus network developed by Xerox, Digital Equipment Corporation, and Intel. Ethernet formed the basis for the IEEE 802.3 standard.

Exchange. A term describing the geographical territory, often a city, filed in an LEC's tariffs. An exchange contains a single rating plan.

Expanded Binary Coded Decimal Interexchange Code EBCDIC). An eight-bit coding scheme used for encoding characters for transmission over a data network.

Expander. A network that has more outputs than inputs. Expansion is the opposite of concentration.

Exponential. A curve that describes the service time of users in a queue.

Exposed. A communication circuit that is subject to contact with lightning or an external electrical voltage or induction source exceeding 300 volts rms.

Extended Area Service (EAS). A system of flat-rate calling among two or more exchanges.

Extended Super Frame (ESF). T-1 carrier framing format that provides 64 kb/s clear channel capability, error checking, 16-state signaling, and other data transmission features.

Facility. Any set of transmission paths that can transport voice or data. Facilities can range from a cable to a carrier system or a microwave radio system.

Facsimile. A system for scanning a document, encoding it, transmitting it over a telecommunication circuit, and reproducing it in its original form at the receiving end.

Fade. A reduction in received signal level in a radio system caused by reflection, refraction, or absorption.

Fade Margin. The depth of fade, expressed in dB, that a microwave receiver can accommodate while still maintaining acceptable circuit quality.

Fast-Connect Circuit Switching. A form of circuit switching that establishes data sessions fast enough to be suitable for data switching.

Fast Packet Switching. A packet switching system intended for voice, data, and video transmission. Fast packet eliminates many of the time consuming link-by-link flow control and error correction procedures that delay the flow of packets.

Fast Select. A packet network service that transmits one packet and a return acknowledgement.

Fault Tolerant LAN. A local area network that has built-in capabilities, such as disk mirroring, uninterruptable power, and redundant hardware, to enable the network to survive a major failure.

Feature Transparency. The ability of a PBX or data system user to have the same features across a network as are available on the local system.

Feeder Cable. A cable originating in a central office that connects distribution cable to the main distributing frame.

Fiber Distributed Data Interface (FDDI). A standard for a 100 mb/s token-passing ring network operating over fiber optics.

Fiber Optics. A medium for transferring electronic signals over a pathway of fibers made of a transparent material such as glass or plastic.

File Server. In a local area network, a host computer or personal computer that acts as a shared repository for files, software, and the network operating system.

Filter. A device used to remove unwanted signals from the pass band of a circuit.

Final Trunk Group. A last choice trunk group that receives overflow from high usage trunks.

Flash. The momentary depression of a telephone switchhook to signal the processor that an additional feature is required.

Flow Control. The process of protecting network service by denying access to additional traffic that would add to congestion.

Flux Budget. In an FDDI network the flux budget is the maximum amount of light that can be lost between two adjacent nodes and still maintain communication.

Footprint. The earth's area that is illuminated by the rf output signal of a satellite.

Forced Disconnect. A feature in a 911 center that enables the emergency operator to forcibly disconnect a line that is deliberately being held up.

Foreign EMF. Any unwanted voltage on a telecommunications circuit.

Foreign Exchange (FX). A special service that connects station equipment located in one telephone exchange with switching equipment located in another.

Foreign Voltage. A voltage imposed on a communications circuit by contact with an outside source.

Forward Error Correction (FEC). A method of correcting errors in a data channel by transmitting overhead bits that enable the receiving end to correct error bits.

Four-Wire Circuit. A circuit that uses separate paths for each direction of transmission.

Four-Wire Terminating Set. A device that combines the separate transmit and receive paths of a four-wire circuit into a two-wire circuit.

Frame. A complete television picture consisting of two fields of interlaced scanning lines. Also, a group of bytes conditioned with header and error correction fields for transmission across a data link.

Frame Alignment. The state in which the frame of the receiving equipment is properly phased with respect to the transmitting equipment.

Frame Relay. A high speed transmission protocol that describes the interface between DTE and a fast packet network.

Free Space Attenuation. The amount of loss, expressed in Db, that a radio signal encounters between the transmitting and receiving antennas.

Freeze-Frame Video. A method of transmitting a video signal over a narrow channel by sending one frame at a time without motion.

Frequency. The number of times per second that an alternating current signal changes state through one complete cycle.

Frequency Agility. The ability of a cellular mobile telephone to shift automatically between frequencies.

Frequency Diversity. Protection of a radio signal by providing a standby radio channel on a different frequency to assume the load when the regular channel fails.

Frequency Division Multiple Access (FDMA). A method of sharing the capacity of a communications satellite by frequency division of the transponder.

Fresnel Zone. An imaginary zone that surrounds a radio or optic wave. If an obstacle is inserted into the first Fresnel zone, it results in attenuation, even if it does not penetrate into the direct path itself.

Frogging. The process of inverting the line frequencies of a carrier system so that incoming low frequency channels leave at high frequencies and vice versa. Frogging equalizes transmission loss between high and low frequency channels.

Front End Processor. An auxiliary computer attached to a network to perform control operations and relieve the host computer for data processing.

Full Duplex. A data communication circuit over which data can be sent in both directions simultaneously.

Fuse. A link in a circuit that is designed to open when the current flowing in the circuit exceeds a specified value.

Fuse Cable. A fine gauge cable, (usually 26-gauge) that is placed in a cable to open if contact with a foreign voltage occurs.

Gain. (1) The increase in electrical power that results from amplification. (2) The increase in power radiated from an antenna compared to the power the would radiate from a dipole antenna.

Gas Tube Protector. A protector that consists of a glass envelope containing a gas that ionizes to discharge a foreign voltage.

Gateway. Circuitry used to interconnect networks by converting the protocol of one network to that used by the other.

Gauge. The physical size of an electrical conductor, specified by American Wire Gauge (AWG) standards.

Generic Program. The operating system in a SPC central office that contains logic for call processing functions.

Geosynchronous. A orbit that positions a satellite at a constant point with respect to a point on the earth's surface.

Gigabits Per Second (gb/s). A unit of data transmission speed measured in billions of bits per second.

Gigahertz (GHz). A unit of frequency measured in billions of cycles per second.

Glare. A condition that exists when both ends of a circuit are seized simultaneously.

Graded Index Fiber (Multimode). Optical fiber that is made with a progressively lower refractive index toward the outer core to reduce the effects of dispersion.

Grade of Service (GOS). The percentage of time or probability that a call will be blocked in a network. Also a quality indicator used in transmission measurements to specify the quality of a circuit based on both noise and loss.

Ground. A connection to a conductor that has the same electrical potential as the earth.

Ground Start. A method of circuit seizure between a central office and a PBX that transmits an immediate signal by momentarily grounding the tip of the line.

Ground Wave. A radio wave that is guided by the earth's surface.

Group. A 12-channel band of frequencies occupying the frequency range of 60 to 108 KHz.

Guard Band. A frequency band that separates the voice channels of circuits from one another.

H Channel. A combination of multiple ISDN B Channels that are used to support a service with a higher speed requirement such as video, high quality audio, and high speed data.

Half Duplex. A data communications circuit over which data can be sent in only one direction at a time.

Handoff. The process of changing radio channels when a mobile unit moves from the coverage area of one cell to another.

Handset. A telephone transmitter and receiver that are mounted as a single piece.

Handshaking. The exchange of signals between two devices preparing to initiate or terminate communications.

Hang-On Queueing. A trunk queueing system in which the switching system signals users that all trunks are busy and allows them to remain off-hook while they are held in queue until the call can be completed.

Hardware. The physical components of a communications or computer system.

Harmonic Distortion. Harmonic frequencies that are present because of non-linearity in a circuit.

Harmonic Ringing. A method of preventing users on a party line from hearing other than their ring by tuning the ringer to a given ringing frequency.

Headend. The equipment in a CATV system that receives television signals from various sources and modulates and applies them to downstream channels.

Heat Coil. A protection device that grounds a circuit when excessive current flows for a specified period of time. A heat coil guards against sneak currents.

Hertz (Hz). The unit of frequency, in cycles per second.

Heterodyning. The process of shifting a radio frequency by mixing it with another frequency and selecting the desired frequency from the resulting modulation products.

Hierarchical Network. A network that includes two or more levels of switching where lower levels home on higher levels to obtain a final trunk route to the destination.

High Definition Television (HDTV). A system for transmitting a television signal with greater resolution than the standard NTSC signal.

High Usage Trunk Group. Trunk groups established between two switching systems to serve as the first choice path between the systems and thus handle the bulk of the traffic.

Holding Time. The time period that a call occupies a telecommunications channel.

Horizontal Wiring. In a wiring system, horizontal wiring is the connection from a distribution frame to the station.

Host. The controlling computer in a communications network.

Hot Standby. A method of protecting a radio system by keeping a duplicate system tuned to the same frequency but decoupled from the antenna.

Hub. A system of multiple headend equipment in a CATV system consisting of master and satellite headends that relay signals to a local distribution area. Also, in a local area network, a device that interconnects workstations at a central location in a star configuration.

Hub Polling. A type of data polling in which polling signals are sent from one terminal to the next in line.

Hundred Call Seconds (CCS). A measure of network load. Thirty-six CCS represents 100% occupancy of a circuit or piece of equipment.

Hybrid. (1) A multiwinding coil or electronic circuit in a four-wire terminating set or switching system line circuit to separate the four-wire and two-wire paths. (2) A customer premises switching system that is a cross between a PBX and a key telephone system. (3) An uninterruptable power supply that is off-line until commercial power fails and which includes power line conditioning equipment.

Hybrid Network. A network that consists of multiple facility ownership, uses, architectures, or other such mixtures of characteristics that take it away from the traditional discrete networks of the past.

Impedance. The ratio of voltage to current along a transmission line or circuit.

Improved Mobile Telephone Service (IMTS). A type of mobile telephone service that allows direct dialing between wireline and mobile units without operator intervention.

Impulse Noise. High level and short duration noise that is induced into a telecommunications circuit.

Inband Signaling. Signaling transmitted within the pass band of the circuit that is used for the transmission.

Independent Company (IC). A non-Bell telephone company.

Induction. The coupling of a current from one circuit to another without direct electrical connection between them.

Ineffective Attempts. Attempts in which a user is unable to access a network.

Insertion Loss. The amount of loss a circuit element introduces into a telecommunications circuit.

Inside Wire. Wiring on customer premises between the public network demarcation point and the station.

Integrated Services Digital Network (ISDN). A set of CCITT standards that provides for an integrated set of voice and data services over an end-to-end digital medium.

Integrated Voice/data. The combination of voice and data signals from a workstation over a communication path to the PBX.

Interactive Voice Response (IVR). See Voice Response Unit (VRU)

Intercept. A service that directs a call placed to a disconnected or invalid number to a recording or operator.

Interexchange Carrier (IEC). A common carrier that provides long distance service between LATAs.

Interface. The interconnection point between two pieces of equipment.

Interframe Encoding. A method of video compression that transmits only changed information between successive frames.

InterLATA Connecting Trunk. A trunk that connects the local exchange carrier's end office or tandem office with the interexchange carrier's switch.

Intermediate Distributing Frame (IDF). A wiring frame located between the main distributing frame and the horizontal wiring to the stations.

Intermodulation Distortion. Distortion or noise generated in electronic circuits when the power carried is great enough to cause non-linear operation.

International Maritime Satellite Service (INMARSAT). The International Maritime Satellite Service that provides communications services to ships at sea.

Internet. A linkage of multiple independent networks.

Interoffice Trunk. A circuit between central offices.

Interrupt. A break in the normal flow of a software routine that enables the routine to resume at the same point at a later time.

Intertoll Trunks. Trunks interconnecting Class 4 and higher switching systems in the AT&T network.

Intra Calling. The capability of a remote line concentrator to interconnect users served by the same concentrator without providing two trunks to the central office.

Intraframe Encoding. A method of video compression that divides the picture into blocks and transmits only changed blocks between successive frames.

Inverter. A device for generating AC from central office battery.

Inward Wide Area Telephone Service (INWATS). A service in which the called party pays for the call. The caller dials a number starting with the area code 800.

Ionospheric Wave. See Sky Wave.

Isochronous. The timing characteristics of an event or signal recurring at known intervals. Digitized voice and video are examples of isochronous signals.

Isotropic Antenna. An antenna that radiates equally in all directions

Jack. A socket that mates with a plug, used to provide access to a test point.

Jitter. The phase shift of digital pulses over a transmission medium.

Jumbo Group. A 3600-channel band of frequencies formed from the inputs of six master groups.

Jumper. Wire used to interconnect equipment and cable on a distributing frame.

Junctor. A link between stages of a switching system.

Key Telephone System (KTS). A method of allowing several central office lines to be accessed from multiple telephone sets.

Kilobits Per Second (kb/s). A unit of data transmission speed measured in thousands of bits per second.

Kilohertz (KHz). A unit of frequency measured in thousands of cycles per second.

LATA Tandem. A tandem switching system provided by an LEC that offers interexchange carriers access to end offices.

Latency. The elapsed time between transmission from one device and its reception by the addressee.

Learning Bridge. A LAN bridge that has the ability to send broadcast messages to learn where addressees are located and to store addresses in a table.

Leased Line. A private line, leased from a common carrier, between two or more points.

Least Cost Routing (LCR). A PBX service feature that chooses the most economical route to a destination based on cost of the terminated services and time of day.

Level. The signal power at a given point in a circuit.

Light Emitting Diode (LED). A semiconductor device that emits light when a voltage is applied.

Line Circuit. The circuitry in a PBX or central office that detects the off-hook/on-hook condition of a line and handles call origination and termination functions.

Line Conditioning. A service offered by telephone companies to reduce envelope delay, noise, and amplitude distortion to enable transmission of higher speed data.

Line Expander. See Voice/Data Multiplexer.

Line Insulation Test (LIT). A central office testing system that automatically measures each line for shorts, grounds, and foreign EMF.

Line Load Control. A control system in an end office that limits the number of users that can receive dial tone. Its purpose is to enable the office to handle temporary overloads caused by emergencies.

Line Status. An indication of whether a line or circuit is busy (off-hook) or idle (on-hook).

Link. A physical or logical circuit between two points.

Link Access Procedure D (LAPD). A link layer protocol specified by CCITT Q.921 that is used in the ISDN D Channel.

Link-by-Link Signaling. A method of connecting signaling equipment so signals are interfaced at intermediate locations between the two ends of the circuit.

L Multiplex (LMX). A system of analog multiplex consisting of combinations of groups, super groups, master groups, and jumbo groups to form a hierarchy of channels that can be transmitted over radio or coaxial cable.

Load Balancing. A process in a switching system whereby heavy and light users are distributed among load sensitive equipment to maintain a uniform distribution of traffic.

Loading. The process of inserting fixed inductors in series with both wires of a cable pair to reduce voice frequency loss.

Local Access Transport Area (LATA). The geographical boundaries within which Bell Operating Companies are permitted to offer long distance traffic.

Local Area Network (LAN). A short range, high speed local network using one of the non-switched multiple access technologies.

Local Exchange Carrier (LEC). A common carrier that delivers local switched services to end users.

Local Loop. A circuit between an LEC's switching center and the customer's premises.

Local Test Desk (LTD). A testing system that testers use to access local loops and central office line equipment from a central location.

Log In. The process of a workstation identifying itself to a host or server on a network.

Logical Link Control (LLC). The portion of the link level protocol in the 802 standards that is in direct contact with higher level layers.

Look Ahead Queueing. A feature in automatic call distributors that enables the system to look ahead to a secondary queue and evaluate congestion before overflowing from the primary queue.

Look Back Queueing. A feature in automatic call distributors that enables the system to look back to the primary queue after the call has overflowed to a secondary queue. If congestion clears in the primary queue, the call is returned.

Loop. The circuit that connects a customer's premises to the telephone central office. Also the condition that exists when the conductors of a cable pair are electrically connected as in a loop start line.

Loopback Test. A test applied to a full duplex circuit by connecting the receive leads to the transmit leads, applying a signal, and reading the returned test signal at the near end of the circuit.

Loop Start. A method of circuit seizure between a central office and station equipment that operates by bridging the tip and ring of the line through a resistance.

Loop Timing. A digital synchronizing method that operates by extracting a synchronizing clock signal from incoming pulses.

Loss. (1) The drop in signal level between points on a circuit. (2) The number of calls lost in a network because of congestion.

Loss Budget. The sum of all factors that introduce loss between the transmitter and receivers.

L-to-T Connector. A unit that interfaces two FDM groups with one TDM digroup to enable a 24-channel band of analog frequencies to interface a DS-1 line.

Luminance. The portion of a video signal that carries brightness information.

Main Distributing Frame (MDF). A connection point that forms the interface between a switching system and outside plant. In a PBX, the MDF connects between the switching system and intermediate distributing frames or station equipment.

Main Feeder. Feeder cable that transports cable pairs from the central office to branching or taper points.

Main Listed Number (MLN). The principal telephone number serving a PBX or key telephone system. Normally the MLN is answered by an attendant.

Manufacturing Automation Protocol/Technical and Office Protocol (MAP/TOP). A set of high level local area network protocols designed for manufacturing and office use.

Mark. In teletypewriter terminology, a mark represents the one level of the signal, usually signified by current on the line or one of two tones in a voice frequency carrier telegraph circuit.

Marker. The logic circuitry in a crossbar central office that controls call processing functions.

Master Group. A 600-channel band of frequencies formed from the inputs of 10 super groups.

Material Dispersion. Broadening of light pulses that occur because of differences in the refractive index at different wavelengths.

Mean Time Between Failures (MTBF). The average time a device or system operates without failing.

Mean Time to Repair (MTTR). The average time required for a qualified technician to repair a failed device or system.

Media Access Controller. The control circuitry in a LAN that converts the protocols of the DTE to those required by the LAN.

Megabits Per Second (mb/s). A unit of data transmission speed measured in millions of bits per second.

Megahertz (MHz). A unit of frequency measured in millions of cycles per second.

Memory. The element of a computer that stores information.

Message Switching. A form of network access in which a message is forwarded from a terminal to a central switch where it is stored and forwarded to the addressee after some delay. A message switch has no direct connection between devices as does a circuit switch.

Message Telephone Service (MTS). A generic name for the switched long distance telephone service offered by all interexchange carriers.

Messenger. A metallic strand attached to a pole line to support aerial cable.

Microwave. A radio frequency in the range of 1 GHz to 300 GHz.

Milliwatt. One one-thousandth of a watt. Used as a reference power for signal levels in telecommunications circuits.

Mixed Mode. A system that is capable of encoding data in both alphanumeric and facsimile form for integrating text and graphics.

Modal Dispersion. Pulse rounding that occurs because of the different paths taken by different light modes that arrive at the detector out of phase.

Mode. The different paths lightwaves can take through a transmission medium.

Modeling. The process of designing a network from a series of mathematical formulas that describe the behavior of network elements.

Modem. A contraction of the terms MOdulator/DEModulator. A modem is used to convert analog signals to digital form and vice versa.

Modem Pool. A centralized pool of modems accessed through a PBX to provide off-net data transmission from modemless terminals.

Modem Turnaround Time. The time required for a half duplex modem to reverse the direction of transmission.

Modified Chemical Vapor Deposit (MCVD). A process for manufacturing a fiber preform by progressively depositing glass chemicals on the inside of a tube under heat.

Modular Plug/Jack. A series of standard plugs and jacks that are used for connecting telephone instruments to the line.

Modulation. The process of imposing information on a carrier signal.

Motherboard. A circuit board that has a group of jacks for receiving printed circuit cards mounted on it.

Mu Law. The coding law used by North American PCM systems.

Multidrop. A circuit dedicated to communication between multiple terminals that are connected to the same circuit.

Multifrequency Signaling. A method of sending pulses over a circuit by using one pair of tones from a total set of five tones to encode each digit.

Multiline Hunt. The ability of a switching system to connect calls to another number in a group when other numbers in the group are busy.

Multipath Fading. A radio system fade caused by reflection of a portion of the transmitted signal so that it takes a longer path to the receive antenna and arrives slightly out of phase. The phase difference results in a reduced receive signal level.

Multiple. The process of wiring several appearances of a terminal in parallel.

Multiple Access. The capability of multiple terminals connected to the same network to access one another by means of a common addressing scheme and protocol.

Multiplexer. A device used for combining several lower speed channels into a higher speed channel.

Multiplexing. The process of combining multiple signals into a single channel.

Narrow Band. A radio system that operates in a bandwidth that is less than the coherence bandwidth.

Network. A group of nodes interconnected by communications channels.

Network Access Unit (NAU). The circuitry and connectors used in local area networks to enable DTE to access the transmission medium.

Network Administration. The process of monitoring loads and service results in a network and making adjustments needed to maintain service and costs at the design objective level.

Network Channel Terminating Equipment (NCTE). Apparatus mounted on the user's premises that is used to amplify, match impedance, or match network signaling to the interconnected equipment.

Network Design. The process of determining quantities and architecture of circuit and equipment to achieve a cost/service balance.

Network Interface Card. A card that plugs into the bus of a computer to interface it to a local area network.

Network Interface Device (NID). A device wired between a telephone station protector and the inside wiring to isolate the customer-provided equipment from the network.

Network Management Control Center (NMCC). A center associated with a network to monitor network service and performance, analyze statistical information, and take maintenance action on failed equipment.

Network Operating System. The software in a local area network that forms the interface between the computer's network basic input/output system and the user.

Network Terminal Number (NTN). The number assigned to a data terminal under the data network identification code system.

Network Termination 1 (NT1). A standard customer premises network termination that provides a physical interface to an ISDN line.

Network Termination 2 (NT2). A standard customer premises network termination that performs the ISDN data link and network layer functions.

Network Termination 12 (NT12) A standard customer remises network termination that performs the functions of both NT1 and NT2 terminations.

Node. The switching system or computer that provides access to the network and serves as the concentration point for trunks.

Noise. Any unwanted signal in a transmission path.

Nonblocking. A network that provides enough paths that all stations can be interconnected.

Nonwireline. A term describing cellular radio service providers that are not operating telephone companies.

Null Modem. A device that interchanges receive and transmit leads so that a DTE-to-DTE or a DCE-to-DCE connection can be made.

Numbering Plan Area (NPA). In the North American telephone system, the first three digits in the 10-digit addressing scheme. NPA boundaries are normally a state or major portion of a state. Also known as area code.

Octet. A group of eight bits. Also known as a byte.

Offered Load. The amount of traffic that is demanded of a switching system or trunk group, including ineffective attempts.

Off-Hook. A signaling state in a line or trunk when it is working or busy.

Off Line UPS. An uninterruptable power supply that operates in the background until commercial power fails and then switches over to carry the load of the protected apparatus. Off line supplies have no power line conditioning equipment. Also known as standby power source.°

Off-Premises Extension (OPX). Any extension telephone that uses public facilities to connect to the main telephone service.

On-Hook. A signaling state in a line or trunk when it is non-working or idle.

On Line UPS. An uninterruptable power supply that continually feeds power to the protected device through an inverter that runs off batteries. The batteries are kept charged by a rectifier that operates when commercial power is working.

Open. A circuit impairment that exists when one or both conductors are interrupted at an unintended point.

Open Network Architecture (ONA). A telephone architecture that provides the interfaces to enable service providers to connect to the public switched telephone network.

Open Switching Interval. A period during which a switching system momentarily opens the path to the user while reswitching to invoke another service such as add-on conferencing.

Open Systems Interconnect (OSI). A seven-layer data communications protocol model that specifies standard interfaces that all vendors can adapt to their own designs.

Operations Support System (OSS). A set of systems used by telephone companies to maintain their networks.

Oscillator. A device for generating an analog test signal.

Out-of-Band Signaling. Signaling within the pass band of a single circuit by tones that are separated from the voice channel by filters.

Outside Plant. A collective term describing the cable and all supporting structures used to provide subscriber loops.

Overhead. Any noninformation bits, such as headers, error checking bits, start and stop bits that are used for controlling a network.

Pacing. A flow control mechanism in a data communications system that prevents a transmitting device from over running the receiving buffer.

Packet. A unit of data information consisting of header, information, error detection, and trailer records that is transmitted across the network layer.

Packet Assembler/Disassembler (PAD). A device used on a packet switched network to assemble information into packets and to convert received packets into a continuous data stream.

Packet Switching. A method of allocating network time by forming data into packets and relaying it to the destination under control of processors at each major node. The network determines packet routing during transport of the packet.

Pad. A device inserted into a circuit to introduce loss.

Pair Gain. The number of circuits added over and above the cable pairs required to support a loop carrier system. For example, a 24-channel system that requires two pairs to operate would have a pair gain of 22.

Parameters. The record in an SPC office's data base that specifies equipment and software quantities, options, and addresses of peripheral equipment for use in call processing operations.

Parity. A bit or series of bits appended to a character or block of characters to ensure that either an odd or an even number of bits are transmitted. Parity is used for error detection.

Partial Dial. A condition that exists when a user hangs up before dialing a complete telephone number.

Patch. (1) The temporary interconnection of transmission and signaling paths. Used for temporary rerouting and restoral of failed facilities or equipment. (2) A temporary change in a software program.

Peak-to-Average Ratio (P/AR). An analog test that provides an index of data circuit quality by sending a pulse into one end of a circuit and measuring its envelope at the distant end of the circuit.

Pedestal. (1) A cable terminal mounted in a slim, above ground enclosure. (2) The device used to mount a pay telephone enclosure on the ground or floor.

Peg Count. The number of times a specified event occurs. Derived from an early method of counting the number of busy lines in a manual switchboard.

Permanent Signal. A permanent seizure of a line or trunk in a switching system.

Permanent Virtual Circuit. A virtual circuit that provides the equivalent of dedicated private line service over a packet switching network. The path between users is fixed.

Personal Identification Number (PIN). A billing identification number dialed by the user to enable the switching system to identify the calling party.

Phantom. A circuit derived by using the simplex of each of two two-wire channels as one leg of the third circuit.

Phase Shift Keying (PSK). A method of digitally modulating a radio signal by shifting the phase of the transmitted carrier.

Phasing. The process of ensuring that both sending and receiving facsimile machines start at the same position on a page.

Picture Element (Pixel). A single element of video information.

Pilot. A single frequency that is transmitted on an L carrier line or microwave radio system to regulate amplifier stability and to actuate alarms.

PIN Diode. A photodiode manufactured with an intrinsic layer of undoped material between doped P and N layers and used as a lightwave detector.

Ping Pong. A method of obtaining full duplex data transmission over a two-wire circuit by rapidly alternating the direction of transmission.

Plesiochronous. The situation that exists when two digital networks are independently timed and no synchronizing signal is passed between them.

Point of Presence (POP). (1) The physical point at which an LEC interfaces with its customer. (2) The physical point at which an IEC interconnects with the LEC.

Point-to-Point. A circuit that directly connects two locations without an intermediate switch or computer.

Poisson. A curve that describes the distribution of arrival times at the input to a service queue.

Poll Cycle Time. The amount of time required for a multidrop data communications controller to make one complete polling cycle through all devices on the network.

Polling. A method of extracting data from remote terminals to a host. The host accesses the terminal, determines if it has traffic to send, and causes traffic to be uploaded to the host.

Positive Action Digit. A digit that a switching system requires to be dialed before it will advance a call to a high cost route.

Postpay. A method of operating a coin telephone in which the calling party inserts coins after the called party has answered.

Power Fail Transfer. A unit in KTS or a PBX that transfers one or more telephone instruments to central office lines during a power or equipment failure.

Power Line Conditioning Equipment. Filtering equipment that is used between commercial power and a sensitive load. Conditioning reduces the effects of surges, spikes, and other power line irregularities.

Preform. A glass rod formed and used as the source material for drawing an optical fiber.

Prepay. A method of coin telephone operation in which a coin must be inserted before dial tone is received.

Presubscription. The process whereby telephone users decides which long distance carrier will carry their calls.

Pressurization. Apparatus that feeds dehydrated air under pressure to a cable to prevent entry of moisture.

Primary Interexchange Carrier (PIC). The IEC that a subscriber has chosen to carry interexchange calls.

Primary Rate Interface (PRI). An interface consisting of 23 64 kb/s B channels and one 64 kb/s D channel that connects high capacity CPE to an ISDN.

Printer. The portion of a facsimile machine that converts a received signal to page copy output.

Printer Redirection. A LAN operating system function that sends output from a personal computer over the LAN to a shared printer.

Private Automatic Branch Exchange (PABX). A term often used synonymously with PBX. A PABX is always automatic, whereas switching is manual in some PBXs.

Private Branch Exchange (PBX). A switching system dedicated to telephone and data use in a private communication network.

Processor. The part of a computer that interprets and executes instructions.

Program. A series of instructions to control the operation of a computer.

Program Store. Permanent memory in an SPC CO that contains the system's generic program, parameters, and translations.

Propagation Delay. The absolute time delay of a signal from the sending to the receiving terminal.

Propagation Speed. The speed at which a signal travels over a transmission medium.

Protector. A device that prevents hazardous voltages or currents from injuring a user or damaging equipment connected to a cable pair.

Protocol. The conventions used in a network for establishing communications compatibility between terminals and for maintaining line discipline while they are connected to the network.

Public Service Answering Point (PSAP). A public agency that is designated to receive and answer emergency calls.

Public Switched Telephone Network (PSTN). A generic term for the interconnected networks of operating telephone companies.

Pulse. A short signal used to transmit information.

Pulse Amplitude Modulation (PAM). A digital modulation method that operates by varying the amplitude of a stream of pulses in accordance with the instantaneous amplitude of the modulating signal.

Pulse Code Modulation (PCM). A digital modulation method that encodes a PAM signal into an eight-bit digital word representing the amplitude of each pulse.

Pulse Link Repeater. A signaling set that interconnects the E & M leads of two circuits.

Quadrature Amplitude Modulation (QAM). A method of digitally modulating a radio signal by combining sine and cosine carrier signals in quadrature.

Quantizing. The process of encoding a PAM signal into a PCM signal.

Quantizing Noise. Noise that results from the inability of a PAM signal to represent each gradation of amplitude change.

Quasi-Synchronous. A system of enabling multiple radio transmitters to operate simultaneously on frequencies that are slightly offset. Also known as Simulcast.

Queuing. The holding of calls in queue when a trunk group is busy and completing them in turn when an idle circuit is available.

Range Extender. A device that increases the loop resistance range of central office equipment by boosting battery voltage.

Raster. The illuminated area of a television picture tube.

Received Signal Level (RSL). The strength of a radio signal received at the input to a radio receiver.

Receiver Sensitivity. The magnitude of the received signal level necessary to produce objective BER or channel noise performance.

Recent Change. Changes to line and trunk translations in an SPC switching system that have not been merged with the data base.

Rectifier. A device that converts alternating current to direct current.

Redirection. The action by a LAN's network operating system that intercepts calls to peripherals and redirects them to another resource such as the file server.

Redundancy. The provision of more than one circuit element to assume call processing when the primary element fails.

Reference Clock. A clock signal of high accuracy and stability that is used to synchronize a network of clocks of lower accuracy.

Reference Noise (rn). The threshold of audibility to which noise measurements are referred, -90 dBm.

Refractive Index. The ratio of the propagation speed of light in free space to its propagation in a given transmission medium.

Registration. The process the FCC follows in certifying that customer premises equipment will not cause harm to networks or personnel.

Regenerator. An electronic digital signal repeater that reshapes incoming pulses into undistorted square waves.

Register. An electronic device used for temporary storage of information. In a switching system, registers are used to store dialed number information.

Relay Rack. Open ironwork designed to mount and support electronic equipment.

Release Link Trunk. A trunk used in a centralized attendant system to enable call information from a PBX to reach a distant attendant. The trunk is released when the attendant extends the call to a station.

Remote Access. The ability to dial into a switching system over a local telephone number in order to complete calls over a private network from a distant location.

Remote Bridge. A LAN bridge that contains two halves connected by a data link. Each interfaces a separate network; the bridge transfers messages between the two networks.

Remote Call Forwarding (RCF). A service offered by most LECs that allows a user to obtain a telephone number in a local calling area and have calls automatically forwarded at the user's expense to another telephone number.

Remote Line Concentrator. A device that switches multiple users' lines to a smaller number of trunks to the central office.

Remote Line Switch. A line unit mounted near a cluster of users and equipped with intracalling capability.

Remote Line Unit. A line unit without intracalling capability mounted near a cluster of users.

Remote Maintenance and Testing System (RMATS). A service offered by PBX manufacturers and vendors that enables the vendor to access a PBX over the PTSN and perform testing and administrative functions.

Remote Office Test Line (ROTL). A testing device that acts with a central controller and a responder to make two-way transmission and supervision measurements.

Remote Switching Unit. A portion of a central office that is extended to a remote location with most of the control circuitry remaining in the host central office.

Reorder. A fast busy tone used to indicate equipment or circuit blockage.

Repeat Coil. Telephone vernacular for an impedance matching transformer.

Repeater. An electronic device that reshapes pulses or adds gain or amplification to a circuit.

Resistance. The property in an electrical circuit that opposes the flow of electricity.

Resistance Design. An outside plant design concept that selects wire gauge based on the length of subscriber loops and the characteristics of the switching equipment.

Resolution. The number of scan lines or picture elements per unit of vertical and horizontal dimension on a document.

Resources. Directories or printers that a server provides to its clients.

Responder. A test line that can make transmission and supervision measurements through its host switch under control of a remote computer.

Response Time. The interval between the terminal operator's sending the last character of a message and the time the first character of the response from the host arrives at the terminal.

Restriction. Limitations to a station on the use of PBX features or trunks based on service classification.

Return Loss. The degree of isolation, expressed in dB, between the transmit and the receive ports of a four-wire terminating set.

Rights. In a local area network, the permissions granted to users by the administrator to read, write, and modify files or directories.

Ring. The designation of the side of a telephone line that carries talking battery to the user's premises.

Ringer Isolator. A device placed on a telephone line to disconnect the ringer when it is in an idle state. It is used for noise prevention.

Ring Trip. The process of removing the ringing tone when a called party answers.

Riser Cable. A cable that connects the main distributing frame to a wiring closet. Usually riser cables connect between floors in a building, but they may also interconnect buildings in a campus environment.

Roamer. A mobile telephone user who uses service in more than one basic service area.

Root Mean Square (rms). The value of an AC voltage that is measured by an ordinary voltmeter. RMS voltage is 0.707 times the peak voltage in an AC circuit.

Rotate Time. The time required for a hard disk to rotate to the sector containing desired information.

Route. The circuits selected by a control system to establish a path for a session.

Router. An active device linking two segments of a LAN through their physical, data link, and network layers.

Routing. The path selection made for a telecommunications signal through the network to its destination.

RS-232 LAN. A local area network that uses the serial port instead of an interface card to connect a device to the transmission medium.

Run-Length Encoding. A facsimile encoding process that converts an expanse of white or black to a code corresponding to the length of the run.

Sampling. The process of periodically examining the amplitude of an analog signal.

Satellite Communications Control (SCC). The earth station equipment that controls such communications functions as access, echo suppression, forward error correction, and signaling.

Satellite Delay Compensator. A device that compensates for absolute delay in a satellite circuit by communicating with data terminal equipment with the DTE's own protocol.

Scanner. The portion of a facsimile system that converts a source document to an electrical signal.

Scattering. The loss that occurs in an optical fiber because of lightwaves striking molecules and imperfections in the core.

Sectoring. The process of dividing a cell into 180 , 120 , or 60 segments to increase capacity of the radio frequencies assigned to the cell.

Security Blanking. The ability of a switching system to blank out the called digits for certain lines so no called number detail is printed.

Seek Time. The time required for a hard disk's read head to move to the track containing desired data.

Segmentation. Division of a LAN into smaller segments to increase range or to isolate portions of the network to reduce contention.

Seize. The process of a switching system's selecting a circuit or item of equipment.

Selective Routing. A 911 service agency feature that enables the agency to route a call automatically to the appropriate serving agency based on the caller's identity.

Selective Signaling. (1) An in-band signaling system used on private line networks to direct equipment to switch a connection. (2) A signaling system used in mobile radio to enable a base station to call mobile units selectively.

Sender. A device used in switching system central offices to store and forward addressing signals.

Serial Interface. Circuitry used in DTE to convert parallel data to serial data for transmission on a network.

Server. A computer in a local area network that offers its resources, such as disk space, files, and printers, to workstations.

Shared Tenant Services. A service provider that offers services to a group of users in an office or apartment complex.

Sheath. The outer jacket surrounding cable pairs to prevent water from entering and to protect against external damage.

Shielding. A protective metallic covering placed around a conductor or conductors to isolate them from interfering signals.

Short. A circuit impairment that exists when two conductors of the same pair are connected at an unintended point.

Sidetone. The sound of a talker's voice audible in the handset of the telephone instrument.

Signal-to-Noise Ratio. The ratio between average signal power and average noise power in a circuit.

Signal Constellation. A two-dimensional diagram that shows the various signal combinations possible with a quadrature amplitude-modulated signal.

Signal Distributor. Circuitry used in electronic switching systems to deliver signals from the common control equipment to other circuits.

Simplex. (1) Information transmitted in only one direction. (2) A signaling system that is derived from the center tap of a repeat coil connected across a physical circuit.

Simulation. The process of designing a network by simulating the events and facilities that represent network load and capacity.

Simulcast. See Quasi-Synchronous.

Singing. The tendency of a circuit to oscillate when the return loss is too low.

Singing Return Loss (SRL). The loss at which a circuit oscillates or sings at the extreme low and high ends of the voice band.

Single-Frequency (SF) Signaling. The use of a single tone (usually 2600 Hz) to indicate the busy/idle status of a circuit.

Single-Mode Fiber. Optical fiber with a small core that propagates only one light mode.

Single-Sideband (SSB). An amplitude modulation method in which the carrier is suppressed and one sideband is filtered out so that only one sideband is amplified and transmitted.

Sky Wave. A radio wave that is reflected by the ionosphere to skip° over great distances before it is reflected to earth.

Slip. The loss or repetition of a frame in a PCM network that occurs when the clocking rates of two network nodes are slightly different.

Sneak Current. A foreign current flowing in a communication circuit. Because the voltage is too low to operate the protector, the sneak current may damage equipment.

Software Defined Network (SDN). A private network that is implemented using the carrier's switched network. The SDN is defined in software as opposed to consisting of discrete circuits.

Space. In teletypewriter terminology, a space represents the zero level of the signal, usually signified by an open on the line or one of two tones in a voice frequency carrier telegraph circuit.

Spacecraft Switched Time Division Multiple Access (SSTDMA). A method of sharing the capacity of a communications satellite by on-board switching of signals aimed at earth stations.

Space Diversity. Protection of a radio signal by providing a separate antenna located a few feet below the regular antenna on the same tower to assume the load when the regular channel fades.

Space Division Switching. Connecting links in a network by the physical connection of the links.

Spanning Tree. The parallel operation of two bridges in a LAN. One bridge is the primary, with the other operating in hot standby ready to assume the load if the primary bridge fails.

Spectral Efficiency. The efficiency of a microwave system in its use of radio spectrum, usually expressed in bits per Hz for digital radios and KHz per voice channel in analog radios.

Speech Synthesis. The process of forming a speech signal from a computer signal.

Speech-to-Text and Text-to-Speech. Converting a speech signal to text and vice versa without manual processing.

Spikes. Short duration excursions of electrical voltage in a power circuit.

Spin Stabilization. A method of preventing a satellite from tumbling by spinning it about an axis.

Split. (1) In an ACD, a subgroup of agents to which calls from a particular source are directed. (2) See Split Pair.

Split Channel Modem. A modem that divides a communication channel into separate send and receive directions.

Split Pair. A situation that occurs in cable splicing when one wire of a cable pair is spliced to a wire of an adjacent pair.

Splitter. A passive device that divides a CATV signal into multiple legs.

Spool. An acronym derived from Simultaneous Peripheral Operation On Line. In a LAN, a spool is a hardware or software device that buffers data before sending it to a printer.

Spot Beam Antenna. A satellite antenna that is capable of illuminating a narrow portion of the earth's surface.

Squelch. The effect of muting the output of a radio receiver when no carrier signal is present.

Standard Metropolitan Statistical Area (SMSA). A metropolitan area consisting of one or more cities as defined by the Office of Management and Budget and used by the FCC to allocate the cellular radio market.

Standby Power Source. See Off Line UPS.

Star Coupler. A device that couples multiple fibers at a central point and distributes the signal from one fiber into all others simultaneously.

Station. A location on a telephone or data network that is wired to give a user access to the network.

Station Keeping. The process on board a satellite for keeping it at its assigned longitude and inclination.

Station Message Detail Recording (SMDR). The use of equipment in a PBX to record called station, time of day, and duration on trunk calls.

Station Range. The number of feet or ohms over which a telephone instrument can signal and transmit voice and data.

Statistical Multiplexing. A form of data multiplexing in which time on a communications channel is assigned to terminals only when they have data to transport.

Step-by-Step. A direct controlled central office that uses Strowger switches to establish a talking path through the network.

Step Index Fiber. A type of optical fiber with a uniform index of refraction throughout the core.

Store-and-Forward. A method of switching messages in which a message or packet is sent from the originating terminal to a central unit where it is held for retransmission to the receiving terminal.

Stored Program Control (SPC). A common control central office that uses a central processor under direction of a generic program for call processing.

Stratum Clock. A particular clock level on the digital network synchronization hierarchy. Each stratum level has a specified stability.

Subnet. The collection of constituent networks in an internet.

Subscriber Loop. The circuit that connects a user's premises to the telephone central office.

Sun Transit Outage. Satellite circuit outage caused by direct radiation of the sun's rays on an earth station receiving antenna.

Super Frame. In T-1 carrier, a repetition of 12 frames with a fixed pattern of framing bits.

Super Group. A 60-channel band of frequencies formed from the inputs of five channel banks or groups.

Superimposed Ringing. A method of preventing users on a party line from hearing more than their ring by superimposing a DC voltage over the ringing signal and using it to fire a tube or semiconductor device in only the selected instrument.

Super Trunk. A trunk between master and hub headends in a hub CATV system.

Supervision. The process of monitoring the busy/idle status of a circuit to detect changes of state.

Suppression. A condition that exists when total service demand in a network is limited by lack of capacity.

Switched Access. A method of obtaining test access to telecommunications circuits by using electromechanical circuitry to switch test apparatus to the circuit.

Switched Multimegabit Data Service (SMDS). A packet switched data service that will be offered by LECs providing LAN-like performance over a metropolitan area. SMDS uses IEEE 802.6 standards.

Switched Virtual Circuit. A virtual circuit composed of a path that is established with each session.

Switchhook. The portion of a telephone set that connects and disconnects the telephone from the line.

Synchronous. A method of transmitting data over a network wherein the sending and receiving terminals are kept in synchronism with each other by a clock signal embedded in the data.

Synchronous Optical Network (SONET). A new suite of fiber optic transmission speeds that will eventually replace the present DS signal levels.

System Gain. The amount of free space path loss that a radio can overcome by a combination of transmitted power and receiver sensitivity.

System Integration. The process of bringing together software and devices from multiple sources and causing them to operate as a unit.

Systems Network Architecture (SNA). An IBM data communications architecture that includes structure, formats, protocols, and operating sequences.

T-1. A multiplexed 24-channel line capable of carrying voice and data signals at a total data rate of 1.544 mb/s.

T-1 Multiplexer. An intelligent device that divides a 1.544 mb/s facility into multiple voice and data channels.

Talk-Off. A circuit irregularity that occurs when sufficient 2600 Hz energy is present in the voice signal to cause the SF set to interpret it as a disconnect signal.

Talk-Through. The ability of a full duplex mobile radio unit to talk to another mobile unit through the base station.

Tandem Switch. A switching system that interconnects local or toll trunks to other switching systems.

Tandem Trunks. Trunks between an end office and a tandem switching system or between tandem switching systems to provide alternate routing capability when direct trunks are occupied.

Tap. A passive device mounted on a feeder cable to distribute a television signal to a user.

Technical Control Center. A testing center for telecommunications circuits. The center provides test access and computer-assisted support functions to aid in circuit maintenance.

Telecommunications. The movement of information by electronic means.

Teleconferencing. An audio-only conference held between multiple parties.

Teletex. A service enabling users to exchange correspondence automatically between machine memories over telecommunication networks.

Teletext. A videotext service that receives information during the vertical blanking interval of a television signal.

Terminal. (1) A fixture attached to distribution cable to provide access for making connections to cable pairs. (2) Any device meant for direct operation over a telecommunications circuit by an end user.

Terminal Adapter. A device that connects non-ISDN equipment to ISDN network terminations.

Terminal Equipment Type 1 (TE1). Terminal equipment that is ISDN compatible.

Terminal Equipment Type 2 (TE2). Terminal equipment that is not ISDN compatible.

Terminal Server. In a local area network, a device that connects multiple asynchronous terminals to the network and buffers and encloses data from the terminals in a packet.

Test Shoe. A device that is applied to a circuit at a distributing frame to gain test access to circuit conductors.

Thermal Noise. Noise created in an electronic circuit by the movement and collision of electrons.

Three-Axis Stabilization. A method of preventing a satellite from tumbling by use of a gyroscope inside the satellite.

Throughput. The effective rate of transmission of information, excluding noninformation (overhead) bits, between two points.

Thunderstorm-Day. Any day in which thunder is heard at a designated observation point. Thunderstorm-days are used to determine the degree of exposure of telecommunications plant to lightning hazards.

Tie Trunk. A privately owned or leased trunk used to interconnect PBXs in a private switching network.

Time Division Multiple Access (TDMA). A method of sharing the capacity of a communications satellite by allotting access to the satellite to earth stations transmitting on the same frequency.

Time Division Multiplexing (TDM). A method of combining several communication channels by dividing a channel into time increments and assigning each channel to a time slot. Multiple channels are interleaved when each channel is assigned the entire bandwidth of the backbone channel for a short period of time.

Time Division Switching. The connection of two circuits in a network by assigning them to the same time slot on a common bus.

Time Domain Reflectometer (TDR). A testing device that acts on radar-like principles to determine the location of metallic circuit faults.

Tip. The designation of the side of a telephone line that serves as the return path to the central office.

Token. A software mark or packet that circulates among network nodes.

Token Passing. A method of allocating network access in which a terminal can send traffic only after it has acquired the network's token.

Toll Call. A call, outside the local calling area, for which the carrier levies a long distance charge.

Topology. The architecture of a network, or the way circuits are connected to link the network nodes.

Traffic. The volume of demand on a telecommunications system.

Traffic Usage Recorder (TUR). Hardware or software that monitors traffic-sensitive circuits or apparatus and records usage, usually in terms of CCS and peg count.

Transceiver. A single device that can both transmit and receive.

Transcoder. A device that combines two 1.544 mb/s bit streams into a single 1.544 mb/s bit stream to enable transmission of 44 or 48 channels over a DS-1 medium.

Transducer. Any device that changes energy from one state to another. Examples are microphones, speakers, and telephone handsets.

Translation. The process of analyzing dialed digits and using them to select a route or equipment features based on information contained in the system's data base.

Transmission. The process of transporting voice or data over a network or facility from one point to another.

Transmission Level Point (TLP). A designated measurement point in a circuit where the transmission level has been specified by the designer.

Transmitter Output Power. The amount of radio frequency energy, usually expressed in dBm, that a transmitter delivers to the antenna.

Transmultiplexer. A device that connects digital and analog transmission lines by signal processing without the need for intermediate voice frequency conversions.

Transponder. A satellite-mounted radio repeater that amplifies and converts the uplink frequency to the downlink frequency.

Trellis-Coded Modulation (TCM). A modulation method often used in modems to reduce the susceptibility of the signal to line impairments.

Tropospheric Wave. A radio wave at VHF frequencies or above that is reflected or scattered by the troposphere.

Trunk. A telephone circuit linking two switching systems.

Trunk Group. A group of trunks of a similar type.

Trunking Radio. A mobile radio station in which multiple mobiles share a group of frequencies. The idle mobiles all tune to a control channel to receive signals and then shift frequency to an assigned channel or trunk.

Twinaxial. A transmission medium consisting of two center conductors surrounded by a shield.

Twisted Pair Wire. Standard telephone cable composed of wires precisely twisted around one another to prevent crosstalk.

Two-Way Trunk. A trunk that can be seized from either end of the circuit.

Underground Cable. A cable that runs through conduit that is buried in the ground.

Unfaded Received Signal Level. The signal level measured at the input to a radio receiver. It is the sum of all gains and losses in the signal except losses due to fading.

Uniform Call Distribution (UCD). A standard feature of many PBXs that distributes incoming calls to an available agent. If no agent is available, the UCD plays an announcement and puts the caller on hold.

Uninterruptable Power Supply (UPS). A power unit that furnishes AC power to a device even when the commercial power source fails.

Uplink. The radio path from an earth station to a satellite.

Upload. To send information from a remote terminal to a host computer.

Upstream Channel. A band of frequencies on a CATV cable reserved for transmission from the user's terminal to the headend.

V & H Coordinates. A system of determining the distance between two points, used for call rating, in which the calling and called cities are assigned coordinates and the distance is calculated by geometry.

Value Added Network. A network in which some form of processing of a data signal takes place or information is added to the signal by the network.

Vertical Blanking Interval. The interval between television frames in which the picture is blanked to enable the trace to return to the upper left corner of the screen.

Via Net Loss (VNL). A design procedure for long haul trunks that controls echo by adding loss to a circuit, based on propagation speed of the transmission medium.

Video Compression. A method of transmitting analog television over a narrow digital channel by processing the signal.

Videotex. An interactive information retrieval service that usually employs the telephone network as the transmission medium.

Virtual Banding. In a WATS systems, the ability of trunks to carry traffic to all WATS bands, with billing based on the terminating points of the call instead of the band over which traffic is carried.

Virtual Circuit. A circuit that is established between two terminals by assigning a logical path over which data can flow. A virtual circuit can be either permanent, in which terminals are assigned a permanent path, or switched, in which the circuit is reestablished each time a terminal has data to send.

Virtual Circuit Switching. A switching system in which the circuit is disconnected during silent periods and reconnected when talking resumes.

Virtual Drive. In a local area network, a disk drive that appears to be installed in the client's workstation, but which is actually installed in the server. A virtual drive is created by the process of linking the client to the server.

Virtual Private Network (VPN). See Software Defined Network.

Voice/Data Multiplexer. A device that compresses voice and integrates it with a data signal for transmission on a digital channel.

Voice Frequency (VF). An audio frequency in the range of 300 to 3000 Hz.

Voice Mail. See Voice Store-and-Forward

Voice Processing. Technologies that capture and use voice signals to perform a specific function. Consists of six features: voice store-and-forward, voice response, speech recognition, speech-to-text, text-to-speech, and speech synthesis.

Voice Response Unit (VRU). A unit that responds to signals from a caller's telephone with recorded prompts and messages.

Voice Store-and-Forward (Voice Mail). A PBX service that allows voice messages to be stored digitally in secondary storage and retrieved remotely by dialing access and identification codes.

Volume Unit. A unit of speech or music level determined by reading an audio signal on a meter.

Voltage. The electrical pressure that forces current to flow through a circuit.

Voting Receivers. A group of mobile base station receivers operating on the same frequency with a control unit to pick the best signal from among them.

Wide Area Telephone Service (WATS). A bulk-rated long distance telephone service that carries calls at a cost based on usage and the state in which the calls terminate.

Waveguide. A rectangular or circular metallic tube capable of coupling a microwave signal from radio equipment to an antenna.

Wavelength Division Multiplexing (WDM). A method of multiplying the capacity of an optical fiber by simultaneously operating at more than one wavelength.

White Noise. Noise frequencies that are equally distributed across all frequencies of a pass band.

Wideband. (1) A channel that has enough bandwidth to carry more than one voice channel. (2) A radio bandwidth that is greater than the coherence bandwidth.

Wink. A momentary interruption in SF tone to indicate that the distant office is ready to receive digits.

Wireline. A term describing cellular radio service providers who are operating telephone companies. Also used to distinguish between mobile radio users and conventional telephone users in a standard telephone-to-mobile call.

Zero Slot LAN. See RS-232 LAN.

Zone-of-Protection. The protection offered to cables between buildings by the proximity of buildings more than 50 feet tall.

Bibliography

Abrahams, John R. *Manager's Guide to Centrex*. Norwood, MA: Artech House, 1988.

Allard, Frederick C., ed. *Fiber Optics Handbook for Engineers and Scientists*. New York: McGraw-Hill, 1990.

American Telephone and Telegraph Co. Bell Laboratories. *Engineering and Operations in the Bell System*. Murray Hill, NJ: AT&T Bell Laboratories, 1983.

American Telephone and Telegraph Co. *Telecommunications Transmission Engineering*, Bell System Center for Technical Education. Vol. 1, 1974, Vol. 2, 1977, Vol. 3, 1975.

American Telephone and Telegraph Co. *Telecommunications Electrical Protection*. 1985.

Archer, Rowland. *The Practical Guide to Local Area Networks*. New York: McGraw-Hill, 1986.

Balin, Frank, and Brent Gale. *KU Band Satellite TV: Theory Installation and Repair*. Indianapolis: Howard Sams, 1986.

Barnett, Richard, and Sally Maynard-Smith. *Packet Switched Networks: Theory and Practice*. New York: John Wiley & Sons, 1989.

Bartee, Thomas, ed. *Data Communications Networks and Systems* Indianapolis: Howard W. Sams, 1985.

Basch, E.E. ed. *Optical Fiber Transmission* Indianapolis: Howard W. Sams, 1987.

Bellamy, John C. *Digital Telephony*. New York: John Wiley & Sons, 1982.

Bertskeas, Dimitri, and Robert Gallager. *Data Networks*. Englewood Cliffs, NJ: Prentice-Hall, 1987.

Beyda, William J. *Basic Data Communications—A Comprehensive Overview*. Englewood Cliffs, NJ: Prentice-Hall, 1989.

Bhargava, V. K., et.al. *Digital Communications by Satellite*. New York: John Wiley & Sons, 1981.

Boithias, Lucien. *Radiowave Propagation*. New York: McGraw-Hill, 1988.

Blahut, Richard E. *Digital Transmission of Information,* Boston: Addison-Wesley, 1990.

Brenner, Aaron. *OS/2 LANS.* New York: Telecom Library, 1988.

Brewster, R. L. *Communication Systems and Computer Networks.* New York: John Wiley & Sons, 1989.

Building Industry Consulting Service International (BICSI). *Telecommunications Distribution Methods Manual.* 1990.

Calhoun, George. *Digital Cellular Radio.* Norwood, MA: Artech House, 1988.

Carson, Ralph S. *Radio Communications Analog.* New York: John Wiley & Sons, 1989.

Caswell, Stephen A. *E-Mail.* Norwood, MA: Artech House, 1988.

Chen, Wai-Kai. *Theory of Nets: Flows in Networks.* New York: John Wiley & Sons, 1989.

Chorafas, Dimitris N. *The Complete Local Area Network Reference Manual.* New York: McGraw-Hill, 1989.

Choudhary, D. Roy. *Networks and Systems.* New York: John Wiley & Sons, 1988.

Comer, Douglas. *Internetworking With TCP/IP: Principles, Protocols, and Architectures.* Englewood Cliffs, NJ: Prentice-Hall, 1988.

Cooper, J. Arlin. *Computer and Communications Security.* New York: McGraw-Hill, 1990.

Cooper, Robert B. *Introduction to Queuing Theory.* New York: North Holland Publishing Co., 1981.

Currie, William Scott. *LANs Explained: A Guide to Local Area Networks.* New York: John Wiley & Sons, 1989.

Datapro. *Reports on Telecommunications.* Delran, NJ: Datapro Research Corp.

Data Communications. *The Local Network Handbook.* 2nd ed. Colin B. Ungaro, ed., New York: McGraw-Hill, 1986.

Davies, D. W., and W. L. Price. *Security for Computer Networks: An Introduction to Data Security in Teleprocessing and Electronic Funds Transfer.* 2nd ed., New York: John Wiley & Sons, 1989.

Deasington, R. J. *X.25 Explained: Protocols for Packet Switching Networks.* 2nd ed. New York: John Wiley & Sons, 1986.

Ditto, Steve. *Buying Short Haul Microwave.* New York: Telecom Library, 1988.

Dordick, H.S. *Understanding Modern Telecommunications.* New York: McGraw-Hill, 1986.

Dordick, Herbert S., and Frederick Williams. *Innovative Management Using Telecommunications: A Guide to Opportunities, Strategies and Applications.* New York: John Wiley & Sons, 1986.

Dunlop, J., and D. G. Smith. *Telecommunications Engineering.* 2nd ed. New York: Van Nostrand Reinhold, 1989.

Edwards, Terry. *Fiber-Optic Systems: Network Applications.* New York: John Wiley & Sons, 1989.

Elbert, Bruce R. *Introduction to Satellite Communication.* Norwood, MA: Artech House, 1987.

Elbert, Bruce R. *Private Telecommunication Networks.* Norwood, MA: Artech House, 1988.

Ellis, Robert L. *Designing Data Networks.* Englewood Cliffs, NJ: Prentice-Hall, 1986.

Feher, Kamilo. *Telecommunications Measurements, Analysis and Instrumentation.* Englewood Cliffs, NJ: Prentice-Hall, 1987.

Flanagan, William A. *The Guide to T-1 Networking.* 3rd ed. New York: Telecom Library, 1988.

Florence, Donne. *Local Area Networks: Developing Your System for Business.* New York: John Wiley & Sons, 1989.

Folts, Harold C., ed. *McGraw-Hill's Compilation of Data Communications Standards.* 3rd ed. New York: McGraw-Hill, 1986.

Folts, Harold C., ed. *The Omnicom Index of Communications Standards,* New York: McGraw-Hill, 1989.

Fortier, Paul J. ed. *Handbook of LAN Technology.* New York: McGraw-Hill, 1988.

Freeman, Roger L. *Reference Manual for Telecommunications Engineering.* New York: John Wiley & Sons, 1985.

Freeman, Roger L. *Radio System Design for Telecommunications.* New York: John Wiley & Sons, 1987.

Freeman, Roger L. *Telecommunications System Engineering.* 2nd ed. New York: John Wiley & Sons, 1989.

Freeman, Roger L. *Telecommunication Transmission Handbook.* 2nd ed. New York: John Wiley & Sons, 1981.

Frenzel, Louise E., Jr. *Communication Electronics.* New York: McGraw-Hill, 1989.

Fthenakis, Emanuel. *Manual of Satellite Communications*. New York: McGraw-Hill, 1984.

Gagliardi, Robert M. *Introduction to Communications System Engineering*. New York: John Wiley & Sons, 1988.

Gasman, Lawrence D. *Manager's Guide to the New Telecommunications Network*. Norwood, MA: Artech House, 1988.

Gayler, Winston D. *Telephone Voice Transmission Standards and Measurements*. Englewood Cliffs, NJ: Prentice-Hall, 1989.

Girard, Andre. *Routing and Dimensioning in Circuit-Switched Networks*. Boston: Addison-Wesley, 1990.

Goeller, Lee, and Gerald Goldstone. *The Business Communication Review Manual of PBXs*. 2nd ed. New York: Telecom Library, 1987.

Green, James H. *The Dow Jones-Irwin Handbook of Telecommunications Management*. Homewood, IL: Dow Jones-Irwin, 1989.

Ha, Tri T. *Digital Satellite Communications*. New York: McGraw-Hill, 1986.

Halley, Pierre. *Fiber-Optic Systems*. New York: John Wiley & Sons, 1987.

Halsall, Fred. *Data Communications, Computer Networks and OSI*. 2nd ed. Boston: Addison-Wesley, 1989.

Hancock, Bill. *Designing and Implementing Ethernet Networks*. 2nd ed. Wellesly, MA: QED Information Sciences, 1988.

Hart, B. L. *Digital Signal Transmission Line Circuit Technology*. New York: Van Nostrand Reinhold, 1989.

Hecht, Jeff. *Understanding Fiber Optics*. Indianapolis: Howard W. Sams, 1987.

Held, Gilbert. *Data Communications Networking Devices*. 2nd ed. New York: John Wiley & Sons, 1989.

Held, Gilbert, ed. *Data and Computer Communications: Terms, Definitions and Abbreviations*. New York: John Wiley & Sons, 1989.

Held, Gilbert, and Thomas Marshall. *Data Compression, 2nd ed.* New York: John Wiley & Sons, 1987.

Henshall, John, and Sandy Shaw. *OSI Explained: End-to-End Computer Communication Standards*. New York: John Wiley & Sons, 1988.

Honig, David A., and Kenton Hoover. *Desktop Communications IBM PC, PS/2, And Compatibles*. New York: John Wiley & Sons, 1989.

Housley, Trevor. *Data Communications & Teleprocessing Systems*. 2nd ed. Englewood Cliffs, NJ: Prentice-Hall, 1987.

Hutchinson, David. *Local Area Network Architectures.* Boston: Addison-Wesley, 1988.

Inglis, Andrew F., ed. *Electronic Communications Handbook,* New York: McGraw-Hill, 1988.

ITT *Reference Data for Radio Engineers. 6th* ed. Indianapolis: Howard W. Sams, 1984

Kao, Charles K. *Optical Fiber Systems: Technology, Design and Applications.* New York: McGraw-Hill, 1982.

Kauffels, Franz-Joachim. *Practical LANs Analyzed.* New York: John Wiley & Sons, 1989.

Keen, Peter G. *Competing in Time: Using Telecommunications for Competitive Advantage.* Ballinger, 1988.

Kim, Gary Y. *Broadband LAN Technology.* Norwood, MA: Artech House, 1988.

Knightson, Keith, and Terry Knowles. *Standards for Open Systems Interconnection.* New York: McGraw-Hill, 1988.

Klinger, D.J., Y. Nakada, and M.A. Menendez. *AT&T Reliability Manual.* New York: Van Nostrand Reinhold, 1989.

Lapatine, Sol. *Electronics in Communication Systems.* New York: John Wiley & Sons, 1986.

Lawson, Robert W. *A Practical Guide to Teletraffic Engineering and Administration.* Chicago: Telephony Publishing Corp., 1983.

Lenk, John D. *Handbook of Data Communications.* Englewood Cliffs NJ: Prentice-Hall, 1984.

Lee, William C. Y. *Mobile Communications Design Fundamentals.* Indianapolis: Howard Sams, 1986.

Lee, William C. Y., *Mobile Cellular Telecommunications Systems.* New York: McGraw-Hill, 1989.

Liebowitz, Jay, ed. *Expert System Applications to Telecommunications.* New York: John Wiley & Sons, 1988.

Lin, Chinlon, ed. *Optoelectronic Technology and Lightwave Communications Systems.* New York: Van Nostrand Reinhold, 1989.

Lindberg, Bertil C. *Troubleshooting Communications Facilities: Measurements and Tests on Data and Telecommunications Circuits, Equipment, and Systems.* New York: John Wiley & Sons, 1990.

Long, Mark. *The KU Band Satellite Handbook.* Indianapolis: Howard Sams, 1987.

Lynn, Paul A., and Wolfgang Fuerst. *Introductory Digital Signal Processing With Computer Applications.* New York: John Wiley & Sons, 1989.

Macpherson, Andrew C. *International Telecommunication Standards Organizations.* Norwood, MA: Artech House, 1990.

Madron, Thomas W. *Local Area Networks, The Second Generation.* New York: John Wiley & Sons, 1988.

Madron, Thomas W. *LANS Applications of IEEE/ANSI 802 Standards.* New York: John Wiley & Sons, 1989.

Malamud, Carl. *DEC Networks and Architecture.* New York: McGraw-Hill, 1989.

Markley, Richard. *Data Communications and Interoperability.* Englewood Cliffs, NJ: Prentice-Hall, 1990.

Martin, James. *Telecommunications and the Computer.* 3rd ed. Englewood Cliffs, NJ: Prentice-Hall, 1989.

McConnell, Kenneth, Dennis Bodson, and Richard Schaphorst. *FAX: Digital Facsimile Technology and Applications.* Norwood, MA: Artech House, 1989.

Meadow, Charles T., and Albert S. Teedesco. *Telecommuications for Management.* New York: McGraw-Hill, 1985.

Meijer, Anton. *Systems Network Architecture: A Tutorial.* New York: John Wiley & Sons, 1988.

Meyr, Heinrich, and Gerd Ascheid. *Synchronization in Digital Communications Vol. 1: Phase-, Frequency-Locked Loops and Amplitude Control.* New York: John Wiley & Sons, 1989.

Miller, Stewart E., and Ivan P. Kaminow, eds. *Optical Fiber Telecommunications II.* San Diego: Academic Press, 1988.

Morgan, Walter L., and Gary D. Gordon. *Communications Satellite Handbook.* New York: John Wiley & Sons, 1988.

Morgan, Walter L., and Denis Rouffet. *Business Earth Stations For Telecommunications.* New York: John Wiley & Sons, 1988.

Muller, Nathan J., and Robert P. Davidson. *LANs to WANs: Network Management in the 1990s.* Norwood, MA: Artech House, 1990.

Murphy, RJ. *Telecommunications Networks: A Technical Introduction.* Indianapolis: Howard W. Sams, 1987.

National Electrical Safety Code, 1987. New York: American National Standards Institute, 1987.

Newton, Harry. *Newton's Telecom Dictionary.* New York: Telecom Library, 1989.

Noll, A. Michael. *Introduction to Telecommunication Electronics.* Norwood, MA: Artech House, 1988.

Noll, A. Michael. *Introduction to Telephones and Telephone Systems.* Norwood, MA: Artech House, 1986.

Noll, A. Michael, *Television Technology: Fundamentals and Future Prospects.* Norwood, MA: Artech House, 1988.

Nussbaumer, Henri. *Computer Communications Systems Volume 1: Data Circuits, Error Detection, Data Links.* New York: John Wiley & Sons, 1989.

Parsons, J.D., and J.G. Gardiner. *Mobile Communications Systems.* Glasgow: Blackie & Sons Ltd., 1989.

Posar, David. *Microwave Engineering.* Boston: Addison-Wesley, 1990.

Powers, John T. *Megabit Data Communications: A Guide for Professionals.* Englewood Cliffs, NJ: Prentice-Hall, 1990.

Pruitt, James B. *T-1 Networks: Design to Installation.* Tulsa: PennWell Books, 1988.

Ranade, Jay, and George Sackett. *Introduction to SNA Networking: A Guide to Using VTAM/NCP.* New York: McGraw-Hill, 1989.

Rees, David W.E. *Satellite Communications: The First Quarter Century of Service.* New York: John Wiley & Sons, 1989.

Ronayne, John P. *Introduction to Digital Communications Switching.* Indianapolis: Howard W. Sams, 1986.

Ronayne, John. *The Integrated Services Digital Network (ISDN): From Concept to Application.* New York: John Wiley & Sons, 1988.

Rose, Marshall T. *The Open Book: A Practical Perspective on OSI.* Englewood Cliffs, NJ: Prentice-Hall, 1990.

Rosner, Roy D., ed. *Satellites, Packets, and Distributed Telecommunications.* Belmont, CA: Lifetime Learning Publications, 1984.

Runge, David. *Winning with Telecommunications.* Washington, DC: ICIT Press, 1988.

Sachnoff, Neil. *Secrets of Installing a Telephone System.* New York: Telecom Library, 1989.

Sarch, Ray, ed. *Integrating Voice and Data.* New York: McGraw-Hill, 1987.

Sarch, Ray, ed. *Telecommunications and Data Communications Fact Book.* New York: McGraw-Hill, 1987.

Schatt, Stan. *Understanding Local Area Networks.* Indianapolis: Howard W. Sams, 1987.

Schatt, Stan, and Steven Fox. *Voice/Data Telecommunications for Business.* Englewood Cliffs, NJ: Prentice-Hall, 1990.

Schwartz, Mischa. *Telecommunication Networks: Protocols, Modeling and Analysis.* Boston: Addison-Wesley, 1987.

Sharma, Roshan La., Paulo T. deSousa, and Ashok D. Ingle, *Network Systems,* New York: Van Nostrand Reinhold, 1982.

Sherman, Kenneth. *Data Communications: A User's Guide.* 3rd ed. Englewood Cliffs, NJ: Prentice-Hall, 1990.

Sioman, Morris. *Distributed Systems and Computer Networks.* Englewood Cliffs, NJ: Prentice-Hall, 1987.

Sokol, Phyllis. *EDI: The Competitive Edge.* New York: McGraw-Hill, 1988.

Stallings, William. *Local Networks: An Introduction.* New York: Macmillan, 1984.

Stallings, William. *Handbook of Computer Communications Volume I.* New York: Macmillan, 1987.

Stallings, William. *Handbook of Computer Communications Volume II.* New York: Macmillan, 1988.

Stallings, William, *Handbook of Computer Communications Volume III,* New York: Macmillan, 1988.

Stuck, B. W., and E. Arthurs. *A Computer and Communications Network Performance Analysis Primer.* Englewood Cliffs, NJ: Prentice-Hall, 1985

Svoboda, Krasna, and Richard L. Godfrey. *The Perfect RFP.* New York: Telecom Library, 1988.

Tannenbaum, Andrew S. *Computer Networks. 2nd ed.* Englewood Cliffs, NJ: Prentice-Hall, 1988. .

Teleconnect Magazine. *Which Phone System Should I Buy?* 7th ed. New York: Telecom Library, 1989.

Thacker, Chet. *Negotiating Telecommunications Contracts.* New York: Telecom Library, 1988.

Tugal, Dogan, and Osman Tugal. *Data Transmission.* 2nd ed. New York: McGraw-Hill, 1989.

Turpin, John, and Ray Sarch, eds. *Data Communications: Beyond the Basics.* New York: McGraw-Hill, 1986.

Waite, Andrew J. *The Inbound Telephone Call Center.* New York: Telecom Library, 1989.

Weik, Martin H., D.Sc. *Communications Standard Dictionary.* 2nd ed. New York: Van Nostrand Reinhold, 1988.

Weik, Martin H., D.Sc. *Fiber Optics Standard Dictionary.* 2nd ed. New York: Van Nostrand Reinhold 1989.

Wallenstein, Gerd D. *Setting Telecommunication Standards: The Stakes, the Players and the Process.* Norwood, MA: Artech House, 1989.

Index

Purging algorithms, 601

Q

Quadrature amplitude modulation, 73, 367
Quantizing, 112
Quantizing noise, 112–13
Quasi-synchronous operation, 425
Queue discipline, 814
Queued Packet Synchronous Exchange, 786
Queuing, 282–84
  automated call distributor, 568
  avoiding, 287
  camp-on feature, 542
  efficiency, 287
  management, 590–91
  overflow, 565–66
  private branch exchanges, 540
  statistics, 285
Queuing theory
  alternate routing, 825
  busy hour determination, 820
  grade of service, 820–21
  network topology, 827
  simulation, 825–27
  traffic load, 814–20
  traffic measurements, 821–24
  variables, 814

R

Radio, 10, 147; *see also* Microwave radio *and*
    Mobile radio
  frequency signal, 362–63
  heterodyning, 915
  modulation, 913–15
  receivers, 915–16
  transmission, 911–16
  transmitters, 912–13
Radio paging, 441–42
Radio relay equipment, 400
Rain absorption, 405
Rain rate fading, 374
Range extenders, 183–85
Reactance, 906
Receive-only satellite services, 407–9
Receivers, 267, 915–16
Receiver sensitivity, 374
Recent change information, 249
Recorded announcements, 237
Redirection, 753
Redundancy, 249–50
Reed relay analog network, 213
Reeves, Alec, 109
Reference noise, 38–39
Refractive index, 337
Refreshed signal, 464
Regional Bell Holding Companies, 1, 51, 889
Regulation, 889–90
Relays, 897–98
Remote access, 282, 289
Remote bridge, 756–57
Remote diagnostics, 488

Remote job entry, 687
Remote maintenance and testing systems, 316–17
Remote office test line, 276
Reorder call progess tone, 294
Repeat coil, 10, 909–10
Repeaters, 12–13, 29–30, 755
Reports, call accounting system, 559
Resistance, 898–99
  series and parallel, 900–901
Resistance design, 167–68
Resonance, 908–9
Responder, 276
Retrofittable telephone instruments, 554–55
Return loss, 33–34, 50, 845
Return to attendant feature, 598
Reverse polling, 634
Ring again feature, 264–65
Ringdown circuits, 306
Ringing, 217, 237
  distinctive, 541
  harmonic, 480
  machines, 315
Ring party, 479
Ring topology, 718
Ring wire, 477
Riser cable, 489
Roamers, 421–22
Roaming, 437
Roll call polling, 657
Root mean square voltage, 902–3
Rotary dials, 477
Rotary line group, 266–67
Routers, 742, 757–58
Routing, 18, 288–89
  alternate, 825
  private tandem switches, 284
  to service facilities, 266

S

SAA, *see* Systems Applications Architecture
Sampling, 111–12
Satellite, 392, 396–400
Satellite Business Services, 392
Satellite circuits, 651–52
Satellite communications, 391–92, 412–14
  advantages, 394–95
  altitude control apparatus, 398–99
  band frequencies, 392–94
  carrier-to-noise ratio, 406
  circuit elements, 396–400
  controller, 401–2
  delay, 403–5
  earth station equipment, 400–403, 414
  interfaces, 406
  limitations, 395–96
  manufacturers, 415
  network management, 415
  paths, 394
  physical structure of satellite, 397
  power supply, 399
  radio relay equipment, 400
  rain absorption, 405

Other Irwin Professional Publishing Titles of Interest:

NEW LIFE FOR OLD PCs
How to Keep Your Company's Computers from Becoming Obsolete
Alfred Poor
Discover the most cost-effective methods for updating your current computer operation. From accelerating your computer operation with hardware/software additions...to upgrading major components or replacing the old with the new, Poor gives you the facts on exactly what your hardware is required to do to improve productivity using the latest software packages.
ISBN: 1-55623-427-9 $29.95 (paper, with disk)

THE USEABLE PORTABLE GUIDES
MS-DOS, WordPerfect and Lotus 1-2-3®
Microsoft® Windows™ 3, Word for Windows™, & Excel™
Jon Haber and Herbert R. Haber
No other book gives an all-in-one, quick-reference solution with step-by-step instructions that follow the work sequence of the software. Features an easy-to-use format that lays flat on a desktop or at the top of a computer keyboard.
ISBN: MS-DOS: 1-55623-617-4 $14.95 (paper)
Windows: 1-55623-618-2 $14.95 (paper)

THE HIGH TECHNOLOGY EDITORIAL GUIDE AND STYLEBOOK
1991 Edition
PC Disk Version or Macintosh® Disk Version
Lewis Perdue
Understand and clearly use high-tech acronyms, buzz words, and ultra-sophisticated definitions. Destined to take its place alongside the *AP Stylebook* and the *Chicago Manual of Style,* this indispensable reference includes a user-friendly disk that will help you to be accurate and credible in your writing.
ISBN: Mac: 1-55623-530-5 $32.50 (paper, with disk)
PC: 1-55623-531-3 $32.50 (paper, with disk)

A GUIDE TO OPTICAL STORAGE TECHNOLOGY
Using CD-ROM, WORM, Erasable, Digital Paper™ and Other High-Density Opto-Magnetic Storage Devices
John A. McCormick
Compares the pros and cons of various optical storage technologies so you can choose the system that best fits your needs.
ISBN: 1-55623-320-5 $40.00

THE SPREADSHEET STYLE MANUAL
David Harrison and John W. Yu
Discover how to create clear, effective spreadsheets. Here's the definitive reference for layout, formatting, and editing of all types of spreadsheets. The practical, information and professional-level spreadsheets in this user-friendly manual can be used with any spreadsheet software or integrated program.
ISBN: 1-55623-267-5 $24.95 (paper)

Prices quoted are in U.S. currency
and are subject to change without notice.

Available at Fine Bookstores or Libraries Everywhere.